D1597180

Fighting Elites

Fighting Elites

A HISTORY OF U.S. SPECIAL FORCES

John C. Fredriksen

 ABC-CLIO

Santa Barbara, California • Denver, Colorado • Oxford, England

Library of Congress Cataloging-in-Publication Data

Fredriksen, John C.
  Fighting elites : a history of U.S. Special Forces / John C. Fredriksen.
    p. cm.
  Includes bibliographical references and index.
    ISBN 978–1–59884–810–6 (hbk. : alk. paper) — ISBN 978–1–59884–811–3 (ebook)
1. Special forces (Military science)—United States—History. 2. Guerrilla warfare—United States—History. 3. Irregular warfare—United States—History. 4. United States Armed Forces—Commando troops—History. I. Title. II. Title: History of U.S. special forces.
UA34.S64F74   2012
356′.160973—dc23   2011036624

ISBN: 978–1–59884–810–6
EISBN: 978–1–59884–811–3

16 15 14 13 12   1 2 3 4 5

This book is also available on the World Wide Web as an eBook.
Visit www.abc-clio.com for details.

ABC-CLIO, LLC
130 Cremona Drive, P.O. Box 1911
Santa Barbara, California 93116-1911

This book is printed on acid-free paper ∞

Manufactured in the United States of America

Contents

Introduction

Ascribe it to the uniquely American penchant for individualism, but the United States, even before its inception, displayed marked proclivities for raising what today are generically deemed "special forces." As early as 1676, the half-English, half–Native American company of Captain Benjamin Church wielded an indelible impact on the field of battle where conventional units had failed and helped decisively end King Philip's War. This was also the first American unit to employ indigenous forces in a direct capacity, a practice since enshrined as a pillar of modern special operations techniques.

The next identifiable phase in the growth and maturation of unconventional warfare occurred in the French and Indian War when Major Robert Rogers organized his famous rangers. Rogers was also the first light infantry leader in American history to codify tactical precepts; hence, his "Rules of Ranging" form the underpinning of many special operations tactics to present times. Next, the Revolutionary War afforded the colonies new vistas for exploring unconventional warfare, and they nuanced it with their famous Minutemen, riflemen, the guerrillas of General Francis Marion, and the 2nd Partisan Legion of Colonel Henry Lee, among others. The war itself was basically won by the hard-slogging Continental Army, which employed conventional tactics not unlike its British adversaries, but homegrown irregulars performed valuable services in their absence, especially in the South.

Nevertheless, while effective in a combat sense, such units found little favor among conventionally minded national leaders, so their recruitment and longevity throughout this seminal period proved at times problematic.

With independence secured, the young nation neglected its conventional military legacy to fixate on the politically expedient militia, a policy harboring grave consequences during the War of 1812. Ironically, it was during this same conflict that the U.S. Army fielded its first, clearly identifiable special forces units, the Regiment of Riflemen and the Regiment of Light Artillery. The war effort here may have been hobbled by military ineptitude, yet both units displayed a tactical effectiveness that belied their relatively small size. These distinguished formations were disbanded in the postwar period, but the onset of the Mexican War in 1846 saw creation of two new elite units—the Regiment of Voltigeurs and the Regiment of Mounted Riflemen—that again rendered distinguished service throughout that conflict. Only the latter unit was retained after 1848, and in 1861 it was redesignated the 3rd U.S. Cavalry and employed like a conventional mounted outfit. However, that same year witnessed creation of the two U.S. Sharp Shooter regiments that, by dint of their unique green uniforms, special weapons, and training, certainly fitted the description and operational motif of a special operations unit. Throughout the nineteenth century, it should also be stressed that Native Americans frequently played important roles as indigenous auxiliaries. During the Creek and Seminole Wars, entire battalions of Indians were raised to fight alongside American forces, albeit with their own unique tactics. This trend crested toward the end of the century when Apaches and other tribes provided valuable detachments of scouts that proved indispensable in tracking down marauding bands led by figures like Geronimo. In 1918, Choctaws provided the army with its first ethnic code talkers, a practice that would be expanded on greatly in World War II. That Native Americans have served so diligently in American employ since 1676 is a theme in national military history that cannot be overlooked or diminished. But the advantages all these units brought to nation's tactical tableau were by and large forgotten, and, once again, their longevity in service proved episodic.

During the latter half of the twentieth century, the expansion of American special forces picked up dramatic pacing and variety. In Europe, Axis forces felt the sting of highly trained units, such as Darby's Rangers, the Devil's Brigade, and the 82nd and 101st Airborne Divisions. In the Pacific, the Marine Raiders, the Paramarines, the Scouts and Snipers, Merrill's Marauders, and the Alamo Scouts joined the Navy's Underwater Demolition Teams to raise havoc among the Japanese, usually with lethal effect. The Army Air Force also demonstrated its flair for special operations by creating the 1st Air Commando Group, while a mercenary outfit, the American Volunteer Group, famously celebrated as the Flying Tigers, also performed valuable services. Ethnic, highly varied allies, such as the Kachin Scouts and the Philippine guerillas, offer proof that the United States had lost none of its talent for recruiting and employing indigenous auxiliaries. Ironically, the persistent American tendency to disband effective special forces was never more manifest than in the postwar period, when even the famous Office of Strategic Service fell by the wayside. Thus, the importance of military capacities afforded by special forces remained overlooked until the initial stages of the Cold War, and the lessons, once again, had to be painfully relearned.

Modern American special forces are a far cry from their historical antecedents, but threads of continuity persist in their tactical mastery of unconventional warfare. Moreover, the extreme dangers posed by the Soviet Union and Red China to the United States finally triggered a lasting resurgence in terms of special operations doctrine, and, for once, the Americans not only raised new special forces units but also grudgingly maintained them as part of the standing military establishment. These include not only storied formations such as the army's Green Berets and Rangers and the navy's SEALs but also lesser-known entities, such as the air force's Air Resupply and Communications Command and the Marine Corps's Force Recon companies. All performed dutifully during the Korean and Vietnamese conflicts, ensuring that, while special forces may not enjoy wide popularity within military institutions, they were no longer considered expendable and subject to immediate disbandment at the end of hostilities. The United States received an abject lesson in the utility of possessing appropriate special operations units for each service and every contingency following the disastrous Iranian hostage rescue attempt of 1980, which exuded dramatic remedial effects to that same end. The interval between the end of the Cold War and the beginning of the War on Terror found special forces employed in minor fare, such as hunting war criminals in the Balkans and Somalia, tasks for which they trained but acquired little distinction. However, the attack against the World Trade Center on September 11, 2001, again spelled in stark relief the growing and sometimes dire necessity of recruiting, training, equipping, and preserving viable special operations capabilities. That the cruel Taliban regime in Afghanistan and their al-Qaeda terrorist consorts were ejected from that rugged country in only three months proffers incontrovertible proof that U.S. Special Forces are a potent factor to reckon with. They currently operate everywhere around the globe, wherever American interests and security are threatened, and scores of dead terrorists, including Osama bin Laden himself, offer mute testimony to their matchless lethality. Given the implications of terrorism to national security, there is little wonder that, over the past two and a half centuries, America's special forces have evolved steadily from tactical novelties into battlefield force multipliers and standing strategic necessities. The twenty-first century may very well prove itself to be a golden age of unconventional warfare and high-tech special warriors who wage it.

The present work is an attempt to provide meaningful coverage of American special forces, particularly from a reference standpoint. This is a somewhat complex subject, given the multiplicity of units involved across time, so I employ a relatively straightforward organization. The first part consists of three chronological chapters discussing various units and individuals associated with special operations during the periods 1676–1918, 1941–1945, and 1946–1991. The first chapter is arranged chronologically, including coverage prior to America's founding, while the next two chapters consist of alphabetical listings of units by service name. Each chapter consists of a broad historical discussion of the unit with a separate section, "Defining Activity," highlighting a particular battle or endeavor with special operations overtones. The chapter ends with an extensive listing of bibliographic citations, including all the latest literature, to promote further research. Part II of the book provides an overview of contemporary special forces and is divided into 13 individual chapters, each covering an individual branch of the Special Forces, alphabetically by service. Each chapter then delineates five major points: introduction for context, organization, training and personnel, weapons and equipment, and known activities. As before, each chapter concludes with a bibliography of the latest available resources. Finally, the book concludes with an extensive chronology of known events in special operations history and a general bibliography covering operations in Afghanistan and Iraq. In sum, I sought to provide a handy, one-stop reference guide to the history of U.S. Special Forces, one that affords extensive historical and bibliographic coverage yet is easy for lay readers to access and inculcate. To that end, I believe I have succeeded. The writer would like to thank editors Padraic Carlin and Andy McCormick for suggesting this topic to me. It proved an arduous task to pursue but also an informative one, and I hope that prospective users find it as enlightening.

John C. Fredriksen, PhD

Part I

Antecedents, 1676 to 1991

1

Special Purpose Units, Colonial Times to 1918

Special purpose units, loosely defined, are any aggregate of military personnel, uniformed or not, operating in manners differently from prescribed tactics or procedures utilized by the majority of other units. Colonial America, given its distance from English institutions and the very different tactical situation confronting its own armed forces, seemed uniquely predisposed to experimenting with unorthodox solutions to military problems seemingly unaddressed by conventional methods. Consequently, in various wars leading up to the American Revolution, that conflict itself, and encounters through 1918, various and sundry special purpose units evolved, fought with distinction, and were unceremoniously disbanded. These include classic guerilla and partisan outfits but also regular members of the standing military establishment who, by dint of special training, attire, or weapons, stood apart from the rest. Many of these units, outlined below, share direct links to today's special forces in the manner in which they trained, fought, or achieved military objectives both on the battlefield or deep behind enemy lines. In at least one instance, special technology facilitating an unconventional naval attack (the submarine *Turtle*) constitutes a legitimate category. This chapter reviews several such units in American employ and clearly identifiable as having a special purpose either on conventional battlefields or beyond them. It should be stressed that special forces, by dint of special training and equipment, are capable of achieving strategic and tactical objectives usually beyond the purview of conventional units, whereby imagination, not military dogma, plays an inordinate role in the planning and execution of said missions.

Army

New England Militia

Ever since English settlers first encountered Native Americans in their New World environment, a far cry from the finely manicured countryside of western Europe, the latter wielded an indelible impact on their subsequent conduct of war. European methods of combat, which in the 17th century consisted of close-order drill with heavily armored cavalry, pikemen, and musketeers, were at a distinct disadvantage when arrayed against lightly armed, fleet-footed adversaries fighting in open order through a heavily forested topography. In fact, Native Americans excelled at ambush and envelopment tactics, honed by centuries of warfare among themselves, and they enjoyed distinct battlefield advantages in hit-and-run tactics or what the colonials unwisely derogated as "a skulking way of war." Success was usually predicated on acute knowledge of local terrain, excellent stealth and marching discipline while approaching an objective, expert concealment up to the point of attack, and an uncanny ability to suddenly retreat and vanish into the woods as circumstances dictated. The Northeast woodland tribes were clear masters of all these operational facets. In fact, entire companies of plodding, heavily armed Englishmen could be engaged, surrounded, and possibly overwhelmed in small-unit wilderness encounters by fast-moving warriors wielding bows and hatchets. Once the Indians began acquiring European firearms through trade, becoming quite as proficient as their opponents, their ability to inflict harm on tightly packed militia formations increased exponentially. That English forces ultimately prevailed during earlier Indian conflicts in Virginia and Connecticut is mute testimony to their own physical hardiness, the lack of political unity among their more numerous opponents, and a rising population occasioned by increased migration to the colonies rather than to any particular battlefield advantage. Western colonialists many have enjoyed societal benefits, such as technology, medicine, and coherent discipline, which did give them a strategic edge, long term, over Native Americans. But on the battlefield, the Indians remained formidable frontier adversaries when engaged on ground of their choosing.

In June 1675, the New England colonies confronted military disaster when the Wampanoags under Metacomet (whose haughty demeanor led to the moniker "King Philip"), rebelled against continuing European encroachment on Indian lands. He was soon after joined by the neighboring Nipmuc, Sakonnet, Pocasset, and Narragansett peoples, whose war bands began raiding and destroying remote English communities throughout the Connecticut Valley. The United Colonies mustered troops and fought back as best they could, although isolated detachments on patrol or marching from one settlement to another were frequently ambushed and roughly handled, or destroyed outright. The biggest colonial reverse happened on September 19, 1675, when Captain Thomas Lathrop and 70 men from Essex County were expertly snared by Indians along the banks of Muddy Brook near the abandoned village of Deerfield and annihilated. Success here emboldened the tribes, and the following October, they attacked and destroyed the settlement of Springfield, then functioning as the main garrison and entrepôt of the Connecticut Valley region. Superior English numbers overall and advanced weaponry availed them little against a foe who could mass at will, strike in overpowering numbers, and suddenly vanished before a counterblow materialized.

Benjamin Church (1639–1718). Benjamin Church was born in Plymouth Colony, Massachusetts, in 1639 and worked as a carpenter at various settlements. In 1675, Church founded Little Compton, Rhode Island, bringing him into daily contact with the Wampanoag Indians. Unlike many contemporaries, he was a keen observer of Indian life and warfare and struck up cordial relations with several chiefs. After King Philip's War commenced that same year, Church commanded a militia company and was badly wounded at the Great Swamp Fight of December 19, 1675, which scattered the powerful Narragansett tribe. The war itself, however, was going badly, so in the spring of 1676, Governor Josiah Winslow of Plymouth appointed Church commander of all militia forces. He immediately recruited and trained an English company in the ways of frontier bush fighting and teamed them up with Christianized Indian warriors. This was the first time

Colonel Benjamin Church raised the first special forces unit in American military history and employed it to decisively end King Philip's War. Unlike most contemporary colonials, he respected Native Americans and had a keen appreciation for their way of warfare. (Library of Congress)

that indigenous forces had been so recruited by the colonials, and Church successfully hunted down hostile tribal leaders. On August 1, 1676, he captured Chief Metacomet's wife and son, then one of his Indians cornered and killed Metacomet himself in Bristol, Rhode Island, on August 12, 1676. Church's actions decisively ended the war in a colonial victory. He subsequently led mixed forces in King William's War (1689–1697) and Queen Anne's War (1702–1713) although with less success and renown than his initial endeavor. His son Thomas published his *Entertaining Passages Relating to King Philip's War* in 1716, one of the earliest colonial military tracts. Church died in Little Compton on January 17, 1718, having raised and commanded the first special forces company in American military history.

It was during this military emergency that the first clearly recognizable special purpose unit in American military history emerged. Benjamin Church of Plymouth, a successful landowner with a long history of dealings with local tribesmen, began pushing superiors to recruit dissident elements from among the tribesmen and enroll them into a mixed Indian/English unit. Given the Puritan attitude toward Indians in general, whom they regarded as the spawn of Satan, this proved a tall order. Fortunately, the exigencies of warfare outweighed theological dictates, and Church finally prevailed. In fact, he was unique among contemporaries for his fair dealing with tribal leaders, his ability to communicate successfully in their own

The First Muster, Don Troiani. English colonial militia of the 17th century, while individually well armed, were at a tactical disadvantage when pitted against more mobile, lightly armed Native Americans in their wooded environment. (Don Troiani © 2011)

dialects, and his open friendship and easy relationships with several local leaders. In sum, Church's respect for indigenous cultures, particularly their mode of combat, facilitated the ultimate colonial victory. Shortly before the onset of hostilities, Church had been forewarned by Awashonks, female sachem of the Sakonnet clan of the Wampanoag, and Weetamoo, a female leader of the Pocassets, that Metacomet was taking up the war hatchet. He dutifully passed the intelligence along to superiors at Plymouth and was commissioned a captain of militia and principal aide to Governor Josiah Winslow in return.

As a military leader, Church was an officer who led from the front. On July 8, 1675, he took 20 Plymouth men on a preliminary peace mission to the Pocasset. No sooner had he reached Tiverton, Rhode Island, that he was directly attacked by an estimated 300 Wampanoags commanded by Metacomet himself. Church beat a hasty retreat to Pease's Field, where his men erected a small fortification from stones and from which they took cover and kept a hot fire on their antagonists. The Indians declined attacking frontally but kept up a steady fusillade upon the defenders. Their fire prevented several English boats offshore from rescuing the garrison. Church subsequently signaled to the vessels to withdraw and send back a smaller sloop with a canoe. The vessel appeared that evening and stealthily began evacuating the militiamen on the canoe, two soldiers at a time, until all were safely on board. Church's inspired leadership enabled them to hold 15 times their number at bay for over six hours and survive. He subsequently accompanied the large preemptive raid against the neutral Narragansett tribe, and on December 19, 1675, he fought with distinction in the Great Swamp Fight (present-day Kingston, Rhode Island). English forces under Governor Winthrop charged headlong against large and well-manned Indian fortification, against Church's advice, and were bloodily repulsed. It was not until Church's own company worked their way around and attacked the rear of their position that the victory was finally clinched. Losses were heavy on both sides, and Church pleaded with superiors not to march back to Wickford in a driving snow to spare wounded men from suffering and not burn the captured Indian dwellings, which were largely intact and well stocked with food. Again, his sound tactical advice was ignored, and the victors endured a grueling midwinter trek back to friendly territory, losing many lives in the freezing temperatures. The amateurish leadership of many colonial officers, who usually lacked prior military experience, was costing the colonies dearly.

Church, an aggressive officer with a flair for self-promotion, nonetheless earned renown as the colonies' most prominent Indian fighter. Having gained the ear of Governor Winthrop, he set about convincing authorities to solicit dissident Native Americans to the colonial cause. Metacomet's overbearing personality produced him many enemies among his fellow tribesmen and these proved more than willing to abandon him. Given the rigid, religious mind-set of the Puritans, Church was nonetheless initially restricted to enrolling converted, or "praying," Indians who, to impress their white neighbors, unhesitatingly plied their martial talents against hostile tribesmen. Church's mixed company, more than any other unit fielded by the colonies, then gained distinction by being employed offensively and taking the war to the enemy. By July 1676, Church's command consisted of 60 Englishmen and 140 Indian auxiliaries, all volunteers and well-versed in irregular warfare. Their several victories in the field convinced Church that he could also recruit defeated Indians into his unit with a generous amnesty that was successfully accomplished. Useful as warriors, these converts proved themselves peerless scouts and invariably relayed useful military intelligence that the English could not garner themselves. Church did, however, incur the wrath of superiors over his insistence that captured Indians be treated fairly after being promised amnesty, and he condemned the practice of selling them into slavery. This racially tinged practice, he argued, was counterproductive, stiffened native resistance, and only prolonged the fighting. Puritan leaders scoffed at the notion. The New England tribes were dangerous, tenacious adversaries, but they lacked both manpower and resources to cope with the steady influx of immigrants into the area and the military manpower they represented. This fact, coupled with the disturbing European ability to conduct winter campaigns because of modern logistical arrangements, sealed the fate of Metacomet's rebellion. After a year of incessant warfare, virtually all the tribes had been either exhausted by continual losses or starved into submission.

Defining Activity

Throughout the summer of 1676, Church's company was eminently successful stalking fleeing parties of warriors, surprising some, and inducing other to surrender without a fight based on his personal promise of good treatment. These irregulars ruthlessly pursued fleeing bands of enemy leaders, killing or capturing them, thus negating the tribal command element. By this time, Metacomet, once a mighty sachem, was now reduced to fugitive with his handful of remaining followers. Ordinarily, the conventionally trained English militias would have been hard pressed to effectively pursue such an elusive opponent, but Church's company was hot on his trail throughout the remaining months of the conflict. On August 2, 1676, they cornered and captured the chief's wife and son near Bristol, Rhode Island, who were promptly shipped off to the West Indies as slaves. Ten days later, on August 12, 1676, John Alderman, a Christian Indian in Church's company, tracked, shot, and killed

Metacomet in his refuge near present-day Mount Hope. The chief's body was subsequently drawn, quartered, and put on public display in Plymouth as a warning to other potential adversaries. Alderman received the severed chief's hand as a grisly trophy. A few weeks later, Church also cornered and subdued Annawon, the last remaining war chief, effectively ending the war. He surrendered on Church's promise of clemency, which the latter sought to uphold, but Puritan leaders overruled him, and the chief was bound, brought to Boston, and executed. For his efforts, Church was roundly praised by Puritan leaders, being voted "their thanks" and awarded a sum of 30 shillings. More significantly, his success effectively demonstrated the viability of ethnically diverse military units drawn directly from indigenous populations. This policy reemerged as a standard tactic of American special forces throughout wars of the 20th and 21st centuries, but it manifested first in the trackless wilderness of New England three centuries earlier.

Rogers's Rangers

In 1754, a minute skirmish over an obscure frontier outpost, dubbed Fort Necessity by its commander, George Washington, precipitated a final showdown between Great Britain and France for control of North America. The British government reacted strongly to the challenge by dispatching General Edward Braddock and 1,500 strongly disciplined infantry and a contingent of local militia to Virginia with orders to capture French-held Fort Duquesne near present-day Pittsburgh. Given the renown battlefield proclivities of the Red Coats in stand-up fighting, few difficulties were anticipated. However, on July 9, 1755, Braddock's column force was ambushed in the act of crossing the Monogahela River by 900 French, Indians, and Canadians and nearly annihilated. The British fought back bravely in their serried ranks but scarcely saw a single adversary lurking in the woods and were shot down in vast numbers. By day's end, 977 British—including Braddock—had been killed or wounded for a loss of only 39 French and Indians. That the French and Indian War began on such a disastrous note underscored the vulnerability of contemporary European-style tactics, whereby massed ranks of infantry traded volleys with each other at close range. In the wilderness, such deployments were completely upended by the looser, Indian-style fighting of their opponents. Hidebound British military leaders were loath to admit it, but new forms of warfare were needed to cope with the heavily forested woodland environment that they found themselves contesting. Such new tactics were never meant to replace conventional styles of combat but were to serve as adjuncts on the battlefield—and behind it.

In 1755, British forces under General William Johnson enjoyed somewhat better success in the vicinity of Lake George, New York, that year, marking the debut of 24-year-old Captain Robert Rogers. He was a rough-hewn New Hampshire militiaman with a somewhat scurrilous reputation but had nonetheless impressed Johnson with his abilities as a scout. The general authorized Roberts to form a company of scouts directly under his own command and act more or less independently in the field. Rogers conducted no fewer than seven reconnaissance missions in the vicinity of Crown Point, including three over the winter months when the rest of the army had gone into quarters. His success induced Governor William Shirley of Massachusetts to commission Rogers to command the first "Independent Company of Rangers"—and a legend was born. As a leader, Rogers had all but dispensed with British-style discipline and instituted a hybrid fighting style grafting Native American woodland tactics onto the colonial sense of strong woodmanship. In 1756, he even established "Rogers's Rules for Ranging," which was the first attempt to codify the rules of irregular warfare and which delineated instructions to be followed at all times. The "rangers," as he termed them, soon established a reputation for efficiency in a number of useful activities, such as deep raiding behind enemy lines, taking prisoners, clandestine reconnaissance, and collecting military intelligence as to enemy strength and intentions.

The specialized military techniques of Rogers's Rangers, as they became famously if informally known, are highly reflected in their uniform, training, and equipment. Rogers was authorized to handpick his volunteers, and, if many shared his roguish, undisciplined nature, they were fearless by nature and capable of doing what was asked of them. Generally, rangers were rough, fit men, inured to fatigue and capable of extended marching for great distances in spite of woods, hills, rain, mud, or snow. They also had to be skilled in woodcraft and in constructing rafts and light boats for lake and riverine transportation when on the trail. Supply wagons being impossible to operate in the wilderness, rangers carried everything they needed to complete a mission on their backs. They also had to be adept at hunting and living off the land in order to reduce the amount of supplies carried. To facilitate cold-weather operations, rangers were also issued snowshoes, skates, and an extra set of blankets, all of which had to be carried unless sleighs or toboggans were available. In contrast to the gaudy and impractical uniforms of British regulars, the rangers received simple, comfortable attire consisting of a green wool jacket, a green beret-style forage cap, buckskin breeches and leggings, and Indian-style moccasins. Not only was this outfit functional and comfortable during constant activity, but it also afforded wearers excellent camouflage, enhancing their ability to blend in with the surrounding terrain. The equipment issued was also somewhat lighter than that carried by regular infantry to increase mobility and speed while marching. The barrels of standard-issue muskets were invariably shortened by several inches to facilitate handling in the field, and each man was issued 60 rounds with ample powder. Moreover, standing up and firing in the open, European style was discouraged. Rogers taught his men the value of "treeing" behind cover while shooting and also pioneered the tactic of aiming and loading while prone. Scalping knives and tomahawks, along with instructions on how to use them in combat, rounded out the ranger's frontier arsenal.

From an operational standpoint, rangers were true light infantry whose tactics stressed nighttime movement and deployments to avoid contact with enemy forces, enhance surprise attacks, and conceal their resting areas. On the trail, they always moved "Indian style," a euphemism for single file, to conceal their numbers if tracked by an enemy. Most important, individual rangers were trained to be ready to march, fully equipped, after only a minute's warning. When moving, especially behind enemy lines, reconnaissance patrols and scouts always deployed ahead of the main force and on either flank to avoid surprise. While encamping, half the men remained on alert half the night while the other half slept and then were relieved. Campfires, if allowed, were dug in pits three feet deep and surrounded by spruce boughs to minimize detection. Rogers was acutely aware that both the French and the Indians preferred to attacking campsites at dawn, so rangers awoke and drew up defensive positions ahead of time. If no attack materialized, the men would breakfast and then resume marching. In sum, Rogers's rangers were one of a few units on the British side capable of year-round field operations and fighting under extreme conditions that would have daunted even the most steadfast European soldiers. Such military unorthodoxy prompted sneering condescension from most British officials, although as his successes piled up, Rogers was instructed to instruct junior officers in his techniques. Ultimately, the

Major Robert Rogers commanded a famous special forces unit which bears his name: Rogers's Rangers. His unit effectively bridged the operational gap between Native Americans and British regulars sometimes with spectacular results. (Library of Congress)

Robert Rogers (1731–1795). Robert Rogers was born in Methuen, Massachusetts, on November 7, 1731, and he was raised in the New Hampshire wilderness. To escape prosecution for forgery, he joined the militia during the French and Indian War and skillfully commanded a scout company in 1755. Three years later he was promoted to major, commanding nine ranger companies, and continued providing excellent screening and reconnaissance work in the Lake George area. To ensure tactical success, he also codified "Rogers' Rules of Ranging," which included ambushes, scouting, intelligence gathering, raiding, encamping, and marching, all of which were based on his experience fighting Native Americans. On March 13, 1758, Rogers was heavily ambushed by French and Indians near Lake George, New York, but he cleverly eluded more numerous pursers and escaped. In September–October 1759, Rogers conducted his most harrowing operation by marching 200 miles through the Canadian wilderness and storming the Indian village of St. Francis on October 5, 1759. Because of rough terrain and endemic supply shortages, only 93 of 180 Rangers survived the long march home. Rogers was subsequently sent west to accept the surrender of Detroit in November 1760, but he ran afoul of English authorities by dint of shady military accounting. Rogers passed in and out of jail until 1775, when he returned from England to fight in the American Revolution, changed sides, and then failed to win support from the British. He died in poverty in London on May 18, 1795, a scurrilous character but in many respects the father of American special operations techniques.

rangers so impressed British authorities that they eventually required all line regiments to possess a light company trained in screening, skirmishing, and outpost work not unlike like rangers.

Captain Rogers's command quickly gained renown throughout the northern colonies for its prowess in the field and its ability to scout enemy positions, take prisoners, and ambush enemy detachments with lethal effect. But even the best-trained units suffer adverse days, and on January 21, 1757, Rogers endured his worst defeat. That day, he took 183 rangers on a scout past French held Fort Carillon (Ticonderoga), where they ambushed a small enemy detachment, capturing seven. However, the remainder fled to the fort and alerted the garrison, at which point the rangers beat a hasty retreat as fast as their snowshoes would allow. En route, they were themselves ambushed by 150 French and Indians who bowled over seven rangers with their first volley. Having formed a rear guard to gain time, Rogers led his surviving men up nearby high ground, where they covered their retreat with alternating lines of volley fire. The rangers were tactically flexile and could employ conventional battle methods when necessary. The French twice rushed their defensive line head on and were as often blasted back. Two attempts to outflank the defenders were thwarted by small parties of rangers who extended the line where threatened. Having held the enemy at bay, Rogers withdrew under the cover of darkness and made his way safely back to Fort William Henry with a loss of 20 rangers. The French, having uncovered his jacket on the field, claimed to have finally killed their hated adversary. The "Battle on Showshoes" was clearly a costly and unexpected reverse, but Rogers, through expert fire discipline and adroit maneuvering, snatched defeat from the jaws of disaster. Consequently, in 1758, he gained promotion to major, and his command was enlarged into nine companies.

Defining Activity

For over a century, the Abenaki tribes had been the scourge of northern New England by dint of their sudden and destructive raids against frontier settlements. By 1759, it had been calculated that their numerous war bands had taken no fewer than 600 English scalps in the present conflict, many of which were hung in public view at their principal town of St. Francis, Lower Canada. Major General Jeffrey Amherst, the new British commander in America, determined to halt such activity prior to his invasion of Canada, and he instructed Major Rogers to draw up plans to attack them. This surprise assault, conducted deep behind enemy lines, encapsulated ranger fighting in its finest tradition. On September 13, 1759, Rogers departed from Crown Point, New York, with 200 rangers and a party of Christianized Stockbridge Indians. They crossed Lake Champlain in whaleboats and landed at Missiquoi Bay, northern Vermont, before proceeding into Lower Canada. The march proved difficult over rough terrain, and the rangers lost one-fourth of their manpower to disease during their approach. Worse, French patrols uncovered and destroyed their camouflaged whaleboats on the shore, depriving them of all waterborne transport. Undaunted by bad luck and the fact that the French were alerted and now out patrolling for him, Rogers summoned a war council that decided to proceed with the raid—followed by an overland withdrawal to the Connecticut River to New Hampshire. The raiders lacked sufficient supplies for such an overland egress, so messengers were sent ahead to have food supplies deposited there in advance.

The rangers stealthily approached their objective on the evening of October 5, 1759, and, with intelligence gathered from newly taken prisoners, Rogers learned that the French expected him to attack elsewhere. Accordingly, in the predawn darkness of October 6, the rangers stormed St. Francis, finding it completely unprepared for an attack. At a signal, they broke into houses and began the deadly work of retribution; men, women, and children were shot, bayoneted, or tomahawked, and all their dwellings were burned, deeds that the Indians had meted out to many a New England community. The rangers then gathered as much Indian food as possible and hastily withdrew up the St. Francis River to the site of present-day Sherbrooke. At that point, all supplies had been exhausted, so Rogers dispersed his men into smaller groups so that they could forage for food easier and avoid pursuit. Vengeful French and Indians did manage to catch and kill several parties of rangers, but Rogers's command constructed rafts, sailed downstream, and eventually straggled into Fort Four (Woodville, New Hampshire) on the Connecticut River. He arrived, only to find that anticipated supplies had not been delivered. Rounding up what food he could, Rogers led a relief expedition back up the river to rescue the survivors, who ultimately numbered 100. Despite the heavy loss of life, Rogers again demonstrated the utility of deep raiding, which, in this instance, ended the Abenaki threat to northern New England. Simply put, the destruction of St. Francis put all Indians settlements on notice that, no matter how remote from the English colonies, they could not escape the long arm of Rogers's rangers.

Rogers continued with his scouting and raiding work until Quebec finally fell to General James Wolfe in the autumn of 1759. The following year, France surrendered all its North American possessions to England, and Rogers's rangers took to whaleboats and paddled down the Great Lakes to take possession of numerous forts and settlements, including Detroit and Michilimackinac. Throughout 1763, Rogers was active in Chief Pontiac's rebellion against the British and returned that year by marching into Philadelphia, where he was greeted as a hero by throngs of admirers. This act concluded Rogers's military activities on behalf of the colonies, although in 1776 he briefly supported England during the Revolutionary War with a Loyalist unit, the Queen's Rangers before being dismissed outright. However, his efficacy in establishing what was the first clearly recognizable special forces unit in North America, replete with acts of tactical prowess, endurance, and daring, is unquestioned. Hereafter, the word, concept, and practice of "rangers" entered the American military lexicon for good.

Minutemen

The famous Minutemen, long viewed as quintessential American militia, actually pre-date their Revolutionary War counterparts by nearly a century. Although the precise term was not in use at the time, in 1645, Massachusetts Bay Colony militia was instructed to have 30 percent of all town levies specially trained to muster quickly in the event of a sudden military emergency. Over the ensuing decades, the process was continually refined, and up through the 1700s, various elite militia formations, variously known as "Snow Shoe Men" or "Picket Guards," arose along the Bay State's western and northern boundaries, largely to counter Indian raids from Canada. Minutemen thus evolved into a separate organization within the colony's standing defenses and was composed generally of young, fit men who were the strongest physically and among the best shots available. It was their stated purpose to muster and deploy first, eventually to be replaced by troops of the regular militia. By 1774, the concept and practice of recruiting Minutemen achieved its final form just prior to the outbreak of hostilities with Great Britain. That September, the Coercive Acts, which closed the port of Boston, coupled with a high-profile buildup of British regulars in that city, induced Whig (radical) leaders of Worcester to completely overhaul their militia force. Known Loyalist officers were unceremoniously expunged from the ranks, and more suitable, politically reliable company-grade leaders were elected in their stead. The seven Worcester regiments, each consisting of nine companies, were then directed to designate one-third of their numbers as Minutemen and prepare for armed musters within a minute's notice should the alarm be raised. On October 26, 1774, the extralegal First Massachusetts Provincial Congress, gathered in Cambridge, mandated that all towns and districts in the colony reorganize their militia along identical lines. Once the designated number of Minutemen was assigned, all ranks were to receive intense drilling and marks-manship at least three times a week; this, again, set them apart from regular levies. This is probably the only time in colonial history when the instruction and disciplining of militia forces was so dutifully implemented. Moreover, towns and districts were obliged to provide all necessary arms and ammunition to indigenous units, another first. Minutemen as a rule did not possess uniforms, and generally they mustered and fought in whatever civilian attire they wore at the time. And, not being equipped or trained with bayonets, they were expected to fight not shoulder to shoulder on open fields like their British counterparts but rather from behind trees, walls, and other cover and then to fall back. As colonial forma-tions go, the whole were comparatively well armed, well trained, and highly motivated and constituted the only first-reaction military force available to the Americans once fighting commenced. Thus, the romantic notion of colonial militiamen, ready to defend home and hearth with the trusty muskets kept securely over the fireplace, was not far from the prevail-ing reality. In concert with rapid dispatch riders of the "Sons of Liberty," Minutemen con-stituted a network of organized units that would greet the impending storm.

Defining Activity

Thomas Gage, former general and now royal governor of Massachusetts, had embarked on a series of military expeditions into the regions surrounding Boston. These armed forays had a twofold purpose: to seize all known arms caches belonging to the radicals and to intimidate the local population with the formidable appearance of British regulars. These crack forces, formally welcomed into the region as saviors during the wars with the French in Canada, were now derided by colonials as "Red Coats" or "lobster backs." Far from intimidating the populace, such activities only convinced many onlookers that an armed showdown with imperial authority was looming and that colonial military preparations should continue apace. On several occasions, large numbers of British troops deployed into the countryside and encountered equally large numbers of well-appointed militia that turned out to meet them. In this heated atmosphere, only a single incident was necessary to trigger a conflagration, and Minutemen were at the very heart of the spark.

On April 19, 1775, Gage dispatched Lieutenant Colonel William Smith with a picked force of 700 elite light infantry and grenadiers to seize 14 colonial cannon known to be sequestered at Concord. The column of Red Coats weathered a difficult night march as church bells pealed in the distance, announcing their approach, and at daybreak Smith's advanced forces confronted the single Minuteman company of Captain John Parker on Lexington Green. Parker's company of roughly 80 men had mustered and deployed, although hearts sank at the sight of British troops marching in precise company formations toward them. Not seeking a fight, Major John Pitcairn of the Royal Marines rode forward and brusquely ordered the rebels to disperse or else face the consequences. Parker wisely ordered his command to stand down and was in the act of withdrawing when a shot from nowhere suddenly rang out. The British, sensing that they were being attacked, fired several volleys at Parker's men, quickly dispersing them, killing eight and wounding nine. Several minutes lapsed before order could be restored, but the fuse had been lit, even as Smith's column resumed marching to Concord for military stores that had long been removed. Thwarted in his objective, Smith ordered his troops to begin their arduous 16-mile trek back to Boston, seemingly oblivious to "the shots heard 'round the world."

Word of the carnage at Lexington electrified the surrounding countryside, and Minutemen units, backed by increasing numbers of regular militia, began filtering into the region. American and Briton confronted each other warily at the south bridge over the Sudbury River as companies of Minutemen under Colonel James Barrett drew themselves up against a force of British light infantry. The Red Coats fired first this time and were driven off with a loss of three dead and eight wounded compared to an American tally of two killed and four wounded. The bloodshed served only to excite greater antipathy towards the British, and several hundred militia and Minutemen drew themselves up alongside the British avenue of march, peppering their column from behind trees and other cover. What followed was a 16-mile running fight with British regulars, deployed in company formation on the road, while the Americans fought Indian-style from the woods on either flank. In practice, the militia sought to catch their adversaries in a deadly crossfire, turning their march into a gauntlet of musketry. It should be noted that the British possessed several light infantry companies trained to fight is similar fashion, and, being equipped with bayonets, they severely punished any rebel unit unfortunate to tangle with them. But the bulk of combat occurred from behind walls and trees, and Smith's casualties continued to mount. By the time that a relief column of 1,000 reinforcements under Lord Hugh Percy arrived at Lexington, site of the original combat, nearly 3,800 Americans were engaged in battle. The British simply took their losses, closed ranks, and continued on in good order to Charlestown. It was a remarkable display of iron discipline for which the British army was justly renown. American musket fire itself had been unremarkable save for the number of bullets fired at British columns but did bring down 250 men killed and wounded, including 14 officers. Colonial losses, reduced by available cover, amounted to 49 dead and 97 wounded. Thus, the Minutemen performed admirably in combat with infantry openly regarded as the world's finest, and they induced an army, all too familiar with victory, into withdrawing. Massachusetts militia continued flocking to the colors outside Boston, where Gage and his regulars found themselves besieged. The ensuing Revolutionary War would ultimately be won by regular soldiers of the new Continental Army, trained, clothed, and equipped in a manner reminiscent of the British. Yet Minutemen of Massachusetts garner laurels for demonstrating to an incredulous world the American resolve to fight their oppressors, if in their own peculiar way. Their unexpectedly rapid mobilization, deployment in superior numbers, and unorthodox battlefield tactics turned what should have been a successful British raid into a near disaster.

American Riflemen

Victory over France in 1763 had precipitated a mass migration of colonists over the Appalachian Mountains and directly into the Indian territories beyond. These incursions were rightfully resented by the inhabitants and occasioned a long series of bloody frontier altercations. The settlers, far removed from centers of civilization, were forced to defend themselves by abandoning the conventional norms of warfare learned from the British and to adopt Indian-style fighting far more attuned with wilderness conditions. This time, the settlers were assisted by a new form of weapons technology, the rifle, which soon became synonymous with—if not the personification of—Indian fighting and frontier living itself. This long arm had been invented in Europe around the middle of the 17th century but had yet to gain widespread acceptance there militarily. A rifle was distinguished from other firearms of this period by possessing grooves spiraling down the length of its barrel. These grooves forced a rifle

Depiction of American riflemen from Colonel Daniel Morgan's *Provisional Rifle Corps at the Battle of Saratoga*, October 7, 1777. These unruly, sharpshooting individualists turned the tide of many a battle throughout the Revolutionary War. (U.S. Army Center of Military History)

ball to spin rapidly after leaving the muzzle, initiating a gyrostabilizing effect that kept it flying straight and true, in effect greatly improving its accuracy. The ball itself was usually inserted into the barrel wrapped in some kind of greased leather patch, which served to better trap propelling gases and allow it extra range during its flight. Compared to contemporary weapons, rifles could shoot farther and with better accuracy, up to 200 to 300 yards in the hands of an expert, but they took longer to load, and consequently the rate of fire was usually in the vicinity of one round per minute. Muskets, possessing inferior range and accuracy at a distance, could handily be discharged at a rate of three shots per minute, a distinct advantage in a stand-up firefight. And after the 1690s, muskets could also be fitted with a bayonet for close-in work, something that rifles could not. Riflemen, therefore, were at a distinct tactical disadvantage given their slow rates of fire and, in American practice, were usually assigned bodies of bayonet-carrying, musket-armed troops to protect them from enemy troops similarly armed.

In the second half of the 18th century, the weapon most clearly identified with the American frontier was the so-called Pennsylvania rifle, or "long rifle." It is commonly believed that the first of these weapons originated with German gunsmiths who had migrated to the frontiers of Pennsylvania, Virginia, and the Carolinas in the 1740s. The weapons quickly found favor among game hunters employed in the fur trade who could bring down quarry at greater ranges and with better success. Being crafted by hand, long rifles were usually inlaid with fine-fitted brass parts and elaborately engraved maple stocks verging on works of art. To conserve lead, they also fired a smaller ball than their musket

Daniel Morgan (1736–1802). Daniel Morgan was born in Hunterdon County, New Jersey, in 1736, fought in the French and Indian War, and in June 1775 he was commissioned a captain of elite riflemen. That fall he accompanied General Benedict Arnold on his ill-fated Quebec campaign and was captured. Once exchanged, he became colonel of 500 picked marksmen known as "Morgan's Rifles" and fought with distinction at the battles of Freeman's Farm and Bemis Heights in September–October 1777. His riflemen were instrumental at picking off British officers at long range and inducing General John Burgoyne to surrender. Morgan endured two years of poor health before transferring South as head of the "flying infantry," a combination of cavalry, light troops, and militia. With them he decisively beat the British at Cowpens on January 17, 1781, inflicting 800 casualties for a loss of 72 men. Ailing health again

Daniel Morgan was a skilled handler of rough-hewn frontier riflemen who scoffed at military discipline but were invaluable as crack shots. (Independence National Historical Park).

forced his retirement, although he took to the field again to help suppress the Whiskey Rebellion in 1794. Morgan, the leading exponent of rifle tactics during the Revolutionary War, died at Winchester, Virginia, on July 6, 1802.

counterparts, usually .36 to .45 caliber. These weapons had seen their combat debut throughout the recent French and Indian conflict, but it was not until the mass western migration following that conflict and the rise of a new generation of frontiersmen who had been handling these fabled weapons since their youth that it began assuming true military significance. Years of conflict with Indians and hunting game for a living produced a surplus of native sharpshooters who could hit targets at greater ranges than many of their contemporaries. This fact was not at all lost on the Continental Congress, then bent on creating the Continental Army, and on June 14, 1775, the first American units authorized were 10 companies of riflemen raised in Pennsylvania, Maryland, and Virginia. Volunteers were readily recruited, and on July 25, 1775, Captain Michael Doudel's rifle company proudly strode into American siege lines outside Boston. Having donned the leather hunting shirts and breeches of the frontier, they presented a distinctly unmilitary counterpoint to the rest of the American army and established them as a breed apart from most Continental troops. The sharpshooters had little chance to demonstrate their combat proclivities at Boston, but they did garner notoriety for insubordination and disregard for the stringent military etiquette of the day. On September 10, 1775, a group of disgruntled Pennsylvania riflemen, chafing under the regular military order imposed on them, briefly mutinied and were forcibly relocated from Cambridge to Prospect Hill. There, they were surrounded by local militia forces until they surrendered up their officers, who were tried for insubordination and fined. Once the latter were reunited with their unruly charges, the whole returned to their siege lines outside Boston, somewhat chastised and more compliant.

The first American officer to gain distinction while fighting with the unruly riflemen was Daniel Morgan, who commanded a company of rough-hewn Virginians outside Boston. He had been tasked by the Virginia House of Burgesses with recruiting and outfitting a company of 96 men, which he accomplished in only 10 days, and then marching them off to Boston. Twenty-one days later, hard slogging brought the riflemen to Massachusetts, where, by dint of expert demonstrations of marksmanship, they quickly acquired the name "Morgan's Sharpshooters." On September 25, 1775, Morgan's company was chosen by to accompany the expedition of Colonel Benedict Arnold to Quebec, and the ensuing wilderness trek would have daunted all but the most grizzled frontiersmen. Nonetheless, the bulk of riflemen survived this perilous trek and were present during the ill-fated assault against Montreal on December 31, 1775. Once General Richard Montgomery had been slain and Arnold was badly wounded, Morgan took command of the troops fighting inside the city until his men were overwhelmed by the defenders. Defeat did not impair his reputation, so, after being exchanged in January 1777, General George Washington entrusted him to raise a "Provisional Rifle Corps" of 500 picked men, each selected by Morgan himself. This force performed useful service throughout the British retreat across New Jersey, and that summer Morgan found himself reassigned to the Northern Department under General Horatio Gates.

Defining Activity

Throughout the late summer and early fall of 1777, a large British army under General John "Gentleman Johnny" Burgoyne was pressing down the Champlain Valley of northern New York in an attempt to separate New England from the rest of the colonies—and potentially end the rebellion. On September 19, 1775, the first major trial of strength between Burgoyne and Gates unfolded at Freeman's Farm (Saratoga), where Morgan's riflemen acted as the forward American force. Emerging from the deep forests, they encountered the advance troops of British General Simon Fraser, and expert shooting quickly dropped all the mounted officers leading them. As the struggle continued, the sharpshooters gave ground before a surging tide of British bayonets until Morgan rallied them on the lip of a woods to the left of the main battle, where they continued picking off officers and men for the rest of the day. Burgoyne's force, badly rattled, withdrew back to their previous position. They did not reemerge again until October 7, 1777, by attempting to turn the American left flank at Bemis Heights. Morgan again encountered light troops under General Frazier and this time broke them. Fraser, a distinct target on horseback, attempted rallying his men until General Arnold pointed him out to Morgan and specifically ordered a marksman to bring him down. Morgan personally selected rifleman Timothy Murphy for the task—it took three attempts at long range, but Fraser was toppled from his saddle, mortally wounded. The loss of so many men and irreplaceable officers forced Burgoyne to retreat a final time. Over the next few days, scouting and sniping parties dispatched by Morgan convinced British leadership that escape was impossible, so on October 17, 1777, Burgoyne yielded his sword up to

Gates at Saratoga. The American army as a whole distinguished itself in combat with Europe's finest soldiers, but Morgan's sharpshooters in particular contributed indelibly by virtue of skill at skirmishing and marksmanship in a heavily wooded environment and severely disrupting British battlefield command-and-control functions by claiming so many officers. This was the American rifleman's finest hour.

Riflemen continued serving in the Continental Army for the remainder of the war in the North, whereby commanders extolled their shooting skills and lamented their gross insubordination. They played similar roles in fighting through the South, particularly at the hard-fought encounter at King's Mountain, South Carolina, on October 7, 1780. Here a large body of 1,100 "over the mountain men" under Colonels William Campbell, Isaac Shelby, Benjamin Cleveland, and John Sevier trapped 900 Loyalists and rangers under Major Patrick Ferguson. Ferguson, a dashing light infantry leader, had previously invented a rapid-fire rifle that was perfectly functional, but the conservative British military hierarchy ignored it. Now his musket-armed troops found themselves in an uneven battle with sharpshooting frontier riflemen who decimated his force with highly accurate fire as they pressed up the slopes. In under an hour, Ferguson was killed and his force annihilated. Riflemen subsequently performed similar work at hard-fought encounters like Cowpens and Guilford Court House in 1781, where they shot down British officers and spontoon-carrying noncommissioned officers with alarming efficiency. However, in the final analysis, the American Revolution was won by musket-armed, bayonet-wielding Continentals who could resist the well-trained professionals of Great Britain in the field. The mythology surrounding riflemen and their seemingly surrealistic shooting ability has traditionally clouded this cold military fact. Nor were the British entirely unfamiliar with riflemen, having recruited several companies of German Jaegers to serve as mercenaries; these, like their American counterparts, served with distinction on many a battlefield. Nonetheless, shirtskin-clad riflemen formed an important part of the tactical matrix inherent in this conflict, and they remain proud purveyors of the special weapons and tactics associated with American long arms.

2nd Partisan Corps

Throughout most of the Revolutionary War, the mounted arm played a relatively small role because of the expense of maintaining horses, the difficulty of finding sufficient forage, and a general lack of open terrain on which to operate tactically. The Americans raised four regiments of Continental Cavalry, while the British shipped over two regiments of light dragoons, and most activities were restricted to traditional outpost work, such as scouting, screening, skirmishing, and occasionally raiding enemy supply convoys. As the war progressed, both sides adopted hybrid formations called "legions," which consisted of units comprised of half horsemen and half light infantry. These were regarded as elite fighting units and more tactically flexible than pure cavalry units because of their mixed nature. In April 1778, cavalry Lieutenant Colonel Henry Lee of Virginia, having distinguished himself on a number of occasions, was authorized to add two companies of horse and three companies of infantry to his existing cavalry company, creating what became known as "Lee's Legion." The men were all hand-picked volunteers enlisted for the duration of the war and subject to Lee's vigorous brand of oversight. First and foremost was his scrupulous attention paid to unit mounts, which were high-quality, thoroughbred stock—expensive to obtain and difficult to replace. Great emphasis was also placed on personal hygiene and cleanliness so that Lee's force remained among the healthiest units in the army. Special care was also toward disciplining the troops to act scrupulously toward civilians and private property and not estrange local populations through errant seizures. Finally, the commander, cognizant of the unit's elite status, placed a high premium on unit cohesion, morale, and esprit de corps and outfitted all ranks with smart green jackets and white doeskin breeches at his own expense. Lee himself was a fierce disciplinarian who continually trained and molded his unit to a fine edge. Consequently, Lee's Legion consistently displayed superior combat capabilities in several noted actions. Foremost among these was the successful raid on Paulus Hook, New Jersey, in August 1779, where the cavalry and infantry stormed a fortified British outpost at night and brought off 150 prisoners. Lee consequently became the only officer of regimental grade to receive a Congressional Gold Medal in this war, and he was allowed to enlarge his command into the new 2nd Partisan Corps as of February 1780. As in similar formations, the troopers could dismount and perform conventional battlefield maneuvers if required, but their real forte was raiding, reconnaissance, and intelligence gathering—all marks of an elite, special operations unit.

In 1780, the tide of American fortunes in the southern theater had soured disastrously with the fall of Charleston and the heavy defeat at Camden. Worse, a mounted force of Loyalist cavalry, the British Legion under the dashing and ruthless Lieutenant Colonel Banastre Tarleton, scoured the surrounding countryside, attacking and stamping out the last bands of organized resistance. General George Washington, unable to spare troops from the northern theater, dispatched Lee to North Carolina to help stabilize the situation and work in concert with surviving partisan bands. To that end, he enjoyed local autonomy in the field and could generally run the campaign as he saw fit. Lee, an aggressive partisan specialist with a knack for devising clever, unorthodox stratagems, took up the challenge and rode south to link up with rough-hewn men the likes of Brigadier General Francis Marion of "Swamp Fox" fame. In this manner, the elite dragoons and light troops of the legion provided badly needed stiffening to the sharpshooting but largely undisciplined militia. And, because each trooper was instructed to carry an infantryman on the saddle behind him, this force enjoyed greater mobility than many British opponents save for Tarleton's own legion. Lee, tasked with conducting partisan warfare, always maneuvered to avoid head-on clashes with British troops and worked in conjunction with guerillas to knock off isolated British outposts in the Carolina countryside. Harassing and threatening British rear-area security became something of a specialty, for more often than not, the 2nd Partisan Corps operated deep behind enemy lines with near impunity. Commencing with an aborted effort against Georgetown, South Carolina, on January 24, 1781, Lee's men facilitated the capture of Forts Watson, Motte, Granby, and Galphin in quick succession. The 2nd Partisan Corps was also designated to cover the withdrawal of General Nathaniel Greene's army across the Dan River into North Carolina, and at one point Lee charged Tarleton's vanguard, annihilating two entire troops. The troopers and light infantry subsequently performed yeoman service at the hard-fought actions of Guilford Court House, Hobkirk's Hill, and Eutaw Springs; while these were American defeats, the actions inflicted far more casualties on the British than they could afford to sustain. Lee remained personally disappointed that, while he continually skirmished with the green-clad Loyalist troopers of the British Legion, he and Tarleton never met face-to-face in open combat. Even so, his valuable work at reducing strong points reduced overall British influence in the Carolinas to the coast and facilitated the eventual Patriot victory. The 2nd Partisan Corps, quite possibly the best-trained and most tactically astute unit of the Continental Army, was unceremoniously disbanded at Winchester, Virginia, on November 15, 1783. Throughout its tenure in the South, it proved how well a regular unit could cooperate, share intelligence, and assist in combat operations with local, indigenous forces.

Defining Activity

The war in the southern theater was in many respects a civil war pitting large numbers of Patriots against Loyalist neighbors and, sometimes, family members. Internecine violence and vengeance between the warring factions was rife and shared little of the battlefield civilities practiced farther north. Prisoners, if taken at all, were routinely abused by captors, and this only fanned animosities following their pardon and release. The British Legion of Lieutenant Colonel Tarleton enjoyed a fearsome reputation for harshness toward captives, even by the region's standards, and was frequently accused of atrocities. The 2nd Partisan Corps also had a full share of this bloody work on February 25, 1781, after it attacked a farm in Orange County, North Carolina, where Tarelton's British Legion was reputedly encamped. The campsite was deserted, but the Americans did capture two British officers who alerted Lee to the fact that a large body of Loyalists was en route to join them at Butler's Plantation. This presented the quick-thinking American commander with an excellent opportunity for a *ruse de guerre*. British General Lord Cornwallis had been summoning Tory troops to join his main force to replenish light troops lost earlier at King's Mountain and Cowpens. Lee, knowing that his troops wore nearly the same green uniform as the British Legion, identified himself as Tarleton to two Loyalist militiamen who had stumbled into his camp and ordered them to have Pyle, encamped a short distance away, clear the road so that he could pass through. Once informed, Pyle quickly obliged, and in a few minutes, the 2nd Partisan Corps was trotting up to the militiamen with Lee in the front posing as the dashing Tarleton. Simultaneously, a force of 400 South Carolina partisans under General Andrew Pickens positioned itself in a woods behind the unsuspecting Tories, preparing to attack. Lee cordially approached in his imposing style, shook Pyle's hand, and began exchanging small talk when fighting suddenly broke out. Whether this was a deliberate signal has never been ascertained, but Lee's troopers fell on the Loyalists with a yell, killing 93 and wounding and scattering the rest; the badly wounded Pyle managed to escape by diving into a nearby pond. Throughout the engagement, many Loyalists shouted out that they were loyal to the king and were being mistakenly attacked. Lee was subsequently criticized by the British (and some Americans) for allowing a massacre to occur, but he insisted that if he had in fact planned a massacre, the remaining two-thirds of Pyle's men would have felt the sword as well. The so-called Pyle's Massacre proved of little consequence tactically, but psychologically it dampened local enthusiasm for the British cause, and despite Cornwallis's repeated entreaties, few Loyalists came forward to join his ranks in time for the major battle at Guilford Courthouse. Having disposed of Pyle, Lee and Pickens resumed their pursuit of Tarleton, who, in any event, received orders to rejoin the main British force and safely withdrew.

American Guerillas

In 1780, the British offensive strategy proffered by General Henry Clinton to conquer the southern colonies commenced brilliantly. Charleston, South Carolina, fell to a siege on

May 12, resulting in the capture of General Benjamin Lincoln and his army of 5,400 men. Subsequently, the British Legion, a ferocious Loyalist unit under Lieutenant Colonel Banastre Tarleton, began roaming the countryside, smashing the various militia bands it encountered. Worse still, on August 10, 1780, General Charles Cornwallis engaged and utterly routed a larger American force under General Horatio Gates at Camden completely dispersed his army of 4,000 men. British forces seemed on the verge of stamping out all organized resistance in the Carolinas, after which a destructive invasion of Virginia appeared imminent. Their success also precipitated a civil war throughout the region whereby long-oppressed Loyalists came to the fore and began striking back at their Patriot neighbors. In time, this civil strife became almost a war within a war whereby atrocities were common and prisoners few. Fortunately for the United States, small bands of guerillas under inspiring leaders such as Andrew Pickens, Thomas Sumter, and, above all, Francis Marion kept the Revolution alive through innumerable small-unit raids and ambushes. Outnumbered and frequently bested, they nonetheless proved relentless, and, thanks to pluck and excellent leadership, neither British lines of communication nor unwary Loyalist units were spared from sudden defeat and possible annihilation. Of the three leaders, Marion proved the most adept practitioner of irregular warfare, along with planning and executing military actions in concert with Continental Army units dispatched to assist him. Not only was he a consummate guerilla leader, but Marion also fully appreciated the value of cultivating local support for manpower and intelligence gathering. For this reason, his men were strictly disciplined to respect private property and pay for any supplies they requisitioned with receipts that could be redeemed after the war. Marion's men soon gained a mythic reputation for self-sufficiency, either growing their own food or subsisting off captured enemy supplies. Virtually everything they owned they carried on their backs, freeing them of fixed bases and rendering them extremely mobile and hard to pin down. Their only formal "base" was located deep in the Great Pee Dee Swamp, an area well known to smugglers in the region but generally inaccessible to the British.

Marion had seen combat in the Cherokee War of the 1760s and also served as a Continental Army officer during the British naval attack on Charleston, South Carolina, in 1776. He had broken his ankle just prior to the second and more successful British siege and was at home recuperating when the city surrendered. A slight man with a seemingly frail physique, Marion was an expert horseman who ate sparingly, seldom drank, and possessed legendary powers of endurance in the saddle. Still limping badly, he recruited a ragtag band of 20 fighters and tendered his service to General Horatio Gates. That haughty officer, eager to rid himself of these armed ragamuffins, simply sent them on an intelligence-gathering mission elsewhere. Marion consequently missed the disaster at Camden in August, then wasted no time demonstrating his flair for slashing guerilla attacks. On August 20, 1780, his men surprised a British detachment at Nelson's Ferry, taking 24 prisoners and freeing 150 American captives previously seized at Camden. On September 4, he followed this up with a devastating attack on a larger Loyalist force at Blue Savannah, where his 50 men ambushed their advanced guard, then pitched full tilt into the remainder, routing them. Marion's band continued their raiding activities through the Pee Dee region and so alarmed General Cornwallis that he ordered his anti-partisan expert, Lieutenant Colonel Tarleton, to track the elusive partisans down and destroy them.

Defining Activity

In terms of escape and evasion tactics, Marion proved himself the most artful dodger of the Revolutionary War. For several days throughout the month of November 1780, the green-clad British Legion of Tarleton rode hard at the heels of Marion's band, who kept retiring deeper and deeper into the surrounding swampland. The Americans waded through swamps, bogs, and woods as far as Benbow's Ferry on the Black River, where they felled trees across the only traversable road and prepared an ambush. Tarleton was not so easily fooled; his men plunged into the morass after Marion, riding 35 miles on a parallel course as far as Ox Swamp, an impassable body of water, before finally giving up. "As for this damn old Fox," Bloody Ban snorted, "the Devil himself could not catch him." Hence, the legend of the "Swamp Fox" was born. The mere act of surviving was important militarily, and the rag-tag partisans lived to fight another day. Before departing, the British Legion attacked and burned the residences of several suspected partisans, behavior that undoubtedly swelled resistance ranks.

Marion subsequently resumed his small-scale warfare against British lines of communications, and in January 1781, he was reinforced by Lieutenant Colonel Henry Lee's 2nd Partisan Corps. To the surprise of many, the homespun Marion and the aristocratic Lee got along famously, and together they proved the bane of British and Loyalist outposts deep in the countryside, including Forts Watson and Motte. On August 31, 1781, his men rode to the rescue of a small American detachment besieged by superior numbers of British and Loyalists; his prompt action led to the Continental Congress voting him their thanks. Marion then cooperated with the forces of General Nathaniel Greene at Eutaw Springs on September 8, 1781, and, though a defeat, his force performed well. He finally mustered out on December 14, 1782, and returned to his plantation, having been a major factor in upending the potentially victorious British strategy to seize the South. Marion's activities pinned down British manpower and resources far out of proportion to his actual numbers and bought valuable time for the shattered Continental Army to regroup. His astonishing grasp of irregular tactics renders him one of the fathers of modern guerilla warfare, and present-day U.S. Army Rangers consider him one of their doctrinal forebears.

The *Turtle*

The United States was generally unprepared for war with Great Britain after independence was declared in July 1776, but there was no shortage of a celebrated quality soon hailed as "Yankee ingenuity." That year, David Bushnell, a noted inventor and tinkerer, produced the world's first functional submarine at Old Saybrook, Connecticut. This primitive yet ingenious device, which he christened the *Turtle*, consisted of two large oak staves caulked together, then bound by iron bands and tarred until it was waterproof. It was six feet high and seven feet long, large enough to fit one human operator who peered out over the water through a win-dowed conning tower. The technology employed included two hand-cranked screw propellers for propulsion, numerous values and ballast weights to control depth, two brass tubes for ventilation (which granted the pilot a roughly 30-minute supply of air underwater), and a compass and a barometer rimmed with Fox Fire (phosphate) to light the instruments. For offensive purposes, the *Turtle* carried a detachable 200-pound "mine" (explosive charge) attached to an outside drill; the theory was that the submarine would station itself beneath an enemy vessel, bore directly into the hull, attach and release the charge, and then withdraw to safety before it exploded. This small yet complicated device seemingly possessed the capacity for undermining the unquestioned naval superiority of the Royal Navy by destroying warships without warning. After successfully demonstrating the device to General Israel Putnam, Bushnell was authorized to mount an attack on the British fleet presently blockading New York City.

Defining Activity

On the evening of September 7, 1776, army Sergeant Ezra Lee piloted the *Turtle* from its sanctuary and toward HMS *Eagle*, the flagship of Admiral Richard Howe, then moored off Governor's Island. Lee, hastily trained for the task because of Bushnell's illness, experienced difficulty controlling the *Turtle* in a strong current, overshot his target, and labored strenuously to return back into position. Once this was achieved, he commenced boring into the *Eagle*'s underside, only to discover that he could not penetrate that vessel's copper sheathing. With daylight approaching, Ezra backed away from his target, released the mine, and returned back safely before the latter item detonated with a tremendous explosion. No damage had been inflicted on the enemy, but Admiral Howe, alarmed over what became condemned by the British as "infernal devices," hoisted his anchor and ordered the fleet repositioned farther out to sea. The *Turtle* was subsequently lost on the Hudson River as New York was being evacuated, but it is a direct precursor of small, highly specialized SEAL delivery vehicles employed in present times.

U.S. Regiment of Riflemen

Despite the near-mythic reputation garnered by American riflemen during the Revolutionary War, they disappeared from the military inventory save for numerous state formations. Rifle companies briefly resurrected as part of the Legion system under Major General Anthony Wayne in 1794. These units provided organic long-range firepower to the regular, musket-armed infantry; however, following the victory at Fallen Timbers, they were abolished by Congress and lapsed back into obscurity. It was not until the wake of the egregious British attack on the American frigate USS *Chesapeake* in 1807 that President Thomas Jefferson authorized the first standing rifle formation in U.S. Army history. On April 12, 1808, Congress sanctioned the creation of the U.S. Regiment of Riflemen, which was organized in 10 companies of 68 privates each. It was envisioned from the outset as an elite formation specialization in forest warfare, skirmishing, and ambushing, as evinced by its distinct uniform of a green, yellow-fringed topcoat and the black collars and cuffs denoting elite status. Moreover, the unit was designated to be armed with the Harpers Ferry Model 1803, a short weapon of Jaeger derivation that was ruggedly constructed and could throw a .54-caliber ball accurately out to 250 yards. This was the first such specialized infantry weapon in U.S. military history, and several preproduction models had previously been issued to the Lewis and Clark Expedition in 1803–1804. Republican Party politics, however, played a major role in the selection of the riflemen's senior officers. Consequently Alexander Smyth, a politician from Virginia, and William Dune, a Philadelphia newspaper editor, became colonel and lieutenant colonel, respectively. The two men despised each other and performed poorly as leaders, so by the advent of the War of 1812, they had been replaced by army veterans Thomas Adams Smith and George W. Sevier.

The Regiment of Riflemen was the first formal United States special forces unit because of its unconventional uniform, weapons, and tactics. It proved so successful during the War of 1812 that three more rifle regiments were raised. (U.S. Army Center of Military History)

Befitting its status as an elite unit, the Regiment of Riflemen proved to be one of a handful of American units capable of successfully tangling with their more veteran British adversaries with reasonable prospects of success. The unit experienced its baptism of fire on November 11, 1811, when a detachment, armed with muskets, performed competently at the Battle of Tippecanoe, Indiana Territory, suffering 1 and wounding 10. In the spring of 1812, several companies under then-Major Smith marched from Georgia into Spanish East Florida to partake of the so-called Patriot War against Spain. Unfortunately, Smith, even when backed by some local militia, lacked sufficient manpower to formally besiege Spanish troops at heavily fortified St. Augustine, so his riflemen established an informal blockade. He was consequently harassed by Spanish gunboats, Seminoles, and escaped African American slaves, and in a heavy exchange fought on October 27, 1812, the riflemen sustained 3 dead and 10 wounded. By the spring of 1813, the bulk of Smith's forces had been transferred from Florida to Canada to fight in the War of 1812. Well trained, well armed, and well led, they were one of the most tactically formidable units deployed by the American side in this conflict.

The first company of riflemen to distinguish themselves in combat belonged to a celebrated leader, Captain Benjamin Forsyth, who gained infamy as the war's most notorious raider. Forsyth, whose men constituted the first regular forces garrisoned in northern New York, directed a successful foray on September 21, 1812, when they crossed by boat from Sackets Harbor into Canada and successfully stormed the village of Gananoque. In a quick action, Forsyth lost 1 dead and 10 wounded while killing 10 and capturing valuable stores of gunpowder and flints. Forsyth then transferred his activities to Ogdensburg, astride the St. Lawrence River, and continued being a nuisance by storming into the settlement of Elizabethtown on February 7, 1813. Many prisoners and muskets stocks, previously captured from the Americans at Detroit, were among the booty hauled back to base. Forsyth's actions made him a distinct threat to already tenuous British supply lines, so a strong riposte was planned. On February 22, 1813, a column of 800 regulars and militia under Lieutenant Colonel George MacDonnell suddenly attacked Ogdensburg and drove his rifle company out with losses of 3 killed and 17 wounded; British losses were heavier—6 dead and 48 wounded—but they had rid themselves of a troublesome and opportunistic freebooter.

Forsyth's company withdrew back to Sackets Harbor, where, two months later, they were designated the shock troops during General Zebulon M. Pike's amphibious descent on York (Toronto) on April 27, 1813. The riflemen paddled ashore, positioned themselves on a sand bank, and then shot the fine grenadier company of the 8th (King's Own) Regiment to pieces at a cost of 7 dead and 17 wounded. Pike was killed in a British magazine explosion, then Forsyth's riflemen disgraced themselves by freeing political prisoners from jail, then helping them plunder and burn the town. In light of his reputation as a peerless fighter, no action was taken against either him or his men. On May 27, 1813, Forsyth again spearheaded the amphibious attack against Fort George, Upper Canada, inflicting numerous casualties on the defenders at a cost of two dead and one wounded. Part of his command subsequently accompanied Brigadier Generals John Chandler and William H. Winder on a foray to Stoney Creek, where, on June 6, 1813, an entire rifle picket was captured after falling asleep in the pews of a church. Forsyth himself remained active in the vicinity of Fort George, frequently skirmishing with enemy light troops and Indians. On August 16, 1813, his riflemen sprung an effective ambush that killed 15 Mohawks, captured 13, in exchange for 2 wounded. Within weeks, Forsyth's command boarded boats and sailed down the St. Lawrence River as part of General James Wilkinson's offensive against Montreal. On November 11, 1813, he led them ashore at Hoople's Creek, Canada, and completely dispersed a large body of militia without loss. That same day, Wilkinson's main force was soundly thrashed at Crysler's Farm, and the riflemen, who wintered at French Mills, New York, endured a period of deprivation and suffering with the rest of the army.

The riflemen also enjoyed tactical successes under other commanders. On October 11, 1813, Colonel Isaac Clark, 11th U.S. Infantry, led a detachment of 102 riflemen on a raid up Lake Champlain against smugglers operating near Massequoi Village (Seignory of St. Armand), Lower Canada. After landing unobserved, Clark personally led a charge that netted 74 militia captives and a mountain of contraband goods at a cost of 2 wounded. Congress, dissatisfied with the conduct of the war thus far, was understandably impressed by the uniform excellent performance of the riflemen, and on February 10, 1814, they authorized three more rifle regiments, numbered consecutively, so that the original Regiment of Riflemen was redesignated the 1st Regiment of Riflemen. Several veteran companies of the latter were present at the aborted attack on March 30, 1814, on LaColle Mill, Lower Canada, where one rifleman was killed and seven wounded. Other companies arrived at Sackets Harbor under Major Daniel Appling, and on May 30, 1814, his men scored one of the regiment's greatest successes by ambushing a large detachment of British sailors and Royal Marines at Sandy Creek, New York, capturing two gunboats and five barges. British casualties in this lopsided affair totaled 19 dead, 28 wounded, and 133 captured against a tally of 1 rifleman wounded. In this engagement, the riflemen were also assisted by 130 Oneida Indians under Lieutenant Ryan, and these had to be restrained from massacring the prisoners.

Forsyth, meanwhile, resumed his raiding activities in the Champlain Valley, where, on June 24, 1814, his green jackets beat off an attack by 200 British light troops and Indians at Odelltown, New York. The dashing commander's luck finally deserted him at the same locale four days later when, having been ordered to lure larger British forces into an ambush, he disobeyed, unwisely stood his ground, and died in a skirmish. His men, grieved by their loss, wasted little time exacting revenge. On August 10, 1814, a rifle detachment under Lieutenant Bennett Riley ambushed Captain Joseph St. Valier Mallioux of the Frontier Light Infantry near Champlain Village, mortally wounding and capturing him. For all their reputation as unruly, fast-fingered malcontents, the riflemen remained formidable adversaries in the art of bush fighting and marksmanship.

Defining Activity

In the wake of the bloody standoff at Lundy's Lane on July 25, 1814, the Left Division under Major General Jacob Brown fell back to Fort Erie at the confluence of the Niagara River and Lake Erie and dug in. Within weeks, they were invested by superior British forces under Lieutenant General Gordon Drummond, who sought to avoid the necessity of a prolonged siege and potentially costly assault by a stratagem. In the early morning of August 3, 1814, he dispatched 700 picked light troops under Lieutenant Colonel John G. P. Tucker to cross the Niagara River, march south, and quickly capture the settlement of Buffalo. This move, if successful, would cut the American garrison at Fort Erie off from its supply line, and it would have no alternative but to surrender or starve. It so happened that Buffalo was then defended by a detachment of 240 men of the 1st and 4th Rifle Regiments under Major Ludowick Morgan and Captain Jonathan Kearsley, two accomplished officers. Morgan closely observed British movements across the river and correctly deduced that they were preparing to cross that evening. Accordingly, he spent the entire day constructing a low-lying breastwork on the south bank of Conjocta Creek, the bridge over which the British would have to pass. He then rounded up his men, paraded them in full view of the enemy, and marched back to Buffalo. Once out of sight, Morgan ordered his men to take a hasty meal and marched them secretly back to their breastwork below the creek. Accordingly, that night Tucker's elite force rowed across the Niagara River, landed, and made their way toward Buffalo in the predawn darkness. They approached the bridge over Conjocta Creek and began crossing, only to discover that Morgan had removed all planks from the lower half. Once the British column convulsed to a halt, Morgan blew his whistle, and his riflemen, exercising superb fire discipline, cut loose with a devastating volley that dropped the front platoons into the stream. The anxious British ran back and fired wildly at the opposite bank, but the riflemen crouched behind their breastwork and let the storm pass harmlessly overhead. Tucker then ordered another charge across the bridge; Morgan allowed them to approach to within close range and blew his whistle, and the riflemen expertly shot down every Red Coat in view. Unable to proceed frontally and his flanking party moving downstream thwarted by another party of riflemen and New York militia, Tucker conceded the action and ordered his command back to their boats. British losses had been 12 dead and 21 wounded to an American tally of 2 killed and 8 wounded. Conjocta Creek was the riflemen's best-conducted action of the war and a clear a strategic triumph for the United States, for, had Drummond's ploy succeeded, Fort Erie would have been isolated and forced to surrender. From a planning and execution standpoint, the battle certainly highlights the superior training, weapons, and marksmanship of riflemen over musket-armed opponents in controlled circumstances. The British now had little choice but to conduct a formal siege of the American fort, an enterprise for which they were ill prepared.

As the siege of Fort Erie unfolded, there commenced a *petit guerre* of outposts in the adjoining woods between the opposing camps whereby the riflemen found themselves in almost daily conflict with the elite Glengarry Fencibles, a green-clad, musket-armed light infantry unit recruited from Canadians. The competing marksmen routinely shot each other to ribbons over the ensuing weeks, and on August 13, 1814, Major Morgan, the "Hero of Conjocta," fell in a heavy skirmish, with three riflemen killed and six wounded. In the early morning of August 15, 1814, the riflemen were active in helping to repulse Drummond's surprise assault on the camp, with an additional three wounded. Costly skirmishing outside the fort resumed until September 17, 1814, when General Jacob Brown, having recovered from his Lundy's Lane wounds, led a violent sortie against the British siege works. The riflemen sustained a further 11 dead and 19 wounded, including Colonel James Gibson, 4th Rifles, the highest-ranking army fatality of the entire campaign, but the attack succeeded in wrecking the British batteries.

Other rifle companies were conspicuously engaged in actions around Plattsburgh, New York. On September 6, Major Appling led a detachment of 100 marksmen alongside the 29th U.S. Infantry of Major John Ellis Wool at Beekmantown Road. In the ensuing skirmish against the vanguard of a huge British invasion force, the Americans managed to inflict 55 casualties and kill Brevet Lieutenant Colonel Willington of the 3rd (Buffs) Regiment. A week later, Appling's men fought with distinction at the September 11, 1814, battle of Plattsburgh, where they successfully repelled several British attempts to force their way over the Saranac River. The final action of the riflemen occurred not far from where its first protracted operations began. On January 13, 1815, Captain Abraham A. Massias found that a British squadron was bearing down on his position at Point Petre, Georgia. Massias had only his company of riflemen and a single company of the 43rd U.S. Infantry to oppose them, and he was quickly overrun by 700 Royal Marines and men of the 2nd West India Regiment. This final action concluded the wartime activities of these skilled marksmen, who were consolidated back into a single Regiment of Riflemen in May 1815.

The postwar career of the riflemen is also worthy of note, for it performed actively throughout the early stages of western settlement and exploration. In 1815, Colonel Smith led them to St. Louis, Missouri, which served as a base camp for several extended frontier forays. By 1817, his riflemen had helped establish Fort Armstrong (on the Mississippi River), Fort Crawford (Prairie du Chien), and Fort Howard (Green Bay). Another detachment under Major William Bradford ventured south along the Arkansas River to establish Fort Smith (in honor of their colonel) in present-day Arkansas. In 1819, several companies constituted the Yellowstone Expedition of Colonel Henry Atkinson, which culminated in the founding of Fort Atkinson in present-day Nebraska. The troops performed useful service in all these capacities, but on March 2, 1821, Congress abolished the regiment to reduce military expenditures. In its 13-year existence, the Regiment of Riflemen, from the standpoint of weapons, distinctive attire, and effectiveness in unconventional warfare, functioned as the nation's first special forces unit. It certainly set the bar high for all similar units that followed for the remainder of the century.

Regiment of Light Artillery

The development and perfection of horse artillery had been under way in Europe since the middle of the 17th century, but that arm had made tremendous strides in the wake of the wars of the French Revolution and Napoleon. Unlike traditional artillery batteries, which consisted of ponderous field pieces and gun crews that walked alongside at an infantryman's pace, horse, or "flying," artillery batteries consisted of smaller-caliber cannon, usually 6-pounders towed by two or three pairs of horses, with all personnel likewise mounted. Thus situated, horse artillery were extremely mobile and usually moved and fought in conjunction with cavalry formations—and with frequent deadly effect. The approach of massed cavalry in a battlefield situation invariably forced infantry to form densely packed "squares" for protection, and these made inviting targets for the cannoneers who unlimbered their pieces at close range and plied the helpless soldiers with canister rounds and grapeshot. Naturally, such close-in fighting required high degrees of training and élan to be successful, so horse artillery units were usually regarded as picked, elite units within the scheme of Napoleonic armies. The French, which pioneered and perfected the latest tactics, were generally attributed as fielding Europe's finest horse artillery, although splendidly mounted batteries of Great Britain's Royal Artillery were also highly capable on the battlefield and any movements up to it.

The Regiment of Light Artillery was an elite formation of the War of 1812 and performed effectively as either artillery or infantry on several occasions. (Center for Military History)

In the United States, awareness of elite horse artillery units and tactics first manifested in 1800 when Thaddeus Kosciusko's treatise *Maneuvers of Horse Artillery* began appearing in English-language editions. No action was taken, however, until April 8, 1808, when Secretary of War Henry Dearborn, as part of a general rearmament program, authorized the Regiment of Light Artillery with a strength of 10 companies. However, in the false military economy characteristic of the Jeffersonian administration, no funding had been provided for either horses or field officers. It was not until Captain George Peter gained appointment as the regiment's senior officer that Dearborn requested funding for one ammunition wagon, a light horse wagon capable of carrying four men, and a small train of horses so that a properly mounted company could deploy. Moreover, in recognition of their designated elite status in the nascent U.S. Army, the 26 men who were selected received new uniforms with blue coatees and black regimental collars and cuffs denoting their status. Peter trained and equipped his charge as best he could, and on July 4, 1808, he dazzled onlookers by marching his two-gun detachment from Baltimore to Washington, D.C., at a speed of six miles per hour. By the fall, Peter had recruited and trained an entire company of light artillery, and he was ordered to New Orleans, via Pittsburgh, as part of the garrison. He completed his trek in 1809, partly overland and partly loaded onto flatboats, and reported his satisfaction at how well his model unit had performed. However, a flinty new secretary of war, William Eustis, was upset at the expense of outfitting an entire regiment of horse artillery, so he ordered Peter to sell off his mounts. Consequently, when the gunners went on maneuvers through the Louisiana mud, they were forced to pull their cannon by ropes. Peter was so distraught over matters that he resigned his commission out of hand and left the service.

It was not until the very cusp of renewed conflict with England in the spring of 1812 that the Regiment of Light Artillery began fleshing out its emaciated ranks. Regimental-grade officers were also finally appointed, and Moses Porter, the army's senior artillerist, became colonel on March 12, 1812. Horses proved almost impossible to come by, so of 10 companies authorized, only around half were ever fully mounted, while the rest were, by necessity, equipped and trained to fight in small detachments as infantry. Nonetheless, the Regiment of Light Artillery was involved in hostilities from the outset and acquired a measure of distinction that belied its relatively small numbers. In the fall of 1812, two companies had mustered at the Niagara frontier under Captains James Gibson and John N. McIntosh, where they served under Lieutenant Colonel John R. Fenwick, himself a Marine Corps veteran. The artillerists, crossing the Niagara River as infantry on October 13, 1812, lost heavily in the defeat at Queenston Heights, where Fenwick, severely wounded, was captured along with 40 of his men. Shortly afterward, the survivors were bolstered by the arrival of Captain Luther Leonard's company, which garrisoned Fort Niagara over the winter. Several other detachments continued gathering strength outside Albany, New York, under Major Abraham Eustis, nephew of the secretary of war. Previously, Luther's company saw action in the November 22, 1812, artillery exchange between Forts Niagara and George, and on November 28, another detachment ferried over to Squaw Island on the Niagara River to assist the failed crossing of Brigadier General Alexander Smyth.

The following spring found men of the Regiment of Light Artillery closely engaged at the capture of York (Toronto) on April 27, 1813, under Major Eustis, while the company of Captain Andrew McDowell fought at Fort George on May 27, 1813, with one killed and one injured. McDowell's men subsequently accompanied the army's advance to Stoney Creek, Upper Canada, where, on June 6, 1813, an additional three were killed and three wounded. This same detachment later passed into captivity at Beaver Dams on June 24, 1813, losing 2 officers and 33 men as prisoners, along with a 12-pounder and a 6-pounder cannon. Several smaller detachments also fought bravely at Sackets Harbor on May 29, 1813, helping to repel a determined British amphibious attack. That September, Colonel Porter arrived with additional companies, and the whole accompanied General James Wilkinson's main force down the St. Lawrence River during his Montreal campaign. Here they formed part of Brigadier Jacob Brown's advance brigade and were deployed mostly as elite infantry. When required, however, they were to also supply the bulk of artillerists for the expedition.

Defining Activity

On November 1, 1813, Brown's brigade debarked at French Creek (Clayton), New York, to engage a force of two Royal Navy brigs, two schooners, and eight gunboats commanded by Captain William H. Mulcaster, a skillful commander. The British vessels worked themselves close to shore in order to damage or possibly capture as many of the American transports as possible covered by their own heavy cannon. The only effective resistance mounted was by three heavy 18-pounder cannon commanded by Captain Robert H. McPherson of the Regiment of Light Artillery. His men, nominally trained to handle much smaller pieces, worked the larger ordnance with adroitness and skill. Mulcaster's vessels made no headway inland under their unerring fire, and he called off the action at sundown. Early the next day, the British resumed the action, only this time McPherson pelted them with a continual stream of red-hot shot—very dangerous to wooden vessels. Once again, the British flotilla proved unable to close with the beached transports, and Mulcaster finally withdrew with a loss of one dead and four wounded on the approach of American warships. Good shooting by these elite gunners spared Wilkinson's expedition the potential loss of valuable transports necessary to continue their sojourn down the St. Lawrence River.

On November 10, 1813, Wilkinson's main force landed on the Canadian shore of the St. Lawrence to engage a sizable force of British infantry who had been shadowing them. The companies of Captains Leonard and MacPherson were then gradually engaged in the hard-fought action at Crysler's Farm on November 11, 1813, during which the horse team of Lieutenant William W. Smith (U.S. Military Academy, 1809) was disabled by musket fire. The British called on Smith to surrender his piece, but he refused and fought on until being mortally wounded. The Regiment of Light Artillery then withdrew back to the flotilla with the main army and wintered at French Mills in northern New York before proceeding to Plattsburgh. In the spring of 1814, several companies of the Light Artillery marched to Sackets Harbor while a detachment was present during the aborted attack on LaColle Mill, Lower Canada, on March 30, 1814, suffering five wounded. The gunners, working in ankle-deep mud and snow, managed to push a 12-pounder and a 5-1/2-inch howitzer to within 200 yards of the stone mill, only to watch their fire glance harmlessly off. Major McPherson, exposing himself recklessly, received a brevet promotion to lieutenant colonel in consequence. Captain George W. Melvin's company subsequently left Sackets Harbor for Buffalo, New York, but was recalled on May 5–6, 1814, with four companies of the 3rd Artillery to Oswego, where it greatly distinguished itself against a British amphibious attack. On May 13, 1814, a detachment of several guns under Lieutenant Arthur W. Thornton, manning a battery of 12-pounders mounted on naval carriages, repelled Royal Navy captain Daniel Pring's squadron at Otter Creek, Vermont. Captain Luther's company also saw action at the Battle of Plattsburgh on September 11, 1814, killing three and wounding one. In the final weeks of active campaigning, the bulk of the regiment, organized as an infantry battalion, accompanied Major General George Izard on his controversial march from Sackets Harbor to the Niagara frontier but saw no additional combat. By war's end, the regiment had relocated back to Greenbush Cantonment outside Albany, where it absorbed the bulk of the 15th, 26th, 30th, 31st, and 45th Infantries into its ranks. The Regiment of Light Artillery continued on as an elite formation under Colonel Porter for six more years until Congress abolished it in a cost-cutting measure on June 1, 1821. While it was almost never deployed in its assigned role as "flying artillery," the Regiment of Light Artillery was among the best-fighting and tactically flexible formations fielded during the War of 1812. Military multi-taskers, they performed equally well as artillerists and infantry at a time when few American formations were competent at either.

The First Long-Range Reconnaissance

The U.S. Army enjoyed a long association with frontier exploration dating back to the Lewis and Clark Expedition of 1803–1804 and the forays of Captain Zebulon M. Pike shortly thereafter. The objective of these missions was to ascertain the topography, climate, and inhabitants of all land acquired in the Louisiana Purchase, which literally doubled the size of the republic. Such scientific expeditions, usually headed by military officers, continued up through the 1830s and were led by men of note such as Major Stephen H. Long and Captain Benjamin Bonneville. However, by the 1840s, the political pressures of Manifest Destiny and desirability of western territory belonging to Mexico changed the nature of these endeavors from exploration to clandestine military reconnaissance. The most adept practitioner in this regard was Major John C. Fremont, himself a noted explorer. In 1846, Fremont was ordered to California, ostensibly for the purpose of establishing overland routes to that region but actually to assess Mexican defenses and stir up English-speaking immigrants against the provincial government. This endeavor, known as the Third Fremont Expedition, began at St. Louis, Missouri, on June 1, 1845, when Fremont assembled 55 men—a composite group from the Corps of Topographical Engineers, some grizzled frontiersmen and scouts (including Kit Carson), and a handful of Indians—to the Far West. Their stated purpose was to find and map the source of the Arkansas River, but on arriving in Arkansas, the party inexplicably turned west, crossed the Rocky Mountains, and entered the Sacramento Valley in early 1846. Fremont, judging Mexican manpower and defenses inadequate, agitated among American settlers for armed resistance if war commenced with Mexico. His none-too-discrete activities were brought to the attention of Mexican General Jose Castro, who, backed by superior numbers of troops, promptly ordered the interlopers out of California. Fremont consequently fled with his small command to Lake Klamath in southern Oregon to await the outcome of events. On May 9, 1846, he received a clandestine visitor in the form of Marine Corps Lieutenant Archibald H. Gillespie, who transmitted verbal instructions from President James K. Polk to foment a California insurrection.

Defining Activity

On June 14, 1846, American settlers had captured Sonoma, ran their "Bear Flag" up the nearest pole, and proclaimed the new California Republic. Fremont arrived there on July 4 and

Lieutenant John C. Fremont led the first long-range reconnaissance patrol in American history by scouting out Mexican positions in California. In military parlance, he functioned as the first "Pathfinder." (California State Military Museum)

John C. Fremont (1813–1890). John Charles Fremont was born in Savannah, Georgia, and he acquired his second lieutenant's commission in the Topographical Engineers in July 1838. He accompanied several western exploring expeditions, and in 1841 he married the daughter of U.S. Senator Thomas Hart Benton of Missouri, who served as a political benefactor. Between 1842 and 1849, Fremont personally conducted four expeditions of the American West of which one, undertaken in 1845, had distinctly military overtones. That year, he arrived in northern California, apparently acting under secret orders, and began fomenting an uprising against Mexican authority. He was ordered out of the region and relocated to Oregon, where he conferred with Marine Corps Lieutenant Archibald Gillespie about the coming conquest of California. Once the Mexican War erupted in 1846, he raised the so-called California Battalion from the indigenous population and assisted Commodore Robert F. Stockton to capture Los Angeles. After the Mexicans surrendered on January 13, 1847, Stockton appointed him governor of California, but Fremont was arrested and court-martialed by General Stephen W. Kearny for failing to step down when ordered. He left the military and pursued politics, becoming the first Republican presidential candidate in 1856, and lost to Democrat James Buchanan. During the Civil War, Fremont held the rank of major general and gained a notorious reputation for insubordination and incompetence. He died in New York City on July 13, 1890, almost penniless. However, Fremont's military reconnaissance of the western frontier greatly advanced the cause of Manifest Destiny. Moreover, it garnered him the nickname "Pathfinder," a term still used to denote elite special forces scouts.

began organizing a military force from the indigenous population, the so-called California Battalion. This consisted of four companies of riflemen numbering 224 men (including 34 Native Americans), with himself functioning as "colonel" and Gillespie installed as his "adjutant." In true American militia tradition, the men proceeded to elect their own officers from the ranks and the military members of Fremont's expedition. A few days later, Commodore Robert F. Stockton, commanding the Pacific Squadron anchored at Monterey, lent official recognition to the battalion, with Fremont officially installed as brevet lieutenant

colonel and Gillespie his major. Since American forces throughout the region were threadbare and amounted to whatever parties of sailors and marines Stockton could spare from
his vessels, Fremont's efforts provided the rebellion an infusion of badly needed organized
manpower. On July 26, 1846, Fremont marched 160 men from his provisional force onto
the sloop USS *Cyane* under Captain Samuel F. Du Pont and sailed south for the conquest
of San Diego. Three days later, the soldiers, assisted by a complement of sailors and marines,
captured the town bloodlessly. Fremont posited 40 soldiers there as a garrison, then sailed
north to Los Angeles with the balance. This settlement also capitulated without a shot being
fired, and an additional 50 men under Gillespie stayed behind to maintain security. Fremont
departed again for northern California until September, when word reached him of a major
revolt in Los Angeles. He continued enlarging the California Battalion to 450 men through
additional recruits, then marched to San Juan Bautista before rejoining the fleet. Los Angeles
was then recaptured by Fremont's men, marines and sailors under Stockton, and newly
arrived dragoons under Brigadier General Stephen W. Kearny, and Fremont was detailed
to seize the settlement of Santa Barbara. He accomplished this on December 24, 1846, by a
forced march over the Santa Ynez Mountains in a driving rainstorm. Many horse and mules
were lost as a consequence, along with some cannon, but the objective was secured without a
struggle. Fremont hastily departed for Los Angeles, where, on January 13, 1847, he accepted
the surrender of General Andreas Pico by signing the Treaty of Cahuenga. Given slender
military resources on hand, the indigenous "California Battalion" certainly weighed heavily
in the ultimate American triumph. In light of his contributions to the conquest of California,
a vast area subjugated on a literal shoestring, Fremont was appointed military governor by
Stockton. Unfortunately, this promotion led him to a direct confrontation with Kearny, who
outranked him and possessed his own orders appointing himself governor. When Fremont
stubbornly and unwisely refused to yield to his superior, he was removed to Fort Leavenworth, Kansas, court-martialed, and found guilty of insubordination. He subsequently
resigned from service rather than endure a mild military rebuke. However, Fremont's long-
established reputation as "The Pathfinder" remained secure, and this precise term remains
in usage to present times and denotes elite reconnaissance personnel within the U.S. Army.

Regiment of Voltigeurs and Foot Riflemen

The onset of war with Mexico in 1846 found the U.S. military establishment lacking in sufficient numbers of troops for the task, so Congress expanded the regular infantry establishment
by eight additional regiments on February 11, 1847. Among these was the Regiment of
Voltigeurs and Foot Riflemen, conceived as a distinctly different kind of formation. They
derived their name from the famous French *voltigeurs* ("vaulters") of the Napoleonic Wars;
these were companies of picked light infantry assigned to each infantry battalion. In recognition of their elite status, these troops wore yellow collars and cuffs on their blue jackets and a
large yellow plume atop their shakos. Their American counterparts were envisioned along
these same lines and were trained to fight either in conventional formations or spread out into
skirmish lines. Moreover, they were armed with the new .54-caliber Model 1841 rifle, being
the first generation of percussion-cap firearms to dispense with traditional flintlocks used to
fire the weapon. Such arrangements made them more reliable than previous firearms, and
as rifled weapons, they enjoyed greater range and accuracy than standard muskets issued to
infantry. In light of the elite status as skirmishers, the men were also accorded smart gray

On September 12, 1847, the Regiment of Voltigeurs particularly distinguished themselves during the storming of Chapultepec. Despite their demonstrated flexibility as either skirmishers or line infantry, they were disbanded immediately after the Mexican War. (Library of Congress)

uniforms, although perpetual shortages of the prescribed cloth meant that they were usually adorned in the same standard blue wool of their infantry counterparts. However, their coat buttons were adorned with a metal "V" for "Voltigeurs."

The Regiment of Voltigeurs and Foot Riflemen were conceived as a standard 10-company formation of 1,104 men and 47 officers, and recruited primarily from Georgia, Kentucky, Maryland, Mississippi, Pennsylvania, and Virginia. The unit was also originally intended as a hybrid formation, with half mounted and the other half deploying on foot. In practice, the foot soldiers were supposed to march rapidly behind the horsemen to assist them but, because the assigned horses never materialized, the regiment fulfilled its service life as pure infantry. On paper, the unit was also supposed to include a company of light mountain howitzers and a rocket battery, but these weapons, while authorized, never accompanied it into the field. In March 1847, the bulk of *voltigeurs* sailed from Savannah, Georgia, and New Orleans, Louisiana, under Colonel Timothy P. Andrews, a former army paymaster. They arrived at Vera Cruz, Mexico, soon after and joined the army of General Winfield Scott as it besieged that Mexican strong point. The *voltigeurs* subsequently accompanied Scott's advance against Mexico City, performing useful service in the battles of Contreras, Churubusco, and Molino del Rey, prior to the assault on the enemy capital itself.

Defining Activity

On September 13, 1847, Scott directed American forces to attack strong Mexican positions around Chapultepec, the capital's last line of defense. At this time, the *voltigeurs* were assigned to the brigade of Brigadier General George Cadwalader, whose task was to storm the formidable south wall of the local castle. A two-battalion assault was planned with Colonel Andrews leading the center column of several companies, while four additional companies accompanied the right assault column under Lieutenant Colonel Joseph E. Johnston. The attack, executed in the face of heavy fire from entrenched Mexican defenders, proved difficult and costly, but the *voltigeurs* seized a sandbag redan, forced their way into the compound, clambered up the walls, and planted their regimental colors in triumph. Losses had been severe, but Johnston's men had all but destroyed the Mexican San Blas battalion obstructing their path. The following day, General Antonio Lopez de Santa

Anna surrendered, and the war ended. The *voltigeurs* remained on garrison duty in the capital for several more months, then sailed off for Fort McHenry in Baltimore, Maryland. The regiment concluded its 18-month service by being formally disbanded on August 25, 1848. Their tenure in uniform had been brief but successful and again demonstrated the unique American proclivity for raising, equipping, and deploying rifle-armed specialty troops in an age when smoothbore muskets and artillery still dominated the battlefield. A decade lapsed, however, before the U.S. Army fielded another sharpshooting specialist infantry unit to carry on the tradition of elite American riflemen.

Regiment of Mounted Riflemen

Having acquired a vast wilderness tract through the Louisiana Purchase in 1803, it took over four decades before Congress decided to raise a unit specifically designated to patrol overland routes to the Pacific coast, which became known as the Oregon Trail. Increasing waves of migration to the region had led to sporadic outbreaks of violence with Native Americans living in that region, and in a rare fit of relevance, funding was appropriated to construct a chain of forts stretching from the Missouri River and the Columbia River along with a specialist sharpshooter unit to patrol all points in between. Because most hostile forces fought on horseback, it made little sense to dispatch foot sloggers to oppose them, so the new entity enjoyed the same mobility as potential adversaries. Thus was born the Regiment of Mounted Riflemen on May 19, 1846, with Persifor F. Smith installed as colonel and the noted explorer John C. Fremont designated as its lieutenant colonel. The outfit initially consisted of 10 companies of 64 privates each, although the following year the total was increased to 70, giving it parity in manpower with the two existing dragoon regiments. Companies were recruited in Pennsylvania, Maryland, Virginia, Texas, Tennessee, Kentucky, Ohio, Indiana, Illinois, and Missouri. As its name implies, it was also armed with the new Model 1841 rifle, a new percussion design also issued to the new Regiment of Voltigeurs and Foot Riflemen. This weapon, in addition to be shorter and lighter than muskets issued to the infantry and the carbines wielded by the dragoons, enjoyed the tactical advantages of greater range and accuracy. However, to also fulfill its capacity as a cavalry regiment, troopers were also issued the heavy Model 1840 dragoon saber ("Old Wristbreaker") and the equally cumbersome Colt pistol, a revolutionary design sporting a revolving cylinder that held five rounds. The riflemen were clad in typical dragoon fashion with blue forage caps, jackets, and trousers, although the later article bore a black stripe down its outer seem, edged in yellow cord, as a mark of distinction. In October 1846, Jefferson Barracks in St. Louis, Missouri, was selected as its headquarters while companies were raised and trained at Columbus, Ohio, and Fort McHenry, Maryland. The majority of troops finally mustered at the barracks by year's end, but instead of riding off to Oregon as planned, the men were co-opted for the war against Mexico as part of General Winfield Scott's army.

The Regiment of Mounted Riflemen deployed to New Orleans, Louisiana, for shipment to Mexico, but en route a storm washed all its horses overboard, and consequently it fought on foot as infantry. They accompanied Scott's brilliant overland drive against Mexico City and participated in several heavy actions under Major William Wing Loring. In general, the regiment was usually broken up into small detachments and used for reconnaissance purposes. Gradually, sufficient Mexican horses were acquired to outfit two complete companies, but the unit continued to performing dismounted. On September 12–13, 1847, various companies fought with distinction at the storming of Chapultepec, a decisive American victory that ended the war. Here Lieutenant B. S. Roberts led the advance storming party, becoming the first officer to raise the American flag on the walls of the enemy bastion. Mexico City was occupied shortly thereafter, and Robert's colors were prominently displayed over the National Palace. General Scott, conducting a post-battle review of his victorious army, noticed the flag, rode up to the regiment, and declared, "Brave rifles! Veterans! You have been baptized in fire and blood and have come out steel!" On July 7, 1848, newly promoted Lieutenant Colonel Loring, who had lost an arm in the fighting, embarked his command at Vera Cruz for New Orleans and began the long ride back to Jefferson Barracks. Consistent with its status as an elite combat formation, the Regiment of Mounted Riflemen had its full share of 18 engagements for which 14 officers received brevet promotions for heroism and 11 enlisted men were likewise singled out for advancement. The troopers lost 4 officers and had 45 men killed in action, 13 officers and 180 were wounded, and a further 1 officer and 240 men succumbed to disease.

Defining Activity

The Regiment of Mounted Riflemen arrived at Jefferson Barracks on July 24, 1848, at which time all volunteers serving in its ranks were discharged. The emaciated unit continued on as part of the postwar establishment, but it remained at Fort Leavenworth, Kansas, for nearly a year awaiting new recruits. It was not until May 10, 1849, that the Regiment of Mounted Riflemen finally departed Kansas and commenced its 2,000-mile trek to Oregon under Lieutenant Colonel Loring. Major General David Twiggs, commanding the Sixth Military District, arrived to personally see them off, for this was the first army unit to venture up the entire length of the Oregon Trail. Loring's entire train consisted on 700 horses and men, 1,200 mules, and 170 wagons. The march of 2,500 miles, unfortunately, was plagued by sickness, and desertion rates skyrocketed in Oregon once information arrived that gold had been discovered in California. With common laborers averaging between $5 and $10 per day, roughly 100 deserters departed en masse up the Willamette Valley 160 miles south of Oregon City, and Colonel Loring set off in hot pursuit, assisted by militia led by Governor Joseph Lane. The majority were caught and rounded up before reaching California, but 35 of these subsequently built a canoe and escaped again. The regiment, consisting of young, rough-hewn men of little breeding, was also particularly obnoxious toward the settlers whom they were assigned to protect. Consequently, after Loring's command transferred from Oregon City to Fort Vancouver, enraged locals torched the building they occupied, undoubtedly to prevent his troops from ever returning. In May 1851, the remainder of the regiment rode back down the Oregon Trail to the Jefferson Barracks, where it was reorganized for the third time in five years. In January 1852, the regiment transferred to Texas, where it fought several skirmishes with Comanche raiders until 1856, then relocated again to New Mexico for additional combat against the Apache. The Regiment of Mounted Riflemen continued patrolling the prairies of the West with little incident until August 3, 1861, when it was renamed the 3rd U.S. Cavalry (today's 3rd Armored Cavalry Regiment). On the cusp of the Civil War, several ranking officers, all southern born (including Loring), handed in their commission to go fight for the Confederacy, but not a single enlisted man left the ranks. The "Brave Rifles" are currently stationed at Fort Hood, Texas.

Texas Rangers

The United States enjoys traditions of partisan/ranger forces dating back to the French and Indian War. These units may or may not have enjoyed direct relationships with the standing military establishment, but they were by and large the creatures of various states. In the instance of Texas, then a Mexican province, mounted ranger units were raised in 1826 before that territory was even associated with the United States. Settlers under Sam Houston, distrusting Mexican authorities to adequately police the frontier and protect settlements from marauding Comanches and banditos, took it on themselves to provide their own armed forces. By 1835, with the rebellion against Mexico in full bloom, local authorities again met and authorized a formal corps of "Texas Rangers" for the purpose of patrolling the Indian frontier in small detachments. In tried-and-tested tradition, these "standing irregulars" were recruited

Captain Samuel Walker of the Texas Rangers for whom the six-shot "Walker Colt" revolving pistol was named. His fellow Texans performed invaluable service as irregular scouts and raiders. (Library of Congress)

from among the hardy denizens of the frontier with demonstrated skills in scouting, tracking, riding, and marksmanship. Such a crowd usually resisted imposition of anything even vaguely resembling military discipline, but they could be kept in line by the presence of a forceful individual who was elected their captain. Irregulars by nature, the rangers wore no uniforms, furnished their own horses and weapons, and also lacked an assigned surgeon or a unit flag. Once independence was won, the rangers continued patrolling the borders of Texas against Indian and Mexican raiders with small bands of well-mounted, heavily armed men. Nominally outnumbered by their adversaries, they nonetheless acquired a reputation for dash and ruthlessness in battle. As the product of gruff frontier conditions, they usually meted out rough justice to all who opposed them. By 1840, the rangers had successfully turned back Comanche raiders in a number of bloody fights, such as Council House and Plum Creek, and they were sought by the U.S. government to serve as scouts after the Mexican War commenced in 1846. The high-spirited Texans, positing themselves as superior to all others in terms of scouting and fighting, remained beholden to no one. Moreover, possessed of an extreme egalitarian outlook, men and officers alike addressed each other on a first-name basis, dressed and ate the same, and shared all deprivation and prizes occasioned in the course of their dangerous duties.

No sooner had the army of General Zachary Taylor began its southward march into Mexican territory in the spring of 1846 than it was beset by swarms of Mexican irregulars (rancheros). These excellent horsemen, armed with lances and lassos (the latter a most dangerous weapon in the hands of expert horsemen), continuously attacked American communication and supply routes, killed their prisoners, and then vanished into the countryside or among the local population. Their success prompted Taylor to recruit several companies of Texas Rangers that April, tasking them with antipartisan warfare and deep reconnaissance missions across the rugged Mexican landscape. The company of Captain Samuel H. Walker excelled at both activities, although they proved as brutal in dealing with Mexicans as the rancheros had been with the invaders. Walker also distinguished himself on two valuable missions as a courier through enemy-infested country, winning a regular army commission in the elite Regiment of Mounted Riflemen. In this capacity, he subsequently ventured to Connecticut to visit arms manufacturer Samuel Colt and helped develop the new six-shot .44-caliber "Walker Colt." This powerful handheld weapon thereafter served as a standard sidearm of the Texas Rangers. During his absence, the Texans, brought up to two complete mounted regiments, fought ferociously in the capture of Monterey on September 20–24, 1846, the approach to which had been expertly scouted by ranger Captain Ben McCulloch. McCulloch performed even more critical work for Taylor in February 1847 after the Polk administration had removed most regular forces from the latter's army to support the amphibious invasion of General Winfield Scott. Taylor now possessed only 4,650 men, mostly volunteers, and he ordered McCulloch to scout below Saltillo to ascertain enemy intentions. On February 20, 1846, the rangers uncovered the army of General Antonio Lopez de Santa Anna, 20,000 strong, heading north to attack and crush Taylor's weakened force. Galloping hard back to headquarters with this intelligence, Taylor was given two days' notice to place his men in stronger defensive positions at Buena Vista, where they decisively repulsed Santa Anna's attack on February 22–23.

Other ranger detachments accompanied Scott's overland drive onto Mexico City, where they guarded his 250-mile supply route to Veracruz from guerillas. On November 23, 1847, the company commanded by Captain Jacob Roberts encountered a force of 200 Mexican lancers in a mountain pass south of Puebla. Despite the odds, the rangers held their ground, blazing away with their Colt pistols, and dropped an estimated 50 lancers before the later finally retreated. After Mexico City capitulated and was occupied, a single ranger strayed into a part of town known as "Cutthroat," where he was murdered. Angry rangers then rode into town, Colts drawn, and departed only after 80 Mexicans died in retaliation. Such brutal behavior resulted in the moniker Los Diablos Tejanos ("Texan Devils") from the inhabitants. Generally, the Mexicans were terrified by their wild-eyed demeanor and disconcerting behavior.

Defining Activity

The Treaty of Guadalupe Hidalgo in January 1848 ended the Mexican War, but many Mexican guerilla bands chose to fight on against the occupiers. One particularly ruthless group, headed by Padre Celestino Jarauta, had successfully dodged the rangers for several months until the detachment under Captain Jack Hays learned that they were ensconced at the village of Zacualtipan. On February 25, 1848, Lane's 250 rangers, accompanied by 130 dragoons under Major William H. Polk (brother of the president), stealthily approached their quarry and attacked at daybreak. The 450 rancheros and lancers, completely surprised, fought back viciously but were overwhelmed by blazing Colt pistols in house-to-house fighting. Jarauta's band had finally been shattered, with 150 killed and 50 taken prisoner. One Texan died of his wounds. This was the final encounter of the Mexican War, and it highlights in bold relief the mobility, firepower, and shock action of the Texas Rangers in combat. The battle also underscored the utter ruthlessness and contempt that Texans held for their adversaries, indicative of strong racial overtones. Their tendency toward brutality may have clouded an otherwise sterling reputation for combat, but, in terms of unconventional warfare techniques and overall success, the jaunty, undisciplined Texans had few peers. During the Civil War, the Texas Rangers fought with distinction for the Confederacy and were disbanded afterward. The rough-and-tumble nature of the western frontier, however, resulted in their speedy resurrection, this time for the purpose of law enforcement and public safety. They continue in these fields to the present day.

U.S. Sharpshooters

By the onset of the Civil War in 1861, the majority of infantry on either side had been equipped with muzzle-loading rifled ordnance of one kind or another. While restricted to roughly two aimed shots per minute, much as the muskets they replaced, these represented a quantum increase in terms of range and lethality over previous military technology. However, high casualty rates were further abetted by the infantry tactics of the day, which still dictated massed, Napoleonic-style formations to attack and defend positions. An important exception to this was the presence of elite companies or even battalions of picked sharpshooters, usually deployed in extended order or to take advantage of the natural cover afforded by the local terrain. Crack shots abounded in either army, and the overwhelming majority of these belonged to state formations with the important exception of the U.S. Sharpshooters, which were trained, armed, and uniformed in the manner of an elite regular unit. The sharpshooters were the brainchild of Hiram Berdan, a successful and wealthy inventor who, since 1846, was also renowned as the best marksman in the nation. Possessing an inventive mind along with a flair for showmanship and egregious self-promotion, Berdan visited Washington, D.C., in the early days of the war and had prevailed on Lieutenant General Winfield Scott, the army's senior commander, to allow him to raise a entire regiment of sharpshooters for the U.S. Army. Scott subsequently convinced President Abraham Lincoln to agree to the scheme, and on June 14, 1861, the 1st U.S. Sharpshooters were authorized as a standard, 10-company infantry formation. Unlike the majority of infantry units in the Civil War that were raised from a single state, the sharpshooters recruited marksmen from New York, Vermont, Michigan, New Hampshire, Wisconsin, and Minnesota. Prospective members were subject to an

Colonel Hiram Berdan, a master of self-promotion, failed to distinguish himself in combat, but his two battalions were probably the best overall marksmen and skirmishers of the Civil War. (Library of Congress)

The 1st and 2nd Regiments of U.S. Sharpshooters are believed to have inflicted more Confederate casualties than any other Union formation. Their distinctive green uniforms effectively blended in with most terrain, while the breech-loading Spencer rifles they toted were extremely accurate at long range. (Library of Congress)

extremely stringent qualification test whereby they had to fire 10 shots at a target 150 yards distant, with no shot farther than five inches from the bull's-eye. Telescopic sights were not permitted, but so many qualified shooters stepped forward that on September 28, 1861, the 2nd U.S. Sharpshooter Battalion was organized with Berdan functioning as colonel of both. Consistent with their elite status, the sharpshooters received uniforms of green jackets, pants, and caps with the brass insignia "USSS," enclosed by wreaths, proudly displayed. Beyond cutting a rather splashy appearance, this attire also served as practical camouflage while fighting in forests. The men were also rigorously drilled to deploy tactically as skirmishers and not in massed lines like the blue-clad infantry. Given their commander's flamboyance and the excellent reputation acquired on many a hard-fought field, both battalions became publicly known by as "Berdan's Sharpshooters" or simply the "Green Coats."

What made the sharpshooters such a deadly unit was their ordnance. Berdan had pushed to have his men armed with the breech-loading Sharps rifles of .52 caliber, a highly accurate weapon capable of loosing 10 rounds a minute. Loaded from the rear, it was an ideal weapon for firing from a prone position, minimizing the shooter to counterfire. However, General James W. Ripley, the army's chief ordnance officer, viewed such weapons as wasting expensive ammunition and sought to issue standard muzzle-loading ordnance to the sharpshooters. A temporary compromise was arranged, whereby the men agreed to accept a five-shot Colt revolving rifled carbines for the time being until sufficient numbers of Sharps rifles had been manufactured. The Colt had been in service since 1855 but had an alarming tendency of shooting off all five rounds from its cylinder. The men, having been promised with Sharps rifles and unhappy with the Colt, clung to their own personal telescoped weapons for several months until the threat of wholesale mutiny induced Secretary of War Edwin M. Stanton to expedite deliveries. The Sharps were finally issued the following spring. Berdan, ever mindful of cultivating favorable publicity, wasted no time establishing a "camp of instruction" for his marksmen. Politicians, dignitaries, news-hungry journalists, and even President Lincoln were all invited to behold the dazzling shooting prowess of his men. Many walked away astonished, but Berdan, having recruited what was probably the most rowdy set of ruffians in the Union army, could scarcely keep them under control. One reason was his perpetual absence from the army to meet with congressmen and manufacturers for none-too-subtle pitches for various inventions and patents belonging to him. Berdan's own lack of military experience was also a consistent sore point with the men: having ordered gray overcoats for his command in winter, these were quickly discarded for making the sharpshooters appear dressed like Confederates.

The sharpshooters proved themselves a garrulous sort, and their commander seemed preoccupied with advancing his personal fortunes, but in combat they were one of the most effective units in the Union army. Tactically, they seldom deployed in formations larger than two or four companies, and they marched ahead of the main line as skirmishers and snipers across a broad front. Battlefield orders were also issued in true light infantry fashion by calls of the bugle. The sharpshooters received their baptism by fire in the Peninsula Campaign of 1862, where they piled up Confederates in heavy engagements stretching from Yorktown to Malvern Hill. During the later engagement, four companies under Lieutenant Colonel William Y. Ripley occupied a ravine and bloodily repelled a larger force of Confederates maneuvering to surround them. As the rebels retreated back to the wood line, a battery—the Richmond Howitzers—rode up the battle line, intending to pound the sharpshooters into submission. Instead, a single volley dropped all the horses and half the crews, sending the rest scampering to the rear. Southerners, who boasted of being the best marksmen on the continent, soon came to respect and dread these green-coated apparitions as they hid behind trees, rocks, and whatever cover was available, blazing away with unerring accuracy and at great range. They repeated their performance at Antietam in the fall, shooting an enemy regiment opposing them to pieces in short order, and quickly secured that front of the bloody battlefield. Subsequent actions at Fredericksburg and Chancellorsville confirmed further their abilities, although Berdan was consistently criticized for repeated absences from the regiment, invariably where the fighting was heaviest.

Defining Activity

On July 2, 1863, the battle of Gettysburg found the 1st Sharpshooters attached to the 3rd Corps of Major General Dan Sickles and deployed just north of the hills called the Round Tops. Anxious as to what the Confederates were doing along the southern edge of Seminary Ridge, Sickles ordered Berdan to take four depleted companies of 100 men, accompanied by 200 soldiers of the 3rd Maine Infantry, on a scout to the front. As Berdan advanced into Pitzer's Wood, he ran headlong into General Cadmus Wilcox's brigade, which promptly attacked with the 10th and 11th Alabama Regiments. The sharpshooters, taking themselves behind trees, blazed away at the exposed southerners for 20 minutes, assisted by the Maine troops, before yielding to superior numbers. They suffered 19 casualties while inflicting 56 on the southerners. Sickles was thus alerted that the division of General A. P. Hill was deploying in the vicinity, and he carefully advanced his own men to Emmitsburg Road to thwart any possible flanking moves. Moreover, during this brief but hot action, the sharpshooters fired off an average of 90 rounds per man, inducing an astonished General Wilcox to report that he had encountered two regiments of sharpshooters instead of four companies. Farther west, the 2nd Sharpshooters deployed closer to Little Round Top near Emmitsburg Road to prevent its capture. At length, they engaged the 4th Texas Infantry of General James Longstreet's corps, wounding both its colonel and the lieutenant colonel near Devil's Den before falling back on the south face of Big Round Top. There they espied the Confederate brigade of Colonel William C. Oates en route to his famous and fateful joust with Colonel Joshua Chamberlain's 20th Maine on Little Round Top and gunned down the lieutenant colonel of the 15th Alabama. Oates felt that he could not leave the sharpshooters in his rear as he outflanked the Union line, so he charged and drove them up and over the crest of the hill, buying valuable time for Chamberlain to prepare his wafer-thin defenses, which held. On July 3, 1863, the sharpshooters were instructed to pry all remaining rebel marksmen still holding out in Devil's Den, accomplishing this by taking several prisoners in the process. In terms of affecting battlefield results, albeit on a very small scale, Gettysburg is probably the regiment's finest moment.

   In the fall of 1863, Berdan, unhappy with his lack of official recognition, left his sharpshooters for good and was succeeded by various subordinates. The unit continued giving good service at Mine Run in 1863, the Wilderness and Spotsylvania in May 1864, and outside the trenches of Petersburg for several months. During the latter engagement, shooting heavy telescoped rifles from prepared sniping positions, the sharpshooters became the bane of southern sentinels, who felt the sting of bullets fired from so far off that they usually failed to hear the rifle's report. The end of the sharpshooters proved anticlimactic, however, and expiring enlistments did more harm to regimental manpower than disease or combat. When the original three-year term expired in August 1864, many of the 1st U.S. Sharpshooters starting going home that fall, and the unit mustered out. In February 1865, the War Department ordered the remaining skeletal companies of the 2nd U.S. Sharpshooters likewise broken up and distributed to other formations. Of the 2,570 men mustered into the elite battalions, 300 had died in combat with another 1,000 wounded, an attrition rate of nearly 40 percent. Fortunately, the unit could also boast, with veracity, that they had killed and wounded more Confederates than any other unit in the Union army.

Andrews Raid of 1862

Not all special forces operations involve uniformed troops, and throughout the Civil War, espionage and sabotage activities were frequently conducted by secret service agents of either government. These could be active or former military personnel, highly trained and motivated to achieve their objectives in question. For the North, the most memorable attempt at a deep, "behind-the-lines" raid by disguised soldiers was the Andrews raid, more famously known as the "Great Locomotive Chase." That railways and trains figured prominently in the scheme is indicative of how valuable that technology had become to the war effort. The story began in April 1862, when Union General Ormsby Mitchel was preparing to advance from Nashville, Tennessee, to Huntsville, Alabama. That done, his forces would then sweep east along the railroad lines to nearby Chattanooga, a vital rail hub in the western Confederacy. To accomplish this objective, he solicited the services of 31-year-old James J. Andrews of Kentucky, a civilian railroad engineer and something of a personal daredevil. In the previous March, Andrews led a small group of Union operatives south on a mission to sabotage the Memphis & Charleston and Western & Atlantic Railroads by stealing a locomotive, racing north, and burning the bridges over the Chickamauga and Tennessee Rivers. The mission was aborted in Atlanta, Georgia, once a key conspirator, a Georgian Union sympathizer, failed to materialize as planned. Unperturbed, Andrews endorsed a similar scheme calculated to assist General Ormsby during his approach to Chattanooga. He proposed taking a party of 23 Union soldiers, all former railroad employees from the 2nd, 21st, and 33rd Ohio Infantry Regiments, behind southern lines. There they would seize a locomotive belonging to the Western & Atlantic Railroad, run it north, and burn every bridge approaching Chattanooga to obstruct Confederate reinforcements as Mitchel attacked. The mission was perilous in the extreme, for the soldiers, if captured in civilian garb, would be tried and executed as spies. But the overall scheme seemed plausible enough, so Mitchel authorized its undertaking.

Defining Activity

Andrews and his men began filtering into enemy territory in groups of two and three and were scheduled to arrive at Marietta, Georgia, no latter than midnight on April 10. However, incessant rains slowed their arrival, and they rendezvoused a day later, that Friday. Two of their number were missing, having been impressed into the Confederate army at Jasper, Tennessee. Despite these setbacks, Andrews determined to carry on with the raid, so on the morning of Saturday, April 12, the men boarded a train at Marietta and departed 6:00 a.m. for Big Shanty (Kennesaw, Georgia), where they would steal the engine. This site was chosen because it lacked a telegraph office and southerners would be slowed in alerting authorities of the theft. The train pulled into the station, the majority of passengers debarked for breakfast, and then Andrews and his men commandeered the locomotive called "*The General*" while others quietly decoupled the passenger cars. The raiders then applied steam and chugged out of the station, much to the consternation of onlookers. One of these, conductor William Fuller, immediately dispatched a rider to the closest telegraph station to report the theft while he and two others ran on foot to Moon' Station. There they grabbed a handcar and began backtracking to Big Shanty to organize a chase. The southerners worked their handcars as far as Etowah, where they absconded with the mine engine *Yonah* and took off after the *General*.

Andrews had failed to anticipate that Fuller's party would react as swiftly to the *General*'s theft as they did. Their dogged pursuit forced the raiders to limit any attempts to inflict damage to the rail line and to concentrate instead on simply evading capture. As a precaution, he stopped the engine and sabotaged some of the rail line to delay any pursuing trains, cut some telegraphs lines, and then resumed the trek north. Unfortunately, recent rains soaked many of the wooden bridges, and they would not burn. Fuller, meanwhile, stopped at Kingston Station and requisitioned a faster engine, the *William R. Smith*, and resumed the chase. He had to stop after encountering some damaged track, then hailed and a freight train coming down the opposite track and reversed it all the way back to Adairsville. There Fuller dropped all the passenger cars and took off with the engine *Texas*, running it backward to avoid the time-consuming process of turning it around. Andrews's men, meanwhile, continually tossed wooden railroad ties onto the track to delay any pursuers. The *General*, however, was running low on firewood and water for its boilers, and it finally creaked to a halt 18 miles south of Chattanooga, which, in any event, remained in southern hands. Mitchel canceled his offensive at the last moment, so the entire effort was for naught. Anderson's escapade lasted 90 miles, and no sooner did they abandon the engine than Fuller and the *Texas* roared up to claim it, and a massive manhunt began throughout the countryside. Over the next two weeks, all 21 of the raiders were apprehended and imprisoned in Atlanta.

On May 31, 1862, Andrews was tried and condemned to hang for spying. The following evening, he and another raider staged a bold escape from prison, but they were caught and executed a week later. Seven more Union soldiers went to the gallows on June 18, but the remaining 14 staged another escape attempt, and eight of these reached the safety of Union lines. In March 1863, Confederate authorities exchanged the remaining six captives for six of their own. Secretary of War Edwin M. Stanton awarded all participants the new Congressional Medal of Honor, becoming the first recipients. James Andrews, the guiding spirit behind the daring raid that bears his name, was a civilian and thus ineligible for the award. In 1887, his body was relocated from Georgia to the national military cemetery in Chattanooga, Tennessee, adorned with a miniature bronze replica of the *General*, the train that he and his men rode to immortality.

Blazer's Independent Scouts

By August 1864, the embarrassing success of Confederate guerillas throughout northern Virginia and the Shenandoah Valley prompted Major General George Crook, 8th Corps commander, to authorize formation of the Union's first dedicated antipartisan unit, Blazer's Independent Scouts. Commanded by Captain Richard Blazer, it was drawn from soldiers of the 5th, 9th, 13th and 14th West Virginia Infantries; the 2nd West Virginia Cavalry; and the 12th, 23rd, 34th, and 36th Ohio Infantries. This was intended as a hard-riding, straight-shooting unit, being especially equipped with highly accurate, rapid-fire Spencer carbines. Their mission was twofold but essential: to protect lengthening Union supply lines as Major General Philip H. Sheridan pressed farther down the Shenandoah Valley and engage and destroy roving bands of Confederate rangers, especially those commanded by Colonel John S. Mosby, the "Gray Ghost." Blazer's Independent Union Scouts, as they were informally known, used their superior firepower to engage and defeat several rebel bands at Myer's Ford and Myerstown. The scouts, who never numbered more than 100, were soon divided into two companies operating on both sides of the Blue Ridge Mountains—and to good effect. In early November, Blazer managed to surprise and rout a ranger detachment under Captain R. P. Mountjoy, one of Mosby's most trusted subordinates, near Berry's Ferry. The Gray Ghost consequently resolved to put an end to this harassment and detached Major A. E. Richards with two companies of rangers to destroy Blazer's command.

Defining Activity

On November 18, 1864, Richards set a trap for Blazer near Myerstown with his 100 rangers. The 62 Federals, having learned of their presence in town, rode up, dismounted, and began a long-range firefight from the wood line favoring their Spencer rifles. Union reconnaissance was apparently poor, for Blazer was apparently unaware that he opposed no mere raiding party but rather a unit twice his size. Suddenly, Richards ordered part of his command, arrayed along a fence, to fall back suddenly as if retreating. Blazer, eager to close with his elusive foe, gave the signal to remount and charge the rebels. As the scouts rode forward into an open field, they were suddenly assailed by Confederates hiding on either flank whose close-range fire with heavy Colt pistols emptied many Union saddles. The scouts were routed, and Blazer, having failed to rally them, was clubbed from his horse and captured. Only 29 surviving scouts made it back to Union lines, and the unit was disbanded the following January. So even a unit as good as Captain Blazer's was capable of having a very bad day indeed. Their defeat left Mosby at liberty to conduct his infamous raids until the end of the war.

John S. Mosby (1833–1916). John Singleton Mosby was born in Edgemont, Virginia, on December 6, 1833, and he practiced law until the Civil War commenced in 1861. He joined the Confederate cavalry and performed competently as a scout for General J. E. B. Stuart through February 1863, after which he became a lieutenant of a mounted ranger company. Mosby, by dint of intelligent and highly innovative tactics, quickly established himself as the scourge of the Shenandoah Valley. His men scouted intensely, hit select targets suddenly, and then dispersed and regrouped at a preas-signed locations. More often than not, the raiders simply blended in with the local population until another raid was scheduled. His most notorious deed happened on March 9, 1863, when, with only 29 men, Mosby stole past Union sentries and accosted General Edwin H. Stoughton in his bed. That summer, his command was designated Company A, 43rd Battalion, Virginia Cavalry, and he rose steadily to colonel by the

Colonel John S. Mosby's raiders proved such a bane to occupying Union forces that the region of Virginia he operated from was touted as "Mosby's Confederacy." His uncanny ability to suddenly appear and then vanish, as if at will, earned him the nickname "The Gray Ghost." (Library of Congress)

end of 1864. Try as they may, numerous Union forces could not stamp out Mosby's raiders, who mounted the only organized Southern resistance in the region. Consequently, his men were declared outlaws, and several of them were hanged outright, leading to Union captives being executed in retaliation. Only then did both sides resolve to spare their respective prisoners. After General Robert E. Lee surrendered in April 1865, Mosby simply disbanded his men and sent them home. He subsequently found favor with several Republican administrations, costing him many southern friendships. Mosby, one of the finest guerilla leaders of American history, died in Washington, D.C., on May 30, 1916.

43rd Battalion, Virginia Cavalry

Throughout the Civil War, both sides fielded 428 units loosely designated as "rangers," including actual guerilla bands, lawless freebooters, and outright criminals. The Confederate States of America, enjoying the same military traditions as its northern counterpart, also recruited regular forces capable of conducting irregular, or partisan, warfare. The most famous and effective of these was the 43rd Battalion, Virginia Cavalry, known better to posterity as "Mosby's Raiders," because its success and operations are inseparable from its leader, John Singleton Mosby. Audacity personified, Mosby had enlisted in the Virginia cavalry when the Civil War commenced in 1861, and he served capably in the command of General J. E. B. Stuart, another celebrated cavalier. On April 21, 1862, Confederate President Jefferson Davis signed an act authorizing the recruitment of partisan rangers as part of the war effort, largely to offset Union advantages in manpower and materiel. Meanwhile, Mosby so impressed his superior with his ability to plan irregular actions that he received his own semiautonomous command in January 1863. Taking only nine men with him, he conducted a series of successful raids against Union outposts in northern Virginia, taking captives and seizing arms and military property. Consequently, the unit was expanded by the addition of a mixed lot of older men, regular soldiers, boys, and even Union deserters, along with some rather shady, self-interested individuals. His main base was at Middleburg in Loudoun County, where members boarded in private homes or lived off the country instead of in formal military campsites. Most importantly, Mosby had the drive and personality to whip his followers into a coherent raiding unit, and the successes continued.

Mosby's most notorious act occurred in March 1863, when he led 29 men on a nighttime raid against the Union outpost at Fairfax Courthouse, Virginia. Having taken a guard and learning from him that Brigadier General Edwin H. Stoughton was sleeping nearby, Mosby crept into the general's bedroom, woke him with a rude slap to his bottom side, and successfully spirited him away, along with 33 prisoners and 58 horses—under the very noses of his armed guard. Frustrated Union forces responded with scorched-earth tactics to smoke out the elusive guerillas, but Mosby, well supported by the local population, simply blended back into the woods until the next strike was planned. In fact, the rangers so dogged Union forces in northern Virginia that the region was commonly referred to as "Mosby's Confederacy." Mosby himself, who displayed an uncanny knack for vanishing into thin air after each raid, became reviled and feared in Union circles as the Gray Ghost.

Given the success of Mosby's raiders, on June 10, 1863, it was formalized at Rectorville, Virginia, as Company A, 43rd Battalion, Virginia Cavalry, now boasting 240 troopers in four companies. The unit clearly bore Mosby's personal stamp of leadership, seeing that he only chose officers on merit, quickly dropped any ineffective members, and imposed strict military discipline on all ranks. In terms of fighting, Mosby abandoned outdated saber tactics and equipped each trooper with a brace of heavy .44-caliber Colt revolvers. Carbines, unwieldy and unsuited for hit-and-run tactics, were likewise abandoned. In combat, Mosby taught his men not to fire at an opponent until they could see the whites of their opponent's eye, leading to many Union saddles being emptied. The result was a mobile and well-motivated raiding force reflexively in tune with their leader's unorthodox tactics. Mosby himself was daring and innovative in planning stages, but he placed a premium on gathering intelligence beforehand, traveled at night with small groups of men, struck hard, and then scampered back to prearranged sanctuaries. The end result was that Union forces detailed thousands of combat troops, better employed elsewhere, to guard rear areas. Ironically, many regular Confederate officers looked down on the rangers, seeing them as little more than opportunistic brigands and "featherbed soldiers." The experiment with rangers ended in February 1864 when the Partisan Act was revoked by the Confederate Congress, but two units, including Mosby's, were allowed to continue on in service. In fact, the popular reputation of the raiders led to a surplus of volunteers, and by war's end Mosby commanded nine companies totaling over 1,000 men. Nor did his pace of attacks slacken. In one particularly galling raid, the rangers attacked General Sheridan's main supply convoy, capturing 75 wagons and several hundred prisoners. By year's end, the rebels had captured 1,600 horses and 230 head of cattle and had killed, wounded, or captured 1,200 Union soldiers.

Defining Activity

The victor of a hundred small actions, Mosby's most prided himself on the so-called Greenback Raid of October 14, 1864, an act he considered his "greatest piece of annoyance." In the predawn darkness, his rangers pulled up a section of track belonging to the Baltimore & Ohio Railroad just west of Harpers Ferry, West Virginia. Once the train's engineers perceived the danger and brought the train to a screeching halt, the raiders suddenly emerged from the nearby woods and boarded at gunpoint. There they robbed all the passengers, stole all its cargo, and set the train afire before galloping off. That night, they counted $173,000 in payroll, dollars (greenbacks) intended for General Philip H. Sheridan's troops that were divided up among the 84 men involved in the raid. Mosby, characteristically, received no share in the plunder. Success here placed greater pressure on Union military authorities to track down Mosby and destroy him.

On November 18, 1864, a special Union outfit called Blazer's scouts, being equipped with the latest rapid-fire Spencer carbines, went scouting for Mosby's unit in the Virginia backcountry. Instead, they were ambushed by their quarry at Myerstown and had 43 men killed or captured and Blazer himself captured. As a rule, Mosby insisted on the humane treatment of all captives unlike other Confederate guerillas operating elsewhere. But by 1864, General Ulysses S. Grant was so vexed by his raiding activities that he ordered any raider caught to be executed after a trial. Colonel George A. Custer subsequently captured and hanged several of Mosby's men, at which point Mosby retaliated by executing a like number of Union captives. Thereafter, both sides agreed to refrain from killing prisoners. The Civil War ended on April 9, 1865, but Mosby, fearing the treatment his men would receive, declined to capitulate formally. He held out until April 21 and did not surrender to Union authorities; rather, he simply disbanded his unit and dismissed his men. For the time they operated in northern Virginia, Mosby's raiders epitomized the detailed planning, fast attack, and lighting withdrawals of irregular warfare, and in the finest traditions of Robert Rogers and Francis Marion.

Marine Corps

Since its founding on March 27, 1794, the U.S. Marine Corps was overwhelmingly preoccupied with providing infantry detachments to U.S. Navy warships. They were expected to fight from the yard arms with muskets, assist gun crews where needed, and help spearhead boarding parties against enemy vessels. In time, they began asserting themselves as elite naval infantry capable of operating effectively onshore as well as at sea. The first major land engagement by the Marines occurred at Bladensburg, Maryland, on August 24, 1814, when Commodore Joshua Barney led a detachment of 400 sailors and 114 Leathernecks under Captain Samuel Miller. The encounter proved disastrous to the Americans when the bulk of their force, largely militia, ran from the disciplined British regulars, but Barney's command offered the only stiff resistance encountered that sorry day. Marines did not come ashore as regular infantry again until the Seminole War, when Commandant Archibald Henderson cobbled together two battalions of shipboard detachments for service in the field. These distinguished themselves in the battle of Wahoo Swamp, Florida, on November 21, 1836. The next time that sizable Marine contingents served on land as elite infantry was during the Mexican War of 1846–1848, and a battalion under Lieutenant Colonel Samuel Watson distinguished themselves during the storming of Chapultepec outside Mexico City. Success here led to the adoption of the phrase "From the Halls of Montezuma" in the Marine Corps hymn. It was not until 1861 that the Marines again campaigned as a battalion, and at the battle of Bull Run on July 21, the newly raised force of 353 marines and 12 officers fought well but, like the majority of formations in the Union army, hastily abandoned the battlefield. The marines had demonstrated their overall excellence in land and sea combat over the past six decades, but on at least two occasions, Marine Corps officers performed clandestine missions reminiscent of special forces operations and in concert with indigenous forces. That both missions generally succeeded demonstrates the utility of marines when tasked with missions ashore.

The Shores of Tripoli

On May 14, 1801, Yusef Karamanli, the pasha of Tripoli, declared war on the United States to secure larger tribute payments intended to restrain that leader from attacking and seizing American commerce in the Mediterranean. President Thomas Jefferson responded by dispatching a series of naval squadrons that blockaded and bombarded that city but otherwise lacked the strength to decisively defeat the pirates. In an attempt to break the impasse, William Eaton, the American consul at Tunis, suggested to Jefferson that he outfit an armed expedition financed by Hamet Karamanli, the pashas disposed brother, and forcibly place him back on the throne. After Jefferson agreed, Eaton proceeded to Syracuse, Italy, where the American Mediterranean squadron was berthed under Commodore Samuel Barron. Barron ordered Lieutenant Isaac Hull of the brig *Argus* to transport Eaton to Egypt, where Hamet resided, and the latter commenced recruiting an armed expedition. It was a hare-brained scheme on the surface, but given the fluid nature of Middle Eastern politics, tribal, and family alliances, Eaton gambled that Yusef could be rendered more tractable toward the United States if his rule was threatened from within.

Present throughout these proceedings was Marine Corps Lieutenant Presley O'Bannon, who commanded a detachment of eight marines onboard the *Argus*. In time, these were joined by 80 Greek mercenaries and 300 Arab followers of Hamet, both of whom had been convinced into compliance by the smooth-talking Eaton. Their caravan also contained 107 heavily loaded camels, themselves regarded as "ships of the desert" and essential for any desert trek. On March 8, 1805, the expedition departed Egypt and plodded across 600 miles of scorching North African desert. The Arabs, fierce fighters but undisciplined, mutinied several times en route, but Eaton's control of the purse strings and food supply managed to induce their return. The presence of Presley's marine contingent, small but firm, implicitly dissuaded their rowdy allies from attempting to raid either. The fractious column recruited additional Bedouin warriors along the way before arriving outside their immediate objective, the coastal city of Derna, on April 25, 1805. Considering the hardships of the march, the lack of water, and the unruly composition of Eaton's force, it was a minor miracle that they had persisted so far. Spirits rose further in the American camp when Hull also appeared in the Bay of Bomba with no less than three vessels, including the sloop *Hornet* and the schooner *Nautilus*.

Eaton reasoned that the capture of Derna, with the assistance Hull's squadron, would induce the pasha into peace negotiations. The city was large and contained 800 defenders and several pieces of artillery, but he and Eaton trusted in the temperament of their marines. Prior to attacking, he requested the governor to surrender peacefully, but his note was returned with the brusque inscription "My head or yours." On April 27, Eaton dispatched Hamet's cavalry against the southern flank of the city while he and O'Bannon took the eight marines and 80 Greeks on a headlong charge against the main enemy battery. Taking heavy fire, the marines and mercenaries bayoneted their way directly into the city. Eaton was wounded in the arm, and three Leathernecks were hit (two were killed), but O'Bannon kept the remainder in action and routed his more numerous opponents. He then personally raised the American flag, the first time it ever fluttered over a foreign rampart. Fighting concluded quickly, and the victors, stunned by their good fortune, occupied the governor's palace. But the pasha, far from intimidated, dispatched an army of 3,000 splendid light cavalry to take the city back. Throughout May, these circumspectly probed the city's defenses and were invariably blasted back by Eaton's cannon, so no full assault ever developed. But stalemated and feeling threatened by the growing prestige of his brother, Hamet Karamanli signed a peace agreement with the United States on June 3, 1805, and the Barbary War concluded. Eaton, O'Bannon, and Hamet, along with their followers, were evacuated by the squadron, with the former returning to the United States, O'Bannon rejoining the fleet at Syracuse, and the ex-pasha resuming his luxurious exile in Egypt. The object of this fantastic "long march" had been defeated by diplomacy, but it demonstrated the flexibility and utility of Marine Corps forces operating far from the vessels on which they served. O'Bannon has since been honored by having three destroyers carry his name. And in light of his contributions at Derna, the stanza "To the shores of Tripoli" is enshrined in the Marine Corps hymn.

California Conquest

By 1846, the United States, under the administration of President James K. Polk, was eager to secure safe ports along the Pacific coast to enhance the growing China trade. To this end, he approached the Mexican government and offered to purchase all their possessions north of the Rio Grande River in Texas as far west as California and as far north as Oregon. Many southern politicians, eager to expand slavery into said territory, were willing to go to war with Mexico should that nation decline to sell. Naturally, the Mexican government refused to surrender any of its territory to the Americans no matter how lucrative the offer, so conflict was clearly in the offing. It turns out that another Marine Corps officer, Lieutenant Archibald H. Gillespie, figured prominently at the center of diplomatic and military subterfuge as events unfolded. A career marine, he had risen from the commission ranks and had performed competently yet possessed no particular talents beyond a good command of Spanish that he acquired while he was stationed at Pensacola, Florida. On October 30, 1845, Gillespie was summoned from the Washington Navy Yard and brought before President Polk for a confidential meeting. There he was entrusted with a sensitive mission of conveying top-secret messages to Thomas O. Larkin, the American consul at Monterey,

California, and Commodore John D. Sloat, commanding the U.S. Pacific Squadron off the coastline. He also received a package of letters for noted army officer and explorer John C. Fremont, then encamped somewhere in northern California. Gillespie then sailed on a ship bound for Santa Cruz, Mexico, disguised as a merchant. En route, he memorized all his dispatches before destroying them. Having debarked at Vera Cruz, he made the four-day journey to Mexico City, carefully noting the ragged conditions of Mexican military forces encountered along the way. A coup by General Mariano Paraedes against President Jose Joaquin Herrera resulted in his being detained in Mexico City for several weeks, and it was not until January 20, 1846, that roads out of the city were opened and he resumed traveling overland to Mazatlan. There he boarded the Pacific Squadron offshore and delivered his secret message to Commodore Sloat. Sloat, cognizant that war with Mexico might erupt at any time, further masked Gillespie's mission by dispatching him to distant Hawaii as additional cover before allowing him to continue onto Monterrey, his final destination.

Gillespie concluded his arduous trek back and forth across the Pacific before finally reaching Monterrey on April 17, 1846. He subsequently conferred with Consul Larkin onboard the warship USS *Cyane*, verbally relaying his secret instructions. These directed Larkin, in the event of war, to coax authorities in California to secede from Mexico peacefully and to ask for annexation by the United States. The latter move was sought to preempt France or Great Britain from stepping in and forming a protectorate under their sway. Gillespie then rode west to Sutter's Fort (present-day Sacramento) to track down the elusive Fremont. Not finding him there, he continued northward into southern Oregon and finally established contact on May 9, 1846, along the Klamath River. Having survived an attack on their campsite by hostile Klamath Indians, Fremont and Gillespie next ventured south into California where, on June 15, 1846, the Bear Flag Rebellion erupted. Here American settlers declared their independence from Mexico, and the "California Battalion" of four companies was authorized, with Fremont as colonel and Gillespie serving as second-in-command. The latter rejoined the fleet back at Monterey, where Commodore Sloat disapproved of his unauthorized actions with Fremont, but insofar as Commodore Robert F. Stockton arrived as the new squadron commander and fully endorsed such machinations, no action was taken against Gillespie. Instead, on August 31, 1846, Gillespie assisted Stockton in occupying Los Angeles, receiving for his effort the somewhat grandiose title of "Military Commandant of the South." The appointment lacked sufficient numbers of men to back it up, and after Gillespie declared martial law in that settlement, the Californios rose in revolt. On September 29, the 140 Americans, outnumbered four to one, accepted peace terms and evacuated the premises, marching to San Pedro to rejoin the fleet offshore.

Within days, Gillespie's small command was reinforced by 50 dragoons under Brigadier General Stephen W. Kearney, and their combined force slogged back overland to recapture Los Angeles. Instead, they were roughly handled by Californio lancers at the battle of San Pascual on December 6, 1846, where Gillespie, badly wounded by lance thrusts, fired off several cannon shots that broke up the attack. Kearney and Gillespie were reinforced by marines and sailors under Commodore Stockton, and Los Angeles finally capitulated on January 10, 1847. Shortly afterward, Gillespie was ordered to rejoin the marine detachment onboard the USS *Columbus* at Monterrey, where he arrived May 26. The new squadron commander, Commodore James Biddle, disapproved of his meddling ashore and relieved him of command responsibilities until he returned to the Marine Barracks in Washington, D.C. Gillespie's escapades in California ended at that point, but his clandestine operations over the preceding four months proved instrumental to the acquisition of California; rarely has such a vast area been subverted by such a threadbare, motley assemblage of frontiersmen, sailors, and marines. The affair certainly demonstrated that Marine Corps officers were not only capable of military subterfuge but also quite adept at it.

Navy

Like the Marine Corps, the U.S. Navy had few opportunities to demonstrate any capacity for special operations since its founding in 1794, save for cutting-out expeditions by small parties of sailors to capture enemy vessels at anchor. The advent of the Civil War in 1861, coupled with advances in steam technology and underwater explosives, promoted its first fledgling steps toward embracing unconventional warfare. The principal agent of this change was Lieutenant Commander William B. Cushing, renowned as "Lincoln's commando" for his grasp of unorthodox tactics and personal daring in their execution. Cushing, who had previously been kicked out of the U.S. Naval Academy for hijinks, subsequently enlisted in the navy as a midshipman. He surprised superiors by acting bravely on several small-scale raids against Confederate forces along the Virginia coast, and on July 16, 1862, Cushing advanced two grades to lieutenant at the age of 19. Over the next year, he continued leading cutting-out expeditions and daring reconnaissance missions behind enemy lines. For instance, on February 29, 1864, he led a party of sailors up the Cape Fear River in North Carolina to capture General Louis Herbert; Cushing's party stormed into his tent at night only to discover the general was absent but did manage to capture his chief engineer. Four months later, Cushing returned up the Cape Fear River intending to attack the southern ironclad CSS *Raleigh*, unaware that it had run aground and sunk previously, so he spent three days reconnoitering the area, sabotaging Confederate installations, and generally terrorizing the local populace. By this time, Cushing was so well-regarded in naval circles that his services as a naval commando were in high demand. In the summer of 1864, Admiral Samuel P. Lee of the South Atlantic Blockading Squadron specifically requested him for his most dangerous assignment yet.

Sinking the *Albemarle*

The objective of Cushing's mission was the huge and dangerous Confederate ironclad CSS *Albermarle*, then the bane of Union blockading forces. With a length of 152 feet and a 34-foot beam and encased by four

Throughout the Civil War, William B. Cushing was the U.S. Navy's foremost practitioner of unconventional warfare. A seemingly endless appetite for dangerous assignments led to his promotion to lieutenant commander while still in his early 20s. (Naval Historical Foundation)

Lieutenant B. Cushing's daring nighttime raid on the giant Confederate ironclad CSS *Albemarle* was the most audacious naval action of the Civil War. (Naval History and Heritage Command)

inches of wrought-iron plate, this Confederate giant was nearly impervious to Union gunfire, while its own pair of 6.4-inch Brooke cannon had sunk or damaged several blockading vessels in two pitched battles that spring. Damage sustained in these encounters required the *Albemarle* to be anchored up the Roanoke River near Plymouth, North Carolina, for repairs. Union authorities nonetheless feared that once this armored monster resumed operational status, it would inflict serious damage on the remaining blockaders, and possibly break the blockade altogether. Cushing, typically, accepted the hazardous mission without an afterthought and received complete latitude in planning, equipping, and executing the mission. He first ventured to New York City to observe two 50-foot-long steam launches outfitted with "torpedoes," or explosive charges mounted on a spar. Cushing elected to employ two of these relatively quiet, speedy craft on a nighttime raid up the river. One vessel was captured on a train while passing through Virginia, but he proceeded on with the remaining launch. On the evening of October 27, 1864, Cushing, accompanied by 15 volunteers, steamed up the Roanoke River in search of his quarry. By this time, the youthful officer had a personal stake in the outcome. Previously, on April 19, 1864, the *Albemarle* engaged the Union steamer *Miami* led by Commander C. W. Flusser, an Annapolis school mate of Cushing's who arranged his midshipman's warrant. Flusser was killed in combat, and the raid presented Cushing with an opportunity to exact personal vengeance.

The early morning of the April 28 was exceedingly rainy and dark, and anxious moments ticked by as the raiders sought out the *Albemarle*. At last, they perceived their target in the distance, put on speed, and began their final approach. Alert Confederate sentries hailed the unidentified craft, began firing their guns, and also lit a bonfire to assist their aim. Cushing, guided by the fire, suddenly observed that the ironclad was surrounded by a protective log boom floating 30 feet away from its hull. Undeterred, he quickly surmised that the logs were probably overgrown with algae and very slimy after soaking in the water for months. Cushing ordered them rammed at high speed, and the steam launch hit the logs, slid effortlessly over the top, and closed with the *Albemarle*. He steadied his torpedo as bullets continuing flying around him, aimed it below the vessel's protective shield, then detonated the device. The explosion completely swamped his launch, but the Confederate warship had been fatally holed and settled to the bottom of the river. Cushing and his entire crew were forced to swim for safety, but only he escaped capture. Stealing a Confederate boat, he paddled alone for nearly 10 hours before reaching the blockading squadron and reported his success to the admiral. He consequently received promotion to lieutenant commander at the age of 21. More important, the city of Plymouth, now robbed of its naval guardian, fell to Union land forces only four days after the attack. Thanks to Cushing, the sounds of North Carolina were finally closed to Confederate blockade runners. The *Albemarle*'s destruction was one of the boldest commando attacks of the entire war, one in which a determined naval leader, armed with special weapons and a well-conceived plan of attack, fearlessly executed, sank a ship and helped capture a city.

Miscellaneous

Native Americans

The use of indigenous forces by the United States in wartime is an old and cherished tradition. In fact, its military annals are replete with instances of large numbers of Native Americans fighting for the government as auxiliaries, bringing their own peculiar martial talents to the battlefield. For several months into the War of 1812, a company of Shawnee scouts under Johnny Logan, a Christian convert, provided useful intelligence to American units in the Old Northwest. One of the larger instances of direct Indian field support occurred in the summer of 1814, when the Seneca tribe under Chief Red Jacket, a famed orator, led a force of 600 warriors into Canada as part of General Jacob J. Brown's Left Division. On July 5, 1814, the Native Americans suffered heavy casualties by fighting Mohawks, allied with the British, at the battle of Chippewa. In light of the fratricidal conflict, the Senecas and Mohawks opted out of the war to curtail further bloodletting. At this time, many southern tribesmen also came forward to support the United States during the Creek War of 1813 and sided against the so-called Red Stick faction of the Upper Creek nation. A battalion that was organized under Chief William McIntosh saw active service in concert with troops from Georgia. Another large force of Choctaws under Pushmataha (another celebrated chief) supported Mississippi militia under General Ferdinand L. Claiborne at the battle of Eccanachaca in 1813. A large number of Cherokees under Chief Junaluska were also present at General Andrew Jackson's victory over the Creeks in March 1814 at Horseshoe Bend, where they swan across the river behind enemy fortifications and removed all their canoes, preventing an escape. The following May, 130 Oneida Indians joined Major Daniel Appling's flotilla on Lake Ontario and helped ambush a large British detachment at Sandy Creek. In 1836 and 1837, another Creek battalion was raised

Native American warriors, such as this group of Sioux photographed on the Pine Ridge Agency in 1891, served the U.S. Army with distinction, especially as scouts and trackers. (Library of Congress)

for service in the Second Seminole War. It was guided by Major David Moniac, the first full-blooded Indian to graduate from the U.S. Military Academy, who led them until his death in battle. During the Civil War, Creek and Seminole Indians residing in the Indian territory (Oklahoma) also contributed several battalions of mounted riflemen to the Confederacy. These fought well under General Stand Watie, a Native American who was also the last senior Confederate officer to lay down his arms. By comparison, the Cherokee remained steadfast, loyal allies of the United States and likewise contributed several hundred warriors to the cause. After the war, increasing frictions with the Plains Indians led to the outbreak of hostilities, principally with the Sioux and Cheyenne, and several companies of Crow warriors eagerly joined the U.S. Army as mounted scouts. They did so more out of a sense of long-standing antipathies toward peoples considered hereditary enemies and possibly to win favorable concession from the whites than out of any great love for the United States. At the time, the nature of Indian warfare was also changing dramatically; conflict at the tribal or battalion level had given way to small raiding parties, pursued by cavalry and elite scouting units. In time, Native American scouts were prized by army commanders for their uncanny ability to read the terrain, skills only acquired over a lifetime while living in a desert clime. Scouting was perhaps the most celebrated use of Indians during the 19th century; the majority were favorably commended by commanding officers, and a handful received Congressional Medals of Honor for bravery under fire.

The process of hiring scouts for the U.S. Army began on July 28, 1866, when Congress formally authorized their recruitment. To that end, prospective recruits received the same service terms as their white counterparts and were issued rations and weapons and drew regular pay. Uniforms varied from tribe to tribe, but most prided themselves on donning a blue coat and a back cavalry hat, adorned with tribal feathers, in addition to their usual garb. Warriors from the Pawnee, Crow, Cheyenne, and even various Sioux bands consequently joined to campaign with soldiers against other warring tribes. One particular Crow scout, "Curley," gained a measure of renown by working closely with General George A. Custer throughout the Little Big Horn Campaign of 1876 and was touted in newspapers as the sole survivor of the infamous battle, an assertion that he vehemently denied. In the Southwest, mounting dissatisfaction about life on reservations convinced several bands of Apaches to bolt and resume their freebooting lives as raiders. The most famous chief, Geronimo, was the subject of no fewer than two intense military campaigns to apprehend him in 1873–1874 and 1885–1886. Fortunately for both sides, General George Crook realized the futility of attempting to track fast-moving fugitives across the harsh terrain of Arizona and northern Mexico with regular cavalry. Embracing the apt dictum that "it takes an Apache to find an Apache," he openly recruited Indian scouts from diverse branches within that nation to excellent effect. This military practice proved eminently successful and presaged the present-day special forces doctrine of recruiting friendly locals to assist in "brushfire" wars. Crook was also unique among contemporaries by dealing and negotiating with Native Americans in good faith. Consequently, Geronimo and his followers were talked into surrendering and returning to the reservation. However, after that chief escaped from the reservation again, Crook was sacked and replaced by hard-line General Nelson A. Miles, who sought to subdue the elusive band with his troopers. In time, Miles was likewise forced to recruit Apache and Navajo mounted scouts to find the fugitive chief and persuade him to return.

The Plains Indian Wars abated by the end of the 19th century, so the army issued General Order No. 28 on March 9, 1891, and reduced the number of Indians scouts to 150. These men were distributed by handfuls among the various western departments. However, provisions were also made to recruit 1,500 Apaches directly into the army as line infantry companies, with one being attached to 14 standing regiments along the frontier. Ambitious plans were also made to raise four complete regiments, numbered the 9th to 12th, entirely of Native Americans. Here the Indians would be subject to regular army discipline and training to turn them into western-style soldiers. General Crook, who had long advocated preserving Indian ways of life, railed against such forced acculturation, for it militated against the Indians' fabled skills as scouts. These could only be acquired by a lifetime in their native environment. Crook, however, was ignored and the entire program was canceled in 1897 because of deep-seated cultural incongruities and a prevailing sense of white superiority among the officers. It was not until World War I that Native Americans were allowed to enlist in large numbers, and they performed with distinction. It is a little-known fact that a small number of Choctaw Indians performed an invaluable service as "code talkers" in the waning days of that conflict in France. It was assumed that crack German code breakers could accurately decipher military codes employed by the U.S. Army, thus anticipating their battlefield maneuvers. It occurred to Colonel A. W. Bloor of the 142nd U.S. Infantry, after overhearing two Choctaw soldiers in his unit conversing in their native tongue, that they could safely transmit military radio signals in this same manner. Given the obscurity of their dialect and German unfamiliarity with it, they could relay military orders quickly from one unit to another without having to decode it. Bloor arranged an experiment on October 26, 1918, in which two companies of the 142nd were ordered to withdraw by Choctaw speakers. The maneuver proceeded safely without German interference, and a captured officer subsequently admitted that they were completely dumbfounded by the Choctaw language. The war ended before this pioneering experiment with indigenous linguistics was used on a wider scale, but the activities of this group anticipated the more famous effort mounted by Navajo code talkers in World War II.

Bibliography

New England Militia

Chet, Guy. *Conquering the American Wilderness: The Triumph of European Warfare in the Colonial Northeast*. Amherst: University of Massachusetts Press, 2003.

Chet, Guy. "The Literary and Military Career of Benjamin Church: Change or Continuity in Early American Warfare." *Historical Journal of Massachusetts* 35, no. 2 (Summer 2007): 105–12.

Church, Benjamin. *Diary of King Philip's War, 1675–1676*. Chester, CT: Published for the Little Compton Historical Society by the Pequot Press, 1975.

Mandell, Daniel R. *King Philip's War: Colonial Expansion, Native Resistance, and the End of Indian Sovereignty*. Baltimore: Johns Hopkins University Press, 2010.

Philbrick, Nathaniel. *Mayflower: A Story of Courage, Community, and War*. New York: Viking, 2006.

Schultz, Eric B. *King Philip's War: The History and Legacy of America's Forgotten Conflict*. Woodstock, VT: Countryman Press, 2000.

Zelner, Kyle F. *A Rabble in Arms: Massachusetts Towns and Militiamen during King Philip's War*. Amherst: University of Massachusetts Press, 2009.

Rogers's Rangers

Black, Robert W. *Ranger Dawn: The American Ranger from the Colonial Era to the Mexican War*. Mechanicsburg, PA: Stackpole Books, 2009.

Brumwell, Stephen. *White Devil: A True Story of War, Savagery, and Vengeance in Colonial America*. Cambridge, MA: Da Capo Press, 2005.

Horn, Bernd. "Hollow of Death: Rogers' Rangers Desperate Fight for Survival, 21 January 1757." *Canadian Military History* 14, no. 4 (October 2005): 5–14.

Lock, John D. *To Fight with Intrepidity: The Complete History of the U.S. Army Rangers, 1622 to Present*. New York: Pocket Books, 1998.

Loescher, Burt G. *Genesis: Rogers' Rangers: The First Green Berets; the Corps and the Revivals, April 6, 1758–December 24, 1783*. Bowie, MD: Heritage Books, 2000.

Loescher, Burt G. *The History of Rogers' Rangers*. Bowie, MD: Heritage Books, 2001.

Mancini, John. "Rogers' Rangers and the Battle of Labarbue Creek." *Military Heritage* 5, no. 3 (December 2003): 76–81.

Rogers, Robert. *The Annotated and Illustrated Journals of Major Robert Rogers*. Fleischmanns, NY: Purple Mountain Press, 2002.

Ross, John F. *War on the Run: The Epic Story of Robert Rogers and the Conquest of America's First Frontier*. New York: Bantam Books, 2009.

Wulf, Matt. *Robert Rogers' Rules for Ranging Service: An Analysis*. Westminster, MD: Heritage Books, 2006.

Wulf, Matt. *North American Frontier Soldier*. Westminster, MD: Heritage Books, 2008.

Minutemen

Breen, T. H. *American Insurgents, American Patriots: The Revolution of the People*. New York: Hill and Wang, 2010.

Cain, Alexander R. *We Stood Our Ground: Lexington in the First Year of the Revolution*. Westminster, MD: Heritage Books, 2004.

Galvin, John R. *The Minute Men: The First Fight: Myths and Realities of the American Revolution*. Washington, DC: Potomac, 2006.

Gross, Robert A. *The Minutemen and Their World*. New York: Hill and Wang, 2001.

Morrissey, Brendan. *Boston, 1775: The Shot Heard Round the World*. Westport, CT: Praeger, 2004.

Ryan, D. Michael. *Concord and the Dawn of Revolution: Hidden Truths*. Charleston, SC: History Press, 2007.

American Riflemen

Callahan, North. *Daniel Morgan, Ranger of the Revolution*. New York: Holt, Rinehart and Winston, 1961.

Cecere, Michael. *They Are Indeed a Very Useful Corps: American Riflemen in the Revolutionary War*. Westminister, MD: Heritage Books, 2006.

Higginbotham, Don. *Daniel Morgan, Revolutionary Rifleman*. Chapel Hill: University of North Carolina Press, 1961.

La Crosse, Richard B. *Revolutionary Rangers: Daniel Morgan's Riflemen and Their Role on the Northern Frontier, 1778–1783*. Bowie, MD: Heritage Books, 2002.

Morgan, Richard L. *General Daniel Morgan: Reconsidered Hero*. Morgantown, NC: Burke County Historical Society, 2001.

Westwood, David. *Rifles: An Illustrated History of Their Impact*. Santa Barbara, CA: ABC-Clio, 2005.

2nd Mounted Partisan Corps

Hartman, John W. *The American Partisan: Henry Lee and the Struggle for Independence, 1776–1782*. Shippensburg, PA: Burd Street Press, 2000.

Hayes, John T. *Massacre: Tarleton vs Buford, May 29, 1780; Lee vs Pyle, February 25, 1781*. Fort Lauderdale, FL: Saddlebag Press, 1997.

Lee, Henry. *The Campaign of 1781 in the Carolinas: With Remarks Historical and Critical on Johnson's Life of Greene*. Cranbury, NJ: Scholar's Bookshelf, 2006.

Troxler, Carole W. *Pyle's Defeat: Deception at the Racepath*. Elon, NC: Alamance County Historical Association, 2003.

American Guerillas

Piecuch, James. *Three People, One King: Loyalists, Indians, and Slaves in the Revolutionary South, 1775–1782*. Columbia: University of South Carolina Press, 2008.

Russell, David L. *The American Revolution in the Southern Colonies*. Jefferson, NC: McFarland, 2000.

Swisher, James K. *The Revolutionary War in the Southern Back Country*. Gretna, LA: Pelican Press, 2008.

Thomsen, Paul A. "The Devil Himself Could Not Catch Him." *American History* 35, no. 3 (August 2000): 46–53.

Wilkins, David K. *The Southern Strategy: Britain's Conquest of South Carolina and Georgia, 1775–1780*. Columbia: University of South Carolina Press, 2005.

The Turtle

Diamant, Lincoln. *Dive! The Story of David Bushnell and His Remarkable 1776 Submarine (and Torpedo)*. Fleischmanns, NY: Purple Mountain Press, 2003.

Lefkowitz, Arthur S. *Bushnell's Submarine: The Best Kept Secret of the American Revolution*. New York: Scholastic Nonfiction, 2006.

Manstan, Roy R., and Frederic J. Frese. *Turtle: David Bushnell's Revolutionary Vessel*. Yardley, PA: Westholme, 2010.

Regiment of Riflemen

Austerman, Wayne R. "This Excellent and Gallant Rifle Corps." *Man at Arms* 3, no. 3 (1981): 18–24, 44.

Berkeley, Lewis. "Early U.S. Riflemen: Their Arms and Training." *American Rifleman* 106, no. 12 (December 1958): 30–33.

Campbell, J. Duncan. "Notes on the Insignia of the Riflemen, U.S. Army." *Military Collector and Historian* 1 (1949): 6–8.

Fredriksen, John C. *Green Coats and Glory: The United States Regiment of Riflemen, 1808–1821*. Youngstown, NY: Old Fort Niagara Association, 2000.

Gerber, William E. "Harper's Ferry Rifles: Comparing the Models 1803 and 1814." *American Society of Arms Collectors Bulletin*, no. 38 (1978): 17–21.

Holt, Richard A. "Pre-1814 U.S. Contract Rifles." *American Society of Arms Collectors Bulletin*, no. 147 (1982): 7–19.

McBarron, H. Charles. "American Military Dress in the War of 1812: Regular Riflemen." *Military Affairs* 5 (1941): 139–40.

Palmer, Richard. "Lake Ontario's Battles, Part 3: The Battle of Sandy Creek." *Inland Seas* 53, no. 4 (1997): 282–91.

Zlatich, Marko, and Detmar H. Finke. "The Uniform of the United States Rifle Regiment, 1808–1812." *Military Collector and Historian* 50 (Spring 1998): 120–26.

Regiment of Light Artillery

"Biographical Notice of Lieut. W. W. Smith." *Analectic Magazine* 8 (July 1816): 52–54.

Campbell, J. Duncan. "Second Pattern Cap Plate, U.S. Light Artillery, 1814." *Military Collector and Historian* 26 (Spring 1974): 6–9.

Chartrand, Rene, and Eric I. Marsden. "U.S. Light Artillery, 1814–1821." *Military Collector and Historian* 48 (Summer 1996): 86–87.

Eustis, Abraham. "The Capture of York." *Massachusetts Historical Society Proceedings* 11 (December 1876): 492–95.

Fredriksen, John C. *The United States Army in the War of 1812: Concise Biographies of Commanders and Operational Histories of Regiments, with Bibliographies of Published and Primary Sources*. Jefferson, NC: McFarland, 2009.

Larter, Harry C. "Material of the First American Light Artillery." *Military Collector and Historian* 4 (1952): 53–63.

Putnam, Alfred A. "General Moses Porter, 1756–1822." *Danvers Historical Society Collections* 15 (1927): 1–25.

Todd, Frederick P. "Notes on the Dress of the Regiment of Light Artillery, U.S.A., 1808–1811." *Military Collector and Historian* 2 (1950): 10–11.

The First Long-Range Reconnaissance

Chaffin, Tom. *Pathfinder: John Charles Fremont and the Course of American Empire*. New York: Hill and Wang, 2002.

Denton, Sally. "Fremont Steals California." *American Heritage* 60, no. 4 (Winter 2011): 30–39.

Fremont, John C. *Memoirs of My Life*. New York: Cooper Square Press, 2001.

Roberts, David. *A Newer World: Kit Carson, John C. Fremont, and the Claiming of the American West*. New York: Touchstone, 2001.

Sherwood, Midge. *Fremont: Eagle of the West*. North Hollywood, CA: Jackson Peak Publishers, 2002.

Walker, Dale L. *Bear Flag Rising: The Conquest of California, 1846*. New York: Forge, 2000.

Regiment of Voltigeurs and Foot Riflemen

Cunningham, Roger D. "The Regiment of Voltigeurs and Foot Riflemen." *On Point* 13, no. 3 (2007): 29–31.

Regiment of Mounted Riflemen

Raab, James W. *W. W. Loring: Florida's Forgotten General*. Manhattan, KS: Sunflower University Press, 1996.

Settle, Raymond W. ed. *The March of the Mounted Riflemen: First United States Military Expedition to Travel the Full Length of the Oregon Trail from Fort Leavenworth to Fort Vancouver, May to October, 1849: As Recorded in the Journals of Major Osborne Cross and George Gibbs, and the Official Report of Colonel Loring.* Lincoln: University of Nebraska Press, 1989.

Wade, Arthur P. "Forts and Mounted Rifles along the Oregon Trail, 1846–1853." *Kansas Quarterly* 10, no. 3 (1978): 3–15.

Wright, John. *Recollections of Western Texas: Descriptive and Narrative, Including an Indian Campaign, 1852–1855, Interspersed with Illustrative Anecdotes, by Two of the U.S. Mounted Rifles.* Edited by Robert Wooster. Lubbock: Texas Tech University Press, 2001.

Texas Rangers

Collins, Michael L. *Texas Devils: Rangers and Regulars on the Lower Rio Grande, 1846–1861.* Norman: University of Oklahoma Press, 2008.

Cutrer, Thomas W. *Ben McCulloch and the Frontier Military Tradition.* Chapel Hill: University of North Carolina Press, 1993.

Moore, Stephen L. *Savage Frontier: Rangers, Riflemen, and Indian Wars in Texas.* 2 vols. Denton: University of North Texas Press, 2006–2007.

Utley, Robert M. *Lone Star Justice: The First Century of the Texas Rangers.* New York: Oxford University Press, 2002.

Wilkins, Frederick. *The Highly Irregular Irregulars: Texas Rangers in the Mexican War.* Austin, TX: Eakin Press, 1990.

Wilkins, Frederick. *The Legend Begins: The Texas Rangers, 1823–1845.* Austin, TX: State House Press, 1996.

U.S. Sharpshooters

Earley, Gerald L. *The Second United States Sharpshooters in the Civil War: A History and Roster.* Jefferson, NC: McFarland, 2009.

Fahle, Michael L. *The Best the Union Could Muster: The True Story of Berdan's Sharpshooters at the Battle of Gettysburg.* Lindsey, OH: Greencoat Publications, 1998.

Giese, Lucretia H., and Roy L. Perkinson. "A Newly Discovered Drawing of Sharpshooters by Winslow Homer: Experience, Image, and Memory." *Winterthur Portfolio* 45, no. 1 (Spring 2011): 61–89.

Greene, William B. *Letters from a Sharpshooter: The Civil War Letters of Private William B. Greene, Co. G, 2nd United States Sharpshooters (Berdan's) Army of the Potomac, 1861–1865.* Belleville, WI: Historic Publications, 1993.

Katcher, Philip R. N. *Sharpshooters of the American Civil War, 1861–65.* Chicago: Raintree, 2003.

Marcot, Roy M. *U.S. Sharpshooters: Berdan's Civil War Elite.* Mechanicsburg, PA: Stackpole Books, 2007.

Matthews, James M. *Soldiers in Green: The Civil War Diaries of James Mero Matthews, 2nd U.S. Sharpshooters*. Sandy Point, ME: Richardson's Civil War Roundtable, 2002.

Murray, R. L. *Berdan's Sharpshooters in Combat: The Peninsula Campaign and Gettysburg*. Wolcott, NY: Benedum Books, 2005.

Ripley, William Y. W. *Vermont Riflemen in the War for the Union, 1861–1865. A History of Company F, First United States Sharpshooters*. Rutland, VT: Tuttle, 1883.

Sword, Wiley. *Sharpshooter: Hiram Berdan, His Famous Sharpshooters, and Their Sharps Rifles*. Lincoln, RI: Andrew Mowbray, 1988.

White, Wyman S. *The Civil War Diary of Wyman S. White: First Sergeant of Company F, 2nd United States Sharpshooter Regiment*. Baltimore: Butternut and Blue, 1991.

Andrews Raid of 1862

Bonds, Russell S. *Stealing the General: The Great Locomotive Chase and the First Medal of Honor*. Yardley, PA: Westholme Publishing, 2006.

Cohen, Stan. *The General and the Texas: A Pictorial History of the Andrews Raid, April 12, 1862*. Missoula, MT: Pictorial Historical Publishing, 1999.

Rottman, Gordon L. *The Great Locomotive Chase: The Andrew's Raid of 1862*. New York: Osprey, 2009.

Blazer's Independent Scouts

Stephenson, Darl L. *Headquarters in the Brush: Blazer's Independent Union Scouts*. Athens: Ohio University Press, 2001.

Walzer, Jordan D. "Chasing the Gray Ghost: Blazer's Independent Union Scouts and the Shenandoah Valley Campaign of 1864." *North and South* 11, no. 2 (December 2008): 54–61.

43rd Battalion, Virginia Cavalry

Ashdown, Paul, and Edward Caudill. *The Mosby Myth: A Confederate Hero in Life and Legend*. Wilmington, DE: Scholarly Resources, 2002.

Black, Robert W. *Ghost, Thunderbolt, and Wizard: Mosby, Morgan, and Forrest in the Civil War*. Mechanicsburg, PA: Stackpole Books, 2008.

Bonan, Gordon B. *The Edge of Mosby's Sword: The Life of Confederate Colonel William Henry Chapman*. Carbondale: Southern Illinois University Press, 2009.

Brown, Peter. *Mosby's Fighting Parson: The Life and Times of Sam Chapman*. Westminster, MD: Willow Bend Books, 2001.

Brown, Peter., ed. *Take Sides with the Truth: The Postwar Letters of John Singleton Mosby to Samuel F. Chapman*. Lexington: University Press of Kentucky, 2007.

Cary, Carolyn C. *William Thomas Overby: Proud Partisan Ranger*. Fayetteville, GA: C. J. Cary and Associates, 2003.

Johnson, Teri. "Mosby's Magic: All Over Northern Virginia the Confederacy's Gray Ghost Spooked His Yankee Prey." *America's Civil War* 23, no. 6 (January 2011): 30–37.

Mewborn, Horace. *"From Mosby's Command": Newspaper Letters and Articles about John S. Mosby and his Rangers*. Baltimore: Butternut and Blue, 2005.

Mosby, John S. *The Memoirs of John Singleton Mosby*. Nashville: J. S. Sanders, 1995.

Ramage, James A. *Gray Ghost: The Life of Colonel John Singleton Mosby*. Lexington: University Press of Kentucky, 1999.

Simson, Jay W. *Custer and the Front Royal Executions*. Jefferson, NC: McFarland, 2009.

March on Tripoli

Fremont-Barnes, Gregory. *The Wars of the Barbary Pirates: To the Shores of Tripoli: The Rise of the U.S. Navy and Marines*. New York: Osprey, 2006.

Lambert, Frank. *The Barbary Wars: American Independence in the Atlantic World*. New York: Hill and Wang, 2005.

London, James E. *Victory in Tripoli: How America's War with the Barbary Pirates Established the U.S. Navy and Built a Nation*. Hoboken, NJ: Wiley, 2005.

Longo, Mark S. "To the Shores of Tripoli." *Military Heritage* 6, no. 6 (June 2005): 40–49.

Martin, Tyrone G. " . . . To the Shores of Tripoli." *Naval History* 19, no. 2 (April 2005): 57–61.

Wheelan, Joseph. *Jefferson's War: America's First War on Terror, 1801–1805*. New York: Carroll and Graf, 2003.

Whipple, A. B. C. *To the Shores of Tripoli: The Birth of the U.S. Navy and Marines*. Annapolis, MD: Naval Institute Press, 2001.

Zacks, Richard. *The Pirate Coast: Thomas Jefferson, the First Marines, and the Secret Mission of 1805*. New York: Hyperion, 2005.

Conquest of California

Kurutz, Gary F. "'The Entire Southern Country Abandoned by American Arms': An Eyewitness Account of the Siege of Los Angeles, 1846." *Southern California Quarterly* 85, no. 2 (June 2003): 117–44.

Marti, Werner H. *Messenger of Destiny: The California Adventures, 1846–1847*. San Francisco: J. Howell, 1960.

Rychetnik, Joe. "Both Old-Fashioned Skullduggery and Brave Fighting Lay behind the U.S. Acquisition of California." *Military History* 11, no. 5 (August 1994): 20–25.

Rychetnik, Joe. "The U.S. Marine's Role in the Conquest of California." *Californians* 13, no. 1 (1996): 12–14.

Santelli, Gabrielle M. *Marines in the Mexican War*. Washington, DC: History and Museums Division, Headquarters, U.S. Marines Corps, 1991.

Sinking the *Albemarle*

Cushing, William B. *The Sea Eagle: The Civil War Memoir of Lt. Cdr. William B. Cushing*. Edited by Alden R. Carter. Lanham, MD: Rowman and Littlefield, 2009.

Hinds, John W. *The Hunt for the Albemarle: Anatomy of a Gunboat War*. Shippensburg, PA: Burd Street Press, 2001.

Schneller, Robert J. *Cushing: Civil War SEAL*. Washington, DC: Brassey's, 2004.

Stempel, Jim. *The CSS Albemarle and William Cushing: The Remarkable Confederate Ironclad and the Union Officer Who Sank It*. Jefferson, NC: McFarland, 2011.

Native Americans

Aleshire, Peter. *The Fox and the Whirlwind: General George Crook and Geronimo*. New York: Wiley, 2000.

Britten, Thomas A. *A Brief History of the Seminole-Negro Indian Scouts*. Lewiston, NY: Edwin Mellen Press, 1999.

Chamberlain, Kathleen. *Victorio: Apache Warrior and Chief*. Norman: University of Oklahoma Press, 2007.

Confer, Clarissa W. *The Cherokee Nation in the Civil War*. Norman: University of Oklahoma Press, 2007

Cozzens, Peter. *The Struggle for Apacheria*. Mechanicsburg, PA: Stackpole Books, 2001.

Dunlay, Thomas W. *Wolves for the Blue Soldiers: Indian Scouts and Auxiliaries with the United States Army, 1860–1890*. Lincoln: University of Nebraska Press, 1982.

Field, Ron. *U.S. Army Frontier Scouts, 1840–1921*. New York: Osprey, 2003.

Gatewood, Charles B. *Lt. Charles B. Gatewood and His Apache Wars Memoir*. Lincoln: University of Nebraska Press, 2005.

Griffith, Benjamin. "Lt. David Moniac, Creek Indian: First Minority Graduate of West Point." *Alabama Historical Quarterly* 43, no. 2 (1981): 99–110.

Hatch, Tom. *The Blue, the Gray, and the Red: Indian Campaigns of the Civil War*. Mechanicsburg, PA: Stackpole Books, 2003.

Kraft, Louis. *Gatewood and Geronimo*. Albuquerque: University of New Mexico Press, 2000.

Lardas, Mark. *Native American Mounted Riflemen*. New York: Osprey, 2006.

McKanna, Clare V. *Court-Martial of Apache Kid: Renegade of Renegades*. Lubbock: Texas Tech University Press, 2009.

Radbourne, Allan, and Joyce L. Jauch. *Micky Free: Apache Captive, Interpreter, and Indian Scout*. Tucson: Arizona Historical Society, 2005.

Robinson, Charles M. *General Crook and the Western Frontier*. Norman: University of Oklahoma Press, 2001.

Spencer, John C. *American Civil War in the Indian Territory*. New York: Osprey, 2006.

Van de Logt, Mark. *War Party in Blue: Pawnee Scouts in the U.S. Army*. Norman: University of Oklahoma Press, 2010.

2

Special Forces of World War II, 1939–1945

Special purpose–type units had all but been forgotten by the United States since 1918, but the advent of World War II witnessed their dramatic rebirth. As its title implies, this conflict was waged across global dimensions and included fighting in desert environments, hostile jungles, mountain ranges, and isolated Pacific islands. This multiplicity of varied climes, coupled with the perfection of modern technologies such as aircraft, submarines, and primitive Aqua-Lungs, facilitated the deployment of special forces in terms of insertion and extraction. Transport aircraft, in particular, played an essential role for deploying behind enemy lines, sometimes as single agents, sometimes in regimental-sized formations, and, most spectacularly, as entire airborne divisions. Other land formations, such as rangers and raiders, specialized in large-scale infiltration, hit-and-run missions, more characteristic of classic guerilla warfare but with a conventional twist. All these activities confirmed the utility of special forces–type units in both combat and intelligence-gathering operations. The creation of the paramilitary Office of Strategic Services (OSS) in 1941, while technically a civilian agency, also employed specially trained uniformed personnel who displayed some operational overlap with bona fide military units. The period of 1939–1945 thus occasioned a blooming of diverse American special forces, although the lessons—and units—were subsequently lost in the immediate postwar period.

Army

Alamo Scouts

As the Sixth U.S. Army continued advancing across the southwestern Pacific, the growing emphasis on amphibious landings required better and more timely intelligence respecting Japanese defenses, capabilities, and intentions. On November 28, 1943, Lieutenant General

A team of Alamo Scouts pose for a photo after completing a reconnaissance mission on Los Negros Island, February 1944. They were among the most successful American reconnaissance units of World War II. (National Archives)

Walter Krueger, the regional commander, signed orders to organize the U.S. Sixth Army Special Reconnaissance unit, or Alamo Scouts, which derive their name from his San Antonio, Texas, origins and his personal admiration for the Alamo there. This detachment was envisioned from the onset as an elite, finely honed group of six- to seven-man teams with specialized skills for operating behind enemy lines in dense jungle foliage. These detachments would ingress by submarine ahead of an anticipated Sixth Army landing area, clandestinely scour the area for relevant information, and then report back without being discovered. In light of the intricate demands of this assignment, an intense volunteer selection process was circulated throughout Sixth Army combat units, and selectees so chosen were authorized to attend a rigorous six-week training program at the Alamo Scouts Training Center on Fergusson Island, New Guinea. Candidates had to successfully master no fewer than eight assigned skills, including rubber boat handling, intelligence gathering, scouting, patrolling, land navigation, weapons, and top physical fitness. The dropout rate was prodigious, and only 30 percent of all graduates, 250 enlisted men and 75 officers, were retained; of these, only 138 actually served in the field.

Despite their relative obscurity, the Alamo Scouts emerged as one of the finest American special forces units of this or any other conflict. During a 17 month period, they conducted 108 penetration missions behind Japanese lines without a single casualty. Moreover, they successfully raided Japanese camps and freed 197 Allied prisoners without loss. They also arrived on Luzon and Leyte in the Philippines to assist and coordinate Filipino guerrillas prior to the Allied invasion there. In January 1945, the scouts performed their most celebrated mission by providing tactical and intelligence support for the 6th Ranger

Battalion during the latter's daring rescue of 500 American captives from Cabanatuan prison camp in Luzon. In the ensuing action, the scouts took 84 Japanese prisoners while sustaining only two wounded. They subsequently formed part of the army of occupation following Japan's surrender in September 1945 and were unceremoniously disbanded at Kyoto the following November. The Alamo Scouts, their outstanding combat record notwithstanding, quickly slipped into obscurity, but in 1988 surviving members received an honorary Special Force Tab. The unit has since been officially co-opted into the lineage of modern U.S. Army Special Forces.

1st Special Service Force (Devil's Brigade)

In the spring of 1942, British scientist Geoffrey Pyke of the British Combined Operations Command opined that the Allies needed a small but elite military force capable of sustained operations in rough winter conditions. He envisioned a commando-type outfit that inserted itself behind enemy lines by land, sea, or air, especially in Nazi-occupied Rjukan, Norway, site of the heavy-water plant used by the Germans for atomic research. Pyke also formulated Project Plough, a large commando-style operation that would parachute this new unit into the Norwegian mountains near Jostedalsbreen to establish its base on a glacier there, then conduct raids against German occupiers. He initially broached the idea to Admiral Lord Louis Mountbatten, chief of Combined Operations Headquarters, but the latter felt that only the United States had the money, manpower, and resources to raise and field it. Fortunately, General George C. Marshall, U.S. Army chief of staff, was receptive to Project Plough and authorized a concept paper to be drawn up. The task fell on Lieutenant Colonel Robert T. Frederick, a relatively obscure officer in the Operations Division of the general staff, and his May 1942 report proved so thorough and so clearly identified its many drawbacks that Mountbatten suggested that Frederick receive the assignment himself. Project Plough was canceled in due course as impractical, but the elite force envisioned to conduct it was allowed to continue.

Frederick accepted the assignment with relish and began assembling what he deemed the 1st Special Service Force. This new unit received top priority in terms of equipment and select training areas. Because it was originally envisioned as a winter-fighting formation, he was allowed to recruit a mixed American-Canadian force from outdoorsmen, including skiers, hunters, or lumberjacks. The volunteers next arrived at Fort William Henry Harrison in Helena, Montana, on July 9, 1942, so chosen for its proximity to mountain ranges for climbing and adjacent flat terrain for parachuting. Here the men endured a grueling regimen that imbued them with infiltration tactics, hand-to-hand combat, parachuting, mountain climbing, and ski warfare. Silent sentry elimination was especially stressed, so much so that the 1st Special Service Force was issued its own knife, the infamous V-42, based on the deadly weapon carried by British commandos. And, as a light infantry unit bereft of heavy weapons, they also received a higher proportion of Thompson and Johnson machine guns for added firepower in stand-up engagements. The 1st Special Service Force gradually expanded into three small regiments of two battalions each, and all ranks wore distinct unit patches consisting of a large red arrowhead with the words "USA" written horizontally and "Canada" vertically. They also received the cross-arrows insignia previously granted to the U.S. Army Indian Scouts. Frederick drilled his men mercilessly until July 4, 1943, when they embarked at San Francisco, California, for service in Alaska's Aleutian Islands. However, the Japanese had

Robert T. Frederick (1907–1970). Robert Tryon Frederick was born in San Francisco, California, on March 14, 1907, and he graduated from the U.S. Military Academy in 1928. In 1941, he transferred to the War Plans Division of the War Department general staff as a lieutenant colonel. There he learned of Prime Minister Winston Churchill's proposal for a special service brigade recruited from the United States and Canada. Frederick was chosen to visit Ottawa to make arrangements, and the Canadian government, impressed by his presentation, insisted that he lead it. Consequently, Frederick advanced to brigadier general in June 1942 and was appointed commander of the 1st Special Service Force, recruiting at Fort William Henry Harrison in Montana. Frederick's command received intense training in hand-to-hand combat, infiltration, amphibious landings, and parachut-

General Robert T. Frederick of the 1st Special Service Force, or "Devils Brigade." (National Archives)

ing, and their elite status was reflected by a red beret and distinctive cross-arrow insignia. Frederick next reported to the Fifth Army in Italy, where, in December 1943, his men quickly captured Monte la Difensa, a strongly held German position that had defied an entire division for a month. In January 1944, the 1st Special Service Force landed at Anzio and guarded their positions with such tenacity that Germans dubbed them the "Black Devils." On June 4, 1944, Frederick's men were among the first Allied troops to enter Rome. The following August, he left the "Devil's Brigade" to command the 1st Airborne Task Force, and subsequently headed up the 45th "Thunderbolt" Division. Afterward, he headed up the Sixth Training Division until 1952, when his eight wounds induced him to retire. Frederick died in Palo Alto, California, on November 29, 1970, once hailed by Churchill as "the greatest fighting general of all time."

expertly evacuated the island of Kiska before they arrived, so the 1st Special Service Force was subsequently diverted to Italy. This transfer came at the request of Lieutenant General Mark Clark, Fifth Army commander, then embroiled in a grueling war of attrition on that rugged peninsula.

The struggle for Italy had been going badly since the initial Allied landing at Salerno in September 1943. The harsh terrain posed serious problems for large-scale offensive operations and veteran German forces, brilliant on the tactical defense, thwarted American and British advances with severe casualties. By December, the drive on Rome had stalled out along the Bernhard Line, erected along a formidable chain of mountaintops that intersected Highways 6 and 7. In November, a concerted attack by the U.S. 3rd Infantry Division and the British 56th Division failed to gain any significant ground over a 12-day period and sustained heavy losses. The key to the German position, Monte la Difensa, was heavily guarded by several companies of the crack 104th Panzer Grenadiers, the 104th Infantry Regiment, and the 115th Reconnaissance Regiments, all of whom employed well-camouflaged machine gun nests and interlocking fields of fire that smothered every avenue of approach. Moreover, as long as the Germans controlled the high ground and directed artillery fire into the valley below, no movement through the Mignano Gap onto Rome was possible. The 1st Special Service Force's combat debut was in every sense a trial by fire, but the action itself constitutes a model of careful planning, thorough preparation, and ruthless execution.

Defining Activity

General Clark requested Colonel Frederick to prepare a plan for the capture of Monte la Difensa, and over the last week of November, the latter made several personal reconnaissance missions, both on foot and from the air, to gauge German defenses. He concluded that the only possible approach meant scaling a 300-meter cliff face on the north side of the mountain, presuming that the enemy regarded such an act as physically impossible; this was an attitude that the 1st Special Service Force counted on. On December 1, 1943, the 2nd Regiment boarded trucks for Presenzano, then marched 10 miles through rain and darkness to the final assembly area. The 1st and 3rd Regiments followed at casual, one-hour intervals so as to not arouse enemy attention. Great care was taken to infiltrate the strike force behind German lines unobserved, and the soldiers were strictly ordered not to use firearms, only knives and grenades, if enemy troops were encountered. At a prearranged time, hundreds of Allied artillery pieces opened up on the German position to give them the impression that another frontal assault was pending. In the early morning hours of December 2, 1943, 300 men of the 2nd Regiment under Colonel D. D. Williamson began scaling the sheer cliffs, straight up behind the German strongpoint. The 1st and 3rd Regiments remained below, functioning as reserves and litter bearers. At a prearranged signal, Allied gunners switched over to high-explosive, white phosphorus shells, providing a tremendous pyrotechnic diversion to the enemy as Williamson's men continued rappelling up the cliff to the crest. The assault force of three companies were deployed in place at 3:00 a.m. on December 3, 1943, and they pitched into the German position shortly before daybreak. The enemy, taken by surprise, quickly sorted themselves out, and the struggle for Monte la Difensa degenerated into a no-holds-barred infantryman's fight. Frederick's men, well versed in small-unit tactics and hand-to-hand combat, steadily eliminated all German resistance they encountered with hand grenades and bayonets. By dawn, the 1st Special Service Force stood triumphantly along the crest of the mountain, having killed 75 Germans and captured another 40. The 1st Regiment came up to join the victors, and together they endured a heavy German artillery bombardment that inflicted heavy losses but never yielded an inch. Thus, the previously impregnable Monte la Difensa, which had defied an entire division for 12 days, fell to 300 men of the 1st Special Service force in two hours. Their losses totaled 500 men—nearly 30 percent—but Frederick's unyielding emphasis on leadership, training, and, above all, surprise carried the day. It is the stuff of legends.

Subsequent attacks on Monte la Remetanea and Monte Vischiataro continued until January 8, 1944, before they were successfully concluded, but by then the 1st Special Service Force had lost 1,400 of its original 1,800 men, and the unit was withdrawn to rest and refit. Frederick's command recuperated until February 1, 1944, when they splashed ashore at Anzio, Italy, as part of Operation SHINGLE. There they absorbed survivors of the 1st and 3rd Ranger Battalions of Colonel William Darby, which had suffered heavily at the Battle of Cisterna. The brigade was required to defend an area usually assigned to an entire division, so Frederick ordered his men to conduct aggressive nighttime patrols and outpost raids to give the impression of greater numbers. They attacked unsuspecting German positions with faces blackened by shoe polish and stilettos silently drawn. Dead enemy soldiers were invariably festooned with a card declaring, "The worse is yet to come" in German. Their penchant for eliminating sentries led to the appellation of "Die schwarzen Teufel," or Black Devils, at which point the 1st Special Service Force became popularly heralded as the Devil's Brigade. Frederick's men remained on the lines for 99 days without relief, then accompanied the breakout from Anzio on May 25, 1944. They subsequently spearheaded the advance on Rome, captured seven bridges from the Germans to prevent their demolition, and were among the first Allied units to occupy the Eternal City. By late summer, the 1st Special Service Force had been culled from the Fifth Army to participate in Operation DRAGOON, the invasion of southern France, as part of the new 1st Airborne Task Force, which General Frederick now commanded. The force was subsequently tapped to storm the offshore islands of Ile de Port Gros and Ill du Levant, where several German batteries were deployed and menaced the invasion's flank. On the evening of August 14–15, Colonel Edwin A. Walker led his men ashore in rubber boats, surprised the Germans, and stormed their positions. The Devil's Brigade then accompanied the main force ashore; captured the village of Villeneuve-Loubet on August 26, 1944, in an extremely tough fight; and then protected the right flank of the Seventh Army as it proceeded inland. They advanced as far as the Franco-Italian border on September 7, 1944, and assumed defensive positions. The elite formation remained idle for three months as Allied leaders decided how to employ them and at length the Canadian Ministry of National Defense requested its personnel back. Accordingly, on December 5, 1944, the 1st Special Service Force returned to Villeneuve-Loubet for disbandment. The Canadians transferred mostly to the 1st Canadian Parachute Battalion, while the Americans enrolled in the new 474th Infantry, 12th Army Group. It was an ignominious ending for such a fighting outfit, for of the 2,400 men recruited, no fewer than 2,300 had become casualties at one point or another, a staggering loss rate of 90 percent. Nonetheless, the training, tactics, and battlefield lessons of the Devil's Brigade have since been inculcated by U.S. Army Special Forces (Green Berets) and Canada's top-secret JTF2 Force.

Rangers

In the early days of World War II, Great Britain found itself bested on the continent by new German tactics involving massed Panzer divisions, close air support, and imaginative use of parachute infantry operating behind the lines. Unable to compete with them in terms of equipment or numbers, the British countered with small-unit specialists capable of striking back unexpectedly, wearing an opponent down, and keeping him off balance along diverse fronts. These specialist troops quickly gained renown as Army and Royal Marine

William O. Darby (1911–1945).
William Orlando Darby was born in Fort Smith, Arkansas, on February 18, 1911, and in 1933 he graduated from the U.S. Military Academy. After World War II commenced, Darby came to the attention of Colonel Lucian K. Truscott, then recruiting volunteers for his new ranger program, and he signed up. Darby first fought during the ill-fated British-Canadian landing at Dieppe, France, in August 1942, then rose to lieutenant colonel, 1st Ranger Battalion, in North Africa. He fought with distinction at Gafsa-El Guettar, Tunisia, on March 21, 1942, and his force was gradually expanded into a brigade. During General George S. Patton's drive on Gela, Sicily, in July 1943, Darby personally knocked out several German vehicles at close range, winning a Distinguished Service Cross. Two months later, his rangers deployed at Salerno, Italy, as conventional infantry, where they sustained heavy losses. Unfortu-

Colonel William Darby led the first Ranger units in World War II with distinction. (Courtesy of the U.S. Army)

nately, his new replacements were not as thoroughly trained as the original rangers. On January 22, 1944, Darby's men landed at Anzio to help break the stalemate in Italy, and six days later the 1st and 3rd Battalions advanced to town of Cisterna while Darby remained with the 4th Battalion in reserve. The Germans anticipated the move, unfortunately, and ambushed the lightly armed rangers, who lost two-thirds of their strength. In April 1944, Darby shipped back to Washington, D.C., as a staff officer but he gained appointment as executive officer in the 10th Mountain Division during final phases of combat in Italy. On April 30, 1945, he was killed by shell fragments only one week before Germany surrendered. Darby consequently received posthumous promotion to brigadier general, being the only American soldier so honored.

Commandos, the Special Air Service, the Special Boat Squadron, and the Special Operations Executive (SOE), which handled clandestine espionage and sabotage affairs. Army Chief of Staff General George C. Marshall, who toured British military establishments prior to American entry into World War II, was singularly impressed by these troops and determined that the United States should raise similar units. He first broached the subject with a personal friend, Colonel Lucian K. Truscott, who, drawing on the army's light infantry tradition, suggested reviving the title "ranger" to denote American-style commando units.

This early photograph depicts U.S. Army rangers, still equipped with World War I–style helmets, training under the aegis of British naval instructors. (Library of Congress)

The idea was approved, and on June 8, 1942, Major William O. Darby, was reassigned from his present position as aide-de-camp to the commanding general of the 34th Infantry Division, organized the 1st Ranger Battalion at Carrickfergus, Northern Ireland. Recruits were drawn from 1,500 volunteers, of whom only 600 passed muster. Consistent with light infantry traditions, these troops emphasized speed and stealth over sheer firepower and were not equipped with standard heavy weapons. Moreover, Darby was authorized to recruit a headquarters company and six line companies of 67 men apiece, and all volunteers were handpicked for their intelligence, good military records, and outstanding physical prowess. Once assembled, the unit shipped to Achnacarry, Scotland, home of the famous commando training base, where they endured a grueling course at the hands of British instructors. Firing drills were conducted with live ammunition, while qualities of common sense, persistence, and teamwork were emphasized until they became second nature. Most significant, all rangers were paired into a "buddy" system where each looked out for the other, on and off the battlefield. This practice culminated in a "no-man-left-behind" policy which endures in ranger units to present times. Once basic infantry operations, such as scouting and patrolling, were mastered, rangers were keenly taught the art of ambushes, cliff assaults, amphibious landings, and full-scale maneuvering at night. Infiltration behind enemy lines under a variety of conditions, was likewise highly stressed. The men were further subject to expert marksmen courses, unarmed combat with knives, rappelling up and down mountainsides, explosive handling, and prisoner snatches. In sum, rangers endured the most complete regimen of any Allied infantry of this conflict, one reflecting their unique role as America's premier special operations force.

1st, 3rd, and 4th Ranger Battalions

The 1st Ranger Battalion experienced its baptism of fire on August 18, 1942, when a party of 50 men accompanied the British-Canadian raid at Dieppe, France. The operation proved disastrous for the Allies and it highlighted operational shortcomings in planning, but the rangers acquitted themselves well, suffering three killed and several captured. Lieutenant E. V. Loustalot thus became the first U.S. Army officer to die in Europe, but Corporal Franklin Koons became the first American soldier to kill an enemy there, winning a Silver Star. That fall, Darby's 1st Ranger Battalion was deemed ready for action, and on October 1942 it spearheaded Major General Terry Allen's 1st Infantry Division landing at Arzew, Algeria, as part of Operation TORCH. Once ashore, it split into two groups and quickly silenced some Vichy French batteries ahead of the main landings. The rangers next saw important action at Sened Station, Tunisia, on February 11, 1943, when Darby infiltrated 32 miles behind Italian lines and successfully stormed the enemy camp, killing

50 enemy soldiers and seizing 10 prisoners. In light of his excellent planning and determined execution, Darby received a Silver Star, while the Italian christened his rangers the "Black Death." They performed similar work on March 21, 1943, at Djebel El Ank Pass east of El Guettar after hiking a 12-mile gorge route around the enemy flank. Darby then scaled steep cliffs behind the enemy position and ordered his rangers forward, clearing the area of enemy troops and seizing 200 additional captives. After advancing to Sfax, where a further 1,400 Italian went into the bag, Darby's rangers endured three days of counterattacks by the German Panzer grenadiers before driving them off. The 1st Ranger Battalion ultimately received its first Presidential Unit Citation (PUC) in light of its operational excellence.

Darby's successes resulted in the recruitment of the 3rd and 4th Ranger Battalions at Nemours, Morocco, which participated in the forthcoming invasion of Sicily with the 6615th Ranger Force (Provisional). Darby, now commanding the 1st and 4th Battalions, spearheaded the 1st Infantry Division's landing outside Gela, which was successfully stormed. The town of San Nicole also fell with the assistance of an armored division, as did the town of Buerta, situated on the very edge of a seaside cliff. Rather than risk heavy losses to a frontal assault, Darby infiltrated a single platoon into the town, convincing the defenders into surrendering en masse. Concurrently, the 3rd Ranger Battalion marched in the direction of Agrigento, seizing the towns of Campobello, Naro, and Favara. The town of Porto Empedocle also fell during a stiff fight, during which Germans and Italians poured a heavy fire down a cliff side, but the rangers seized their objective before an assisting infantry battalion landed to assist. Darby received a Distinguished Service Cross for his actions in Sicily; however, he turned down a promotion offered by Major General George S. Patton rather than be separated from his rangers.

The rangers subsequently garnered additional laurels during the difficult and costly invasion of the Italian mainland. Darby's troops landed near Salerno on September 9, 1943, where they embroiled in costly mountain fighting against entrenched German defenders along the Winter Line. Being deployed by superiors as line infantry, a task for which they were not well-suited, the rangers took heavy losses in securing and defending the Chiunzi Pass for two weeks, assisted by naval gunfire from offshore. Pushing inland, they next fought at the Mignano Gap and sustained further casualties while butting up against the heavily defended German line at Cassino. Casualty rates topped 40 percent by the time Darby and his men withdrew from action, given an infusion of new recruits, and prepared for their greatest battle yet. Unfortunately, the rangers' well-honed skills, especially in terms of nighttime infiltration, had deteriorated since their heady days on the British Isles. These newest additions, while eager and earnest, lacked the same degree of training imparted into the casualties they replaced. As late as January 17, 1944, during a landing rehearsal at Pozzuoli Bay, umpires roundly criticized the rangers for numerous mistakes during their nighttime maneuvers, especially a tendency for making too much noise.

Defining Activity

On January 22, 1944, the Allies commenced Operation SHINGLE at Anzio, an amphibious landing intended to outflank German defenses on the peninsula and quickly seize Rome. However, timid leadership allowed the enemy time to consolidate their defenses, and the entire campaign bogged down into a slugfest. On January 30, 1944, Darby led the 1st,

3rd, and 4th Ranger Battalions forward, intending to infiltrate the town of Cisterna de Lattoria and facilitate an Allied breakout. The 1st and 3rd Battalions threaded their way through a series of dry irrigation canals, believing themselves undetected. However, radio communication began breaking down, and the 3rd Battalion also became lost and separated from the 1st Battalion. The impact of poorly trained replacements was now making itself felt. Meanwhile, Darby led the 4th Battalion by a different route and encountered stiff resistance outside the town. By daybreak, it was obvious that the Germans had anticipated the Americans' approach, for they surrounded Cisterna with armor and elite airborne troops. Darby and his 4th Ranger Battalion attacked heroically to reach the cut-off 1st and 3rd Battalions, but he was blasted back by tanks of the Hermann Göring Panzer division. Darby finally yielded after a desperate four-hour struggle and retreated with 50 percent casualties. The Germans, meanwhile, surrounded the ditches of Cisterna with tanks and fired point blank into ditches occupied by survivors of the 1st and 3rd Battalions. It was a massacre; by day's end, only six of the 767 rangers escaped back to American lines. The disaster at Cisterna further highlighted the folly of allowing lightly armed rangers to be ensnared by heavier, conventional formations. The rangers, for their part, managed to inflict over 5,000 casualties on the Germans, forcing them to delay their counterattack against the Anzio beachhead by two precious days. The survivors from all three battalions were then broken up and subsequently distributed to the 1st Special Service Force (Devil's Brigade) and some parachute infantry units. The army ultimately deactivated the 1st, 3rd, and 4th Ranger Battalions at Camp Burner, North Carolina, on October 26, 1944. Prior to disbandment, they had been publicly hailed as Darby's Rangers because of the reputation of their leader.

2nd and 5th Ranger Battalions

As events played out in Italy, the 2nd and 5th Ranger Battalions completed their training at Camp Forrest, Tennessee, and arrived in England as the Ranger Assault Group under Lieutenant Colonel Max Schneider. They continued receiving intensive training in cliff climbing, amphibious raiding, and night tactics as the invasion of Europe dawned. Grandiose schemes were cooked up for them, including raids against Norway and a prisoner snatch mission near Calais, France, but these were canceled because of high seas and fears that such activity might arose German suspicions. Instead, on D-Day, they were tasked with eliminating an enemy battery at Pointe du Hoc, four miles west of Omaha Beach, that threatened the landing force coming ashore below it. Taking these gun entailed scaling a 100-foot cliff up from the beach itself, most likely in the face of determined German resistance. Lieutenant Colonel Schneider, ignoring the perils facing his command, ordered all training measures stepped up and intensified ahead of the invasion.

Defining Activity

On June 6, 1944, Lieutenant Colonel James E. Rudder, commanding 230 men of Companies C, D, E, and F, 2nd Ranger Battalion, led his men ashore in rough weather and moved toward Ponte du Hoc in the predawn darkness. To scale the imposing cliff from the beachhead, rangers carried special rocket-propelled launchers that tossed a grappling hook and rope ladders up the heights. En route, high seas soaked men and equipment alike, while and rough currents placed them far from their scheduled landing zone. The dripping rangers consequently arrived 35 minutes late, but on reaching the base of the cliff, they fired off their grappling rockets and began clambering up. German infantry began firing down from above, and tossed hand grenades over in buckets. Rangers toppled in heaps, but within 10 minutes, Rudder personally led the survivors across the top and overpowered the defenders—only to discover that the German guns had been moved. The cannon were subsequently found further inland, and the rangers neutralized them as ordered. Rudder, who defied direct orders not to accompany his men into combat, commanded rangers inland and held off German counterattacks for two additional days before being relieved. Hereafter, his command became known as "Rudder's Rangers."

Meanwhile, the 5th Ranger Battalion, bolstered by two companies of the 2nd Battalion, stormed ashore at Dog Green Beach (Vierville sector, Omaha Beach) with the 29th Infantry Division. Schneider and his men were quickly pinned behind a seawall under heavy fire, and casualties mounted. At this juncture, Major General Norman Cota suddenly bellowed "Rangers, lead the way!" (since adopted as their official motto), and, accompanied by the 166th Infantry, the 5th Battalion clawed its way forward and carried the heights. Fighting at Normandy cost the 2nd Ranger Battalion 200 out of 350 men, while the 5th Battalion lost 62 out of 130 men present. Given the small numbers for such a big mission, it was a bravura performance.

After D-Day, the rangers assisted in the August–September struggle for the port city of Brest. During the fighting, the 5th Rangers knocked out several pillboxes with high explosives and gasoline, which burned furiously and convinced the Germans defending similar positions to simply surrender. On December 7, 1944, the 2nd Rangers participated in the ongoing fiasco at the Heurtegen Forest, where they were to seize ground overlooking the Schmidt and Roer Dams. Rudder's men infiltrated and captured the position, then withstood repeated counterattacks until relief arrived on March 9, 1945. The 2nd Rangers, now misused as line infantry, lost half their remaining strength in the struggle for Bergstein. On February 23, 1945, the 5th Battalion also executed a difficult infiltration mission to establish a blocking position across the Irsch-Zerf road. The Germans counterattacked immediately, although the rangers held out until rescued by friendly armor on February 26; in this final action, they accounted for 299 enemy dead and 328 prisoners. For the remainder of the war in Europe, rangers found themselves increasingly employed as regular infantry, a task for which they were poorly suited, and they suffered accordingly.

6th Ranger Battalion

For several months, General Douglas A. MacArthur and 6th Army commander Walter E. Kruger bemoaned the fact they lacked specialist units capable of performing large-scale raiding and intelligence-gathering missions behind enemy lines. The famous Alamo Scouts, while brilliant in their role, simply lacked the manpower for such larger, sustained endeavors. Consequently, in January 1943, the 6th Ranger Battalion arose at Hollandia, New Guinea, when it was culled from the 98th Field Artillery Battalion by Major Henry A. Mucci. These men, mostly tall, fit farm boys from the Midwest, were tired of hauling pack howitzers around the jungle on mules and volunteered in droves. Once assembled at Port Moresby, they endured a rigorous physical training routine, led by Major Mucci himself, while also polishing their skills in reconnaissance, patrolling, scouting, weapons, and nighttime maneuvers. Moving from there to Finschafen, the rangers practiced amphibious landings in rubber boats. Senior leaders were so pleased by Mucci's progress that they formally activated the 6th Ranger Battalion on September 26, 1944, in time for the upcoming invasion of the Philippines. On October 17, 1944, the rangers landed on Homonhon, Suluan, and Dinagat Islands guarding the entrance to Leyte Gulf, the Philippines, three days ahead of the main American invasion force. Resistance proved light, so they any destroyed radio or communication facilities useful to the Japanese before departing. On Dinagat, Company B under Captain Arthur D. "Bull" Simons encountered a Japanese force garrisoned in a lighthouse, surrounded on three sides by imposing cliffs and accessible only by a steep trail. Undeterred, his rangers silently scaled the cliffs at night, struck the garrison from the rear, and wiped them out. The rangers spent the next two months unglamorously providing rear-area security and guarding supply dumps until the next special mission arose.

Defining Activity

As the invasion developed, senior American leaders expressed concern that the Japanese might transfer the captives from the Cabanatuan prison camp in Luzon or even execute them. The camp itself was located deep behind enemy lines and along a main road used by Japanese forces for supplies and reinforcements. The 6th Ranger Battalion was consequently entrusted with their rescue, and several days were spent planning and collecting military intelligence from Filipino guerillas and the famous Alamo Scouts. On January 29, 1945, a reinforced ranger company of 107 men skillfully infiltrated 29 miles behind Japanese lines. They finished the final mile by wading through a flooded rice paddy on their stomachs to avoid detection. The rangers attacked the prison at dawn on January 30, killing 200 Japanese soldiers and securing 500 American half-starved prisoners within half an hour. Good intelligence, a stealthy approach, and hard-hitting tactics rendered Cabanatuan one of the most daring prisoner rescues in American military history, and the 6th Ranger Battalion had only two killed and seven wounded. Success here also triggered a wave of emotional and favorable publicity stateside, for the captives were originally taken when Bataan surrendered in 1942 and were subject to horrific mistreatment. The rangers continued fighting in the Philippines and performed mop-up operations against isolated pockets of resistance but were never employed as line infantry and were spared the heavy losses characterized by like units in western Europe. They were disbanded in Japan on December 30, 1945.

5307 Composite Unit (Provisional)

Commencing in January 1942, the Japanese launched an aggressive and highly successful campaign to eject the British from northern Burma, thereby cutting China's last remaining supply link over the so-called Burma Road. The British subsequently mounted a slapdash offensive in the Arakan region in late 1942 that was completely thwarted by dense jungle conditions and tenacious Japanese tactics. It appeared that Burma might be lost for the duration of the war, but in February 1943, eccentric British military leader Colonel Orde Wingate led a deep raid behind enemy lines that was partially supplied by air and linked to headquarters by radio. The raiders became known as "Chindits," taken from a mythical

Burmese griffin that guarded temples. Wingate's effort was only partially successful and returned to British lines minus one-third its numbers, but they demonstrated that, with air-to-ground cooperation and unconventional strategies, the Japanese could be defeated. Allied leaders determined to retry Wingate's experiment on a larger scale, and at the Quebec Conference of August 1943, discussions arose concerning an American long-range penetration unit to act in concert with the Chindits. Wingate, who was present during the proceedings, argued for the establishment of a series of strong points deep behind enemy lines that could be supplied and reinforced by air—an unprecedented military feat. American leaders were impressed, and Operation GALAHAD arose as a raid deep in enemy-held territory and made in concert with several Chinese divisions from northern Burma. Because this unit represents the only purely American ground force on the Asian landmass, it would be assigned to Lieutenant General Joseph Stillwell, senior American leader of the China-Burma-India (CBI) theater. Furthermore, it received the rather grandiose title of the 5307th Composite Unit (Provisional) to disguise its actual intent. Stillwell appointed one of his protégés, Brigadier General Frank D. Merrill, to command it. Merrill, a former cavalry officer, envisioned his force as a form of strategic cavalry that would envelop Japanese formations from behind once they were pinned frontally by the two Chinese divisions present.

On September 18, 1943, the War Department issued a preliminary draft for the this new penetration force, which would be cobbled together from seasoned troops already versed in jungle warfare. These veterans were culled from garrisons across the Army Ground Forces (in the United States), the Caribbean Defense Command, the South Pacific Command, and the Southwest Pacific Command once President Franklin D. Roosevelt personally asked for 3,000 volunteers to step forward. The men were to deploy at bases in India no later than October to commence training. Only the highest-quality candidates were sought, but when many of the Pacific commands simply emptied out their stockades and sent a fair share of misfits, and these were simply absorbed into the unit. The whole arrived at Bombay, India, on October 31, 1943, and commenced a rigorous light infantry regimen under Brigadier General Wingate himself. Quick movements and slashing attacks were emphasized, for the 5307th Composite Unit (Provisional), like any ranger-type unit, lacked the organic fire-power (cannon and heavy mortars) inherent in regular infantry formations. In fact, no weapon heavier than 60-mm mortars were issued, and these were carried across the difficult terrain by mules. Merrill's unit was never intended for "stand-up" engagements, even though a greater proportion of automatic weapons was issued. The men also became adept at scouting, patrolling, stream crossing, land navigation, demolition, camouflage, and radio techniques to facilitate supply airdrops, which was the very lifeline of the unit. The three battalions of the 5307th were subsequently organized into six self-contained combat teams (Red, White, Blue, Khaki, Green, and Orange) for a total of 2,750 men. Training continued at Deogarh, India, until the end of January 1944, then they began assembling for their offensive into Burma. The ensuing campaign, in which the 5307th displayed an uncanny knack for rapidly traversing terrain considered impassable, proved a military trek worthy of Xenophon himself.

On February 24, 1944, Merrill led the 5307th down the Ledo Road from India and into Burma, a march of 1,000 miles. Throughout they were assisted continually by several hundred Burmese Kachin rangers, lithe, little warriors who performed invaluable services as scouts and screeners. Once behind Japanese lines, the Americans made themselves felt by ambushing patrols, cutting enemy communications, and harassing enemy rear areas.

Brigadier General Frank D. Merrill, commander of the jungle outfit known as "Merrill's Marauders," at his headquarters behind enemy lines in Burma on June 16, 1944. Merrill commanded the first U.S. combat unit on the Asian mainland during World War II. (Bettmann/Corbis)

Frank D. Merrill (1903–1955). Frank Dow Merrill was born in Hopkinton, Massachusetts, on December 4, 1903, and he joined the U.S. Army in 1922. He was allowed to attend the U.S. Military Academy, from which he graduated in 1929, and served as a career cavalry officer. Following American entry into World War II, Merrill accompanied General Joseph W. Stillwell out of Burma, and in October 1943 he gained promotion to temporary brigadier general with orders to raise a ranger-style outfit. This was the origin of the 5307th Composite Unit (Provisional), subsequently hailed as "Merrill's Marauders," a name they themselves never used. In January 1944, Merrill led them deep into the Burmese jungle on a 100-mile raid, all the while supplied by air. He heavily defeated the veteran Japanese troops encountered, but his men suffered heavily through disease and malnutrition. Nonetheless, Stillwell now ordered them to capture the Japanese airfield at Myitkyina, entailing another difficult slog over the Kuman Mountains and across some of Asia's most foreboding terrain. The Marauders endured their march, infiltrated the settlement, and stormed the airfield in May 1944. Fanatical Japanese resistance kept the town out of their hands until August, when it fell with the assistance of Chinese troops. The 5307th Composite Unit (Provisional) was then so disease ridden that it was unceremoniously disbanded. Merrill, meanwhile, had been evacuated after two heart attacks and was reassigned to the Allied Southwest Asia Command. After the war, he served as chief of staff with the 6th Army in San Francisco and also functioned with the U.S. Military Mission to the Philippines. Merrill, an outstanding special forces commander, died in Fernandina Beach, Florida, on December 11, 1955.

However, unexpected problems in coordinating Chinese movements left the crack Japanese 18th Infantry Division of Lieutenant General Shinichi Tanaka free to attack the American roadblocks with superior numbers. During the battle at Walawbum on March 7, 1944, the outnumbered 3rd Battalion found itself completely surrounded but demonstrated acute tactical prowess by mowing down 500 Japanese. The Americans withstood numerous attacks with machine gun fire and accurate mortars yet suffered heavy losses in a protracted firefight that they were supposed to avoid. Expert maneuvering allowed the Japanese to bypass Merrill's roadblocks, and they fell back to new positions along the Jambu Bum mountain range. By late March, the Marauders had cut enemy supply lines in the Hukawng Valley as planned, and they were expecting to be relieved. Stillwell, however, suddenly changed their tactical mission from flanking to blocking and ordered them to dig in at Nhpum Ga. Lightly armed and irregularly supplied by air, this was a mission that the 5307th was not designed for, but Merrill organized his three battalions into mutually supporting fire zones. Consequently, when large numbers of Japanese troops flooded around the 2nd Battalion, they were invariably blasted back over the course of 11 days. By April 9, 1944, the Marauders accounted for 400 Japanese while losing 57 dead and 302 wounded. Another 379 were so sick from malaria, dysentery, and other jungle maladies that they were officially incapacitated. However, when the press got wind of their impressive achievements in the depths of Burma, they pronounced them "Merrill's Marauders," a name they never applied themselves.

Defining Activity

By the late spring of 1944, the British had successfully contained a determined Japanese thrust at their lines of communication at Kohima-Imphal. Stillwell then sought to capitalize on enemy weakness by launching Operation END RUN, a sudden march through mountainous jungle territory to capture Myitkyina, site of a strategic Japanese airfield. A committed Anglophobe, he apparently conceived this plan as much to embarrass the British as to defeat the Japanese. The men of the 5307th, decimated from heat exhaustion and disease, and fully expecting some well-deserved rest, were suddenly ordered back into the field. They wearily mustered 1,400 men and traversed 65 miles through some of the worst terrain imaginable long before any any offensive operations could commence. The slopes of the 6,000-foot Kumon mountain range were steep and muddy because of recent rains, and hundreds of mules—along with the supplies they carried—were lost as they slid over the cliffs. Ongoing rains and dense jungle foliage also interfered with resupply efforts, and the men suffered from a lack of food. Nonetheless, once informed by Kachin scouts that the garrison at Myitkyina was not alerted, the tired, disease-ridden Marauders successfully stormed the airfield on May 17, 1944. Merrill lacked the strength to tackle the town itself, even with the assistance of Chinese troops, and the 4,600 Japanese defenders defied every attempt to evict them. Stillwell nevertheless ordered Myitkyina to be taken. The siege dragged onto into the monsoon season, and sickness rates skyrocketed once exhausted soldiers began sleeping in the mud. The siege was another activity that the 5307th was neither designed nor equipped for, and Colonel Charles N. Hunter, who replaced Merrill after the latter suffered a second heart attack, protested loudly to Stillwell. Myitkyina was finally captured on August 3, 1944, the same day that Hunter was relieved of command but only after the Americans airlifted in an entire Chinese division to assist. Only 600 Japanese escaped its fall, and an estimated 3,800 died in combat. The Marauders, for their part, had an additional 287 killed, 955 wounded, and 980 so ill that they were medically evacuated. Success here also terminated the 5307th as a combat unit, for it was unceremoniously discharged at Myitkyina on August 10, 1944; of 2,250 men originally mustered, only 130 officers and men remained combat effective. These survivors were enrolled into the new 475th U.S. Infantry, which, when attached to the 124th Cavalry Regiment, constituted the new Mars Task Force. Stillwell, for his part, both embarrassed his allies and was roundly criticized for pushing the Marauders beyond their physical and mental limits. Operation GALAHAD may have been successful tactically and facilitated the final Japanese collapse in Burma, but it proved a horrendous experience for the troops involved.

The litany of achievements was impressive: during their five-month service life, the Marauders marched over 750 miles through incredibly harsh mountainous jungles and won five major battles and most of the 32 lesser engagements against veteran Japanese troops. As such, they became the first U.S. combat unit to fight on the Asian mainland since the 1900 Boxer Rebellion in China and consequently received a Distinguished Unit Citation award. Furthermore, each of the surviving Marauders, having slogged longer in jungle terrain than any other U.S. Army unit of the war, received the Bronze Star, an unprecedented event. In 1954, the 475th Infantry was redesignated the 75th Infantry, a lineal descendant of today's 75th Ranger Regiment.

10th Mountain Division

The U.S. Army gained an increased awareness of winter-weather troops during the 1939 Soviet invasion of Finland, where highly trained and athletic ski troops of the Finnish army destroyed several Soviet formations despite terrible operating conditions. However, it fell on Charles Minot Dole, president of the National Ski Patrol, to finally broach the subject with the War Department. In September 1940, Dole ventured to Washington, D.C., and conferred with Army Chief of Staff General George C. Marshall to make the case for a unit specifically trained to conduct mountain warfare. Marshall was sufficiently impressed to authorized creation of the 87th Mountain Infantry Battalion on December 8, 1941, and the unit initially trained atop of Mount Rainier. The National Ski Patrol took on responsibility for recruiting prospective members, mostly highly disciplined athletes, including rock climbers, skiers, or forest rangers. The regiment first saw action in August 1943 on Kiska, the Aleutians, where the only casualties sustained were by friendly fire. Fortunately, senior army commanders envisioned the utility of such a formation, and on July 10, 1943, the 10th Light Division (Alpine) was created and activated at Camp Hale, Colorado. The 87th Mountain Infantry Battalion was redesigned the 87th U.S. Infantry, now the core of the new formation, and it was joined by the 85th and 86th Infantries. Throughout 1943–1944, the 10th Light Division trained at Seneca Rocks, West Virginia, with troops receiving intense instruction on climbing, hand signals, and proper use of muffled piton hammers. Advanced instruction was imparted back at Camp Hale and included mass movement on skies and snowshoes in brutal weather and camping in deep snow without tents. On November 6, 1944, the unit received its new designation as the 10th Mountain Division, and members toted blue and white "Mountain" uniform tabs denoting their elite status. The 10th Mountain Division shipped for Italy in late 1944 and debarked there on January 6, 1945. At this point, German defenses were sequestered behind the so-called Gothic Line, which stretched 120 miles across the northernmost fringes of the Apennine Mountains. It was manned by units of the crack LI Mountain Corps, who were well armed and tactically astute in defensive warfare. After some preliminary skirmishing near Cutigliano and Orsigna, the 10th Mountain Division was earmarked for serious combat near Monte Castello in concert with troops of the Brazilian Expeditionary Force. As such, it was also among the final U.S. Army combat divisions to see action during World War II.

Defining Activity

In February 1945, Allied planners had decided to crack the line of German defenses by storming 3,876-foot-high Mount Belvedere, which overlooked and controlled access to Highway 64 into the heart of western Europe. To accomplish this, it was necessary to first secure nearby Riva Ridge and deny enemy troops observation points from which they could rain down mortar and artillery fire. This position in question was a three-and-a-half-mile-long massif of peaks and was unapproachable during daylight hours. The mission fell to General George Hays and his 10th Mountain Division, which was well trained but still untested. Several night patrols were dispatched to ascertain the best way up the sheer cliffs, and leaders decided that Riva Ridge and Mount Belvedere could be taken in two consecutive nighttime assaults. On the evening of February 18, 1945, 700 soldiers from the 86th Infantry began climbing up toward the crest with full packs and combat equipment, moving quietly so as to not alert the defenders. By daybreak on February 19, all four assault companies were successfully entrenched on Riva's summit, and the Germans launched determined counterattacks to throw them off. At one point, batteries of the 605th Field Artillery, acting in support of the 86th, brought plunging fire to within 10 yards of American positions. The defenders repelled several attacks over the next 36 hours before the enemy finally abandoned the attempt. On the evening of February 19, 1945, several battalions of the 85th and 87th Infantry also began scaling up the cliff sides of Mount Belvedere, only this time against an opponent that was thoroughly aroused and waiting. Germans of the 1044th Regiment withheld their fire until the Americans were within a few yards, then suddenly cut loose. The attack staggered to a halt until air strikes silenced several strong points, then men of the 10th Mountain Division flooded over remaining resistance. Sporadic mountain fighting continued without interruption until February 25, when the Americans finally crowned the crest of Mount Belvedere. Meanwhile, the Brazilian Expeditionary Force had also stormed nearby Mount Castello. The 5th Army was now better positioned to batter its way up through the remainder of the Apennines and into southern Austria.

After their victory at Mount Belvedere, the 10th Mountain Division continued fighting its way to within 15 miles of Bologna during March, and that April it launched a new offensive that captured Mongiorgio in the Po Valley. They then forded the Po River on April 23, 1945; captured Verona two days later; and then made an amphibious crossing of Lake Garda to seize Porto di Tremosine on the April 30. Germany formally capitulated on May 2, 1945, at which point General Fridolin Von Senger und Enterlin, commanding all German units in the region, insisted that he surrender personally to General Hays. The division was slated for service in the Pacific, but Japan surrendered in August 1945, and the men shipped back to the United States for demobilization. The 10th Mountain Division, America's premier rough-terrain experts, was deactivated at Camp Carson, Colorado, on November 30, 1945. In 114 days of sustained combat, the 10th Mountain Division suffered 992 dead and 4,154 wounded, and it received two campaign streamers.

11th Airborne Division

The 11th Airborne Division was activated at Camp Mackall, North Carolina, on February 25, 1943, under the command of Major General Joseph M. Swing. It consisted of the 511th

Parachute Infantry Regiment and the 187th and 188th Glider Infantry Regiments, the whole with an assigned strength of 8,321 officers and men. Like all airborne formations, it received a more rigorous training regimen and higher pay rates than standard infantry formations, consistent with its elite status. However, at this time, senior commanders of the U.S. Army were seriously questioning the utility of airborne troops in general, following the poor performance of the 82nd Airborne Division during Operation HUSKY on Sicily. However, Army Chief of Staff General George C. Marshall directed General Dwight D. Eisenhower to establish a review board for the purpose of evaluating airborne operational techniques and to hold a large-scale maneuvers before a final verdict was rendered. The 11th Airborne Division was chosen as the test formation, while General Swing was appointed head of the Swing Board to decide the fate of airborne units in the U.S. Army. As the test formation, the 11th Airborne participated in the simulated capture of Knollwood Army Auxiliary Airfield near Fort Bragg, North Carolina. Among those observing the proceedings was Lieutenant General Leslie J. McNair, commander of U.S. Army ground forces and a decided skeptic of parachute infantry. On December 7, 1943, however, the 11th Airborne Division, capitalizing on improved navigation and deployment techniques developed since Sicily, executed their mission flawlessly. That evening, a force of 200 C-47 transports and 234 Waco gliders landed their paratroopers, then launched a simulated ground attack while supplied by aircraft of the Army Air Force. McNair, impressed by the smoothness of the Knollwood Maneuver, recommended the retention of airborne forces, and all were preserved intact.

The 11th Airborne Division continued training stateside in reserve until June 1944, when it shipped out to Milne Bay, New Guinea, to prepare for service in the Philippines. Over the next four months, the troops were acclimatized and schooled in jungle tactics until it deployed for combat operations on Leyte on November 18, 1944. As part of the 24th Corps, they went into action against dug-in Japanese forces in the Burauen-La Paz-Bugho region, although fighting as regular infantry, not paratroopers. On December 6, 1944, the Japanese managed to drop airborne troops of their own on Burauen Airfield, headquarters of the 11th Airborne, but these were mopped up by ad hoc forces assembled by General Swing in person. On January 22, 1945, the division shipped north for service on Luzon, with the glider regiments coming ashore in light amphibious craft, while the 511th Parachute Infantry arrived at Mindoro by air transport. Hard fighting against entrenched, fanatical defenders ensued, and it was not until February 3, 1945, that the 11th Airborne Division finally made an aerial drop against Tagaytay Ridge. The 511th Parachute Infantry was delivered in three waves because of a lack of transport aircraft, and landing zones were scattered, but the troops consolidated themselves and linked up with the 187th and 188th Glider Infantries pushing inland. Even harder fighting erupted as the 11th Airborne Division was ordered to penetrate the Japanese Genko Line north of Manila on February 5, 1945, and the defenders were not completely silenced for another two weeks of intense combat.

Defining Activity

On February 22, 1945, Company B, 511th Parachute Infantry, was chosen to make an airborne assault against the Los Banos prison camp on Luzon, located near the Agricultural College of the Philippines, where many civilian captives, mostly missionaries, clergymen, and civilian professionals, were interred. In fact, the 11th Airborne Division had been personally tasked by General Douglas A. MacArthur for the mission, and it was planned by General Swing and his staff. It was decided that as the paratroopers stormed the camp, two additional companies would traverse a nearby lake in amphibious Amtracs for support. Prior to this, the divisional reconnaissance platoon would also arrive by lake to secure a large adjacent field for the paratroopers to land. Various detachments of Filipino guerillas were also operating in the area to provide intelligence. Once Company B had landed, they quickly overcame the defenders with machine gun and bazooka fire. All 2,147 civilian internees were then quickly rounded up for immediate evacuation. The operation proceeded smoothly, and the rear guard, consisting of Company B and the guerillas, were likewise removed back to American lines without incident.

At length, the Sixth U.S. Army headquarters assigned the 11th Airborne Division the task of mopping up final Japanese resistance on southern Luzon. Between February and May, the paratroopers fought a bloody battle with 80,000 members of the Japanese Shimbu Group, which flatly refused to surrender. Fighting was so fierce that the paratroopers required the assistance of Filipino guerillas and the 1st Cavalry Division before all resistance ended. The following June, the division transferred up to northern Luzon to deal with the 52,000-strong Shobu Group near Aparri, which was subdued only by four divisions. On June 25, 1945, Gypsy task force, consisting of the 1st Battalion, 511th Infantry, G and I Companies, the 2nd Battalion, and a battery from the 457th Parachute Field Artillery battalion, airdropped near Camalaniugan Airfield in stiff winds, greatly disrupting the landing patterns. The men quickly sorted themselves out and proceeded to eliminate a large part of the Shobu Group before linking up with the 37th Infantry Division. The 11th Airborne Division engaged in sporadic combat against pockets of fanatical resistance until August 1945, when it transferred to Okinawa prior to occupation duties on the Japanese homeland. An advance party secured Atsugi Airfield outside Yokohoma, while the balance of the 11th Airborne and 37th Infantry Divisions were airlifted in place. It continued on in Japan until May 1949 and returned to Fort Campbell, Kentucky, to serve as a training formation. The 11th Airborne Division was the sole formation of its kind assigned to the Pacific theater, and it fully upheld the fighting traditions of the American parachute infantry.

17th Airborne Division

The 17th Airborne Division was activated at Camp Mackall, North Carolina, on April 15, 1943, one of five airborne divisions raised by the United States. It initially consisted of the 513th Airborne Infantry Regiment and the 193rd and 194th Glider Infantry Regiments, all under Major General William M. Miley. As such, several detachments participated in the important Knollwood Maneuver of December 1943, where the U.S. Army elected to keep its airborne formations as valid tactical units.

The 17th Airborne Division finally completed its training in Match 1944 and deployed to Great Britain on August 26, 1944, as part of the new 18th Airborne Corps under General Matthew B. Ridgway. However, because it was still collecting assigned equipment and lacked combat experience, it did not participate in Operation MARKET GARDEN alongside the 82nd and 101st Airborne Divisions. The 17th Airborne Division remained in Britain and continued training. However, on December 16, 1944, the Germans launched their famous Ardennes offensive through Belgium, ripping through several unprepared American

General Matthew B. Ridgway was America's leading exponent of airborne forces during World War II. (National Archives/Corbis)

Matthew B. Ridgway (1895–1993). Matthew Bunker Ridgway was born in Fort Monroe, Virginia, on March 3, 1895, the son of an army colonel. He graduated from West Point in 1917, and, over the next two decades he fulfilled a typical regimen of far-ranging appointments in China, Nicaragua, and the Philippines. Following American entry into World War II, Ridgway rose to major general commanding the 82nd Infantry Division and supervised its conversion to a parachute unit. In July 1943, Ridgway spearheaded the invasion of Sicily with his 82nd Airborne division, and in June 1944 he jumped over Normandy, France, as part of Operation OVERLORD. He subsequently assumed control of the Allied XVIII Airborne Corps of American, British, and Polish units in time for the ill-fated Operation MARKET GARDEN in the Netherlands, and in December 1944, his paratroopers helped blunt the northern shoulder of the German Battle of the Bugle offensive in the Ardennes, Belgium. During the postwar period, Ridgway served with the Military Staff Committee of the United Nations from 1946 to 1948, and in 1950 he replaced the late General Walton Walker as head of the 8th Army in Korea. In May 1952, he was tapped to succeed General Dwight D. Eisenhower as commander of the North Atlantic Treaty Organization, and the following year Eisenhower made him army chief of staff in Washington, D.C. Ridgway retired from active service in 1955 and died in Pittsburgh, Pennsylvania, on July 26, 1993. From the standpoint of strategy and tactics, he is regarded one of the most adept American military leaders of the 20th century.

formations, and the division was ordered to the continent to help stem the tide. The 82nd and 101st Airborne Divisions, already present in France, were readily trucked to the scene of combat and garnered additional fame to their reputations. However, the 17th Airborne Division remained sidelined by bad weather and could not be flown in until December 23, 1944. After assembling at Reims, France, it was assigned to the U.S. 3rd Army under General George S. Patton and ordered to defend a 30-mile stretch of terrain along the Meuse River at Charleville. The division remained in place until January 1, 1945, then advanced to the region southwest of Bastogne and relieved the 11th Armored Division. The paratroopers finally experienced combat on January 4, in concert with the 87th Infantry Division, as it fought to prevent German units from surrounding that vital road junction a second time. At this time, the 513th Parachute Infantry Regiment and the 194th Glider Infantry Regiment constituted the division's assault element, while the 507th Parachute Infantry Regiment and 193rd Glider Infantry Regiment prepared defensive measures to thwart any possible counterattacks. Combat along a stretch of elevated road known as "Dead Man's Ridge" proved particularly brutal and cost the 17th Airborne Division nearly 1,000 casualties. By January 26, 1945, the division finally pierced German lines and linked up with the British 51st Highland Division. The town of Espeler, Belgium, fell soon after, at which point the 17th Airborne Division disengaged to rest and refit in France.

Defining Activity

For several weeks into the spring of 1945, the Allies toyed with the idea of Operation ECLIPSE, which involved dropping the 17th, 82nd, and British 6th Airborne Divisions directly into Berlin, Germany, to capture the city, but on March 28, 1945, General Dwight D. Eisenhower signaled to Marshal Josef Stalin that the Nazi capital remained a Soviet prerogative. Around that time, the Allied high command also conceived Operation VARSITY, a large airborne drop into Germany to accompany an amphibious crossing of the Rhine River by the British 21st Army Group of Field Marshal Bernard Montgomery. This would involve the entire 18th U.S. Airborne Corps, consisting of the 13th, 17th, and British 6th Airborne Divisions, but the 13th was subsequently omitted because of insufficient transport aircraft available and its lack of combat experience. At length leaders determined that the last two formations would drop in the vicinity of Wesel to upend enemy defenses and link up with the British 2nd Army. Furthermore, to avert the high loss rate experienced by airborne forces during Operation MARKET GARDEN, the jump would be made only after Allied forces were across the Rhine and even then in close proximity to them. Once landed, the paratroopers were simply to hold their positions and wait to be relieved within a few hours.

On March 24, 1945, Operation VARSITY commenced as the 17th Airborne Division boarded 541 transport aircraft and 1,050 aircraft towing 1,350 gliders. It successfully landed 9,387 men of the 507th and 513th Parachute Infantries plus support troops north of Wesel. A thick ground haze scattered several formations, but the 507th quickly secured its objectives around Diersfordt. Meanwhile, the 513th, which lost 22 transports to German ground fire, came down virtually on top of the British 6th Airlanding Brigade. Together, the two units cleaned out pockets of resistance nearby, then jointly stormed into Hamminkeln. The 194th Glider Infantry Regiment also touched down across the Rhine, having lost 12 transports to antiaircraft fire. Having landed adjacent to several German batteries bombarding British forces crossing the Rhine, they traded point-blank fire with enemy troops before silencing 42 cannon, 10 tanks, two mobile flak wagons, and five self-propelled guns. By nightfall, American and British paratroopers secured all their objectives, including bridges over the Ijssel River and the nearby Diersfordter Forest, and they were relieved by the British 15th Infantry Division. By the time combat operations concluded on March 29, 1945, the 17th Airborne Division sustained 1,346 casualties.

Once in Germany, the paratroopers continued fighting on foot as regular infantry and pushed into Wesel, Essen, and Munster before Germany surrendered on May 7, 1945. The 17th Airborne Division was subsequently tapped for occupation duties in northern parts of the country, but the following June, it transferred several component units to the 13th Airborne Division for service in the Pacific and to the 82nd Airborne Division in

Berlin. Japan surrendered before the move could be effected, and the 17th Airborne Division was formally inactivated at Camp Myles Standish in Taunton, Massachusetts, on September 16, 1945. During its relatively brief service life of five months, the division suffered 314 dead and 4,904 wounded. It was briefly reactivated as a training division in July 1948 but was permanently struck from the army rolls as of June 19, 1949.

82nd Airborne Division

In May 1940, German forces startled the world with a massive airborne invasion of the Netherlands and Belgium; despite heavy losses, this completely upset local defenses through the new tactic of "vertical envelopment." Their success sufficiently impressed U.S. Army leadership to acquire airborne divisions of their own. The first experimental parachute test platoon was culled from volunteers at Fort Benning, Georgia, and, on August 16, 1940, Lieutenant William T. Ryder conducted their first successful test jump. The initial formation was expanded, and the following October, the 501st Parachute Battalion under Major William M. Miley conducted the first large-scale drop from Douglas C-33 transports. The Japanese attack on Pearl Harbor on December 7, 1941, lent greater urgency to the creation of airborne units, and on August 15, 1942, the 82nd Infantry Division was redesignated the 82nd Airborne Division under Major General Matthew B. Ridgway. This was the latest incarnation of a unit first raised for service in World War I, and because it contained units from around the country, it adopted a moniker as the "All Americans." That fall, the 82nd Airborne relocated to Fort Bragg, North Carolina, where it received final training and organization. At length, it consisted of the 504th and 505th Parachute Infantry Regiments, the 325th Glider Infantry Regiment, and various artillery support units. By April 1943, the division was deemed combat worthy, and it shipped out for Casablanca, Morocco, to continue training for the upcoming invasion of Sicily.

On July 9, 1943, Operation HUSKY commenced as Colonel James M. Gavin led the 505th Parachute Infantry, assisted by the 3rd Battalion, 504th Parachute Infantry, on its first combat drop. They paratroopers arrived over their objective, Gela, but were widely scattered by adverse winds. The crack Hermann Göring Panzer division promptly counterattacked but was stopped cold by Gavin's men along Biazza Ridge. On July 11, the balance of the 504th Parachute Infantry assembled on transport aircraft to support Gavin, but as they passed over the American fleet, they were mistaken for German aircraft and fired on. No fewer than 23 transports were downed, killing 81 soldiers, including Brigadier General Charles Keerans, the assistant division commander. Despite this disaster, the 82nd Airborne Division continued fighting on Sicily and even spearheaded General George S. Patton's drive west to Trapani and Castllemare. The men covered 150 miles over the next five days, netting 23,000 German and Italian prisoners. The 82nd Airborne subsequently remained in reserve during the Salerno landings the following September, but when these were threatened by stiff German resistance, General Mark Clark ordered the 505th Parachute Infantry on a combat jump over Paestum south of the city. Having driven German forces in the vicinity back into the foothills, the 3rd Battalion, 504th Parachute Infantry, accompanied the 25th U.S. Infantry on a supporting amphibious landing near Salerno. Continued heavy

Paratroopers of the 82nd Airborne Division inspect each others' equipment prior to a training maneuver in England during World War II. They emerged as one of the most decorated American units of this conflict. (Library of Congress)

fighting saw the fall of Naples in October, and the 82nd Airborne Division became the first American unit into the city. The unit subsequently cleared out German units from the Volturno River, then shipped off to England to partake of the invasion of France. In January 1944, the battalions of the 504th Parachute Infantry remained behind to fight at Anzio, where one German officer pronounced them "devils in baggy pants." In March 1944, this unit also joined its parent organization in England.

Defining Activity

While in England, the 82nd Airborne Division was bolstered by the new 507th and 508th Parachute Infantries arriving from Fort Bragg. However, only 11 hours from D-Day, General Ridgway was informed that the Germans had moved their 91st Division into the 82nd's drop zone. Ridgway immediately scrapped existing plans and scheduled new ones closer to the beachhead to prevent the 91st Division from interfering with Allied landings. In the early morning hours of June 6, 1944, Operation NEPTUNE, the air assault phase of Operation OVERLORD, commenced as the 505th, 507th, and 508th Parachute Infantries leapt from aircraft over their objectives at St. Mere Eglise and Le Fiere. The 505th descended in good order, but the 507th and 508th were badly scattered. Men of the 82nd were among the very first Allied soldiers to land on French soil, and St. Mere Eglise became the first French town liberated by the 3rd Battalion, 505th Parachute Infantry. The paratroopers quickly unfurled an American flag first flown by them over liberated Naples. Over the next few hours, the 505th was reinforced by men and equipment of the 325th Glider Infantry as the paratroopers held the bridge over the Merderet River. The Germans, who needed to cross the bridge in order to reach the beaches, attacked relentlessly with tanks and infantry but were blasted back by the 1st Battalion, 505th Parachute Infantry. It was not until June 7 that a company of American tanks finally clanked up from the beachhead, and the division finally drew its scattered detachments together. Men of the 82nd Airborne Division next fought nonstop over the next 33 days and spearheaded the American advance across the base of the Cotentin Peninsula. Having won a PUC, they were finally relieved on July 8, 1944, and returned to England to rest and refit. Sustained combat cost the division 5,245 men killed, wounded, or missing in action.

Back in England, the 82nd Airborne Division joined the 17th and 101st Airborne Divisions to form the new 18th Airborne Corps, which, when combined with two British airborne divisions, constituted the First Allied Airborne Army. The unit then conducted its fourth wartime aerial assault on September 17, 1944, by participating in Operation MARKET GARDEN in Holland. The attack was carried out by the 504th and 508th Parachute Infantries alone since the 507th had been assigned elsewhere. Its objectives were bridges over the Maas and Waal Rivers along with the high ground between Nijmegen and Groesbeek. At the city of Grave, the paratroopers secured the Maas bridge on the first day, but it was not until the September 20 that an attack pressed through Nijmegen to secure the south end of the Waal River bridge. The north end of the bridge fell to a combined assault by the 504th Parachute Infantry and C Company, 307th Engineers, although troops involved incurred 50 percent casualty rates. The overall operation was cancelled once when British airborne units were overwhelmed by German Panzers at Arnhem and the Americans withdrew. The 82nd Airborne Division, having sustained 56 uninterrupted days in combat, was sent to Reims, France, on November 11, 1944, to refit. A month later, the Germans launched their famous Ardennes offensive against American forces in Belgium, and the "All Americans" were hastily dispatched to Webermont. There they constituted the northern shoulder of the bulge in American lines and dug in along the Salm River. The paratroopers defied every effort of Marshal Gerd von Rundstedt's Panzers to evict them, and the Germans made scant progress along this front. The enemy offensive collapsed by January, and the 82nd Airborne Division went on the attack, crossing into the heavily fortified Siegfried Line and deploying along the Roer River by February 1945.

Its final combat operation of the war transpired on April 30, 1945, when it crossed the Elbe River near Bleckede, Germany. Major General Galvin subsequently accepted the surrender of 150,000 German troops belonging to Lieutenant General Kurt von Tippelskirch's 21st Army, and paratroopers also liberated the Woebbelin Concentration Camp. The 82nd Airborne Division, having participated in six campaigns, including 442 days in sustained combat, suffered a grand total of 1,619 killed and 6,560 wounded. It spent the last few months of 1945 performing garrison duty in Berlin behind Soviet lines, and General George S. Patton bestowed on it the title of "America's Honor Guard." The division sailed for home aboard the *Queen Mary* and led a ticker-tape victory parade in New York City on January 12, 1946. This outstanding unit was not demobilized but, rather, returned to Fort Bragg to function as a strategic deployment force in the event of hostilities with a former ally, the Soviet Union.

101st Airborne Division

The 101st Airborne Division ("Screaming Eagles") was activated at Camp Claiborne, Louisiana, on August 15, 1942, having been split off from the 82nd Airborne Division. It was assigned the 501st, 502nd, and 506th Parachute Infantry Regiments and, in light of its junior status, Commanding General William C. Lee reminded his charge that the new formation had "no history but a rendezvous with history." Operationally, it turned out to be one of America's preeminent combat units of World War II. On the evening of June 5–6, 1944, the 101st Airborne Division loaded onto transports in England, crossed the English Channel, and parachuted on the Cotentin Peninsula, France, as part of Operation ALBANY, the air assault phase of Operation OVERLORD. Its objective was to land ahead of Utah Beach and destroy a German coastal battery at Saint-Martin-de-Varreville. That done, the paratroopers would obstruct several highway bridges over the Douve River to sever German communications and prevent reinforcements from attacking the beachheads. Once this was accomplished, the Screaming Eagles would link up with the 82nd Airborne Division at Les Forces and establish a defensive line. In Drop Zone A, the 502nd Parachute Infantry scattered upon landing, but it hurriedly reassembled and stormed all its objectives at Saint-Martin-de-Varreville by daylight, then held on tenaciously until relieved by the 4th Infantry Division advancing inland from Utah Beach. The 506th Parachute Infantry Regiment, assigned to land at Drop Zone C near Sainte Marie-du-Mont, had a much rougher time by comparison. En route, it encountered stiff antiaircraft fire that claimed three C-47s, and the 2nd Battalion landed far to the west of its objective. The various detachments spent several hours sorting themselves out under Major General Maxwell D. Taylor but did manage to evict the German 1058th Grenadier Regiment from Pouppeville in a stand-up fight. The 501st Parachute Infantry, constituting the third wave, lost an additional six aircraft to flak, then landed under preregistered mortar and machine gun fire that killed many paratroopers and some battalion-level commanders. The survivors worked their way inland to seize the bridges over the Douve River at Saint-Come-du-Mont but were halted by stiff enemy resistance from the elite 6th Fallschirmjager Regiment–German paratroopers. The bridges were seized, but the town's defenses rebuffed them despite long-range naval gunfire from the cruiser *Quincy* offshore. By day's end, Taylor and his second in command, Brigadier General Anthony C. McAuliffe, had assembled 2,500 out of 6,000 men in the

In this iconic photograph, General Dwight D. Eisenhower gives encouragement to pathfinders of the 101st Airborne Division on the eve of D-Day. They will be the first American forces to land in Nazi-occupied France. (National Archives)

vicinity of Culoville, and these were strengthened by the arrival of the 327th Glider Infantry; Brigadier General Don F. Pratt was killed while landing. All told, the division fought continuously for 33 days before being relieved, and several units received a PUC for their capture of Carentan, in this instance carried at bayonet's point.

The 101st Airborne Division's second combat jump occurred on September 17, 1944, when the new 18th Airborne Corps of Major General Matthew B. Ridgway participated in Operation MARKET GARDEN in Holland. The division was assigned to secure several bridges between Eindhoven and Nijmegen. The 101st quickly captured Eindhoven, the first Dutch city liberated in World War II, although stiff German resistance prevented them from crossing the bridge over the Wilhelmina Canal, then seizing another bridge across the Maas River until September 20. They also could not overcome the Germans a few miles away at Best, which kept another bridge out of their hands. On September 18, the paratroopers linked up with 30th Corps, whose attack was also stalled by fierce fighting with enemy infantry and armor. At length, a Bailey bridge was thrown across the Wilhelmina Canal, and the British pushed on, while a part of the roadway seized by the 101st between Eindhoven and Zon became known as "Hell's Highway" because of the losses incurred. Overall, the Screaming Eagles fought for 73 days nonstop before being relieved.

Defining Activity

On December 16, 1944, the Germans launched a major offensive in the thickly wooded Ardennes region of Belgium to split the British and American lines in half, capture the strategic port of Antwerp, and greatly prolong the war. Their initial attack completely overran the 28th Infantry Division, at which point the 8th Corps ordered Combat Command B, 10th Armored Division, to secure the vital road junction of Bastogne from eminent capture. This town controlled access to no fewer than seven major roadways and, in American hands, constituted a serious roadblock to any German advance. Concurrently, the 101st Airborne Division, stationed at Reims, France, in reserve, boarded a convoy of 380 trucks and made for Bastogne on December 17. The situation was so grave that that the 11,000 soldiers traveled the entire 107 miles that night with their lights on, completely disregarding the possibility of German aerial attacks. The entire division, consisting of the 501st, 502nd, 506th Parachute Infantries and 327th Glider Infantry, hastily assembled on December 19 and took up defensive positions around the town. Two days later, they were surrounded by parts of the 2nd Panzer, Panzer Lehr, 26th Volksgrenadier and 5th Fallschirmjager divisions, who captured the entire medical detachment during an initial attack against the perimeter. The 101st, assisted by the shot-up remains of Combat Command B and three batteries of heavy artillery, nonetheless repelled all subsequent attempts to overrun the town. The Germans responded with continual artillery barrages and night attacks by far-ranging bomber aircraft. On December 22, Generalieutenant Heinrich Freiherr von Luuwitz switched tactics and sent a deputation to General McAuliffe to demand his surrender. In a celebrated display of bravado, McAuliffe brusquely told the Germans "Nuts!" and sent them back to their own lines. The expression was eventually explained to the bewildered Germans as "Go to Hell!" Additional German attacks made no further progress, and two Panzer divisions of the 47th Panzer Corps departed Bastogne for another actions farther west. The 101st Airborne Division then squared off against the 26th Volksgrenadier Division, bolstered by a Panzergrenadier regiment from the crack Panzer-Lehr Division. Through it all, men on both sides were forced to eat, sleep, and die in the freezing-cold snow. Fortunately, the Americans began receiving airdrops of food, medicine, and ammunition as the weather began to clear. Swarms of American fighter-bombers also began pounding German troop formations and supply routes, increasing their discomfiture. On December 24, 1944, the Germans nonetheless struck at several places along the American perimeter in a final onslaught but were again rebuffed. The attack was fiercely renewed Christmas Day, and, while some local penetrations were achieved, the 101st held firm. The following day, tanks of the 4th U.S. Armored Division broke through German lines in the south, ending the 22-day siege. American positions around the town were littered with burned-out remains of 148 German tanks and 26 halftracks. all destroyed during intense small-unit encounters. On January 9, 1945, the 101st Airborne Division assumed the offensive and seized Noville and Bourcy from the retreating Germans. Their epic stand in the face of tremendous odds remains a vital part of American military tradition.

The division was placed in reserve for the balance of the war and it was finally disbanded on November 30, 1945. In light of an excellent combat record across Normandy, Holland, and Belgium, the Screaming Eagles also received four campaign streamers and two PUCs This was also the first time that the War Department awarded a PUC to an entire division. This soaring accomplishment came at a cost of 1,766 dead and 6,388 wounded.

Army Air Force

1st Air Commando Group

The fall of Burma to Japanese troops in the spring of 1942 induced British colonel Ord C. Wingate to suggest creation of long-range penetration (LRP) groups to infiltrate behind enemy lines and raise havoc with their supply lines and communications. Previously, the first Chindit incursion, Operation LONGCLOTH, was a mixed success tactically but also psychologically debilitating since all wounded soldiers had to be abandoned in the jungle. Any future offensive would now be supplied and reinforced wholly by airpower, with all sick and wounded personnel safely removed. Wingate's superior, Admiral Lord Louis Montbatten, broached the issue with commanding general of the Army Air Force Henry H. Arnold during the Quebec Conference of August 1943. Arnold was impressed by the plan and suggested that the mobile LRP force be assigned its own air transportation, supply, and support service with an appropriate variety of aircraft to enhance mission flexibility. Thus was born Project Nine, which would be based in India under two individuals hand-picked by Arnold himself: Lieutenant Colonels Phillip G. Cochran, a noted P-40 fighter pilot in North Africa, and John R. Alison, a former 23rd Fighter Group pilot. The organization began assembling and training its 1,000 men at bases in India, and on November 29, 1943, it was renamed the 5318th Provisional Unit. As such it received diverse aircraft such as L-1 and L-5 "grasshoppers," P-51A Mustangs, B-25 medium bombers, C-47 Skytrains, and Waco CG-4A gliders. Significantly, their roster included the first six Sikorsky YR4s, America's first operational helicopter. Cochran and Alison also began training with Wingate's Chindits in preparation for a major offensive action. Administratively, the unit was part of the U.S. 10th Air Force, although it was operationally hinged to the British 14th Army in Burma.

The Sikorsky R-4 Hoverfly, the first operational American helicopter, saw active duty in Burma with the 1st Air Commando Group. (National Museum of the US Air Force)

Philip G. Cochran (1910–1979). Philip Gerald Cochran was born in Erie, Pennsylvania, on January 29, 1910, and, after graduating from Ohio State University in 1935, he became a pilot in the Army Air Corps. In 1941, he befriended cartoonist Milton Caniff, who modeled a character, (Flip Corkin) after Cochran in the comic strip *Terry and the Pirates*. During World War II, Cochran commanded a P-40 squadron in North Africa to good effect and acquired the reputation of a driven but highly innovative leader who got results. For this reason, he advanced to lieutenant colonel and was handpicked by Army Air Force commander General Henry H. Arnold to lead a daring new unit, the 1st Air Commando Group. This was to be done in concert with another distinguished flier, Lieutenant Colonel John R. Alison. The new unit represented a radical departure in conventional thinking, for it employed fighters, medium bombers, trans-

Colonel Philip G. Cochran pioneered many innovative aerial tactics over the skies of Burma. His 1st Air Commando Group demonstrated the extreme flexibility of airpower, imaginatively applied, even in the most remote theaters of operation. (Bettmann/Corbis)

ports, light planes, and new helicopters, all of which flew and fought in close coordination with ground units. Cochran and Alison also pioneered the art of deep-penetration flights whereby British raiders under General Orde C. Wingate, the famous Chindits, were supplied andtactically supported in the Burmese jungle. Among the unorthodox tactics pioneered by Cochran was having fighter aircraft fly close to the tree line, dip a wing to one side, and then sever telephone and telegraph wires from their poles. Thanks to Cochran's outstanding performance, British and American special forces in the region, including Merrill's Marauders, were continually supplied, while their wounded were evacuated, entirely by air. Cochran retired to his hometown in 1945 and left the service. He worked several years as a businessman at Geneseo, New York, before dying on August 26, 1979, the godfather of today's Air Force Special Operations Command.

Defining Activity

On March 5, 1944, Operation THURSDAY commenced as aircraft and gliders of the 5318th Provisional Unit arrived at point "Broadway," 165 miles behind Japanese lines, to deliver 539 men and 33 tons of equipment (including a baby bulldozer) to construct an airfield. To underscore the dangers of operating under such primitive conditions, only 37 out of

52 gliders remained operational, while 31 men died and 40 were injured in crashes. One C-47 was lost after it taxied into a water buffalo during a night landing. Incredibly, the field was operational within 24 hours, at which point 10,000 armed Chindits and 1,000 mules were flown in for military operations. Shortly after, B-25s and P-51s began flying missions directly from the airstrip and in support of the Chindits. The fighters, in particular, utilized a special technique whereby a weighted cable was dangled from the aircraft to cut Japanese telephone wires. Wingate was killed in a B-25 crash on March 24, 1944, and four days later the unit that he inspired was redesignated the 1st Air Commando Group. On April 4, rocket-armed P-51s came on a concentration of Japanese aircraft parked at an airfield in northern Burma, destroying 26 of them. On April 21, 1944, another four Mustangs, armed with 1,000-pound bombs, successfully destroyed a strategic bridge that had defied all previous attempts to neutralize it. The aircraft continued supporting the raiders until the onset of the monsoon season of 1944, at which point the Chindits were evacuated by air along with all their sick and wounded—a first for aerial operations. On April 24–26, 1944, a YR4 made the first helicopter-borne evacuation by rescuing the crew of a downed L-5 from the jungle. Because of limitations in its lifting capacity, four trips were necessary to remove one crew member at a time over a two-day period. In the spring, the Japanese launched a strong offensive against British supply lines and surrounded parts of the 14th Army at Kohima and Imphal, India. The 1st Air Commando Group responded by delivering 28,120 tons of supplies and 61,000 men to the threatened region, effectively breaking the siege.

In light of its numerous contributions to Operation THURSDAY, the 1st Air Commando Group received a PUC. The success of the 1st Air Commando Group led to the creation of 2nd and 3rd Air Commando formations, which performed similar service in Burma, New Guinea, and the Philippines before disbanding at war's end. The 1st Air Commando Group, the world's first aerial special operations formation, was deactivated on November 3, 1945, and finally disbanded on October 8, 1948.

801st Bombardment Group (Heavy)

Whereas aerial special operations in the Pacific more or less gravitated toward sustaining military actions in the bush, those undertaken in Europe exhibited a decidedly covert flair. Commencing in November 1943, the OSS prevailed on Army Air Force leaders to lend aircraft and other assets to facilitate clandestine activities throughout occupied Europe. The first special missions were handled by the 5th Bombardment Wing, 12th Air Force, which operated out of North Africa with a small collection of modified B-17, B-24, and B-25 bombers. These initial forays usually consisted of dropping psychological warfare leaflets behind enemy lines and were gradually expanded into agent drops. The unit eventually relocated to Brindisi, Italy, where it continuously flew a further 3,769 sorties into the Balkan region, delivering 2,149 tons of weapons and supplies to various partisan groups. C-47 transports also landed and rescued downed allied pilots and also delivered agents and saboteurs.

The largest effort along these lines was based in England, where, in September 1943, the Combined Chiefs of Staff directed that inactivate elements of the Army Air Force antisubmarine command be cobbled together into the new 801st Bombardment Group (Heavy) (Provisional) at Harrington Field. Using the code name Operation CARPETBAGGER, this unit operated specially modified B-24 Liberator bombers with undersides painted black for nocturnal flights over occupied Europe. Moreover, they had most of their armament removed and were fitted with special radars, navigation systems, and radio sets to both locate and communicate with partisan units far behind enemy lines. The aircraft were further modified by having their ventral ball turret removed and replaced by a "Joe door," whereby teams of OSS agents ("Joes") could rapidly parachute to the ground. The 801st was therefore central to the success of Operation JEDBURGH, the largest introduction of intelligence agents into western Europe during

(National Museum of the U.S. Air Force)

the entire war. The unit was eventually bolstered by two squadrons of similarly modified B-17s that performed similar work. The 801st, which prided itself on the moniker "The Carpetbaggers," conducted its first mission on the evening of January 4–5, 1944, and

The Carpetbaggers operated Consolidated B-24 Liberator heavy bombers while transporting agents and their supplies over occupied Europe. These craft were specially modified for the dangerous, nocturnal operations essential to their mission. (Library of Congress)

routinely operated in weather so bad that most aircraft were grounded. Flying such large bombers close to the ground—only 600 feet and in complete darkness—was inherently risky and no fewer than 25 Liberators were lost to accidents, ground fire, or enemy night fighters; 208 personnel were killed or missing in action. Nonetheless, the Carpetbaggers air-dropped 4,680 containers and 62 agents into France prior to Operation OVERLORD, the Allied invasion of France, and continued similar work up through September 17, 1944. By that time, totals had increased to 1,860 sorties and 20,495 containers and 1,000 agents delivered.

In August 1944, the squadrons of the 801st were absorbed into the new 492nd Bombardment Group (Heavy), which were co-opted into performing night bombardment of enemy positions. However, in December, Carpetbagger missions resumed over the skies of Germany and continued up through May 1945. That spring, the Carpetbaggers were infused by A-26 Invader light attack aircraft for the speedier delivery (350 miles per hour) of agents and supplies at low altitude. A pair of British-manufactured DeHaviland Mosquito light bombers also performed high-altitude radio missions to receive coded messages from agents on the ground. After the war, the 492nd Bomb Group returned to Kirtland Field, New Mexico, where it was disbanded on October 17, 1945. They were clearly successful at abetting aerial special operations, but no Army Air Force or, after 1947, U.S. Air Force unit could assume such duties until the Korean War five years hence.

Marine Corps

Marine Corps Amphibious Reconnaissance Battalion

The war in the Pacific revolved largely around amphibious landings on islands held by fanatical, well-trained, and well-equipped Japanese forces. Therefore, accurate military intelligence became a vital prerequisite for victory—and avoiding potential military disasters. By necessity, such intelligence had to be gathered in as clandestine as fashion to avoid alerting enemy garrisons that an attack was pending. On January 7, 1943, Major General Holland M. Smith, commanding general of the 5th Amphibious Corps, ordered the Amphibious Reconnaissance Company of six officers and 92 men activated at Camp Elliott, California. This was a small but highly trained and specialized unit consisting of a service platoon and four reconnaissance platoons, each containing a lieutenant and two six-man squads. They were commanded by Captain James L. Jones, formerly of the now defunct Observer Group. Consistent with their mission, they were especially equipped with lighter armament, noiseless foot attire, and no insignia on their uniforms. They were also tactically flexible and could ingress to a target area at night by submarine, rubber dingy, PBY flying boats, destroyer transports, and even motor patrol (PT) boats. In addition to gathering strictly military intelligence as to island defenses, they were also scientifically versed in hydrology and topography, charting and measuring water depths, collecting soil samples, and identifying submerged coral reefs. Moreover, the men trained intensively in amphibious reconnaissance techniques over the next nine months and learned to evaluate landing areas in terms of emergency exists if retreat became necessary. The company deployed in the Pacific with the 5th Amphibious Corps (VAC) as the 5th Amphib Recon

Company. On November 19, 1943, they performed their first mission when the transport submarine USS *Nautilus* disembarked them off Tarawa Atoll, Gilbert Islands, where they uncovered an 11-degree compass error on old British charts that the navy utilized, intelligence that proved vital to the subsequent invasion. On November 20, 1943, the company landed on Apamama Island, which they secured four days later at a cost of two dead and two wounded. On January 3, 1944, the unit expanded with the addition of new personnel to an authorized strength of seven officers and 101 men, two navy corpsmen, and an attached mortar section of 22 marines. On February 1, 1944, the transport destroyer USS *Kane* landed them on Majuro Atoll to ascertain whether Japanese forces were present in strength; they were not, and the islands were subsequently utilized as a fleet anchorage for the central Pacific region. On February 17, 1944, the company was again transported by the *Kane* to Aitsu, part of Eniwetok Atoll, which again uncovered no Japanese garrison. They spent the next week scouting nearby islands, and on February 22, 1944, Jones took his men ashore at Parry Island, losing four men wounded in a sudden night action but killing 15 enemy soldiers.

The VAC Amphibious Company, despite its demonstrated utility, was still deemed too small to perform amphibious reconnaissance missions at the corps level, so Major General Smith broached the subject of expanding them into a battalion with Marine Commandant Alexander Vandegrift. Vandegrift gave his blessings, and on April 14, 1944, the VAC Amphibious Reconnaissance Battalion was authorized at a strength of 303 men divided into two companies, each with a weapons platoon and a headquarters company. The battalion was commanded by newly promoted Major Jones, who formerly headed up the reconnaissance company. On June 15, 1944, the force debarked off of Saipan and spent several days in mopping-up operations and reducing enemy sniper nests. On July 11, 1944, the men came ashore on Tinian with some underwater demolition teams (UDTs) to reconnoiter two promising landing zones. They reported that the beaches, while narrow, were nearly undefended and ideal for the amphibious assault that followed on July 24, 1944. A month later, the unit designation was upgraded to Fleet Marine Force Amphibious Recon Battalion. On the evening of February 17, 1945, B Company, under Lieutenant Russell Corey, landed on Iwo Jima, once again accompanied by UDT swimmers. They made a detailed survey of Japanese defenses along several beaches and returned under fire from hidden artillery batteries. They landed again during the evening of February 20 and scouted around the base of Mount Suribachi. The following month, the battalion withdrew to Saipan to rest and refit. On the evening of March 25, A and B Companies snuck ashore at Kerama Retto and Keise Shima off Okinawa to seize enemy offshore artillery batteries ahead of the main landing. They subsequently scoured the six islets guarding the entrance to Chimu Wan, encountering heavy resistance from entrenched Japanese defenders. Because mortar fire had damaged several of the rubber dingies, many marines dropped their equipment and swam several miles to their troops destroyers. The battalion next appeared on Minna Shima on April 15, 1945, finding it free of enemy forces, and it subsequently participated in the capture of Ie Shima. The men performed their final wartime mission on June 26, 1945, on Kume Shima west of Okinawa, capturing an enemy radio relay station. By war's end, the reconnaissance battalion was back at Pearl Harbor, Hawaii, having successfully completed over 150 vital reconnaissance missions, more than any other unit of the Pacific War. It was formally deactivated on September 24, 1945.

Marine Corps Scout and Sniper Companies

The idea of scout and sniper companies originated in 1941 with Lieutenant Colonel William Whaling, 5th Marine Regiment. He argued that such tactical organization were necessary to conduct specialized reconnaissance missions beyond routine battalion-level scouting and patrolling. However, it was not until February 1943 that Major General Alexander Vandegrift, commanding the 1st Marine Division, granted permission to form a unit from Marine veterans of the Guadalcanal campaign. The were authorized at a strength of one platoon per regiment, and tasked with guiding units ashore and confirming their position in dense jungle foliage. They were also expected to execute independent patrols deemed critical to whatever division they were attached. Like any elite unit, scout and sniper companies received intense, specialized training, in this instance an eight-week course held at Mornington peninsula, Australia. To the usual regimen of scouting, patrolling, and land navigation were added new skills as ingress using rubber boats and amphibious reconnaissance techniques in general. Officers assigned intelligence functions with the companies also studied sophisticated ambushes and raids at the navy's Amphibious Scouts School to enhance combat efficiency. All marines are required to be marksmen by mandate, but candidates for scout and sniper companies were picked from the very best in this field. By 1944, most Marine regiments possessed scout/sniper formations and ground and amphibious reconnaissance platoons. In time, many of these lightly armed formations were usually attached to a platoon of light or medium tanks for great mobility and firepower. By this time, the bulk of personnel were drawn from former Marine Raiders and Paramarines, who were already adept at several of these functions.

One particular unit of note was the scout and sniper company under Major Anthony Walker, which was culled from the 29th Marine Regiment at Okinawa. On April 1, 1945, Major General Lem Shepherd instructed that Company H of the 29th would organize a scout company for the entire 6th Marine Division. Transported by tanks to the battlefield, its purpose was to reconnoiter ahead of the main force and uncover any hidden Japanese defenses. It was anticipated that such tactical reconnaissance in force missions would also promote better coordination with supporting artillery, air, and naval gunfire support where needed. The new company was constituted on April 2, 1945, and immediately rode tanks to the northern parts of Okinawa. In its first action, the scout and sniper company performed mop-up activities between the Ishikawa Isthmus Line and the Yakadsa-Yaka Line. That accomplished, they performed useful work reconnoitering the west coast of the Motobu peninsula in front of the 29th Marines. On April 12, 1945, they seized the town of Bise, where a radar unit was placed to warn the fleet against incoming kamikaze raids. After the northern part of Okinawa was declared secure on April 21, 1945, the scout and sniper company advanced to the city of Naha, where it engaged in antisniper activity. General Shepherd subsequently ordered them to assess beach defenses along the Oruku peninsula. The men came in under heavy fire but concluded that Japanese preparations were far from extensive, and on June 5 the region fell to an amphibious assault by the 4th Marines. The scout and sniper company spent the remainder of the campaign seizing various offshore islands on June 23–24, 1945. Despite excellent reconnaissance work, Walker's company was disbanded along with the 6th Marine Division shortly after the Pacific War ended.

Marine Raiders

During the early days of American involvement in World War II, President Franklin D. Roosevelt expressed interest in raising a force based on the famous British commandos. Such a unit would naturally enjoy elite status and perform small raiding actions behind enemy lines. The president felt that the Marine Corps was a natural recruiting ground for the new formation, but the idea did not sit well with Commandant Thomas Holcomb. He strongly argued that creating an elite unit within an organization that already prided itself as elite was superfluous and, worse, might generate resentment among line units. The president nonetheless prevailed, and in an initial move, the 1st Battalion, 5th Marines, was detached from its parent organization as the 1st Separate Battalion, while the 2nd Separate Battalion was cobbled together from other units. Both had an authorized strengths of 850 officers and men. The need to create commando-style units assumed greater urgency once Admiral Chester W. Nimitz, commander of the Pacific Fleet, opined that they would prove useful for lighting raids against lightly defended Japanese-occupied islands throughout the region. Holcomb complied as requested, but he rejected the British name "commando" in favor of the generic term "raider." The units were tasked with three specific missions: to spearhead amphibious landings ahead of the main force, to conduct "hit-and-run" raids on enemy-held islands, and to launch deep penetration raids behind enemy lines.

U.S. Marine Raiders gathered in front of a Japanese dugout on Cape Totkina on Bougainville, Solomon Islands, which they helped to take in January 1944. They were ultimately disbanded despite a tremendously effective combat record. (National Archives)

Consistent with their elite status, the raiders enjoyed first pick of the best equipment available to marines and were recruited only from handpicked volunteers. In addition to standard weapons, they were also authorized to carry shotguns and bangalore torpedoes and were extensively trained to employ rubber dingies for transportation.

The 1st Raider Battalion was authorized at Quantico, Virginia, on February 16, 1942, under the aegis of Lieutenant Colonel Merritt A. Edson. It was assigned to the 1st Marine Division during the invasion of Guadalcanal, and it performed its first mission on August 7, 1942, by seizing the nearby island of Tulagi from its Japanese garrison. The latter was wiped out in a hard fight by the following evening, and Major General Alexander Vandegrift praised Edson and his men for their élan under fire. The 1st Raider Battalion subsequently transferred to Guadalcanal itself, where, on September 8, 1942, it launched a successful raid on Major General Kiyotake Kawaguchi's 35th Infantry Brigade at Tasimboko. Edson had caught the Japanese in the act of landing supplies ashore, so his own force disembarked from destroyers, worked their away around the enemy's rear, and drove them into the jungle, capturing tons of supplies. On the evenings of September 13–14, Edson's raiders particularly distinguished themselves in the defense of Henderson Field. A larger force of 4,000 Japanese veterans attacked them along "Bloody Ridge" and were repelled with heavy losses. The raiders, assisted by the 1st Parachute Battalion and the 2nd Battalion, 5th Marines, 700 men in all, were completely spent after three continuous days of combat, but they clearly demonstrated that Japanese forces, heretofore regarded as invincible at night, could be defeated. Edson subsequently led the 1st Raider Battalion into action on Tulagi and Dragon's peninsula, New Georgia, where they mauled Japanese army and special naval landing forces deployed there. Of the 2,800 men who passed through the formation, 312 had been killed in combat by February 1944, and the 1st Raider Battalion received a PUC for its sterling performance under fire.

The 2nd Raider Battalion was authorized at Camp Elliott, California, on February 19, 1942, and entrusted to the command of Lieutenant Colonel Evans F. Carlson. Unlike its more conventional stablemate, the 2nd Battalion was very much a product of Carlson himself, who had spent years in China observing communist guerrillas in fighting against Japan. He consequently inculcated their egalitarian approach to discipline by treating officers and men with little difference respecting rank while also instituting group self-criticism and adopting the Chinese slogan "Gung-ho" ("Work together") as a form of military indoctrination Carlson also modified the usual Marine organization by substituting six rifle companies with two platoons each, all of which utilized three-man "fire teams" as the standard tactical unit. Carlson, who enjoyed particularly cordial relations with the president, picked Major James Roosevelt, his son, to serve as his executive officer.

Defining Activity

In May 1942, the 2nd Battalion transferred to Oahu, Hawaii, where it was placed under the direct command of Admiral Nimitz, the naval commander in chief. Carlson spent several weeks honing his men's skill in combat and landing tactics, a task made difficult by faulty motors on their rubber dingies that usually stalled in rough surf. Nonetheless, the admiral's staff began planning a large-scale raid on Makin Island in the Gilberts for the purpose of taking prisoners, obtaining intelligence, and providing a diversion for the upcoming Guadalcanal operation. The raiders trained on simulated mock-ups of the island's wharves, roads, and buildings, and on August 8, 1942, 222 officers and men embarked on the large,

Evans F. Carlson (1896–1947). Evans Fordyce Carlson was born in Sidney, New York, on February 26, 1896, and he joined the U.S. Army in 1912. He served until 1919, then resigned, but when he tried and failed to get reinstated at his previous rank, Carlson joined the U.S. Marines in 1922. Over the next two decades, he held down various stints in China as a military observer and wrote extensively about the Red Chinese Army of General Chu Teh. Carlson was singularly impressed by their egalitarian methods, particularly the closeness of officers to their men. His seemingly procommunist sympathies resulted in trouble with superiors, but following American entry into World War II, Carlson was allowed to command the elite 2nd Marine Raider Battalion. He scrupulously trained this handpicked force in the manner of the Chinese communists, incorporated democratic principles, abolished

Colonel Evans F. Carlson helped pioneer unconventional tactics in the U.S. Marine Corps based on his observation of communist forces fighting in China. (National Archives)

officer's mess privileges and uniform distinctions, and instituted group discussions of tactics and objectives. On August 17, 1942, Carlson's raiders were conveyed by submarines to the Japanese outpost on Makin Island, where they stormed ashore and wiped out the 85-man garrison. Carlson subsequently saw action on Guadalcanal, and his men routed the Japanese 228th Regiment in a running jungle fight of several days, killing 488 enemy soldiers. Carlson was then felled by illness and placed on leave. However, his superiors were angered by his unorthodox methods, so his battalion was incorporated into the new Raider Regiment, then disbanded outright. Carlson saw additional service at Tarawa and Saipan, being severely wounded at the latter engagement, before mustering out in 1946. He died in Portland, Oregon, on May 27, 1947, an enterprising special forces leader.

troop-carrying submarines *Argonaut* and *Nautilus*, bound for Makin. For all Carlson's intense planning and preparation, the ensuing raid proved a near fiasco. On the evening of August 16, 1942, they disembarked from the submarines in heavy swells that scattered the landing parties. Worse, one of the raiders' weapon accidentally discharged and alerted the 160-man Japanese garrison ashore. Carlson nevertheless gathered up his men as they came landed and attacked. The defenders were wiped out in a fierce firefight, and Carlson radioed one of the submarines to surface and sink two enemy vessels in the harbor. A pair of large Japanese seaplanes arrived later that day, dropped a few bombs, and attempted to land reinforcements, but both were shot down. However, in a completely unexpected development, the high, pounding tide prevented the raiders from returning to the submarines for another 24 hours. Carlson, having failed to secure any captives and believing that large numbers of Japanese were still afoot, granted his men the option of surrendering. Few took him up on the offer, and the bulk of the raiders gradually made it back to the submarines offshore. The Americans had sustained only 30 casualties, although nine raiders were inadvertently left behind. and these were subsequently captured and executed by the Japanese. In return, they killed or wounded 160 enemy troops, destroyed several radio stations, and burned 1,000 barrels of aviation gasoline along with a large quantity of military supplies. The fumbled attack on Makin was inconsequential in terms of results and may have even induced the Japanese to fortify the nearby garrison at Tarawa, which would cost the Marines dearly in 1943. But, coming at the time that it did, Carlson's actions constituted America's first offensive action of the Pacific War and greatly boosted morale at home. His force was popularly heralded as "Carlson's Raiders," a name the modest leader never applied himself.

The 2nd Raider Battalion arrived at Guadalcanal on November 4, 1942, and deployed at Aola Bay to secure a landing zone from which an airfield would be constructed. When it became apparent that the swampy ground could not serve the purpose intended, Carlson led his men on an epic 150-mile raid behind enemy lines. Over the next 37 days, his raiders harassed, ambushed, and pinned down the enemy's 228th Infantry Regiment in a long-running engagement, killing 488 Japanese at a cost of 16 dead and 18 wounded. The action finally concluded by December 15, 1942, at which point Carlson's men arrived on Espiritu Santo Island to rest and refit. By this time, the storied success of Marine raiders led to the 3rd and 4th Battalions being raised, which campaigned alongside their predecessors in heavy fighting along the Upper Solomons. The raiders then returned to Espiritu Santo, where, on March 15, 1943, the four battalions were consolidated into the 1st Marine Raider Regiment. This new formation incorporated ideas from both Edson's and Carlson's experiences and were organized with a weapons company and four rifle companies per battalion. Each company further consisted of a weapons platoon and three rifle platoons. The 1st Marine Raider Regiment subsequently fought with distinction at Bairoko, New Georgia, while the 2nd and 3rd Raider Battalions were grouped into the 2nd Marine Raider Regiment (Provisional) for additional fighting on Bougainville. During the last two encounters, the raiders were mistakenly utilized as line infantry and suffered heavy losses because of their lack of heavy weapons. Both units still enjoyed excellent reputations, but inasmuch as the Marine Corps was experiencing manpower problems fleshing outs its six authorized divisions, Commandant Alexander Vandegrift felt that they had become a superfluous luxury, and lacking a clearly defined mission. In fact, the nature of Pacific combat had shifted toward large-scale amphibious operations against heavily fortified islands, and long-range raids were no longer considered relevant. Moreover, the raiders were basically light infantry that lacked the organic firepower of a regular infantry formation and always suffered disproportionate casualties in stand-up engagements. Accordingly, on January 8, 1944, both the raiders and the paramarines were ordered broken up and their manpower distributed to the 4th Marine Regiment, then part of the 6th Marine Division. It was an ignominious end for one of the Pacific War's most effective fighting formations, but on June 20, 2003, the Marine Corps Special Forces Command paid homage to the raiders by incorporating the Raider's unit insignia into their own.

Observer Group

In January 1941, Major General Holland M. Smith of 1st Corps (Provisional), U.S. Atlantic Fleet, and his chief of staff, Colonel Graves B. Erskine, U.S. Army, originated a plan to organize a joint-force unit specializing in clandestine reconnaissance of enemy shorelines prior to an amphibious landing. This was the first such unit in either service, and it received greater urgency following American entry into World War II that December. Initially designated the Observer Group, it consisted of 22 enlisted men and two officers drawn from the 1st Infantry Division and the 1st Marine Division. Specialized training was received at Little Creek, Virginia, and the Chesapeake region, with additional instruction at the Naval Submarine Base at New London, Connecticut. In this context, the Observer Group also began experimenting with doctrines and procedures involving inflatable rubber boats that could deploy through a submarine hatch. A Momsen lung, an early form of Aqua-Lung, also allowed users to remain in the coning tower as observers while submerged. At the individual level, all personnel received intense hand-to-hand knife-fighting instruction from famed British commando instructor Lieutenant Colonel William E. Fairbairn and employed the noted Fairbairn-Sykes dagger, which was also adopted by Marine raiders and the paramarines. The Federal Bureau of Investigation (FBI) further contributed to training with jujitsu and pistol firing from the hip. However, in August 1942, the army and navy concluded their joint effort, and the Observer Group disbanded. The following month, the navy founded its scouts and raiders, along with a specialized school for their instruction. The Observer Group saw no combat during its brief existence but it pioneered reconnaissance methodologies and specialized technologies necessary for such clandestine tasks. In this context, they are spiritual forebears of the OSS, UDTs, army special forces, and air commandos.

Paramarines

Immediately before American entry into World War II, the U.S. Marine Corps, like the U.S. Army, developed interest in developing and deploying airborne-capable forces. The Marines established the 1st Marine Parachute Battalion at Naval Air Station Lakehurst, New Jersey, in October 1940, followed by the 2nd Battalion in December. Early in 1941, the 3rd Battalion was raised and trained at Camp Kearney, San Diego, California. Like all paratroopers, the training was daunting, even by Marine Corps standards, so the program weathered dropout rates approaching 40 percent. However, there was no shortage of unmarried volunteers because of the higher rates of pay and the elite status paramarines enjoyed. The 1st Parachute Battalion formed part of the 1st Marine Division during Operation SHOESTRING, the landing on Guadalcanal, and on August 7, 1942, it performed an amphibious assault on nearby Gavutu and Toanambogo Islands in concert with other Marine units. The battalion subsequently transferred to Guadalcanal itself in time to see action in the Tasimboko raid and the battle of Bloody Ridge alongside the 1st Battalion, Marine Raiders. The 1st Parachute Battalion performed well but suffered high casualties against resilient Japanese forces, and by September 1942, it was transferred to Tontouta, New Caledonia, to rest and refit. Meanwhile, the 2nd Parachute Battalion arrived in theater subsequently and performed a diversionary raid against Japanese-held Choiseul Island in

October 1943 before uniting with the 1st and 3rd Battalions on Bougainville. There, all three formations were consolidated into the 1st Marine Parachute Regiment, 3,000 men strong, and attached to the I Marine Amphibious Corps. By this time, however, senior Marine leadership questioned the utility of such specialized, expensive, and hard to train units, especially seeing that the Marine Corps lacked resources to conduct massed parachute drops in any case. Commandant Thomas Holcomb ordered the units terminated and their personnel was absorbed into other units as of December 30, 1943; they officially ceased to exist as of February 29, 1944. Ironically, the only paramarines to actually be dropped in harm's way were a small group of OSS operatives under Captain Peter J. Ortiz, who landed in France. Corporals Harlon H. Block and Ira H. Hayes, both former paramarines, were also photographed during the iconic flag-raising ceremony on Iwo Jima in February 1945.

Navy

Beach Jumpers

Lieutenant Douglas Fairbanks Jr., a noted Hollywood actor and U.S. Navy officer, completed a tour of staff duty with Admiral Lord Louis Montbatten's commandos in England. Having participated in several cross-channel raids, he returned to the United States in 1942, convinced that the navy could incorporate British operational facets into navy tactical doctrine. Fairbanks found their use of diversion and deception operations, particularly ahead of amphibious landing, noteworthy and broached creation of a specific unit capable of performing such tasks with superiors. The suggestion was favorably received, and on March 5, 1943, naval commander in chief Admiral Ernest J. King issued secret orders creating a unit commonly referred to as the Beach Jumpers. The vice chief of naval operations was tasked with recruiting 180 officers and 300 enlisted men for the secret unit, and members were handpicked for immunity to seasickness, experience in handling small boats, knowledge of electronics and radio technology, and ability to conduct celestial navigation. Later than month, all personnel reported to the Amphibious Training Base, Camp Bradford, Virginia, where Beach Jumper Unit One was organized. The men trained extensively in boat handling, seamanship, ordnance gunnery, demolition, pyrotechnics, and meteorology. They were to operate 10 high-speed, all-plywood air-sea rescue boats equipped with specialized deceptive equipment, including a wire recorder, amplifier, 100-watt speaker, and several naval balloons fitted with radar-reflecting metal strips. With all this training and equipment, they were tasked with giving an enemy the radio, audio, and radar signatures of an incoming amphibious force, one much larger than the handful of vessels emitting such electronic disinformation. By diverting enemy attention, it was calculated that the real amphibious force, landing elsewhere, would be enabled to take shore defenses by surprise.

Defining Activity

The Beach Jumpers were initially employed during Operation HUSKY, the Allied invasion of Sicily, on July 10, 1943. That evening, Beach Jumper Unit One arrived off Cape San Marco, 100 miles west of the actual landing zones, and unleashed their electronic diversions. The vessels accordingly began laying down smoke and running parallel to the supposed beachhead with their equipment blaring, giving the distinct impression that an invasion flotilla was hovering offshore. Two nights later, they conducted similar work off the same point with more boats, and German shore batteries were duped into opening fire on them. Consequently, the actual landing came off with little opposition, while the German high command, unsure as to where the actual landing would occur, unnecessarily withheld an entire division in reserve. Beach Jumper units remained active in the Mediterranean theater well into 1944, and a handful of units also operated in the Pacific with reasonable success. All Beach Jumper units were immediately disbanded in 1945 at the end of World War II.

In 1951, the Beach Jumper program was reactivated for service in the Korean War, although the program was further expanded during the Vietnam conflict. With better equipment, their mission expanded to include psychological operations in addition to the usual deception and electronic warfare activities. Operating from the helicopter assault ships USS *Iwo Jima* and *Tripoli*, they continually monitored Soviet signal intelligence trawlers shadowing the American flotilla in the Gulf of Tonkin, working to jam their signals and feed them false yet seemingly credible electronic disinformation. The term "Beach Jumper" was eventually discarded, and by 1986, "Fleet Tactical Deception Group" became the present-day designation.

Naval Combat Demolition Units

In September 1942, a group of 17 unattached navy salvage personnel attended the Amphibious Training School in Little Creek, Virginia, for a crash course in underwater demolitions, cable cutting, and related activities. Two months later, they participated in Operation TORCH by venturing up the Sebou River, Algeria, to reach Port Lyautey, site of a strategic airfield coveted by the Allies. Their mission was to sever a boom laid across the river by French forces. On the evening of November 8, the team piloted their Higgins boat in very rough water up the Sebou River, where they were detected by the French halfway to their objective. Heavy machine gun fire forced them to abandon the attempt and withdraw, so they repeated the mission on the evening of November 9. This time, the Higgins boat reached the cable without interference, at which point the salvage operators successfully cut the cable. The following morning, the destroyer USS *Dallas* conveyed a party of scouts and raiders near the Port Lyautey airfield, which was successfully secured. The various units then returned to their camp in the United States for additional training. The success of the salvage operators convinced navy officials of their need for bona fide demolition experts capable of clearing beach obstacles ahead of planned amphibious landings. The Germans were known to construct entire belts of defenses along potential landing areas, so it became militarily imperative to neutralize all threats to Allied landing craft. On May 6, 1943, Admiral Ernest J. King, naval commander in chief, addressed this impending problem by authorizing specialized "naval demolition units" for obstacle clearance. The following day, Lieutenant Commander Draper Kaufman was tasked with establishing a naval demolitions school at Fort Pierce, Florida, and the following month he began recruiting the first naval combat demolition units. The men received extensive physical training to weed out those less capable of prolonged, strenuous exertions, along with the expected regimen of handling underwater explosives and removing obstacles. Equally important was

Rear Admiral Draper L. Kaufman was a pioneering underwater demolitions expert who organized the navy's first team of "frogmen." His efforts foreshadowed what eventually became today's SEALs. (Courtesy of the U.S. Navy)

Draper L. Kaufman (1911–1979). Draper Lawrence Kaufman was born in San Diego, California, on August 4, 1911, and in 1933 he graduated from the U.S. Naval Academy. Denied a commission because of poor eyesight, he joined a steamship company, was taken prisoner by the Germans in France in 1940, and subsequently made his way to England. After serving as a sublieutenant in the Royal Navy Reserve, Kaufman transferred to the U.S. Naval Reserve in November 1941 to serve as a bomb disposal expert and ordnance officer. He managed to disarm the first Japanese bomb retrieved for examination following the attack on Pearl Harbor, winning a Navy Cross. In light of his technical expertise, Kaufman was next appointed the first commander of the Naval Combat Demolition Unit, Naval Amphibious Training Base, Fort Pierce, Florida. The techniques he pioneered and perfected established the first special operations force in U.S. Navy history: the so-called frogmen. In June 1943, he organized the first underwater demolition team (UDT), and in July 1944 he led UDT 5 into action on Saipan and Tinian, winning his second Navy Cross. Kaufman subsequently directed submerged operations off Iwo Jima and Okinawa in 1945. His many successful actions demonstrated the viability and practicality of amphibious warfare, but most UDT teams were disbanded after the war. Kaufman nonetheless rose through the ranks and held several destroyer commands. He became a rear admiral in July 1960, and in 1965 he served as the 44th superintendent of the U.S. Naval Academy. Kaufman, whose pioneering efforts eventually led to creation of the famous Navy SEALs, died on August 18, 1979.

their ability to reconnoiter and evaluate a prospective landing zone and determine where the troops could best advance toward the interior. Each team consisted of an officer and five enlisted men in a seven-man rubber boat; the place for the seventh man was occupied by explosives for the mission. The men wore steel helmets, dungarees, and heavy boots and were expected to paddle and walk to their objectives, not swim. Draper, who had the full cooperation of the Navy Department and a free hand at selecting recruits and devising their curricula, deployed 34 naval combat demolition units (NCDUs) in England by April 1944. The men trained continually in anticipation of Operation OVERLORD, the Allied invasion of Europe scheduled for June 1944.

Defining Activity

In the predawn hours of June 6, 1944, finely honed NCDU members went ashore at Normandy to mark and disable German explosives and all potential menaces to incoming landing craft. Exposed to heavy enemy fire at Omaha Beach, they nonetheless managed to blast eight gaps through German defenses at a loss of 31 killed and 60 wounded. Casualties proved less of a problem at Utah Beach, and 1,500 yards of beachhead was cleared by noontime at a cost of six dead and 11 injured. Thanks to their intense training, not a single member was lost through mishandling of explosives. The Utah Beach teams subsequently performed similar work for Operation DRAGOON in southern France the following August, the last time they were employed in western Europe. Two other demolition teams, NCDU 2 and NCDU 3, were attached to the Seventh Amphibious Force in the Pacific, and they made repeated landings along the New Guinea coast, Biak, and Borneo with excellent results. By war's end, the majority of NCDUs had also received underwater training and were absorbed into the new UDTs.

Scouts and Raiders

By the middle of 1942, the joint Army/Marine Corps Observer Group had been broken up and returned to the respective services. The Marines went on to raise and train their own scout and sniper teams in the Pacific, but that left the Atlantic Fleet lacking an intelligence-gathering unit to facilitate amphibious operations in North Africa or Europe. Consequently, Admiral Henry K. Hewitt, commander of Amphibious Force, Atlantic Fleet, ordered that a new school be established at the Naval Amphibious Base at Little Creek, Virginia. The new institution was christened the Scout and Raider School (Joint), and it was headed by U.S. Army Lieutenant Lloyd Peddicord, formerly of the Observer Group, who was instrumental in developing the seven-man rubber boat employed by that force. Prospective personnel were to master intense training in the scouting, swimming, boat-handling, and raiding techniques essential for their mission. The initial training class of 40 sailors arrived on September 1, 1942, and were divided into 10 scout boat crews of four men and one officer. A small contingent of army personnel was also present, although these received greater emphasis on land tactics than their naval counterparts. All ranks were intended to ingress onto a hostile shore at night, reconnoiter the area, and then establish signaling locations to guide in landing craft for an invasion.

Defining Activity

No sooner had Scout and Raider Team One been activated than it deployed with the Atlantic Fleet in time for Operation TORCH, the Allied invasion of North Africa. On November 8, 1942, the unit went ashore to mark the landing beaches just ahead of the invasion. Potential resistance from Vichy French units proved light, and 10 officers received the Navy Cross for their actions. On July 7, 1943, a second group of scouts and Raiders, designated Special Service Unit #1, was raised for service in the Pacific. That September, they guided landings ashore at Finschafen, New Guinea, with subsequent operations at Cape Gloucester and along the coast of New Britain, without loss. Non-navy personnel were reassigned after operational matters arose, and the new unit was renamed the 7th

Amphibious Scouts. These were retrained to go ashore in assault boats, mark channels with buoys and markers, detonate obstacles to landing craft, and communicate with troops onshore and those still on transport vessels. This unit successfully conducted over 40 amphibious landings without serious mishap. A third and final scout and raider group was handpicked and especially trained at Fort Pierce, Florida, for the purpose of operating in China and conducting amphibious guerilla warfare with local resistance units. Their only wartime activity was surveying the upper Yangtze River and, in the spring of 1945, conducting a three-month survey of the coast from Shanghai to Hong Kong while disguised as coolies. All scout and raider units were disbanded by war's end.

UDTs

On November 23, 1943, Operation GALVANIC, the amphibious assault on Tarawa Atoll, unfolded with extremely heavy losses to the U.S. Marines involved. Despite careful reconnaissance and intelligence work, unexpectedly treacherous tides and unseen coral reefs stopped many landing craft far from the beach, leaving marines to wade ashore under heavy fire. Admiral Richmond K. Turner, commanding the Tarawa invasion, decided that a specialized unit capable of handling underwater demolitions to remove any obstacles to landing forces, natural or man-made, was a military necessity. Shortly afterward, the first group of 30 officers and 150 enlisted men reported to the Waimanalo Amphibious Training Base at Oahu, Hawaii, to begin training as UDTs. Armed only with knives for personal defense and a bag of explosives, it was their mission to stealthily approach enemy-held beaches at night, reconnoiter and neutralize all potential threats to landing craft, and then egress undetected. Unlike previous demolition units employed by the navy, these were true amphibians employing the Lambertsen Underwater Respiratory Unit (an early form of Aqua-Lung), along with rubber fins to enhance swimming. This is the origin of the slang word "frogman"; being clad only in swim trunks, although they jocularly referred to themselves as the "naked warriors." After a period of intense demolition and underwater instruction, UDT Teams One and Two deployed for combat operations in the central Pacific. Normally, UDT teams were housed onboard converted troop-carrying destroyers and deployed to a given area on a ramped Higgins-type landing craft.

Defining Activity

On January 31, 1944, the frogmen partook of Operation FLINTLOCK, the invasion of the Marshall Islands, and their success at detecting and removing underwater obstacles near Roi, Namur, and Kwajalein gave the UDT program greater impetus. Consequently, in February 1944, existing UDT teams were broken up as training cadres, and the new Naval Combat Demolition and Experimental Base arose at Kihei, Maui. Here, 34 UDT teams were ultimately trained, and they saw action in virtually all major amphibious landings, such as Eniwetok, Saipan, Guam, Tinian, Angaur, Ulithi, Peleliu, Leyte, Iwo Jima, and Okinawa. Their final operation of the war occurred at Balikpapan, Borneo, on July 4, 1945, and virtually all UDT teams would have been involved in Operations OLYMPIC and CORONET—the invasion of Japan—had not the war concluded that September. Only two UDT teams of seven officers and 45 enlisted men apiece were retained in the peacetime establishment, but as a military unit, they had repeatedly demonstrated their tactical utility and value to the navy.

OSS

Prior to World War II, U.S. intelligence-gathering procedures and institutions were episodic endeavors at best. The State, Treasury, Navy, and War Departments all possessed intelligence capabilities through various agencies under their purview, but the nation lacked a single, unified entity to collect, analyze, and disseminate information at the highest levels. In fact, MI-8, the original code-breaking office of the State Department, had been disbanded in 1929 by Secretary of State Henry Stimson through the simple expedient that "gentlemen do not read each other's mail." This informational malaise persisted for over another decade until July 1940, when President Franklin D. Roosevelt dispatched New York attorney William J. Donovan, a highly decorated army officer, to England to assess

Major General William J. Donovan headed up the Office of Strategic Services, the first clandestine paramilitary agency in American history and a precursor to the Central Intelligence Agency. He was an attorney by training and among the most highly decorated American soldiers of World War I. (Library of Congress)

that island's ability to resist Nazi Germany. There Donovan encountered William S. Stephenson, chief of British security coordination, who convinced him that the United States had to drastically improve its intelligence functions because of the likelihood of American involvement in World War II. Donovan reported as much back to Roosevelt, who, on July 11, 1941, authorized creation of the new office of Coordinator of Information (COI). Donovan was appointed head of that post and granted a budget of $10 million. This groundbreaking agency consisted of four distinct branches: Secret Intelligence, which conducted covert gathering operations; Research and Analysis, which interpreted and summarized information procured in the field; the Foreign Information Service, which distributed governmental, or "white," propaganda; and Special Operations, authorized to execute armed covert action operations abroad. Ironically, despite the significance of COI to American national security, it enjoyed far closer ties to British intelligence services simply because the FBI, the navy, the army, and the State Department engaged in an internecine turf war and refused to acknowledge or coordinate their efforts with them.

The sorry state of American intelligence was instantly rectified by the Japanese attack on Pearl Harbor on December 7, 1941, where the COI, the State Department, and the military were finally forced to work together. In order to transfer jurisdiction of Donovan's agency from the executive branch to the newly formed Joint Chiefs of Staff (JCS), on June 13, 1942, Roosevelt signed an order recasting it as the new Office of Strategic Services, or

OSS This entity was tasked with clandestinely collecting and analyzing foreign intelligence to assist the JCS in formulating and executing high-level strategies. The OSS, while technically a civilian agency, included many uniform personnel, and Donovan himself received the rank of major general. Once operational, it was authorized to conduct clandestine missions abroad, including sabotage, which strictly intelligence agencies did not. Over the next three years, Donovan and his carefully crafted body of agents accumulated economic, political, and military information about Nazi Germany, fascist Italy, imperial Japan, and their allies that proved of enormous use to the Allied war effort. Its spy network also included political and conscientious dissidents, with the most important being Fritz Kolbe, a high-level German diplomat. Trains and boats were frequently used by OSS agents, although it was not uncommon for them to parachute into their destination or paddle ashore from a submarine. They also infiltrated various antifascist groups in Austria, Hungary, and Germany, using them to spread unfavorable propaganda against the native regimes. OSS operatives, fluent in the languages and cultures of their assigned targets, worked through Europe and Asia, cultivating intelligence contacts and, more important, armed and trained a host of resistance movements. Agents were also responsible for assisting Chinese units in China and Kachin guerrillas in Burma to fight effectively against Japanese occupiers. In March 1945, one OSS team even established formal contacts with Ho Chi Minh of the communist Viet Minh in French Indochina (Vietnam), supplying his ragtag force with guns and radios to combat the invaders. OSS medical aid man Paul Hogland went so far as to treat the ailing Ho, whom he found dying of malaria and dysentery, and kept him alive. Following the German surrender on May 8, 1945, OSS leader Allen Foster Dulles also helped personally arrange the surrender of all German units in Italy to the Allies. At the height of its influence, the OSS employed roughly 24,000 people with the multiplicity of sundry skills necessary to complete its various tasks. It was one of the most successful spy agencies to that date and acquired intelligence from a global reach.

Defining Activity

Of all the actions undertaken by the OSS, none was more celebrated than Operation JED-BURGH, which derives its name from a Scottish highland town near their main training camp. The Jedburghs consisted of 93 three-agent teams, or operational groups; usually one Frenchman of the Central de Renseignements et d'Action; and two American OSS operatives or two British SOE agents. These men would be parachuted into occupied France, Belgium, and Holland at night to link up with regional resistance groups (Marquis) and serve as their conduit to Supreme Headquarters Allied Expeditionary Forces. All teams were equipped with a Type B Mark II radio, or "Jed Set," through which close contact was maintained with Special Force Headquarters in London. Moreover, they were thoroughly trained in the use of codes, ciphers, parachutes, homing beacons for incoming aircraft, explosive and demolition equipment, and all other tricks of the trade. Of particular use was the explosive designated Compound C, a precursor of modern plastic explosives that was powerful and could destroy train rails with charges the size of a golf ball. Finally, despite their highly clandestine function, OSS operatives remained clad in military attire to circumvent their execution as spies, if caught. Operation JEDBURGH also marks the first time that the OSS enjoyed the opportunity for a mass insertion of assets into western Europe and to coordinate its efforts on such a large scale with the SOE. Politics never remain far from below the surface, however, and for expediency's sake, General Dwight D. Eisenhower diplomatically placed Operation JEDBURGH under French control.

The Jeds arrived in France just prior to Operation OVERLORD, the invasion of western Europe, slated for June 6, 1944. Having contacted their requisite Marquis cells, the next phase was arranging airdrops of supplies and weapons to resistance fighters: some 6,000 tons were eventually delivered in 4,000 missions. Still, the overwhelming emphasis of their mission was not sabotage, which only provoked German reprisals, but rather reconnaissance and intelligence with respect to troop dispositions and coastal fortifications. After D-Day, the Jeds and Maquis carried on a campaign of sabotage behind German lines to slow the flow of reinforcements against the Normandy beachheads. The exact military impact of such activity has never been accurately assessed, but it undoubtedly tied down thousands of troops to guard communication and supply routes, men who could be better employed elsewhere. Similar attacks occurred along the French Riviera as part of Operation DRAGOON, the Allied invasion of southern France, with similar results. Another important function of Jeds was to hide and smuggle downed Allied airmen out of France and to safety. Jedburgh teams continued working in France, Holland, and Belgium up through October 1944, when they were recalled to England.

The OSS enjoyed a proven track record of success in the field, and its activities undoubtedly hastened the end of the war, potentially saving thousands of Allied lives. General Donovan pleaded this fact to Roosevelt's successor, President Harry S. Truman, but the latter nonetheless ordered the agency disbanded on October 1, 1945. Thereafter, the intelligence-gathering functions so painstakingly constructed over the previous three years were shared between the State Department and the Department of War. It took the onset of a new struggle, the Cold War with the Soviet Union, for a single, highly coordinated clandestine body to arise once more. Accordingly, the National Security Act of 1947 founded the nation's first permanent spy apparatus, the fabled Central Intelligence Agency (CIA). Many former OSS operatives went on to enjoy distinguished careers, including William Colby, a future CIA director; Lucien Conein, a central CIA operative during the Vietnam War; Army General John Singlaub; and Colonel Aaron Bank, who helped to found the famous Green Berets. The U.S. military subsequently inculcated many of the special operational techniques and technologies pioneered by the OSS between 1943 and 1945 in its own special operations forces.

Miscellaneous

American Volunteer Group

The onset of hostilities between Japan and China in 1937 was, in many respects, the opening round of a gradually expanding global conflict. Japan had been intent on securing an empire in Asia since it emerged from isolation under the Meiji Restoration of 1868, and for the past seven decades it imported and inculcated the very best of Western military technologies, adapting them for their own use and, in many instances, improving upon them. This was especially true in the field of military aviation, for in 1937 the Japanese fielded some of the world's most advanced fighters and bombers, flown by pilots who were thoroughly trained and fanatically devoted to the pursuit of victory. Their lopsided advantage over the tottering Nationalist Chinese Air Force, still struggling to achieve parity with the invaders, led to a profusion of foreign military advisers into the region, with many seeking employ in the service of Chinese leader Chiang Kai-shek. Most of these proved fraudulent adventurers who inflicted more harm on Chinese aeronautics than anything else, but one name stands out as the world's greatest exponent of aerial guerilla warfare: Claire Lee Chennault. Not only were his advisory efforts capable and exemplary, but the clandestine unit he molded together blazed its way into the history books as the famous "Flying Tigers." This colorful outfit, while never an official part of the U.S. military establishment, provided the West with its only uplift and inspiration during dark, initial phases of war in the Pacific.

Like many successful irregulars, Chennault, a former fighter pilot, came from a nondescript background with little in his mien to suggest anything other than obscurity. While attending the Air Corps Tactical School at Langley Field, Virginia, in 1935, he had authored a notable treatise, *The Role of Defensive Pursuit*, which postulated that properly handled fighter aircraft would always inflict grievous losses on attacking bombers. His theories did not sit well with prevailing Army Air Corps doctrine, then beholden to the "flying battleship" concept, whereby bombers like the new B-17 bomber could fend for themselves without fighter escort. In 1937, ill health and lack of recognition prompted Chennault to resign his commission. Fortuitously, he encountered the formidable Madam Chiang Kai-shek, who spoke fluent English with a Georgian accent, and convinced him to accompany her back to China and conduct a "survey" of the Chinese air force. What he saw appalled him: the air school, run by Italians, would grant a pilot's license to any aristocrat's son regardless of his abilities, while aircraft maintenance by foreign mechanics was shoddy, if that. It was little wonder that crack Japanese aircrews easily dispersed all aerial opposition and ranged freely across Chinese skies. Jiang grew so desperate that his regime contracted with Josef Stalin and acquired Soviet "volunteers" to man two light bomber groups and four fighter groups. Chennault, who dealt with the Soviets directly, was impressed by their skill and professionalism, and they, in turn, expressed interest in his aeronautical theories. The Soviets enjoyed several tactical air victories in 1937 and 1938 over the Japanese, but by 1940 they were ordered home in light of mounting fears of a German attack. Chennault, fortunately, proved himself an astute observer of Japanese airpower. Casting a professional eye, he appreciated their prowess as airmen—then began dissecting them for weaknesses. He quickly deduced that Japanese aircraft were lightly constructed to enhance maneuverability, and their pilots placed a premium on combat maneuvering. In Chennault's estimation, the Japanese were superbly trained and equipped—to refight World War I. He passed these observations back to aerial leaders in Washington, D.C., who either disbelieved him or ignored his advice outright. In the summer of 1940, the Japanese navy deployed it famous Mitsubishi A6M "Zero" fighter, which simply obliterated any remaining Chinese opposition. Chennault examined a captured example that had been downed by ground fire and sent off frantic intelligence cables to the War Department warning of its sterling dogfighting abilities. American military authorities nonetheless refused to believe that the Japan's aviation industry was anything but amateurish and its aerial arm of little consequence.

By 1941, Japanese bomber formations were hammering China's industrial and population centers with virtual impunity. Given the vast disparity between Chinese and Japanese aeronautical infrastructures, Jiang convinced Chennault that the only way to counter this

Claire L. Chennault (1890–1958). Claire Lee Chennault was born in Commerce, Texas, on September 6, 1890, and he joined the Aviation Section, Signal Corps, in 1920, gaining his wings. Chennault, a natural-born flier, held a number of important assignments over the next two decades. In 1935, he also published an important book titled *The Role of Defensive Pursuit*. Deafness in one ear removed him from flying status, so he resigned in April 1937 and was hired by Madam Chiang Kai-shek to serve as an aviation adviser to the Nationalist Chinese government. Chennault spent the next four years scrutinizing Japanese aerial capabilities, and he issued repeated warnings to Washington, D.C., that were ignored. In 1941, he prevailed upon the American government to allow him to organize a group of mercenar-

General Claire L. Chennault was the first aerial guerrilla strategist, and his "Flying Tigers" were among the most celebrated aviation units of World War II. (National Archives)

ies, officially named the American Volunteers Group, to fight the Japanese directly. That December, Chennault's three squadrons began winning air battles against heretofore invincible Japanese aircraft, and they became regaled in the press as as the "Flying Tigers." Chennault's group is credited with over 100 Japanese aircraft for the loss of 12 pilots, but it was disbanded in July 1942. He rose to major general in March 1943 as head of the newly created 14th Air Force and, by war's end, claimed 2,600 enemy planes downed and 1.2 million tons of shipping sunk. Denied his third star, he resigned from the army in August 1945 and remained in China as head of the Civil Air Transport, which was eventually sold to the Central Intelligence Agency. Chennault died in New Orleans, Louisiana, on July 27, 1958, aviation's first guerilla fighter.

aerial blitzkrieg was with a unit of experienced foreign pilots equipped with modern aircraft. Chennault consequently visited Washington, D.C., with Madam Chiang and noted financier T. V. Soong to obtain direct American assistance for the plan. Given strictly observed American neutrality at the time, his plea for what amounted to a group of flying mercenaries was scoffed at by the military establishment. Fortunately, the scheme caught the ear of President Franklin D. Roosevelt, who was overtly sympathetic toward the plight of China. At length, Roosevelt ordered that a "special unit" of volunteer pilots and mechanics drawn from army, navy, and Marine Corps personnel. They would be allowed to resign their commissions and sign up with the Central Aircraft Manufacturing Company for service in China. The pilots were lavishly paid by contemporary standards, roughly $600 per month, with a further $500 bonus for each Japanese aircraft downed, and at length 109 fliers and 186 ground personnel volunteered. Furthermore, they would operate 100 Curtiss Tomahawk IIB fighters (P-40Bs) previously earmarked for the Royal Air Force (RAF). All these arrangements dangerously skirted existing neutrality and export laws, but given the seriousness of the situation, Roosevelt assigned two close associates, Lauchlin Curry and Thomas G. Corcoran, to smooth out arrangements. The unit would operate under the ambiguous designation of "American Volunteer Group" (AVG) once its three squadron's became operational. As a further mark of distinction, all P-40Bs received the famous "shark mouth" decoration on the bottom half of their engine cowling, copied from RAF squadrons operating in North Africa.

Throughout the summer and fall of 1941, Chennault's clandestine operatives and their equipment unpacked at Rangoon, Burma, and threaded their way to the RAF base at Toungoo for orientation. Here they were exposed to Chennault's innovative theories of air combat, especially as it related to fighting the Japanese and exploiting their tactical rigidity. He lectured how the enemy, by virtue of training and equipment, were virtually unbeatable in "classic" dogfighter tactics, namely, a contest of slow turns along a horizontal plane. Instead, he instructed his men to capitalize on the P-40's strengths, its high speed and heavier weight, that allowed it to dive down and zoom up faster than their antagonists. The Japanese, flying much lighter, slower aircraft, could not follow. In tactical parlance, this entailed avoiding the enemy where he was strongest and focusing on his weaknesses. Chennault ordered all pilots to disregard their previous aerial training and concentrate on flying and fighting in pairs, especially along the vertical axis. They were to climb to an altitude advantage, dive on their quarry, and then break away and climb again for another pass. Thus, the time-honored guerilla expedient of "hit-and-run" warfare received a decidedly new twist. Chennault also appreciated the significance of early warnings against bombing raids, and he established a clandestine network of radios, telephones, and telegraphs through the southern China countryside that could relay the size, speed, and direction of enemy armadas along with probable targets. Chennault offered his tactical expertise to the RAF, but many officers, veterans of fighting the Germans and Italians, simply scoffed at his notion of hit-and-run attacks. By November 1941, Chennault had two AVG squadrons stationed at Kunming, China, while a third deployed at Mingaladon, Burma, for the defense of Rangoon. Their intended opponent was the Japanese Army Air Force, which, while not equipped with the legendary Mitsubishi A6M Zero carrier fighter, still possessed good aircraft and pilots of its own. The AVG's baptism under fire did not occur until December 20, 1941, two weeks following the Japanese attack on Pearl Harbor. Chennault's early warning net advised him that a force of 10 Ki-48 light bombers were en route to Kunming, so he scrambled two squadrons of P-40s, bagging four of the intruders. The lesson was taken to heart by the Japanese, who never raided Kunming again as long as the AVG operated there.

Defining Activity

The scene of action quickly shifted southward once Japanese aerial forces began a concerted bombing campaign of Rangoon, an important British dock facility. Chennault continually rotated a single squadron of 18 fighters there, and between December 23, 1941, and February 27, 1942, they routinely engaged large bomber forces and their escorts.

The AVG was assisted by several determined RAF squadrons flying outdated Hawker Hurricanes and Brewster Buffalos. In virtually every engagement, the American and British fliers were heavily outnumbered by their opponents, and while the latter gave a good account of themselves, the Flying Tigers made world headlines by drawing prodigious quantities of enemy blood. Japanese light and medium bombers suffered from the same tactical deficiencies as Japanese fighters and could not withstand the concentrated firepower of the P-40s. For example, on January 12, 1942, a force of six Ki-21 Sally medium bombers appeared over Rangoon escorted by Ki-27 Nate fixed-wheeled fighters; the AVG bagged all the bombers without loss. This pattern of punishing attacks continued until British forces retreated in the face of a Japanese ground offensive, and Rangoon was abandoned. Still, in contrast to Allied fighter units elsewhere in the Pacific, the AVG scored heavily against their opponents, claiming over 50 Japanese aircraft downed for a loss 20 P-40s. Success in the skies of Burma greatly heartened the American public, still reeling from disasters in Hawaii and the Philippines. The AVG's renown was such that the famous Walt Disney Studios designed a distinct insignia for the Flying Tigers consisting of a Bengal tiger flying through a "V" for "Victory." In terms of press coverage, Chennault also became the most famous airman of the war.

With Rangoon's fall impending, the AVG retreated to Magwe in northern Burma, where they continued wracking up tactical successes against Japanese aircraft. Heavily outnumbered and weakened by attrition, Chennault subsequently withdrew them to Loiwing in southern China to regroup and then again to Baoshan after Burma finally fell. In true guerilla fashion, he constantly rotated his base of operations from various make-shift airfields, constructed by thousands of Chinese coolies, to preclude any chance of Japanese air raids. At that point, the AVG's basic mission also changed from aerial defense to ground assault, and they bombed and strafed Japanese columns traversing the Salween Gorge into southern China. This dangerous work caused a minor mutiny among pilots that Chennault quashed by dint of his fierce personality, and the attacks resumed. Given that the Army Air Force was rapidly expanding, all former military personnel were also recalled home for active duty, and on July 4, 1942, the AVG was formally disbanded at Kunming after seven months of action. Only five of the original pilots and a handful of ground personnel elected to remain behind as part of the new 23rd Fighter Group, China Air Task Force (CATF), but by dint of Chennault's aerial guerilla tactics, they had carved their name into aviation history and succeeded where comparably equipped Allied units failed disastrously. In sum, they dramatically proved that the Japanese were not invincible and could be bloodied. The AVG's three squadrons were officially attributed with 299 aerial victories, but historians have since rounded down their tally to 115. This reduction hardly derogates their accomplishments, for Japanese army aviation was at the top of its game at the onset of World War II and, considering the quality of the opposition, Chennault's success over Burma and southern China is still remarkable. No fewer than 19 individuals became aces with five or more victories. In exchange, 14 AVG pilots were either killed, missing in action, or captured. Memory of the AVG, the most famous clandestine aerial organization in history, is perpetuated by today's 23rd Fighter Group, which adorns their aircraft with the same "Shark Mouth" markings. In 1991, the AVG also received a prestigious PUC, even though, officially at least, it constitutes part of the Nationalist Chinese Air Force.

Kachin Rangers

A mixed force of U.S. troops and Kachin scouts advance through the jungles of Burma. Kachin operations against occupying Japanese forces were among the most successful campaigns mounted by the Office of Strategic Services. (Library of Congress)

During the opening days of World War II, imperial Japanese forces lashed out with astonishing speed and efficiency across the Pacific and the Asian landmass. Nowhere was this more apparent than in British-held Burma, which fell to a rapid Japanese onslaught in March 1942. This act cut the so-called Burma Road into southern China, the sole remaining over- land supply route for the Nationalist Chinese regime of Chiang Kai-shek. While the British frantically shored up their defenses in northern India and pre- pared to mount a counterattack, the OSS created Unit 101 on April 14, 1942, for the purpose of mobilizing the indigenous local peoples of northern Burma, or Kachins, to assist the Allied war effort. This unit came in response to a staff study by Colonel Preston Goodfellow of the Coordinator of Information, the precursor of the OSS. Lieutenant General Joseph W. Stillwell, the newly appointed American commander of the CBI theater, was suitably impressed by the plan, given the direness of the situation, and the mission unfolded. This proved no mean feat, considering that everything, from instruct- ing the backward locals on modern military methods to supplying the entire operation by air, was experimental. Still, from his headquarters in Assam, India, Colonel Carl F. Eisler began infiltrating small teams of American-trained Burmese operatives back into Kachin areas for recruiting and supplying local guerilla bands. The Kachins, who resented the strong-arm tactics of Japanese occupiers, were all too willing to volunteer and filtered back to Assam for military and communications training. These people in question were friendly, good natured, yet grimly earnest in their work. Moreover, they proved highly adaptable to terrible jungle conditions and became adept at using coded radio messages and automatic weapons. Kachins, in particular, were experts at ambushes and routinely lined killing zones with hidden sharpened stakes (*pungyi* sticks) on either side. Once an attack was sprung, Japanese soldiers invariably flung themselves into the bushes—only to be painfully impaled on the stakes. Each Kachin also carried his traditional short swords, or *dah*, into battle. The Americans recoiled over the Kachin practice of cutting off ears from dead Japanese soldiers with *dahs* and keeping them as trophies. When their training was completed, the volunteers parachuted back into Kachin areas in small groups and began clandestine intelligence- gathering missions from remote villages. Highly skilled in hit-and-run tactics, they also proved to be the bane of Japanese patrols and supply routes throughout northern Burma; they wiped out several small enemy units and cut several important railroad bridges in this inhos- pitable terrain. The no-nonsense Eisler was suitably impressed by the Kachins "rangers," as he deemed them, and he prevailed on General Stillwell to expand their size and mission.

The first American-led Kachin ranger operations did not commence until January 1943, and these were tasked with establishing guerrilla bases at Ngumla, just north of Myitkyina, the site of a major Japanese airfield. While ambushes and sabotage were important, the basic mission of Kachin rangers was as agent/radio operators teams along Japanese transportation routes leading to northern Burma. The data they collected were relayed back to headquarters in Nazira, India, 500 miles away, and aircraft of the U.S. 10th Air Force were dispatched on bombing and strafing runs should supply convoys be sizable. If an aircraft was lost to ground fire, the Kachins also proved especially helpful in smuggling the crews back to Allied lines; over 300 American and British personnel were rescued in this fashion. By year's end, Detachment 101 was coordinating no fewer than six intelligence bases behind enemy lines, all regularly supplied at night through airdrops. The information they relayed respecting enemy troop concentrations proved invaluable once the major Allied counteroffensive in Burma was being planned. However, Colonel Eisler's performance had grown increasingly erratic after he had been accidentally struck on the head during one operation, and in December 1943, OSS chief William Donovan replaced with him Lieutenant Colonel William R. Peers.

Defining Activity

By the spring of 1944, the Allies shifted over from a defensive posture in Burma to the offense, intent on driving the Japanese out from the region. That April, Operation GALAHAD commenced as three battalions of Merrill's Marauders advanced into the jungle to seize the enemy airfield at Myitkyina. This was an important enemy position, for Japanese aircraft stationed there harassed vital cargo airlifts over the Himalayan Mountains, or the "Hump." The Japanese naturally ascribed great importance to this airfield, and it was defended by members of the elite 18th Infantry Division, the former conquerors of Singapore. Fortunately, the Marauders were accompanied by no fewer than 3,200 armed Kachin rangers acting as scouts and guides throughout this mountainous jungle terrain. Given their expertise at jungle warfare, nimble Kachins greatly boosted American morale in this steamy, hellish environment. They unerringly provided reliable intelligence, scouted ahead of the main column, secured their flanks, and screened movements in such a manner as to deceive the enemy into thinking that only guerillas were moving through the area. Still, the GALAHAD force weathered an arduous 65-mile passage through the 6,000-foot Kumon mountain range, slippery with mud, while losing half its pack animals and equipment. At one point, the only Kachin guide familiar with the area was bitten by a poisonous snake, but rather than be evacuated, he received a tourniquet and continued leading while strapped to a horse. On May 14, 1944, other Kachin scouts slipped unobserved into enemy positions and reported that no special defensive measures had been taken. The airfield was quickly seized on May 17, although the campaign to secure the town dragged on through August. In light of their important contribution to the final victory, Stillwell authorized expanding the Kachin force to 10,000 guerillas. These were to be distributed among no fewer than three new area commands and would coordinate large-scale operations against the Japanese.

From August to December 1944, the Kachin rangers supported the Allied advance from Katha to Bhamo, the later finally falling on December 15, 1944. Once again, the natives distinguished themselves by infiltrating enemy lines, staging ambushes, and relaying accurate military intelligence. The Kachin rangers were subsequently employed in the state of Shan to mop up Japanese defenders along the Taunggyi-Kengtung Road, but enemy resistance was fierce and fanatical. Fortunately, by June 15, 1945, the Kachins managed to capture the strategic strong points of Lawsawk, Pangtara, and Loilem killing 1,200 Japanese at a cost of 300 dead and scores more wounded. These represent the heaviest losses sustained by the Kachins during the war years, although they ultimately received help from hundreds of armed Karen, Gurhka, Chan, and Chinese volunteers. Unit 101 was formally deactivated in Simlumkaba, Burma, on July 12, 1945, and it received a PUC for orchestrating America's best-executed guerilla campaign of the war. Each Kachin fighter also received a Citation for Military Assistance Award, although the very bravest fighters kept Japanese swords and weapons as souvenirs. Over the previous two years, no fewer than 162 native agent/radio teams had deployed behind enemy lines by land, sea, and air. The Kachin rangers thus provided 75 percent of military intelligence utilized by the 10th Air Force in India and 85 percent of all intelligence relayed to Stillwell's Northern Combat Area Command. They also managed to sabotage 57 bridges and nine trains and destroyed 272 Japanese trucks, along with 15,000 tons of enemy supplies. Moreover, Kachin activities forced hard-pressed Japanese forces to assign combat troops to protect rear-area echelons and lines of communication. The 10,800 armed guerilla fighters and their 120 American handlers also accounted for 5,428 enemy dead and over 10,000 wounded along with 78 prisoners. Unit 101 losses amounted to 27 Americans and 338 Kachins killed in action, while a further 40 native intelligence agents also died in the line of duty. All told, this was a stirring display of unconventional warfare waged through indigenous forces and one strongly mirrored by the modern Green Berets.

Native Americans

The advent of improved communications in World War II opened up new avenues for clandestine linguistics on the battlefield, a tactic that had been successfully demonstrated in 1918 with native Choctaw speakers. Success on the modern battlefield is largely contingent on secure military communications transmitted rapidly yet remaining beyond the grasp of enemy intelligence. The standard practice of encrypting messages usually ensures a measure of security, although valuable time must be expended decoding them, a luxury not always afforded in the heat of frontline operations. Therefore, the most desirable method of real-time, secure communication is voice transmission via radio or telephone employing a language or dialect undecipherable to all but a handful of native speakers. The principle had been successfully demonstrated in 1918 with a handful of Choctaw, but the practice had all but been forgotten during the interwar period.

During World War II, the most celebrated use of military linguists were the Navajo code talkers, who were employed largely by the U.S. Marine Corps and the U.S. Navy in the Pacific. Early in 1942, Philip Johnston, the son of a missionary to the Navajo nation and fluent in that dialect, approached Major General Clayton B. Vogel about the possibility of employing native speakers for battlefield communications. This language, spoken only by Navajo living in the southwestern United States, is extremely complex and subtle in its tonal qualities and requires a lifetime of use for an outsider to gain meaningful fluency. The language is also unwritten, like virtually all Native American dialects, and so is even harder to study. Because only about 30 non-Indian Navajo speakers were extant at the time, Johnston considered the language relatively secure from German, Japanese, or Italian translators. Vogel, as head of Amphibious Corps, Pacific Fleet, recognized what a boon this held for on-site radio communications, and he arranged extensive testing under simulated battle conditions. Not surprisingly, it took trained Navajo code talkers only 20 seconds to accurately translate a three-line English message, whereas an encrypted message required up to 30 minutes. Vogel, suitably impressed by the Native Americans, approached the Marine Corps commandant by recommending that Navajo be employed for military communications training, and in May 1942, the first 29 Navajo arrived at Camp Pendleton, California. By war's end, no fewer than 420 Navajo served in this capacity, and they performed invaluable work on battlefields across the Pacific. Prior to shipping out, all had to memorize a specially developed dictionary of military terms and phrases and codes to be used in combat. Here, simple native words, such as "dah-her tie-hi" (hummingbird), were used in place of "fighter plane." The Navajo code talkers performed their work with astonishing speed and accuracy at Guadalcanal, Tarawa, and Pelelieu. During the battle for Iwo Jima in January 1945, they sent and received over 800 codes messages or the 5th Marine Division alone, facilitating the final American victory. After the war, several Japanese intelligence officers admitted to being flummoxed by Native American dialects. The Navajo fulfilled a similar task during the Korean War in 1950–1953 until the program was finally terminated in the early days of the Vietnam struggle. Navajo code talkers went largely unrecognized by the military establishment until September 1992, when a group of survivors were formally honored by ceremonies held at the Pentagon in Washington, D.C.

In Europe and elsewhere, the U.S. Army also employed Native American code talkers, including Pawnee, Creek/Seminole, Cherokee, Meskwaki, Lakota (Sioux), and Comanche. The 4th Signal Company in particular hosted a number of the latter in particular, and these compiled a dictionary of over 100 precise military terms based on their dialect. No fewer than 14 Comanche were present during Operation OVERLORD on June 6, 1944, and they splashed ashore with the 4th Infantry Division during the landings at Normandy. Two speakers were usually assigned to each regiment arriving at Utah Beach, and like their Navajo counterparts, they completely baffled German radio intelligence. This was despite that fact that, in the 1930s, Adolf Hitler instructed German anthropologists to learn Indian dialects, including Comanche, to thwart their possible use in wartime.

Nisei Translators

While the U.S. military employed Native American speakers to ensure their own battlefield communications, they also used Nisei (second-generation Japanese Americans) to eavesdrop on enemy transmissions. This became a national security imperative given the complexity and intense subtlety of the Japanese language and the glaring lack of fluent speakers and readers back in the United States. In fact, as relations between the two nations deteriorated prior to 1941, the government began rounding up Japanese linguistic authorities, including several American citizens of Japanese extraction, to serve as instructors. Only a handful of students graduated, and this scheme became impractical after 1942 once President Franklin D. Roosevelt consigned millions of Japanese Americans to interment camps on the West Coast for security reasons. Consequently, many Nisei-language instructors were removed from teaching positions and sent off as detainees. The dire emergency of the Pacific War largely reversed this overtly racist practice, and many Nisei were actively sought out by the army and navy as translators and radio-intercept operators. Most of these subsequently served with the Military Intelligence Service with the War Department's blessing. By war's end, the Japanese-language program had expanded to 160 instructors, 3,000 students, and 125 classrooms. Graduates of the program served actively throughout the Pacific and South Pacific regions and were regarded as the "front line" of military intelligence gathering for combating the Japanese Empire. For example, one unit, the 8th Radio Squadron Mobile (8th RSM), part of the Joint Army Navy Radio Analysis Group, employed Nisei translators to intercept and decipher Japanese air and ground transmissions. No fewer than 10 accompanied B-29 bombing missions over Japan and continually alerted aircrews of enemy activities. In light of their efficient work, men of the 8th RSM were highly commended by Admiral Chester W. Nimitz for invaluable contributions to the war effort.

By war's end, Nisei linguists translated no fewer than 18,000 captured enemy documents, composed 16,000 propaganda leaflets for Japanese consumption, and interrogated over 10,000 prisoners of war. Their service was regarded as indispensable for securing the final victory, and no fewer than three top-secret Nisei translators accompanied the battleship USS *Missouri* during surrender ceremonies in Tokyo Harbor on September 2, 1945. Immediately afterward, many Nisei translators served as cultural liaisons during the American occupation of Japan and smoothed out ruffled edges occasioned by the disparate parties. Steeped in the cultural and linguistic nuances of both cultures, the Nisei helped lay the foundation for a harmonious occupation along with the goodwill and rapprochement that exists between both nations today. Because the activities of Nisei translators were so militarily sensitive, they received no public attention relative to the incomparable 442nd Regimental Combat Team, the all Japanese American "Go for Broke" unit that became the most decorated army outfit of the war. It is nonetheless widely acknowledged that Nisei translators advanced the course of Allied victory in the Pacific by at least two years.

Philippine Scouts

Having liberated the Philippines from Spain in 1898, the U.S. Army became embroiled in its first large-scale guerilla war in Asia once Filipino patriot Emilio Aguinaldo refused to accept anything less than immediate independence. As the conflict dragged on, American military leaders in the field came to respect the fighting prowess of their adversaries on these islands and set about recruiting the first non–North American ethnic units in U.S. Army history. The first Philippine scouts were organized in 1898 to help suppress the ongoing insurgency, and 50 companies of 100 men each were deployed. They were formally inculcated into the U.S. military establishment by an act of Congress in February 1901, and a month they later scored a spectacular success by aiding in the capture of Aquinaldo while inside his own headquarters. They quickly gained the reputation as elite fighting units and performed capably in various outlying islands up through the 1930s. Beginning in 1919, the various companies were grouped into identifiable regiments within the U.S. Army as the 43rd, 45th, and 57th Infantries; the 24th and 25th Field Artillery Regiments; the 26th Cavalry Regiment; and the 91st and 92nd Coast Artillery Regiments. Collectively, all these units included the suffix "PS," denoting their status as Philippine scouts. Like standing U.S. formations, these included the requisite number of service and support detachments, including military police, medical, engineer, and quartermaster units. These were also organized, along with the U.S. 31st Infantry Regiment, to form the new

Captain Arthur Wermuth, the noted "One Man Army of Bataan," is pictured here with one of his elite Philippine scouts. Man for man, they were probably the best indigenous soldiers who ever fought for the United States. (Library of Congress)

Philippine Division. During this formative period, the army began dispatching at least one qualified Filipino to study at the U.S. Military Academy at West Point, 26 of whom subsequently graduated and served with the regular Philippine establishment. The scouts themselves were recruited solely from handpicked individuals, well motivated and eager to serve for half the pay of their American counterparts. By the advent of the Pacific War in 1941, there were no fewer than 11,972 Philippine scouts. These troops were well trained and lavishly equipped in comparison to the hastily raised and equipped soldiers of the regular Philippine army, who had scarcely completed basic training when war commenced.

On December 22, 1941, the crack Japanese 14th Army under Lieutenant General Masaharu Homma splashed ashore at Lingayen Gulf, northern Luzon, and began pressing south toward Manila. All these 40,000 troops were veterans of fighting in China and possessed a fanatical combat creed that made no allowance for defeat. Nonetheless, they encountered fierce opposition from the 26th Cavalry (PS) who, despite four-to-one odds, successfully delayed their advance long enough for General Douglas MacArthur to pull his force into more defensible positions on the Bataan peninsula. By early January 1942, 80,000 Filipinos, stiffened by 10,000 Americans and 9,500 Philippine scouts, occupied the so-called Abucay-Mauban Line. Between January 9 and 14, 1942, superior numbers of Japanese veterans attacked the 57th Infantry (PS) along the coastal highway that paralleled Manila Bay. For three days, the outnumbered scouts blasted back the first banzai attacks of the war, killing over 300 of the enemy. The scouts sustained serious losses, but the 57th's Lieutenant Alexander R. Nininger also won the first posthumous Congressional Medal of Honor for his sacrifice near Abucay. Sergeant Jose Calugas and Lieutenant Willibald C. Bianchi also received the coveted award for related actions in this vicinity. Thwarted to their front, the Japanese shifted their axis of attack through the jungle and routed the poorly trained 51st Philippine Division along the slopes of Mount Natib on January 16, 1942. The U.S. 31st Infantry and the 45th Infantry (PS) were rushed to the area to plug the gap, and fierce fighting raged over the next six days. On January 22, the Japanese attacked in overwhelming numbers, forcing the defenders, seriously weakened by disease and food shortages, farther back down the peninsula.

Defining Activity

Having been thwarted in front by a series of costly frontal assaults, General Homma switched strategy by landing sizable Japanese detachments on the west coast of the Bataan peninsula between Quinauan and Anyasan. This rough, hilly terrain provided excellent cover from which fanatical Japanese infantry could fight to the end, and they defied numerous attempts by an ad hoc battalion of sailors, grounded members of the U.S. Army Air

Corps, and local constabulary troops to evict them. Veterans of the 45th and 57th Infantries (PS) were consequently culled from slender American reserves and ordered to secure the area. The scouts pitched into the stubborn enemy on January 28, and by the following day, they had mopped up 300 Japanese at a cost of 11 dead and 40 wounded. A more protracted struggle unfolded against an estimated 600 Japanese troops who landed at Anyasan Point, dug in, and were reinforced. Once more, skeletal battalions of the 45th and 57th Infantries (PS) cordoned off the area and began rooting them out. Fighting in the dense foliage continued until February 8, 1942, at which point 1,500 enemy troops had been slain; American-Filipino losses totaled 800 men, and one battalion of Philippine scouts that went into battle 500 strong mustered only 212 survivors. As this struggle unfolded, the enemy managed to infiltrate 1,000 troops behind the 1st Corps line. Their position was quickly cordoned off by the 1st Battalion, 45th Infantry (PS), which eliminated them in three weeks of fierce, no-quarter combat. Only 300 Japanese managed to escape back to their own lines. The Philippine scouts had literally saved overstretched American defenses by dint of ferocity in combat and heavy sacrifice in lives. As good as the Japanese were at jungle warfare, they had met their match in the Philippine scouts.

Throughout March–February 1942, fighting mostly died down along the lines as the Japanese withdrew to regroup and make up for severe losses. Incredibly, men of the Philippine scouts, backed by the U.S. 31st Infantry, did the bulk of the fighting, took the heaviest losses, yet still held the line against superior numbers of veteran combat troops. The strategic impasse on Bataan lasted until April 3, 1942, when General Homma, strongly reinforced, commenced a five-hour aerial and artillery bombardment followed by a massive frontal assault. The defenders, ravaged by starvation and disease, finally crumbled under the onslaught. The surviving Philippine scouts fought bravely but were too few to stem the tide. The end came on April 9, when 78,000 men of the Luzon force finally capitulated, including 8,000 scouts. However, a further 1,500 Philippine scouts from various detachments were evacuated to Corregidor Island in Manila Harbor, where they held out for another 27 days. Like all the survivors, they were herded by the Japanese into harsh captivity, and thousands perished before being gradually paroled. Many scouts immediately joined the underground guerilla movement, while others waited under General MacArthur made his fabled return to the Philippines. Once MacArthur arrived in the fall of 1944, former scouts joined the newly reconstituted 12th Philippine Division. The "new" scout units included the 43rd, 44th, 45th, and 57th Infantries (PS); the 23rd, 24th, and 88th Field Artillery (PS) Battalions; and the 56th Engineer Battalion. These fought with their accustomed ferocity in the closing phases of the Luzon reconquest, served as military peacekeepers to help restore order, and then performed occupation work on Okinawa prior to the war's end. The Philippines received its full independence from the United States on July 4, 1946, but the Americans offered Philippine scouts full citizenship in light of their exemplary service, and over 1,000 transferred their allegiance to the U.S. Army. Many of these served over the next two decades up through the Vietnam War. In 1947, President Harry S. Truman ordered the Philippine scouts disbanded, eliminating the most accomplished indigenous combat unit in United States employ.

Philippine Guerrillas

No sooner had Japan occupied the Philippine Islands in May 1942 than renegade bodies of American soldiers and former Philippine scouts began organizing an armed resistance.

Their efforts at recruiting, training, and equipping guerrillas behind enemy lines bore all the marks of special operations and enjoyed a considerable degree of success. The Japanese penchant for treating Filipinos harshly only hastened additional volunteers into the guerilla ranks, and their 228,000-man army of occupation was soon spread so thin that sustained counterinsurgency operations proved impossible. Various guerilla various groups existed throughout the islands, but some individuals enjoyed greater success than others. For example, Colonel Russell Volckmann managed to outfit the equivalent of five regiments on Luzon, while Major Wendell Fertig, on Mindanao, commanded an estimated 36,000 fighters by the time General MacArthur stormed back ashore.

Filipino guerrillas armed with bolo knives and bad attitudes. These fighters were indispensable adjuncts in jungle warfare against equally ruthless Japanese troops. They are depicted here assisting Americans to raid a prisoner-of-war camp. (Center for Military History)

Fertig's effort on Mindanao was subsequently hailed as a model for subsequent special forces operations. He was an imaginative civil engineer by profession and an army reserve officer. Fertig worked in the Philippines as a civilian when the Japanese invaded in December 1941, and he was called back to the colors on Luzon. He transferred to the southern island of Mindanao just prior to the American surrender in May 1942, and, determined to fight on, he established contacts with embryonic guerilla forces then forming. Many of these were little more than gangs of armed bandits, but Fertig, by dint of his forceful personality and acute understanding of Filipino honor, persuaded them to take up the resistance cause. He even grew a beard signifying his age, seeing how Filipino culture equated old age with wisdom. Fertig, given his prior engineering experience, next directed his followers in salvaging machinery for valuable parts and constructing weapons, brewing battery acid from coconut palms, and cannibalizing Japanese sea mines towed ashore for gunpowder. However, his most daunting task was constructing a working transmitter and receiver to contact the outside world. After several fits and starts, his guerillas, the self-styled "United States Forces in the Philippines," finally radioed a U.S. Navy monitoring station, and supplies began arriving by submarine. In between raids and ambushes, Fertig also played close attention to civil action and worked hard to establish efficient civil governance to bind the populace closer to the resistance. As a rule, Fertig avoided pitched battles with large Japanese formations, but his men were experts at surrounding and knocking off smaller detachments pursuing them into the jungles. This prompted the Japanese to launch several punitive raids throughout Mindanao, but atrocities committed against Filipinos only swelled guerrilla ranks. By 1945, the 18,000 enemy troops on the island controlled only settlements along the coast, while Fertig's guerillas commanded

95 percent of the island's interior. The resistance also assisted the forthcoming American invasion by providing military intelligence to submarines lurking offshore, performing coast-watching duties, and seizing several beachheads long enough for American landing forces to land. Fertig even managed, by dint of his engineering expertise, to construct a 7,000-foot landing strip, then camouflage it with topsoil and plants. His guerillas proved useful auxiliaries to the army by performing scouting, screening, and reconnaissance missions and they are regarded as one of the most successful guerilla efforts of World War II. They also accounted for an estimated 7,000 Japanese troops and were a constant drain on their manpower and resources. None of this could have been accomplished without Fertig's thoughtful, considerate leadership, which understood and respected the indigenous culture, and motivated them to take up arms against a hated invader. In light of his success, he became one of the guiding spirits behind the new Army Special Warfare School at Fort Bragg, North Carolina.

Bibliography

General

Hogan, David W. *U.S. Army Special Operations in World War II*. Washington, DC: Center of Military History, Department of the Army, 1991.

Paddock, Alfred H. *U.S. Army Special Warfare: Its Origins: Psychological and Unconventional Warfare, 1941–1952*. Lawrence: University Press of Kansas, 2002.

Thompson, Leroy. *U.S. Special Forces, 1941–1987*. New York: Blandford Press, 1987.

Thompson, Leroy. *America's Commandos: U.S. Special Operations Forces of World War II and Korea*. Mechanicsburg, PA: Stackpole Books, 2001.

Warner, Philip. *Secret Forces of World War II*. Barnsley: Pen & Sword, 2004.

Alamo Scouts

Alexander, Larry. *Shadows in the Jungle: The Alamo Scouts behind Japanese Lines in World War II*. New York: NAL Caliber, 2009.

Zedric, Lance Q. *Silent Warriors of World War II: The Alamo Scouts behind Japanese Lines*. Venture, CA: Pathfinder Publications of California, 1995.

1st Special Service Force

Adleman, Robert H., and George Walton. *The Devil's Brigade*. Annapolis, MD: Naval Institute Press, 2004.

Burhans, Robert D. *The First Special Service Force: A Canadian/American Wartime Alliance: The Devil's Brigade*. Washington, DC: Infantry Journal Press, 1947.

Cottingham, Peter L. *Once upon a Wartime: A Canadian Who Survived the Devil's Brigade*. Neepawa, MB: P. L. Cottingham, 1996.

Hicks, Anne. *The Last Fighting General: The Biography of Robert Tryon Frederick.* Atglen, PA: Schiffer Military History, 2006.

Hope, Tom, ed. *Bonding for Life: The Post World War II Story of the Elite Strike Brigade, First Special Service Force.* Helena, MT: First Special Service Force Association, 2007.

Joyce, Kenneth H. *Snow Plough and the Jupiter Deception: The Story of the 1st Special Service Force and the 1st Canadian Special Service Battalion, 1942–1945.* St. Catharines, ON: Vanwell, 2006.

Joyce, Kenneth H. *Crimson Spearhead: The History, Uniforms, and Insignia of the First Special Service Force, and Related Units.* Ottawa, ON: Service Publications, 2010.

Nadler, John. *A Perfect Hell: The True Story of the Black Devils, the Forefathers of Special Forces.* New York: Presidio Press, 2006.

Nelson, Mark J. *With the Black Devils: A Soldier's World War II Account with the First Special Service Force and the 82nd Airborne.* Atglen, PA: Schiffer Military Books, 2004.

Ross, Robert T. *The Supercommandos: First Special Service Force, 1942–1944, an Illustrated History.* Atglen, PA: Schiffer, 2000.

Springer, Joseph. *The Black Devil Brigade: The True Story of the First Special Service Force.* Pacifica, CA: Pacifica Military History, 2001.

Werner, Brett. *First Special Service Force 1942–1944.* New York: Osprey, 2006.

Wood, James A. *We Move Only Forward: Canada, the United States, and the First Special Service Force, 1942–1944.* St. Catharines, ON: Vanwell, 2006.

Rangers

Altieri, James. *Darby's Rangers: An Illustrated Portrayal of the Original Rangers, World War II, in Training and in Action.* Arnold, MO: Ranger Book Committee, 1977.

Altieri, James. *The Spearheaders: A Personal History of Darby's Rangers.* Washington, DC: Zenger, 1979.

Black, Robert W. *Rangers in World War II.* New York: Ivy Books, 1992.

Black, Robert W. *The Battalion: The Dramatic Story of the 2nd Ranger Battalion in World War II.* Mechanicsburg, PA: Stackpole Books, 2006.

Black, Robert W. *The Ranger Force: Darby's Rangers in World War II.* Mechanicsburg, PA: Stackpole Books, 2009.

Breuer, William B. *Great Raid on Cabanatuan: Rescuing the Doomed Ghosts of Bataan and Corregidor.* New York: Wiley, 1994.

Darby, William O., and William H. Baumer. *We Led the Way.* Novato, CA: Presidio Press, 1993.

DeFelice, Jim. *Rangers at Dieppe: The First Combat Action of U.S. Army Rangers in World War II.* New York: Berkley Caliber, 2008.

Dunstan, Simon. *Allied Special Forces.* Edison, NJ: Chartwell Books, 2007.

Edlin, Robert L., Marica Moen, and Margo Heinen. *The Fool Lieutenant: A Personal Account of D-Day and World War II.* Elk River, MN: Meadowlark, 2003.

Gorman, John W. *Compass: U.S. Army Ranger, European Theater, 1944–45*. New York: iUniverse, 2009.

Heefner, Wilson A. *Dogface Soldier: The Life of General Lucian K. Truscott*. Columbia: University of Missouri Press, 2010.

Jeffers, H. Paul. *Onward We Charge: The Heroic Story of Darby's Rangers in World War II*. New York: NAL Caliber, 2007.

Jeffers, H. Paul. *Command of Honor: General Lucian Truscott's Path to Victory in World War II*. New York: NAL Caliber, 2008.

King, Michael J. *William Orlando Darby, a Military Biography*. Hamden, CT: Archon Books, 1981.

King, Michael J. *Rangers: Selected Combat Operations in World War II*. Fort Leavenworth, KS: Combat Studies Institute, U.S. Army Command and General Staff College, 1985.

Ladd, James D. *Commandos and Rangers of World War II*. Newton Abbot: David and Charles, 1989.

Not for Glory: The Memoirs of Sgts. Evan J. "Tommy" Thompson, Ronald "Rip" Peterson, and Roger Twigg, A, D, and F Companies, First Ranger Battalion, as told to William E. Staab. New York: Vantage Press, 2009.

O'Donnell, Patrick. *Beyond Valor: World War II's Ranger and Airborne Veterans Reveal the Heart of Combat*. New York: Free Press, 2001.

Prince, Morris. *The Road to Victory: The Story of WWII's Elite 2nd Battalion Rangers*. Elk River, MN: Meadowlark, 2001.

Ross, Robert T. *U.S. Army Rangers and Special Forces of World War II: Their War in Photographs*. Atglen, PA: Schiffer, 2000.

Rottman, Gordon T. *U.S. Army Rangers and LRRP Units, 1942–87*. London: Osprey, 1987.

Sadler, Michael. *Army Rangers in Action*. New York: Bearport, 2008.

Saloman, Sidney A. *2nd U.S. Ranger Infantry Battalion: Germeter-Vossenach–Hurtgen–Bergstein–Hill 400, Germany*. Doylestown, PA: Birchwood Books, 1991.

Sasser, Charles W. *Raider: The True Story of the Legendary Soldier Who Performed More POW Raids Than Any Other American in History*. New York: St. Martin's Press, 2002.

Westwell, Ian. *U.S. Rangers: "Leading the Way."* Hersham: Ian Allan, 2003.

Merrill's Marauders

Astor, Gerald. *The Jungle War: Mavericks, Marauders, and Madmen in the China-Burma-India Theater in World War II*. Hoboken, NJ: Wiley, 2004.

Baker, Alan D. *Merrill's Marauders*. New York: Ballantine Books, 1972.

Bjorge, Gary J. *Merrill's Marauders: Combined Operations in Northern Burma in 1944*. Fort Leavenworth, KS: Combat Studies Institute, U.S. Army Command and General Staff College, 1996.

George, John B. *Shots Fired in Anger: A Rifleman's View of the War in the Pacific, 1942–1945, Including the Campaign on Guadalcanal and Fighting with Merrill's Marauders in the Jungles of Burma*. Washington, DC: National Rifle Association of America, 1981.

Hopkins, James E. T., and John M. Jones. *Spearhead: A Complete History of Merrill's Marauder Rangers*. Baltimore: Galahad Press, 1999.

Hoyt, Edwin. *Blood in the Jungle*. New York: iBooks, 2004.

Hunter, Charles N. *Galahad*. San Antonio, TX: Naylor, 1963.

Kearney, Cresson H. *Jungle Snafus . . . and Remedies*. Cave Junction: Oregon Institute of Science and Medicine, 1996.

Latimer, John. *Burma: The Forgotten War*. London: John Murray, 2004.

McClean, Donald B. *Merrill's Marauders, February–May, 1944*. Forest Grove, OR: Normount Armament Co., 1968.

McGee, William E. *Men of Granite: True Stories of New Hampshire's Fighting Men*. Portsmouth, NH: Peter Randall, 2007.

O'Donnell, Patrick K., ed. *Into the Rising Sun: In Their Own Words, World War II's Pacific Veterans Reveal the Heart of Combat*. New York: Free Press, 2002.

Ogburn, Charlton, Jr. *The Marauders*. Woodstock, NY: Overlook Press, 2002.

Randle, Fred E. *Hell on Land, Disaster at Sea: The Story of Merrill's Marauders and the Sinking of the Rhona*. Paducah, KY: Turner, 2002.

Randolph, John. *Marsmen in Burma*. Houston: Gulf, 1946.

Weston, Logan. *The Fightin' Preacher*. Cheyenne, WY: Vision Press, 2004.

Young, Edward M. *Merrill's Marauders*. New York: Osprey, 2009.

Airborne Forces

Arnold, James. *Operation Overlord: Utah Beach & US Airborne Divisions, 6 June 1944*. Lincolnshire: Ravelin, 1994.

Blair, Clay. *Ridgway's Paratroopers—The American Airborne in World War II*. New York: Dial Press, 1985.

Crookenden, Napier. *Airborne at War*. New York: Scribner, 1978.

Davis, Brian L. *U.S. Airborne Forces Europe, 1942–45*. London: Arms and Armour Press, 1974.

Deschodt, Christophe. *D-Day Paratroopers: The Americans*. Paris: Histoire & Collections, 2004.

Devlin, Gerard M. *Paratrooper! The Saga of U.S. Army and Marine Parachute and Glider Combat Troops during World War II*. New York: St. Martin's Press, 1979.

Ellis, Chris, and Mike Verier. *Airborne at War*. Edison, NJ: Chartwell Books, 2007.

Flanagan, E. M., Jr. *Airborne—A Combat History of American Airborne Forces*. New York: Ballantine Books, 2003.

Harclerode, Peter. *Wings of War—Airborne Warfare, 1918–1945*. London: Weidenfeld and Nicolson, 2005.

Howard, Gary. *America's Finest: U.S. Airborne Uniforms, Equipment, and Insignia of World War Two*. Mechanicsburg, PA: Stackpole Books, 1994.

Huston, James A. *Out of the Blue: U.S. Army Airborne Operations in World War II*. West Lafayette, IN: Purdue University Studies, 1972.

Laughlin, Cameron P. *U.S. Airborne Forces of World War Two*. Poole: Arms and Armour Press, 1987.

Marshall, S. L. A. *Night Drop: The American Airborne Invasion of Normandy*. Boston: Little, Brown, 1962.

O'Donnell, Patrick M. *Beyond Valor: World War II's Ranger and Airborne Veterans Reveal the Heart of Combat*. New York: Free Press, 2001.

Rentz, Bill. *Geronimo! U.S. Airborne Uniforms, Insignia, and Equipment in World War II*. Atglen, PA: Schiffer, 1999.

Ross, Kirk B. *The Sky Men: A Parachute Rifle Company's Story of the Battle of the Bulge and the Jump across the Rhine*. Atglen, PA: Schiffer, 2000.

Thompson, Leroy. *U.S. Airborne in Action*. Carrollton, TX: Squadron/Signal Publications, 1992.

Tugwell, Maurice. *Airborne to Battle—A History of Airborne Warfare, 1918–1971*. London: William Kimber, 1971.

Whitlock, Flint. *If Chaos Reigns: The Near-Disaster and Ultimate Triumph of Allied Airborne Forces on D-Day, June 6, 1944*. Havertown, PA: Casemate, 2011.

Wright, Robert K. *Airborne Forces at War: From Parachute Test Platoon to the 21st Century*. Annapolis, MD: Naval Institute Press, 2007.

Zaloga, Steve. *U.S. Airborne Divisions in the ETO, 1944–45*. New York: Osprey, 2007.

11th Airborne Division

Bailey, Maxwell C. "Raid at Los Banos." *Military Review* 63, no. 5 (May 1983): 51–66.

Burgess, Henry A. *Looking Back*. Missoula, MT: Pictorial Histories Publishing, 1993.

Flanagan, E. M. *The Angels: A History of the 11th Airborne Division*. Novato, CA: Presidio Press, 1989.

Flanagan, E. M. *Angels at Dawn: The Los Banos Raid*. Novato, CA: Presidio Press, 1999.

Roberts, Donald J. "Angels to the Rescue." *Military Heritage* 3, no. 1 (September 2001): 78–86.

Rottman, Gordon L. *U.S. Airborne Units in the Pacific Theater, 1942–45*. Oxford: Osprey, 2007.

Salecker, Gene E. *Blossoming Silk against the Rising Sun: U.S. and Japanese Parachutists at War in the Pacific in World War II*. Mechanicsburg, PA: Stackpole Books, 2010.

Wiegand, Brandon T. *Index to the General Orders of the 11th Airborne Division in World War II*. Brackenridge, PA: D-Day Militaria, 2004.

17th Airborne Division

Breuer, William B. *Storming Hitler's Rhine: The Allied Assault, February–March 1945*. New York: St. Martin's Press, 1985.

Clark, Lloyd. *Crossing the Rhine: Breaking into Nazi Germany 1944 and 1945—The Greatest Airborne Battles in History*. New York: Atlantic Monthly Press, 2008.

Hagerman, Bart, and Gardner Hatch. *17th Airborne Division*. Paducah, KY: Turner, 1987.

O'Rourke, Frank F. "A Gliderman across the Rhine." *World War II* 19, no. 1 (April 2004): 42–48.

Pay, Don R. *Thunder from Heaven: Story of the 17th Airborne Division, 1943–1945*. Nashville: Battery Press, 1980.

Rawson, Andrew. *Rhine Crossing: Operation Varsity—30th and 79th US Divisions and 17th US Airborne Division*. Barnsley: Pen & Sword, 2006.

Ross, Kirk B. *The Sky Men: A Parachute Rifle Company's Story of the Battle of the Bulge and the Jump across the Rhine*. Atglen, PA: Schiffer, 2002.

Seelinger, Matthew J. "Operation Varsity: The Last Airborne Deployment of World War II." *On Point* 10, no. 3 (December 2004): 9–17.

Therrien, Mel. *17th Airborne Division History*. St. Paul, MN: 17th Airborne Division Association, 1993.

Wiegand, Brandon T. *Index to the General Orders of the 17th Airborne Division in World War II*. Brackenridge, PA: D-Day Militaria, 2004.

Wilson, Robert L. *A Paratrooper's Panoramic View: Training with the 464th Parachute Field Artillery Battalion for Operation Varsity's "Rhine Jump" with the 127th Airborne Division*. Bloomington, IN: AuthorHouse, 2005.

Wright, Stephen L. *The Last Drop: Operation Varsity, March 24–25, 1945*. Mechanicsburg, PA: Stackpole Books, 2008.

82nd Airborne Division

Alexander, Mark. *Jump Commander: In Combat with the 82nd Airborne in World War II*. Havertown, PA: Casemate, 2010.

Anzunoi, Robert P. *I'm the 82nd Airborne Division! A History of the All American Division in World War II after Action Reports*. Atglen, PA: Schiffer Military History, 2005.

Baugh, James E. *From Skies of Blue: My Experiences with the Eighty-Second Airborne during World War II*. New York: iUniverse, 2003.

Booth, T. Michael. *Paratrooper: The Life of Gen. James M. Gavin*. New York: Simon and Schuster, 1994.

Breuer, William B. *They Jumped at Midnight: The "Crash" Parachute Missions That Turned the Tide at Salerno*. St. Louis, MO: Zeus, 1983.

Buriss, T. Moffatt. *Strike and Hold: A Memoir of the 82nd Airborne in World War II*. Washington, DC: Brassey's, 2000.

Burns, Dwayne, and Leland Burns. *Jump into the Valley of the Shadow*. Philadelphia: Casemate, 2006.

Carter, Ross S. *Those Devils in Baggy Pants*. New York: Appleton-Century-Crofts, 1951.

Cooksey, Jon. *Crossing the Waal: The U.S. 82nd Airborne Division at Nijmegen*. Barnsley: Pen & Sword, 2005.

Covington, Henry L. *A Fighting Heart, An Unofficial Story of the 82nd Airborne Division*. Fayetteville, NC: T. Davis, 1949.

Dawson, W. Forrest. *Saga of the All American*. Nashville: Battery Press, 2004.

Francois, Dominique. *82nd Airborne in Normandy: A History in Period Photographs*. Atglen, PA: Schiffer Military History, 2004.

Garrison, Chester A. *An Ivy-League Paratrooper*. Corvallis, OR: Franklin Press, 2002.

Gavin, James M. *On to Berlin: Battles of an Airborne Commander, 1943–1946*. New York: Viking Press, 1978.

Lebensen, Leonard. *Surrounded by Heroes: Six Campaigns with Division Headquarters, 82nd Airborne Division, 1942–1945*. Drexel Hill, PA: Casemate, 2007.

Lelendais, Benoit. *From Heaven to Hell: Men Like No Others: HQ/1 508 PIR, a Company of the 82nd Airborne*. Cully: Orep Edition, 2007.

LoFaro, Guy A. *Sword of St. Michael: The 82nd Airborne Division in World War II*. Cambridge, MA: Da Capo Press, 2011.

McCann, John P. *Passing Through: The 82nd Airborne Division in Northern Ireland, 1943–44*. Newtonards: Colourpoint Books, 2005.

Megallas, James. *All the Way to Berlin: A Paratrooper at War in Europe*. New York: Ballantine Books, 2003.

Mitchell, George C. *Matthew B. Ridgway: Soldier, Statesman, Scholar, Citizen*. Mechanicsburg, PA: Stackpole Books, 2002.

Mrozek, Steven J. *The 82nd Airborne Division*. Paducah, KY: Turner, 1997.

Murphy, Robert M. *No Better Place to Die: Ste-Mere Eglise, June 1944: The Battle for La Fiere Bridge*. Havertown, PA: Casemate, 2009.

Nordyke, Phil. *All American, All the Way: The Combat History of the 82nd Airborne Division in World War II*. St. Paul, MN: Zenith Press, 2005.

Nordyke, Phil. *Four Stars of Valor: The Combat History of the 505th Parachute Infantry Regiment in World War II*. St. Paul, MN: Zenith Press, 2006.

Nordyke, Phil. *More Than Courage: Sicily, Naples-Foggia, Anzio, Rhineland, Ardennes-Alsace, Central Europe: The Combat History of the 504th Parachute Infantry Regiment in World War II*. Minneapolis: MBI, 2008.

Richlack, Jerry L. *Glide to Glory: 325 Glider Infantry Regiment, 82nd Airborne Division*. Chesterland, OH: Cedar House, 2002.

Rottman, Gordon L. *U.S. Airborne Units in the Mediterranean Theater, 1942–44*. Oxford: Osprey, 2006.

Ruggero, Ed. *Combat Jump: The Young Men Who Led the Assault into Fortress Europe, July 1943*. New York: HarperCollins, 2003.

Saunders, Dave. *Nijmegen, Grave, and Groesbeck*. Barnsley: Leo Cooper, 2001.

Thompson, Leroy. *The All Americans: The 82nd Airborne*. Newton Abbott: David & Charles, 1988.

Tucker, William H. *Parachute Soldier: Based on the 1942 to 1945 Diary of Sergeant Bill Tucker*. Athol, MA: Haley's, 1994.

Verier, Mike. *82nd Airborne: "All American."* Hersham: Ian Allan, 2001.

Wurst, Spencer F., and Gayle Wurst. *Descending from the Clouds: A Memoir of Combat in the 505 Parachute Infantry Regiment, 82nd Airborne Division*. Havertown, PA: Casemate, 2004.

101st Airborne Division

Allen, Patrick H. F. *Screaming Eagles: In Action with the 101st Airborne Division (Air Assault)*. London: Hamlyn, 1990.

Antal, John F. *Hell's Highway: The True Story of the 101st Airborne Division during Operation Market Garden, September 17–25, 1944*. Minneapolis: MBI and Zenith Press, 2008.

Bando, Mark. *The 101st Airborne: From Holland to Hitler's Eagle Nest*. Osceola, WI: Motorbooks International, 1995.

Bando, Mark. *The 101st Airborne: Screaming Eagles at Normandy*. Osceola, WI: MBI, 2001.

Bando, Mark. *Vanguard of the Crusade: The 101st Airborne Division in World War II*. Bedford, PA: Aberjona Press, 2003.

Bando, Mark. *101st Airborne: The Screaming Eagles in World War II*. St. Paul, MN: Zenith Press, 2007.

Bowen, Robert. *Fighting with the Screaming Eagles: With the 101st Airborne from Normandy to Bastogne*. Mechanicsburg, PA: Stackpole Books, 2001.

Burgett, Donald R. *Currahee! A Screaming Eagle at Normandy*. Novato, CA: Presidio Press, 1999.

Burgett, Donald R. *The Road to Arnhem: A Screaming Eagle in Holland*. Novato, CA: Presidio Press, 1999.

Burgett, Donald R. *Seven Roads to Hell: A Screaming Eagle at Bastogne*. Novato, CA: Presidio Press, 1999.

Burgett, Donald R. *Beyond the Rhine: A Screaming Eagle in Germany*. Novato, CA: Presidio Press, 2001.

Francois, Dominique. *101st Airborne Division in Normandy: A History in Period Photographs*. Atglen, PA: Schiffer Military History, 2006.

Guarnere, William. *Brothers in Battle, Best of Friends: Two WWII Paratroopers from the Original Band of Brothers Tell Their Story*. New York: Berkley Caliber, 2007.

Hojris, Rene. *Anthony "Nuts!" McAuliffe: A Portrait of the U.S. General Who Became World Famous by Replying "Nuts!" to the German Demand for Surrender at Bastogne during the Battle of the Bulge in WWII*. Bronshoj: Roger Publishing House, 2004.

Houston, Robert J. *D-Day to Bastogne: A Paratrooper Recalls World War II*. Smithtown, NY: Exposition Press, 1980.

Koskimaki, George E. *D-Day with the Screaming Eagles*. Madelia, MN: House of Print, 1970.

Koskimaki, George E. *The Battered Bastards of Bastogne: A Chronicle of the Defense of Bastogne (December 19, 1944–January 17, 1945)*. Sweetwater, TN: George E. W. Koskimaki, 1994.

Koskimaki, George E. *Hell's Highway: Chronicle of the 101st Airborne Division in the Holland Campaign, September–November 1944*. Havertown, PA: Casemate, 2003.

Marshall, S. L. A. *Bastogne: The Story of the First Eight Days in Which the 101st Airborne Division Was Closed within the Ring of German Forces.* Washington, DC: Center of Military History, United States Army, 2004.

McManus, John C. *Alamo in the Ardennes: The Untold Story of the American Soldiers Who Made the Defense of Bastogne Possible.* New York: NAL Caliber, 2008.

Mitchell, Ralph M. *The 101st Airborne Division's Defense of Bastogne.* Fort Leavenworth, KS: U.S. Army Command and General Staff College, Combat Studies Institute, 1986.

Nibley, Hugh. *Sergeant Nibley, Ph.D.: Memories of an Unlikely Screaming Eagle.* Salt Lake City: Shadow Mountain, 2006.

Rapport, Leonard. *Rendezvous with Destiny: A History of the 101st Airborne Division.* Washington, DC: Infantry Journal, 1948.

Rice, Thomas M. *Trial by Fire: A Paratrooper of the 101st Airborne Division Remembers the 194 Battle of Normandy.* Bloomington, IN: AuthorHouse, 2004.

Saunders, Tim. *Hell's Highway.* Barnsley: Leo Cooper, 2001.

Shapiro, Milton J. *The Screaming Eagles: The 101st Airborne Division in World War II.* New York: Messner, 1976.

Simms, James B. *A Soldier's Armageddon.* Manhattan, KS: Sunflower University Press, 1999.

Taylor, John M. *General Maxwell Taylor: The Sword and the Pen.* New York: Doubleday, 1989.

Taylor, Thomas. *Behind Hitler's Lines: The True Story of the Only Soldier to Fight for Both America and the Soviet Union in World War II.* New York: Ballantine Books, 2004.

True, William. *The Cow Spoke French: The Story of Sgt. William True, American Paratrooper in World War II.* Bennington, VT: Merriam Press, 2002.

Walker, James W. *Fortune Favors the Bold: A British LRRP with the 101st.* New York: Ivy Books, 1998.

Whiting, Charles. *American Eagles: The 101st Airborne Assault on Fortress Europe, 1944/ 45.* York: Eskdale, 2001.

10th Mountain Division

Baumgardner, Randy, ed. *Tenth Mountain Division.* Paducah, KY: Turner, 1998–2003.

Brooks, Robert R., and John Imbrie. *Mission Undine: The 10th Mountain Division at the Yugoslav Border, May 19 to July 17, 1945.* Forest Hills, NY: National Association of the 10th Mountain Division, 2005.

Brown, Donald G. *Love Letter to Americans: Observations of a Ski Trooper and Journalist.* Victoria, BC: Trafford, 2003.

Burton, Hal. *The Ski Troops.* New York: Simon and Schuster, 1971.

Casewit, Curtis W. *The Saga of the Mountain Soldiers: The Story of the 10th Mountain Division.* New York: J. Messner, 1981.

Dole, Robert J. *One Soldier's Story: A Memoir.* New York: HarperCollins, 2005.

Dusenbery, Harris. *North Apennines and Beyond: With the 10th Mountain Division*. Portland, OR: P. Ware, 1998.

Ellis, Robert B. *See Naples and Die: A World War II Memoir of a United States Army Ski Trooper in the Mountains of Italy*. Jefferson, NC: McFarland, 1996.

Feuer, A. B. *Packs On! Memoirs of the 10th Mountain Division*. Westport, CT: Praeger, 2004.

Imbrie, John. *10th Mountain Division Campaign in Italy, 1945*. Forest Hills, NY: National Association of the 10th Mountain Division, 2002.

Jenkins, McKay. *The Last Ridge: The Epic Story of the U.S. Army's 10th Mountain Division and the Assault on Hitler's Europe*. New York: Random House, 2003.

Johnson, Norma T. *Soldiers of the Mountain: The Story of the 10th Mountain Division of World War II*. Baltimore: PublishAmerica, 2005.

Kohlman, Oley. *Up Hill with the Ski Troops*. Walden, CO: O. Kohlman, 1995.

Meinke, Albert H. *Mountain Troops and Medics: Wartime Stories of a Frontline Surgeon in the U.S. Ski Troops*. Kewadin, MI: Rucksack, 1993.

Parker, Robert W. *What'd You Do in the War, Dad? A Personal Look at 34 Months in the 10th Mountain Division*. Santa Fe, NM: Rio Grande, 2005.

Pote, Winston. *Mountain Troops, 10th Mountain Division, Camp Hale, Colorado*. Camden, ME: Down East Books, 1982.

Putnam, William L. *Green Cognac: The Education of a Mountain Fighter*. New York: AAC Press, 1991.

Reining, Harry J. *My Story: A World War II Memory*. Richardson, TX: Printed by RedEx Kinko's, 2004.

Shelton, Peter. *Climb to Conquer: The Untold Story of World War II's 10th Mountain Division Ski Troops*. New York: Scribner, 2003.

Sherwood, Frank P. *It Wasn't All Combat: A Soldier's Life in World War II*. New York: iUniverse, 2007.

Whitlock, Flint. *Soldiers on Skies: A Pictorial Memoir of the 10th Mountain Division*. Boulder, CO: Paladin Press, 1992.

Wolf, Tom. *Ice Crusaders: A Memoir of Cold War and Cold Sport*. Boulder, CO: Roberts Rinehart, 1999.

1st Air Commando Group

Baisden, Charles. *Flying Tiger to Air Commando*. Atglen, PA: Schiffer, 1999.

Chinnery, Philip D. *Any Time, Any Place: Fifty Years of the USAF Air Commando and Special Operations Forces, 1944–1994*. Annapolis, MD: Naval Institute Press, 1994.

Eason, W. Robert. *WW II Air Commandos: Photo Supplement to Volumes I and II*. Madison, VA: W. R. Eason, 1996.

King, Barbara P., and Edward M. Leete. *The First Air Commando Group of World War II: An Historical Perspective*. Maxwell Air Force Base, AL: Air Command and Staff College, 1977.

Mason, Herbert A., Randy G. Bergeron, and James A. Renfrow. *Operation THURSDAY: Birth of the Air Commandos*. Washington, DC: Air Force History and Museums Program, 1994.

Masters, John. *The Road Past Mandalay: A Personal Narrative*. New York: Harper, 1961.

Thomas, Lowell. *Back to Mandalay*. New York: Greystone Press, 1951.

Van Wagner, R. D. *Any Place, Any Time, Any Where: The 1st Air Commandos in WWII*. Atglen, PA: Schiffer, 1989.

Y'Blood, William T. *Air Commandos against Japan: Allied Special Operations in World War II*. Annapolis, MD: Naval Institute Press, 2008.

Young, Edward M. *Air Commando Fighters in World War II*. North Branch, MN: Specialty Press, 2000.

801st Bombardment Group (H)

Fesmire, Robert H. *Flight of a Maverick: In the Secret War against Hitler*. Nashville: Eggman, 1995.

Parnell, Ben. *Air Commandos: The Saga of the Carpetbaggers of World War II: A Story of the 801st/492nd Bombardment Group (H), U.S. Army, Eighth Air Force*. New York: iBooks, 2004.

Marine Corps Amphibious Reconnaissance Battalion

Melson, Charles D., and Paul Hanon. *Marine Recon, 1940–1990*. London: Osprey, 1994.

Meyers, Bruce F. *Swift, Silent, and Deadly: Maritime Amphibious Reconnaissance in the Pacific, 1942–1945*. Annapolis, MD: Naval Institute Press, 2004.

Marine Corps Raiders

Alexander, Joseph H. *Edson's Raiders: The 1st Marine Raider Battalion in World War II*. Annapolis, MD: Naval Institute Press, 2000.

Beau, Jerome C., and Robert A. Buerlein. *The U.S. Marine Raiders of WWII: Those Who Served*. Richmond, VA: American Historical Foundation, 1996.

Daley, LaVarre. *United States Marine Corps Raiders: A Personal Account*. Erie, CO: M. J. Clark, 2002.

Feuer, A. B. "Carlson's Raiders at Makin Island." *Military Heritage* 1, no. 2 (March 1999): 87–87.

Gaddis, David. "Defending Bloody Ridge." *Naval History* 13, no. 1 (February 1999): 47–49.

Gilbert, ed. *U.S. Marine Corps Raider, 1942–1943*. New York: Osprey, 2006.

Gleason, James D. *Real Blood! Real Guts! U.S. Marine Raiders and Their Corpsmen in World War II*. N.p.: Raider, 2003.

Hoffman, Jon T. *Once a Legend: "Red Mike" Edson of the Marine Raiders*. Novato, CA: Presidio Press, 1994.

Hoffman, Jon T. *From Makin to Bougainville: Marine Raiders in the Pacific War*. Washington, DC: History and Museums Division, Headquarters, U.S. Marine Corps, 1995.

Hoffman, Jon T. *Marine Raiders: More than a Few Good Men*. Paducah, KY: Turner, 1999.

Hoyt, Edwin P. *The Marine Raiders*. New York: Pocket Books, 1989.

Ludwig, Verle E. *Archie Smallwood and the Marine Raiders: A Rifleman's Brief .30-Caliber History of the 20th Century*. Santa Barbara, CA: Fithian Press, 1998.

O'Donnell, Patrick K. "Raid on Makin." *MHQ* 14, no. 3 (Spring 2002): 56–59.

Rosenquest, R. G., Martin J. Sexton, and Robert A. Buerlein. *Our Kind of War: Illustrated Saga of Marine Raiders of WWII*. Richmond, VA: American Historical Foundation, 1990.

Rottman, Gordon L. *US Special Warfare Units in the Pacific Theater, 1942–45: Scouts, Raiders, Rangers, and Reconnaissance Units*. Oxford: Osprey, 2005.

Sexton, Martin J. *The Marine Raiders' Historical Handbook*. Richmond, VA: American Historical Foundation, 1987.

Smith, George W. *Carlson's Raid: The Daring Marine Assault on Makin*. Novato, CA: Presidio Press, 2001.

Smith, Michael S. *Bloody Ridge: The Battle That Saved Guadalcanal*. Novato, CA: Presidio Press, 2000.

Sweeney, John B. "Battle of Bloody Ridge." *Marine Corps Gazette* 88, no. 9 (September 2004): 93–96.

Updegraph, Charles L. *U.S. Marine Corps Special Units of World War II*. Washington, DC: Historical Division, Headquarters, United States Marine Corps, 1972.

Wiles, Tripp. *Forgotten Raiders of '42: The Fate of Marines Left behind on Makin*. Washington, DC: Brassey's, 2007.

Wukovits, John F. *American Commando: Evan Carlson and His WWII Marine Raiders, and America's First Special Forces Mission*. New York: NAL Caliber, 2009.

Marine Corps Paramarines

Christ, James F. *Battalion of the Damned: The 1st Marine Paratroopers at Gavutu and Bloody Ridge, 1942*. Annapolis, MD: Naval Institute Press, 2007.

Cole, Merle T. "The Paramarines: Organization and Training of USMC Parachute Troops, 1940–1944." *American Aviation Historical Society Journal* 34, no. 4 (December 1989): 242–49.

Haney, Ken. *U.S. Marine Corps Paratroopers, 1940–1945: An Illustrated History*. Jackson, TN: K. Haney, 1990.

Mason, Chris. *Paramarine! Uniforms and Equipment of Marine Corps Parachute Units in World War II*. Atglen, PA: Schiffer, 2004.

Marine Corps Scout Sniper Companies

Senich, Peter R. *U.S. Marine Corps Scout-Sniper: World War II and Korea*. Boulder, CO: Paladin Press, 1993.

Navy Beach Jumpers

Dwyer, John B. *Seaborne Deception: The History of the U.S. Navy Beach Jumpers*. New York: Praeger, 1992.

Navy Scouts and Raiders

Dwyer, John B. *Scouts and Raiders: The Navy's First Special Warfare Commandos*. Westport, CT: Praeger, 1993.

Rottman, Gordon L. *US Special Warfare Units in the Pacific Theater, 1942–45: Scouts, Raiders, Rangers, and Reconnaissance Units*. Oxford: Osprey, 2005.

Navy Underwater Demolition Teams

Berry, Erick. *Underwater Warriors: Story of American Frogmen*. New York: D. McKay, 1967.

Best, Herbert. *The Webfoot Warriors: The Story of UDT, the U.S. Navy's Underwater Demolition Team*. New York: John Day, 1962.

Blassingame, Wyatt. *The U.S. Frogmen of World War II: Illustrated with Photographs and Maps*. New York: Random House, 1964.

Bush, Elizabeth K. *America's First Frogman: The Draper Kauffman Story*. Annapolis, MD: Naval Institute Press, 2004.

Camp, Dick. *Iwo Jima Recon: The U.S. Navy at War, February 17, 1945*. St. Paul, MN: Zenith Press, 2007.

Cunningham, Chet. *The Frogmen of World War II: An Oral History of the U.S. Navy's Underwater Demolition Teams*. New York: Pocket Star Books, 2005.

Dockery, Kevin. *Special Warfare, Special Equipment: The Arms and Equipment of the UDT and SEALs from 1943 to the Present*. Chicago: Emperor's Press, 1996.

Dockery, Kevin. *Navy Seals: A Complete History: From World War II to the Present*. New York: Berkley Books, 2004.

Dwyer, John B. *Commandos from the Sea: The History of Amphibious Special Warfare in World War II and the Korean War*. Boulder, CO: Paladin Press, 1998.

Fane, Francis D. *The Naked Warriors: The Story of the U.S. Navy's Frogmen*. Annapolis, MD: Naval Institute Press, 1995.

Higgins, Edward T. *Webfooted Warriors: A Story of a "Frogman" in the Navy during World War II*. New York: Exposition Press, 1955.

Kaine, Francis R. *Reminiscences of Captain Francis R. Kaine, U.S. Naval Reserve*. Annapolis, MD: Naval Institute Press, 1990.

Karl, S. W. *Too Deep, Too Late*. New York: Manor Books, 1978.

O'Dell, James D. *The Water Is Never Cold: The Origins of the U.S. Navy's Combat Demolition Units, UDTS, and SEALs*. Washington, DC: Brassey's, 2000.

Young, Darryl. *SEALS, UDT, Frogmen: Men under Pressure*. New York: Ivy Books, 1994.

Office of Strategic Services

Aldrich, Richard J. *Intelligence and the War against Japan: Britain, America, and the Politics of Secret Service*. New York: Cambridge University Press, 2000.

Bartholomew-Feis, Dixee. *The OSS and Ho Chi Minh: Unexpected Allies in the War against Japan*. Lawrence: University Press of Kansas, 2006.

Bevan, Colin. *Operation Jedburgh: D-Day and America's First Shadow War*. New York: Viking, 2006.

Delattre, Lucas. *A Spy at the Heart of the Third Reich: The Extraordinary Story of Fritz Kolbe, America's Most Important Spy of World War II*. New York: Atlantic Monthly Press, 2005.

Fenn, Charles. *At the Dragon's Gate: With the OSS in the Far East*. Annapolis, MD: Naval Institute Press, 2004.

Ford, Roger. *Steel from the Sky: The Jedburgh Raiders, France, 1944*. London: Orion, 2004.

Freeman, Gregory A. *The Forgotten 500: The Untold Story of the Men Who Risked All for the Greatest Rescue Mission of World War II*. New York: NAL Caliber, 2007.

Hassell, Augustino von, Sigrid von Hoyningen-Huene MacRae, and Simone Ameskamp. *Alliance of Enemies: The Untold Story of Secret American and German Collaboration to End World War II*. New York: Thomas Dunne Books, 2006.

Irwin, Will. *The Jedburghs: The Secret History of the Allied Special Forces, France, 1944*. New York: Public Affairs, 2010.

Katz, Robert. *The Battle for Rome: The Germans, the Allies, the Partisans, and the Pope, September 1943–June 1944*. New York: Simon and Schuster, 2003.

Kloman, Erasmus H. *Assignment Algiers: With the OSS in the Mediterranean Theater of Operations*. Annapolis, MD: Naval Institute Press, 2005.

Liptak, Eugene. *Office of Strategic Services, 1942–1945: The World War II Origins of the CIA*. New York: Osprey, 2009.

Lucas, Peter. *The OSS in World War II Albania: Covert Operations and Collaboration with Communist Partisans*. Jefferson, NC: McFarland, 2007.

Macpherson, Nelson. *American Intelligence in War-Time London: The Story of the OSS*. Portland, OR: Frank Cass, 2003.

Mauch, Christof. *The Shadow War against Hitler: The Covert Operations of America's Wartime Secret Intelligence Service*. New York: Columbia University Press, 2003.

Moon, Tom. *This Grim and Savage Game: OSS and the Beginning of U.S. Covert Operations in World War II*. Cambridge, MA: Da Capo Press, 2000.

Nelson, Wayne. *A Spy's Diary of World War II: Inside the OSS with an American Agent in Europe*. Jefferson, NC: McFarland, 2009.

O'Donnell, Patrick K. *Operatives, Spies, and Saboteurs: The Unknown Story of the Men and Women of World War II's OSS*. New York: Free Press, 2004.

O'Donnell, Patrick K. *The Brenner Assignment: The Untold Story of the Most Daring Spy Mission of World War II*. Cambridge, MA: Da Capo, 2008.

O'Donnell, Patrick K. *They Dared Return: The True Story of Jewish Spies behind the Lines in Nazi Germany*. Cambridge, MA: Da Capo Press, 2009.

Perdue, Robert E. *Behind the Lines in Greece: The Story of OSS Operations Group II*. Bloomington, IN: AuthorHouse, 2010.

Persico, Joseph E. *Roosevelt's Secret War: FDR and World War II Espionage*. New York: Random House, 2001.

Pinck, Daniel C. *Journey to Peking: A Secret Agent in Wartime China*. Annapolis, MD: Naval Institute Press, 2003.

Reynolds, E. Bruce. *Thailand's Secret War: The Free Thai, OSS, and the SOE during World War II*. New York: Cambridge University Press, 2005.

Rudgers, David F. *Creating the Secret State: The Origins of the Central Intelligence Agency, 1943–1947*. Lawrence: University Press of Kansas, 2000.

Smith, R. Harris. *OSS: The Secret History of America's First Central Intelligence Agency*. Guilford, CT: Lyons Press, 2005.

Waller, Douglas. *Wild Bill Donovan: The Spymaster Who Created the OSS and Modern American Espionage*. New York: Free Press, 2011.

Warner, Michael. *The Office of Strategic Services: America's First Intelligence Agency*. Washington, DC: Central Intelligence Agency, 2001.

Yu, Macchun. *OSS in China: Prelude to Cold War*. Annapolis, MD: Naval Institute Press, 2011.

American Volunteer Group

Armstrong, Alan. *Preemptive Strike: The Secret Plan That Would Have Prevented the Attack on Pearl Harbor*. Guilford, DE: Lyons Press, 2006.

Bishop, Lewis S. *Escape from Hell: An AVG Flying Tiger's Journey*. Bloomington, IL: Tiger Eye Press, 2004.

Bond, Charles R. *A Flying Tiger's Diary*. College Station: Texas A&M University Press, 1984.

Byrd, Martha. *Chennault: Giving Wings to the Tiger*. Tuscaloosa: University of Alabama Press, 1987.

Chennault, Claire L. *Way of a Fighter*. New York: G. P. Putnam's Sons, 1949.

Clements, Terrill J. *Sharks of the Air: Camouflage and Markings of the American Volunteer Group, August 1941–July 1942*. Seattle: T. J. Clements, 1998.

Cornelius, Wanda. *Ding Hao: America's Air War in China, 1937–1945*. Gretna, LA: Pelican, 1980.

Ford, Daniel. *Flying Tigers: Claire Chennault and His American Volunteers, 1941–1942*. New York: Smithsonian Books/Collins, 2007.

Heiferman, Ronald. *Flying Tigers: Chennault in China*. New York: Ballantine Books, 1971.

Hill, David L. *"Tex" Hill: Flying Tiger*. Spartanburg, SC: Honoribus Press, 2003.

Losonsky, Frank S. *Flying Tiger: A Crew Chief's Story: The War Diary of a Flying Tiger American Volunteer Group Crew Chief with the 3rd Pursuit Squadron*. Atglen, PA: Schiffer Military/Aviation History, 1996.

Nalty, Bernard C. *Tigers over Asia*. New York: Elsevier-Dutton, 1978.

Pistole, Larry M. *The Pictorial History of the Flying Tigers*. Orange, VA: Publisher's Press, 1981.

Scott, Robert L. *Flying Tiger: Chennault of China*. Garden City, NY: Doubleday, 1959.

Smith, Robert M. *With Chennault in China: A Flying Tiger's Diary*. Blue Ridge Summit, PA: Tab Books, 1984.

Sperry, Roland. *China through the Eyes of a Tiger*. New York: Pocket Books, 1990.

Toland, John. *The Flying Tigers*. New York: Random House, 1963.

Kachin Rangers

Barrett, Neil R. *Chingpaw*. New York: Vantage Press, 1962.

Dunlop, Richard. *Behind Japanese Lines, with the OSS in Burma*. Chicago: Rand McNally, 1979.

Fellowes-Gordon, Ian. *Amiable Assassins: The Story of the Kachin Guerillas of North Burma*. London: R. Hale, 1957.

Fellowes-Gordon, Ian. *The Magic War: The Battle for North Burma*. New York: Scribner, 1972.

Moon, Thomas N., and Carl F. Eifler. *The Deadliest Colonel*. New York: Vantage Press, 1975.

Oatts, Lewis B. *The Jungle in Arms*. London: W. Kimber, 1962.

Peers, William R., and Dean Brelis. *Behind the Burma Road: The Story of America's Most Successful Guerrilla Force*. Boston: Little, Brown, 1963.

Native Americans

Bernstein, Alison R. *American Indians and World War II: Towards a New Era in Indian Affairs*. Norman: University of Oklahoma Press, 1991.

Bixler, Margaret T. *Winds of Freedom: The Story of the Navajo Code Talkers of World War II*. Darien, CT: Two Bytes Publishing, 1992.

Brandon, Lee E. *The Proudest Moment of Their Lives: Navajo Code Talkers and the Battle of Iwo Jima*. Brevard, NC: Brevard College, 2004.

Franco, Jere B. *Crossing the Pond: The Native American Effort in World War II*. Denton: University of North Texas Press, 1999.

Gilbert, Oscar E. *Native American Code Talkers in World War II*. New York: Osprey, 2008.

Kawano, Kenji. *Warriors: Navajo Code Talkers*. Flagstaff, AZ: Northland Publishing, 1990.

Mack, Stephen. *It Had to Be Done: The Navajo Code Talkers Remember World War II*. Cortaro, AZ: Whisper Dove Design, 2008.

McClain, Sally. *Navajo Weapon*. Tucson, AZ: Rio Nuevo Publishers, 2002.

Meadows, William C. *The Comanche Code Talkers of World War II*. Austin: University of Texas Press, 2002.

Nez, Chester, and Judith S. Avila. *Code Talker*. New York: Berkley Caliber, 2011.

Townsend, Kenneth W. *World War II and the American Indian*. Albuquerque: University of New Mexico Press, 2000.

Viola, Herman K. *Warriors in Uniform: The Legacy of American Indian Heroism*. Washington, DC: National Geographic, 2008.

Nisei Translators

Dingman, Roger. *Deciphering the Rising Sun: Navy and Marine Codebreakers, Translators, and Interpreters in the Pacific War*. Annapolis, MD: Naval Institute Press, 2009.

Harrington, Joseph D. *Yankee Samurai: The Secret Role of Nisei in America's Pacific Victory*. Detroit: Pettigrew Enterprises, 1979.

Hays, Otis. *Alaska's Hidden Wars: Secret Campaigns on the North Pacific Rim*. Fairbanks: University of Alaska Press, 2004.

McNaughton, James C. *Nisei Linguists: Japanese Americans in Military Intelligence Service during World War II*. Washington, DC: Department of the Army, 2006.

Secret Valor: M.I.S. Personnel, World War II, Pacific Theater, Pre-Pearl Harbor to Sept. 8, 1951: 50th Anniversary Reunion, July 8–10, 1993. Honolulu: Military Intelligence Service Veterans Club of Hawaii, 1993.

Philippine Scouts

Linn, Brian M. *Guardians of Empire: The U.S. Army and the Pacific, 1902–1940*. Chapel Hill: University of North Carolina Press, 1997.

Milligan, W. D. *Lest We Forget: The Brave and Honorable Guerillas and Philippine Scouts of World War II*. Quezon City: Central Book Supply, 2010.

Olson, John, ed. *The Philippine Scouts*. Daly City, CA: Philippine Scouts Heritage Society, 2002.

Rottman, Gordon L. *World War II US Cavalry Units: The Pacific*. New York: Osprey, 2009.

Sorley, Lewis. *Honorable Warrior: General Harold K. Johnson and the Ethics of Command*. Lawrence: University Press of Kansas, 1998.

The Philippine Scouts, Prepared by the Philippine Scouts Heritage Society. Fort Sam Houston, TX: The Society, 1996.

Whitehead, Arthur K. *Odyssey of a Philippine Scout: Fighting, Escaping, and Evading the Japanese, 1941–1944*. Bedford, PA: Aberjona Press, 2006.

Philippine Guerrillas

Guardia, Mike. *American Guerilla: The Forgotten Heroics of Russell W. Volckmann*. Philadelphia: Casemate, 2000.

Holmes, Virginia H. *Guerrilla Daughter*. Kent, OH: Kent State University Press, 2009.

Hunt, Ray. *Behind Japanese Lines: An American Guerrilla in the Philippines*. Lexington: University Press of Kentucky, 2000.

Keats, John. *They Fought Alone*. Philadelphia: Lippincott, 1963.

Lukacs, John D. *Escape from Davao: The Forgotten Story of the Most Daring Prison Break of the Pacific War*. New York: Simon and Schuster, 2010.

Mills, Scott A. *Stranded in the Philippines: Professor Bell's Private War against the Japanese*. Annapolis, MD: Naval Institute Press, 2009.

Norling, Bernard. *The Intrepid Guerillas of North Luzon*. Lexington: University Press of Kentucky, 1999.

Ramsey, Edwin P. *Lieutenant Ramsey's War: From Horse Soldier to Guerilla Commander*. Washington, DC: Brassey's, 2004.

Volckmann, Russell W. *We Remained: Three Years behind Enemy Lines in the Philippines*. New York: Norton, 1954.

3

Special Forces of the Cold War, 1946–1991

No sooner had World War II ended than the United States and its Western allies became embroiled in a global ideological conflict with the Soviet Union and its communist satellites, the Cold War. The perfection of atomic weapons in 1945 convinced many leaders on both sides that large-scale, conventional conflicts were no longer practical and, in fact, might trigger nuclear exchanges capable of extinguishing all humanity. It fell on the communists to devise guerrilla-based wars of "national liberation" in colonial nations to destabilize them as part of a worldwide ideological conquest. Direct confrontation with the West was thus preempted by Moscow-inspired and -supported insurgencies intending to drain Western nations of men, resources, and, ultimately, the political will to resist. Thus an age of global strife continued on, only this time with self-imposed restraints. Conventional-style conflicts, such as in Korea, 1950–1953, thwarted the potential use of nuclear weapons by being cast as regional conflicts, even if competing superpowers were directly involved. Korea proved a costly draw to the communists, so afterward they more fully articulated and orchestrated low-level "brushfire" wars, usually with a colonial, anti-imperialist spin, throughout Southeast Asia, Africa, and Latin America. The United States took up the challenge with massive counterinsurgency, or COIN, operations that required expansion of special forces across all four services. This process began in June 1952 when Congress passed the so-called Lodge Bill authorizing creation of the first bona fide special operations units since World War II. Their record in combat was outstanding, but their overall impact remained mixed in light of political, diplomatic, and other nonmilitary realities beyond their control. The "defeat" in Vietnam gave an overall false impression of American special warfare capabilities, which otherwise continued enjoying success in other parts of the world, if on a reduced scale. Nonetheless, special forces were in a very real sense America's tip of the spear throughout the struggle against communist totalitarianism and proved a major factor in the West's ultimate victory.

Air Force

Air Resupply and Communications Service

By 1948, it was apparent that the Cold War with the Soviet Union was very real and the new U.S. Air Force lacked any unconventional capability or equipment to assist the Central Intelligence Agency (CIA) in its clandestine operations. In fact, such aerial assets as the 1st Air Commando Group in Asia and the 801st Bombardment Group (Heavy) in Europe had been unceremoniously disbanded at the end of World War II. However, in 1947, following the outbreak of the Huk (communist) rebellion in the Philippines, another ad hoc unit was cobbled together by Colonel Edward G. Lansdale with surplus C-47s, P-51s, L-5s, and AT-6s. They also pioneered aerial psychological warfare with airborne speakers, another first. The unit was successful operationally and a major contributor to victory over the rebels by 1954. Consequently, given this novel communist emphasis on "national liberation," American military authorities correctly deduced that the Cold War would be won or lost largely in the minds of those engaged. In February 1948, the Air Force Air Staff created the Psychological Warfare Division, tasked with developing new forms of warfare (psychological warfare) to thwart the Soviets and their relentless propaganda campaign. However, it was not until 1950 that the service authorized two special air wings capable of actually undertaking these very missions. On January 5, 1951, the Military Air Transport Service (MATS) was ordered to organize, man, and equip such formations, known as Air Resupply and Communications Wings (ARCWs). The first ARCW wing was activated at Andrews Air Base, Maryland, on February 23, 1951, and it represented the first embrace of aerial special operations since the heady days of World War II. The wings, despite an organizational affiliation with MATS, were under the close supervision of the Psychological Warfare Division, Directorate of Plans, Headquarters, U.S. Air Force. Each wing consisted of six active and support squadrons, rendering them operationally self-sufficient. The purpose of the ARCW was to assist the CIA in covertly delivering and extracting human assets behind enemy lines, along with supplies for armed resistance groups, support for commando-type ranger raids, strategic intelligence collection missions, and psychological warfare activities. The mission profiles called for medium to long-range, low-level penetration of enemy airspace, usually at night, for the purpose of delivering or supplying the requisite assets.

As a unit, the Air Resupply and Communications wings operated a mélange of World War II leftovers, along with some newer amphibians and helicopters. The largest of these aircraft, 12 surplus B-29 bombers, were painted black on the underside to conduct nocturnal operations in hostile skies. Taking a leaf from World War II "Carpetbagger" operations, they were also stripped all of armament, save for tail guns, and had a special exit installed at the belly turret to allow agents ("Rabbits") to parachute directly down. Other modifications included the HTR-13 obstruction-warning radars, essential for handling large aircraft during low-level airdrops. The 580th ARCW, once activated at Mountain Home Air Force Base, Idaho, deployed at Wheelus Air Base, Libya, for service in the Middle East and eastern Europe. Commencing in 1955, they acted in concert with top secret U-2 flights over the Soviet Union, and in 1956 their HU-16 amphibians rescued two pilots after their planes crashed in the Black and Caspian Seas. The 581st ARCW, also activated in Idaho, arrived in July 1951 at Clark Air Base, the Philippines, where it compromised communist-held territories by dropping millions of propaganda leaflets. The unit's four Sikorsky H-19 Chickasaw helicopters were likewise utilized by inserting and extracting covert special forces teams behind enemy lines. By war's end, the crews logged 1,100 hours of combat time during more than 300 missions. On January 15, 1953, an H-19 piloted by Captain Lawrence A. Barrett traversed 100 miles into North Korean airspace to rescue a downed F-51 pilot, which he accomplished under heavy ground fire. However, one unlucky ARCW B-29, designated Stardust Four Zero, was downed near the Chinese border during a covert leaflet drop, and its crew endured harsh captivity until 1956. These men were the last prisoners of the Korean conflict to be released. Other ARCW crews were drawn directly into the raging conflict in Indochina (Vietnam) by piloting C-119 Flying Boxcars, sporting French national markings, in and out of combat zones. They frequently returned to Clark Air Base with shot-up aircraft, still in French colors, but, raised eyebrows notwithstanding, no questions were asked. A third unit, the 582nd ARCW, was activated in Idaho in September 1951 and deployed to Molesworth, England. There it assisted ongoing clandestine operations against the Soviet Union and its Warsaw Pact allies in the Baltic region.

The end of the Korean War signaled a commensurate drop in funding for the U.S. Air Force. That service, now overwhelmingly concerned with acquiring nuclear armed jet bombers for the Strategic Air Command, dropped its prior emphasis on psychological warfare. Moreover, in April 1953, the Air Staff ordered all ARCW wings to restrict themselves to air force projects only and all cooperation with the CIA was terminated. That September, new directives reduced the wings to group size (ARGs), now consisting of one active and one support squadron apiece. These units muddled along at their respective bases until 1956, when the 580th ARG was disbanded in Libya on October 12, and the 582nd ARG was axed on October 18. Their missions were taken over largely by the 42nd Troop Carrier Squadron in England and the 322nd Troop Carrier Squadron in the Pacific until these units were themselves disbanded in 1958. The air force consequently lacked genuine special operations capacity until 1964, when Air Commando units were resurrected for use in the Vietnam conflict.

Pararescuemen

As early as 1922, Colonel Albert E. Truby, U.S. Army Medical Corps, predicted that aircraft outfitted as "air ambulances" would one day deliver medical personnel to the battlefield and speedily evacuate patients back to treatment facilities. The primitive state of aviation technology at the time meant that two decades lapsed before true pararescue operations became viable. In 1940, a new, maneuverable parachute was successfully demonstrated by two U.S. Forest Service rangers, and, thus outfitted, army doctor Captain Leo P. Martin became the first medic to qualify as a "paradoctor." As World War II progressed, ad hoc air rescue units were formed by local commanders, while in the continental United States such missions were assumed by the Civil Air Patrol (CAP). Once patrolling CAP aircraft espied a plane wreck, parachute rescue teams would drop there to assist potential survivors. The first official pararescue training program was founded in Edmonton, Alberta, by Canadian expatriate Wop May in 1943 when he instructed several American forestry smoke jumpers to assisting crews who crashed while ferrying aircraft to Alaska. Ironically, the remote and hostile China-Burma-India ultimately gave rise to the first bona fide

Sikorsky HH-3E "Jolly Green Giant" helicopters were often employed in search-and-rescue operations to locate pilots downed in Vietnam or in the South China Sea. (Department of Defense)

pararescue services. These became essential operational assets seeing how hundreds of transport pilots and crews, operating over the inhospitable "Hump" (the Himalayas) risked certain death if they survived a crash due to harsh weather, the sheer distance back to civilization, or a lack of food and medicine. To Captain John L. Porter goes the distinction of commanding the first organized air rescue unit in August 1943, operating out of Chabua, India, with two C-47 transports. Several teams of parajumpers, or "PJs" as they called themselves, were carried to the scene by Porter's planes, and several marooned aircrews were rescued. By 1944, General William H. Tunner had organized the 3352nd Air Search and Rescue Squadron in India and appointed Major Donald C. Pricer to lead it. This unit made aviation history by operating Sikorsky Hoverflies, the first helicopters in the American aerial inventory, and they succored several downed pilots with them.

The drive for standing search-and-rescue units achieved greater impetus on May 29, 1946, when the Army Air Force finally established the Air Rescue Service. This unit was specifically tasked with rescuing aircrews involved in crashes on land and ditchings at sea, near operational bases or anywhere abroad. The protocol that arose mandated that a base commander could employ Local Base Rescue helicopter units, limited by range restrictions to a 135-mile radius, to be first on the scene. For crashes farther away, the first pararescue teams, delivered by aircraft, were established on July 1, 1947. Each team was comprised of a paradoctor and four medical technicians—specialists in medicine, survival, rescue, and tactics—and were intended to assist crews of long-range bomber and transport missions or support other agencies where rescue functions were necessary. Soon after, the 5th Rescue Squadron introduced the Pararescue and Survival School at MacDill Air Force Base, Florida. Later that same year, the B-29 bomber "Clobbered Turkey" struck a mountain top in Alaska on December 21, 1947, and crashed, further highlighting the need for professionally qualified pararescue men. The wreckage was spotted six days later, and a team of three medical volunteers, not trained pararescuers, dropped in to assist, but all three perished in the low temperatures and harsh weather. Ground rescue crews arrived two days later and brought out the remaining six survivors. The demand for air rescue missions grew exponentially with the Korean War in 1950, and within three years, they transported over 8,000 casualties from the front and rescued a further 1,000 pilots and crewmen from behind enemy lines. A decade later, pararescue teams were again expanded during the Vietnam War because of the sheer scope of air force activity throughout Southeast Asia. The new generation of helicopters then in use, faster and possessing greater range than their predecessors, also resulted in new tactics involving forward air controllers, armed helicopter gunship escorts, and protective fighter combat air patrols (CAP). HH-3 Jolly and HH-53 Jolly Green Giant helicopters made routine armed forays into North Vietnam or communist-controlled regions of South Vietnam to assist downed airmen. Pararecsuers were closely engaged throughout this conflict and, significantly, of 19 airmen awarded the Air Force Cross for bravery, no fewer than 10 went to pararescuers.

Special Operations Command

After a long hiatus, the air force revived its special operations capability after the administration of President John F. Kennedy began touting its new "flexible response" doctrine to combat communist-inspired insurgencies. This approach rendered low-intensity conflict as the new centerpiece of U.S. military doctrine and was a direct counterpoint to the nuclear-oriented "massive retaliation" policies of the Eisenhower administration. In 1961, the 4400th Combat Crew Training Squadron (CCTS) arose under Colonel Benjamin H. King for implementing this new counterinsurgency (COIN) doctrine. Their code name was "Jungle Jim." The new unit was again equipped with aging aircraft, including RB-26 Invaders, C-47s Dakotas, and marginally modern T-28 Nomad trainers, heavily modified to carry .50-caliber machine guns and 2.75-inch rocket pods under each wing. In August 1961, the 4400th CCTS executed Operation SANDY BEACH 1, its first overseas deployment, by dispatching Detachment 1 to the African nation of Mali. There it conducted an airlift of Malian paratroopers on maneuvers and convinced President Modiba Keita to remain in the American fold. By March 1962, the 4400th CCTS had been enlarged to a group and subordinated to the newly created Air Force Special Air Warfare Center at Eglin Air Force Base, Florida. This outfit managed the 1st Air Commando Group, the 1st Air Combat Applications Group, and other combat support groups. These combat elements were initially equipped with Douglas A-1E Skyraiders, a former U.S. Navy carrier-based bomber adapted for air force use. There appeared marginally obsolete compared to modern jets but, because their bomb loads were so prodigious and so much larger than many World War II heavy bombers Skyraiders received the fitting moniker of "Dumptrucks."

Meanwhile, Detachment 2, another classified unit, arrived in South Vietnam on November 6, 1962, to initiate Operation FARMGATE and instruct the fledgling Vietnamese air force in counterinsurgency tactics. FARMGATE also executed the first covert air support and resupply missions for units fighting communist Vietcong, and the ostensibly slow and outdated RB-26s and T-28s proved valuable as close-air-support aircraft. On November 26, 1962, an Invader flown by Lieutenant Colonel Philip O'Dwyer and Major Robert P. Guertz espied communist troop activity along a canal near Can Tho, bombed a large warehouse nearby, and then strafed the tree line from which ground fire was observed. South Vietnamese Army (ARVN) troops subsequently arrived and counted nearly 300 communist bodies, along with 20 wrecked sampans and other small vessels. Concurrently, FARMGATE-assigned C-47s performed up to 70 supply sorties per week, typically delivering 70,000 pounds of food and ammunition to ARVN units in the field, while T-28s flew nearly 100 ground support missions. Despite its relatively small size, the 4400th CCTS made a costly and unheralded impact on communist insurgents in South Vietnam, who heretofore enjoyed a free reign. Vietnam was also the first conflict where the air force did not provide supply missions for operations run by the CIA, the latter having acquired its own air force, Air America, for that purpose.

To provide counterinsurgency aerial units with vastly increased firepower, the air force also began experimenting with a new concept in ground support: the fixed-wing gunship. Project Tailchaser unfolded at Wright-Patterson Air Force Base, Ohio, with the idea of fitting a C-47 Dakota with three SUU-11A 7.62-mm Gatling guns (or miniguns) from fixed fuselage mounts, aimed over the left wing. Firing as a single battery, these weapons spewed 6,000 rounds per minute into a relatively small area, literally saturating it with bullets. On May 2, 1964, Captain Ronald W. Terry broached the project with General Curtis E. LeMay, the air force chief of staff, who wished to have a 4400th CCTS C-47 armed and combat tested in Vietnam. LeMay endorsed the concept, and the following December, Terry arrived in South Vietnam with two test aircraft. Each plane carried a crew of seven air force members and a single Vietnamese observer. In as series of initial daylight missions, Terry's aircraft caught several Vietcong detachments in the open, hosed them down, and literally reduced them to mincemeat. They C-47s proved equally effective at night, dropping magnesium flares to illuminate the target area, while miniguns emitted what was described as a wispy tongue of fire skirting along the ground. In light of their supernatural appearance at night, the gunships acquired the nicknames of "Spooky" and "Puff the Magic Dragon." Additional modified C-47s began arriving in greater numbers, and several were delivered to the newly established 4th Special Operations Squadron (SOS) to expand the work pioneered by the 4400th CCTS. Over the next few years, Spookies proved themselves the bane of any Vietcong unit attacking U.S. Special Forces outposts along the northern border, day or night. Their success prompted the top-secret Studies and Observations Group (SOG) of the Military Assistant Command, Vietnam (MACV), to interdict communist supply efforts along the Ho Chi Minh Trail from North Vietnam. On January 10, 1966, a section of Spookies arrived at Udorn Royal Thai Air Base, Thailand, for that express purpose. In addition to strafing missions, the aircraft were now tasked with armed reconnaissance and forward air control profiles to assist other aircraft attacking the convoys. The AC-47s enjoyed considerable success as truck destroyers and littered the jungle with hundreds of wrecks with an "orbiting strike maneuver," circling overhead as they destroyed the first and last vehicles in a convoy, then blasting everything trapped in between. The interdiction campaign was managed by the 14th SOW, which conducted 150,000 combat missions before AC-47s retired from active service in November 1969. These aircraft were then refurbished and handed over to the South Vietnamese and Laotian air forces, who continued supply interdiction attacks of their own up through 1975.

By 1966, air force special operations forces crested at 10,000 personnel and 550 aircraft divided into 19 squadrons. Moreover, the success of the relatively primitive C-47 as an airborne gunship prompted the air force to develop more sophisticated battle platforms as a follow-on. This became essential after the communists emphasized resupply missions at night, as the United States lacked true night-vision capabilities. This deficiency prompted Project Gunship II, in which a Lockheed C-130 Hercules four-engine transport was rigged with several minigun batteries, two M61 20-mm Vulcan Gatling guns, and a host of nocturnal detection and navigation systems. The first version also employed early starlight magnification systems, along with equally primitive infrared illuminators hooked directly into the fire control system. The net result was an aerial firing platform capable of accurately dispensing concentrated firepower from on high into any given area. The first C-130 gunship prototypes, nicknamed "Spectres," deployed to South Vietnam in September 1969 and proved immediately successful. Over the next three months, they accounted for 38 trucks during a handful of night flights and were rated four times more effective than the AC-47s they replaced. The prototypes returned home that winter for further modifications, returned to South Vietnam in February 1969, and over the next 10 months accounted for

The Fairchild AC-119 Shadow was another transport aircraft reconfigured as a ground-attack weapon. However, it was not highly successful as an firing platform and was ultimately replaced by the AC-130 Specter. (National Museum of the U.S. Air Force)

a further 228 communist trucks and 32 sampans destroyed. No sooner were they recycled back to the United States that fall than the first-production AC-130 Specters deployed to take their place. Meanwhile, the North Vietnamese sought to counter nighttime intrusions along the Ho Chi Minh Trail with radar-guided 37-mm cannons. A handful of aircraft were damaged with one or two downed over the jungle, but by April 1969, Specter gunships racked up kill rates of 100 percent per target per sortie. On May 8, 1969, the world's most unique aircraft interception took place when Specter No. 629's radar detected an object moving slowly over the jungle canopy beneath it that turned out to be a communist helicopter. The craft was tracked to a clearing where it landed, then the Spector obliterated it with volleys of 20-mm cannon fire. The air force conducted AC-130 missions with considerable success up through 1972, when they were finally withdrawn. The final variants to see service in this conflict had been further upgraded with computerized 40-mm cannon and a 105-mm airborne howitzer, exponentially increasing its lethality as a flying gunnery platform. However, in an attempt to retain the majority of C-130 aircraft as transports and preserve airlift capability, Secretary of Defense Harold Brown ordered that older Fairchild C-119 Flying Boxcars be brought out of mothballs and modified as gunships. The new AC-119 Shadow conducted its first mission in January 1969; it displayed inferior flight performance to the AC-47s and was gradually withdrawn from active duty. The 5th Air Commando Squadron also attempted psychological operations against the Vietcong using loudspeakers and leaflet drops, but their four C-47s and 10 U-10 Courier light aircraft invariably drew heavy gunfire in response, and the missions were canceled. Like all the services, air force special operation forces suffered severe cutback in the postwar period and were reduced to roughly one-third of their previous size in terms of personnel and equipment.

An important but little-appreciated component of air force special operations were civic endeavors aimed at winning "hearts and minds' of indigenous peoples. In 1963, the newly resurrected 1st Air Command Wing dispatched mobile training teams to six Latin American countries to assist local air force personnel in honing their own civic action skills and diluting guerrilla local influence. Specially trained teams air commandos also flew from various points within Bolivia, Guatemala, the Dominican Republic, Honduras, Ecuador and Paraguay to deliver medical supplies, perform basic dentistry, and provide inoculations against disease. In 1966, a milestone was reached in the scale of operations when air commandos delivered 50,000 pounds of medical supplies to Laos to contain outbreaks of typhus, malaria, dysentery, and tuberculosis. Over 8,000 patients were treated over a six-month span, underscoring air force emphasis on mercy missions that, along with covert activities, form the core of most special operations.

Defining Activity

Despite the secretive nature of air force special operations, they were involved in several high-profile missions of varying success. The earliest recorded sortie occurred in May 1970, when Lieutenant General Leroy Manor and Colonel Arthur "Bull" Simons led an army special forces in a rescue raid against the Son Tay prison camp outside Hanoi, North Vietnam. The air force provided highly trained aircrews flying MC-130 Combat Talons, HC-130 tankers, and H-3 and H-53 helicopters. The troops successfully landed and quickly disposed of the garrison, only to discover that the captives had been relocated some time previously. However, the planning and execution of the raid proved that joint special operations were both practical and desirable.

On May 13, 1975, an AC-130 Specter gunship of the 16th SOS was dispatched from a base in Thailand to assist a U.S. Marines rescue of the American freighter *Mayaguez*, which had been hijacked in international waters by communist Khmer Rouge guerrillas. That eve-ning, the Specter repeatedly swooped in low over Koh Tang island, using infrared detectors to ascertain body heat readout of all people present and indicating a sizable human pres-ence. At dusk on May 13–15, the aircraft served as a command-and-control platform that directed air strikes by air force F-111s and navy A-7s, sinking a Cambodian gunship. In the early morning hours of May 15, 1975, that same AC-130 again supported a Marine Corps aerial assault as several CH-53 helicopters bore in to land and rescue the hostages. They were greeted by heavy fire, and several helicopters were lost, at which point the Spec-ter swooped low and raked the tree line with 40-mm cannon fire. An aerial observer on the beachhead next called in for a 105-mm howitzer strike against a bothersome antiaircraft battery, and they silenced it with a single round. As this fighting transpired, the American crewmen were released through diplomatic efforts at Kompong Som, and all troops and air-craft in the vicinity of Koh Tang island were ordered withdrawn. The AC-130 laid down a sheet of fire from which the remaining CH-53s flew the marines back to safety. Because of poor intelligence, the American high command remained convinced that the *Mayaguez* crew was still on the island when in fact they had been transferred to the port of Kompong Som. This botched and hastily assembled rescue attempt cost several American lives and underscored the need for better planning in special operation sorties.

The next air force special operations mission of note transpired four years later—and proved to be an even bigger setback. On November 4, 1979, militants loyal to the Ayatollah Khomeini seized the American embassy in Tehran, Iran, and took 54 hostages. By November 15, Air Force Colonel James Kyle and army special forces leader Colonel Charles Beckwith formulated Operation RICE BOWL, a daring plan to fly into the city and rescue the hostages with a reasonable prospect of success. This entailed AC-130 Specter gunships and MC-130E Combat Talon transports from the 1st Special Operations Wing (1st SOW), Hurlburt Field, Florida, rendezvousing with Delta Force commandos who would arrive on Marine Corps CH-53 helicopters from the carrier USS *Nimitz* in the Indian Ocean. The MC-130Es, which possessed aerial refueling capabilities, would gas up the helicopters at a desert landing site near Tehran while the AC-130s provided top cover during the actual rescue. The operation would be conducted under total radio blackout conditions. However, the plan adopted was wrought with intrinsic flaws, not the least of which was that the navy and marine helicopter pilots lacked meaningful experience flying in the dark with night-vision goggles. The CH-53 helicopters were themselves barely suited for the mission at hand, being designed more or less for minesweeping operations, not long-range insertions and extractions. Nonetheless, President Jimmy Carter, to circumvent charges that he was being "soft" on Iran, approved the mission on April 11, 1980, and it was launched five days later. Eight CH-53s were launched from the *Nimitz* as planned, but hydraulic problems forced two of the giant craft to turn back. The rest were damaged by flying through an unscheduled sandstorm, or haboob, at which point a third machine aborted. The rest managed to land at the designated landing zone, Desert One. They were joined there by the EC-130s and began refueling when additional helicopters malfunctioned. At this juncture, the mission was abandoned altogether, but disaster struck as another sandstorm engulfed the helicopters as they lifted off, and one struck a C-130 on the ground. The ensuing explosion wrecked both aircraft, killing five airmen and three marines, at which point all helicopters were abandoned and surviving assault team members evacuated on the remaining transports. The disaster at Desert One was humiliating but constitutes a dramatic turning point in the development of aerial special operations. Hereafter, better planning, coupled with specialized training and equipment, negated future reverses on this scale.

In fact, the failure at Desert One proved something of a catharsis, for the ensuing Holloway Commission recommended greater interoperability between all the services. This, in turn, resulted in the consolidation of all–air force special operation units into the 1st SOW at Hurlburt Field, on March 1, 1983, with the whole falling under the purview of the commander of the 23rd Air Force at Scott Air Force Base, Illinois. This new entity included the 8th, 16th, and 20th Special Operation Squadrons, with the 8th SOS operating MC130 Combat Talon transports and HC-130 Hercules tankers, the 16th AC-130 Specter gunships, and the 20th MH-53 Pave Low and HH-54 Jolly Green Giant helicopters. An armed ranger-style infantry component was provided by the 1720th STG, also based at Hurlburt. To these must be added several special operations units active in the reserves, including the 919th SOG, flying AC-130 Specters, and the 302nd Special Operations Group with their EC-130E Volo Solant psychological warfare aircraft. Commencing in April 1983, these newly configured special operation units became involved in President Ronald Reagan's campaign to interdict the drug trade from the Caribbean, particularly from the Bahamas. Aircraft of the 1st SOW were tasked with flying Drug Enforcement Agency agents into offending areas to make arrests.

These aircraft remained in the field up through 1985 and scored continual success against smuggling operations.

A major turning point in air force special operations was Operation URGENT FURY against the bloody communist clique that had seized power on the Caribbean island of Grenada in 1983. To rescue hundreds of American students being held hostage on a medical campus, MC-130 Combat Talons of the 1st SOW were tasked with airdropping U.S. Army rangers over the Point Salinas airfield and delivering close air support to American units across the island as needed. These aircraft would be guided in by elite Combat Control Teams who clandestinely arrived and deployed overhead before the main assault developed. Early on the morning of October 25, 1983, an MC-130 piloted by Major Michael Couvillon flew high over the Point Salinas airfield, surveying it closely with infrared and other sensory detectors. He concluded that it was guarded with Soviet-supplied ZU-23 antiaircraft cannon and that the landing strips were blocked by heavy construction equipment. Military leaders surmised that the Cuban defenders knew that rangers routinely jumped from an altitude of 1,000 feet, and anticipated that they had calibrated their weapons to fire accordingly, so the soldiers were ordered dropped from only 500 feet. This caused the communist weaponry to overshoot their targets. The rangers arrived safely, then Major Couvillion's aircraft silenced a ZU-23 battery with 40-mm cannon fire. His MC-130 also shot up a communist machine gun position that was obstructing the American advance, despite some onboard computer malfunctions. The aircraft loosed its barrage of 20-mm and 40-mm shells within 50 feet of the rangers' position, but the enemy battery fell silenced. The gunships provided close air support as needed over the next two days and took no losses. Operation URGENT FURY was an operational success and marks a resurgence of air force special operations since the drastic budget cuts of 1975. Moreover, their basic mission of inserting armed assets into a hostile environment and then providing them with accurate close air support remains unchanged to present times.

In 1989, the air force followed up its success in Grenada with another successful display of prowess during Operation JUST CAUSE, the invasion of Panama. Here, AC-130 Specters of the 4th and 16th SOSs, based at Hurlburt, were called on to deliver precision fire in heavily populated urban areas to minimize civilian casualties. In the early morning hours of December 20, 1989, gunship Air Papa 05 loosed a lethal barrage against the Pacora River Bridge to keep Panamanian reinforcements from crossing. Heavy and accurate fire from on high stopped an enemy convoy in its tracks, then special forces arrived by helicopter and secured the bridge. Concurrently, theAC-130 codenamed Air Papa 03 circled the Rio Hato airfield in concert with two U.S. Army Apache attack helicopters, seeking targets. They knocked out a ZPU 23mm battery with a single infrared-directed cannon shot while the MC-130s dropped ranger contingents to seize the field. Two additional AC-130s were delegated to attack La Commandancia, the headquarters of dictator Manuel Noriega. Guided by sensors, they commenced firing 105-mm howitzer shells at numerous barracks, destroying several; however, it is suspected that at least some of the 26 casualties suffered by Delta Force operators nearby were inflicted by friendly fire. All told, no fewer than nine AC-130 Specters facilitated Operation JUST CAUSE and were closely integrated into the overall battle plan. Furthermore, most were carefully guided by elite Combat Control Teams on the ground who ensured accurate delivery of aerial fire and reduced fratricidal casualties. All told, air force special operations aircraft performed 27 separate and simultaneously actions at divers parts of Panama at H-hour—and this after flying 1,500 miles from their main base in Florida. The final mission associated with JUST CAUSE occurred when an MC-130 Combat Talon from the 1st SOW flew former dictator Noriega from Panama to a jail in the United States to face trial for drug smuggling.

On May 22, 1990, three decades of experimentation and refinement culminated in renaming the 23rd Air Force as the Air Force Special Operations Command (AFSOC) at Hurlburt Field. Having finally acquired a major command status, it now consisted of the 1st, 39th, and 353rd SOWs and the 1720th Special Tactics Group (STG). These, in turn, were a fully integrated component of the new U.S. Special Force Command. This new, multifaceted agency was entrusted with organizing, training, equipping, and educating the appropriate forces for deployment around the globe for purposes of unconventional warfare, special reconnaissance, direct action, counterterrorism, and humanitarian assistance. Tactically, this translates into providing quick and reliable air transport and fire support to special operations forces of the army and navy. Only three months into its service life, the AFSOC kicked into high gear following the Iraqi invasion of Kuwait in August 1990. MC-130 Combat Talon and MH-53 Pave Low aircraft from the 8th and 20th SOSs were immediately dispatched to Saudi Arabia as part of Operation DESERT SHIELD, followed by the 21st SOS to Turkey and HH-3 helicopters the 71st SOS (Air Force Reserve). Compared to the ill-equipped and ad hoc units assembled at Desert One a decade before, the AFSOC units were now well equipped with the latest sophisticated technologies and trained in tactical resourcefulness to a degree heretofore thought unimaginable. When Operation DESERT STORM commenced the following January, the men and aircraft were basically tasked with getting in and out of hostile airspace undetected as quickly as possible as well as rescuing downed pilots and delivering missiles, bombs, and other precision-guided munitions, along with leaflets, without loss. One weapon of note was the BLU-82, a 15,000-pound bomb nicknamed "Daisy Cutter," dropped out the rear doors of MC-130s to clear Iraqi minefields ahead of ground forces.

The aerial component of Operation DESERT STORM commenced on January 16, 1991, when Task Force Normandy, consisting of two MH-53 Pave Low helicopters from the 20th SOS ("Green Hornets"), specially equipped for operating with night-vision goggles, guided two flights of army AH-64 Apache attack helicopters against a pair of sophisticated Iraqi early-warning radars. Hellfire missiles fired by the Apaches obliterated the system; hence, Baghdad and other cities were unprepared for the massive coalition air strike that followed. Over the next few weeks, AFSOC helicopters were also called on to perform pilot rescue missions under extremely harrowing conditions. For example, on January 21, 1991, a MH-53 Pave Low helicopter raced in 180 miles behind Iraqi lines to rescue a downed F-14 navy pilot. The chopper dipped low and flew 160 miles per hour only 10 feet off the ground to avoid detection, then located and successfully rescued the pilot. On February 19, 1991, another Pave Low, accompanied by two MH-3Es from the 20th SOS, delivered 13 Navy SEALs to Kubbar Island in the Persian Gulf, then extracted them safely the following day. However, the 1st SOW suffered the largest single airplane loss of the war on January 31, 1991, when the AC-130 Spirit 03 was shot down by a missile, killing all 14 crewmembers. The gunship had been specifically tasked with destroying an Iraqi rocket launcher near Khafji and did so with a single volley of 40-mm and 105-mm fire but was probably struck by a shoulder-fired surface-to-air missile. The loss of Spirit 03 induced air force leaders to cancel all further gunship missions during the Gulf War. Otherwise, Air Force special forces performed their assigned tasks with efficiency and courage.

Army

1st Special Forces Operational Detachment—Delta (Delta Force)

Continuing tension between Israel and the Arab states in the Middle East led to a global upswing in terrorism by militant Muslim groups. The most notorious example of this trend occurred during the Summer Olympic Games of 1972, when gunmen took several Israeli athletes hostage and murdered them before a rescue mission could be mounted. In 1976, Palestinians held several Israelis hostage an Entebbe Airport in Uganda until they were dramatically freed by specially trained Israeli commandos. In light of these developments, several European nations, especially France and Germany, began raising designated antiterrorist units as part of their standing military establishments, while Great Britain placed its increasing reliance on its existing Special Air and Boat Service squadrons. The United States, by contrast, waited until 1975 to begin contemplating elite antiterror units above and beyond the special forces (Rangers and Green Berets) already extent. It fell on Colonel Charles Beckwith, a distinguished and highly decorated Vietnam War veteran, to push for such an organization. Beckwith, who commanded the Special Forces School at Fort Bragg, North Carolina, suggested a small handpicked outfit that was highly trained, specially equipped, and capable of engaging and defeating terrorists before they could attack American assets. Moreover, having served with Britain's renown and highly successful Special Air Service (SAS) as an exchange officer, he determined to use them as his inspiration and model. Moreover, the new unit would be expected to excel at a full spectrum of tricky missions, including hostage rescue and other rapid-response operations missions where planning was, by necessity, at a minimum. The argument won favor at the Pentagon, but after Beckwith conceded that he needed at least two years to make his unit operational, a small detachment from the 5th Special Force Group (SFG) under Colonel Robert Montell, code-named "Blue Light," trained to fill the gap. Beckwith envisioned a highly skilled, highly unconventional force whose members execute antiterrorist tactics but were likewise capable of unorthodox tasks, such as clandestine reconnaissance, rappelling from helicopters, cracking safes, and hot-wiring vehicles. In sum, he determined to carry the original concept of special forces to new operational heights—even extremes.

In October 1977, the 1st Special Forces Operational Detachment—Delta, popularly called "Delta Force," finished recruiting and training functions and became fully operational. Then, as now, its existence was highly classified, and few details have emerged. At the time, it was thought to have consisted of six small Alpha (or simply A) teams, which, in turn, constitute a Bravo (B) team company-sized formation under a major. The largest known detachment, a Charlie (or C) team, is battalion-sized under the purview of a colonel. The next letter in military nomenclature being D, or "Delta," it became the unit designation. Delta's first known combat foray occurred during Operation EAGLE CLAW on April 25–26, 1980. Their deployment came in response on November 4, 1979, to the Iranian seizure of the American embassy in Tehran, Iran, where a rescue mission was planned. For several months, a force of Delta troopers trained on a life-size mock-up of the embassy at Yuma Army Airfield, Arizona. The assault force of nearly 100 men was divided into Red, White, and Blue teams, with Red being tasked with taking the embassy compound, Blue taking the ambassador's residence, and White securing the streets and approaches outside. Ingress

Charles A. Beckwith (1929–1994). Charles Alvin Beckwith was born in Atlanta, Georgia, on January 22, 1929, and he was commissioned a second lieutenant through the University of Georgia's ROTC program in 1952. Three years later, he joined the 82nd Airborne Division and also completed ranger training in before transferring to U.S. Army Special Forces in 1957. He first deployed to Vietnam and Laos as a military adviser in 1960 and two years later transferred to the elite British Special Air Service as an exchange officer during the Malaysian Emergency. Beckwith carefully noted British special operations procedures and, following his return to the United States, agitated constantly for creation of an elite, direct-action unit. His recommendations were ignored by superiors, so he transferred back to the 7th Special Forces Group as an operations officer at Fort Bragg,

Colonel Charles A. Beckwith was the inspiration behind today's Delta Force commandos. An aggressive, hard-hitting infantry officer, he acquired the apt moniker "Charging Charlie." (Courtesy of the U.S. Army)

North Carolina. Using his British experience, he completely revitalized training methods for the Green Berets, laying the foundations for what became the noted Qualifications Course. Beckwith subsequently returned to Vietnam in 1965 with Project Delta, and he was seriously wounded the following year. He returned in 1968 commanding the 2nd Battalion, 327th Infantry (Airborne), in a series of hard-fought battles west of Hue. Afterward, he served as a trainer at Fort Bragg until November 1977, when he was finally asked to create a new elite unit, Delta Force. This formation saw its initial debut during Operation EAGLE CLAW, and Beckwith subsequently recommended to Congress that the 160th Special Operations Aviation Regiment and the Joint Special Operations Command also be created to support them. "Charging Charlie" retired from active duty in 1980 and died in Dallas, Texas, on June 13, 1994, a celebrated and thoroughly unconventional warrior.

was to be made in helicopters provided by the Marine Corps and navy, supported by air force C-130 and MC-130 transports and tankers. However, this overly complicated scheme met with disaster at the Desert One rendezvous point, south of Tehran, after several helicopters aborted because of mechanical problems arising from an unexpected sandstorm. With only five helicopters functional, one below the minimum of six needed deemed necessary, Beckwith decided to abort. Unfortunately, as the Americans departed, a chopper accidentally collided with an MC-130 transport on the ground. Five airmen and three marines died in the inferno, but the Delta team emerged intact. A thorough investigation pinpointed

23 problems relative to operations, communications, and command-and-control incongruities between the different services involved. Luckily no blame was ever attached to Delta, arrayed in casual civilian attire of blue jeans, boots, and field jackets for the mission. By 1980, the Joint Special Operations Command, which Colonel Beckwith had long advocated, also came into being, and he gained appointment as its first leader. One of his first acts was to codify Delta operational procedures and mission profiles, along with personnel selection and training routines into a document known as the "Black Book." The picked force was also expanded to 300 men arrayed into 16-man squadrons and enjoyed the best personnel available from a small pool of qualified volunteers and the first shot at state-of-the-art equipment. By now the Defense Department bureaucracy had finally determined that future disasters involving its special forces were not politically or militarily acceptable and they embraced changes heretofore long contested.

Defining Activity

Even from their inception, very little can be confirmed about Delta Force activities. Its operators are suspected of playing major roles in helping suppress the communist-inspired civil war in El Salvador and assisting, directly and indirectly, anticommunist Nicaraguan guerrillas, or "Contras," in their struggle against the Marxist Sandinista dictatorship. On October 19, 1983, the Caribbean island of Grenada was also rocked by a communist-inspired revolution leading to the death of Prime Minister Maurice Bishop and the installation of a radical Revolutionary Council with uncomfortably close ties with Cuba and the Soviet Union. Not only were hundreds of American medical students studying on the island taken hostage, but the communists began working on a 10,000-foot runway capable of accommodating Soviet nuclear-armed bombers. President Ronald Reagan acted with dispatch by formulating Operation URGENT FURY to rescue the students and rid the region of this menace. The Deltas received the dangerous, "direct-action" assignment of arriving ahead of the main assault force (rangers and 82nd Airborne Division) to a target area outside the Point Salinas airfield. Their objective was the Richmond Hill Prison, where numerous political dissenters were incarcerated, but poor reconnaissance led to the loss of a UH-60 Black Hawk helicopter with 11 Delta casualties, as it was unexpectedly ringed with Cuban troops and heavy 23-mm antiaircraft cannon. The troopers attempted rappelling down ropes from the helicopters but were caught in a crossfire from the ground and driven off. Another objective, Fort Rupert, was successfully stormed. All told, Grenada was a somewhat shoddy example of poor intelligence and planning, and corrective measures addressed both operational facets. On a lesser note, a team of troopers proved a measure of antiterrorist security during the 1984 Summer Olympic Games in Los Angeles, California, completing their rounds in a disguised beer truck. During this same interval, a force of Delta types successfully executed a direct-action rescue mission in Venezuela on July 29, 1984, freeing all hostages on an airliner. During this time frame, it was suspected that a Delta Force sniper assassinated Colombian drug lord Pablo Escobar, although the act is officially attributed to Colombian security forces.

The next sizable opportunity for action came in December 1989 during Operation JUST CAUSE. Once the decision was made to overthrow Panamanian dictator and drug kingpin Manuel Noriega, Delta was tasked with freeing radio host Kurt Muse, an American citizen, from the notorious Modelo Prison. This building was directly adjacent to the Comandancia,

Noriega's military headquarters. Early in the morning on December 19, 1989, an MH-6 Little Bird helicopter from the 160th Special Operations Aerial Squadron (SOAR) delivered a crack Delta assault team to the prison's roof. Concurrently, all electricity from the emergency generators was also cut, leaving the defenders in the dark. As AC-130 Specter gunships pounded the Comandancia next door, the Deltas fought their way inside, found Muse unhurt, and freed him. As the MH-6 flew off with the commandos and their guest, it was damaged by gunfire and made a soft landing between two tall buildings. Four Deltas were wounded in the action, but the entire party was secured by a helicopter gunship and an armored personnel carrier that raced to the scene. This particular maneuver was a textbook success and added to Delta's reputation for efficiency under fire. Meanwhile, Operation NIFTY PACKAGE, the capture of Noriega himself, was undertaken by an eight-man Delta team dressed in civilian garb, but they failed to snare the elusive dictator.

By far the most important work performed by Delta Force during the Cold War period happened during Operation DESERT STORM, the campaign to free Kuwait from occupying Iraqi forces. Once the coalition aerial campaign commenced in January 1991, Iraqi dictator Saddam Hussein ordered his Soviet-supplied SCUD medium-range missiles fired at Israel to draw them into the war. This act would have severely strained the anti-Iraq coalition, as it contained several Muslim nations. On January 18, 1991, seven unguided missiles struck an urban complex in Haifa and Tel Aviv, inflicting 50 civilian casualties and destroying 1,587 apartments. Any Israeli retaliation was sure to inflame Arab opinions, so it became a strategic imperative to knock out the SCUDs before the Jews gave into provocation. Many launching sites were deep behind enemy lines, so Delta operatives were delivered through HALO (high-altitude, high-opening) parachute jumps from 30,000 feet, then deployed utilizing a double-canopy parachute capable of pinpoint maneuvering to a select landing site. Thus outfitted, Delta members can control their descent for up to 60 miles and land precisely where desired. Once on the ground, they were tasked with locating SCUD launchers, which were large-wheeled vehicles, then "painting" them with laser target designators for an incoming air strikes by coalition aircraft. Several targets of opportunity, such as bunkers, radar sites, and supply depots, were also destroyed in this manner. When forced to move, the teams did so only at night and spent daylight hours well camouflaged to escape Iraqi detection. Delta also worked closely in concert with British SAS members and helped eliminate most missile launchers in western Iraq, sometimes with their own handheld weapons. On February 21, 1991, a helicopter from the 160th SOAR crashed during a sandstorm, killing four crewmen and three Delta passengers; these were the only known Delta losses of Desert Storm. Whether or not the unit fulfilled other missions within Iraq proper remains speculative, and whatever else they did, it remains highly classified. Ironically, General Norman Schwarzkopf, the coalition commander, steadfastly rejected offers by the 1st and 5th SFGs to participate in the ground war. Political pressure from Washington, in light of the SCUD attacks, forced his hand on the issue, and those Delta units (and others) committed to combat demonstrated their operational worthiness by acquitting themselves well.

Rangers

Despite the obvious success of ranger-type formations throughout World War II, all were summarily disbanded by the U.S. Army at the conclusion of that conflict. It was not until the outbreak of the Korean War in 1950 that rangers experienced a limited revival. Apparently, Army Chief of Staff Lawton J. Collins, impressed by communist infiltration abilities in their first encounters with U.S. troops, informed Army Operations in Washington, D.C., that rangers should be raised for similar purposes. However, unlike the full battalions mobilized during World War II, the new rangers were restricted to company-sized units and attached to infantry divisions as organic special forces. The ranger training program was consequently resurrected at Fort Benning, Georgia, under the aegis of Colonel John G. Van Houten, and 16 rangers companies were trained over the ensuing seven months. Each consisted on a headquarters section of six men and three platoons of one officer and 32 men each. This organization was larger than ranger companies of the previous war but still half the size of a regular infantry company. For this reason, rangers received a higher proportion of automatic weapons, bazookas, and grenade launchers than other. However, they still lacked the organic heavy firepower of line infantry and, for that reason, could not sustain that work for long. Only six ranger companies actually arrived in Korea and these were attached to the 1st Cavalry and 2nd, 3rd, 7th, 24th, and 25th Infantry Divisions. Among them, the 2nd Ranger Company, culled from the 505th Airborne Infantry Regiment and the 82nd Airborne Division's 80th Antiaircraft Artillery Battalion, remains the only purely African American ranger unit in American military history. As before, prospective recruits underwent a thorough six-week training regimen at Fort Benning to acquire specialized skills of demolition, land navigation, hand-to-hand combat, infiltration, and communications. Successful candidates were further expected to hike between 40 and 50 miles cross country in 12 to 18 hours, while carrying a full combat load. Rangers also trained for cold-weather conditions at Camp Carson, Colorado, after which they were marched to a local corral to learn mule handling for, in rough terrain, these docile, rugged beasts were still a ranger's best friend.

As these preparations transpired, the hard-pressed 8th Army independently organized its own ranger company under Lieutenant Ralph Puckett, a former airborne officer, for raiding and reconnaissance missions around the Pusan perimeter. The unit, the 8213th Provisional Company, better known as the 8th Army Raider Company, was attached to the 25th Infantry Division. It saw active duty in the advance toward the Yalu River in North Korea and was nearly wiped out by Chinese forces near Ipsak. With its commanding officer severely wounded, the company was withdrawn from the line and supported the Turkish Brigade until its disbandment in March 1951. Another ad hoc ranger formation was the 8245th Army Unit, raised from X Corps troops at the behest of Major General Edward M. Almond. They staged an amphibious landing at Kusan Bay on September 12, 1950, which was a ruse intending to deflect attention from the main landing at Inchon three days later. That November, the rangers shipped to the eastern coast of North Korea, where they performed reconnaissance operations around the port of Hamhung.

Meanwhile, the U.S.-raised ranger companies finally reached Korea in the wake of the Chinese winter offensive, and they bore dramatic if small-scale roles in rolling back the tide. In March 1951, a party of 11 men was entrusted with destroying an enemy railroad tunnel in Wonsan, North Korea, but they were discovered by innumerable Chinese troops, who killed or captured eight. On March 13, 1951, the 2nd and 4th Ranger Companies participated in Operation TOMAHAWK, an airborne assault with the 187th Regimental Combat Team near Munsan-ni, north of Seoul. While failing to trap retreating communist units, the jump displayed their capability for deploying anywhere. Combat now degenerated into a static contest of outposts and defensive lines, and rangers distinguished themselves with ambushes, patrols, and nighttime raids behind enemy positions. In one sudden attack, the 1st Ranger Company destroyed the headquarters of the 12th North Korean Division during a well-conducted nocturnal foray. In time, such actions became less and less frequent, and ranger companies were once again pressed into service as regular infantry, taking heavy losses. Worse, despite their demonstrated utility, commanders complained that rangers absorbed the very best officers and men from regular units and, becoming a superfluous luxury that the army could not afford. The general consensus of the U.S. high command also felt that rear-area raids and reconnaissance missions were better handled by South Korean guerrillas led by U.S. Army officers, so as of August 1951, ranger companies were broken up and all personnel were shunted over to airborne units. Fortunately, the Ranger Training Command survived as the new U.S. Army Ranger School, now tasked with imparting specialized light infantry skills to those officers and noncommissioned officers (NCOs) willing to learn them. Seventeen years lapsed before the military again fielded traditional-style ranger units.

The United States was heavily involved in the Vietnam War in January 1969, and army leadership decided that those units capable of conducting long-range reconnaissance patrols (LRRPs) would convert them into ranger companies and part of the new 75th Infantry Regiment (Ranger). Previously, these six-man LRRP teams functioned as elite light infantry in the bush, performing many ranger-type functions at much greater distances than before. They were tasked with reconnaissance, intelligence gathering, directing air strikes from the ground, assisting conventional ground operations with surprise attacks, conducting hunter-killer sweeps through the jungles, ambushing Vietcong and North Vietnamese Army (NVA) units, while highly trained snipers among them killed enemy soldiers from afar. Deep behind enemy lines, it was not uncommon for rangers to also attempt prisoner snatches, rescue allied captives, tap into communist wire communications along the Ho Chi Minh Trail, and secretly mine enemy transportation routes. Their mission completed, LRRPs quietly repaired to a prearranged landing zone and egress by helicopter back to friendly lines. For many years, LRRPs performed with an effectiveness that belies their relatively small numbers.

In light of this new directive, however, Ranger Company A formed at Georgia, while a new Company B arose at Fort Carson, Colorado. These two units remained stateside for training purposes and were ultimately disbanded. Fortunately, in the post-Vietnam era, senior military leaders became cognizant that the U.S. Army lacked viable light infantry capable of rapidly deploying across a variety of terrain and under difficult operating conditions. Such tasks are an American military specialty, and shows how far army doctrine had drifted from its roots. Accordingly, Army Chief of Staff General Creighton Abrams authorized creation of the 1st Ranger Battalion (Fort Stewart, Georgia) and the 2nd Ranger Battalion (Fort Lewis, Washington) in January 1974. The new unit was conceived as an elite assault force capable of storming fixed, heavily defended positions, putting up a tough firefight in the process and were a far cry for the small-team, reconnaissance-oriented doctrine of the Vietnam War.

The new ranger units were first committed to action during Operation EAGLE CLAW, the ill-fated hostage rescue attempt in Iran. Here Company C, 1st Battalion, 75th Ranger Regiment, was to accompany men of the 1st Special Forces Operational Detachment—Delta to Egypt and provide security for the men and their equipment. From these, a 12-man detachment would also accompany the Delta Force into Iran as a road team and secure the Desert One landing site as the helicopters on which they flew were being refueled. The balance of the rangers were scheduled for an airdrop on an airfield at Manzariyeh 35 miles south of Tehran, seize it, and hold it long enough for C-141 Starlifters to land and pick up the American hostages and their Delta rescuers. However, the attempt was abandoned after three helicopters aborted from mechanical failures, while another collided on the ground with a MC-130 tanker aircraft. Company C never left Egypt and returned to the United States with the Delta members, rather discouraged.

Defining Activity

In November 1983, the Caribbean island of Grenada experienced a sudden and bloody coup once Prime Minister Maurice Bishop was toppled and murdered by a violent communist clique under General Hudson Austin. As events played out, the new regime took several hundred American medical students studying there as hostages. This act triggered a violent response, Operation URGENT FURY, on the orders of President Ronald Reagan. On October 24, 1983, rangers had only received a few hours' warning by the time they assembled on C-130 transports at Army Air Field, Alabama, under Lieutenant Colonel Wesley Taylor. These men were tasked with seizing Point Salinas airfield, known to be garrisoned by hundreds of Cuban troops, before moving onto St. Georges University's True Blue Campus to free the hostages. The rangers, once reinforced by members of the 82nd Airborne Division, would then storm the Grenadian army barracks at Calivigny, completing their conquest. However, events began going awry, largely on account of hasty planning. First, given the lack of available airlift, the two battalions selected went into action understrength and took only their best and most capable soldiers. En route, reliable intelligence revealed the Salinas airstrip blocked with obstacles, meaning that the rangers would have to parachute down to their objective. The presence of nearby Soviet ZU-23 antiaircraft weapons was also confirmed, and these were probably preregistered to fire at the known ranger drop altitude of 1,000 feet. Consequently, orders were issued to deplane at only 500 feet, which not only caused the Cubans to overshoot their targets but also reduced the descent time to a mere 17 seconds. This required them to jump without a reserve parachute, but no rangers were killed or injured while deploying. As their aircraft approached Grenada through driving rain squalls, the lead aircraft suffered internal navigation problems, and the armada straggled in out of their assigned order. The rangers requested then permission to make a mass drop and get as many men on the ground in as little time as possible, but air force authorities refused, so the rangers were parachuted in several waves.

At 5:30 a.m. on October 25, 1983, the first detachments of the 1st Battalion, 75th Rangers, drifted down over Salines without incident, although an hour passed before the troops formed up. The 2nd Battalion needed another hour to deploy, then the combined force advanced on their objectives, receiving scattered fire. Several abandoned bulldozers were hot-wired and used by the rangers to clear the airfield, and by 10:00 a.m., the runway was secured and made operable. A Company, 1/75th, also began advancing on the True Blue Campus. Over 100 Cubans surrendered to the rangers at the airfield, although at 5:30 p.m. they counterattacked with three BTR-60 armored vehicles, all of which were destroyed. All told, five rangers were killed and six wounded at Salines. However,

C Company, 1/75, flying on UH-60 Black Hawk helicopters of the 160th SOAR, encountered stiff antiaircraft fire from the Richmond Hill Prison, and two crashed with some casualties among rangers and Delta troops. On the morning of October 25, rangers packed into several navy and Marine Corps CH-46 helicopters for an assault on the True Blue Campus, which fell without resistance. On October 27, Company C, 1 /75, and Company B, 2/75, joined with the 82nd Airborne Division and stormed into the Calivigny army barracks, which was found abandoned. Three rangers died and four injured when a Black Hawk crashed on landing. Grenada was declared secure shortly afterward, at which point the rangers were loaded up on transports and returned to the United States. In light of their success on Grenada, the 3rd Ranger Battalion was authorized on October 3, 1984. This move culminated in founding the new 75th Ranger Regiment in 1986, which consisted of three battalions, and encapsulated the elite status and specialized missions of all previous formations. Grenada also imparted many lessons on the military respecting joint military actions, so that same year, the *U.S.* Special Operations Command was created to help ensure smoother operations.

On December 19, 1989, the 75th Rangers again rushed into action during Operation JUST CAUSE, enacted to root out thuggish drug lord Manuel Noriega from his roost in Panama. A day previous, they began assembling at Pope Air Force Base, North Carolina, with orders to secure Torillos International Airport, Tocumen Military Airfield, and Rio Hata Military Airfield. This accomplished, they would also pay an unannounced visit to Noriega's personal beach house to try and apprehend him. The rangers thus constituted the backbone of Task Force Red, the special forces assault group. In the early morning hours of December 19, the first 500 rangers jumped low over Rio Hata amidst some sporadic antiaircraft fire from the Panamanian Defense Force (PDF). Once deployed, they received support from AC-130 Specter gunships orbiting overhead and quickly subdued all opposition. Within two hours, Rio Hata airfield was used to land additional troops and equipment for the invasion. The rangers subsequently advanced inland to deal with Panamanian special forces, the so-called Mountain Troops, who either surrendered or quickly withdrew into the jungle. By the fifth day of URGENT FURY, the rangers had also liberated Calle Diez, 25 miles from Panama City, from Noriega's paramilitary "Dignity Battalions," which likewise fled without ceremony. All the rangers were withdrawn back to the United States within three weeks of the initial invasion. Better communications and control resulted in a smoother overall action than at Grenada; five rangers were killed and 50 injured, mostly through friendly fire.

The rangers next saw action during Operation DESERT STORM, January/February 1991, in the wake of the Iraqi invasion of Kuwait. During the buildup to the liberation of that country, General Norman Schwarzkopf unilaterally rejected all special forces offers to assist the general ground campaign. However, Iraqi use of SCUD missiles against Israel forced him to change his tack. Precious little is known of special forces activities, but apparently Delta Company, 4th Ranger Training Battalion, instructed members of the 24th Infantry Division in long-range surveillance techniques while operating in a desert environment. More directly, parts of Companies B and C, 1 /75, were involved in actions against Iraqi radar and communications installations far inland and also assisted Delta and SAS teams in hunting down SCUD missile launchers. It is conjectured that other detachments seized airfields for use by different special operations troops, but this cannot be verified with certainty. The

A former Office of Strategic Services operative, Aaron Bank was considered to have been the driving force behind modern American special forces, commencing with the Green Berets. He was one of the first military leaders to see the need for clandestine, culturally fluent operatives who were not civilians (Lena Olson, NSS. www.lenaolson.com)

Aaron Bank (1902–2004). Aaron Bank was born in New York City on November 23, 1902, and educated in Switzerland, gaining fluency in both French and German. He joined the U.S. Army in 1939 and was deemed too old for combat operations, but he subsequently transferred to the Office of Strategic Services (OSS) and found his niche. As part of the Special Operations Branch, he led a Jedburgh team into southern France on July 31, 1944, in concert with Operation ANVIL, and liberated several towns. Bank was then directed to conduct Operation IRON CROSS, an attempt to capture Adolf Hitler with German army deserters, but it was called off shortly before Germany surrendered. Bank next transferred to the Pacific theater, where he parachuted into French Indochina (Vietnam) and struck up cordial relations with communist revolutionary Ho Chi Minh. He was impressed by Ho's popularity and advised the Truman administration to allow the latter into a coalition government, but he was ignored. This unfortunate act set the stage for the future Vietnam War. However, in 1952, Bank was ordered to form the 10th Special Force Group, the first such unit in the army's history. Training was based on his OSS experience and called for intense language and cultural fluency along with unconventional training in sabotage and espionage. Bank retired in 1958 to San Clemente, California, but lax security at a local nuclear power plant led him to testify before Congress for improved measures. He died in Dana Point, California, on April 1, 2004, aged 101 years, renowned as the father of army special forces.

balance of the 75th Rangers remained in reserve for the balance of DESERT STORM and were not engaged. Subsequently, to underscore American resolve to defend Kuwait, Company C, 1/75, performed an unusual daylight airdrop into the desert in December 1991 that was carried on national television. The unprecedented maneuver undoubtedly gave pause to Saddam Hussein for any aggression he may have contemplated.

U.S. Army Special Forces (Green Berets)

As the war in Korea raged, the army decided to revitalize its clandestine capabilities and activated the 10th SFG (Airborne) at Fort Bragg, North Carolina, on June 19, 1952. Concurrently, the Psychological Warfare School was also established at the same time and locale as part of the former's overall mission. Commanded by Colonel Aaron Bank, a former Office of Strategic Services (OSS) operative, the 10th SFG was originally tasked with unconventional warfare in western Europe after it had presumably been overrun by Soviet forces. The new unit enjoyed an initial authorized strength of 2,300 officers, NCOs, and men, but mustered only 10 soldiers at its first assembly. Bank sought only the best-qualified, most experienced personnel, including former rangers, paratroopers, and OSS operatives like himself, from the ranks of junior officers and veteran NCOs. Drawing on his own clandestine experience, Bank not only instituted routine classes in infiltration, espionage, small-unit ambushes, and sabotage but also recruited language-proficient eastern European expatriates, now U.S. citizens, who could blend in with the native populations they assisted. There was also great emphasis placed on psychological warfare to win over indigenous populations, and all special force members had to be proficient in the cultural nuances of the region in which they were assigned. In this context, the new special force drew direct lessons learned from the "Jedburgh" teams sent into western Europe during World War II, and they were expected to raise partisan troops, conduct guerilla raids, and generally raise havoc in Soviet rear areas. In some respects, their physical training and abilities overlapped those of U.S. Army Rangers, but whereas rangers functioned as elite, light infantry assault troops, special forces would live behind enemy lines in a self-sustaining fashion for months at a time and filter into regions by means of land, sea,

U.S. Special Forces move past knocked out enemy tanks and equipment in Vietnam, 1969. (AP/Wide World Photos)

An American green beret lobs a grenade at a nearby North Vietnamese position near the Thuong Duc special forces camp, Vietnam, 1968. (AP/Wide World Photos)

or air. The training regimen that Bank devised was considered extremely demanding for its time and ensured high dropout rates for those seeking to volunteer. Once prospective recruits successfully completed parachute training, they could enter one of five career specialties—intelligence, weapons, demolitions, medicine, or communications—in all of which outstanding proficiency was required.

In June 1953, a violent uprising in East Germany was brutally crushed by Soviet forces, and the 10th SFG deployed to Bad Tölz, West Germany, to be better positioned should the Russians invade. These teams would be responsible for destroying bridges and railway tunnels to impair Soviet supply lines, so they carried special 60-pound atomic demolition charges capable of leveling any known structure. Gradually, the new 77th SFG (subsequently renamed the 7th) also began training at Fort Bragg, and in 1957 it was posted in Hawaii for eventual operations throughout Asia. In June 1956, the first men from the 14th Special Forces Operational Detachment, 1st SFG, arrived in South Vietnam to begin training the newly established South Vietnamese Army. This new 1st Observation Group suffered its first loss on October 21, 1957, of that year, whereby Captain Harry G. Cramer became the first American special forces soldier killed in action. However, a suspicious military establishment, which traditionally distrusted elite units, basically sidelined Bank's command until the ascension of President John F. Kennedy in 1961. Kennedy embraced new notions of "flexible response" for dealing with communist-inspired wars of national liberation around the globe, and he felt that unconventional forces were the key to victory. During his 1962 visit to Fort Bragg, Kennedy also authorized special forces to wear a green beret, one of the most iconic headgears in military history. The beret itself had been originally designed in 1953, but the army refused its use until the president intervened.

Furthermore, Kennedy expanded special forces by adding the 3rd (Africa), 6th (Middle East), and 8th (Latin America) Groups, each with it own geographic areas of responsibility. To these were eventually added the 11th and 12th Groups in the Army Reserve and the 19th and 20th Groups in the National Guard. Overall manpower likewise soared dramatically from 1,800 men to over 10,500 in this period. By the advent of Kennedy's assassination in November 1963, over 1,500 Green Berets were already operating throughout Southeast Asia, demonstrating in no uncertain terms American resolve to confront communist aggression.

The first special force teams deployed to Southeast Asia were connected with Project White Star, the first mobile training teams (MTTs) functioning in Laos. Typically, these men were entrusted with imparting counterinsurgency skills on local forces to combat communist Pathet Lao guerrillas in the north. Kennedy also enlarged the special forces commitment by dispatching the new 5th SFG to South Vietnam and expand counterinsurgency efforts by co-opting indigenous mountain people—Chams, Montagnards, and Nungs—into the war effort. Once trained, these fierce auxiliaries were expected to root out and destroy the communist infrastructure throughout South Vietnam's remote countryside, assisted by local defense forces. The 5th SFG established its headquarters at Nha Trang, where they remained until 1971. It proved a long and costly endeavor, conducted largely in the shadows, but throughout their tenure in Southeast Asia, Green Berets demonstrated their uncanny mastery of unconventional warfare. They deployed in small teams as part of the Civilian Irregular Defense Group (CIDG), which included South Vietnamese soldiers and local tribesmen instructed in counterinsurgency techniques. These joint forces were tasked with defending their own hamlets and villages, if occasionally stiffened by a small American detachment. Special forces were also heavily engaged in winning "hearts and minds" through extensive civil action projects whereby medical care to villagers and the construction of schools and hospitals received high priority. The Green Berets also enjoyed success against lightly armed Vietcong forces but proved ill equipped to tangle with regulars of the NVA, now increasingly operating on South Vietnamese soil. The Vietcong also traditionally resorted to terrorism to extract compliance from the peasantry, and the Green Berets, in concert with the CIA, enacted Operation PHOENIX to neutralize communist operatives living among the civilian populace and pay them back in kind. Throughout all these expedients, Green Berets gained a reputation as peerless exponents of unconventional warfare becoming the tip of the spear in the struggle against global communism.

Defining Activity

One of the most important camps established and defended by the Green Berets was Nam Dong, Thua Thien Province, near the Laotian border. This sizable position was situated between two mountain valleys and interdicted several infiltration routes. It also lent a measure of security to 5,000 Montagnard villagers residing nearby. Nam Dong was garrisoned by the A-726 Team of Green Berets, 381 CIDG soldiers, and 50 Nung (Chinese) mercenaries under Captain Roger H. C. Donlon. Army authorities evinced concerns that Nam Dong was exposed to enemy attack because of its remoteness, and plans were afoot to close it down. However, in the early morning hours of July 6, 1964, a fierce mortar barrage suddenly hit the campsite, then a Vietcong battalion attacked en masse, intending to overrun it. Donlon, severely wounded in the initial attack, remained active in the camp's defense and rushed

Captain Roger Donlon's heroic defense of Nam Dong resulted in the first Medal of Honor awarded during the Vietnam War. He is also the first Green Beret so honored. (U.S. Army Military History Institute)

about to threatened parts of its perimeter. For five hours, his Montagnards and Nungs fought back fiercely, killing scores of Vietcong before they breached the inner defenses. Donlon sustained a fourth wound by the time the attack finally abated, becoming the first special forces soldier awarded a Congressional Medal of Honor. Five other Special Forces men received Silver Stars. Having sustained heavy losses, the communists pulled back into the jungle, but Nam Dong was nonetheless abandoned on September 4, 1964, and its functions were transferred elsewhere. Another disaster occurred on the evening of February 7–8, 1968, when the special forces camp at Lang Vei was attacked by North Vietnamese forces employing light tanks and overrun. Of 24 Green Berets present, seven were killed, 13 were wounded, and three captured. All told, the introduction of regular NVA forces against lightly guarded border camps, however ably manned and defended, led to their gradual abandonment. Green Berets and their ethnic allies, however skillful at small-unit reconnaissance and ambush maneuvers, simply lacked the firepower, even when backed by gunships, to long contest heavily armed regular troops.

Once special forces began making inroads against the Vietcong, North Vietnam enlarged its influx of regular army units down the Ho Chi Minh Trail. To counter this sustained infiltration, Project Delta was born in 1965 as a countrywide strategic reconnaissance effort. This plan utilized six reconnaissance/hunter-killer teams of eight South Vietnamese Airborne Special Forces under two American officers that would infiltrate communist-held areas of the jungle, identify enemy units, snatch prisoners, call in artillery and air strikes, and then retire undetected. Concurrently, a "Roadrunner" platoon, dressed in enemy garb, traversed the roads in broad daylight, gathering intelligence and monitoring communist intentions. Delta's impressive success led to the creation of Projects Omega and Sigma, which applied similar operating principles to the southernmost regions of South Vietnam. By 1966, the CIDG forces had also become sufficiently adept in fighting skill to allow formation of mobile strike teams, or Mike Forces, to reinforce border camps under attack. Their finest hour occurred on March 9, 1966, when two NVA battalions attacked Camp A Shau. This was defended by Detachment A-102, 5th SFG, under Captain John D. Blair, who commanded his own 12 men and 200 South Vietnamese and militia troops. Just prior to the attack, a Mike Force consisting of 143 Nung fighters under Captain Tennis Carter arrived by helicopter as reinforcements. The communists struck throughout the predawn darkness, recklessly throwing themselves against the barbed wire defenses despite murderous defensive fire. At length, repeated air strikes by B-57 bombers drove the North

Vietnamese back into the jungle. However, Blair decided that his motley force were too outnumbered to survive, and he evacuated them by helicopter, covered by the Mike Force. Five Americans died along with 75 Nung; communist casualties were calculated in the range of 700 to 800 from a single regiment of 2,000. A victory of sorts, perhaps, but the North Vietnamese remained undaunted by the prospect of heavy losses.

One of the more significant subsets of the MACV was the highly classified SOG, which commenced in 1964. This unit was equipped for, among other things, fomenting political dissent within North Vietnam (an impossible task given the iron-fisted nature of the regime) and sowing psychological discord through clandestine radio stations. In this capacity, they reported accurate North Vietnamese casualty counts to the public and also exposed corrupt communist officials who, in several instances, were removed from power. However, the most significant directorate was Operation 35 (Op-35), the concerted effort by the 5th SFG to monitor and interdict traffic along the Ho Chi Minh Trail from Laos and Cambodia into South Vietnam. This campaign, known as Operation SHINING BRASS, was orchestrated by Colonel Arthur D. ("Bull") Simons, a veteran of the earlier White Star project in Laos. Reconnaissance members of special forces and indigenous allies, known as Spike teams, would deploy at critical road junctions by helicopter, then perform scouting mission for several days before being extracted through the jungle canopy. This was usually through use of the "Maquire rig," a special sling lifted from the ground by low-flying aircraft or helicopters. Such missions might be followed by the insertion of so-called Hatchet teams, consisting of Green Berets and Nung mercenaries, which eliminated small communist units as they moved along the trail. Larger targets might require an attack by a South Vietnamese ranger battalion that would be transported to the scene by the 281st Assault Helicopter Company. These actions were hardly intended to halt the flow of communist traffic southward but, rather, to rob the North Vietnamese of their sense of security in these neutral countries. Special forces and their local allies proved highly effective in this harassment role, but generally speaking, the campaign lacked sufficient resources and manpower to impact the course of the war. Still, for their size, they proved highly destructive and distracting to enemy forces, who deployed thousands of troops to deter their activities.

As the war in Southeast Asia ground on, the need for additional special forces troops became paramount, and recruitment efforts expanded. However, these newest additions lacked the intense indoctrination of the initial cadre and were concerned more with projecting an outsized "macho" image of Green Berets as killers rather than highly trained cultural adjuncts. Such grandstanding was appreciably resented by other members of the U.S. military who derided special forces as "snake eaters" and exhibited professional disdain for them. At a time when special operations greatly facilitated the containment of communist aggression, the very forces entrusted with their execution were viewed with increasing suspicion from the highest command centers. In May 1969, Colonel Robert B. Rheault was appointed commander of the 5th SFG, and two months later he was implicated in the murder of a captured North Vietnamese intelligence operative. General Creighton Abrams, the supreme American commander, had long questioned the value of special forces to the war effort, and he brooked no delay in having Rheault arrested and relieved of command for the alleged misdeed. All told, Rheault's case served as a convenient pretext for clamping down on the entire special forces mystique. The fresh-faced image of U.S. Special Forces was also compromised in public opinion and making it politically palatable for Abrams to begin easing them out of the picture altogether. In March 1971, final elements of the 5th SFG had

Arthur D. Simons (1918–1979). Arthur D. Simons was born in New York City on June 28, 1918, and raised in Missouri. After graduating from the University of Missouri in 1937, he was commissioned a second lieutenant through ROTC and served in the artillery. During most of World War II, his battery fought in the jungles of New Guinea, but Simons subsequently joined the new 6th Ranger Battalion under Lieutenant Colonel Henry Mucci and found his calling: unconventional warfare. Simons distinguished himself in several actions, especially the 1945 raid on Cabanatuan Prison to rescue survivors of the Bataan Death March, winning a Silver Star. He left the military after the war but rejoined in 1951 to serve as a ranger trainer at Fort Benning, Georgia. In 1958 he joined the 77th Special

U.S. Army Special Forces officer Colonel Arthur D. "Bull" Simons. A longtime special forces operator, Simons led the heroic Son Tay prison raid in 1970. (National Archives)

Force Group, rising to lieutenant colonel, and in 1961 he departed for Laos to command the "White Star" training team. A tour of Panama ensued from 1962 to 1964, after which Simons was reassigned to the highly classified Studies and Observations Group during the Vietnam War. In 1970, he was handpicked to lead Operation IVORY COAST, an ambitious prisoner-of-war rescue attempt against the Son Tay prison camp in North Vietnam. The mission liberated no captives but inflicted numerous casualties on the enemy and boosted the morale of American prisoners. For his effort, "Bull" Simons received the Distinguished Service Cross from President Richard M. Nixon. He died in Vail, Colorado, on May 21, 1979; a 12-foot-tall bronze statue of him was erected at the John F. Kennedy School of Special Warfare, Fort Bragg, North Carolina, in his honor.

transferred back to Fort Bragg, closing a controversial but illustrious chapter in Green Beret history. Small teams from the 1st SFG remained behind as advisers, but the heyday of special operations throughout Southeast Asia had passed.

One final activity of the Green Berets in Vietnam was among the most controversial. On May 9, 1970, American intelligence perceived a prisoner-of-war camp at Son Tay, 23 miles west of Hanoi and deep behind enemy lines. Consequently, the Joint Chiefs of Staff began formulating plans for a daring rescue operation under the name Operation KINGPIN. Task Force Ivory Coast, the intended strike force, consisted of 56 Green Berets from Fort Benning and Fort Bragg, all under the command of veteran hard-slogger Colonel Arthur D. "Bull" Simons. Preparations were extensive and included rehearsals on a life-size mock-up of the camp and its environs constructed at Eglin Air Force Base, Florida, that cost

$60,000. For three months, the team meticulously trained for their mission before deploying to Takhli, Thailand, on November 20, 1970. The following evening, the raiders helicoptered into Son Tay prison, hosing down enemy gun towers with a fusillade of 7.62-mm minigun fire. An HH-3 helicopter deliberately crash-landed inside the enemy compound, and the assault troops fanned out only to find that the entire complex had been abandoned for some time. The only real fighting occurred when another party of raiders mistakenly but wholeheartedly attacked a North Vietnamese barracks just south of the camp, killing scores of Chinese or Soviet-bloc military advisers. The troops, quite crestfallen, boarded their helicopters safely egressed back to Thailand; one American had been injured in the crash landing. The Son Tay raid may have been thwarted in its objective, but it certainly put the North Vietnamese on notice that Americans could mount attacks at virtually any time or place of their choosing. Moreover, they would incur great risks to secure the welfare of any captive troops. The communists responded by gathering up all American prisoners from dispersed camps and concentrating them at secure holding facilities in Hanoi.

For the Green Berets, the war in Southeast Asia symbolically ended on March 5, 1971, when the 5th SFG completed its redeployed to Fort Bragg. In many significant respects, Vietnam was a catalyst for U.S. Army Special Forces, and it went a long way to both define and refine the organizations and doctrines extant. The strategic and long-range reconnaissance techniques they perfected were subsequently incorporated in a variety of regular and special operations doctrines that continue to present times. Vietnam also firmly cemented the concept of special forces operations as a part of U.S. global policies, especially with respect to developing nations. By the end of the war, Green Berets of the 5th SFG had received no fewer than 17 Congressional Medals of Honor, making them the most highly decorated unit of its size from that struggle. They were also the recipients of one Distinguished Service Medal, 60 Distinguished Service Crosses, 814 Silver Stars, 13,234 Bronze Stars, 235 Legions of Merit, 232 Soldier's Medals, 6,908 Army Commendation Medals, and 2,658 Purple Hearts. Their heroic sacrifices were not lost on the American people, and seldom in American history has a military unit become more inculcated by popular culture as the Green Berets. Their legendary activities inspired a best-selling fictional book, *The Green Berets*, by Robin Moore; the hit-single "Ballad of the Green Berets" by Barry Sadler; the movie *The Green Berets* produced by and starring John Wayne; and a comic strip of the same name drawn by cartoonist Joe Kubert. They were possibly the only segment of the American military to enjoy public recognition in the wake of an otherwise unpopular conflict.

Following the drawdown in Southeast Asia, the military establishment experienced a spate of fiscal retrenchment and cutbacks. For special forces, this entailed disbandment of the 1st, 3rd, 6th, and 8th SFGs as the army shelved counterinsurgency warfare and reverted back to conventional tactics intended to defeat the Red Army in western Europe. The election of Ronald Reagan as president in 1980, fortunately, led to an overall resurgence of military spending and renewed emphasis on special operations. Special forces were among the foremost beneficiaries of this resurgence given the administration's determination to thwart communist-inspired insurgencies throughout Latin and Central America. As early as October 1967, Green Berets of the 8th SFG made their presence felt in Bolivia, where they trained and assisted the local Army Ranger battalion to track down and kill the bloodthirsty insurgent Che Guevara. Unlike distant Vietnam, here was a Soviet-supplied and -orchestrated war of subversion in America's own backyard, and Reagan responded with an appropriate urgency. MTTs were dispatched to perform instruction duties in Honduras and El Salvador, and special counterinsurgency battalions were raised locally and deployed against particularly brutal gangs of Marxist guerillas. The troops also forced insurgents of the Farabundo Marti National Liberation Front in El Salvador to sign a cease-fire with the government in 1992. Green Berets were concurrently dispatched to Colombia throughout the 1980s to confront major drug trafficking and terrorist problems, and these teams raised and trained three counternarcotics battalions to oppose well-armed drug lords. These activities are still ongoing and, while enjoying impressive success, have yet to completely root out the problem. Concurrently, Green Berets enjoyed an extension of qualification courses to ensure that only the finest personnel gained admittance, and as of June 1983, they were allowed to wear a special forces tab on their uniforms as a mark of professional pride. Moreover, special forces became a separate and distinct career field within the military as of October 1984, and on April 9, 1987, a unique Special Force Branch was established for officers.

On December 20, 1989, Green Berets were prevalent throughout Operation JUST CAUSE, the overthrow of Panamanian dictator Manuel Noriega, and they worked in small hand-picked units to defeat the PDF. In one instance, a team of Green Berets turned back an entire PDF convoy attempting to cross the Pacora River Bridge with just a handful of rockets. These teams subsequently raided command-and-control centers and accepted the surrender of enemy forces in more distant regions of the country. In 1990, Green Berets were also highly active throughout Operation DESERT SHIELD against Iraqi dictator Saddam Hussein. Teams deployed deep inside Kuwait and Iraq months before the coalition campaign began, conducted highly classified reconnaissance missions over several months, and relayed invaluable military intelligence to coalition leaders. They also rescued downed pilots and trained local Kuwaiti forces in the skills of guerrilla warfare. However, the overwhelming bulk of their activities remains a closely guarded secret. No fewer than 109 special forces teams were active throughout Operation DESERT STORM, January/February 1991, and they were among the first coalition units to enter newly liberated Kuwait City.

82nd Airborne Division (All Americans)

The 82nd Airborne Division, having returned in triumph from Europe, deployed back to Fort Bragg, North Carolina, on January 19, 1946. In light of the rapidly unfolding Cold War with the Soviet Union, it was retained as a strategic rapid-deployment reserve force, and in 1948 it finally joined the standing military establishment as part of the regular army. As such, it underwent continual training and tested new transport aircraft possessing greater range and troop-carrying capacities. With the possibility of all-out war against the Soviets looming, the 82nd Airborne was not committed to combat operations in Korea and remained at home. The division underwent a major transformation once it adopted the new Pentomic structure and was reorganized into five self-sufficient airborne groups, better suited for fighting in a nuclear environment. In 1964, the division next reverted to the new ROAD (Reorganization Objective Army Division) organization of three infantry brigades, each consisting of three battalions and an artillery brigade of three batteries. The "All Americans" also demonstrated tactical flexibility by conducting training exercises in varied environments throughout Alaska, Panama, and the Far East. In 1965, the 82nd Airborne

Division was in the vanguard of U.S. foreign policy when it deployed to the violence-wracked Dominican Republic as part of Operation POWERPACK. Here the 3rd Brigade, reinforced by the 1st Battalion, 508th Parachute Infantry, secured the Duarte Bridge over the Ozama River and linked up with marines in Santo Domingo to cordon off rebel forces. By June 17, 1965, the paratroopers mopped up any remaining insurgents after two days of heavy fighting. With order restored to the island, divisional elements began shipping back to Fort Bragg, with the final units arriving in September 1966. Other noncombat functions include two small deployments to Congo in 1964 and 1967 and the suppression of civil unrest in Detroit and Washington, D.C., in 1967 and 1968.

Unlike Navy SEALS, U.S. Army special forces worked closely with their South Vietnamese counterparts. Here they are parachuting into the mountainous Central Highlands region to observe Communist troop movements. (AP/Wide World Photos)

In February 1968, the 82nd Airborne Division resumed direct combat operations when the 3rd Brigade was sent to South Vietnam in the wake of the bloody Tet Offensive. Operation ALL AMERICAN resulted in paratroopers deploying to Chu Lai and Phu Bai, and over the next few months, they fought alongside the 101st Airborne Division during Operation CARENTAN 1. Over the next 22 months, the 3rd Brigade distinguished itself during intense combat operations along Highway 1, up the Song Bo River to Hue and Saigon. The paratroopers waged their last battle during Operation YORKTOWN VICTOR in September 1969, then deployed back to Fort Bragg on December 12, 1969, after 22 months overseas and sustaining 227 killed and 1,009 wounded. Back home, the 82nd Airborne was repeatedly placed on full alert throughout the 1970s because of successive international crises, and parts of the unit deployed abroad for war games held in South Korea, Turkey, and Greece. A small antitank detachment armed with the new TOW missile, a tube-launched, optically guided antitank weapon, also returned to South Vietnam in the spring of 1972 to counter the communist Easter Offensive there. Members of the 82nd Airborne Division were also among the first U.S. Army troops deployed to the Sinai region between Egypt and Israel as part of the United Nations Multinational Force and Observers peacekeeping mission. In 1979, the division went on alert for a possible rescue attempt of American hostages in Tehran, Iran. This mission was subsequently assigned to Delta Force and the rangers, but around this time, the United States also created a new strategic entity, the Rapid Deployment Force. This consisted of elite mobile units, like the 82nd Airborne Division, that could be deployed en mass to trouble spots worldwide in a matter of hours.

On October 25, 1983, the 82nd Airborne Division resumed combat operations during Operation URGENT FURY on the Caribbean island of Grenada. After a 17-hour warning notice,

C-141 Starlifters conveyed the 2nd Battalion, 325th Airborne Infantry Regiment, to the Point Salinas airfield, then in the hands of U.S. Army rangers, then pressed inland to engage fleeing members of the People's Revolutionary Army and Cuban forces. They were soon after joined by the 1st Battalions, 505th and 508th Parachute Infantry Regiments, who likewise arrived by jet. After rescuing American students on the Lance aux Epines peninsula, the paratroopers concluded their participation by assisting in the capture of General Hudson Austin, commander of the People's Revolutionary Army. Grenada was declared secure shortly afterward and the division redeployed back to Fort Bragg on December 12, 1983. Communist activities in Central America also resulted in the 1st Battalion, 504th Parachute Infantry, being landed in Honduras as part of Operation GOLDEN PHEASANT, while the 2nd Battalion parachuted in a day later. Their presence was calculated to deter aggression from communist Sandinista forces in Nicaragua who had made previous incursions into Honduran territory. On December 20, 1989, 2,200 members of the 82nd Airborne Division conducted its first combat airdrop since World War II during Operation JUST CAUSE, aimed at restoring the duly elected government in Panama. The 1st Brigade Task Force (1st and 2nd Battalions, 504th Parachute Infantries) under Major General James Johnson airlifted in and helped subdue Forts Cimmarron, Tinajitas, and Panama Viejo amidst light resistance. The paratroopers were joined on the ground by the 3rd Battalion, already deployed there, and follow-on air assaults were executed against targets in Panama City, including the home of dictator Manuel Noriega. All armed opposition collapsed quickly, and the 82nd Airborne members returned home by January 12, 1990.

Defining Activity

The final Cold War deployment of the "All Americans" occurred shortly after the August 2, 1990, invasion of Kuwait by Iraqi dictator Saddam Hussein. Six days later, elements of the 82nd Airborne Division's 2nd Brigade under Major General James Johnson were rushed to Saudi Arabia as part of Operation DESERT SHIELD, and it guarded the border with M551 Sheridan light tanks, AH-64 Apache helicopters, and batteries of TOW missiles. Incredibly, this movement was completed only 31 hours after receiving the initial alert. Iraqi armored forces, massed just over the line, never tested their resolve. Within weeks, the entire division deployed en masse as part of a large coalition army. Operation DESERT STORM commenced on January 16, 1991, with a massive aerial interdiction campaign against Iraqi defenses, and the ground offensive was launched on February 24, 1991. At this time, the 82nd Airborne Division occupied the allied left flank and rode trucks deep into Iraqi territory. A 2nd Brigade Task Force also found itself attached to the French 6th Light Armored Division as it advanced and helped secure thousands of Iraqi prisoners in only 100 hours of combat. With Kuwait liberated, the paratroopers returned to Fort Bragg by April 1991 to await their next overseas assignment.

101st Airborne Division (Screaming Eagles)

Following its deactivation at the end of World War II, the 101st Airborne Division was repeatedly reactivated at Camp Breckinridge, Kentucky, as a training unit in 1948, 1950, and 1954. After spending two years at Fort Jackson, South Carolina, it finally transferred to Fort Campbell, Kentucky, for eventual organization as a combat formation in

At Little Rock, Arkansas, in 1957, Screaming Eagles of the 101st Airborne Division enforce President Eisenhower's desegregation order at bayonet's point. (Library of Congress)

September 1956. The following year, it was drastically reorganized along new Pentomic lines into five independent battle groups that were substituted for regiments and battalions. The unit conducted the usual spate of training exercises until the fall of 1957, when the 101st Airborne Division was called in to enforce civil rights actions at Little Rock, Arkansas. There, in a high-profile exercise meant to underscore President Eisenhower's determination to end segregation, members escorted nine African American schoolchildren into newly desegregated Central High School. The division subsequently assumed a prominent role within the new Strategic Army Corps, a large operational reserve as the Cold War unfolded.

Defining Activity

The 101st Airborne resumed combat operations in 1965 once the 1st Brigade arrived in South Vietnam, and the rest of the formation joined it there in 1967. The "Screaming Eagles" fought for seven years and participated in no fewer than 15 campaigns, mostly in the hotly contested I Corps Tactical Zone, just south of the Demilitarized Zone (DMZ). It was concerned mainly with interdicting communist infiltration routes through Laos and the A Shau Valley, a daunting proposition considering the foreboding terrain and fanatical opposition. In August 1968, the Screaming Eagles were completely reorganized as a new Airmobile Division employing massed helicopters for the vertical envelopment of enemy forces, and they lost their paratrooper status. Thus augmented, the division performed well during the 1968 Tet Offensive and Counteroffensive during which their 3rd Brigade ("Rakkasans") distinguished themselves in heavy fighting at Hill 932, the infamous

"Hamburger Hill," which fell after 10 days of incessant combat. In July 1970, this same unit fought well at the siege of Firebase Ripcord, inflicting heavy losses on Vietnamese units at a cost of 250 members killed. The following year, the Screaming Eagles supported Operation LAM SON 719, a large South Vietnamese incursion into neighboring Laos. Having accruing a distinguished combat record, the 101st Airborne Division became the last American combat unit to depart in 1972. It had sustained 4,011 killed and 18,259 wounded, twice as many casualties as in all of World War II, but no fewer than 17 of its soldiers received Congressional Medals of Honor.

In February 1974, the Airmobile Badge became an authorized part of the 101st Airborne's uniform. This was subsequently modified to the Air Assault Badge, and by October 1978, the formation was officially redesignated the 101st Airborne Division (Air Assault). The division was then tapped to serve in the Sinai Desert as part of an international peacekeeping force, commencing in March 1982. On December 12, 1985, a chartered commercial airliner connected to this duty crashed near Gander, Newfoundland, killing all 248 paratroopers on board. The 101st Airborne Division next was deployed in harm's way during Operation DESERT SHIELD, August 1990–January 1991, becoming one of the first units deployed to Saudi Arabia to prevent Iraqi attacks on that oil-rich kingdom. On January 17, 1991, two flights of AH-64 Apache helicopters attached to the division fired the opening shots of Operation DESERT STORM, knocking out an enemy early-warning radar site. Next, from its position on the coalition army's left flank, helicopter-borne infantry and equipment of the 1st Brigade Task Force under Colonel James T. Hill made a deep aerial penetration of Iraqi territory. This was the largest operation of its kind in military history with over 2,000 men, 50 vehicles, artillery pieces, and tons of fuel and ammunition delivered intact and 50 miles behind enemy lines. These troops established Forward Operating Base Cobra, while land vehicles conveyed an additional 2,000 men into Iraqi territory on Kuwait's western flank. After 100 hours of ground fighting, a cease-fire was declared; five Screaming Eagles had died in combat. The entire division returned to Fort Campbell by May 1, 1991, and awaited its next overseas assignment.

173rd Airborne Brigade (Sky Soldiers)

The first incarnation of the 173rd Infantry Brigade occurred in 1915, when it was organized as part of the 87th Infantry Division. It ventured to western Europe in September 1918, but arrived too late for combat and spent several months providing laborers and reinforcements for other units. The brigade disbanded in 1919, then was reconstituted as the headquarters company of the 173rd Infantry Brigade in 1921. During World War II, the unit was initially redesignated the 87th Reconnaissance Troop in December 1942, then reactivated as a brigade, and it saw fighting in central France, the Rhineland, and the Ardennes. In the Pacific, the 503rd Parachute Regimental Combat Team, a unit with future ties to the brigade, greatly distinguished itself during the airborne assault on Corregidor Island on February 16, 1945. After the war, brigade remnants assumed reserve status as a troop with the 87th Infantry Division until another demobilization on December 1, 1951. The 173rd Airborne Brigade was activated on March 26, 1963, under the army's new ROAD scheme, which reintroduced brigade-sized formations within divisional structures. At that time, it was singled out to serve as a separate brigade and a special airborne task force equipped to deploy and fight independently. It was therefore the only formation of its kind to have permanently assigned artillery and support units. The 173rd Airborne Brigade gradually assembled on Okinawa under Brigadier General Ellis W. Williamson, where it functioned as a quick-reaction force for the entire Pacific region. Williamson intensely trained his unit for mass parachute deployments, and they acquired the nickname "Sky Soldiers" from the Taiwanese paratroopers they trained with. Like all paratroopers, the brigade openly touted itself as one of the toughest—if not the toughest, unit in the region—and subsequent actions bore this out.

In May 1965, the 173rd Airborne Brigade, 3,000 men strong, became the first major American combat unit deployed to South Vietnam. It was posted with the II Corps Tactical Zone, serving six years there with distinction. It also became the first unit to introduce small-unit LRRPs behind Vietcong lines and performed aggressively against all communist units it encountered. The brigade partook of Operation HUMP on November 8, 1965, by sweeping through the region north of Bien Hoa near Saigon where a company was heavily ambushed, losing 48 soldiers killed. The following year, it fought in Operation CRIMP, designed to eliminate communists from the Cu Chi tunnel system, and later that same year, it participated in Operation ATTLEBORO, a large search-and-destroy mission north of the capital region. On February 22, 1967, the brigade made history during Operation JUNCTION CITY by performing the Vietnam War's sole combat parachute jump into Tay Ninh Province. Hard fighting there helped eliminate the 9th Vietcong Division as a fighting force.

Defining Activity

By the summer of 1967, the scene of fighting shifted to the Central Highlands region of Kontum Province, where engagements with the People's Army of North Vietnam (PAVN) were increasingly common. On June 17, the 173rd Airborne Brigade under Brigadier General John R. Deane committed two battalions on a jungle sweep through to the Dak To area as part of Operation GREELEY. Three days later, Alpha Company, 503rd Airborne Infantry, was decimated in a heavy ambush near Hill 1338, with 76 killed and 23 wounded. Other units bolstered the 173rd Airborne Brigade in consequence, while the communists built up their own troop strength to four infantry regiments and one artillery regiment, totaling 6,000 men. The battle for Dak To commenced once the 4th Battalion, 173rd Airborne Brigade, stormed onto Hill 823 under heavy fire, at which point Task Force Black fanned out into the wilderness to hunt down enemy formations. On November 11, 1967, they were heavily ambushed, with 20 killed and 154 wounded, before being relieved. Shortly after, the 2nd Battalion, 503rd Airborne Infantry, attacked Hill 875, only to receive heavy artillery and rocket fire as communist infantry moved in from behind to strike their rear. Reinforcements were summoned, and several battalions of the 503rd charged ploughed forward in the face of stiff resistance, but the hill crest did not fall until November 23, long after the communists had fled. Severe fighting here cost the 173rd Airborne Brigade 340 casualties, and, though defeated in these large engagements, the North Vietnamese remained full of fight.

The 173rd continued fighting in the north until it transferred to An Khe and Bong Son in 1968 to rest and refit. Little action ensued, but the unit did execute an amphibious assault along the Bong Song River—the first by a parachute unit in this war. In April 1969, the brigade transferred to Binh Dinh Province, remaining in place until August 1971. The "Sky Soldiers" then redeployed back to Fort Campbell, Kentucky, representing the first time it served in the United States at brigade strength since 1942. Throughout its six-year tenure in South Vietnam, the173rd Airborne Brigade reaped 14 campaign streamers, four unit citations, and a Presidential Unit Citation (PUC), while individual paratroopers collected 13 Medals of Honor, 32 Distinguished Service Crosses, 1,736 Silver Crosses, and over 6,000 Purple Hearts. The toll for this achievement came to 1,533 combat deaths and over 6,000 wounded. After Vietnam, the United States ended the military draft and resorted to a more traditional all-volunteer force. At that time, military authorities decided to rebuild the 101st Airborne Division, so the 173rd Airborne Brigade was deactivated on January 14, 1972, and transferred to the Screaming Eagles as their 3rd Brigade.

187th Infantry Regiment (Rakkasans)

The 187th Glider Infantry Regiment arose at Camp Mackall, North Carolina, on February 25, 1943. It deployed to the Pacific in March 1944 as part of the 11th Airborne Division and spent an additional six months training on New Guinea before finally seeing combat in the Philippines. It fought exceedingly well during the Leyte and Luzon campaigns, winning a PUC for bravery under fire. In September 1945, the 187th Glider Infantry was handpicked by General Douglas A. MacArthur to become one of the first Allied units landed in Japan for occupation duties. It was during this service that they obtained the nickname "Rakkasans" (Japanese slang for "falling down umbrella," or parachute), which has served as a point of pride ever since. The 187th transferred back to Camp Campbell, Kentucky, in 1949, where it was redesignated an airborne infantry regiment and reattached to the 11th Airborne Division. The following year, it participated in Operation SWARMER, the largest peacetime airborne maneuver up to that point, and a fine performance led to its selection to head up an airborne force in Korea. In June 1950, the 187th shipped to the theater as a pioneering Airborne Regiment Combat Team under Colonel Frank S. Bowen Jr. The Rakkasans lived up to their reputation as an elite fighting unit by wracking up another PUC in six grueling campaigns, including the landing at Inchon, and the war's first parachute jump over Sukchon-Sunchon, north of Pyongyang, North Korea, on October 20, 1950. Here they caught the North Korean 239th Regiment in a pincer between themselves and the 27th British Commonwealth Brigade, killing 805 enemy troops and capturing 681; Rakkasan losses were 66 killed and wounded. On March 23, 1951, the 187th made the second and final combat jump of the war by parachuting over Munsan-ni to cut off fleeing Chinese communist units. The 187th then rotated to Japan as a strategic reserve and returned to Korea to help suppress a prisoner uprising at the Koje-do prisoner-of-war camp in June 1952. The unit rotated back to Fort Campbell by way of Fort Bragg in 1956, there to serve as the combat test group of the newly resurrected 101st Airborne Division. It also adopted the new Pentomic organization of five independent battle groups to facilitate combat in a nuclear environment. The 187th Airborne Infantry briefly rejoined the 11th Airborne Division in 1958 as part of peacekeeping forces sent to Lebanon, and in 1963 it helped develop the army's new airmobile assault concept using massed helicopters. The following year, they resumed their assignment back with the 101st Airborne Division.

Defining Activity

A major turning point in the Rakkasans' history occurred in December 1967, when the 3rd Battalion arrived in South Vietnam as part of the 3rd Brigade, 101st Airborne Division.

Over the next four years, the unit distinguished itself in combat across 12 major campaigns and demonstrated its mastery of air assault and search-and-destroy missions. Its most famous engagement was the struggle for Hill 973 in the A Shau Valley on May 10, 1969, infamously known as "Hamburger Hill." Here the 3rd Battalion, 187th Infantry Regiment, was airlifted into Dong Ap Bia as part of Operation APACHE SNOW. The A Shau Valley, near the Laotian border, sat astride a major communist infiltration route, and the 29th Regiment, NVA, determined to make a stand. A and B Companies advanced under Lieutenant Colonel Weldon Honeycutt, and over a 10-day period, the Rakkasans committed four frontal assaults up the steep slopes. The well-entrenched NVA resisted from their intricate series of bunkers, spider holes, and other interlocking defenses, defying every attempt to dislodge them. Despite incessant close air support and artillery fire, the fight degenerated into an infantryman's battle at close range and was settled with grenades and rifle fire. Progress remained slow and costly, and it was not until the arrival of the 2nd Battalion, 506th Airborne Infantry, that the Americans forced carried the top of the ridge. Victory here cost them 56 dead and 420 wounded to a communist tally of 700 known killed. However, the hard-won position was abandoned only two days later and subsequently reoccupied by the North Vietnamese, occasioning considerable outcry in the United States. In 1971, the Rakkasans came home to Fort Campbell, having accrued two additional PUCs and two Valorous Unit Awards and emerging as the Vietnam conflict's most highly decorated airborne battalion.

The 187th Airborne Infantry functioned as the 3rd Brigade, 101st Airborne Division, over the next 19 years, and on November 21, 1984, a total of five battalions were activated. This number was reduced again to three in 1987, and in August 1990 it participated in Operation DESERT SHIELD against Iraq. On February 20–21, 1991, as part of Operation DESERT STORM, two companies of the 1st Battalion stormed Objective Weber, seizing 484 Iraqi captives. Then, on February 25, 1991—the 48th anniversary of the regiment's founding—the unit performed the largest air assault in military history as helicopters carried men and equipment 175 miles behind Iraqi lines and deposited them at key blocking points along the Euphrates River valley. This action isolated several units of Saddam Hussein's Republican Guards and was a key factor in the overwhelming land victory that followed. By the time a cease-fire was arranged, the Rakkasans stood only 150 miles from the capital of Baghdad, the closest that any coalition unit would come.

10th Mountain Division

The U.S. Army's only division-level light infantry force was quiescent for most of the Cold War period. Following its disbandment on November 30, 1945, the unit was reactivated at Fort Riley, Kansas, on July 1, 1948, as the 10th Training Division. As such, the elite "mountain tab" was removed, and it assumed the task of instructing large numbers of recruits destined for other formations. The pace of instruction accelerated with the advent of war in Korea, and between 1948 and 1953, the 10th Training Division processed 123,000 men. Things changed in January 1954, when the secretary of the army declared that the 10th Training Division would be reconfigured as a regular infantry division and deployed to Europe as part of the North Atlantic Treaty Organization (NATO). After receiving equipment from the 37th Infantry Division, the 10th Infantry Division was reactivated and assigned to replace the 1st Infantry Division at Würzburg, West Germany. Here it occupied a 75-mile arc stretching from Frankfurt to Nuremburg, the strategic center of NATO's main defense line. At this time, it mustered nine infantry battalions, four artillery battalions, and one tank battalion. The 10th Infantry Division remained in place until 1958, when it was replaced in turn by the 3rd Infantry Division; and sent to Fort Benning, Georgia; where it was again deactivated on June 14, 1958.

The 10th Mountain Division (Light Infantry) was finally resurrected at Fort Drum, New York, on February 13, 1985, being the first formation of its kind since 1945 and also the first such formation stationed in the Northeast since World War II. This latest incarnation configured it as an extremely mobile light infantry force capable of rapid deployment anywhere in the world. For this reason, much of its equipment was of lighter weight than standard designs to accentuate tactical mobility. Moreover, the new force was grouped around two self-sustaining brigades instead of regiments and was also nominally assigned to administer the National Guard's 27th Infantry Brigade. A new insignia, denoting its revitalized elite status, was also issued. During Operation DESERT SHIELD in 1990, the 10th Mountain Division contributed 1,200 soldiers of the 548th Supply and Services Battalion in support of the 24th Mechanized Infantry Division in Kuwait. These were active during Operation DESERT STORM, January–February 1991, and then all soldiers had returned back to Fort Drum by June of that year. The 10th Mountain Division's first mass deployment came in the wake of Hurricane Andrew, which slammed into southern Florida on August 24, 1992, causing extensive damage and loss of life. Task Force Mountain arrived at the scene on September 27, 1992, to oversee the erection of relief camps ands distribution of food, clothing, and medical supplies to the survivors. The 6,000 soldiers engaged completed their assignment and returned to Fort Drum as of October 1992 with much gratitude from the local inhabitants.

Central Intelligence Agency

The highly successful OSS did not long survive the end of World War II, and its intelligence-gathering functions were handed off to the State Department, while paramilitary activities were absorbed by several military agencies. However, the exigencies of Cold War politics prompted the Truman administration to pass the National Security Act of 1947, which created a new clandestine body, the Central Intelligence Agency, famously known by its abbreviations, CIA. In addition to the usual authorization surrounding spying and espionage, this entity possessed a Special Activities Division (SAD) charged with executing "direct-action" paramilitary missions much in the same manner as the old OSS operational groups. They are also tasked with conducting covert activities relative to political influence, psychological warfare, and training armed ethnic operatives to function behind enemy lines. Given the sensitivity of these missions, the CIA recruits SAD personnel only from former special forces members who possess both the physical skills and the mental aptitude to execute them. In time, such operations became standard fixtures in the ongoing struggle against Soviet and Chinese communism.

The first known CIA covert mission to arm ethnic paramilitaries occurred in 1950, when teams of agents were dispatched to Tibet, recently occupied by communist China. Selected Tibetan men were then secreted out of the country to receive special commando-style training in the United States. On returning home, they began recruiting fellow dissidents and began training a national resistance to Chinese rule. CIA operatives were also responsible for safely spiriting the 14th Dalai Lama out of the country to India, rescuing him from certain execution. American assistance to Tibetan guerillas persisted until 1972, when the United States and China finally normalized relations, and such activity became diplomatically unfeasible. The CIA was also active during the Korean War, 1950–1953, and sponsored numerous naval operations and raids behind communist lines. From their base on Yong Do Island, American-trained South Korean operatives would ingress North Korea for purposes of espionage, ambushes, assassinations, and the destruction of bridges, tunnels, and other transportation targets. Other teams assisted maritime operations conducted by indigenous surrogates along the North Korean coast, including prisoner rescues in the interior. These operations fell under the collective purview of the Joint Advisory Commission, Korea, which was administered by the CIA. Other operatives went ashore prior to the landings at Inchon in September 1950 to provide timely intelligence on communist defenses. Overall, the experience in Korea cut an operational template that both the CIA and American special followed in subsequent conflicts throughout Asia and elsewhere. This was especially true if the recruitment of local surrogate forces were in the offing.

Defining Activity

It is a curious fact that in 1945, OSS operatives parachuted into French Indochina (Vietnam) to provide aid and assistance to communist guerillas under Ho Chi Minh. Once the Japanese had surrendered, Ho attempted to maintain good relations with the United States, but that became impossible in light of Cold War tensions with the Soviet Union. In 1961, the Americans returned to the region to halt communist attempts to unite North and South Vietnam by subversion and force of arms. By now, the North Vietnamese had established an extensive network of spies, saboteurs, assassins, and propagandists throughout South Vietnam and virtually every level of political life. Members of the National Liberation Front, or Vietcong, were notorious for assassinating uncooperative tribal chiefs and civilian authorities as well as waging a terror campaign against innocent civilians. To obviate their plight, Project Phoenix was born, being a joint CIA/special force "pacification" mission to identify and neutralize known communist Vietcong sympathizers through either apprehension or elimination. It drew its name from the Phung Hoang, the mythical Vietnamese bird associated with prosperity and good luck. Between 1969 and 1971, U.S. and South Vietnamese agents seized 81,470 suspected Vietcong operatives, of which 26,369 were subsequently killed. This activity, along with devastating losses suffered during the 1968 Tet Offensive, devastated the Vietcong's political base and its ability to wage guerilla warfare. One unsavory consequence of the Phoenix program was a demand by North Vietnamese authorities that Vietcong units maintain a quota of killing 400 South Vietnamese authorities per month, thereby ratcheting up the terror campaign. Moreover, given the rising impotency of the Vietcong for sustained military action, more and more regular units of the PAVN were shipped south to confront the Americans, usually with staggering losses to the latter. The CIA was also directly involved with the top-secret Studies and Observations Group (SOG) which orchestrated highly classified and diplomatically sensitive reconnaissance missions into neighboring Laos and Cambodia. Paramilitary CIA officers also trained, equipped, and led Laotian Hmong tribesmen to detect North Vietnamese and Pathet Lao (communist) assets in their country and then attack them. This ground effort was backed by Air America, a CIA-operated airline that handled all logistics, combat, and search-and-rescue functions in that region. These activities remain shrouded in secrecy and are generally not well known but are nonetheless regarded as strikingly successful, especially in the utilization of employing indigenous forces for intelligence gathering and interdiction purposes. Critics of the Phoenix program countered that the communist infrastructure at the time was simply too entrenched to be completely neutralized and that, whatever success the CIA and special forces achieved, it was essentially a case of too little and too late. There is truth behind both assertions.

As communist-inspired "national wars of liberation" spread their tentacles into Central and Latin America, CIA special activity personnel were frequently at the forefront of arranging their containment. Operating in tandem with soldiers of the 8th SFG, they actively identified, tracked, and eliminated known guerillas and subversives, usually in concert with local military establishments. The best-known example was Bolivia, long beset by a terrorist movement headed by bloody Argentine radical Ernesto "Che" Guevara. By the mid-1960s, the SAD teams and special forces were in theater and training Bolivian special forces. Their success can be gauged by the arrest and execution of Guevara on October 9, 1967. A thornier task was the case of Nicaragua, whose conservative regime had been overthrown by a bloody and violent communist dictatorship in 1979. SAD teams were dispatched to the region and began arming anticommunist freedom fighters, or contras, to oppose their oppressors by force. Operating in small teams from neighboring Costa Rica and Honduras, the contras managed, against great odds, to fight the Soviet-trained and Cuban-equipped Sandinistas to a draw, at which point war-weary electorate tossed the communists from power in a 1990 national election. Moreover, success was achieved only by skirting various shortsighted U.S. laws, such as the 1983 Boland Amendment, which forbade any form of military intervention in the region. Throughout the Cold War, the CIA remained on the cutting edge of anticommunist efforts, and, collectively, their efforts bore conspicuous roles in the ultimate overthrow of the Soviet Union in 1991.

Marine Corps

Force Reconnaissance Companies and Battalions

All the Amphibious Reconnaissance Battalions were demobilized in the wake of World War II, and their personnel was reabsorbed into line units or newly established division reconnaissance companies. During the interwar period, the Marine Corps consequently lacked Fleet Marine Force reconnaissance capabilities, as these were executed by whatever smaller units were on hand. Designated reconnaissance formations were not resurrected on a large scale until the Korean War, and in December 1950, the 2nd Amphibian Recon Battalion arose at Camp Lejeune, North Carolina. However, the bulk of reconnaissance missions was still handled by special units attached to various divisions. These performed extremely valuable services by scouting ahead of the main landing force at Inchon in September 1950, and the time-sensitive intelligence they relayed enhanced operational planning and saved scores of lives. After the war concluded in 1953, most battalion-level reconnaissance units were again disbanded, although many company-sized formations carried on as separate entities.

In 1950, the 1st Marine Division Reconnaissance Company was temporarily assigned to the 1st Marine Brigade, and in this capacity it performed scouting activities throughout the defense of the Pusan Perimeter, July–August 1950. On August 12–16, 1950, marines from the 1st Recon Company were tapped to conduct seven raids into North Korea from the troop destroyer USS *Horace A. Bass*, accompanied by 25 Underwater Demolition Team (UDT) frogmen. These frequented the Posung-Myon region and destroyed three tunnels and two bridges without a single loss. In September, the company accompanied the 1st Marine Division ashore at Inchon, after which it was reorganized into a motorized unit of four jeep teams. They subsequently performed deep reconnaissance patrols from Wonsan on the east coast of Korea and as far north as Hungnam, 40 miles distant. In January 1951, the company helped suppress communist guerilla activities in the Andong area and also directed air strikes down on enemy cavalry and infantry patrols.

After the Korean War subsided, the 1st Reconnaissance Battalion returned to Camp Pendleton, California, where it remained until the Cuban missile crisis of 1962. As conflict with the Soviet Union seemed pending, it deployed to Guantanamo Naval Base, Cuba, in the event of an American invasion. When the crisis subsided, the unit returned to California. The 1st Battalion next saw service in the I Corps Tactical Zone of South Vietnam in June 1966, where it conducted extensive scouting missions in the vicinity of Tam Ky and Hiep Duc as part of Operation KANSAS. On June 13, six marine teams were helicoptered into various positioning sites, being tasked with reporting on enemy movements and, if possible, calling in air strikes or artillery fire to demolish them. As these bombardments occurred, a large Vietcong force attacked the team headed by Staff Sergeant James L. Howard, who radioed for an immediate extraction. This proved impossible because of enemy ground fire, so Howard's men dug in and held their ground for a full day until the 1st Battalion, 5th Marines, were transported to Nu Vui and fought their way up to the beleaguered unit. Howard lost six out of 18 marines, and they held off the final Vietcong attack by throwing rocks and firing off captured AK-47s; the communists left 42 bodies on the field. By the time Operation KANSAS concluded on June 22, 1966, marine recon teams had made 141 sightings with a requisite number of air and artillery strikes called in. Between July 6 and 14, 1966, a company of the 1st Recon Battalion also participated in Operation WASHINGTON around Hau Doc, 25 miles west of the main marine base at Chu Lai. The marines extensively searched the region over eight days, making 46 enemy sightings through the triple-canopy jungle terrain that was impervious to aerial reconnaissance. Their last known field operation was Operation SCOTT ORCHARD in April 1971, when men of the 1st Recon Battalion helicoptered into an abandoned firebase in the Que Son Mountains. This region was secured after a brief firefight, and the unit was eventually replaced by artillerymen of the 1st Battalion, 11th Marines.

The 3rd Reconnaissance Battalion, which enjoyed a distinguished service record during World War II, was reactivated at Camp Pendleton, California, on March 1, 1952, as the Reconnaissance Company, Headquarters Battalion, attached to the 3rd Marine Division. After serving three years in Japan and Okinawa, on April 15, 1958, they were reconstituted as the 3rd Reconnaissance Battalion, 3rd Marine Division. In April 1965, Company D, 3rd Reconnaissance Battalion, patrolled southwest of the main marine base of Da Nang, skirmishing heavily with local Vietcong units. The remainder of the battalion arrived at Da Nang shortly afterward and assumed active operations. On July 12, 1965, Company A launched an 18-man patrol under Lieutenant Frank S. Reasoner that was struck by heavy communist mortar and automatic weapons fire; Reasoner was killed while aiding his injured radioman, becoming the first marine to win a posthumous Congressional Medal of

Honor in this war. On June 4, 1969, another six-man reconnaissance team from D Company, code sign "Flight Time," was helicoptered onto Hill 471 south of Khe Sanh, where it was attacked by superior Vietcong forces. The team requested an immediate extraction but the reactionary force arrived too late to help, and all six marines of the patrol were killed in action. This was the only full recon team lost by marines in Vietnam. The 3rd Reconnaissance Battalion continued on in the western Pacific following the American withdrawal from Southeast Asia in 1975 and was deactivated in 1992; four members of this unit received posthumous Congressional Medals of Honor.

In September 1965, the 3rd Force Reconnaissance Company was reactivated at Camp Lejeune, North Carolina, for service in the Vietnam War. It received intense training in the Caribbean and various fleet exercises before finally deploying at Phu Bai, South Vietnam, in September 1966. There the company was attached to the 3rd Reconnaissance Battalion and spent the next six months patrolling Thua Thien Province. In January 1967, members were culled into a "Special Purpose group" organized for a prisoner rescue attempt, while the rest deployed in the vicinity of Khe Sanh to monitor the buildup of communist forces. All three platoons of the 3rd Force Reconnaissance Company were then reunited in time to help repel a North Vietnamese attempt to seize Quang Tri Province, and it actively reconnoitered the vicinity of the Cobi Than Tan Valley before being reassigned to Dong Ha. There it assumed responsibility for patrolling Highway 9 as far north as the DMZ until its parent unit, the 3rd Marine Division, rotated back to the United States. The company performed similar services under the 3rd Marine Amphibious Force until the mid-1970s, when it too was deactivated. Throughout this period, one particularly effective tactic executed by Marine Force Recon units was the so-called Stingray operation. This involved infiltrating small radio-equipped teams into known communist staging areas where they would identify the precise location of enemy units and call down concentrated air- and artillery strikes on them. Not only were many Vietcong and North Vietnamese army units surprised in the open, but they also incurred heavy losses from these sudden, unexpected attacks.

Marine Corps Test Unit 1

With the advent of nuclear weapons in 1945 and the arrival of helicopter technology shortly thereafter, the Marine Corps Commandant instructed that an elite test unit be organized to develop new methods of insertion, extraction, and reconnaissance. This is the origin of many special operation styles of tactics and procedures employed by the U.S. Marine Corps to present times. On July 1, 1954, the Marine Corps Test Unit 1, a battalion-sized formation, arose to explore new venues and methodologies relative to future Marine Corps reconnaissance activities. However, it was not until September 1955 that a reconnaissance platoon under Captain Joseph Z. Taylor was added to refine amphibious reconnaissance tactics within the Fleet Marine Force. It was further tasked with updating all reconnaissance techniques established during World War II and to now include parachutes and helicopters as means of insertion. Thus disposed, it functioned as an antecedent of the Force Reconnaissance companies that followed, and helped pioneer deep recon techniques. For this reason, the 20 assigned members were cross trained with U.S. Air Force Escape and Evasion courses in the belief that such skills would be useful for operating behind enemy lines. A handful of marines also attended the U.S. Army Airborne School at Fort

Benning, Georgia, to acquire meaningful experience with parachute insertions. In August 1956, four marines from the recon platoon made the first parachute jump from a jet aircraft by exiting from a Douglas F3D-2 Skyknight. With all this preparation in hand, the recon platoon began developing new pathfinding methods that involved arriving at a scheduled landing zone, marking it with visual and radio aids, and guiding in helicopters to a successful landing. On June 19, 1957, Marine Corps Test Unit 1 was officially disbanded and replaced by the 1st Force Reconnaissance Company, which continued experimenting with imaginative techniques for insertion and extraction for select teams behind enemy lines.

Navy

Navy Mobile Riverine Force

The U.S. Navy was no stranger to large-scale riverine naval operations. During the Civil War, 1861–1865, flotillas of steam-powered gunboats and ironclads operated on the Mississippi River and other western waters, where they cut the Confederacy in half and provided supporting fire to army units operating ashore. Throughout the 1920s and 1930s, the period of "gunboat diplomacy," the navy also operated numerous vessels on the Yangtze River in China to protect American interests. It is no surprise that, in 1965, a study commissioned by the Naval Advisory Group, MACV, highlighted the need for heavily armed, highly mobile forces to patrol the Mekong River and its delta to curtail infiltration by communist Vietcong units. Hence was born the "brown water navy," a force distinct from the traditional "blue water navy," being tasked with operating far from the ocean and in constricted river environments. This new special operations force was equipped with a variety of specially designed craft, ranging from fast, lightly armored swift boats to heavily armed and armored monitors. The workhorses were the fiberglass Patrol Boat River (PBRs), which employed water jet propulsion instead of propellers, and these were eventually joined by aluminum-hulled Patrol Craft Fast on various missions. Moreover, in 1967 they became a joint-force operation with units of the army's 2nd Brigade, 9th Infantry Division, under Major General William Fulton. The infantry constituted the landing component of the new River Assault Groups for operations beyond the riverbank. Four Navy Assault Squadrons were ultimately created to work in tandem with the army, and a fixed base was dredged out of the Song Ham Luong River and christened "Dong Tam." That same year, the entire operation was also redesignated the Mobile Riverine Force, or Task Force 116.

The brown water navy drew heavily on similar French forces employed during the First Indochina War (1945–1954) with all the advantages of more modern technology. As a special operations force, the brown water navy was tasked with interdicting communist supply routes into the southernmost reaches of South Vietnam. This implied aggressively patrolling up and down numerous waterways, including creeks, rivers, canals, and streams—in short, anywhere that enemy sampans could float—and landing troops or SEAL teams ashore to destroy caches of supplies and even fortifications ashore. The unit was also expected to engage any enemy unit willing to confront them on the water's edge. For this reason, river patrol boats bristled with armament, usually .50-caliber machine guns and

81-mm mortars, and operated in tandem with helicopter gunships or warplanes overhead. Some specially fitted gunboats were also capable of projecting napalm like giant flamethrowers. These actions were usually followed up with the landing of U.S. or South Vietnamese troops from a variety of World War II–vintage landing craft, all heavily modified for riverine warfare. Protracted operations were further assisted by a floating Mobile Riverine Base, a collection of barracks vessels, repair ships, and support vessels that hovered in close proximity to each other (usually moored together) and capable of moving up and down waterways in support of ongoing actions. Between 1965 and 1969, the brown water navy enjoyed considerable success in reducing the flow of communist troops and supplies into the Mekong Delta region, and in 1970 the navy turned over all its riverine assets to the South Vietnamese navy. While little heralded, the brown water navy was one of the resounding military successes of the Vietnam War and one of few bright spots in an otherwise dismal conflict.

A river patrol boat navigates inland waterways in Vietnam in an offensive against Vietcong forces. Riverine craft were specially designed to operate in shallow rivers and canals. (National Archives)

Defining Activity

Combat and death in the Mekong Delta waterways was invariably unpredictable, unexpected, and swift. On October 13, 1966, a pair of PBRs commanded by Boatswain's Mate James Williams ran headlong into parts of two North Vietnamese regiments traveling down the same river at night. Although badly outnumbered, James's vessels made three complete passes through the enemy formation, firing every machine gun into their packed ranks. No fewer than 64 sampans were sunk and 1,000 communist casualties inflicted in this lopsided three-hour battle. James consequently received a Congressional Medal of Honor. Countless other men of the brown water navy were never officially classified as special forces, yet their close working relationship with SEALs and other elite units, in addition to the highly specialized nature of their work and the extreme talents it demanded, render them honorary members of a rather exclusive club.

SEALs

In 1961, President John F. Kennedy ushered in new perspectives relative to national security by breaking with the prevailing dogma surrounding "massive retaliation" (nuclear weapons) by embracing unconventional brushfire warfare and counterinsurgency. It so happens that in March of that year, Admiral Arleigh Burke, the chief of naval operations, sounded a call for creation of elite naval special forces capable of operating behind enemy lines and also effectively waging campaigns to suppress guerillas. By this time, the U.S. Navy's UDTs were already evolving in that direction, having conducted land operations during the Korea War. Moves were then undertaken to create new naval units roughly analogous to the army's new Green Berets. Thus was born the Sea-Air-Land (SEALs) concept on January 1, 1962. As their name implies, they had to be militarily proficient in two distinct climes—land and water—and dually capable of insertion and extraction by air. Two SEAL teams were authorized initially, with Team One constituted at Naval Amphibious Base (NAB) Coronado, California, and Team Two arising at NAB Little Creek, Virginia. Many of the initial enlistees were already UDT veterans and highly proficient in underwater techniques. However, to these skills was added new training in language, hand-to-hand combat, firearms, small-unit tactics, high-altitude parachuting, and demolitions. Prospective candidates attended the SEAL Basic Indoctrination class held at Camp Kerry in the Cuyamaca Mountains, after which they would be assigned a platoon and endure the rigors of intensified field training. SEALs were also schooled to function closely with new Special Boat Units responsible for their speedy ingress and egress to and from hostile environments. The concept of maritime special operations had no sooner coalesced than it was tested during the Cuban missile crisis of 1962 and then the iron crucible of war in Southeast Asia.

Defining Activity

The first SEAL teams reached Da Nang, South Vietnam, in March 1962, just as UDTs conducted clandestine hydrographic surveys of the coast. At this time, all special operations units were consolidating within the MACV. for expanded service throughout the region SEALs initially served as instructors for Republic of Vietnam frogmen (Lien Doc Nguoi Nhia) until the CIA co-opted them for covert actions along the North Vietnamese coast. These highly classified missions usually staged out of Da Nang, where teams of SEAL-trained commandos were inserted and extracted by high-speed patrol boats, submarines, and sometimes even junks. The men also pioneered the use of attack dolphins for use against enemy frogmen which may have accounted for up to 60 divers. However, in 1965, the SEALs found their niche as counterinsurgency troops operating deep within labyrinth reaches of the Rung Sat Special Zone near Saigon. This jungle-and-river-infested area was heavily used by Vietcong operatives who acted with near impunity because of the shelter provided by the inhospitable terrain. Two platoons from SEAL Team One were introduced in small hunter-killer teams of six to seven men and, received orders to detect and ambush communist forces, the conduct a quick extraction. The SEALs, packing grenade launchers, submachine guns, and machine guns, were taught to stealthily approach an enemy unit, then obliterate it at close range with overwhelming firepower. On certain special missions, 60-mm mortars could also be employed. In combat with Vietcong irregulars, they exhibited terrible lethality and help break the communist strangle hold over villagers in the region. However, they differed from their Green Beret counterparts by declining to work closely with South Vietnamese forces, believing them to be infiltrated or politically untrustworthy. They also preferred gathering and acting upon their own tactical

Richard Marcinko (1940–). Richard Marcinko was born in Lansford, Pennsylvania, on November 21, 1940, and he enlisted in the U.S. Navy in 1958. After serving in Naples, Italy, as a teletype operator, Marcinko joined an underwater demolition team and subsequently became one of the first Navy SEALs. He was spectacularly successful as a raider during the Vietnam War, and on May 18, 1967, his attack on Ilo-Ilo Island killed several Vietcong and destroyed six enemy sampans. At the commencement of his second tour, Marcinko became leader of the Eighth Platoon, SEAL Team Two, and heavily engaged assisting other U.S. Special Forces in the struggle for Chau Doc. His SEAL team gained such notoriety among the Vietcong that they offered a reward of 50,000 piasters for Marcinko's death. In 1973, he rose to commander and served as naval attaché to the Cambodian government. Eighteen months later, he returned stateside to serve as commanding officer of SEAL Team Two. In the wake of the failed Iranian hostage attempt in 1979, Marcinko convinced superiors to create a dedicated counterterrorist unit that emerged as SEAL Team Six—and under his command. In 1982, he was tapped by Vice Admiral James Lyons, deputy chief of naval operations, to create a unit to test the navy's defenses against terrorists. The new outfit, Red Cell, which was handpicked from SEAL Team Six and Marine Force Recon, embarrassed navy officials on several occasions by breaking into high-security installations and nuclear submarines. Marcinko's unstinting criticism of the navy's bureaucracy also made him unpopular with the brass. Since leaving the service in 1988, Marcinko continues on as a popular author, lecturer, radio host, and consultant on national security issues.

Commander Richard Marcinko distinguished himself as a Navy SEAL in Vietnam and elsewhere. He also founded and led the original SEAL Team Six, so named to confuse Soviet intelligence. (Courtesy of the U.S. Navy)

intelligence for field operations rather than relying on the army or air force assistance, hence theirs usually proved timely and accurate. In this manner, the local Vietcong infrastructure, including leadership and fortification, were fair game for sudden, devastating attacks. In fact, annihilating nighttime ambushes became something of an operational forte for SEALs as well as their calling card.

SEALs subsequently expanded operations into an even more challenging region: the Mekong Delta, home to an estimated 80,000 Vietcong soldiers and sympathizers. This swampy, mangrove-choked morass, inundated with rivers and rice paddies, covered 16,000 square miles and was accessible only by boat. Hence, it was not uncommon to insert SEAL squads at night, then retrieve them a week later once their mission was complete. If small boats could not access a certain site, SEALs would rappel down ropes from helicopters to execute their task. Missions of this sort were extremely trying and required the greatest degree of stealth, discipline, and physical hardiness as resupply missions were impossible. Among the litany of tasks performed by the SEALs were long-range reconnaissance, ambushes, sabotage, and assassinations associated with the CIA Phoenix program. In this last capacity, SEALs were also responsible for training and leading the Provincial Reconnaissance Units throughout the region, again with good effect. For many months, SEALs disrupted communist supply and transportation routes along the inland waterways previously considered secure. The Vietcong, thoroughly rattled by this new and formidable adversary, dubbed them "the men with green faces" because of their distinct and effective camouflage. It was not uncommon for individual SEAL platoons to conduct over 100 ambush-style missions during a single six-month deployment. A total of 34 SEALs died over nine years of low-intensity warfare, during which time they amassed an impressive kill ratio of 50 dead communists for every American casualty.

As clandestine operations grew beyond South Vietnam's borders into neighboring Laos and Cambodia, SEAL members were frequently assigned to MACV's highly classified SOG to conduct reconnaissance forays. Members of Team Two were also assigned to work with South Vietnamese commandos in the field, always a dicey proposition considering the extent of communist infiltration. Still, between 1970 and 1972, SEALs also participated in Operation BRIGHTLIGHT to free prisoners held by the Vietcong in the Mekong Delta. No Americans were ever liberated, but many of Vietcong's captives were rescued and released. By 1970, however, public opinion of the war induced President Richard M. Nixon to begin "Vietnamization," whereby indigenous forces assumed larger and larger roles in their own national defense as U.S. forces went home. The last SEAL adviser was withdrawn in March 1973, although some team members are thought to have remained behind as clandestine operations as late as April 1975, when South Vietnam was finally overrun. Their 14-year tenure in Southeast Asia was nonetheless illustrious, for SEALs were among the most highly decorated small units in this conflict. No fewer than two Navy Crosses, 42 Silver Stars, 402 Bronze Stars, two Legions of Merit, 352 Commendation Medals, three PUCs, and three Medals of Honor were awarded to SEAL members. In sum, SEALs enjoyed a well-deserved reputation as among the toughest special forces to perform service and survive the hard school of Southeast Asia. Like the Green Berets, their reputation transcended the overall negative feelings associated with this war.

In May 1983, the Naval Special Warfare command finally absorbed the remaining UDT units into its structure, along with their many tasks for which SEALs are also trained to perform. That year, the SEALs also made their Middle Eastern debut by coming ashore at Beirut, Lebanon, to assist a large Marine peacekeeping force. A civil war then raged throughout the city, and hostile factions, when not shooting at each other, randomly and periodically shelled the American position. The SEALs responded with accurate long-range fire from the .50-caliber Special Application Sniper Rifle, making several kills at ranges up to 1,000 yards. By 1987, the ongoing war between Iraq and Iran also induced the

U.S. Navy to deploy SEAL teams in the Persian Gulf region to ensure freedom of navigation through the Strait of Hormuz. Once the Iranians began secretly mining strategic gulf waters to obstruct U.S.-flagged tankers from trading with Iraq, Operation PRIME CHANCE was enacted to stop them. This entailed deployment of SEAL Teams One and Two in the Gulf region, backed by Special Boat Units. On September 21, 1987, an Iranian landing craft was attacked by U.S. Army helicopters and boarded by SEALs who seized several mines waiting deployment; three Iranians were killed and 26 captured. This reverse failed to mitigate Iranian behavior, however, and on April 18, 1988, in response to the frigate USS *Samuel B. Roberts* striking a mine, Operation PREYING MANTIS was unleashed in retaliation. Here SEAL teams captured and destroyed several Iranian gulf oil platforms being used for military purposes. This debacle convinced Iran that it could not win a confrontation with the United States, so its behavior moderated thereafter.

The next opportunity for SEALs to mount combat operations was on October 23, 1983, during Operation URGENT FURY, the liberation of Grenada from a bloody Marxist clique. They were tasked with rescuing and extracting Governor General Paul Scones from captivity in his mansion, and seizing of the island's only radio transmitter. This being an emergency action, summoned with only a few hours' notice, the missions were not adequately planned and lacked meaningful real-time intelligence before the teams were sent in. Consequently, command-and-control problems arose from the onset, and the SEALs experienced several close brushes with disaster. For example, the platoon from SEAL Team Six was ordered to parachute to the sea, then paddle ashore and reconnoiter communist defenses on Point Salines. A spate of delays made them deploy six hours late, and they arrived over their rendezvous point in complete darkness. One of the C-141 Starlifter transports missed the drop zone by several miles. The other dropped an eight-man squad that came to grief when their boat's parachute failed to open and three members, heavily loaded with equipment, drowned. The survivors jettisoned their equipment and floated on open water for several hours until daybreak, when they were rescued by naval vessels. The two SEAL teams that manage to land completed their insertion and advanced inland. Governor General Scoon was successfully freed from house arrest in his mansion, but the SEALs were suddenly surrounded by Grenadian troops and BTR-60 armored cars. At this critical juncture, their short-range tactical radios had run out of power, so the SEALs were forced to use a regular telephone to call in air support from a circling AC-130. A heavy suppressing fire allowed them to remain in the mansion until the following day, when they were relieved by Force Recon Marines. Meanwhile, the detachment sent to seize the Beausejour radio station was also surrounded by Cubans and Grenadians in their BTR-60s. After beating off several attacks, theyfell back upon some seaside cliffs and hid among them for several hours. The enemy troops eventually gave up the search, at which point the SEALs took to the open ocean and swam for several hours until being spotted by a reconnaissance aircraft and rescued. Fortunately, a platoon from SEAL Team Four did manage to successfully execute their reconnaissance of the beach area near Pearls Airport, finding the region both unsuitable for an amphibious landing by marines, and defended scores of heavily armed Grenadians. They reported these findings back to vessels offshore before the marines landed, sparing many lives.

Once the lessons of Grenada were incorporated into SEAL tactics and technology, they were again deployed during Operation JUST CAUSE in Panama. On December 29, 1989, Task Force White, consisting of SEAL Teams Two and Four were ordered to destroy PDF vessels in Balboa Harbor along with the personal Lear jet of dictator Manuel Noriega at Paitilla Airport to prevent his escape. In the former objective, five SEALs of Task Unit Whiskey swam underwater for several miles using Dreager LAV-V rebreathers. After arriving, they fixed C4 explosive charges to Noriega's personal yacht, the *Presidente Porras*, and a 65-foot patrol boat, destroying both. Meanwhile, several SEAL platoons of Task Unit Papa, 80 men in all, came ashore on the beach outside Paitilla Airport and advanced inland. En route they were detected by PDF forces nearby who opened fire, killing four SEALs and wounding 13. Fortunately, the Noriega's aircraft was destroyed, and the defenders were driven off. While SEAL performance in JUST CAUSE was somewhat smoother than in URGENT FURY, its still revealed rough patches in their operational doctrine that would be addressed in subsequent deployments.

The final Cold War mission of the SEALs came in January/February 1991 as part of Operation DESERT STORM against Iraq. On January 30, 1991, a platoon from SEAL Team One, manning a border observation post at the Saudi town of Khafji, was suddenly attacked by large numbers of Iraqi troops. They radioed in for air strikes, then successfully slipped away unharmed. During the land portion of Operation DESERT STORM, SEALs performed over 200 naval special warfare missions in and around the Persian Gulf near Kuwait. These involved mostly reconnaissance but included the capture of Qaruh Island and several oil platforms as well as the rescue of a downed coalition F-16 pilot. Their biggest accomplishment was in convincing two Iraqi armored divisions that a Marine Corps amphibious landing was imminent on the beaches near Kuwait City. The SEALs took their high-speed craft offshore at night, paddled to the beach in rubber boats, and then deposited haversacks full of C4 explosives times to detonate in rapid sequence. The Iraqi high command, noting the explosions and feeling that a landing had commenced, detained the two formations on the spot, removing them as a threat to coalition forces advancing from the south. Since 1962, the SEALs repeatedly demonstrated their skill, adaptability, and courage in numerous and dangerous missions that would have daunted the most hardened regular soldiers or frogmen. Their success guaranteed that the Sea-Air-Land concept for elite naval infantry in global special operations would certainly carry over into the 21st century, where even greater challenges await.

UDTs

In the mass demobilization following World War II, the Navy's finely honed UDT force was reduced to four half-strength teams, with UDT 1 and 3 at NAB Coronado, California, and UDT 2 and 4 at NAB Little Creek, Virginia. They remained operationally marginalized over the next five years but did pioneer new techniques and technologies pertaining to underwater and shallow-water operations, in many respects anticipating what eventually emerged as the SEALs. The greatest technological innovation was the adoption of the new Aqua-Lung breathing apparatus, which, while leaving a trail of telltale bubbles on the water's surface, was deemed safer to use than the Lambertson Amphibious Respiratory Unit of World War II. In 1948, a test group headed by Lieutenant Commander Francis Fane successfully demonstrated lockout and reentry techniques for frogmen from the submerged submarine USS *Grouper*, which was the navy's first direct application of the Aqua-Lung. Concurrently, UDT teams began experimenting with skills and procedures relevant to commando-style operations far inland from strictly coastal regions. The newly emerging helicopter technology also led to experiments in aerial deployments, such as jumping into water from a moving aircraft offshore or rappelling down ropes to the ground. All this was a far cry from their reconnaissance/beach-clearing missions of World War II and a harbinger of things to come.

Despite their small size, the two UDT teams found immediate employment during the Korean War, and a new team, UDT 5, was also commissioned. They were employed during large mine-clearing operations along the North Korean coast, although teams sometimes accompanied South Korean commando teams ashore to destroy railroad tunnels and bridges. Such endeavors raised the ire of senior UDT officers who felt that such assignments strayed too far from the traditional employment of frogmen, but they also highlighted tactical capabilities beyond the beachhead. UDT teams were also conspicuously employed during the September 1950 landings at Inchon, South Korea, where they performed vital roles of scouting, demolishing obstacles, marking points in the channel, and detecting minefields. The frogmen also subsequently cleared Wonsun Harbor for UN operations to good effect. In another first, the frogmen engaged in economic warfare by sabotaging the nets of North Korean fishermen. Korea amply demonstrated that, however small in numbers, UDT members wielded considerable military impact and that they were still capable of expanding tactical parameters into new venues. Moreover, the cold operating conditions off the Korea coast necessitated the development of watertight insulated rubber suits to preserve body heat and prevent hypothermia, leading in turn to more specialized equipment.

Frogmen destroy North Vietnamese fishing nets during Operation FISHNET, a mission designed to destroy main source of communist forces food supply, 1962. By this period, their mission was being absorbed by a new formation, the SEALS. (U.S. Department of Defense)

During the immediate postwar period, the frogmen were again were reduced to only three commissioned teams between 1956 and 1962. However, U.S. Navy intervention in the Vietnam War by 1960 granted the UDTs additional avenues for distinction. Initially employed to deliver small vessels up the Mekong River into Laos, they were soon co-opted into training South Vietnamese sailors as frogmen and conducting an extensive hydrographic survey of that nation's coastal waters. They subsequently accompanied ARGs up Vietnam's numerous rivers, where they manned riverine patrol craft and landed to eliminate obstacles and bunkers. By this juncture, the navy found it desirous to expand their horizons with a new operational concept, SEALs, in January 1962. UDTs still remained a viable part of the navy, and, in fact, many SEAL personnel were initially trained as frogmen. They continued working alongside SEALs during insertion and extraction operations until May 1983, when their functions were officially coopted by the latter. In a nod to their illustrious ancestors, all SEALs still endure the same basic underwater demolition training course originally pioneered by the UDTs.

Miscellaneous

Hmong

Commencing in 1954, the kingdom of Laos began experiencing civil war at the instigation of communist Pathet Lao forces, backed by troops infiltrated in by the Democratic Republic of Vietnam (North Vietnam). The battle ebbed and flowed over the next few years, but by 1962 the situation appeared serious enough to warrant indirect intervention by the CIA, a dicey proposition seeing that Laos was officially neutral. This was the commencement of the so-called Secret War waged by the CIA's SAD and U.S. Special Forces against North Vietnam and Laotian communist operatives. In effect, Laos had become the latest proxy war waged between the United States, the Soviet Union, and Red China, with massive amounts of military aid provided by both sides. In April 1961, the first White Star MTT arrived in Laos under Lieutenant Colonel Arthur D. "Bull" Simons. Central to this effort was the recruitment of Hmong soldiers into a clandestine fighting force independent of the Royal Laotian Army. Hmong are an ethnic minority domiciled in the highlands and mountain ranges of Laos and are believed to have migrated there 2,000 years ago from southern China, where sizable populations still reside. Hmong leadership centered around General Vang Pao, a charismatic figure and a capable leader in guerilla warfare. As the campaign unfolded, arms and supplies intended for the Hmong were provided by Air America, Inc., the CIA's proprietary airline. The 4802nd Joint Liaison Detachment was also established in neighboring Thailand to funnel Thai military operatives into the region and coordinate reconnaissance and military activities against communist forces lurking inside Laos. This became doubly essential once all U.S. Army White Star operations ceased in October 1962 following a second declaration of Laotian neutrality—which neither side respected—so the CIA moved in to pick up the slack. Ultimately, 30,000 Hmong fighters were enrolled in Special Guerilla Units, and after 1968, they were equipped and trained to fight more and more like conventional infantry, backed by massive American aerial support. In this respect, the Secret War became the largest clandestine CIA operation until the Soviet invasion of Afghanistan.

The principal role of the Hmong resistance was monitoring the Ho Chi Minh Trail, constructed illegally on Laotian territory, for transporting men and supplies into South Vietnam. On the basis of their intelligence, U.S. Air Force and Navy warplanes routinely bombed truck convoys and supply dumps to stem the flow. In retaliation, the North Vietnamese unleashed brigade-size conventional attacks against the Hmong, who were only lightly equipped and sustained heavy losses. Combat focused on a region known as the Plain of Jars, which changed hands several times over the years. The impasse continued until 1973, when the Laotian government signed an agreement with the Pathet Lao, granting them equal representation, and the United States halted aerial bombing and supplies to the Hmong. On April 27, 1975, Pathet Lao and NVA forces attacked the Hmong and finally drove them out of their northern strongholds. The communist onslaught proved relentless, and they achieved total victory on August 23, 1975. The Hmong, the staunchest adversaries of the communists, were marked for extermination, so the CIA arranged an air evacuation of thousands of fighters and their families. By the time hostilities finally ceased, roughly 12,000 Hmong had been killed in a losing struggle against communism. Aided and abetted by American special forces, they nonetheless performed well against tremendous odds.

Kit Carson Scouts

Among the ethnic groups that American special operations in the Vietnam War devolved on were the Vietnamese themselves. In May 1966, several officers of the 1st Marine Division broached the possibility of cultivating and employing Vietcong and North Vietnamese defectors. The commanding officer, Major General Herman Nickerson, agreed in principle, and the program known as the Kit Carson Scouts was formally established on November 10, 1966. The unit derived its name from the famous scout, who excelled at working with Native Americans and whom Nickerson, a western history buff, widely admired. Two defectors were initially assigned to work in the field with the 7th Marine Regiment along the coast plain region of the I Corps Tactical Region. They were paired with a Vietnamese-speaking marine and accompanied him on various patrols throughout the region. As hoped, the defectors proved useful in pointing out Vietcong infiltrators in nearby civilian populations, identifying booby traps, and helping to uncover arms caches hidden in the jungle. They also served useful purposes as prisoner-of-war interrogators and translators for captured enemy documents. Success here led to an expansion of the Kit Carson Scouts throughout the I Corps, with more or less good results. Many new recruits were brought into the program through the South Vietnamese government's Chieu Hoi program, which actively solicited disgruntled Vietnamese communists to change sides.

By 1967, General William Westmoreland, the supreme commander in South Vietnam, ordered that all American units employ communist defectors in their field operations with up to 100 operating in each infantry division. Within a year, over 700 former communists were in American employ and were even allowed to accompany the highly classified LRRPs along the Cambodian border. They proved especially useful in uncovering hidden Vietcong camps and jungle trails during search-and-destroy missions conducted in dense countrysides. From a political standpoint, they were also extremely useful as propaganda tools in dealing with indigenous populations and convinced many peasants not to side with the communist insurgency. As the United States continued withdrawing military units after

1971, many Kit Carson Scouts were enrolled in regular South Vietnamese units. Those captured after the final communist victory in April 1975 were usually sent off to "reeducation camps" as punishment, or simply executed.

Montagnards

No sooner did the United States become militarily involved in thwarting the communist insurgency against South Vietnam than it began soliciting support from the large Montagnard (French for "Mountaineer") population residing in the strategic Central Highlands region. They constituted a large grouping of 30 distinct tribes, with many subdivisions among them. Historically, they viewed themselves as different from the Vietnamese inhabiting the coastal regions and had always been scorned by the latter as savages. However, the governments of both North and South Vietnam sought their military assistance in the present struggle, and the majority of Montagnards, given their antipathy toward all Vietnamese in general, remained aloof. Things changed dramatically following American intervention. In 1961, Gilbert Layton of the CIA suggested that Montagnards could be protected from the Vietcong through an extensive village defense program that came to be known as CIDG. This was a comprehensive strategy that combined self-defense capabilities with social and economic programs to win over "hearts and minds." The tribesmen, distrusting the South Vietnamese government, generally welcomed the Green Beret teams that were sent to fortify their villages. Commencing in February 1962, American special forces organized a force of 40,000 militia in 27 heavily fortified CIDG camps across the

A U.S. Special Forces officer yells instructions to Montagnard mercenaries as they move forward to retake a hilltop outpost near Ha Thanh, some 325 miles northeast of Saigon, South Vietnam, September 5, 1968. This outpost had been overrun by communist North Vietnamese troops three days earlier, and two previous attempts to retake it had been pushed back. (AP/Wide World Photos)

Central Highlands. Each camp was uniformly organized with three companies of 132 men each, three reconnaissance platoons, two supporting 105-mm howitzers, and, all told, a garrison strength of 530 men. An elite force of specially trained Montagnards, or Mike Forces, also functioned as a mobile reserve to reinforce and assist threatened points within this jurisdiction. Occasionally, the Americans would be accompanied by members of the Luc Luong Dac Biet, or South Vietnamese special forces, who despised Montagnards. Despite the best efforts at cultivating goodwill between them, tensions persisted and in 1964 a major uprising of Montagnards occurred to reclaim lands previously seized by the Vietnamese. Once this was suppressed, the CIDG program was largely disbanded, and only the elite strike force continued existing under the direct supervision of special forces. These troops and their handlers deployed in 25 base camps along the Laotian and Cambodian borders for the purpose of monitoring, harassing, and occasionally interdicting communist supplies moving south along the Ho Chi Minh Trail.

Defining Activity

Montagnards traditionally enjoyed a reputation for martial prowess, and they worked exceedingly well with their American handlers. As such, they distinguished themselves in a number of actions connected with the CIDG program. On July 6, 1964, Vietcong forces attacked the Nam Dong CIDG base camp near the Laotian border in an attempt to overrun it. The camp was defended by a Green Beret A-Team under Captain Roger H. Donlon, 300 Montagnards, and 60 Nung mercenaries who steadfastly rebuffed 900 communist troops for five hours. The Vietcong withdrew into the jungle, leaving 62 bodies behind, and Donlon became the first Green Beret to receive the Congressional Medal of Honor. On June 10–11, 1965, the Vietcong also stormed into the camp at Dong Xoai, 55 miles northeast of Saigon. This posted was defended by Green Beret Detachment A-342 under Lieutenant Charles Q. Williams, South Vietnamese special forces, and several hundred Montagnards. Communists of the 273rd Regiment charged directly into the camp perimeter, breaching the first line of defense until they came under fire from gunships and helicopters. A battalion of the ARVN 42nd Ranger Battalion was airlifted and landed outside the camp, but they could not dislodge the Vietcong. The decision was made to airlift the surviving garrison members, although the Montagnard units present fought well. On March 9–10, 1966, the CIDG border camp at A Shau, 30 miles west of Hue and adjacent to the Ho Chi Minh Trail, also came under attack. The Montagnards were led by their usual special forces advisers, a Mike Force company, and some Marine Corps snipers but were vastly outnumbered by the North Vietnamese. The latter overran the camp in spite of heavy resistance and attacks by helicopters, and the camp was ordered evacuated. American losses were five killed and 12 wounded, the Montagnards lost 47 dead or missing, while communist casualties were estimated in the vicinity of 800.

Montagnard units in American service continued fighting with distinction both as Mike Forces and as members of highly classified LRRPs, but as the United States continued withdrawing combat units in 1971, they were gradually shifted over to South Vietnamese control The Montagnards were usually incorporated into ranger units, but old animosities were flickered anew and fighting between the two occurred. In March 1975, the Montagnards refused to alert South Vietnamese officials that North Vietnamese units were massing in the vicinity of Ban Me Thuot, contributing to the ultimate communist victory. By the time hostilities ceased, an estimated 200,000 Montagnards had been killed and 85 percent of their villages leveled. Afterward, the tribesmen continued resisting the North Vietnamese up through 1979, at which point the United States accepted thousands of refugees from the region. As a rule, Montagnards they exuded far more affinity toward Green Berets leading them than the Vietnamese, North and South alike.

Studies and Observations Group

As the United States was drawn deeper into anticommunist efforts throughout Southeast Asia, the Joint Chiefs of Staff felt it prudent to create units and design programs capable of sustained and clandestine counterinsurgency operations. Such missions were conducted in South Vietnam but also in Laos, Cambodia, and even North Vietnam itself. Secrecy was essential, for General William Westmoreland, commanding U.S. forces in South Vietnam, was under strict orders not to expand operations beyond their nation's boundaries. From 1961 to 1964, these activities were consequently handled by the CIA under Operation Leaping Lena, in concert with teams of Vietnamese operatives. The effort was subsequently judged a failure, giving rise to calls for a strictly U.S. military–directed effort. Accordingly, the MACV founded SOG on January 24, 1964, entrusting it with highly classified cross-border reconnaissance missions into neighboring countries—a politically and diplomatically untenable proposition. Unlike the rest of army forces in Southeast Asia, SOG reported directly to the Joint Chiefs of Staff back in Washington, D.C. Operationally, their missions were planned and executed by mixed groups of American special forces—Green Berets, Navy SEALs, Air Force Combat Control Teams, and Marine Corps Force Reconnaissance personnel—assisted by groups of ethnic allies, including Montagnards, Nungs (Chinese Vietnamese) and Khmer Kroms (Cambodian Vietnamese). The Montagnards, always eager to kill Vietnamese, be they northern or southern, provided cheerful cooperation, along with the largest manpower totals. They were also useful in accessing the large numbers of Montagnards dwelling in Laos and northern Cambodia for military intelligence and prospective recruits. The overall effort fell under the rubric of Op-35, whose charter included unconventional warfare, maritime operations, psychological warfare, and training agents for insertion into restricted areas. SOG was further tasked with captive rescue missions, prisoner snatches, and equipment retrieval. As additional political cover, all Green Beret personnel involved were officially listed as part of the 5th SFG when, in fact, they answered to directly to SOG. Ultimately, an estimated 2,000 to 2,500 Americans served under Op-35 up through 1972, along with 7,000 to 8,000 indigenous troops.

Commencing on September 21, 1965, and continuing for the next six years, SOG operatives performed highly classified missions into Laos and Cambodia as part of Operation SHINING BRASS. This was for the purpose of ascertaining communist activity in those regions, monitoring military traffic along the Ho Chi Minh Trail into South Vietnam with acoustic or seismic sensors, and tapping into enemy communication lines. One of the most hazardous undertakings assigned to these elite troops were SLAM (seek, locate, annihilate, and monitor) missions, aimed at inflicting heavy casualties among all enemy units encountered. The SOG teams invariably caused losses to communist forces, but they themselves sustained deaths and injuries as well. Many of these remain classified and undocumented to present times. Operation SHINING BRASS (later called PRAIRIE FIRE) invariably dispatched "Spike

Teams" of six to 12 men as cross-border scouts conveyed to the region and inserted by Marine Corps helicopters from the 1st Corps Tactical Zone. These units monitored communist activities, ambushed enemy units where possible, and enabled U.S. Army intelligence to better ascertain enemy activities and intentions in that region. Teams frequently included an air force air controller to act as a ground liaison to air force warplanes. Thus apprised, jets of the 7th Air Force conducted their own clandestine bombing campaign against enemy supply dumps and truck convoys. Between September 1965 and April 1972, SOG authorized no fewer than 1,579 reconnaissance patrols, 216 platoon-sized patrols, and three multiplatoon actions into Laos from CIDG camps such as Kham Duc, Khe Sanh, and Kontum. Once in the field, the teams were restricted to 20-kilometer penetrations of the countryside and no farther. The North Vietnamese understood the nature of these activities perfectly and constantly attacked CIDG base camps to disrupt reconnaissance operations emanating there. Concurrent with operations in Laos was a parallel effort in Cambodia known as Operational DANIEL BOONE (later known as SALEM HOUSE). This endeavor succeeded ongoing efforts such as Projects Sigma and Omega run by the 5th SFG and were now greatly expanded. SOG teams were permitted to penetrate no farther than 20 kilometers past the Cambodian border, although they remained authorized mine any trails used by communists forces. As the war ground on, this range was extended out to 185 miles, a good indication of how seriously the Americans regarded communist sanctuaries in neutral Cambodia. Between 1967 and April 1972, SOG is known to have authorized 1,398 reconnaissance missions into Cambodia, along with 38 platoon-sized operations as 12 multiplatoon undertakings.

Special operations ground units in Southeast Asia also received extensive assistance from the 15th Air Commando Squadron, SOG's designated Air Operation Group. They had been outfitted with specially modified MC-130 Combat Talon transports along with smaller C-123s to transport supplies and insert agents. These were joined in due course by CH-3 Jolly Green Giant helicopters of the 20th SOS, operating from Nakhon Phanom Royal Thai Air Force Base, which assisted SOG teams in Laos and elsewhere. All these units performed heroic (if highly classified) missions throughout this dabbling beyond South Vietnam's borders, and pioneered many of the techniques and tactics employed by present-day special forces.

The surprise communist Tet (Lunar New Year) Offensive in the spring of 1968 led to a drastic revamping of SOG operations in Laos, with greater emphasis on larger-sized units. This new campaign, Operation COMMANDO HUNT, also placed a premium on ambushing North Vietnamese units and implanting electronic sensors along the Ho Chi Minh Trail. The Special Commando Units of mixed special forces and indigenous soldiers proved adept at inflicting casualties on unwary enemy units, but by 1969, the Americans had 20 dead, 199 wounded, and nine missing, while their allies sustained 57 killed, 270 wounded, and 31 missing in 404 combat missions. This attrition prevailed until the program was finally canceled in 1972. Moreover, as good as most SOG operations were, intelligence efforts entrusted to purely South Vietnamese units were frequently compromised by communist infiltrators working within them. Consequently, the extensive SOG campaign to insert agents within the communist North failed, leading to the death or imprisonment of 456 South Vietnamese operatives. Overall, SOG failed to change the course of the conflict in Southeast Asia, but, operationally, it was highly successfully in terms of intelligence gathering and cost the North Vietnamese several thousand casualties to contain. For the special forces involved, it also represents a high point in the adroit handling of indigenous forces during a period of protracted unconventional warfare. SOG was formally deactivated as of May 1, 1972, and at its height, it officially employed 394 American personnel. These were further assisted in the field by 1,041 army, 476 air force, 17 Marine Corps, and seven CIA personnel, along with 3,068 ethnic allies and 5,402 South Vietnamese, a total of 12,210 soldiers and civilians. From this aggregate, one air force member, two Navy SEALs, and nine Green Berets received Congressional Medals of Honor (including three posthumous) for their role in special operations throughout Southeast Asia. All told, SOG's legacy lends additional credence to the growth, maturation, and sophistication of U.S. special operations and special forces since the end of World War II.

Bibliography

General

Barker, Geoffrey T. *A Concise History of U.S. Army Special Operations Forces, with Lineage and Insignia*. Fayetteville, NC: Anglo-American Publishing, 1988.

Brown, Jeremy M. *Explaining the Reagan Years in Central America: A World System Perspective*. Lanham, MD: University Press of America, 1995.

Buschmann, Klaus. *United States Army Special Forces, 1952–1974*. Las Vegas, NV: Lang, 1978.

Colby, Carroll B. *Special Forces, the U.S. Army's Experts in Unconventional Warfare*. New York: Coward-McCann, 1964.

Collins, John M. *Green Berets, Seals, and Spetsnaz: U.S. and Soviet Special Military Operations*. Washington, DC: Pergamon-Brassey's, 1987.

Duncan, Don. *The New Legions*. New York: Random House, 1967.

Edwards, Paul M. *Combat Operations of the Korean War: Ground, Air, Sea, Special and Covert*. Jefferson, NC: McFarland, 2010.

Evanhoe, Ed. *Darkmoon: Eighth Army Special Operations in the Korean War*. Annapolis, MD: Naval Institute Press, 1995.

Fitzgerald, Tom. *Get Tough! The U.S. Special Forces Physical Conditioning Program*. New York: St. Martin's Press, 1985.

Ives, Christopher K. *U.S. Special Forces and Counterinsurgency in Vietnam: Military Innovation and Institutional Failure, 1961–63*. New York: Routledge, 2007.

Lenahan, Rod. *Crippled Eagle: A Historical Perspective of U.S. Special Operations, 1976–1996*. Charleston, SC: Narwhal Press, 1998.

Neillands Robin. *In the Combat Zone: Special Forces since 1945*. London: Weidenfeld and Nicolson, 1997.

Paddock, Alfred H. *U.S. Army Special Warfare: Its Origins: Psychological and Unconventional Warfare, 1941-1952*. Washington, DC: Government Printing Office, 1982.

Spies, Scouts, and Raiders: Irregular Operations. By the Editors of Time-Life Books. Alexandria, VA: Time-Life Books, 1985.

Thompson, Leroy. *De Oppresso Liber: The Illustrated History of the U.S. Army Special Forces*. Boulder, CO: Paladin Press, 1987.

Thompson, Leroy. *U.S. Special Forces, 1941–1987*. New York: Blandford Press, 1987.

Thompson, Leroy. *U.S. Special Operations Forces in the Cold War*. Mechanicsburg, PA: Stackpole Books, 2002.

Vanderbroucke, Lucien S. *Perilous Options: Special Operations as an Instrument of U.S. Foreign Policy*. New York: Oxford University Press, 1993.

Walker, Greg. *At the Hurricane's Eye: U.S. Special Forces from Vietnam to Desert Storm*. New York: Ivy Books, 1994.

Walmer, Max. *An Illustrated Guide to Modern Elite Forces*. New York: Prentice Hall, 1986.

Zimmerman, Dwight J., and John D. Gresham. *Beyond Hell and Back: How America's Special Operations Forces Became the World's Greatest Fighting Unit*. New York: St. Martin's Press, 2007.

Air Resupply and Communications Service

Baumer, William H. *The Extended Mission of Stardust Four Zero*. Apollo, PA: Closson Press, 1999.

Brown, Wallace L. *The Endless Hours: My Two and a Half Years as a Prisoner of the Chinese Communists*. New York: Norton, 1961.

Haas, Michael E. *Air Commando! 1950–1975: Twenty-Five Years at the Tip of the Spear*. Hurlburt Field, FL: U.S. Air Force Special Operations Command, 1995.

Haas, Michael E. *Apollo's Warriors: U.S. Special Operations during the Cold War*. Maxwell Air Force Base, AL: Air University Press, 1997.

Haas, Michael E. *In the Devil's Shadow: UN Special Operations during the Korean War*. Annapolis, MD: Naval Institute Press, 2000.

Kelly, Orr. *From a Dark Sky: The Story of U.S. Air Force Special Operations*. Novato, CA: Presidio Press, 1996.

Kiba, Steve E. *The Flag, My Story: Kidnapped by Red China*. Bloomington, IN: 1st Books Library, 2002.

Marchio, James. "Casualties of the Cold War: "Operation Think: And the Air Resupply Communications Service." *Air Power History* 39, no. 4 (Winter 1992): 19–23.

Thigpen, Jerry L. *The Praetorian STARship: The Untold Story of Combat Talon*. Maxwell Air Force Base, AL: Air University Press, 2001.

Air Force Pararescuemen

Brehm, Jack. *That Others May Live: The True Story of a PJ, a Member of America's Most Daring Rescue Force*. New York: Crown, 2000.

La Pointe, Robert L. *PJs in Vietnam: The Story of Air Rescue in Vietnam as Seen through the Eyes of Pararescuemen*. Anchorage, AK: Northern PJ Press, 2001.

Air Force Special Operations Command

Chinnery, Philip D. *Any Time, Any Place: Fifty Years of the USAF Air Commando and Special Operations Forces, 1944–1994*. Annapolis, MD: Naval Institute Press, 1994.

Gleason, Robert L. *Air Commando Chronicles: Untold Stories from Vietnam, Latin America, and Back Again*. Manhattan, KS: Sunflower University Press, 2000.

Haas, Michael E. *Apollo's Warriors: U.S. Air Force Special Operations during the Cold War*. Maxwell Air Force Base, AL: Air University Press, 1997.

Halliday, John T. *Flying through Midnight: A Pilot's Dramatic Story of His Secret Missions over Laos during the Vietnam War*. New York: Scriber, 2005.

Mutza, Wayne. *Green Hornets: The History of the U.S. Air Force 20th Special Operations Squadron*. Atglen, PA: Schiffer, 2007.

Padden, Ian. *U.S. Air Commando*. New York: Bantam, 1985.

Thigpen, Jerry L. *AFSOC: The Air Force's Newest Command*. Carlisle Barracks, PA: U.S. Army War College, 1991.

Trest, Warren A. *Air Commando One: Heinie Aderholt and America's Secret Air Wars*. Washington, DC: Smithsonian Institute Press, 2000.

Delta Force

Beckwith, Charlie A., and Donald Knox. *Delta Force: The Army's Elite Counterterrorist Unit*. New York: Avon Books, 2000.

Boykin, Jerry. *Never Surrender: A Soldier's Journey to the Crossroads of Faith and Freedom*. New York: Faith Works, 2008.

Griswold, Terry. *Delta, America's Elite Counterterrorist Force*. Osceola, WI: Motorbooks International, 1992.

Green Berets

Archer, Chalmers. *Green Berets in the Vanguard: Inside Special Forces, 1953–1963*. Annapolis, MD: Naval Institute Press, 2001.

Bank, Aaron. *From OSS to Green Berets: The Birth of Special Forces*. Novato, CA: Presidio Press, 1986.

Coppola, Vincent. *Uneasy Warriors: Coming Back Home: The Perilous Journey of the Green Berets*. Atlanta: Longstreet Press, 1995.

Cornett, Alan G. *Gone Native: An NCO's Story*. New York: Ballantine Books, 2000.

Craig, William T. *Lifer! From Infantry to Special Forces*. New York: Ivy Books, 1994.

Dix, Drew. *The Rescue of River City*. Fairbanks, AK: Drew Dix, 2000.

Donlon, Roger H. C. *Outpost of Freedom*. New York: McGraw Hill, 1965.

Donlon, Roger H. C. *Beyond Nam Dong*. Leavenworth, KS: R. N. Publishers, 1998.

English, Adrian, et al. *The Green Beret: U.S. Special Forces from Vietnam to Delta Force*. New York: Villard Books, 1986.

Fitzgibbon, Daniel H. *To Bear Any Burden: A Hoosier Green Beret's Letters from Vietnam.* Indianapolis: Indiana Historical Society Press, 2005.

Gargus, John. *The Son Tay Raid: American POWs in Vietnam Were Not Forgotten.* College Station: Texas A&M University Press, 2010.

Gill, H. A. *Soldier Under Three Flags: Exploits of Special Forces Captain Larry A. Thorpe.* Venture, CA: Pathfinder Publications, 1998.

Gregory, Barry. *The Vietnam War/2, the Green Berets.* New York: Marshall Cavendish, 1988.

Gritz, James. *A Nation Betrayed.* Boulder City, NV: Lazurus, 1989.

Halberstadt, Hans. *Green Berets: Unconventional Warriors.* Novato, CA: Presidio Press, 1988.

Halberstadt, Hans. *War Stories of the Green Berets.* St. Paul, MN: Zenith Press, 2004.

Hoe, Alan. *The Quiet Professional: Major Richard J. Meadows of the U.S. Army Special Forces.* Lexington: University Press of Kentucky, 2011.

Kelly, Francis J. *U.S. Army Special Forces, 1961–1971.* Washington, DC: Government Printing Office, 1973.

Kelly, Francis J. *The Green Berets in Vietnam, 1967–71.* Washington, DC: Brassey's, 1991.

Kureth, Elwood J. C. *Reflections of a Warriors: Six Years as a Green Beret in Vietnam.* New York: Pocket Books, 2007.

Marvin, Daniel. *Expendable Elite: One Soldier's Journey into Covert Warfare.* Waterville, OR: TrineDay, 2003.

Meissner, Joseph P. *The Green Berets and Their Victories.* Bloomington, IN: AuthorHouse, 2005.

Paddock, Alfred H. *U.S. Army Special Warfare: Its Origins.* Lawrence: University Press of Kansas, 2002.

Patton, Charles D. *Colt Terry, Green Beret.* College Station: Texas A&M University Press 2005.

Pristash, David J. *Diary of a Special Force Trooper in Vietnam, 1967.* Brecksville, OH: Publishing Systems, 1997.

Ray, Morris. *The Ether Zone: U.S. Army Special Forces Detachment B-52, Project Delta.* New York: Midpoint Trade Books, 2011.

Rottman, Gordon L. *Green Beret in Vietnam, 1957–73.* Oxford: Osprey, 2002.

Sasser, Charles W. *Always A Warrior: The Memoir of a Six-War Soldier.* New York: Pocket Books, 1994.

Shachnow, Sidney, and Jann Robbins. *Hope and Honor.* New York: Forge, 2006.

Shelton, Henry H. *Without Hesitation: The Odyssey of an American Warrior.* New York: St. Martin's Press, 2010.

Simpson, Charles M. *Inside the Green Berets: The First Thirty Years, a History of the U.S. Army Special Forces.* Novato, CA: Presidio Press, 1983.

Stanton, Shelby L. *U.S. Army Special Forces A-Team Vietnam Combat Manual*. Boulder, CO: Paladin Press, 1988.

Stanton, Shelby L. *Green Berets at War: U.S. Army Special Forces in Southeast Asia, 1956–1975*. New York: Ivy Books, 1999.

Rangers

Ankony, Robert C. *Lurps: A Ranger's Diary of Tet, Khe Sanh, A Shau, and Quang Tri*. Lanham, MD: Hamilton Books, 2006.

Arnold, James R. *Rangers*. New York: Bantam Books, 1988.

Black, Robert W. *Rangers in Korea*. New York: Ivy Books, 1989.

Black, Robert W. *A Ranger Born: A Memoir of Combat and Valor from Korea to Vietnam*. New York: Ballantine Books, 2002.

Burford, John. *LRRP Team Leader*. New York: Ballantine Books, 1994.

Burford, John. *LRRPs in Action*. Carrollton, TX: Squadron Signal Publications, 1994.

Chambers, Larry. *Death in the A Shau Valley: L Company LRRPs in Vietnam, 1969–70*. New York: Ivy Books, 1998.

Chambers, Larry. *Recondo: LRRPs in the 101st Airborne*. London: Greenhill, 2004.

Cold Steel Third: 3rd Airborne Ranger Company, Korean War (1950–1951). Assembled from Records and Letters of Company Members. Edited by Bob Channon. Franklin, NC: Genealogy Publishing Service, 1993.

Emanuel, Ed. *Soul Patrol: The Riveting True Story of the First African-American LRRP Team in Vietnam*. New York: Presidio Press, 2003.

Field, Ron. *Ranger: Behind Enemy Lines in Vietnam*. London: Military Illustrated, 2000.

Goshen, Bill. *War Paint*. New York: Ballantine Books, 2001.

Hall, Don C. *I Served*. Bellevue, WA: A. D. Hall, 2001.

Harrison, Benjamin L. *Hell on a Hill Top: America's Last Major Battle in Vietnam*. New York: iUniverse, 2004.

Hogan, David W. *Raiders or Elite Infantry? The Changing Role of the U.S. Army Rangers from Dieppe to Grenada*. Westport, CT: Greenwood Press, 1992.

Johnson, Frank. *Diary of an Airborne Ranger: A LRRP's Year in the Combat Zone*. New York: Ballantine Books, 2001.

Jorgenson, Kregg P. J. *LRRP Company Command: The Cav's LRP Rangers in Vietnam, 1968–1969*. New York: Ballantine Books, 2000.

Kiper, Richard L. *Army Raiders: The Special Activities Group in Korea*. Kent, OH: Kent State University Press, 2011.

Landau, Alan M. *Airborne Rangers*. Osceola, WI: Motorbooks International, 1992.

Lanning, Michael L. *Insides the LLRPs: Rangers in Vietnam*. New York: Presidio Press, 2006.

Linderer, Gary A. *Phantom Warriors*. 2 vols. New York: Ballantine Books, 2000.

Martin, Michael N. *The Black Tigers: Rangers of the Second Indochina War*. South Bend, IN: Carleton Graphics, 1998.

Martinez, Reynel. *Six Silent Men: 101st LRP/Rangers*. Book 1. New York: Ivy Books, 1997.

Miller, Kenn. *Six Silent Men: 101st LRP/Rangers*. Book 2. New York: Ivy Books, 1997.

Miraldi, Paul W. *Uniforms and Equipment of U.S. Army Infantry, LRRPS, and Rangers in Vietnam, 1965–1971*. Atglen, PA: Schiffer, 1999.

Posey, Edward L. *The U.S. Army's First, Last, and Only All-Black Rangers: The 2nd Ranger Infantry Company (Airborne) in the Korean War, 1950–1951*. New York: Savas Beattie, 2009.

Puzzo, John J. *K/75th Rangers, "The Highlanders," in the Viet Nam War*. Plainville, CT: Minutes to Midnight Press, 2009.

Roper, Jim. *Aardvarks and Rangers*. Baltimore: PublishAmerica, 2004.

Rottman, Gordon L. *U.S. Army Long-Range Patrol Scout in Vietnam, 1965–71*. New York: Osprey, 2008.

Rotundo, John L. *Charlie Rangers*. New York: Ballantine Books, 1989.

Shanahan, Bill. *Stealth Patrol: The Making of a Vietnam Ranger*. Cambridge, MA: Da Capo Press, 2003.

Sizer, Mona D. *The Glory Guys: The Story of the U.S. Army Rangers*. Lanham, MD: Taylor Trade, 2010.

Stanton, Shelby L. *Rangers at War: Combat Recon in Vietnam*. New York: Orion Books, 1992.

Thompson, Leroy. *America's Commandos: U.S. Special Operations Forces of World War II and Korea*. Mechanicsburg, PA: Stackpole Books, 2001.

Walker, James W. *Fortune Favors the Bold: A British LRRP with the 101st*. New York: Ivy Books, 1998.

82nd Airborne Division

Barker, Geoffrey T. *A Concise History of U.S. Army Airborne Infantry, with Lineage and Insignia*. Brandon, FL: Anglo-American Publishing, 1989.

Ellis, John. *A History of the Airborne Command and Airborne Center*. Sharpsburg, MD: Antietam National Museum, 1979.

Thompson, Leroy. *U.S. Airborne Forces of the Cold War*. Mechanicsburg, PA: Stackpole Books, 2003.

Toomey, Charles L. *XVIII Airborne Corps in Desert Storm: From Planning to Victory*. Central Point, OR: Hellgate Press, 2004.

101st Airborne Division

Anderson, Christopher J. *Screaming Eagles: The 101st Airborne Division from D-Day to Desert Storm*. Mechanicsburg, PA: Stackpole Books, 2000.

Borroel, Roger. *With the "Screaming Eagles" in Vietnam: A Personal Narrative of a Soldier in the 101st Airborne Division, 1968–1969*. East Chicago, IL: La Villita, 1995.

Burns, Richard R. *Pathfinder: First In, Last Out*. New York: Ballantine Books, 2002.

Dustan, Simon, and Mike Sharp. *Airborne in Vietnam*. Edison, NJ: Chartwell Books, 2007.

Flanagan, E. M. *Lightning: The 101st in the Gulf War*. Washington, DC: Brassey's, 1994.

Garcia, Rafael J. *Paladin Zero Six: A Desert Storm Memoir by a 101st Airborne Attack Helicopter Company Commander*. Jefferson, NC: McFarland, 1994.

Linderer, Gary A. *Eyes behind the Lines*. New York: Ivy Books, 1991.

Linderer, Gary A. *The Eyes of Eagles*. New York: Ballantine Books, 1991.

Miller, Randy K. *Troubled Hero: A Medal of Honor, Vietnam, and the War at Home*. Bloomington: Indiana University Press, 2006.

Nolan, Keith W. *Ripcord: Screaming Eagles under Siege, Vietnam, 1970*. Novato, CA: Presidio Press, 2000.

Sharpe, Mike. *101st Airborne Division in Vietnam: The "Screaming Eagles."* Hersham: Ian Allan, 2005.

Taylor, Thomas. *Lightning in the Storm: The 101st Airborne Air Assault Division in the Gulf War*. New York: Hippocrene Books, 1994.

Wiknik, Arthur. *Nam-Sense: Surviving Vietnam with the 101st Airborne Division*. Havertown, PA: Casemate, 2005.

173rd Airborne Brigade

Arthurs, Ted. *Land with No Sun: A Year in Vietnam with the 173rd Airborne*. Mechanicsburg, PA: Stackpole Books, 2006.

Berry, Clifton F. *Sky Soldiers*. New York: Bantam Books, 1987.

Bradley, James R. *173rd Airborne Brigade: Sky Soldiers*. Paducah, KY: Turner, 1993.

Breen, Bob. *First to Fight: Australian Diggers, N.Z. Kiwis, and U.S. Paratroopers in Vietnam, 1965–66*. Boston: Allen and Unwin, 1989.

Flannigan, E. M. *Corregidor, the Rock Assault Force, 1945*. Novato, CA: Presidio Press, 1988.

Hendrix, Dennis. *Head Hunter—One Kilo*. Bloomington, IN: AuthorHouse, 2006.

Leppelman, John. *Blood on the Risers: An Airborne Soldier's Thirty-Five Months in Vietnam*. New York: Ballantine Books, 2006.

McDonough, James L. *Platoon Leader: A Memoir of Command in Combat*. Novato, CA: Presidio Press, 2003.

Murphy, Edward F. *Dak To: America's Sky Soldiers in South Vietnam's Central Highlands, June-November 1967*. New York: Ballantine Books, 2007.

Sanford, Gene W. *Sky Soldier: Airborne, the Long Way Home*. Evansville, IN: Sky Soldier's Ministry, 1992.

187th Airborne Infantry

Bond, James E. *Rakkasans: A History and Collection of Personal Narratives from Members of the 3rd Battalion (Airborne), 187th Infantry, 101st Airborne Division, Republic of Vietnam, 1968*. Baltimore: Gateway Press, 2008.

Flanagan, E. M. *The Rakkasans: The Combat History of the 187th Airborne Infantry*. Novato, CA: Presidio Press, 1997.

Gill, Kirk, L. *3rd Brigade, 101st Airborne Division (Air Assault): Rakkasans*. Paducah, KY: Turner, 1992.

Waterhouse, Fred J. *The Rakkasans: Airborne, 187th Steel Berets*. Paducah, KY: Turner, 1997.

Zaffiri, Samuel. *Hamburger Hill, May 11–20, 1969*. Novato, CA: Presidio Press, 1988.

Central Intelligence Agency

Ahern, Thomas L. *Vietnam Declassified: The CIA and Counterinsurgency*. Lexington: University Press of Kentucky, 2010.

Briggs, Thomas L. *Cash on Delivery: CIA Special Operations during the Secret War in Laos*. Rockville, MD: Rosebank Press, 2009.

Conboy, Kenneth J. *Shadow War: The CIA's Secret War in Laos*. Boulder, CO: Paladin Press, 1995.

Cook, John L. *The Advisor: The Phoenix Program in Vietnam*. Atglen, PA: Schiffer, 1997.

Herrington, Stuart A. *Stalking the Viet Cong: Inside Operation Phoenix: A Personal Account*. Novato, CA: Presidio Press, 1997.

Kelly, Joseph B., and Ben R. Games. *Confessions of a CIA Interrogator*. Bloomington, IN: AuthorHouse, 2007.

Leary, William M. *Perilous Missions: Civil Air Transport and CIA Covert Operations in Asia*. Washington, DC: Smithsonian Institution Press, 2002.

Milton, Bearden, and James Risen. *The Main Enemy: The Inside Story of the CIA's Final Showdown with the KGB*. New York: Random House, 2003.

Monje, Scott C. *The CIA: A Documentary History*. Westport, CT: Greenwood Press, 2008.

Moyar, Mark. *Phoenix and the Birds of Prey: Counterinsurgency and Counterterrorism in Vietnam*. Lincoln: University of Nebraska Press, 2007.

Nashel, Jonathan. *Edward Lansdale's Cold War*. Amherst: University of Massachusetts Press, 2005.

Rosenau, William. *The Phoenix Program and Contemporary Counterinsurgency*. Santa Monica, CA: RAND, 2009.

Smith, Warner. *Covert Warrior: Fighting the CIA's Secret War in Southeast Asia and China, 1965–67: The Vietnam Memoir of Warner Smith*. Novato, CA: Presidio Press, 1996.

Marine Corps Force Reconnaissance

Baumgardner, Randy. *3rd Reconnaissance Battalion: Vietnam War, 1965–1969*. Paducah, KY: Turner, 2003.

Delezen, John E. *Eye of the Tiger: Memoir of a United States Marine, Third Force Recon Company, Vietnam*. Jefferson, NC: McFarland, 2003.

Dillon, George T. *My Duty As I Saw It: U.S.M.C.* Baltimore: PublishAmerica, 2005.

Floyd, W. C. *Green Ghosts: Personal Accounts of Reconnaissance in the DMZ by Marines and Corpsmen Who Bet Their Daily Lives in the Most Dangerous Combat Environment in Vietnam*. Lincoln, NE: iUniverse, 2006.

Goodson, Barry L. *CAP Mot: The Story of a Marine Special Forces Unit in Vietnam, 1968–1969*. Denton: University of North Texas Press, 1997.

Henderson, Charles. *Marshaling the Faithful: The Marines' First Year in Vietnam*. New York: Berkley Books, 1993.

Hildreth, Ray. *Hill 488*. New York: Pocket Books, 2003.

Hodgins, Michael C. *Reluctant Warrior*. New York: Fawcett Columbine, 1997.

Lanning, Michael L., and Ray W. Stubbe. *Inside Force Recon: Recon Marines in Vietnam*. New York: Ivy Books, 1989.

Lee, Alex. *Force Recon Command: A Special Marine Unit in Vietnam, 1969–1970*. Annapolis, MD: Naval Institute Press, 1995.

Meyers, Bruce F. *Fortune Favors the Brave: The Story of First Force Recon*. Annapolis, MD: Naval Institute Press, 2000.

Norton, Bruce H. *Force Recon Diary, 1969–1970*. New York: Ivy Books, 1992.

Peters, Bill. First *Force Recon Company: Sunrise at Midnight*. New York: Ivy Books, 1999.

Rhodes, John R. *Rejoice or Cry: A Vietnam Diary*. Edison, NJ: John R. Rhodes, 1996.

Roberts, Craig. *The Walking Dead: A Marine's Story of Vietnam*. New York: Pocket Books, 1989.

Yerman, Ron. *Lead, Follow, or Get the Hell Out of the Way!* New York: Vantage Press, 1997.

Young, Paul. *First Recon—Second to None: A Marine Reconnaissance Battalion, 1967–1968*. New York: Ivy Books, 1992.

Navy Mobile Riverine Force

Callaway, Joseph W. *Mekong First Light*. New York: Ballantine Books, 2004.

Carrico, John M. *Vietnam Ironclads: U.S. Navy River Assault Craft, 1966–1970*. Morrisville, NC: J. M. Carrico, 2007.

Cutler, Thomas J. *Brown Water, Black Berets: Coastal and Riverine Warfare in Vietnam*. Annapolis, MD: Naval Institute Press, 1988.

Friedman, Norman. *U.S. Small Combatants, Including PT-Boats, Subchasers, and Brown-Water Navy*. Annapolis, MD: Naval Institute Press, 1987.

Fulton, William B. *Mobile Riverine Force: America's Mobile Riverine Force Vietnam*. Paducah, KY: Turner, 1997.

Goldsmith, Wynne. *Papa Bravo Romeo: U.S. Navy Patrol Boats at War in Vietnam*. New York: Ballantine Books, 2001.

McAbee, Ronald L. *River Rats: Brown Water Navy: U.S. Naval Mobile Riverine Operations, Vietnam*. Spartanburg, SC: Honoribus Press, 2001.

Mesko, Jim. *Riverine: A Pictorial History of the Brown Water Navy in Vietnam*. Carrollton, TX: Squadron/Signal Publications, 1985.

O'Neill, John E. *Unfit for Command: Swift Boat Veterans Speak Out against John Kerry*. Washington, DC: Regnery, 2004.

Rottman, Gordon L. *The Vietnam Brown Water Navy: Riverine and Coastal Warfare, 1965–1969*. Hong Kong: Concord, 1997.

Rottman, Gordon L. *Vietnam Riverine Craft, 1962–75*. Oxford: Osprey, 2006.

Steffes, James. *Swift Boat Down: The Real Story of the Sinking of PCF-19*. N.p.: Xlibris, 2006.

Symmes, Weymouth D. *War on the Rivers: A Swift Boat Sailor's Chronicle of the Battle for the Mekong Delta*. Missoula, MT: Pictorial Histories, 2004.

Navy Underwater Demolition Teams

Bosiljevac, T. L. *SEALs: UDT/Seal Operations in Vietnam*. Boulder, CO: Paladin Press, 1990.

Carrico, Phillip E. *Exploits of Navy Frogmen in Korea: Pioneers of U.S. Navy Special Warfare*. Hemphill, TX: Dogwood Press, 2004.

Dockery, Kevin. *Special Warfare: Special Weapons, the Arms and Equipment of the UDT and SEALs from 1943 to the Present*. Chicago: Emperor's Press, 1996.

Fane, Francis D., and Don Moore. *The Naked Warriors: The Story of the U.S. Navy's Frogmen*. Annapolis, MD: Naval Institute Press, 1995.

Kaine, Francis R. *Reminiscences of Captain Francis R. Kaine, U.S. Naval Reserve*. Annapolis, MD: Naval Institute Press, 1990.

Melson, Charles D., and Bruce Vanderhort. *The Water Is Never Cold: The Origins of the U.S. Navy's Combat Demolition Units, UDT, and SEALs*. Washington, DC: Brassey's, 2000.

Nickelson, Richard G. *Hooyah! UDT/SEAL Stories of the 1960s*. Westminster, MD: Eagle Editions, 2006.

Waterman, Steven L. *Just a Sailor: A Navy Diver's Story of Photography, Salvage, and Combat*. New York: Ballantine Books, 2000.

Young, Darryl. *SEALs, UDT, Frogmen: Men under Pressure*. New York: Ivy Books, 1994.

Navy SEALs

Couch, Dick. *SEAL Team One*. Annapolis, MD: Naval Institute Press, 2008.

Cummings, Dennis J., ed. *The Men behind the Trident: SEAL Team One in Vietnam*. Annapolis, MD: Naval Institute Press, 1997.

Dockery, Kevin. *SEALs in Action*. New York: Avon Books, 1991.

Dockery, Kevin. *Free Fire Zones: The True Story of U.S. Navy SEAL Combat in Vietnam.* New York: Harper Torch, 2000.

Dockery, Kevin. *Navy SEALs: A History of the Early Years.* New York: Berkley Books, 2001.

Dockery, Kevin. *Navy SEALs: A History, Part II: The Vietnam Years.* New York: Berkley Books, 2002.

Dockery, Kevin. *Navy SEALs: A Complete History: From World War II to the Present.* New York: Berkley Books, 2004.

Dockery, Kevin. *Operation Thunderhead: The True Story of Vietnam's Final POW Rescue Mission—and the Last SEAL Killed in Country.* New York: Berkley Caliber, 2008.

Enoch, Barry W., and Gregory A. Walker. *Teammates, SEALs at War.* New York: Pocket Books, 1996.

Fawcett, Bill, ed. *Hunters and Shooters: An Oral History of the U.S. Navy Seals in Vietnam.* New York: William Morrow, 1995.

Gardner, Bill. *Hell Week: U.S. Navy SEALs.* Victoria, BC: Trafford Press, 2004.

Gormly, Robert A. *Combat Swimmer: Memoirs of a Navy SEAL.* New York: Dutton, 1998.

Hutchins, Joel. *Swimmers among the Trees: SEALs in the Vietnam War.* Novato, CA: Presidio Press, 1996.

Jordan, David. *The U.S. Navy SEALs: Sea, Air, and Land Specialists.* San Diego: Thunder Bay Press, 2003.

Keith, Thomas H. *SEAL Warrior: Death in the Dark: Vietnam, 1968–1972.* New York: St. Martin's Press, 2009.

Keith, Thomas H. *SEAL Warrior: The Only Easy Day Was Yesterday.* New York: St. Martin's Griffin, 2010.

Kelly, Daniel E. *U.S. Navy Seawolves: The Elite HAL-3 Helicopter Squadron in Vietnam.* New York: Ballantine Books, 2002.

Kelly, Orr. *Brave Men . . . Dark Waters: The Untold Story of the Navy SEALs.* Novato, CA: Presidio Press, 1992.

Kelly, Orr. *Never Fight Fair! Navy SEALs Stories of Combat and Adventure.* Novato, CA: Presidio Press, 1995.

McPartlin, Greg. *Combat Corpsmen.* New York: Penguin, 2005.

Marcinko, Richard. *Rogue Warrior.* New York: Pocket Books, 1992.

Micheletti, Eric. *SEALs in Vietnam.* Paris: Histoire & Collections, 1997.

Miller, Rad. *Whattaya Mean I Can't Kill 'Em: A Navy SEAL in Vietnam.* New York: Ivy Books, 1998.

Miller, Rad. *SEAL Stories: Tango Platoon 1969 Vietnam.* Bloomington, IN: AuthorHouse, 2007.

Smith, Gary R. *Death in the Jungle: Diary of a Navy SEAL.* Boulder, CO: Paladin Press, 1994.

Vistica, Gregory L. *The Education of Lieutenant Kerrey.* New York: Thomas Dunne Books/St. Martin's Press, 2003.

Walsh, Michael J. *SEAL! From Vietnam's PHOENIX Program to Central America's Drug Wars: Twenty-Six Years as a Special Operations Warrior*. New York: Pocket Books, 1994.

Watson, James, and Kevin Dockery. *Point Man: Inside the Toughest and Most Deadly Unit in Vietnam by a Founding Member of the Elite Navy SEALs*. New York: Morrow, 1993.

Young, Darryl. *The Element of Surprise: Navy SEALs in Vietnam*. New York: Ivy Books, 1990.

Hmong

Churchill, Jan. *Classified Secret: Controlling Airstrikes in the Clandestine War in Laos*. Manhattan, KS: Sunflower Press, 2000.

Curry, Robert, et al. *Whispering Death "tuag nco ntsoov": Our Journey among the Hmong in the Secret War for Laos*. New York: iUniverse, 2004.

Halliday, John T. *Flying through Midnight: A Pilot's Dramatic Story of His Secret Missions Over Laos during the Vietnam War*. New York: Scribner, 2005.

Hathorn, Reginald. *Here There Are Tigers: The Secret Air War in Laos, 1968–69*. Mechanicsburg, PA: Stackpole Books, 2008.

Leary, William M. *Perilous Missions: Civil Air Transport and CIA Covert Operations in Asia*. Washington, DC: Smithsonian Institution Press, 2002.

Morrison, Gayle. *The Sky Is Falling: An Oral History of the CIA's Evacuation of the Hmong from Laos*. Jefferson, NC: McFarland, 1999.

Nalty, Bernard C. *The War against Trucks: Aerial Interdiction in Southern Laos, 1968–1972*. Washington, DC: Air Force History and Museums Program, 2005.

Pao Vang. *Against All Odds: The Laotian Freedom Fighters*. Washington, DC: Heritage Foundation, 1987.

Quincy, Keith. *Harvesting Pa Chay's Wheat: The Hmong and America's Secret War in Laos*. Spokane: Eastern Washington University Press, 2000.

Kit Carson Scouts

Brown, F. C. "Kit Carson Scouts in the Vietnam Conflict." *Military Collector and Historian* 30, no. 3 (September 1978): 109–12.

Cowan, William V. "Kit Carson Scouts." *Marine Corps Gazette* 53, no. 10 (October 1969): 30–32.

Tovy, Tal. "From Foe to Friend" *Armed Forces and Society* 33, no. 1 (October 2006): 78–93.

Montagnards

Barnes, H. Lee. *When We Walked above the Clouds: A Memoir of Vietnam*. Lincoln: University of Nebraska Press, 2011.

Blondell, Anthony J. *Honor and Sacrifice: The Montagnards of Ba Cat*. Central Point, OR: Hellgate Press, 2000.

Burruss, L. H. *Mike Force*. Lincoln, NE: iUniverse, 2000.

Donlon, Roger H. *Beyond Nam Dong*. Leavenworth, KS: R and N Publishers, 1998.

Donahue, James C. *No Greater Love: A Day with the Mobile Guerilla Force in Vietnam*. Canton, OH: Daring Books, 1988.

Dooley, George E. *Battle for the Central Highlands: A Special Forces Story*. New York: Ballantine Books, 2000.

Moore, David K. *Tribal Soldiers of Vietnam: The Effects of Unconventional Warfare on Tribal Populations*. Philadelphia: Xlibris, 2007.

Philips, William R. *Night of the Silver Stars: The Battle of Lang Vei*. Annapolis, MD: Naval Institute Press, 1997.

Rottman, Gordon L. *Special Forces Camps in Vietnam, 1961–70*. New York: Osprey, 2005.

Rottman, Gordon L. *Mobile Strike Forces in Vietnam, 1966–70*. New York: Osprey, 2007.

Sherman, Steve. *U.S. Army Special Forces Participation in the CIDG Program: Vietnam, 1957–1975*. Houston: Radix Press, 2000.

Wade, Leigh. *Tan Phu, Special Forces Team A-23 in Combat*. New York: Ivy Books, 1997.

Wade, Leigh. *Assault on Dak Pek: A Special Forces A-Team in Combat, 1970*. New York: Ivy Books, 1998.

Wade, Leigh. *The Protected Will Never Know*. New York: Ivy Books, 1998.

Yedinak, Steven M. *Hard to Forget: An American with the Mobile Guerilla Force in Vietnam*. New York: Ivy Books, 1998.

Studies and Observations Group

Benavidez, Roy P., and John P. Craig. *Medal of Honor: One Man's Journey from Poverty and Prejudice*. Washington, DC: Potomac Books, 2005.

Blessing, Leonard D. *Warrior Healers: The Untold Story of the Special Forces Medic*. Lincoln, NE: iUniverse, 2006.

Burkins, Lee. *Soldier's Heart: An Inspirational Memoir and Inquiry of War*. Bloomington, IN: 1st Books, 2003.

Carpenter, Stephen A. *Boots on the Ground: The Story of Project Delta*. Scotts Valley, CA: Createspace, 2010.

Conboy, Kenneth J., and Dale Andrade. *Spies and Commandos: How America Lost the Secret War in North Vietnam*. Lawrence: University Press of Kansas, 2000.

Donahue, James C. *Blackjack-33: With Special Forces in the Viet Cong Forbidden Zone*. New York: Ivy Books, 1999.

Garner, Joe R. *Code Name, Copperhead: My True-Life Exploits as a Special Forces Soldier*. New York: Simon and Schuster, 1994.

Gillespie, Robert M. *Black Ops, Vietnam: The Operational History of MACVSOG*. Annapolis, MD: Naval Institute Press, 2011.

Gole, Henry G. *Soldiering: Observations from Korea, Vietnam, and Safe Places*. Washington, DC: Potomac Books, 2005.

Greco, Frank. *Running Recon: A Photo Journey with SOG Special Ops along the Ho Chi Minh Trail*. Boulder, CO: Paladin Press, 2004.

Greco, Frank. *Kontum: Command and Control: Select Photographs of SOG Special Ops during the Vietnam War*. Philadelphia: Xlibris, 2005.

Hoe, Alan. *The Quiet Professional: Major Richard J. Meadows of the U.S. Army Special Forces*. Lexington: University Press of Kentucky, 2011.

Jackson, Walter J. *Shades of Daniel Boone: A Personal View of Special Ops during the War in Vietnam*. Westminster, MD: Eagle Editions, 2005.

Meyer, John S. *Across the Fence: The Secret War in Vietnam*. Oceanside, CA: SOG Publishing, 2011.

Miller, Franklin D., and Elwood C. Kureth. *Reflections of a Warrior*. Novato, CA: Presidio Press, 1991.

Morris, R. C. *The Ether Zone: U.S. Army Special Forces Detachment B-52, Project Delta*. Ashland, OR: Hellgate Press, 2009.

Nicholson, Thom. *15 Months with SOG: A Warrior's Tour*. New York: Ivy Books, 1999.

Parnar, Joe, and Robert Dumont. *SOG Medic: Stories from Vietnam and over the Fence*. Boulder, CO: Paladin Press, 2007.

Plaster, John L. *The Secret War's of America's Commandos in Vietnam*. New York: Simon and Schuster, 1997.

Plaster, John L. *SOG: A Photo History of the Secret Wars*. Boulder, CO: Paladin Press, 2000.

Plaster, John L. *Secret Commandos: Behind Enemy Lines with the Elite Warriors of SOG*. New York: Simon and Schuster, 2004.

Reske, Charles F., ed. *MAC-V-SOG Command History, Annex B, 1971–1972*. 2 vols. Sharon Center, OH: Alpha Press, 1990.

Rottman, Gordon. *US MACV-SOG Reconnaissance Team in Vietnam*. New York: Osprey, 2011.

Saal, Harve. *SOG, MACV Studies and Observations Group: Behind Enemy Lines*. Ann Arbor, MI: Edwards Brothers, 1990.

Shultz, Richard H. *The Secret War against Hanoi: And Johnson's Use of Spies, Saboteurs, and Covert Warriors in North Vietnam*. New York: HarperCollins, 1999.

Singlaub, John K., and Malcolm McConnell. *Hazardous Duty: An American Soldier in the Twentieth Century*. New York: Summit Books, 1991.

Stein, Jeff. *A Murder in Wartime: The Untold Spy Story That Changed the Course of the Vietnam War*. New York: St. Martin's Press, 1992.

Part II

U.S. Special Forces, 1992 to the Present

4

Air Force Air Commandos

Any time, any place.

The U.S. Air Force Special Operations Command (AFSOC) was founded on May 22, 1990, from the existing 23rd Air Force. It is the junior member of all special forces groups and the one placing the greatest emphasis on high technology for navigation, communications, and fire control. It also represents the first time that the vaunted Air Commandos, which have existed in various ad hoc formations since World War II, finally acquired a command of their own. Based at Hurlburt Field, Florida, AFSOC is tasked with a multiplicity of special operation profiles, all of which can be conducted anywhere around the world with speed, precision, and efficiency. Many of these same missions are also executed in close concert with special operations personnel from other branches, including rangers, SEALs Delta Force, and so on. Such mission profiles include unconventional warfare, special reconnaissance, counterterrorism, foreign internal defense, and psychological warfare. AFSOC is also capable of undertaking classified direct-action missions, namely, small-scale tactical assaults from the sky with highly trained shock troops to eliminate enemy positions, personnel, or even individual leaders. More mundane but equally vital activities, such as combat search and rescue to secure downed airmen deep behind enemy lines, are also prescribed. Presently, AFSOC fields an estimated 25,000 men, all collectively known by the rubric of "air commandos," a concept harkening back to operations over Burma during World War II. Although their actual inventory is not precisely known, AFSOC apparently operates approximately 100 specially equipped aircraft, including gunships, tankers, transports, and helicopters. These represent the most highly sophisticated machines of their class, anywhere.

Of special note among AFSOC are the Special Tactics Squadrons (STS), which serve as an elite infantry component for air force special operations. They consist of heavily armed and highly trained Combat Controller Teams (CCTs) and pararescuemen, each with their own distinct preparation and functions. Both categories, by necessity, have to be extremely

(Library of Congress)

proficient at the mind-boggling variety of insertion techniques employed. CCTs principally function as forward air controllers, who usually land by parachute, then establish landing zones for helicopters by providing the requisite air traffic control. To facilitate this, they employ the latest state-of-the-art communications equipment and air navigation aids. More important, they serve as the ground-to-air link to AFSOC aircraft flying close support missions to assist special forces below. This is usually accomplished by "painting" ground targets with a special laser beam target indicator that guides aircraft munitions, either cannon fire or smart weapons, precisely to the target. By comparison, pararescuers, or "PJs" (parajumpers) as they call themselves, are rigorously trained, medical rescue personnel who provide emergency treatment to battlefield casualties, then oversee their evacuation from combat zones. There are presently only six STS units extant; each consists of three teams of 18 men and two officers each. All are equally divided between controllers and pararescuers and are among the most highly trained specialists in American special operations.

Aside from their military expertise, AFSOC places a high emphasis on humanitarian and civic assistance around the world. Being specially trained to respond to any crisis on short notice, they are usually the first military units at a disaster scene and function as America's ambassadors in poor and frequently politically unstable nations. Food delivery, disaster evacuation, and medical treatments all figure prominently in this important public relations function, albeit on a global scale.

Organization

Presently, AFSOC consists of six active-duty units, with an additional two in the reserves. These are as follows:

U.S. Air Force Special Operations School, headquartered at Hurlburt Field, Florida
This institution is designed to impart special operations theory and training on 7,000 students a year, including American service personnel, select government agencies, and officers from allied nations. A wide variety of classified subjects are covered relative to the conduct of special operations, including current global affairs, civil action, antiterrorism, and unconventional warfare.

1st Special Operations Wing, stationed at AFSOC headquarters, Hurlburt Field, Florida
It consists of seven special operations squadrons equipped with AC-130U Specter gunships, MC-130E Combat Talon II transports, HC-130M/P Combat Shadow aircraft, and MH-53J Pave Low helicopters. This select unit, previously known as the 16th Special Operations Wing, is the most senior and experienced formation within AFSOC. In 2011,

Variants of the AC-130 Specter aerial gunship have seen distinguished service since the Vietnam War. They are equipped with a vast array of radars, sensors, and communications equipment for all-weather operations. (U.S. Department of Defense)

the first deliveries of the MC-130J, even more sophisticated and fuel-efficient than their predecessors, were accepted.

352nd Special Operations Group, stationed at Royal Air Force Base Mindenhall, United Kingdom

Designated part of Special Operations Command, Europe, this unit consists of three special operations squadrons equipped with MC-130H Combat Talon II transports, HC-130N/P Combat Shadow aircraft, and MH-53 Pave Low helicopters. Units of the crack 321st Special Tactics Squadron, elite air force assault troops, also reside there.

353rd Special Operations Group, based at Kadena, Japan

This is the designated air force member of the Special Operations Command, Pacific. It consists of three special operations squadrons utilizing MC-130E Combat Talon II transports, the HC-130N/P Combat Shadow aircraft, and the MH-53J Pave Low III helicopter.

720th Special Tactics Group, stationed at Hurlburt Field, Florida

This unit deploys its constituent units across the United States, Europe, and the Pacific. It contains four highly trained special operations squadrons, including elite CCTs, combat weathermen, and pararescuers.

18th Flight Test Squadron, based at Hurlburt Field, Florida

This unit is tasked with evaluating new equipment and technologies, concepts, and strategies, all of which are calculated to enhance the performance of AFSOC units. In this capacity, it frequently conducts joint command projects with elite units drawn from other branches of the service.

Air force commandos include specially trained ground controllers who can accurately direct laser-guided bombs and other ordnance from aircraft circling overhead. (U.S. Department of Defense)

The reserve component of AFSOC presently consists of two units in the Air National Guard:

193rd Special Operations Group, stationed at Harrisburg International Airport, Pennsylvania

Despite its reserve status, this unit handles all AFSOC television and radio broadcasting from the air and operates specially equipped EC-130E Commando Solo aircraft. As such, it is frequently deployed around the world to fly psychological operations warfare missions along with humanitarian assistance where needed.

919th Special Operations Wing, flying from Duke Field, Florida

This unit specializes in the insertion of special operations forces and under daylight or nocturnal conditions and is specially outfitted to operate at low levels in hostile airspace.

One constituent unit, the 5th Special Operations Squadron, operates HC-130N/P Combat Shadow tankers for the refueling of special operations aircraft in the air and resupply missions on the ground.

Personnel and Training

All AFSOC personnel must successfully complete routine air force boot camp before proceeding into a special forces field, although anyone can volunteer. For flight personnel, this includes advanced technical training in flying, navigating, and equipment maintenance, reflecting the complicated equipment at the heart of special forces missions. Prospective candidates are expected to display above-average flying and navigation skills, problem-solving abilities, and a knack for working with individuals or small groups of individuals in hostile combat environments.

Membership in the highly elite STS, however, requires quantum jump in training, endurance, and all-around pain. To weed out undesirables, volunteers first endure the rigors of the dreaded Physical Abilities and Stamina Test (PAST), a gruesome regime intended to push future members to their limits—and beyond. This commences with a 25-meter underwater swim without surfacing; those who fail are immediately disqualified. Survivors next endure a 1,000-meter surface swim that must be successfully concluded in only 26 minutes. As before, any recruit pausing to rest is ejected from the program. Following a 30-minute respite, recruits are next subjected to a 1.5-mile run to be completed in 10 minutes, 30 seconds; a 10-minute rest; and then a series of four concentrated calisthenics sets interspersed by three-minute rest periods. Older commissioned officers attempting to enter the STS face enhanced physical challenges to bring them up to parity with their younger charges. These are also required to write extensive essays explaining exactly why they chose special operations and must submit three letters of recommendation from superiors. With the PAST having run its course, the survivors are then trundled off to Lackland Air Force Base, Texas, to attend the Indoctrination Course.

The 12-week Pararescue/Combat Control Indoctrination Course brings physical and mental discomfiture to new heights. Here candidates must master the nuances of airborne training and basic underwater demolition techniques not unlike Army Rangers and Navy SEALs. It commences with two weeks of intense physical endeavors, followed by a period of unvarnished pain endowed with the deceptively tame title of Motivation Week. The ensuing seven days of mental and physical challenges usually cuts class sizes down dramatically, sometimes up to 90 percent, and include water confidence tests, firearms handling, marksmanship, and physiological training in atmospheric and dive chambers. These ordeals are specifically calculated to reaffirm existing mental and physical endurance—then expand them. Additionally, all candidates are required to successfully execute a series of complex tasks under duress, all the while closely monitored by their superiors. Only those fortunate enough to persevere are allowed to enroll in specialty training, better known as the "Pipeline." Here, candidates arrive at the U.S. Army Combat Divers School in Key West, Florida, to familiarize themselves with a variety of underwater respiratory equipment. Through this expedient, air force personnel gain exposure to the tactics and methodologies of Navy SEALs, with whom they will one day deploy. Exercises are conducted in both day and night conditions and include submarine operations and underwater demolitions. From here, the men report to the U.S. Navy Underwater Egress Center at Pensacola, Florida, for a ride in the so-called Helicopter Underwater Egress Trainer. This is basically a helicopter mock-up plunged upside down into water with the recruits blindfolded, at which point they have to release their seat belts and fumble their way to the exit.

With all this torment under their belts, the men report to Fort Benning, Georgia, for three weeks of basic airborne training, another demanding routine. Those passing receive the Silver Wings denoting their airborne-qualified status and then proceed to Fort Bragg, North Carolina, to attend the U.S. Army Military Freefall Parachutist School. In addition to military static line techniques, the recruits practice free-fall, high-altitude, high-opening parachuting, which allows them to ingress into enemy positions and guide their actual landing for several miles. This is accomplished through the MC-5 Ram-Air Parachute System, a rectangular device allowing for pinpoint accuracy during their descent. The Yuma Proving Grounds in Arizona is the next stop for a bout of continual jumping from every conceivable altitude and weather condition, including night descents while strapped to several hundred pounds of field equipment. Assuming that this phase of the training is accomplished, the recruits next proceed to the Colville and Kaniskau National Forests in Spokane, Washington, for a three-week visit with the 22nd Training Squadron, specializing in cold-weather, outdoor survival techniques, including land navigation, ground-to-air signaling, and helicopter hoist training. The last remaining hurdle is the Survival Escape Resistance and Evasion training to avoid capture, which is also the final time that officers and enlisted men train in concert. Survivors of the previous 55 weeks attend a graduation ceremony before pursuing their individual combat specialty. Still even more arduous work is required before they can join the select ranks of the Special Tactics STS.

Those men intending to become combat controllers report to Keesler Air Force Base in Mississippi to attend the 15-week Combat Control Operator Course. This regimen is jointly taught by civilian and military instructors to impart basic flight rules, radar approach and control techniques, air navigational aids, weather forecasting, and all the nuances of air traffic control to their charges. Graduates next attend the Combat Control School at Pope Air Force Base in North Carolina for exposure and hands-on training in communications equipment, fire support, combat air traffic control, and properly preparing a landing zone. Concurrently, candidates endure continual physical conditioning throughout the 87-day training period, including six-mile runs, swimming, marching with field packs, and calisthenics. Once the basics have been mastered, the men attend Camp McKall in North Carolina to endure the so-called Q-Course. This involves mastering the use of laser designators to "paint" enemy targets for destruction as well as additional techniques for prepping landing zones. The device in question, the 70-pound Special Operations Force Laser Acquisition Market (SOFLAM), allows "smart bombs" dropped by AFSOC from any American military aircraft to land a safe distance with a minimum risk to either the aircraft or laser operator. Properly employed, the designator virtually ensures a direct hit every time. As students near the end of their training, they plan and execute a mock mission, ingress into the area by parachute, and then execute a select mission profile over a 10-day period. That done, they march back to the Combat Control School lugging the SOFLAM in their rucksack prior to reporting for ranger-style training to acquaint themselves with army special forces. The final phase of combat controller training is undertaken at Eglin Air Force Base in Florida for the Initial Familiarization Course. This requires candidates to train with pararescuers and acquire the skill and cohesion inherent in all air commandos. They also practice constantly on a variety of aircraft and helicopters operated by AFSOC to gain familiarity and operational proficiency. The final obstacle is a joint mission with ranger units in a simulated airfield seizure exercise. The handful of volunteers still present are finally granted Special Operations Tactical Air Control certification, which marks them as members of one of the world's most elite fighting forces.

Volunteers intending to become pararescuers weather a similar ordeal at Fort Bragg, where the Special Operations Combat Medic Course unfolds. This regimen is designed to impart comprehensive medical training over the course of 24 weeks and includes four-week stints in urban areas of New York City. Here they are constantly exposed to patients suffering from knife and gunshot wounds, burns, crash injuries, and conditions similar to those found under battlefield conditions. Phase I, also known as the Emergency Medical Technician Basic, prepares future pararescuers on how to prepare trauma patients for evacuation while attending to lesser though still life-threatening, injuries. A further 17 weeks of Phase II training ensues whereby minor surgery, pharmacology, trauma management, and other emergency treatments are inculcated. Successful candidates obtain emergency medical personnel status, which indicates that they have been certified in cardiac training by the American Heart Association and basic paramedical techniques endorsed by the National Registry of Emergency Technicians. They are then herded to Kirtland Air Force Base in New Mexico for the 90-day Pararescue Recovery Specialist Course. The first, or Ground Phase, teaches field craft, woodcraft, and wilderness survival techniques and ends with a 10-day jaunt in the nearby Pecos Mountains. During the second, or Medical Phase, trainees are issued the All-Purpose Lightweight Individual Carrying Equipment (ALICE) rucksack, which is standard equipment for Green Berets, rangers, and combat controllers, although in this instance it is crammed with medical impedimenta. The men also gain instruction on the Rapid Extraction Deployment System, a set of portable hydraulic jaws for cutting away parts of aircraft fuselages to rescue trapped crew members. This is followed by the Air Operations Phase, whereby recruits familiarize themselves with the aircraft and helicopters they will be riding in. They are taught various insertion/extraction techniques using ropes, ladders, hoists, and rappelling. The men also make numerous parachute jumps over water and land under various conditions. Jumpers must also don the Parachutist Rough Terrain System, a bulky, padded suit designed to protect them from hard landings in wooded areas. Given the highly demanding nature of their work, successful candidates must then demonstrate unflagging proficiency in rescue operations, parachuting, medicine, navigation, and weapons usage. Once they do, they are finally accorded pararescue status, along with the distinctive maroon beret denoting their station.

Equipment

The main aircraft in the AFSOC inventory is based on the legendary Lockheed C-130 Hercules transport, which has been in service since 1956 and continues flying to the present. The latest variant is the AC-130U Specter, an aircraft that first performed air support missions during the Vietnam conflict. This aircraft is heavily armed with a GAU-12/U 25-mm Gatling gun in the nose, which is completely traversable and capable of loosing 1,800 rounds a minute at ranges up to 12,000 yards. Generally, this weapon is employed against infantry, small buildings, and light vehicles, usually with devastating effect. For larger ground targets, the Specter also carries a 40-mm Bofors gun on the port (right) side of the fuselage, firing high-explosive, incendiary, or conventional ammunition. However, the biggest punch comes from its M1A1 105-mm howitzer cannon, which handles armor-piercing, white phosphorus, and incendiary rounds. The reason behind all this concentrated firepower is that the AC-130U, unlike speedy jet fighter-bombers, is a relatively slow aircraft with considerable loiter time above the battlefield and can select, attack, and destroy targets in almost leisurely fashion, especially at night. The aircraft itself is packed with modern, state-of-the-art sensors and computerized aiming devices in the Battle Management Center, whereby all potential targets are illuminated through special televised monitors. Onboard gunners can employ a variety of infrared and radar detection devices to see a target, even if obscured by dense smoke. Moreover, they are at liberty to point all three weapons at three different targets and engage them all simultaneously. AC-130Us (and the earlier AC-130Hs) possess top speeds in excess of 300 miles per hour, a range of 2,200 miles, and a service ceiling of 30,000 feet. Because the AC-130 can be refueled in flight by a variety of tanker aircraft, its range is virtually unlimited. Both models are presently operated by the 4th and 16th Special Operations Squadrons; 13 aircraft are known to be in operational use. While lethal when properly deployed, the low, slow-flying AC-130s are nonetheless vulnerable to ground fire and hostile aircraft, so they perform primarily support missions at night and only in low-threat environments. AFSOC have made its desire known that any successor aircraft should be equipped with stealth technology to enhance survivability and be armed with smart missiles and possible laser weapons.

An equally important variant is the MC-130H Combat Talon II, which is specially designed for the clandestine insertion and extraction of large special operation teams. As such, it can be rigged to accommodate 77 seated passengers, 57 medical litters, or 52 fully equipped parachutists. Like the gunship version, the Combat Talon is outfitted with high-tech radars and advanced delivery equipment to allow low-level flight in hostile airspace. The aircrews are also especially trained to successfully perform night and bad-weather operations. The MC-130H can also be outfitted for offensive purposes by dropping the huge 15,000-pound BLU-82 "Daisy Cutter" bomb through its cargo doors. This highly destructive device is generally used to clear minefield and landing zones, although it can also be used to level enemy positions in caves and other natural fortifications. Another important subtype is the MC-130P Combat Shadow, which serves as an aerial tanker. It is designed to refuel special operations helicopters at night while also flying in formation at low altitudes to avoid detection. The aircraft is also capable of conveying small rubber boats and their teams into hostile regions and parachuting them into the water.

The wear and tear of constant use in Iraq, Afghanistan, and elsewhere has pushed the MC-130H aircraft to the limits of their service life, so in 2011 the first of the newer MC-130J variants started arriving. This aircraft, equipped with newer and efficient engines, is both cheaper and easier to maintain and generates 29 percent greater thrust while consuming 15 percent less fuel. Upgraded avionics have also reduced the crew size from four to three men, and the large rear ramp can now be opened in flight at speed of up to 300 miles per hour. Despite all these advantages, the MC-130J is expected to cost 20 percent less than its predecessors. It has also been revealed that 16 of these aircraft will also be converted into gunships to replace aging AC-130 gunships.

A final version employed by AFSOC is the EC-130E River Rider Command Solo specifically employed by the 193rd Special Operations Group, a National Guard unit. This is essentially a psychological operations platform equipped with AM/FM radio, HF/shortwave, and television facilities capable of transmitting messages from outside the range of enemy guns and antiaircraft missiles. Jamming devices are also available to confuse and interrupt enemy communications. In essence, the Command Solo is literally a flying television and radio station combined in one high-tech media package.

The standard rotary-wing aircraft employed by AFSOC is the Sikorsky MH-53J/M Pave Low III, a large flying platform with a crew of six. Like all special operations aircraft, it is crammed with sophisticated electronics and is capable of performing safely at night and in bad weather. The Pave Low is tasked with executing a low-level, long-range clandestine ingress behind enemy lines, usually for the purpose of inserting or extracting teams of special forces. To this end, it employs the Interactive Defensive Avionics System/Multi-Mission Advanced Tactical Terminal, which sports a color display console with digital night vision. This allows the helicopter to traverse at low altitudes in the dark while still navigating clear of telephone poles and other dangerous barriers. For assault missions, the Pave Low also carries up to 38 troops and is armed with two 7.62-mm miniguns and a .50-caliber machine gun. However, because the Pave Lows are aging, they are destined for gradual replacement by an exciting new form of aerial technology.

The newest aircraft in the AFSOC arsenal is the radically different CV-22 Osprey tiltrotor transport, which lifts off and lands like a helicopter, yet flies like a conventional aircraft. It accomplishes this by having the wingtip-mounted engines tilt upward to rise then level out to fly straight. Several have already been deployed in Afghanistan. The Osprey is capable of hauling 24 full equipped troops or 12 casualty litters at speeds up to 310 miles per hour. It is flown by two officers and two flight engineers, yet it exceeds every flight profile of all the machines it replaces. Give the speed and flexibility of these new aircraft, it is now theoretically possible for special forces teams to perform several select missions in a single day or night. Such technology is extremely pricey, and at $50 million each, only 32 machines will be acquired to replace all AFSOC helicopters by 2012. The Osprey is designed to adequately meet all air force special operations requirements well into the 21st century, and follow-on models will undoubtedly enhance that capability exponentially.

Known Activities

Because of the classified nature of air force special operations, the exact time, date, and nature of air commando missions are not generally known. Throughout the 1990s, they participated in NATO operations in Kosovo and the Balkans and assisted in the rescue of downed coalition airmen. From September 2001 through November 2004, no fewer than 8,500 of AFSOC's 20,000 air commandos have been deployed across the globe in the war against terror. Special Tactic Teams were certainly present in Afghanistan in October 2001 during the commencement of Operation ENDURING FREEDOM, when they guided in air strikes to assist Army Special Forces Operational Detachment-Alphas on the ground. Al-Qaeda and Taliban formations were simply decimated in this fashion no matter where they hid. Such attacks could be delivered by jets, attack helicopters, and even such high-flying bombers as B-52s. Enemy resistance simply wilted, and troops of the Northern Alliance took control of the country by December 2001. Large bodies of Army Rangers were also delivered to the theater by

MC-130 H Combat Talons, while MC-130P Combat Shadows refueled continual special forces helicopter missions. In March 2002, air commandos participated in Operation ANACONDA above the mountains of southern Afghanistan. Accidents apparently claimed one Pave Low helicopter in November 2001 and a Combat Talon II in June 2002, while other losses of aircraft and personnel remain speculative. AFSOC is nonetheless highly engaged in the war against global terror, and their silent contributions should be acknowledged as such.

Bibliography

Call, Steve. *Danger Close: Tactical Air Controllers in Afghanistan and Iraq*. College Station: Texas A&M University Press, 2007.

Carney, John T., and Benjamin F. Schemmer. *No Room for Error: The Tactics behind the USAF Special Tactics Unit*. Novato, CA: Presidio Press, 2003.

Fleming, Edward. *Heart of the Storm: My Adventures as a Helicopter Rescue Pilot and Commander*. Hoboken, NJ: Wiley, 2004.

Hebert, Adam J. "The Air Commandos." *Air Force Magazine* 88, no. 3 (March 2005): 32–38.

Hebert, Adam J. "The Ground Warriors of Airpower." *Air Force Magazine* 88, no. 9 (September 2005): 32–37.

Hirsch, Michael. *None Braver: U.S. Air Force Pararescuemen in the War on Terrorism*. New York: New American Library, 2003.

Jolly, Randy. *Air Commandos: The Quiet Professionals, Air Force Special Operations Command*. Garland, TX: Aero Graphics, 1994.

Kelly, Orr. *From a Dark Sky: The Story of U.S. Air Force Special Operations*. Novato, CA: Presidio Press, 1996.

Llinares, Rick, and Andy Evans. *U.S. Air Force Special Operations Command*. Bedford: SAM, 2010.

McCullough, Amy. "Air Commando U: The Air Force Special Operations Center Is Discovering New Ways to Turn Out Highly Trained Airmen." *Air Force Magazine* 94, no. 7 (2011): 47–51.

McKinney, Mike. *Chariots of the Damned: Helicopter Special Operations from Vietnam to Kosovo*. New York: Thomas Dunne Books/St. Martin's Press, 2002.

Mutza, Wayne. *Green Hornets: The History of the U.S. Air Force 20th Special Operations Squadron*. Atglen, PA: Schiffer Military History, 2007.

Pushies, Fred. *U.S. Air Force Special Ops*. St. Paul, MN: Zenith Press, 2007.

Pushies, Fred. *Deadly Blue: Battle Stories of the U.S. Air Force Special Operations Command*. New York: American Management Association, 2009.

Yancy, Madonna. *United States Air Force Commandos*. Paducah, KY: Turner, 2000.

5

1st Special Forces Operational Detachment—Delta (Delta Force)

Since their founding on November 21, 1979, the 1st Special Forces Operational Detachment—Delta, also known as the Combat Applications Group or, more popularly, Delta Force, is the nation's premier counterterrorism unit. Specifically, it is tasked with the surgical application of brute military force during hostage situations but is also highly capable while performing clandestine reconnaissance and intelligence-gathering missions, lightning-quick commando-style attacks against specific objectives, and the wide variety of tasks usually associated with special operations. From a personnel standpoint, Delta Force is a deft combination of brawn and brains, handpicked from only the most accomplished military volunteers and survivors of training and constant preparation that can best be described as excruciating. Delta Force thus constitutes the vanguard in America's struggle against terrorism outside the United States. Given the startling rise of organized malevolence worldwide, their existence has seldom been so cogent to national security interests. Moreover, in fulfilling this capacity, they maintain close links with similar units across the globe, such as the 22 Special Air Squadron (Britain), the GIGN (France), the GSG-9 (Germany), the Sayeret Matkal/Unit 269 (Israel), and the Australian SAS. Versatile by design and deadly by necessity, Delta Force is uncannily quick and lethal when authorized to act.

Organization

Delta Force is nominally under the control of the U.S. Army Special Operations Command, but because of the sensitive nature of their missions, they are kept under the tight reins of the Joint Chiefs of Staff. Consequently, most facts surrounding Delta's exact size, manpower levels, and operations—past and present—remain closely guarded secrets. What

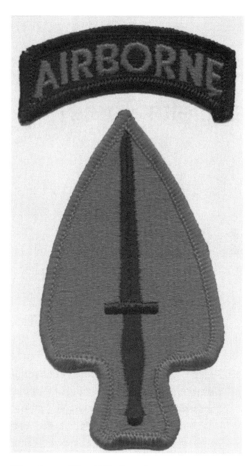

(Courtesy of the U.S. Army)

little known about them is as follows: Delta Force is more or less patterned after Britain's highly successful Special Air Service Regiment "Sabre Squadron" and consists of three squadrons (A, B, C) of 75 to 85 men who go by the precise term "operators." Each squadron is made up of one reconnaissance/sniper troop and two direct-action/assault troops. These, in turn, can be broken down into functioning groups as small as four to six men each. Recent congressional testimony by Delta Force members implies that a fourth squadron will be added and that the entire organization will be expanded by one-third to meet their commitments in the war against terror. In manpower terms, Delta Force is thought to number around 1,000 officers and men, with the whole divided up into various detachment designations, including the following:

D—*Command and Control* Headquarters.

E—*Communications, Intelligence and Administrative Support*
Handles financial, logistical, medical, research, and technological concerns.

F—*Operational Arm* Operators in the Field.

Medical
Small teams of specialized medics housed at Fort Bragg and deployed with the operators as necessary.

Operational Support Troop
This is the intelligence section of Delta Force that consists of highly trained operators capable of infiltrating into countries prior to the commencement of direct-action missions. Because this is the only part of Delta Force to allow female operators, it is jocularly known as the "Funny Platoon."

Aviation Squadron
A small force of specially equipped helicopters and aircraft, distinct and separate from the 160th Special Operations Aviation Regiment (Airborne), who usually ferries them about. These men and machines are tapped to provide Delta Force with tactical airlift on specific missions. Their aircraft are also decorated in civilian markings and with false registration numbers to blend in with local air traffic of a given region.

Personnel and Training

Delta Force is one of the most exclusive military clubs in the world, and while its physical and mental standards are stellar in the extreme, recruitment methods curiously range from direct invitations to plain homespun advertising. In fact, it is euphemistic that no one simply joins Delta; Delta has to join them first. Recruiting standards are appreciably among the most stringent in the world, with exacting qualifications for the mental, physical, and leadership skills to be a successful "operator." The bulk of prospective recruits are usually successful soldiers from the 75th Ranger Regiment, U.S. Army Special Forces (Green Berets), with a smattering of accomplished Army reservists and National Guard troops. Basically, all volunteers must be male, at least 21 years of age with a rating of E-4 to E-8, representing at least two and a half years of service in the ranks, and possess fairly high ratings on the Armed Services Vocational Aptitude Battery test. All these qualification must be met before an interview from Delta recruiters is even considered. Having met these prerequisites, recruits must also provide relevant letters of recommendation from superiors. However, a fair share of candidates have previously been identified by Delta officials as possessing a specific skill (language, mechanical aptitude, and so on) that would benefit the force, and these are usually approached by Delta recruiters directly and encouraged to apply. Finally, the force also solicits new members through advertising in select military magazines, with appropriate contact information list for any interested parties. All volunteers are carefully screened in advance for past criminal records, drug abuse, or disciplinary problems, any one of which courts immediate disqualification. The ability to keep one's mouth shut and skill at maintaining a low profile is also highly prized. Further culling of the volunteer pool occurs as candidates submit to extensive batteries of psychological and physical tests, including minute eye examinations. The exact number of students admitted is classified, but the number is thought to tally 100 annually.

Those individuals fortunate enough to pass the preliminary Delta Force screening are then subject to an initial round of physical training. The timing constraints for these are precise and unyielding. They includes a 40-yard inverted crawl under some kind of obstacle in under 25 seconds, 37 sit-ups in 60 seconds, 35 push-ups in 60 seconds, traversing a jump-and-dodge course in 25 seconds, a two-mile run in only 16 minutes, a 100-meter swim fully clothed, and then an 18-mile speed march to be completed in 10 hours or less. Those retained are then trundled up and sent to camps in either West Virginia or New Mexico to complete a 40-mile speed march, compass navigation courses, and a wilderness survival regimen. Here candidates are summarily dropped off into the woods or deserts alone with a 60-pound rucksack of food, a compass, and a map and told to reach specific areas in a given sequence. They must successfully complete all objectives within 24 hours without any encouragement or knowledge of having passed or failed the test. In any case, this ordeal pales in comparison to what follows: the dreaded five-hour interrogation by a board of Delta veterans, better known as "The Interview." In fact, Delta Force prizes mental toughness more than physical agility. Candidates grilled by the board are subject to barrages of personal and general questions and are gauged not simply by answers but also by their reactions under extreme stress. In this manner, they can better assess the totality of the

Delta Force operators are superbly drilled and equipped shock troops who incessantly train to storm almost any objective, especially in hostage situations. (U.S. Army)

individual, his potential for handling himself in a tight situations, and his ability to work independently and without clear instructions. By the time this grueling process transpires, only 10 percent of candidates are still standing, and these are shunted off to the next phase of training.

Trainees are now subjected to the six-week Operator Training Course at Fort Bragg, North Carolina, Special Operations Training Facility. This is also home to the Close Quarter Battle House (better known as the "Haunted House"), where mock rescue attempts are continually staged and restaged against pop-up terrorists lurking behind furniture, and spread among "hostages." Assaults are rehearsed and evaluated, with all members assigned to differing tasks within the same operation until each man is proficient. The men also train on mock airliners to help resolve skyjackings. Through all these tactical expedients, members gradually master all the nuances of counterterrorism tactics and techniques, which basically boil down to three main considerations:

Insertion Because Delta Force operators are designed with countering terrorist/hostage situations in distant lands, most likely at a U.S. embassy, they are required to infiltrate into the host country quickly and unobtrusively. Beforehand, all cultural and political factors inherent in the region must be evaluated in the event that they may weigh against "direct-action" solutions from taking place. A high degree of real-time intelligence quickly gathered and evaluated must also be in hand before an operation commences.

Preparation In the brief period leading up to a Delta Force operation, it is essential that the military enjoy clear channels of authority to conduct itself without interference from competing government agencies or even host governments and officials. Consensus must be speedily reached with authorities as to who, precisely, is in charge of events. While these factors are being resolved, Delta members also conduct close surveillance of the intended target while all facets regarding command and control, including intelligence of the facilities in question, are verified.

Execution Here is the payoff for months of intense training and preparation by Delta Force operators. Direct action against terrorists must be boldly planned and swiftly executed to succeed, with virtually no margin for error. Delta commanders are continually training to formulate devastating attack plans—and quickly—on surveying the scene, Moreover, his operators must also possess an intuitive grasp of exactly what do to at each precise moment of the raid. Unlike the usual military mind-set, flexibility and unorthodox approaches to tactical problems are encouraged. If the action proves successful, the terrorists are neutralized, the hostages are freed, and damage to facilities is limited.

Precise maneuvering under fire requires precise training, and Delta operatives rehearse specialized techniques throughout their tenure as operators. They learn how to correctly enter a building, seize or free captives, and then exfiltrate quickly and safely. To accomplish this, they practice rapid rappelling from helicopters by rope, blowing doors off their hinges with explosives, and effectively fighting their way through a building floor by floor. Delta teams, by necessity, also shoot instantly and accurately at clearly identified targets to lessen the risk of harm to captives or themselves. They must fire, move quickly, and then crouch and drop to the floor before firing again. Effective close-quarter combat with automatic weapons is therefore doubly stressed. One particularly lethal technique is the "double tap," a sharpshooting technique placing two bullets between a terrorist's forehead and nose from up to 50 feet away. Various types of smoke and stun grenades are also employed as distractions and cover during the fighting. In addition, operators must endure the rigors of parachute training, including HALO high-altitude, low-opening and HAHO high-altitude, high-opening jumps for aerial descents where helicopters are impractical. Other skills, such as scuba diving and miniature submersibles, round out the training routine. The net result is a well-adapted individual who excels in numerous counterterrorist skills and is capable of successfully engaging objectives under varied conditions. No fewer than two years of relentless instruction are necessary to become a successful Delta Force operator, and while many of the techniques employed remain classified, they are unquestionably lethal and effective. In many respects, Delta teams epitomize the image of the modern, high-tech warrior.

Equipment

In terms of uniforms, Delta Force is devoid of any distinct cut of clothing. While routine attire is adorned on military bases, operators enjoy a wide latitude of clothing, hairstyles, and facial hair to choose from on duty. This emphasis on nondescript civilian dress allows members to avoid being identified as elite special operations members and facilitates their blending in with local populations. During actual takedowns, operators can don modern Kevlar body armor, including helmets and vests, but this is at the discretion of the operators in question. The usual uniform, when worn, consists of a green or sand-colored flight suit that is light, comfortable, and flameproof. Each individual operator also carries a close-fitting microphone placing him in instant communication with his entire unit. To these are added specialized equipment, such as flashlights, grenades, radios, knives, and medical pouches, the sum total of which presents a bulky appearance but one that underscores the bloody business at hand.

Personal choice also applies to the weapons employed. Delta personnel are nominally proficient with a wide variety of American and foreign firearms, including the M-4 carbine (shortened M-16), the Mossberg automatic shotgun, or the German-made Heckler & Koch MP5 submachine gun. Operatives are also known for their marksmanship, and they can achieve miraculous kills at extreme ranges with their .50-caliber Barrett and McMillan sniper rifles. They may also tote the famous Russian-built Kalashnikov AK-47 assault rifle, which is common across the globe. In short, if it shoots and the operator approves, Delta Force employs it.

Known Operations

Given the extreme secrecy surrounding Delta Force, most of their activities are speculative at best. However, they are known to have participated in Operation GOTHIC SERPENT in Somalia to apprehend renegade warlord Mohamed Farrah Aidid and several ranking henchmen. On October 3–4, 1993, Delta operators accompanied men of the 75th Ranger Regiment into downtown Mogadishu, but disaster struck when ground fire downed two MH-60L Black Hawk helicopters. At one point, Sergeants Gary I. Gordon and Randall Shugart rappelled down a to a crash site where they fought off an armed mob of angry Somalis. They remained in place to save the sole survivor of the Black Hawk, but both men were eventually killed after inflicting scores of casualties in this one-sided battle. No fewer then five Delta operators paid the supreme sacrifice that day. However, several of Aidid's lieutenants were successfully snared by other teams of operators elsewhere in town.

Delta Force has also been conspicuously engaged in the war against terror, commencing with Operation ENDURING FREEDOM in Afghanistan. Small teams of operators deployed in country around October 2001, and at one point they assisted rangers in a surprise attack on the headquarters of renegade Mullah Mohammed Omar, spiritual head of the Taliban. While the raid failed to snare the elusive Omar, the troops did capture valuable intelligence information; several Delta members were wounded by Taliban forces during the extraction process. Their activities since remain generally classified, but by 2009 it was acknowledged that Delta operators have been active in eastern Afghanistan throughout 2009, usually in concert with Navy elite SEAL Team Six. Several successful actions against the Haqqani/Taliban network are attributed to their handiwork, and it is suspected that Delta operators remain active along both sides of the Pakistani border.

Not surprisingly, Delta Force has also seen active duty during Operation IRAQI FREEDOM, commencing in March 2003. It is admitted that several teams of operators, acting with the Central Intelligence Agency's Special Activity Division, had infiltrated into the country prior to the outbreak of hostilities. When war commenced, they undoubtedly performed their usual routine of intelligence gathering, guiding air strikes with laser target designators, and sabotaging Iraqi communications. In April 2004, Delta operators were known to accompany Marine Corps scout/sniper companies although to what end has not been ascertained. Other operators are suspected to have been present in Mosul on July 22, 2003, the day that Saddam Hussein's sons Uday and Qusay were killed and also accompanied the task force that captured the dictator himself in Tikrit on December 13, 2003. Reports have since surfaced that Delta members were in place near Baquba on June 7, 2006, searching for the wanted terrorist leader Abu Musab al-Zarqawi, and they successfully called in air strikes on the safe house that killed him. It is assumed that Delta Force remains active in Iraq despite the ongoing American pullout and clandestinely acts with British and Australian special forces in their ongoing struggle against terrorism and its perpetrators.

Bibliography

Beckwith, Charlie A., and Donald Knox. *Delta Force: The Army's Elite Counterterrorist Unit.* New York: Avon Books, 2000.

Blaber, Pete. *The Mission, the Men, and Me: Lessons Learned from a Former Delta Force Commander*. New York: Berkley Caliber, 2008.

Bowden, Mark. *Black Hawk Down: A Story of Modern War*. New York: Atlantic Monthly Press, 1999.

Boykin, Jerry. *Never Surrender: A Soldier's Journey to the Crossroads of Faith and Freedom*. New York: Faith Words, 2008.

Fury, Dalton. *Kill Bin Laden: A Delta Force Commander's Account of the Hunt for the World's Most Wanted Man*. New York: St. Martin's Press, 2008.

Griswold, Terry, and D. M. Giangreco. *Delta: America's Elite Counterterrorist Force*. St. Paul, MN: Zenith Press, 2005.

Haney, Eric L. *Inside Delta Force: The Story of America's Elite Counterterrorism Unit*. New York: Delacorte Press, 2006.

Pushies, Fred J. *Weapons of Delta Force*. St. Paul, MN: MBI, 2002.

6

U.S. Army Special Forces (Green Berets)

De Oppresso Liber (To Liberate the Oppressed)

There are few such storied units in military history as the U.S. Army Special Forces: the Green Berets. Since their inception in 1952, they function as the nation's preeminent exponents of unconventional warfare and channel it in diverse theaters throughout the world. As such, they serve under the United States Special Operations Command and are usually independent of the theater commands in which they reside. Once committed, their activities touch on guerilla activities, foreign internal defense, special reconnaissance, direct-action assaults, hostage rescues, and counterterrorism. In pursuit of these goals, Green Berets remain the only American special operations unit overwhelming given to linguistic and cultural training along with training skills for instructing indigenous forces or foreign troops. So flexible and adaptive have they proven that they serve around the world to perform peacekeeping, humanitarian assistance, manhunts, and counternarcotics operations, aside from purely military considerations. Their peculiar brand of training renders them well equipped to conduct civic action and help local populations help themselves. The intense nature of Green Beret preparation is also highly prized among other clandestine units, and it is not uncommon for the highly classified Special Operations Group of the Central Intelligence Agency (CIA) to recruit these soldiers into their very selective ranks.

While it is true that Green Berets are highly capable warriors and capable of executing direct-action missions like U.S. Army Rangers and hostage rescue missions like Delta Force operators, their operational forte is as cultural liaisons with indigenous forces, invariably far behind enemy lines. To this end, they eschew military attire on station and generally don whatever is in fashion with the locals. They are carefully matched to blend in with native populations in terms of both physical appearance and cultural/sociological fluency. In this sense, they can trace their ancestry directly back to the Office of Strategic Services

(Courtesy of the U.S. Army)

Jedburgh teams in western Europe, Detachment 101 in Burma, and the Alamo Scouts of the western Pacific. Simply put, they are among the most supremely adaptable special operations units in the world and, in terms of results, among the most effective.

Organization

Presently, the U.S. Army Special Forces consists of five active-duty groups and two National Guard groups. Unique to Green Berets in general, each group is assigned to a specific world region and especially steeped in the requisite language and cultural nuances dominate there. Each group currently consists of three battalions, but commencing in 2012, U.S. Army Special Forces Command has authorized a fourth battalion. This comes down to roughly 1,200 rank and file per group for a total of 10,000 Green Berets worldwide. The organizations are as follows:

1st Special Force Group (Joint Base Lewis-McCord, Washington)
Being tasked with the Pacific region, the three battalions of this group are forward deployed at Torri Station, Okinawa. Two battalions are currently rotating, on a six-month basis, to Iraq as part of the Combined Joint Force Special Operations Task Force—Arabian Peninsula, to Afghanistan with the CJSOTF—Afghanistan, and to the Philippines with the CJSOTF—Philippines. They are also subordinated to the Pacific Command.

3rd Special Forces Group (Fort Bragg, North Carolina)
This force is responsible for all of sub-Saharan Africa, save for the eastern Horn of Africa. It presently rotates two of its battalions on six-month tours with the Combined Joint Special Task Force—Afghanistan. They report to the Central Command (CENTCOM).

5th Special Force Group (Fort Campbell, Kentucky)
This group specializes in the Middle East, central Asia, and the Horn of Africa. Two of its battalions are constantly rotated in and out of Iraq as part of the Combined Joint Special Operations Task
Force—Arabian Peninsula. Like the 3rd Special Forces Group, they also report to CENTCOM.

7th Special Forces Group (Eglin Air Force Base, Florida)
This group is oriented toward Central and South America and the Caribbean. However, it deploys two of its battalions on a six-month rotational basis to Afghanistan as part of the Combined Joint Special Operations Task Force—Afghanistan. They report to the Southern Command.

Green Berets on parade during a change of command ceremony at Fort Bragg, North Carolina. These troops constitute the senior branch of American special forces and can trace many operational procedures back to the Office of Strategic Services of World War II. In addition to being combat proficient, they place a high priority on language and cultural fluency. (Leif Skoogfors/Corbis)

10th Special Forces Group (Fort Carson, Colorado)
This force forward deploys three of four battalions at Boeblingen, Germany, and is oriented toward central and eastern Europe, the Balkans, Turkey, Israel, Lebanon, and northern Africa. It currently deploys two of three battalions to Iraq on a six-month rotational basis as part of the Combined Joint Special Operations Task Force—Arabian Peninsula. They are nominally part of the Europe Command.

19th Special Forces Group (Draper, Utah)
This National Guard force deploys companies in Washington, West Virginia, Rhode Island, Colorado, California, and Texas and orients itself toward Southwest Asia with the 5th Special Force Group and Southeast Asia with the 1st Special Force Group.

20th Special Forces Group (Birmingham, Alabama)
This National Guard force has battalions in Alabama, Mississippi, and Florida with additional companies in North Carolina, Illinois, Kentucky, and Maryland. Its area of responsibility covers no fewer than 32 countries, including Latin America, the Caribbean, and the southwestern Atlantic, which it shares with the 7th Special Force Group.

Within each battalion, the organization of a special forces company reflects its unique training and operations in the field. Battalion consists of four companies designated Alpha, Bravo, Charlie, and Headquarters/Support, each with its own tailor-made functions. Companies are further subdivided into at least six Operational Detachments Alpha (ODAs), commonly but unofficially known as "A-Teams." Each ODA specializes in a given infiltration or military skill, including high-altitude, low-opening (HALO) parachuting; mountain fighting; diving; urban combat; and maritime operations. Teams nominally consist of 12 men—two officers and 10 sergeants—each cross trained within their own occupational specialty to cover operations, intelligence, weapons, engineering, medicine, or communications. On specific missions, ODAs can be split into six-man teams, each still containing the same levels of cross training and skills. The next-higher level is the ODB ("B-Team"), a command element consisting of 11 to 13 soldiers. This formation is also capable of combat operations but is better situated to support A-Teams while in garrison or the field. B-Teams are nominally run by a major and several senior sergeants although without a weapons or engineering noncommissioned officers (NCOs) because of their supportive nature. The final battalion element is the ODC, or "C-Team," which functions as a headquarters element to the three subordinate companies. In this capacity, it handles the most important planning, training, signal, and logistics functions concomitant in most field operations. The C-Team is administered by a lieutenant colonel and the battalion command sergeant major, who is also the senior battalion NCO.

Recruitment and Training

Given the acutely sensitive nature of Green Beret's to unconventional warfare, namely, operating for extended periods behind enemy lines in a foreign culture, recruiting standards and training imposed on prospective candidates are excruciatingly high. For this reason, Green Berets consider only seasoned soldiers with accomplished records, mostly sergeants and captains, although promising corporals and lieutenants can be given due consideration should their talents and attitude be deemed relevant. Outstanding physical condition is a major factor, and individuals with uncanny powers of strength and endurance are sought out, but the most important consideration is intellectual.

Simply put, the ideal candidate for the Green Berets is as mentally tough and inured to physical hardship as possible. Moreover, individuals wishing to wear the coveted beret must possess foreign language skills and an innate ability to conduct personal diplomacy, military instruction, and weapons handling along with a penchant for decisive leadership as individuals. This is an exceedingly tall order, and the Green Berets enact one of the most bruising regimens ever devised to weed out the weak and push even the gifted and strong to their utmost limits. Standards are so stringent that only an estimated 5 percent of all prospective candidates can even qualify to gain admittance to the training.

Volunteers joining the Green Berets must first endure the preliminary "Special Forces Selection and Assessment" (SFSA) process, which consists of 24 days of intense psychological and physical testing. Recruiters generally gravitate toward more mature, experienced soldiers, usually seasoned captains and sergeants with an occasional lieutenant if he appears promotable. Those individuals not already airborne qualified are required to obtain their Silver Wings at the U.S. Army Airborne School at Fort Benning, Georgia, by the time they graduate. Soldiers of a certain ethnic backgrounds or appearances are always sought, as this facilitates "blending in" with native populations abroad. Language skills are also essential in this regard, and the more fluent a speaker, the more valuable he is to the service.

Finally, candidates must demonstrate high degrees of communication and instructional abilities, for teaching indigenous populations is a core responsibility of U.S. Army Special Forces.

The first hurdle to be passed is the grueling SFSA routine, consisting of obstacle courses, marches, running, orientation and field craft exercises, and situational and reaction drills. Not only does this impart valuable skills to recruits, but it also eliminates the less capable, physically and mentally, who are free to quit with no stigma attached. The prescribed abuses include sleep deprivation, limited food intake, and unending physical and mental challenges, all of which must be successfully met if a candidate is to advance to the next stage of training. Naturally, attrition rates are exceedingly high, so it is not uncommon for half of a 300-man class to depart before the 24th day.

Having survived the SFSA course, a recruit's ordeal is only just beginning; now he has to confront the grueling Qualification Course, more simply known as the Q Course. This is a three-part nightmare of endurance and deprivation from which only 3 percent of surviving recruits are expected to surmount. Phase I transpires at Camp Mackall and the Colonel Nick Rowe Training Facility at Fort Bragg. It involves 21 days of field craft/land navigation exercises in the wilderness, being armed only with a compass, a map, and a protractor. As the program progresses, recruits must learn the art of ambushing, reconnaissance, and other military skills. The first part concludes on the 39th day with students forming up into 12-man teams and graded on various mock missions.

Phase II of the Q Course focuses on each soldier's chosen military specialty and unfolds at various facilities over period ranging from six months to a year. The specialty field courses cover officer training, weapons training, medical training, engineering, communications, and operations/intelligence. All courses are demanding and thorough, and those flunking out are allowed to try a second time, but a second failure means returning to their previous unit.

Phase III constitutes the most demanding part of the Q Course and is the most tactically oriented part of a recruit's instruction. Officer candidates are expected to completely master all nuances of battlefield intelligence related to terrain and targets, while sergeants must grapple with every facet of operational planning. A refresher course on parachute and helicopter insertions is mandatory, as is additional instruction on cross-cultural communication and weapons instruction. The latter is essential, for candidates must demonstrate complete mastery of every weapon in the U.S. arsenal, along with weapons found in inventories across the globe. Days 16 to 22 concentrate on preparations for the final exam and include simulations and exercises, all performed in isolation.

The meaning and significance of the Q Course culminate during the Robin Sage Field Exercise, held four times a year. This is a two-week, full-scale mock exercise replete with every combination of special operation scenarios imaginable. As such, it deliberately challenges participants to meet—and surpass—their physical and mental limits. It also involves hundreds of instructors, National Guardsmen, and reservists, and even local town members living in the Uwharrie Forrest of North Carolina participate as "natives."

Candidates are expected to successfully ingress into an imaginary country called Pineland link up with sullen guerilla bands (played by army reservists), then win them over. That done, demanding tactical missions must be successfully planned and executed while the teams are also being stalked by military reservists acting as aggressors.

Throughout the entire process, training teams are obliged to call in supplies from air force and army aviation units without revealing their location to potential enemies, including partisan bands whose actual alliances can best be problematic. Thus, the full tableau of Green Beret skill and expertise undergoes severe testing that approximates wartime conditions with zero tolerance for failure. Any individual failing to measure up flunks the course and has spent the past year toiling in vain. Those fortunate enough to pass attend a graduating ceremony at Camp Mackall where they receive their iconic badge of military identity: the green beret.

The mere act of graduating does not signify any letup in the pace of instruction, for the new special forces troopers are shunted off for additional language instruction along with intensive escape and evasion courses at Fort Bragg. This is followed up by a stint at Yuma, Arizona, to attend the Military Free-Fall Course, where various tribes within the special forces clan gather to master advanced arts of parachuting. Only then are individual Green Berets assigned to ODAs on the front lines, wherever in the world that may take them.

Equipment

Green Berets employ a variety of equipment operated by all other U.S. forces and are also capable of using similar devices fielded by foreign armies. One piece that stands out is the Ground Mobility Vehicle (GMV), a highly modified versions of the army's standard HUMMV, or "Hummer." This machine is basically employed during long-distance desert missions and has been upgraded with improved suspension, a stronger motor, and an open bed for lugging additional water, fuel, and other equipment deemed relevant to a mission. The cupola atop the cabin is also capable of hosting a TOW antitank missile system, a .50-caliber M3 machine gun, or a Mark 19 40-mm automatic grenade launcher. Three Green Berets are allotted to each GMV, with four vehicles constituting an operational detachment. These rugged, versatile machines add speed, endurance and flexibility to highly demanding desert missions.

Known Operations

Since the end of the Cold War in 1991, the Green Berets have been highly active in many parts of the globe, but inasmuch as their duty is highly classified and decidedly low profile, little can be said of them. These activities range from civic action duties in Haiti to hunting down war criminals in Bosnia and Kosovo. However, their most notable actions occurred in October 2001 during the initial phases of Operation ENDURING FREEDOM in Afghanistan. Several ODA teams and CIA paramilitary officers from the Special Activities Division were clandestinely flown in from Uzbekistan to establish contacts with the anti-Taliban Northern Alliance. The most celebrated of these was ODA 555, which infiltrated at Bagram, north of Kabul, on October 19, 2001, to link up with alliance fighters under General Baba Jan. Once deployed, they immediately adapted to the most common mode of local transportation—

horses—and they even requested old cavalry field manuals on mounted operations. Now augmented for the Middle Ages, the men, assisted by a highly trained U.S. Air Force Air Controller, plied their advanced aiming technologies for precision-guided air strikes against Taliban and al-Qaeda targets. They were particularly distinguished during the capture of Mazar-i-Sharif by the Taliban on November 9–10, 2001, allowing for one of the heaviest aerial bombardments of the war. However, during a prison uprising in the city on November 25–28, an errant bomb accidentally wounded five special forces soldiers. Tragedy struck again on December 5, 2001, when bombs dropped by B-52 bombers from high altitude killed three Green Berets and five Afghan allies. These deaths underscore the hazards of working closely with indigenous forces in unconventional warfare. However, ODA 555 enjoyed the honor of being the first special forces team inside liberated Kabul only 25 days after their deployment. One of their first tasks was reoccupying the long-abandoned U.S. embassy compound, now open for business after a long hiatus. Little else is known of their actions, but on August 4, 2010, a Taliban force estimated at 45 men ambushed ODA 31216, 3rd Special Forces Group, a mixed Green Beret/Afghan commando team, in southern Afghanistan. The team sergeant was wounded then rescued by Sergeant 1st Class Chad E. Lawson, a communications soldier darted ahead under machine gun and rocket fire to rescue him. Lawson then rallied the Afghans and defended the MEDEVAC helicopter as it arrived. On February 14, 2011, the quick-acting sergeant received a Silver Star, the nation's third-highest military decoration, from General David Petraeus, the U.S. commander. However, on May 29, 2011, three Green Berets were killed in Wardak Province when their vehicle was struck by an improvised explosive device, which only underscores the unforgiving and unpredictably dangerous nature of warfare in that part of the world.

Over the past eight years, Green Berets still conduct highly classified missions throughout Afghanistan, all the while shabbily clad in the same long beards, hair, scarves, and belts of their hosts.

Typically, they meet with tribal elders to gain respect and trust, provide medical treatment to civilians, and orchestrate humanitarian assistance where it is desperately needed to win "hearts and minds." Teaching the multiethnic, multilingual Afghan military would be a nightmare for any contingent other than Green Berets. Their success here results in many willing recruits wishing to to serve as adjuncts in the field and against the terrorists. Their service is vital because of their thorough knowledge of local topography and known Taliban sympathizers in given regions. The Green Berets also conduct their own miniature war against the insurgents by ambushing supply columns and drug convoys, clearing out Taliban safe havens, and in every way bringing the war to the enemy—on both sides of the Afghanistan/Pakistan border.

Green Berets were also heavily involved during the initial phases of Operation IRAQI FREEDOM against dictator Saddam Hussein. In fact, special operations forces engaged in Operation COBRA II represent the largest use of clandestine units in history, more numerous than those at the Normandy invasion of June 6 1944. Long before war erupted on March 20, 2003, ODA 551 (2nd Battalion, 5th Special Forces Group) under Captain Dan Runyon was ordered to occupy forward scouting positions along the strategic Karbala Gap, 350 miles behind Iraqi lines and only 50 miles due south of Baghdad. This placed the men adjacent to the Iraqi Republican Guard's crack Medina Division—a very dangerous proposition for such lightly armed soldiers. Their mission was to observe and report on enemy military traffic through this valuable choke point, especially if they noticed Iraqi chemical weapons being deployed. All told, a daunting proposition, but on the evening March 21–22, 2003, ODA 551 and their three GMVs were conveyed by helicopters from Kuwait into the desert below the gap and deposited far enough from their destination to avoid detection. Pushing forward into the darkness, Runyon's team assumed a "day-over" hiding spot, then resumed traveling the following night until they encountered a dried-out wadi (riverbed) near Lake Bahr al Milh. This terrain feature afforded them excellent cover, and they promptly deployed and began observations.

Between March 23 and 30, ODA 551 kept close tabs on events around the Karbala Gap, just as the American 5th Corps began pushing up from the south. They managed to call in selected air strikes against military targets, although not enough to raise Iraqi suspicions. Their mission concluded on March 30, but they decided to exfiltrate overland seeing that the region was deemed too hostile for helicopters. The teams carefully retraced their steps through an Iraqi minefield until they encountered forward elements of the 3rd Infantry Division (Mechanized). For flawlessly executing a highly classified, dangerous endeavor, Runyon received promotion to major. His effort has since become known in special forces circles as the "Immaculate Mission" for its near-perfect execution.

During the planning stages of Operation IRAQI FREEDOM, American strategists intended to have the 4th Mechanized Infantry Division invade northern Iraq from Turkey. At the last minute, the Turkish parliament voted against such measures, and the Americans altered decided to make northern Iraq an exclusively special forces operation. Accordingly, Joint Special Operations Task Force—North, consisting of the 173rd Airborne Brigade ("Sky Soldiers"), two battalions of the 10th Special Forces Group, and the 3rd Battalion of the 3rd Special Forces Group, arrived in northern Iraq for the express purpose of tying down approximately 20 Iraqi divisions and preventing them from interfering with the coalition offensive advancing from the south. A critical part of this mission was Task Force Viking, comprised of ODAs 391, 392, and 044, whose purpose was to coordinate their efforts with local Kurdish *peshmerga* ("those who face death") guerillas. Kurds enjoy sterling reputations as mountain fighters, and they happily embraced U.S. Special Forces from the onset. However, no sooner had Task Force Viking established itself in the Debecka Pass to block Route 2, a strategic highway junction, than they were set on by the Iraqi 34th Division. For several hours, a handful of Green Berets and GMVs withstood an onslaught of enemy tanks and personnel carriers, inflicting heavy losses on them with Javelin antitank missiles. This was rapidly becoming an unorthodox and dangerous mission for ODAs 391 and 392, for they were supposed to operate undetected and avoid direct actions. Their last-ditch defense was further complicated when navy F-14s accidentally bombed a convoy of Kurdish vehicles, killing 16 guerillas and wounding 45 more. Fortunately, the Iraqis finally withdrew with heavy losses, and, the handful of Green Berets who were engaged suffered no fatalities. Within days, men of the 3rd Battalion, 3rd Special Forces Group, were among the first troops to liberate the Kurdish city of Kirkuk. Their stand at Bedecka Pass remains one of the greatest achievements by U.S. Special Forces and adds further luster to an already formidable reputation.

Meanwhile, in western Iraq, an entire battalion from the 5th Special Forces Group infiltrated into the country before the invasion commenced, where it helped organized anti-Saddam forces and inflicted considerable losses on the Iraqi army. Their activities also convinced the Iraqis that the main coalition drive was advancing from that direction instead of from the south. Since 2003, men of the 5th and 10th Special Forces Groups have been instrumental in hunting down terrorists, identifying and apprehending Baath Party hold-outs, and tracking the fugitive Saddam Hussein and his sons. In August 2010, the combat role of U.S. Army and Marine Corps forces in Iraq was officially handed over to the new Iraqi defense forces, but Green Berets remain on hand as military instructors and, unoffi-cially at least, are still engaged in the shadowy war to stop al-Qaeda groups from commit-ting atrocities against civilians.

Bibliography

Antenori, Frank, and Hans Halberstadt. *Roughneck Nine-One: The Extraordinary Story of a Special Forces A-Team at War*. New York: St. Martin's Press, 2006.

Blehm, Eric. *The Only Thing Worth Dying For: How Eleven Green Berets Forged a New Afghanistan*. New York: Harper, 2010.

Blessing, Leonard D. *Warrior Healers: The Untold Story of the Special Forces Medic*. New York: iUniversal, 2006.

Bradley, Rusty, and Kevin Mauer. *Lions of Kandahar: The Story of a Fight against all Odds*. New York: Bantam Books, 2011.

Couch, Dick. *Chosen Soldier: The Making of a Special Forces Warrior*. New York: Crown, 2007.

Grey, Stephen. *Into the Viper's Nest: The First Pivotal Battle of the Afghan War*. Minneapolis: MBI, 2010.

Halberstadt, Hans. *Green Berets: Unconventional Warriors*. Novato, CA: Presidio Press, 1988.

Isby, David C. *Leave No Man Behind: Liberation and Capture Missions*. London: Cassell, 2005.

Johnson, Ronald W. *Honduras to Haiti: Five Years in the Life of a Special Forces Sergeant*. Bloomington, IN: 1st Books, 2004.

McNab, Chris. *Survive in the Jungle with the Special Forces "Green Berets."* Broomall, PA: Mason Crest, 2003.

Meissner, Joseph P. *The Green Berets and Their Victories*. Bloomington, IN: AuthorHouse, 2005.

Moore, Robin. *The Green Berets: The Amazing Story of the U.S. Army's Elite Special Forces Unit*. New York: Skyhorse Press, 2007.

Moore, Robin. *The Wars of the Green Berets: Amazing Stories from Vietnam to the Present*. New York: Skyhorse Press, 2007.

Pushies, Fred J. *U.S. Army Special Forces*. St. Paul, MN: MBI, 2001.

Schumacher, Gerald. *To Be a U.S. Army Green Beret*. St. Paul, MN: Zenith Press, 2005.

Simons, Anna. *The Company They Keep: Life inside U.S. Army Special Forces*. New York: Free Press, 1997.

Stanton, Doug. *Horse Soldiers: The Extraordinary Story of a Band of U.S. Soldiers Who Rode to Victory in Afghanistan*. New York: Scribner, 2009.

Strozzi-Heckler, Richard. *In Search of the Warrior Spirit: Teaching Awareness Discipline to the Green Berets*. Berkeley, CA: North Atlantic Books, 2003.

7

75th Ranger Regiment

Sua Sponte (Of Their Own Accord)

The 75th Ranger Regiment is the world's premier light infantry formation and also the largest direct-action force within the U.S. Army Special Operations Command. Operationally, they are something of a hybrid unit, uniting special operations capabilities with airborne mobility and extreme physical prowess. Like their illustrious forebears, rangers specialize in unconventional infantry tactics and missions, including air assault; raiding; infiltration by air, sea, and land; airfield seizure; prisoner rescues; and support of conventional line infantry. In sum, rangers function as highly capable light infantry specialists, and at least one of their four battalions is kept as the Ranger Ready Force and capable of deploying anywhere in the world within 18 hours. To maintain razor-sharp levels of proficiency, rangers drill constantly and spend several months of the year in the field. Their skills are much sought after by other parts of the special forces community, so it is not uncommon that a successful tour with rangers leads to subsequent recruitment by Green Berets or Delta Force.

Unlike conventional land forces, which are heavily armed with organic firepower in the form of tanks and attached artillery, rangers are lightly equipped and carry everything necessary to execute their missions. For this reason, they are trained to move rapidly over the most foreboding terrain (even under nocturnal and bad-weather conditions), make excellent use of all available cover, and then strike hard and quickly with overwhelming force. Once their mission is accomplished, rangers usually make a hasty if well-executed egress from the scene of action before larger and more heavily armed enemy units can react. Tactical surprise, the most valued battlefield commodity, is by necessity one of their most sterling attributes.

When combat is not required, rangers are also completely versed in clandestine reconnaissance deep behind enemy lines. Some of these assignments range from a few days to several weeks and hinge completely on their ability to hide and move frequently without

(Courtesy of the U.S. Army)

detection. To all these formidable capabilities must be added strategic flexibility, for rangers can enter a battle area on foot, in helicopters, on boats, or by parachute then depart in an entirely different method, depending on the circumstances. It is a standard ranger practice to maintain a minimum of one battalion on constant alert for a solid month, with the two months on stand-down. This active battalion is expected to deploy anywhere at full strength within hours of an alert. In emergency situations, one rifle company and battalion-level command and control can go in with only nine hours' notice. Consequently, ranger equipment and supplies must be quickly palleted for air shipment and loaded onto transport planes for parachute delivery when needed. More than any other American special operations unit, rangers have a disturbing penchant for appearing suddenly and in strength, usually where an adversary least expects them.

Organization

The 75th Ranger Regiment presently consists of 2,000 men divided into four equal-strength battalions station at the following locales:

1st Battalion (Fort Benning, Georgia)

2nd Battalion (Hunter Army Airfield, Georgia)

3rd Battalion (Joint Base Lewis-McCord, Washington)

Special Troops Battalion (dispersed)

Battalions are the standard tactical unit, but because of their specialization as light attack infantry, the regimental command also includes a communications specialist, a fire support officer, a surgeon, and a permanently assigned U.S. Air Force tactical air control officer to channel aviation matters. Battalions consist of three companies and one headquarters company, each with 152 and 125 men, respectively, for a grand total of 580. Each rifle company contains three rifle platoons and one weapons platoon. At the lowest levels, each rifle platoon contains three rifle squads of three teams each and one machine gun squad. In addition, there is a higher proportion of seasoned noncommissioned officers (NCOs) in a ranger battalion, with staff sergeants running squads and sergeants commanding fire teams. Classic American military discipline stresses individual initiative, and with rangers this is even more so, thus it is not uncommon to find junior NCOs, such as corporals, serving as team leaders.

Pat Tillman (1976–2004). Patrick Daniel Tillman was born in San Jose, California, on November 6, 1976, and he excelled at football while in high school. He was admitted to Arizona State University on a scholarship in 1994 and four years later was drafted by the Arizona Cardinals. Tillman played until May 2002, then allowed his contract to expire in consequence of the 9/11 terror attacks in New York City. The following June, he joined the U.S. Army to help combat terrorism. After completing basic training with his younger brother Kevin, both attended the Ranger Indoctrination Program and were assigned to the 2nd Battalion, 75th Ranger Infantry, at Fort Lewis, Washington, as recruits. At the time, Tillman was held up as a national hero for abandoning his lucrative sports career to fight abroad. In September 2003, he participated in Operation IRAQI FREEDOM, then finally passed through the Ranger School

Pat Tillman ended a lucrative sports career to serve in Afghanistan as a Ranger, but his death by friendly fire stirred charges of a cover-up. (Courtesy of the U.S. Army)

at Fort Benning, Georgia, on November 28, 2003. Tillman, now a corporal, subsequently deployed to Afghanistan as part of Operation ENDURING FREEDOM and, on April 22, 2004, was killed in a firefight near the town of Sperah. A controversy arose after the military, having initially announced that Tillman died fighting bravely in action, later admitted that friendly fire was the probable cause. A political uproar ensued, and Tillman's death was investigated by the U.S. Army Criminal Investigation Command. On March 19, 2007, they concluded that he was, in fact, killed after one allied group fired on his group in the heat of battle. However, the controversy surrounding Tillman's demise does not detract from his heroic service and sacrifice.

One pervasive shortfall inherent in ranger organization is their lack of medical evacuation personnel. This is because, due to the nature of their classified missions, any attempted air evacuation might tip off an enemy as to their location. Consequently, rangers carry an extensive array of medical supplies into the field with them, and all team, squad, and platoon leaders have mastered basic first-aid techniques, such as administering hypodermic needles to wounded soldiers. Qualified medics are also found at the squad level, but when not tending the injured, these men carry rifles and fight like any other ranger. A new development in ranger organization occurred on July 17, 2006, when, due to the necessity for expanded special operations capability, the Regimental Special Troops Battalion was organized to better more specific intelligence, reconnaissance, and maintenance missions.

Such activities were previously handled by small, specially trained detachment attached to battalion headquarters.

Recruitment and Training

To become a ranger, volunteers are subject to one of the most brutally exacting training regimens ever devised. Only about 20 percent of all candidates come from the army, while half of the remainder come from other services and the other half from foreign nations. Of these, many have already passed through the rigors of airborne school, which is a ranger prerequisite, and know what lays in store for them.

Prospective recruits are trundled off to Camp Rogers at Fort Benning, Georgia, for the first phase of training, the Ranger Indoctrination Program (RIP), which comes courtesy of the 4th Ranger Training Battalion. This is an intensive 26-day program of marches, physical training, land navigation testing, and other preliminaries to eliminate the weak and unqualified. Other obstacles include a combat water survival test (a 15-minute swim in full equipment and boots) followed by a five-mile run, three-mile runs over obstacle courses, a 16-mile foot march, and rifle, bayonet, and combat classes. All these endeavors are calculated to instill or improve on traditional ranger qualities of physical and mental endurance, confidence, and personal initiative. Surviving recruits next report to Phase II at nearby Camp William O. Darby, which focuses on squad-level operations, including combat and patrolling. This training includes drills, mock ambushes, reconnaissance patrols, and airborne assaults, in all of which students must be proficient. Furthermore, the men conduct their affairs out in the open, regardless of the weather, to approximate real-life operating conditions. Ranger tradition also asserts that individual soldiers are assigned "buddies" with whom they train for the rest of the entire course; both men are charged with looking out for and assisting each other.

Having survived Fort Benning, the recruits arrive at Dahlonega, Georgia, for mountain training with the 5th Ranger Training Battalion. Here they are repeatedly drill and redrilled in squad- and patrol-sized maneuvers over extremely harsh terrain. The cold weather, skimpy rations, and realistic drills push all hands past their mental and physical limits. Moreover, the art of tying knots, climbing, and rappelling must all be mastered in only five days before the next phase of instruction begins on Yonah Mountain. Over the next 48 hours, recruits are placed through the wringer as they apply skills learned in rugged field-training exercises. This includes simulated combat with teams of conventional "enemy" troops in simulated low-intensity warfare. To make things more interesting, students may be required to stop training and make a sudden airborne assault on a mountaintop or complete a 10-mile march with a 75-pound rucksack across the Tennessee Divide.

Instructors might also single out tired and hungry soldiers to lead selected combat missions at random; all these challenges must be successfully met before moving on to another round of instruction.

The next phase occurs at Eglin Air Force Base, Florida, with the 6th Ranger Training Battalion. Here trainees acquire real-time experience in Florida's storied swamps replete with poisonous snakes and man-eating alligators. Nevertheless, all ranks are expected to maintain proficiency while executing combat missions in difficult junglelike environments, including the usual airborne, air assault, Zodiac (rubber boat), ship to shore, and foot patrols against simulated hostile forces. The fast pace and relentless challenges, leavened

Members of the U.S. Army Rangers, Special Operations, Special Forces, 1st Battalion, 75th Regiment, prepare to attack an abandoned building in an urban environment. The 75th Ranger Regiment forms the largest part of America's antiterrorist arsenal, and these highly mobile, light infantry specialists can deploy anywhere across the globe within hours. They nominally operate behind enemy lines and specialize in assault missions. (Corbis)

throughout with food and sleep deprivation, run roughshod over all candidates throughout this 10-day period. In fact, the biggest obstacle trainees have to surmount is their own fatigue and stress, abetted by endless ambushes, insertions, extractions, and every variety of maneuver by air, sea, or land. Candidates also endure harsh-weather training at Fort Bliss, Texas, with the 7th Ranger Training Battalion, then its onto desert fighting and reconnaissance techniques, along with water procurement and preservation and other essential survival skills. Food rations are reduced to one per day, with little slackening of the pace or intensity. Only after completing this final round of abuse—to the satisfaction of superiors—can the surviving candidates wear the proud black-and-gold ranger tab and a distinct tan beret. This newly minted status notwithstanding, soldiers train continuously throughout their tenure with the rangers by honing old skills and refining new ones. No less than 48 weeks every year is spent in the field to ensure that rangers remain the finest light infantry force in the world. Given the regimen involved, a drop out rate of 70 percent is considered average.

Equipment

As light infantry, rangers carry standard-issue American firearms, including M-4A1 (M-16) rifles, usually fitted with the ACOG 4X sight and AN/PVS-14 night-vision devices; the M203 40-mm grenade launcher; and M181A1 Claymore mines. For heavier, sustained firepower, the M249 SAW (squad automatic weapon), which fires the same 5.56-mm bullet as the M-4, is deployed. The newer M240B utilized the heavier 7.62-mm NATO round fired by the older M-60 machine gun, which is also still in use. Soldiers also carry the 9-mm Beretta semiautomatic pistol as a sidearm. To these are added a variety of sniper rifles, such as the M24 or the .50-caliber Haskins sniper rifle, to enhance tactical situations at very long range. Rangers also employ a variety of antitank and antiaircraft missiles, such as the Viper and Stinger, along with light 60-mm mortars, but these weapons approximate organic artillery, which is heavy and precludes rapid mobility. Therefore, each battalion is issued a dozen Ranger Special Operations Vehicles, based on the famous British Land Rover. This modestly sized machine carries six rangers and their equipment, is air transportable by MH-47 and MH-53 helicopters, and has a range of 200 miles. It is rugged, reliable, and capable of traversing a variety of environments. The vehicle usually mounts a .50-caliber M-2 machine gun on its cabin roof for defense. Ranger battalions also deploy 10 Kawasaki KLR 250 motorcycles for security and mobility during airfield seizures.

Known Operations

One of the most daunting episodes in 75th Ranger Regiment history happened on October 3, 1993, during Operation GOTHIC SERPENT. On this date, a select force of rangers and Delta Force operators (Task Force Ranger) helicoptered into Mogadishu, Somalia, to apprehend local warlord Mohamed Farrar Aidid and several of his senior lieutenants.

However, once these had fast roped down into the Bakara sector of the city near the Olympic Hotel, the men were surrounded by thousands of hostile militiamen (or "technical"), and a huge, running firefight erupted.

Several helicopters of the 160th Special Operations Aviation Regiment (SOAR) were downed, and rescue attempts were made to secure the surviving crewmen. The rangers, badly outnumbered, nonetheless stood their ground by dint of superior firepower and tactics for the next 18 hours until they were rescued by an armored UN convoy. Six rangers were among the 18 Americans killed that day, along with an estimated 1,000 Somalis. This was also one of the fiercest engagements waged by rangers since the Vietnam War.

Other, less dramatic deployments followed. In 1994, the 2nd and 3rd Battalions were next deployed to Haiti during Operation RESTORE DEMOCRACY, where they helped restore and maintain order once General Raoul Cedras peacefully relinquished power. This occasion also marked the first time that rangers had deployed from a navy vessel, in this instance the carrier USS *America*. The next major deployment unfolded on November 24, 2000, when the Regimental Reconnaissance Team 2 and a command element joined Task Force Falcon for service in Kosovo.

Formal combat operation for rangers came in the wake of the terror attack against the World Trade Center on September 11, 2001. On October 19, 2001, a detachment from the 3rd Battalion flew from Pakistan on four air force MC-130 Combat Talon transports and made a nighttime parachute assault against Taliban positions west of Kandahar, Afghanistan. The rangers, assisted by Delta operators, seized and searched a house formally used by Mullah Omar, their spiritual leader, then safely evacuated. Objective Rhino, a local landing strip, was also seized from hostile operatives for use by U.S. Marines; it was later dubbed Camp Rhino and used as a forward operating area. The rangers were subsequently extracted by helicopters of the 160th SOAR without loss, although one helicopter lost part of its landing gear after striking an unseen obstacle. Rangers also partook of Operation

Aanaconda on March 3–4, 2002, and engaged in a heavy firefight during maneuvers around Takur Ghar.

The 75th Ranger Regiment also actively participated in Operation IRAQI FREEDOM. On the evening of March 25–26, 2003, they performed a dramatic, nighttime air assault against "H-1," an airfield near the Syrian border, and were delivered by C-17 Globemaster transports. However, their most celebrated role was in helping to rescue Private Jessica Lynch from an Iraqi hospital in Nasiriya on April 1, 2003, along with Delta Force operators and Air Force Special Tactics members. Other activities remain classified, but on March 23, 2003, the 3rd Battalion performed an air assault against "Objective Serpent" during Operation IRAQI FREEDOM; the results of this action have never been publicized. However, on May 26, 2008, part of Company A, 2nd Battalion, 7th Rangers, were assigned to storm a Taliban position in Paktia, Afghanistan. Resistance was fanatical and several rangers were wounded, when Sergeant 1st Class Leroy A. Petry sprang into action. Ignoring his own injuries, he killed several Taliban with hand grenades, then lost his own right hand when tossing an enemy grenade back at the owner. Petry continued on, killing several more Taliban with his rifle. On July 12, 2011, President Barak Obama awarded Petry the Congressional Medal of Honor, the nation's highest honor. Over the past decade, rangers have acknowledged taking 412 casualties in the war against terror, including 32 fatalities. This tally is proportionately lower than other special operation branches, and reflects their intense training in flat-out combat operations.

Bibliography

Bryant, Russ. *75th Rangers*. St. Paul, MN: MBI, 2005.

Bahmanyar, Mir. *Shadow Warriors: A History of U.S. Army Rangers*. Westminster, MD: Osprey Direct, 2006.

Bowden, Mark. *Black Hawk Down: A Story of Modern War*. New York: Atlantic Monthly Press, 1999.

Bryant, Russ. *To Be a U.S. Army Ranger*. St. Paul, MN: Zenith Press, 2003.

Bryant, Russ, and Susan Bryant. *Weapons of the U.S. Army Rangers*. St. Paul, MN: Zenith Press, 2005.

Combs, David A. *Black Chinook: An Army Ranger's Story*. N.p.: Bouna Books, 2006.

Couch, Dick. *Sua Sponte*: *The Forging of a Modern American Ranger*. New York: Berkley Books, 2012.

Hohl, Dean. *Rangers Lead the Way: The Army's Rangers' Guide to Leading Your Organization through Chaos*. Avon, MA: Adams Media Corp., 2003.

Krakauer, Jon. *Where Men Win Glory: The Odyssey of Pat Tilman*. Garden City, NY: Doubleday, 2009.

Le Storti, Anthony J. *When You're Asked to Do the Impossible: Principles of Business Teamwork and Leadership from the U.S. Army's Elite Rangers*. Guilford, CT: Lyons Press, 2003.

Lock, John D. *To Fight with Intrepidity: The Complete History of the U.S. Army Rangers, 1622 to Present*. Tucson, AZ: Fenestra Books, 2001.

MacPherson, Malcom. *Roberts Ridge: A Story of Courage and Sacrifice on Takur Ghar Mountain*. New York: Bantam Dell, 2006.

Barber, Brace E. *No Excuse Leadership: Lessons from the U.S. Army's Elite Rangers*. Hoboken, NJ: Wiley, 2004.

Puckett, Ralph. *Words for Warriors: A Professional Soldier's Notebook*. Tucson, AZ: Wheatmark, 2007.

Struecker, Jeff. *The Road to Unafraid: How the Army's Top Ranger Faced Fear and Found Courage through Black Hawk Down and Beyond*. Nashville: W. Publishing Group, 2006.

Taylor, Thomas. *Rangers, Lead the Way*. Paducah, KY: Turner, 1996.

U.S. Army Ranger Handbook. New York: Skyhorse, 2007.

Westwell, Ian. *U.S. Rangers: "Leading the Way."* Hersham: Ian Allan, 2003.

8

Airborne Forces

All the way!

Most but not all U.S. parachute units are assigned to the 18th Airborne Corps. This formation constitutes the nation's largest strategic-level quick-reaction force and is capable of fielding brigade-sized units in direct combat operations, anywhere around the globe, in only 18 hours. Rangers may get to crises zones faster, but they lack the sheer number of the paratroopers. And, because the operational manifesto of airborne units is contingency based, they can field a variety of specialty formations to meet or contain any emergency. Presently, the corps consists of one airborne division, one heavy division, one air assault division, and one light division, a total of 88,000 combat-capable soldiers and their sophisticated equipment. The high levels of training exhibited by constituent units render them very close to special forces, and, in fact, several units are capable of performing special operations. Thus the army's designated "Contingency Corps," which is also its largest war-fighting organization, stands ready to protect American interests and can engage in armed conflict at both tactical and strategic levels. It remains the nation's premier power projection force abroad—and for good reason.

The 18th Airborne Corps was initially activated as the 11th Armored Corps at Fort Bragg, North Carolina, on January 17, 1943. However, its armored designation was dropped by the time it began assembling at Monterey, California, where, on October 9, 1943, it was reactivated as the 18th Airborne Corps. However, nearly a year lapsed before any units obtained their blue airborne tab at Orbourne, England, on August 25, 1944, after it assumed control of the 82nd and 101st Airborne Divisions. The following month, General Matthew B. Ridgway led the 18thAirborne Corps into action during Operation MARKET GARDEN, where, despite a heavy allied defeat, all hands performed exceptionally well. In the spring of 1945, the 18th Airborne Corps, now strengthened by the 13th Airborne Division, completed Operation VARSITY, the largest airborne drop of World War II. In June 1945, the

(Courtesy of the U.S. Army)

corps relocated back to Fort Campbell, Kentucky, where it was deactivated as of October 15 that year. With the onset of the Korean War, the 18th Airborne Corps was again reactivated as a strategic reserve on May 21, 1951. Since then, it has been active in a number of international crises. Most notably, the corps provided the bulk of force employed during Operation URGENT FURY, the 1983 liberation of Grenada, which overthrew a bloody Marxist dictatorship and rescued scores of American medical students. On December 20, 1989, the 18th Airborne Corps figured prominently in Operation JUST CAUSE, the liberation of Panama from dictator Manuel Noriega, and as part of Joint Task Force South, it struck 27 targets simultaneously and also conducted two nighttime parachute assaults. On August 9, 1990, member units were the first ground forces to reinforce Saudi Arabia during Operation DESERT SHIELD. The following February, 1991, the 18th conducted the largest-ever airborne assault by the 101st Airborne Division, while the 82nd Airborne Division, assisted by the French 6th Light Armored Division, commenced the overland ground offensive. Assisted by the 24th Infantry Division (Mechanized) and the 3rd Armored Cavalry Regiment, the 18th Airborne Corps effectively demolished Iraqi forces occupying Kuwait in less than 100 hours of one-sided combat. Closer to home, several major units of the 18th Airborne Corps deployed to Dade County, Florida, in the wake of Hurricane Andrew to provide immediate medical and disaster assistance to thousands of stranded residents. Up through 1998, the formation participated in no fewer than 79 exercises and deployments to 27 different countries for training and stabilization purposes. In January 2005, it fought in Iraq as part of Operation IRAQI FREEDOM and functioned within the Multi-National Corps Iraq. It rotated back to the United States in January 2006 to undergo a number of cost-cutting measures, specifically, discarding most of its airborne certifications for all formations larger than a brigade. However, its component parts remain active in deployments abroad for training purposes in various countries.

Organization

Presently, the 18th Airborne Corps is headquartered at Fort Bragg, North Carolina, home to both airborne and special operations forces. In addition to the 3rd Infantry Division (Mechanized) (Fort Stewart, Georgia) and the 10th Mountain Division (Light) (Fort Drum, New York), its airborne component consists of the following:

U.S. Army paratroopers with the 82nd Airborne Division prepare to board a C-130 Hercules aircraft during the Large Package Week/Joint Operational Access Exercise at Pope Air Force Base, North Carolina, 2011. The army and air force held the exercise to practice large-scale personnel and equipment airdrop missions. (U.S. Department of Defense)

82nd Airborne Division ("All Americans") (Fort Bragg, North Carolina)

This is presently the world's largest pure airborne force, numbering 18,000 men and women. It maintains a constant state of high readiness and can deploy anywhere in the world within 18 hours. For this reason, the men constantly train and practice their war-fighting skills throughout most of the year. Significantly, all ranks, from the colonel to the cooks, are airborne qualified, and virtually every piece of equipment required by the division is also air deliverable. The five-brigade structure reflects the army's new "modular" approach to modern combat, which is best executed at the brigade level. The division consists of the following:

1st Brigade Combat Team ("Devil Brigade")

Headquarters Company

1st Battalion, 504th Parachute Infantry Regiment

2nd Battalion, 504th Parachute Infantry Regiment

3rd Squadron, 73rd Cavalry Regiment

3rd Battalion, 319th Field Artillery (Airborne)

1st Brigade Special Troops Battalion

307th Brigade Support Battalion

2nd Brigade Combat Team ("Falcon Brigade")

Headquarters Company

1st Battalion, 325th Airborne Infantry Regiment

2nd Battalion, 325th Airborne Infantry Regiment

1st Squadron, 73rd Cavalry Regiment

2nd Battalion, 319th Field Artillery (Airborne)

2nd Brigade Special Troops Battalion

407th Brigade Support Battalion

3rd Brigade Combat Team ("Panthers")

Headquarters Company

1st Battalion 505th Parachute Infantry

2nd Battalion, 505th Parachute Infantry

5th Squadron, 73rd Cavalry Regiment

1st Battalion, 319th Field Artillery (Airborne)

3rd Brigade Special Troops Battalion

82nd Brigade Support Battalion

4th Brigade Combat Team ("Fury from the Sky")

Headquarters Company

1st Battalion, 508th Parachute Infantry

2nd Battalion, 508th Parachute Infantry

4th Squadron, 73rd Cavalry

2nd Battalion, 321st Field Artillery (Airborne)

508th Special Troops Battalion

782nd Brigade Support Battalion

82nd Combat Aviation Brigade ("Too Easy")

Headquarters Company

1st Squadron, 82nd Aviation (Recon)

2nd Squadron, 82nd Aviation (Assault)

3rd Squadron, 82nd Aviation (General Support)

1st Squadron, 17th Cavalry

122nd Aviation Support Battalion

101st Airborne Division (Air Assault) ("Screaming Eagles") (Fort Campbell, Kentucky)

The 101st Airborne Division (Air Assault) is the only dedicated air assault unit of its size in the U.S. Army. It consists of 16,000 soldiers and 281 helicopters (including three battalions of AH-64 Apache attack helicopters) and transports every piece of necessary equipment to

U.S. Army General David H. Petraeus, commanding general of the NATO International Security Assistance Force and U.S. Forces Afghanistan, smiles for a photo with U.S. Army Specialist Don Ellen after administering the oath of reaffirmation and reenlistment to 235 U.S. service members during a ceremony called "Operation Enduring Commitment—The Red, White and True," held at Kandahar Airfield in Kandahar, Afghanistan, July 4, 2011. The general points to a unit patch that he knows something about! (AP/Wide World Photos)

a battlefield by air. It thus has the mobility to conduct operations 100 to 200 miles behind enemy lines, and for this reason it is one of few military formations to require daily theater-level intelligence. The soldiers carried are especially trained to rapidly rappel by rope to the ground, although they can also jump off onto a landing zones as required. The division constitutes the largest air mobile formation of its kind and represents a flexible, formidable component of American strategic response. The division consists of four self-sufficient combat brigades, two aviation brigades, and requisite supporting units:

1st Combat Brigade Team ("Bastogne")

Headquarters Company

David H. Petraeus (1952–). David Howell Petraeus was born in Cornwall-on-Hudson, New York, on November 7, 1952, and he graduated from the U.S. Military Academy in 1974. His first assignment was with the 509th Airborne Battalion Combat Team, and his career has been closely associated with airborne forces ever since. By 1993, Major General Petraeus was commanding the 101st Air Borne Division during Operation IRAQI FREEDOM, and he assisted in the capture of Mosul. Afterward, he proved equally successful at counterinsurgency operations and civic action before rotating back to the United States in February 2004. He returned to Iraq shortly after as a lieutenant general in charge of the Multi-National Security Transition Team. Petraeus then rose to full general in January 2007, assumed control of the entire Multi-National Force—Iraq, and then orchestrated the 20,000-man "troop

General David H. Petraeus orchestrated the successful "troop surge" in Iraq before taking charge of the war in Afghanistan. He presently serves as head of the Central Intelligence Agency. (U.S. Army)

surge" that wrested most of that country from the hands of terrorists. The key factor to his success was the so-called Sunni Awakening, which brought traditional Iraqi leaders and their private militias on the side of the government. In 2008, he handed off responsibility for Iraq to General Raymond T. Odierno and transferred as head of the U.S. Central Command in Tampa, Florida. Here he orchestrated the worldwide U.S. campaign against global terrorism with various special forces. In June 2010, Petraeus was next tapped to replace the disgruntled General Stanley McChrystal as head of the International Security Assistance Force in Afghanistan. He stepped up military pressure on Taliban forces throughout the country but also encouraged dialogue between the Afghan government and the militants to secure a broad-based peace. On September 6, 2011, he replaced Leon Panetta as director of the Central Intelligence Agency.

1st Battalion, 327th Infantry Regiment

2nd Battalion, 327th Infantry Regiment

3rd Battalion, 327th Reconnaissance, Surveillance, and Target Acquisition

2nd Battalion, 320th Field Artillery Regiment

326th Brigade Special Troops Battalion

426th Brigade Support Battalion

2nd Brigade Combat Team ("Strike")

Headquarters Company

1st Battalion, 502nd Infantry Regiment

2nd Battalion, 502nd Infantry Regiment

3rd Battalion, 502nd Reconnaissance, Surveillance, and Target Acquisition

1st Battalion, 320th Field Artillery Regiment

311th Brigade Special Troops Battalion

526th Brigade Support Battalion

3rd Brigade Combat Team ("Rakkasans")

Headquarters Company

1st Battalion, 187th Infantry Regiment

2nd Battalion, 187th Infantry Regiment

3rd Battalion, 187th Reconnaissance Squadron

3rd Battalion, 320th Field Artillery Regiment

81st Brigade Special Troops Battalion

626th Brigade Support Battalion

4th Brigade Combat Team ("Currahee")

Headquarters Company

1st Battalion, 4th Brigade Combat Team

2nd Battalion, 4th Brigade Combat Team

3rd Battalion, 4th Reconnaissance, Surveillance, and Target Acquisition

4th Battalion, 320th Field Artillery Regiment

4th Brigade Special Troops Battalion

801st Brigade Support Battalion

101st Aviation Brigade ("Wings of Destiny")

Headquarters Company

2nd Battalion, 17th Cavalry Regiment (OH-58D Little Birds)

1st Battalion, 101st Aviation Regiment (AH-64D Apaches)

2nd Battalion, 101st Aviation Regiment (AH-64D Apaches)

5th Battalion, 101st Aviation Regiment (UH-60L Black Hawks)

6th Battalion, 101st Aviation Regiment (UH-60L Black Hawks)

159th Aviation Brigade ("Eagle Thunder")

1st Battalion, 17th Cavalry Regiment (OH-58D Little Birds)

3rd Battalion, 101st Aviation Regiment (AH-64D Apaches)

4th Battalion, 101st Aviation Regiment UH-60L Black Hawks)

7th Battalion, 101st Aviation Regiment General Support (CH-47D Chinooks)

9th Battalion, 101st Aviation Regiment (UH-60L Black Hawks)

Recruitment and Training

The arduous nature of airborne operations requires soldiers to be in very peak condition in terms of physical fitness. Mentally, participants also have to show initiative and innovation under battlefield conditions, usually in the absence of higher authority. For this reason, volunteers alone are accepted into the parachutist and air assault ranks. Prospective recruits must successfully pass the army's basic training course before applying for army airborne training. After submitting DA Form 4187 and requisite documentation, each candidate must meet or exceed the strict physical standards imposed on all paratroopers: 42 push-ups in less than two minutes, 53 sit-ups in under two minutes, and running two miles in 15 minutes or less. Successful applicants report to the airborne training center at Fort Benning, Georgia, for three weeks of intense paratrooper training. The first phase, or Ground Week, focuses on honing the superbly fit recruits even further and consists of running extended distances at seven to nine miles per hour. The next phase, Tower Week, habituates recruits to practice jumping off a series of successively higher jump towers whereby they slide down wires in simulated parachute jumps. The final phase, Jump Week, is the payoff, and recruits must perform several live jumps from an actual aircraft at altitudes of 1,500 feet. Five jumps are required to graduate, and these are performed with so-called static lines attached to the aircraft that automatically deploy the parachutes. The chute breaks their controlled fall to speeds of 20 feet per second, and the paratroopers are carefully trained to hit the ground precisely to avoid broken limbs. At the conclusion of these rigors, soldiers receive the Silver Wings denoting airborne status along with the divisional red beret. Present personnel includes the 250 female soldiers attached to the 82nd Airborne; these are excluded by law from direct combat roles but nonetheless achieve and maintain their airborne status.

For soldiers attempting to enter the 101st Air Assault Division, training is radically different for they will deploy by helicopter, not parachute. Since 1974, when the division was rated an air assault unit, the parachute qualification was no longer mandatory. Air assault candidates report to the Sabalauski Air Assault School at Fort Campbell, Kentucky, for indoctrination and familiarization with this highly technical form of modern warfare. Strict order is imposed from the onset of what is known as "Zero Day": prospective candidates observe a packing list of items that are either mandatory, optional, or prohibited from the school grounds. Any violations following arrival result in immediate dismissal. The wearing of berets is forbidden, and all recruits sport standard-issue Kevlar helmets at all times. Students are subsequently subject to rigorous physical training to eliminate individuals who are afraid of heights or unnerved by stressful conditions. The men are also required to pass through a severe obstacle course, double-timing it between each obstacle and crying out "Air Assault!" after each challenge is successfully negotiated. This is followed up by a two-mile formation run to be completed in 18 minutes or less. Zero Day usually forces 10

Paratroopers from the 82nd Airborne Division jump from a C17 Globemaster at Fort Bragg, North Carolina, during Exercise Joint Forcible Entry. (U.S. Department of Defense)

to 15 percent of recruits to drop out, then the survivors attend graded courses covering combat air assault, sling load operations, rappelling, and a 12-mile road march with a full rucksack. All candidates must receive passing grades to receive their coveted Air Assault Badge. Courses are also interspersed with daily three-mile runs to maintain fitness standards. Some individuals will be allowed to attend the three-week Pathfinder School at Fort Benning, which imparts skills necessary for establishing landing zones, pickup zones, and drop zones.

Equipment

Airborne infantry carry the same basic weapons as regular infantry, but in some respects these have been lightened for ease of carrying and operation. Troopers receive the standard T-10 parachute, which can safely deliver loads of up to 250 pounds. It consists of a nylon canopy and 30 suspension wires, 25½ feet in length, connected to the parachutist's harness. Each soldier also carries an emergency reserve parachute on his chest in case of main chute failure and a 55-pound rucksack lowered down a special line before impact. Add to this an M-4 carbine (M-16) with a 40-mm grenade launcher slung under the barrel or a SAW (squad automatic weapons) or antitank rockets, plus enough food to sustain the soldier for 72 hours in the field, and his burdensome load becomes comprehensible. A host of smaller items, ranging from bayonets to canteens to GPS navigation systems, finally round out their battlefield array. Small motorcycles and all-terrain vehicles are also airdroppable either by parachute or on a pallet shoved out the rear of transport aircraft. Several lightweight 105-mm and 155-mm howitzers are also available to the 82nd Airborne as needed to enhance organic firepower. Otherwise, paratroopers are lightly armed by modern standards. For this reason, they are designed to seize fixed objectives in anticipation of being rapidly reinforced by ground forces rather than wage sustained conventional combat.

Unlike the 82nd Airborne Division, the 101st Air Assault Division does not rely on large transport aircraft to reach their objectives. Instead, they are entirely move and deploy on the helicopters of two combat aviation brigades. These aircraft are among the most technologically advanced machines of their kind anywhere in the world:

> *AH-6/MH-6 Little Bird*. This small helicopter is not dissimilar from machine utilized by the 160th Special Operations Aviation Regiment, although its configuration here is less specialized. The AH-6 is an attack variant capable of supporting troops on the ground with direct fire. It can carry a wide variety of weapons, including 70-mm Hydra rocket launchers, 7.62-mm miniguns, and air-to air Stinger missiles. The new AH-6J model is also air transportable by C-130 aircraft and can be made operational within five minutes after arrival. The MH-6 version, by contrast, is fitted with special operations equipment and is designed for the insertion and extraction of combat teams behind enemy lines. Both versions carry crews of two at speeds of up to 250 miles per hour for a range of 400 miles.

> *MH-60 Black Hawk*. This versatile machine sees duty with a number of army and air force special operations units but also serves as a standard medium-sized utility helicopter. The MH-60 employed by the 101st Air Assault Division comes in various versions according to the specific mission fulfilled. Most Black Hawks serve as troop-carrying transports and can lift a fully equipped squad directly into a combat zone. The MH-60L also carries ballistic armor and is equipped with Hellfire missiles for close support missions. The MH-60K is further crammed with specialized electronic equipment for nighttime operations and nap-of-the-earth flying and can easily accommodate special operations. The newest addition to the Black Hawk family is the Direct Action Penetrator, which touts a fully integrated fire control system, 70-mm rocket pods, miniguns, 30-mm chain guns, Hellfire rockets, and Stinger missiles. Thus configured, it is ideal for fire support missions and armed escorts.

> *CH-47 Chinook*. This is the army's long-distance, heavy-lift helicopter, and the early models participated in the Vietnam War. Today's MH-47E version carries 1,000 gallons of fuel in internal tanks, allowing it to perform six-hour missions nonstop. Its also contains the same advanced avionics as the MH-60 Black Hawk and is suitable for nocturnal missions, fast-rope rappelling, and in-flight refueling. It can carry between 33 and 55 fully equipped soldiers or two high-mobility wheeled vehicles (Hummers) or a single Hummer and a 105-mm howitzer. The rear ramp is designed to allow vehicles to drive directly out of the fuselage upon landing. The CH-47 is flown by a crew of two and also sports three gunners manning 7.62-mm miniguns— one on each side of the cabin and one on the rear ramp. Finally, Chinooks are fitted

with a triple-hook system that can hoist external loads weighing several thousand pounds.

AH-64 Apache. This fast and lethal machine is the army's prime fast-attack helicopter, which engaging and destroying targets using advanced Hellfire missiles. It carries advanced flying and sensing technology, such as a target acquisition designation sight and pilot night-vision sensors that allow Apaches to successfully operate in low-light and nighttime conditions. The crew consists of a pilot and a weapon operator fitted with advanced cockpit displays and integrated helmet and display sighting systems. The helicopter itself weighs in at 17,650 pounds, has twin motors driving a four-bladed rotor, and can remain airborne for over three hours. In addition to Hellfire missiles, it can deploy 76 2.75-inch aerial rockets and a 30-mm automatic cannon. In a battlefield situation, Apaches are employed primarily for destroying enemy tanks, which remain a paratrooper's greatest threat. Coming in fast, low, and unseen, they are the bane of armored vehicles.

Known Operations

82nd Airborne Division

Since the end of the Cold War, the 82nd Airborne Division has fulfilled numerous combat and humanitarian missions consistent with its role as the premier quick-reaction force. In August 1992, a brigade was dispatched to southern Florida to assist victims of Hurricane Andrew, and they provided food, shelter, and medical relief for 30 days. Two years later, on September 16, 1994, the 82nd Airborne Division participated in Operation RESTORE DEMOCRACY in Haiti, where the mere word of its approach induced General Raoul Cedras, who had overthrown the duly elected civilian government, to resign from office. In December 1994, the 2nd Battalion, 505th Parachute Infantry, arrived in Panama to provide security for numerous Cuban refugees growing restless in confinement there. In March 1999, the same unit was deployed to Albania as part of Operation ALLIED FORCE in Kosovo, and it was soon after joined the 3rd Battalion; these departed by March 2000. In September 2005, the 3rd Brigade deployed to New Orleans, Louisiana, in the wake of destructive Hurricane Katrina, operating out of the international airport there. In 2010, the 82nd Airborne Division contributed numerous troops to Haiti, where they distributed food and medical supplies in the wake of a destructive earthquake.

In the wake of the attack on the World Trade Center in New York, the division resumed combat operations by contributing several formations to Operation ENDURING FREEDOM in Afghanistan, most of which deployed in October 2001. In June 2002, these were joined by the headquarters company and the 3rd Brigade, and relieved in turn by the 1st Brigade in January 2003. During this period, 70 men from Company B, 3rd Battalion, 504th Parachute Infantry, performed a classified aerial jump over western Afghanistan the purpose and results of which remain classified. In September 2004, the 1st Battalion, 505th Parachute Infantry, was alerted for a possible deployment to provide security and support during Afghanistan's first free elections. In January 2007, the headquarters, 4th Combat Brigade Team, and the Aviation Brigade deployed as part of Combined Joint Task

Force-82; it rotated back to Fort Bragg in March 2008. They began a second tour of duty there as of August 2009 and returned back home to base as of August 2010.

On March 21, 2003, the 82nd Airborne Division bore an indirect role in Operation IRAQI FREEDOM, with the 2nd Brigade and headquarters acting as the theater reserve. Various brigades have since rotated into and out of Iraq on a regular basis, with the majority of units departing by April 2005. This first tour of duty cost the division 36 killed and 400 wounded from the 12,000 paratroopers committed. Since then, the 1st and 2nd Brigade Combat Teams have arrived in Iraq and departed with little ceremony. The 82nd Airborne Division still retains its high-alert status and is ready to deploy anywhere, literally, that American interests are threatened.

101st Airborne Division (Air Assault)

The 101st Airborne Division (Air Assault) has enjoyed a particularly active service life since the end of the Cold War, with several humanitarian missions in the fold. In October 2000, the 2nd Battalion, 327th Infantry Regiment, departed Fort Campbell, Kentucky, and was flown to Kosovo to provide security during national elections held there. The following month, its 3rd Battalion arrived in Montana to assist firefighting efforts in the Bitterroot National Forest. Significantly, the division resumed active combat operations in the wake of the attack on the World Trade Center in September 2001. Almost immediately, the 2nd Brigade ("Strike") deployed in Kosovo to shore up peacekeeping operations there in concert with a detachment from the 5th Special Forces Group already present. The following month, elements of the 3rd Brigade ("Rakkasans") became the first divisional unit participating in Operation ENDURING FREEDOM against the Taliban and al-Qaeda in Afghanistan. Their participation is discussed below. In 2008, the 4th Brigade Combat Team ("Currahee") deployed its 1st and 2nd Battalions, 506th Infantry, to the same region. They were joined shortly after by the 101st Combat Aviation Brigade, which arrived at Bagram Air Base as part of Task Force Destiny. In 2009, the 159th Combat Aviation Brigade rotated in to replace them as part of Task Force Thunder. A year later, in March 2010, the 101st Combat Aviation Brigade commenced its second tour of Afghanistan by positioning itself at Kandahar Airfield as part of the Regional Command—South.

Large-scale, conventional military operations also resumed with Operation IRAQI FREEDOM, when the 1st Brigade, 101st Air Assault Division, under Major General David H. Petraeus formed part of the 5th Corps in Kuwait. It was tasked with supporting the 3rd Infantry Division (Mechanized) as it cleared out Iraqi strongpoints during the advance toward Saddam International Airport, particularly in storming the city of An Najaf, where it killed hundreds of militant fedayeen fighters. Once combat operations ceased in April, the city of Mosul became their base of operations, from which numerous sweeps against Baath Party holdouts and insurgent groups were conducted. The 101st returned to Fort Campbell in the spring of 2004, where it underwent the army's modular transformation into four combat brigade teams, two aviation combat brigades, and one sustainment brigade. This new organization renders the Screaming Eagles the largest standing formation in the U.S. Army. In the summer of 2005, the 101st Air Assault Division commenced its second formal tour in Iraq by replacing the 42nd Infantry Division as Task Force Band of Brothers. Later that year, division personnel also accepted responsibility for training Iraqi security forces in Ninevah and Dahuk provinces. Concurrently, the 2nd and 4th Brigades formed part of Task Force Baghdad, alongside the 3rd Infantry Division, to conduct security operations. The 1st Battalion, 506th Infantry, was also detached from the latter to serve with U.S. Marines in Al Anbar Province, regarded as one of the country's most dangerous, while the 1st and 3rd Brigades reported to Kirkuk and Salah ad Din, respectively. In addition to routine combat operations, personnel of the 101st have been active in numerous civic action programs, including the renovation of schools, clinics, and police stations, throughout Iraq. The 2nd and 3rd Brigades have since rotated back to Fort Campbell from Iraq in November 2008, while the 4th Brigade recently completed a second tour of duty in Afghanistan as of March 2009.

187th Infantry Regiment ("Rakkasans")

Although nominally a part of the 101st Airborne Division, the 187th Infantry Regiment has a long and distinguished history of detached service from its parent formation. Most recently, it was one of the first conventional units to arrive in Afghanistan as part of Operation ENDURING FREEDOM. It experienced its baptism of fire on March 2, 2002, during Operation ANACONDA. This was an air assault operation in the Shahi-Kot Valley intended to entrap and destroy lingering Taliban and al-Qaeda bands operating there. That day, CH-47 Chinook helicopters landed Task Force Rakkasan along the eastern edges of the valley, where they came under enemy fire from the high ground. Consequently, only two of eight helicopters could disgorge troops, and for the next 16 hours, C Company, 1st Battalion, 187th Infantry Regiment, fought off superior numbers of enemy troops. Fire support was also provided by two AH-64D Apache attack helicopters from the 3rd Battalion, 101st Aviation Regiment. By the time the Rakkasans were successfully evacuated that evening, they had sustained 19 casualties and won a Presidential Unit Citation (PUC). Enemy casualties are not known but are presumed to have been much larger.

In March 2003, the 3rd Battalion, 187th Infantry Regiment ("Iron Rakkasans"), under Colonel Mike Linnington, was attached to the 3rd Infantry Division (Mechanized) during the opening phases of Operation IRAQI FREEDOM. By dint of hard fighting a solid maneuvering, they were among the first coalition units to enter Baghdad, winning another PUC. They subsequently conducted security sweeps northwest of Ninevah Province with the 1st Battalion, while the 2nd Battalion concentrated on matters in the vicinity of Sinjar and Biaj. The Rakkasans rotated back to Fort Campbell in 2004 for a well-deserved respite, then commenced a second tour of Iraq in the fall of 2005. This time, they focused their attention on Salah ad Din Province under Colonel Michael D. Steele and played a prominent role in Operation SWARMER, one of the largest combat operations in Iraq since the beginning of the war. In concert with Iraqi security forces, they defeated Sunni insurgent bands and al-Qaeda cells, capturing several weapons and explosives caches in the process. Another trip home followed, but in October 2007, the 187th Infantry Regiment, now part of the newly modularized 3rd Brigade Combat Team, commenced a third tour of duty in Iraq by deploying near Baghdad. They were tasked with performing security sweeps throughout the Tigress and Euphrates River valleys, an area that encompassed the notorious "Triangle of Death." This area was successfully patrolled with numerous insurgent bands defeated or captured, so when the Rakkasans returned to Fort Campbell in November 2008, they handed over the region to Iraqi security forces, thereby cementing the growing trend toward national sovereignty.

173rd Airborne Brigade Combat Team ("Sky Soldiers")

This unit is actually an independent airborne brigade and not associated with the 18th Corps. However, its troops perform many of the same tasks as the former and utilize the same equipment and training. The brigade currently consists of the following:

1st Battalion, 503rd Infantry Regiment (Airborne) (Vicenza, Italy)

2nd Battalion, 503rd Infantry Regiment (Airborne) (Vicenza, Italy)

319th Airborne Field Artillery Battalion (Bamberg, Germany)

173rd Special Troops Battalion (Bamberg, Germany)

1st Squadron, 91st Cavalry Regiment (Schweinfurt, Germany)

Since 1991, the 173rd Airborne Brigade Combat Team has confirmed its reputation as one of the foremost units of its kind. In fact, the Sky Soldiers have been extremely active around the globe since the end of the Cold War. They served as a de facto third brigade of the 101st Air Assault Division until June 12, 2000, when it was reconstituted as an independent brigade at Vicenza, Italy, as part of the Southern European Task Force. This action was consistent with U.S. Army Chief of Staff General Eric Shinseki's new policy of emphasizing brigade-level units and operations instead of larger, more ponderous divisional ones. The new formation executed several training deployments to Bosnia, Kosovo, Hungary, Morocco, and the Czech Republic to hone their abilities. After acquiring its second maneuver battalion, the 173rd Airborne Brigade was declared operational as of March 14, 2003. Only 12 days later, it participated in Operation IRAQI FREEDOM by performing an airborne assault in concert with the 10th Mountain Division and members of the 10th Special Force Group already present.

In northern Iraq, the Sky Soldiers formed part of Task Force Viking under Colonel William C. Mayville and were ordered to assist Kurdish resistance forces around the oil-rich city of Kirkuk. On March 26, 2003, 1,000 men jumped over Bashur Airfield as part of Operation NORTHERN DELAY, although the men were scattered over a 10,000-yard area and took nearly 15 hours to assemble. Once the airfield was secured, the rest of the brigade was airlifted into place, and by March 29, 2003, the Sky Soldiers commenced offensive operations. On the following day, Operation OPTION NORTH commenced as the brigade began flooding into local oil fields to control them. In the course of this activity, they met and defeated parts of the Iraqi 2nd, 4th, 8th, and 38th Infantry Divisions along with Ansar al-Islam terrorists. Kirkuk itself was secured on April 10, following a skirmish that cost the Sky Soldiers nine casualties. During subsequent postwar operations, the 173rd Airborne Brigade uncovered over 2,000 bars of gold belonging to the previous regime, and as part of Operation PENINSULA STRIKE, they helped to crush lingering resistance from Baath Party holdouts and other terrorists. Then, as Task Force Bayonet, the brigade functioned in and around the Kirkuk region, where it became involved in the arrest and detention of Turkish special forces operating illegally against Kurdish civilians. Continuing activities, such as Operation BAYONET LIGHTNING, led to the capture of several weapons caches, and kept the Sky Soldiers occupied until they rotated back to Italy on February 21, 2004.

In March 2005, the 173rd Airborne Brigade arrived in Afghanistan under Colonel Kevin Owens as part of Operation ENDURING FREEDOM. Deploying as Task Force Bayonet, the Sky Soldiers took up positions as in Regional Command—South, including parts of Zabol, Kandahar, Helmand, and Nimruz provinces. In this capacity, they waged a constant low-intensity conflict with numerous Taliban, al-Qaeda, and outlaw gangs, losing 17 soldiers. In March 2006, the 173rd Airborne Brigade returned to Italy, where, the following October, they were redesignated the 173rd Airborne Brigade Combat Team, consistent with the army's modularized unit force restructuring. Such modifications allowed the brigade to sustain itself in action for longer periods, being backed by new elements to keep all ground forces supplied and moving. On June 8, 2006, the Special Troops Battalion was also created and attached to the brigade. This new formation consists of three companies plus a headquarters company. In February 2007, the Sky Soldiers commenced their second tour of Afghanistan, where they relieved the 3rd Brigade Combat Team, 10th Mountain Division, and the 4th Brigade Combat Team, 82nd Airborne Division. This combat tour brought them into the eastern reaches of that country, particularly Nangarhar, Nuristan, Kunar, Paktika, and Laghman provinces, where they conducted over 9,000 patrols throughout their 15-month deployment. Contact with the enemy proved sporadic and basically successful, with one important exception.

On July 13, 2008, a force of 200 Taliban fighters attacked Vehicle Patrol Base Kahler in Wanat, Nuristan Province, which was garrisoned by the 2nd Platoon, Chosen Company, 503rd Infantry Regiment (Airborne). This poorly situated base was positioned below surrounding high ground, allowing Taliban gunners to knock out its heavier mortar emplacements with the opening rounds. The fighters then concentrated on overrunning a nearby observation post, where the majority of the nine dead and 27 wounded occurred. The Taliban were on the verge of breaching the main camp's barbed wire when helicopter gunships and jet fighters suddenly bombed the enemy into withdrawing. Other troops were rushed in and pursued the Taliban into a nearby town from which they fled. This attack represents the heaviest loss of American lives since Operation RED WINGS in 2005. All told, a further 43 Sky Soldiers laid down their lives during this deployment abroad.

However, another minor skirmish held more positive results for the Sky Soldiers. On the evening of October 25, 2007, Taliban forces attacked an isolated outpost in the Korengal Valley guarded by a detachment of B Company, 2nd Battalion, 503rd Infantry Regiment (Airborne). Fortunately, Staff Sergeant Salvatore Giunta repelled the attackers with grenades and shot down two fighters who were dragging a wounded American away. On September 10, 2010, the government announced that Sergeant Giunta would receive the Congressional Medal of Honor for his actions; he is the first living recipient of this distinction since the Vietnam War.

Bibliography

Clancy, Tom. *Airborne: A Guided Tour of an Airborne Task Force*. New York: Berkley Books, 1997.

Flanagan, E. M. *Airborne: A Combat History of American Airborne Forces*. New York: Ballantine Books, 2003.

Schrader, Richard K. *Pride of America: An Illustrated History of the U.S. Army Airborne Forces*. Missoula, MT: Pictorial Histories Publishing, 1991.

Smith, W. Thomas. *Alpha Bravo Delta Guide to American Airborne Forces*. Indianapolis,: Alpha, 2004.

Wright, Robert K. *Airborne Forces at War: From Parachute Test Platoon to the 21st Century*. Annapolis, MD: Naval Institute Press, 2007.

82nd Airborne Division

Anzuoni, Robert P. *The All American: An Illustrated History of the 82nd Airborne Division, 1917 to the Present*. Atglen, PA: Schiffer, 2001.

Caraccilo, Dominic J. *The Ready Brigade of the 82nd Airborne in Desert Storm: A Combat Memoir by the Headquarters Company Commander*. Jefferson, NC: McFarland, 1993.

Francois, Dominique. *82nd Airborne Division, 1917–2005*. Bayeux: Heimdal, 2006.

Grey, Stephen. *Into the Viper's Nest: The First Pivotal Battle of the Afghan War*. Minneapolis, MN: Zenith Press, 2010.

Mrozek, Steven J. *82nd Airborne Division: America's Guard of Honor*. Paducah, KY: Turner, 2004.

Pushies, Fred J. *82nd Airborne*. Minneapolis: MBI, 2008.

Verier, Mike. *82nd Airborne: "All American."* Hersham,: Ian Allan, 2001.

Zinsmeister, Karl. *Boots on the Ground: A Month with the 82nd Airborne in Battle for Iraq*. New York: Truman Talley Books/St. Martin's Press, 2003.

101st Airborne Division

Atkinson, Rick. *In the Company of Soldiers: A Chronicle of Combat in Iraq*. New York: Henry Holt, 2004.

Bryant, Russ, and Susan Bryant. *Screaming Eagles: 101st Airborne Division*. St. Paul, MN: Zenith Press, 2007.

Chambers, Larry. *Recondo: LRRPs in the 101st*. New York: Random House, 2004.

Day, Thomas L. *Along the Tigris: The 101st Airborne Division in Operation Iraqi Freedom: February 2003 to March 2004*. Atglen, PA: Schiffer, 2007.

Frederick, Jim. *Black Hearts: One Platoon's Descent into Madness In Iraq's Triangle of Death*. New York: Harmony Books, 2010.

Friedman, Brandon. *The War I Always Wanted: The Illusion of Glory and the Reality of War: A Screaming Eagle in Afghanistan and Iraq*. St. Paul, MN: Zenith Press, 2007.

Gericke, Bradley T. *David Petraeus: A Biography*. Santa Barbara, CA: Greenwood, 2011.

Grey, Stephen. *Into the Viper's Nest: The First Pivotal Battle of the Afghan War*. Minneapolis, MN: Zenith Press, 2010.

Hughes, Christopher P. *War on Two Fronts: An Infantry Commander's War in Iraq and the Pentagon*. Drexel Hill, PA: Casemate, 2007.

Jones, Robert E. *The History of the 101st Airborne Division Screaming Eagles: The First 50 Years*. Paducah, KY: Turner, 2005.

Mast, Gregory, and Hans Halberstadt. *To Be A Paratrooper*. St. Paul, MN: Zenith Press, 2007.

Moore, Robin. *Hunting Down Saddam: The Inside Story of the Search and Capture*. New York: St. Martin's Press, 2004.

Skiba, Katherine M. *Sister in the Band of Brothers: Embedded with the 101st Airborne in Iraq*. Lawrence: University Press of Kansas, 2005.

Tucker, Mike. *Among Warriors in Iraq: True Grit, Special Ops, and Raiding Mosul and Fallujah*. Guilford, CT: Lyons Press, 2005.

187th Airborne Infantry Regiment

Conklin, Ryan A. *An Angel from Hell: Real Life on the Front Lines*. New York: Berkley Caliber, 2010.

Naylor, Sean. *Not a Good Day to Die: The Untold Story of Operation Anaconda*. New York: Berkley Books, 2005.

173rd Airborne Brigade Combat Team

Bradley, James. *173d Airborne Brigade: Sky Soldiers*. Paducah, KY: Turner, 2006.

Junger, Sebastian. *War*. New York: Twelve, 2010.

9

10th Mountain Division (Light Infantry)

Climb to Glory

As presently configured, the 10th Mountain Division (Light Infantry) is America's premier rough-terrain fighting formation. It is also one of few specially tailored infantry divisions capable of rapid deployments around the globe by strategic airlift, with mission profiles ranging from combat action to humanitarian relief. Consequently, it maintains a high degree of readiness and can deploy within 96 hours of an alert. To accomplish this, the division designates one of its four brigades as the "First Infantry Brigade to Deploy," with one battalion task force within that formation assigned as the first unit to deploy. This stance reflects the unit philosophy to commit whatever troops and equipment are on hand whenever notification is given. Commencing in 2005, the 10th Mountain Division adopted the new U.S. Army modular structure to bring its organization in line with other infantry divisions, but it nonetheless remains a highly flexible formation. Significantly, it has performed more overseas assignments than any army division in recent history.

(Courtesy of the U.S. Army)

267

In combat, it exudes high mobility in rough-terrain battlefield situations and packs tremendous firepower and up-to-date equipment despite its otherwise light infantry designation. As part of the 18th Airborne Corps, they remain a significant part of America's foremost quick-reaction force.

Organization

The 10th Mountain Division (Light Infantry) presently consists of four combat brigades, to which are added a Combat Aviation Brigade (flying UH-60 Black Hawk helicopters) and a Special Troops Battalion. Its special training, equipment, and flexible formations render it capable of adapting to the most adverse terrain and weather conditions while under fire.

10th Mountain Headquarters and Headquarters Battalion

Headquarters and Headquarters Company

Network Support Company

10th Mountain Division Band

1st Brigade Combat Team ("Warrior")

1st Battalion, 87th Infantry

2nd Battalion, 22nd Infantry Regiment

1st Squadron, 71st Cavalry Regiment

3rd Battalion, 6th Field Artillery Regiment

1st Brigade Special Troops Battalion

10th Brigade Support Battalion

2nd Brigade Combat Team ("Commandos")

2nd Battalion, 14th Infantry Regiment

4th Battalion, 31st Infantry Regiment

1st Squadron, 89th Cavalry Regiment

2nd Battalion, 15th Field Artillery Regiment

2nd Brigade Special Troops Battalion210th Brigade Support Battalion

3rd Brigade Combat Team ("Spartans")

1st Battalion, 32nd Infantry Regiment

2nd Battalion, 87th Infantry Regiment

3rd Squadron, 71st Cavalry Regiment

4th Battalion, 25th Field Artillery Regiment

3rd Brigade Special Troops Battalion

710th Brigade Support Battalion

4th Brigade Combat Team ("Patriots")

2nd Battalion, 4th Infantry Regiment

2nd Battalion, 30th Infantry Regiment

3rd Battalion, 89th Cavalry Regiment

5th Battalion, 25th Field Artillery Regiment

4th Brigade Special Troops Battalion

94th Brigade Support Battalion

Combat Aviation Brigade ("Falcons")

1st Battalion, 10th Aviation Regiment

2nd Battalion, 10th Aviation Regiment

3rd Battalion, 10th Aviation regiment

6th Squadron, 6th cavalry Squadron

277th Aviation Support Battalion

Personnel and Training

Consistent with their designation, personnel of the 10th Mountain Division (Light Infantry) are authorized to wear the "mountain" tab on their uniform denoting their elite status. In reality, they train to fight effectively in a variety of harsh climes, and not simply mountains. After completing basic training, prospective recruits alternatively report to Fort Drum, New York; the Army Mountain Warfare School, Vermont; and Fort Greely, Alaska, to master their mountain-climbing abilities. This includes instruction in snow skis, snowshoes, *ahikio* sleds, rappelling up and down ice walls, and working with specialized Small Unit Support Vehicles capable of traversing deep snow. Physical conditioning is rigorously enforced through running, hiking, and marching along steep terrain regardless of weather or temperature conditions. This is essential, as the soldiers are expected to traverse rocky ground while carrying heavy packs and weapons, climbing gear and snow-traversing skies. Despite this encumbrance, they are taught to move and attack quickly to secure designated objectives.

Equipment

As a light infantry force, the 10th Mountain Division employs standard infantry weapons, such as the M-16 rifle, usually affixed with an M203 40-mm grenade launcher. Their status as the most high-tech fighting formation in the world is amply demonstrated by the wide variety of electronic gadgets employed. These include night-vision goggles, mortar control fire systems, GPS to enhance navigation, and the Dismounted Soldier System, patterned after the IBM Thinkpad. At the low-tech end of things, good-fitting boots, warm uniforms, and a dry change of socks remain essential to the well-being of the troops, along with maps and compasses.

Men of the 10th Mountain Division are mobile light troops specializing in all-weather/rough terrain operations. They have performed extremely difficult and valuable work in the mountains of Afghanistan. (David Bathgate/Corbis)

Known Operations

The end of the Cold War did not signal any letdown in the 10th Mountain Division's activities. On December 1993, it was assigned as part of Operation RESTORE HOPE in Somalia under Major General Steven L. Arnold, the division commander. The men were tasked with providing security for major cities in roads while providing safe passage for relief supplies to the population, then caught in the grips of a protected and bloody civil war. Factional fighting generally decreased with the new influx of food and medicine, and A Company, 41st Engineer Battalion, also constructed a 160-foot-long Bailey bridge above Kismayo, the largest such structure built since the Vietnam War. Despite this progress, Somalia was beset by various private armies of armed militias, or technicals, who still roamed parts of the capital, Mogadishu, shooting and robbing people at will. On October 3, 1993, Special Operations Task Force Ranger was assembled to capture Mohamed Farrah Aidid, a particularly odious warlord. However, several helicopters were shot down over the city, and the 10th Division, 2nd Battalion, 14th Infantry, deployed to secure their safe evacuation. They encountered a buzz saw of armed militiamen and were required to fight from house to house in order to reach the Olympic Hotel and the rangers isolated there. After a three-hour running gun battle, the 2nd Battalion, reinforced by Pakistani armor, relieved the rangers, then fought their way back out. The 10th Mountain Division suffered one dead and 29 wounded in six and a half hours of continuous gunfire, the most protracted firefight since Vietnam. The last divisional unit

U.S. Army Sergeant John Martek looks down the sights of his M4 carbine in an effort to locate enemy positions after taking fire during a patrol in the village of Mereget, Kherwar District, Logar Province, Afghanistan, 2011. Martek is with Delta Company, 2nd Battalion, 30th Infantry Regiment, 4th Brigade Combat Team, 10th Mountain Division. (U.S. Department of Defense)

to leave Somalia arrived back at Fort Drum on March 12, 1994, at which point 7,300 had performed duty there.

Later that year, the 10th Mountain Division was selected to partake of Operation UPHOLD DEMOCRACY in Haiti, and it formed the nucleus of the Multinational Force Haiti and Joint Task Force 190. This entity consisted of soldiers from 20 nations, of which 8,600 came from the 10th Mountain Division. On September 19, 1994, the 1st Brigade conducted the army's first air assault from a navy carrier as 54 helicopters transported 2,000 soldiers to Port-au-Prince International Airport. This was also the largest army air operation from an aircraft carrier since the Doolittle Raid of May 1942. The men were tasked with enforcing a stable environment for deposed President Jean-Bernard Aristide to return, and new national elections to unfold. Once this transition manifested, the 10th Mountain Division turned control of the island to the 25th Infantry Division on January 15, 1995, and transferred troops and equipment back to Fort Drum.

Between 1997 and 2000, the 10th Mountain Division saw additional deployment in the Balkans as part of Task Force Eagle, a peacekeeping force for Bosnia and Herzegovina. Once in place, the division was divided into two distinct operations: Task Force Drum for the northern sector and Task Force Eagle in Bosnia. By the summer of 2000, the division had handed off its assignment to the 49th Armored Division, Texas National Guard, and returned to Fort Drum. At this juncture, the 10th Mountain Division had become the most-deployed-abroad army formation since the end of World War II.

Commencing in 2001, the War on Terror afforded the 10th Mountain Division additional venues for distinction. During Operation ENDURING FREEDOM in Afghanistan, the special troops battalion and the 1st Battalion, 87th Infantry, arrived to secure forward operating bases; they secured and screened 3,500 Taliban captives at Sherberghan Prison and fought in the capture of Mazar-i-Sharif, the battle at Qala-i-Jangi, and Operation ANACONDA. During the latter, soldiers of the 10th Mountain Division accounted for several hundred armed al-Qaeda fighters in open combat, and also destroyed a large enemy base in the Shahi-Kot Valley, 100 miles to the southeast of Kabul. These forces returned to Fort Drum by the summer of 2002, but commencing in May 2003, the division began another mass deployment in Afghanistan, with headquarters providing command-and-control functions for Coalition Joint Task Force 180. Moreover, through Operations AVALANCHE, MOUNTAIN RESOLVE, and MOUNTAIN VIPER, the 1st Brigade conducted combat operations to root out Taliban and terrorist units in their region, while the 2nd Brigade assisted in training the new Afghan national army. By year's end, no fewer than 6,000 soldiers were in Afghanistan, and in September 2003, the unit formally accepted the army's new modular format. This division next deployed units to Baghdad for the first time in April 2008 as the division headquarters took up stations south of Baghdad, while the 4th Brigade Combat Team joined the 4th Infantry Division northeast of the city. The 3rd Brigade Combat Team was slated to join them, but they were instead shunted off to Afghanistan in January 2009 and deployed in Logar and Wardak to relieve the 101st Airborne Division. They were soon joined the 2nd Brigade Combat Team, while the 1st Brigade Combat Team was slated to arrive in the spring of 2010. In 2009, Jared C. Monti became the first 10th Mountain Division soldier to win a Congressional Medal of Honor for his role in Operation ENDURING FREEDOM.

Bibliography

Casper, Lawrence E. *Falcon Brigade: Combat and Command in Somalia and Haiti.* Boulder, CO: Lynne Rienner, 2001.

Le, Sandra. *18 Hours: The True Story of an SAS Hero's Bloodiest Battle against Al Qaeda in Afghanistan.* London: John Blake, 2007.

McNab, Christopher. *Survive in the Mountains with the U.S. Army Rangers and Army Mountain Division.* Broomall, PA: Mason Crest, 2003.

Pushies, Fred J. *10th Mountain Division.* Minneapolis: MBI, 2008.

Sasser, Charles W. *None Left Behind: The 10th Mountain Division and the Triangle of Death.* New York: St. Martin's Press, 2009.

Stanton, Martin. *Somalia on Five Dollars a Day: A Soldier's Story.* Novato, CA: Presidio Press, 2001.

Tucker, Mike. *Among Warriors in Iraq: True Grit, Special Ops, and Raiding in Mosul and Fallujah.* Guilford, CT: Lyons Press, 2005.

10

160th Special Operations Aviation Regiment (Airborne)

Night Stalkers never quit!

One of the most painful lessons of the disastrous Iranian hostage rescue attempt was the lack of dedicated aviation units for the stealthy insertion and removal of special forces, especially on short notice. The U.S. Army responded to this lacuna in June 1980 by culling volunteers from the 158th Aviation Battalion, 229th Aviation Battalion, and 159th Aviation Battalion, 101st Aviation Brigade (101st Airborne Division), at Fort Campbell, Kentucky, and began assembling an elite, special operations formation from scratch. The men were tasked with pioneering new tactics, techniques, and technologies, especially those related to night flying using the first generation of night-vision goggles. On April 1, 1982, the ad hoc ensemble was formally christened the 160th Aviation Battalion, although in subsequent operations it acquired the moniker Task Force 160. It became apparent to military authorities that, had such a unit been available two years earlier, the disaster at Desert One could have been avoided. On October 16, 1986, it was upgraded to an official airborne unit.

The 160th Aviation Battalion witnessed its baptism of fire during Operation URGENT FURY, the liberation of Grenada. It helicopters were tasked with conveying rangers and Delta Force members on a mission to rescue Governor General Sir Paul Scoon and also to assist in storming the Richmond Hill Prison. Both objectives were met, but heavy ground fire resulted in one helicopter being downed. Task Force 160's next notable assignment was in the Persian Gulf, where several AH-6 Little Bird helicopters operated off the decks of U.S. Navy vessels for the first time. To do so safely, the crews trained assiduously by flying only 30 feet above the waters, relying solely on night-vision goggles. On September 21, 1987, an AH-6 flying from the frigate USS *Jarrett* espied the Iranian vessel *Iran Ajr* illegally laying mines in international waters, then attacked and disabled the craft. On October 8 of that same year, another Little Bird from the frigate USS *Ford* was fired on by Iranian speedboats and shot back, sinking one. This marks the first time that helicopters engaged in combat through the use of night-vision goggles

(Courtesy of the U.S. Army)

and forward-looking infrared devices. In June 1988, Operation MOUNT HOPE II was launched in Chad, where two MH-47 Chinooks from the 160th traversed 490 miles of jungle and recovered a crashed Soviet-built Mi-24 Hind helicopter gunship. In December 1990, Task Force 160 participated in Operation JUST CAUSE in Panama, and over 440 men and machines were deployed from Fort Campbell without major mishap. In December 1989, several MH-60 Black Hawks inserted teams of special forces at the Torrijos-Tocumen Airport while four AH-6 Little Birds attacked the Panamanian Defense Force headquarters; one AH-6 was shot down, although the crews escaped capture. The Night Stalkers suffered a total of two combat casualties and two machines lost but garnered additional luster to their increasingly formidable reputation.

The performance of the 160th Aviation Battalion exceeded all expectations, so on May 16, 1990, they were reconstituted as the 160th Special Operations Aviation Regiment (SOAR), now placed under the purview of the new U.S. Special Operations Command. At that time, they also adopted the official moniker Night Stalkers, given their proclivity for nocturnal operations. They were soon put to the test during Operation DESERT SHIELD by deploying to King Khalid International Airport on September 3, 1990, in response to the Iraqi invasion of Kuwait. In January 1991, Operation DESERT STORM commenced, where the Night Stalkers performed fire support missions against Iraqi targets before the coalition ground offensive began. As it transpired, the 160th's men and machines aerially refueled AH-64 Apache attack helicopters of the 101st Airborne Division during innumerable sorties. They also recovered a downed F-16 pilot some 60 miles behind Iraqi lines, an even more impressive feat considering that the rescue was performed strictly through the use of night-vision goggles. Presently, it functions as America's premier nocturnal/all-weather special operations combat formation. It also remains the U.S. Army's sole special operations aviation unit, with a strength of roughly 1,800 men. Unannounced and slashing nighttime attacks are the Night Stalkers' operational specialty.

Organization

The 160th Special Operations Aviation Regiment (Airborne) represents the first time that army special operations unit did not look outside their parent organization for insertion and extraction capabilities. They are tasked with organizing, training, and equipping army special operations aviation assets, then deploying them anywhere in the world on short notice. It presently consists of four battalions, a headquarters company, and a dedicated training company. The machines employed are also specially fitted with a dazzling array of electronic sensors and devices to facilitate special operations under a variety of conditions.

Headquarters (Fort Campbell, Kentucky)

Headquarters and Headquarters Company

Systems Integration and Maintenance Office

Special Operation Aviation Training Company

1st Battalion (Fort Campbell, Kentucky)

Headquarters and Headquarters Company

Light Attack Helicopters Company (AH-6J Little Birds)

Light Assault Helicopters Company (MH-6J Little Birds)

Medium Assault Helicopters Company (MH-60K/L Black Hawks)

Medium Assault Helicopters Company (MH-60K/L Black Hawks)

Medium Assault Helicopters Company (MH-60K/L Black Hawks)

2nd Battalion (Fort Campbell, Kentucky)

Headquarters and Headquarters Company

Heavy Assault Helicopters Company (MH-47G Chinooks)

Heavy Assault Helicopters Company (MH-47G Chinooks)

Aviation Maintenance Company

3rd Battalion (Hunter Army Airfield, Georgia)

Headquarters and Headquarters Company

Medium Assault Helicopter Company (MH-60K/L Black Hawks)

Heavy Assault Helicopters Company (MH-47G Chinooks)

Heavy Assault Helicopters Company (MH-47G Chinooks)

Aviation Maintenance Company

4th Battalion (Fort Lewis, Washington)

Headquarters and Headquarters Company

Medium Assault Helicopters Company (MH-60K/L Black Hawks)

Heavy Assault Helicopters Company (MH-47G Chinooks)

Heavy Assault Helicopters Company (MH-47G Chinooks)

Aviation Maintenance Company

Personnel and Training

The Night Stalkers pride themselves on their ability, once a sortie is launched, to reach any objective on target and within 30 seconds of assigned scheduling. Moreover, they are required to fly anywhere on the globe, day or night, under any weather conditions, with high expectations for success. Such levels of proficiency can be acquired only by intense training and a professional "can-do" attitude from all ranks. For this reason, the Night Stalkers accept only the best and most qualified recruits, including aviators, crew members, and support personnel. Prospective candidates have to pass through not only the army's basic training but also the rigors of airborne training and additional specialized instruction for the regiment itself, including a grueling seven-day psychological and physical assessment. Pilot candidates must also possess at least 1,000 flight hours in helicopters, including 100 with night-flying equipment. Those so selected next pass through the Basic Mission Qualification courses, or Green Platoon, which is meted out by the Special Operations Aviation Training Company. This instruction lasts five weeks for enlisted men and 20 to 28 weeks for officer candidates. Night Stalkers are subject to intense tactical drills and exercises through their tenure with the unit and must continually familiarize themselves with the incessant flow of new technologies adapted to their mission profiles. Consequently, depending on individual abilities, new members become fully mission qualified in one or two years following training, while three to five years are required to earn a flight-leader qualification. Combat readiness thus becomes a by-product of rigorous, realistic training. Aviation personnel of the 160th are understandably rated as among the best-trained in the world.

Equipment

Boeing AH-6/MH-6. The "hot rod" of the 160th Special Operations Aviation Regiment is the AH/MH-6 Little Bird, a lineal descendant of the old OH-6 "Loach" (light observation helicopter) of the Vietnam War. This diminutive aircraft wields classified capabilities that belie its rather benign, egg-shaped appearance. In fact, its attack, assault, and surveillance abilities remain closely guarded secrets. Suffice to say that it can deliver a squad of special operations troops into hostile airspace quietly, at low altitude and high speed, then extract them in the same stealthy manner. Its small size also allows operations in relatively crowded urban settings, and can hover between buildings while onboard troops rappel down ropes. For offensive missions, the MH-6 version can be mounted with batteries of air-to-ground missiles as well as a 7.62-mm Gatling gun. It is also ideal for conveying up to four Delta Force commandos into action, strapped to the outboard of the fuselage, whereupon they either jump or rope themselves down, depending on the height from the ground. As a flying platform, the Little Bird is propelled by a single jet turbine engine and flown with dual controls by a crew of two. Of special note is the complete absence of a tail rotor to keep it from spinning. Instead, the Little Bird employs a NOITAR (no tail rotor) system utilizing a tail-mounted cool-air jet thruster to control boom movements.

Sikorsky MH-60L. The Black Hawk is a highly modified troop-carrying helicopter that usually ferries men of the 75th Ranger Regiment into harm's way. To facilitate these missions, it is sumptuously equipped with infrared imagers, omnidirectional jammers, and a missile detector with M130 flare/chaff dispensers. It can also carry with two machine guns firing out of doors on either side. The MH-130L Direct Action Penetrator version also sports an array of offensive weapons systems and can perform any mission usually associated with an attack helicopter. Like all special forces machines, the Black Hawk is fully operational at day, at night, or in adverse weather conditions.

Boeing MH-47D/E. The Chinook is an upgraded variant of a troop-carrying helicopter that debuted during the Vietnam War. Powered by twin rotors, its fuselage frame has been carefully rebuilt and modified to pack the very latest in electronic devices and sensors, including terrain-following radar, forward-looking infrared scanners, and an electronic suite to elude and confuse enemy radars and defensive systems. These arrays allow it to operate normally in low-light and low-visibility conditions that other aircraft might find daunting. It also features a conspicuous probe on the nose to allow in-flight refueling and extend mission ranges. The Chinook is capable of hauling 20 fully equipped special operations troops to a combat zone and letting them rappel quickly to the ground without landing. Operationally, the Chinook performs covert infiltration, exfiltration, air assault, resupply, and other specialized tasks. Highly stable during approach, landing, and takeoffs, it is further capable of operating off the decks of U.S. Navy vessels with sufficient space. The newer G models are extensively refitted with a fully integrated digital avionics package and data-processing units for safe, efficient operations in the most dangerous aerial environments.

Known Operations

The Night Stalkers have rendered continuous and distinguished service to the United States since the end of the Cold War in 1991, although many operations remain shrouded in secrecy. The most notorious episode in the unit history was during Operation GOTHIC SERPENT in Somalia, undertaken to rein in or capture the bloody local warlord Mohamed Farrah Aidid. On October 3, 1993, the 160th contributed a flight of MH-60 Black Hawks (Task Force Ranger) that conveyed 140 elite rangers and Delta Force troops over downtown Mogadishu, the nation's war-torn capital. The troops were safely deposited in this crowded urban setting, but the helicopters came under fire from local militias, and two were brought down by rocket-propelled grenades. Two other Black Hawks sustained heavy damage and subsequently crash-landed at their base. Three pilots died, and the fourth was injured, captured, and used as a bargaining chip for several weeks. Some Delta Force commandos subsequently rappelled down to secure the surviving crewman but they were also killed. As the troops held literally thousands of enraged Somalis at bay, a quick-reaction force of American, Pakistani, and Malaysian UN troops advanced overland to rescue the whole, which was successfully accomplished. Meanwhile, several Night Stalker gunships made repeated strafing runs against armed Somali mobs, mowing down hundreds. The entire episode saw 19 Americans killed (including five from the 160th) and 84 wounded, while Somali losses are estimated at nearly 1,000. This was the most intense firefight experienced by American ground forces since Vietnam. Fortunately, not all interventions in Africa were exclusively military in nature. For example, in April 1996, the 160th SOAR participated in Operation ASSURED RESPONSE in Liberia. This entailed the dismantling and shipment of four MH-47 Chinooks on C-5B Galaxy transports, then their hasty reassembling, in only 72 hours of the alert notice. Over the next 10 days, these crews and machines worked ceaselessly in the evacuation of 2,500 civilians from a disaster area.

Commencing September 11, 2001, the 160th Special Operations Aviation Regiment has borne conspicuous roles in the global war against terror. Men and helicopters gradually arrived in Afghanistan as part of Operation ENDURING FREEDOM to overthrow the Taliban regime and hunt down surviving al-Qaeda terrorists. Commencing on October 19, 2001, an MH-47E carried a special forces team 150 miles from Karshi-Khanabad, Uzbekistan, to Dehi, Afghanistan, formalizing their deployment there. Several weeks later, two MH-47s were

Lithe, fast, and lethal, the MH-6 "Little Bird" attack helicopter is the principal offensive weapon of the "Night Stalkers." (Courtesy of the U.S. Air Force)

known to have participated in the capture of Mazar-i-Sharif by the Northern Alliance. That December, additional helicopters carried 150 American and British special forces into the Tora Bora Mountains to locate terrorist fugitive Osama bin Laden. On March 3, 2002, two MH-47Es operated over the Shahi-Kot Valley while inserting special forces observation teams when one aircraft, Razor1, was downed by a rocket-propelled grenade. The surviving crew and rangers came under heavy fire from the surrounding hills, killing five Americans. The survivors were saved by constant air support and a quick-reaction force that the 160th deposited off in the distance and which advanced up the slopes. On June 28, 2005, tragedy struck again during Operation RED WINGS, the rescue of a besieged Navy SEAL team in the mountains. Another rocket-propelled grenade struck an MH-47 Chinook carrying a SEAL team, killing all eight, along with eight members from the 160th SOAR. On April 1, 2003, the Night Stalkers were also actively engaged in Operation IRAQI FREEDOM, their most celebrated action being the conveyance of special forces to rescue Private Jessica Lynch from an Iraqi hospital in Nasiriya. On August 19, 2009, an MH-60 Black Hawk from the 1st Battalion crashed during maneuvers at Leadville, Colorado, killing all four men on board and further underscoring the hazards of working with cutting edge, high-tech machinery. For the Night Stalkers, the risks are inherent in their daily routine, and worth taking.

Defining Activity

Shortly before midnight on the evening of May 1, 2011, Night Stalkers piloted two HH-60 Black Hawks and three MH-47E Chinooks from the Joint Operations Center at Bagram Airfield, Afghanistan, and entered Pakistani airspace. They adopted a low-signature flight profile by deliberately hugging the ground, assisted by advanced terrain-mapping radar and infrared visual technology that rendered this very dangerous ingress acceptably safer. Their destination was the military garrison town of Abbottabad, home of the Pakistan Military Academy—and a high-walled compound apparently occupied by terrorist mastermind Osama bin Laden. It is not known how the Americans conducted what appears to have been a leisurely stroll through 90 miles of Pakistani airspace without detection, and it has been suggested that their aircraft transponders may have been altered to mimic the electronic signature of local helicopters. Or the Pakistani government may have been complicit and simply looked the other way. More likely is the fact that the rotocraft were outfitted with special sound-suppressing equipment and radar-defeating stealth technology, rendering them invisible in the nighttime sky. Either way, they arrived undetected in the nighttime sky.

Apparently, the actual assault team went in aboard the two Black Hawks while backup teams remained on the Chinooks, the latter setting down in a deserted area roughly two-thirds the distance to the objective. Once alerted, these SEALS could intervene if needed. The Night Stalkers' approach proved uneventful and undetected, but nature intervened in unexpected ways. Abbottabad is 1,200 meters above sea level, which renders the air relatively thin. Moreover, the hot temperature that night also interfered with the ability of these heavily laden helicopters to generate sufficient lift. The plan was to hover over the target building and have 21 SEALs and their trained dog rappel quickly to the ground but, on stationing itself above the compound courtyard, the blowback (or "vortex") generated from rotor's downdraft rebounded off the 18-foot-high walls, causing one HH-60 to make an unexpected "hard landing." No injuries resulted, and the assault team carried out its raid as planned, but the damaged craft could not be reflown. Consequently, toward the end of the 40-minute raid, the SEALs packed the Black Hawk with explosives and departed on the remaining HH-60 and an MH-47E that flew in. The helicopter was blown to pieces save for the tail rotor section, now draped ignominiously over the compound wall. The egress back to Afghanistan also held special terrors of its own, for by now the Pakistani Air Force had scrambled several jets to investigate what was apparently a large-scale military operation on their soil. However, they failed to detect the stealthy intruders, who arrived safely back at Bagram. For the Night Stalkers, this had been yet another successful insertion and extraction, replete with the usual close calls and brushes with disaster.

This successful affair held unforeseen technical and diplomatic ramifications, however. On the following morning, pictures of the Black Hawk wreckage were released around the world, and the decidedly unfamiliar features of the tail rotor section, still intact, generated intense speculation within aviation circles. It was deduced by authorities that the stealth-inducing configuration of the tail assembly and boom were not standard features on HH-60 Black Hawks, so this aircraft had apparently been especially modified. The unique shape of the short, multiple tail rotors, coupled with the odd, dish-shaped hub fairing, are indicative of a noise reduction arrangement heretofore unseen on any helicopter. The Pentagon was quick to neither confirm nor deny any special attributes involved, but the American government was concerned that this technology, whatever it actually represented, might end up in hostile hands. Pakistan had been cultivating closer ties with China recently, and it was feared that the classified wreckage would be examined or purchased by the latter. Equally serious from a diplomatic standpoint was that the Pakistani government, unadvised of the raid beforehand, considered it a flagrant violation of national sovereignty. Angry demonstrators took to the streets while the government contemplated reducing its already strained cooperation with the United States in the War on Terror. It took a visit by Senator John Kerry, chairman of the Senate Foreign Relations Committee, who arrived in Islamabad two weeks after the raid, to smooth over the ruffled feathers. On May 21, 2011, Pakistan finally agreed to release the helicopter wreckage back to the United States. Conjecture as to the precise nature and capabilities of the Night Stalker's HH-60 continues, as does growing suspicion that their heavy-lift Chinooks involved were also similarly outfitted with special sound-suppressing rotors. This development is hardly surprising since the MH-47E, renown for being big and loud was never detected on this particular Night Stalker mission.

Bibliography

Bowden, Mark. *Black Hawk Down: A Story of Modern War*. New York: Atlantic Monthly Press, 1999.

Durant, Michael J., and Steven Hartov. *The Night Stalkers: Top Secret Missions of the U.S. Army's Special Operations Regiment*. New York: G. P. Putnam's Sons, 2006.

Pushies, Fred J. *Night Stalkers: 160th Special Operations Aviation Regiment*. St. Paul, MN: Zenith Press, 2005.

11

Intelligence Support Activity

Veritas Omnia Vinucla Vincit (Truth Overcomes All Bonds)

The shadowy world of special forces seldom gets more opaque than with the Intelligence Support Activity, one of the tightest-kept secrets in the American special operations community. Their sole purpose is providing real-time intelligence to direct action and other counterterrorist activities, usually in concert with Delta Force and SEALs of the Naval Warfare Development Group, elites among the elite. As such, all operatives must be highly skilled in human intelligence (spying) and signal intelligence (SIGNIT, or electronic eaves-dropping) to be successful.

The agency's genesis dates back to 1979 in the wake of Operation EAGLE CLAW, the failed Iranian hostage mission. That summer, it initially manifested as the Field Operations Group (FOG) under its founder, Colonel Jerry King. This unit was created to gather intelligence for an anticipated second attempt to free the hostages and actually had operatives on the ground and in place when the mission was scrubbed for want of air assets. Despite this setback, FOG was retained and expanded, and on March 3, 1981, it was reconstituted with the new moniker Intelligence Support Activity (ISA). Presently, it is a standing department within the U.S. Army, has a secret headquarters in Arlington, Virginia, and enjoys a yearly black (classified) budget in excess of $7 million. Most current operations have focused on Latin America and the Middle East, but they also dabble in East Africa, Southeast Asia, and Europe when necessary.

Several stories are associated with ISA operations but cannot be confirmed. One of the first successes came in 1982 when a team of SIGNIT operators arrived in Italy to help rescue Brigadier General James L. Dozier, who had been kidnapped by the communist Red Brigades. SIGNIT provided by the ISA alerted the rescuers as to Dozier's precise location, and he was successfully freed on January 28, 1982. Later that year, SIGNIT teams arrived in El Salvador to help combat a communist-inspired insurgency under the name Operation QUEEN HUNTER. Here a highly modified Beechcraft 100 King Air passenger plane flown by

(Courtesy of the U.S. Army)

ISA operators closely monitored leftist guerillas operating in that nation along with similar bands in neighboring Honduras. The information they retrieved resulted in successful actions by the Salvadoran and Honduran militaries over the next three years, leading to the eventual defeat of the insurrection. They are also rumored to have been part of the campaign to locate missing American prisoners of war in Southeast Asia under the aegis of Major James G. "Bo" Gritz, a former special forces trooper, although this mission, too, was cancelled by the government. In November 1993, the ISA enjoyed immeasurably better success when a SIGNIT team intercepted a careless phone call by cocaine kingpin and druglord Pablo Escobar; once his location had been pinpointed to Colombian authorities, their special forces teams, aided by Delta Force, cornered and killed him.

Organization

Little is known as to the actual size of the ISA, although rumors circulate that it consists of between 100 and 200 highly qualified agents. Their exact organization and mode of operations, however, appreciably remain highly classified.

Recruitment and Training

It is suspected that all ISA personnel originate from other special operations branches, primarily Delta Force and SEALs but the Special Activities Division of the Central Intelligence Agency (CIA) are also fertile recruiting grounds. Prospective members have to be highly accomplished special operators from the onset. Apparently, the CIA and ISA work closely together, and their personnel appear interchangeable during various mission profiles. If true, all ISA members are extremely qualified in the usual nuances of special operations, including weapons, communications, surveillance, reconnaissance, and foreign language expertise. Moreover, the candidates undoubtedly receive new training in other "black" fields, especially communications intercepts, to successfully fulfill their mission.

Equipment

It is safe to assume that ISA operatives employ many of the same weapons, communications gear, parachutes, and other ingress/egress technologies available to all American special forces. Given their expertise at gathering SIGNIT, the devices they field are unquestionably state of the art and most likely "above top secret," in design and function.

Known Operations

In 1993, ISA agents participated in Operation GOTHIC SERPENT in Somalia, and they provided timely intelligence as to the whereabouts of wanted warlord Mohamed Farrah Aidid in Mogadishu. On October 3, 1993, the main mission of U.S. Army Rangers and Delta Force operatives came to grief when two helicopters were downed by Somalia militiamen, but other special forces guided by ISA SIGNIT teams snared Omar Salad Elmi and Mohammed Hassan Awale, two of Aidid's biggest henchmen, along with 24 other captives. Three years later, they arrived in Bosnia as part of the greater UN effort to track down Serbian leaders Ratko Mladic and Radovan Karadzic, who were wanted for the "ethnic cleansing" of Muslims and Croats throughout the region. On July 10, 1997, the intelligence they provided to British Special Air Service (SAS) teams resulted in the capture of Milan Kovacevic, Sisa Drljaca, and Spiro Milanovic near Lake Gradine. The most daring prisoner snatch occurred on September 27, 1998, when ISA teams accompanied the SAS 50 miles behind Serbian lines to retrieve Stevan Todorovic, also wanted for war crimes. Several of these Serbian captives have since been tried for crimes against humanity at The Hague Netherlands.

Prior to the terrorist attack against the World Trade Center on September 11, 2001, the ISA provided the CIA with accurate fixes as to the location of wanted terrorist Osama bin Laden, but several snatch missions planned to capture him in Afghanistan were invariably canceled by the Clinton administration for political reasons. After 9/11, however, the ISA was kicked into high gear for Operation ENDURING FREEDOM, and teams were hastily flown into Afghanistan. Operation JAWBREAKER commenced in concert with the CIA, and the hunt for bin Laden was on. However, that elusive terrorist escaped a closing noose laid for him in his Tora Bora Mountains stronghold, and he apparently fled to Pakistan. Nonetheless, on November 3, 2001, a SIGNIT team picked up senior al-Qaeda leader Qa'ed Sunyan al-Harethi in Yemen, outside the town of Harib. He and four other terrorists were apparently going to bomb the residence of U.S. Ambassador Edmund J. Hull. Fortunately, the CIA was alerted in time, and it placed an armed Predator drone in orbit over where their Land Rover was expected to appear. When it did, a Hellfire missile obliterated the vehicle along with its passengers. The exact role and number of ISA teams in Afghanistan to date remain classified, but they undoubtedly highly active and effective in whatever they do.

Not surprisingly, ISA also played a major, if covert, role in Operation IRAQI FREEDOM. Activity operators and British special forces were present in Mosul, where they successfully tracked down Saddam Hussein's two cruel sons, Uday and Qusay. On July 22, 2003, they guided a detachment of the 101st Airborne Division toward their safe house downtown, where both were killed in a firefight with ISA and British operatives. Task Force 121 was subsequently established to snare Hussein himself, and this was accomplished on Saturday, June 13, 2003, when the dictator was hauled out of his "spider hole" near a farm at al-Dawr. On June 7, 2006, ISA teams were also heavily involved in pinpointing the safe house used by bloodthirsty terrorist Abu Musab al-Zarqawi in the village of Hibhib north of Baghdad. A Delta Force reconnaissance team painted the house with a laser target designator, at which point an F-16 dropped guided 500-pound bombs on it, killing Zarqawi and several occupants. The ISA's continuing activities, despite the decided drop in terrorist activities throughout Iraq, is unknown. What is known is that ISA plays a prominent role behind the scenes, providing accurate information to facilitate direct-action missions by other special forces where necessary. The results speak for themselves.

Bibliography

Berntsen, Gary, and Ralph Pezzullo. *Jawbreaker: The Attack on Bin-Laden and al-Qaeda. A Personal Account by the CIA's Key Field Commander*. New York: Crown, 2005.

Geraghty, Tony. *Black Ops: The Rise of Special Forces in the C.I.A., the S.A.S., and the Mossad*. New York: Pegasus Books, 2010.

Smith, Michael. *Killer Elite: The Inside Story of America's Most Secret Special Force Unit*. New York: St. Martin's Griffin, 2011.

12

Marine Corps Force Reconnaissance/Special Operations Battalions

Celer, Silens, Mortalis (Swift, Silent, Deadly)

Few military organizations in world history can lay claim to such a fabled legacy as the U.S. Marine Corps, a branch that has always regarded itself as an elite fighting force. That legacy has garnered even more acclaim since special operations have been added to its tactical milieu. Since the Cold War ended, there have been handpicked reconnaissance companies at the divisional level, subject to even more rigorous training than marines already receive. They would, however, studiously deny that such units differed in tenor or outlook from any other unit in the corps. But, with the advent of the 21st century and the struggle against terror, some formations have accepted the convention of being more elite than others by formally being designated special operations capable (SOC). This is a significant development, organizationally, considering that the Marine Corps did not become part of the U.S. Special Operations Command until February 24, 2006. Prior to that date, there existed two separate reconnaissance entities, Recon and Force Recon, tasked with providing military intelligence before and during amphibious or ground operations. But, whereas Recon units conduct division-level reconnaissance activities, usually within the range of the navy's guns offshore, Force Recon units are especially trained for deep reconnaissance behind enemy lines and report directly to the expeditionary force commander. After 1998, both units were jumbled together into two designated Recon Battalions, with one assigned to both the Fleet Marine Force Atlantic and Pacific. This arrangement persisted up through March 2006, when personnel of the 1st and 2nd Force Reconnaissance Companies transferred to the newly created Marine Corps Special

(Courtesy of the U.S. Marine Corps)

Operations Command (MARSOC) as the 1st and 2nd Marine Special Operations Battalions. Generally, MARSOC units are capable of missions ranging from foreign internal defense, special reconnaissance, and direct action like any other special operations outfit. Furthermore, all Marine Corps reconnaissance and special forces are parachute and scuba qualified and may deploy into hostile territory by land, sea, or air, and deep behind enemy lines. In the event that a recon team is compromised, they can be speedily extracted from jungles and forests by helicopters equipped with a Spie Rig (a special harness). Interestingly, Force Reconnaissance units were instrumental in pioneering submarine locking-in and locking-out methods, along with high-altitude, low-opening and high-altitude, high-opening parachuting, long before the Green Berets and Navy SEALs adopted them. And, despite the Marine Corps' longstanding disassociation with special operations, its reconnaissance companies contain some of the most adept practitioners of unconventional warfare in the world today.

Basically, marine divisional reconnaissance units are trained to execute two kinds of missions. So-called Green Operations involve traditional preliminary and postassault reconnaissance (both amphibious and ground), along with battle damage assessment or placing/recovering remote sensors or beacons. The companies embark for the sole purpose of gathering military intelligence relating to enemy positions troop strengths and intentions, and they may also initiate terminal guidance procedures for establishing landing zones and drop zones for helicopters and parachutists, respectively. Stealth and silence are essential to the success of Green Operations, so no firing is allowed unless in self-defense; at that point their mission is considered compromised. In contrast, Force Recon companies attached to an expeditionary unit are authorized to conduct Green Operations in "deep-reconnaissance" style, far beyond the range of friendly field artillery and naval gunfire support. Once committed inland, Force Recon units are literally on their own until their mission successfully concludes.

The next level of Marine Corps reconnaissance activity is so-called Black Operations. Here, divisional and Force Recon units engage enemy units or individuals in direct action with military force, usually by calling in gunfire support or air strikes by "painting" targets with laser target designators. Given the need for security and stealth, Force Recon forward observers usually conduct their mission from deep "spider holes" dug just for that purpose. Other mission profiles might entail the seizure of gas/oil platforms at sea and the visit, board, and search and seizure of vessels during maritime interdiction operations. Force Recon detachments can also provide personal security details for important individuals and are versed in hostage rescue situations, as needed. Overall, Force Recon units excel in the escape, evasion, and small-unit combat activities associated with most special operation units. They can perform direct action missions and engage enemy units when required, but clandestine battlefield/theater surveillance remains their principal forte.

Organization

Prior to 2006, Marine Corps Reconnaissance Battalions consisted of three distinct companies, each with its own assigned purpose. The A Company has a training functions and painstakingly instructs all prospective recruits in the art of reconnaissance. Graduates are then assigned to into the B Company for rehearsing routine operations at the division level until they are proficient. Only then can exceptional marines apply for service with C Company, specializing in special operations/deep-reconnaissance missions following another period of intense training. However, once MARSOC arose on August 11, 2006, the 1st and 2nd Force Recon deactivated and their personnel were rolled over into new D Companies within the existing reconnaissance battalions. These units are responsible for the Deep Reconnaissance Platoons assigned to specific expeditionary forces. The companies themselves are organized as follows:

Headquarters Platoon

1st Platoon (Direct Action)

2nd Platoon (Direct Action)

3rd Platoon (Deep Recon)

4th Platoon (Deep Recon)

5th Platoon (Scout/Sniper)

On December 19, 2008, the new Force Reconnaissance Company was activated to provide force-level capabilities within the II Marine Expeditionary Force, and was added to the roster of the 2nd Marine Division's 2nd Reconnaissance Battalion. Presently, Force Recon companies are attached to individual Marine Expeditionary Units (MEUs), which are the smallest versions of Marine Air-Ground Task Forces. These consist of a reinforced battalion and are designed for short-term intervention in natural disasters, police-style actions, and lower-priority assignments. Each of the seven MEUs contain 1,500 to 3,000 marines and are forward-deployed on naval vessels within an Amphibious Ready Group. MEUs can also put ashore in self-sustained fashion for 30 days, and most enjoy SOC ratings. Force Recon companies attached to an MEU answer to the expeditionary commander and are expected to provide amphibious reconnaissance, surveillance, and direct-action missions as needed. Here, companies consist of six operational platoons of three six-man team each. Each headquarters platoon is also staffed by a captain, a gunnery sergeant, a radio operator, a special reconnaissance corpsman, and a platoon equipment rigger/armorer. The reason the six-man team is preferred over a more traditional four-man squad is utility: the extra two members allow the team to secure adequate rest while allowing for sufficient security. In addition, if one member is injured, the casualty can be carried by some members while others convey his valuable and expensive equipment back to safety.

In April 2009, a Marine Special Operations Regiment was founded to execute special operations beyond those routinely handled by the Force Recon units. This new unit provides specialized military combat skills and adviser support to select foreign forces. The sailors and marines involved all train, advise, and assist allied and friendly host nation forces, including military, naval, and paramilitary components, to bolster internal security, enhance political stability, and counter violence from terrorism and other internal threats.

All orders are cut directly from MARSOC in accordance with the wishes of the U.S. Special Operations Command, which places it beyond the usual chain of Marine Corps command. The regiment itself is organized into four separate battalions, each consisting of four Special Operations Companies of 14 men each and led by a captain.

1st Marine Special Operations Battalion (Camp Pendleton, California)
The 1st Marine Special Operations Battalion, activated on October 26, 2006, consists of four companies and is equipped to quickly deploy abroad as per orders from MARSOC. Their personnel is uniquely situated to impart training in communications, reconnaissance, special equipment, intelligence, and fire support to other recon marines.

2nd Marine Special Operations Battalion (Camp Lejeune, North Carolina)
The 2nd Marine Special Operations Battalion, activated on May 15, 2006, consists of five Marine Special Operations Companies, with all personnel highly skilled in the fields of equipment, intelligence, and fire support.

3rd Marine Special Operations Battalion (Camp Lejeune, North Carolina)
The 3rd Marine Special Operations Battalion is responsible for training personnel all Marine Special Operations Forces for deployment overseas.

Recruitment and Training

All individuals who successfully pass Marine Corps basic training—among the most demanding in the world—are eligible to apply for service with Force Recon. Once a prospective recruit has been examined to ascertain his mental and physical readiness, he begins the five-phase Mission Training Plan in his quest for SOC certification. This two-year program is extremely intensive and systematic, in accepted Marine Corps fashion, and emphasizes training recon members in the exact manner they expect to fight. Like all special forces schools, the recon course seeks candidates who are as tough mentally and hardy in terms of endurance as they may be physically fit.

Phase 1: Individual Training

Force Recon training begins within an MEU Predeployment Training Program to enter the "accession pipeline." This requires prospective trainees to successfully pass the Infantry Rifleman Course, the Basic Reconnaissance Course, the SERE School (Level C), the USMC Combatant Diver Course, the Basic Airborne Course, the Special Operations Training Group (SOTG), and the Military Free Fall School. Marine Corps instructors are not exactly renown for their tender sympathies, and failure at any one of these courses results in reassignment back to a line unit.

Phase 2: Unit Training

The second phase of the Mission Training Plan also occurs onboard a Marine Expeditionary Unit as part of its Predeployment Training Plan. Here candidates are assigned to a training cell (T-cell) overseen by experienced noncommissioned officers of the recon

Marines with Individual Training Course, Marine Special Operations School, Marine Corps Forces, Special Operations Command, slowly work through tall grass during a fire and maneuver exercise, 2010, at Camp Lejeune, North Carolina. The exercise was the culminating event of a weapons and tactics package the course conducted that week. (U.S. Department of Defense)

company's Operations Section (S-3). This allows sergeants to train directly with their men in the absence of officers, who remain back at the headquarters platoon. The T-cell also serves as a recruiting ground for future recon platoon sergeants, an essential part of the process. The courses, or "packages," tendered include Advanced Long Range Communications, Weapons and Tactics, Threat Weapons Familiarization, Forces Fire (close air and naval gunfire support), Mobile Reconnaissance, Advanced Airborne, Combat Trauma, Amphibious Training, and Combat Diving. Recruits are also expected to distinguish themselves during long-range patrolling across desert areas, mountainous terrain, and other harsh environments. At the end of six months, the entire unit has worked closely as a team and presumably mastered all the operational facets of deep reconnaissance.

Phase 3: SOC Training

Prospective recon marines now report to the SOTG for hands-on instruction in "black operations," mastery of which is essential to their craft. Over the next six months, they tackle objectives in maritime and urban environments with emphasis on close-quarters combat techniques, demolitions, gas/oil platform seizures, shipboard assaults, and the like. Lesser but equally useful undertakings, such as cordon-and-search missions and humanitarian operations, are also stressed.

Phase 4: SOC Deployment

Once a candidate is judged SOC, he is certified and accompanies his platoon into the field as part of a functioning force. They then embark with their respective MEU on a six-month operational deployment, contingent on where they serve. This means the I MEU on the West Coast for a tour of the Pacific region, the II MEU on the East Coast for a tour of either the Mediterranean of Persian Gulf, or the III MEU on Okinawa, distinct in being the only recon unit on standby alert for immediate deployment worldwide. While shipboard, recon marines stay focused on discipline and training sessions, including live fire drills from the decks of ships coupled with intense physical conditioning. Despite their trainee status, they may nonetheless be called on to conduct joint exercises with British marines, Royal Thai marines, and Australian forces when so ordered.

Phase 5: SOC Postdeployment

When the 18 months of intense military and physical training end, each recon marine obtains a 30-day leave. During this period, they must decide whether to remain with their Force Recon company and its respective MEU or be released from reconnaissance duties and return to their original assignment with the infantry, administration, or motor transport. Roughly 50 percent of all successful recon marines decline to remain longer Force Recon and transfer back to an easier assignment. Significantly, all MEU units hold their SOC designation for only for one year at a time, after which each is retested and/or retrained to be recertified.

Scouts/Snipers

One shot, one kill.

A vital subset of marine reconnaissance units are the scout/sniper platoons who, as their name implies, are adept at both surveillance and marksmanship. This designation is unique among modern militaries, including the U.S. Army, that have traditionally separated scouting and sniping functions. As snipers, marines must be highly skilled in field craft, concealment, and marksmanship to deliver accurate, long-range fire from concealment. In battlefield parlance, they deny freedom of movement to enemy forces by neutralizing officers, crew-served weapons, radio operators, and other key military figures with single, well-placed shots. Marine scout/snipers are among the foremost of American special forces, if the least known, in service, and must conform to exacting physical, mental, and shooting standards simply to join.

Recruitment and Training

Any marine can volunteer for scout/sniper service once he successfully completes basic training and has fulfilled routine duties in an infantry battalion. However, all individuals must have attained the rank of lance corporal to qualify. The process usually involves an extensive physical fitness exam, followed by an interview with a platoon sergeant or officer. If he is judged acceptable for a training platoon, the candidate receives the official designation as Professionally Instructed Gunman (PIG). However, the waiting list to enter the

Marine Corps Scout/Sniper School can take up to three years depending on available slots. In the meantime, prospective candidates continually rehearse skills and attitudes necessary for passing the school. In fact, the Scout Sniper Basic Course is among the most arduous regimens in the entire Marine Corps, with washout rates of 60 percent. Once accepted, the recruit passes through one of four service schools at Camp Pendleton, California; Camp Lejeune, North Carolina; Quantico, Virginia; or the Marine Corps Base Camp in Hawaii. The ensuing eight-and-a-half-week course is followed by a Team Leader Course of four additional weeks.

Phase 1: Marksmanship and Basic Field Craft

Here the candidates receive instruction on mandatory skills as concealed movement, camouflage, observations, known distance range, and weapons system. Marines must be able to strike targets at ranges of 300, 500, 600, 700, 800, 900, and 1,000 yards while with another marine uses an M49 spotting scope or binoculars to call out wind factors. A score of 28 out of 35 hits is necessary to qualify for the next phase of training. Observation skills, especially practiced from behind dense bushes and vegetation, is also stressed.

Phase 2: Unknown Distance and Stalking

This part of scout/sniper training entails engaging targets at unknown distances through range cards and outright estimation. Recruits are required to spread out steel targets at ranges of 300 to 800 yards, then successfully knock them over. The stalking phase of the course is also challenging and requires them to move from 1,200 to 200 yards of a given target without being detected. This must be accomplished within three to four hours, at the conclusion of which the trainee assumes the final firing position and looses two rounds without being seen by a keen-eyed instructor.

Phase 3: Advanced Field Skills and Mission Employment

During this phase of instruction, prospective scouts/snipers report to units in the field for hands-on training under actual operational conditions. Successful candidates should be able to deliver precision rifle fire against select targets from concealed positions and with reasonable prospects of success. At this juncture, he also sheds his designation of PIG and is officially as a Hunter of Gunmen.

Equipment

Force Recon companies are capable of deploying behind enemy lines by air, sea, and land and are issued a wide variety of equipment necessary for their requisite ingress. In terms of firearms, most marines receive standard-issue M16A2 rifles, a modified version of the famous weapon first introduced during the Vietnam War. However, depending on the mission, troopers can substitute the shortened M4A1 carbine version, which fires the identical 5.56-mm round. At 33 inches in length, it is six inches shorter than the standard M-16 and can be fitted with plastic foregrips and sound suppressors for close-quarter combat and the silent elimination of sentries. In addition to adjustable iron sights, the M4A1 mounts an ACOG Day Optical Sight for sniping and an AN/PVS-17 Night Vision Sight for nocturnal operations. Higher up the tech scale, the carbine can be fitted with an AN/PEQ-2 Infra-Red Target Pointer/Illuminator for improved accuracy in the dark. Firepower is further enhanced by the addition of the QDM203 40-mm grenade launcher under the barrel, which

U.S. Marines learn skills for mountain warfare at the Marine Corps Mountain Warfare Training Center through a number of courses, including rock climbing, high-angle sniper training, mountain rescue, and multiday mountaineering expeditions. In addition to being outstanding marksmen, scout/snipers attached to Force Reconnaissance units can conceal themselves in with any environment. They are usually accompanied by a spotter who calls out target, distance, and shooting conditions. (Ed Darack/Science Faction/Corbis)

weighs only three pounds. Each marine also carries an M9 9-mm pistol as a sidearm, although the older .45-caliber M1911 pistol remains much in demand. Shotguns of various sorts can likewise be issued depending on mission requirements, as is the M249 SAW (Squad Automatic Weapon), a magazine-fed weapon with a cyclic rate of 750 rounds per minute. However, the reconnaissance version of the SAW has to be being broken down into parts for deploying by parachute and must be reassembled on the ground. Thus, it is not readily available if hostile contact is made on landing, an extreme disadvantage. More exotic weaponry befitting of Force Recon special operations is also available. Foremost among these are various sniper rifles, ranging from standard 7.62-mm M40A1 rifles to the larger 12.7-mm Special Application Scoped Rifle, which has a range of 1,800 yards and armor-piercing capability. Another vital piece of equipment issued to Force Recon squads is the AN/PEQ-1A Special Operations Forces Laser Marker, which is used to "paint" targets at a distance so that they can be taken out by laser-guided missiles or bombs. It weighs 34 pounds and can illuminate targets up to three miles distant.

In addition to weapons, marine reconnaissance units can also carry the 28-pound Close Quarter Battle Equipment Assault Vest for protection although, in practice, this item proved so heavy that lighter, more flexible designs are being evaluated to replace it. Marines might also be required to wear the bulky Kevlar Modular Integrated Communications Helmet for protection and continual radio links. In terms of motor vehicles, Force Recon sometimes deploys the Mercedes-Benz Improved Fast Attack vehicle, a diesel-powered

Paul Scheppf, right, uses Afghan interpreter, Mati Ullah, left, to talk to an Afghan policeman at a security checkpoint in Khan Neshin, Afghanistan, 2011. Scheppf, assigned to the 2nd Light Armored Reconnaissance Battalion, is visiting the Afghan policemen manning the checkpoint. (U.S. Department of Defense)

all-terrain vehicle, while the more familiar M998 HMMWV, or Hummer, is utilized as a logistics support vehicle. For ingress over water, marines field the Combat Rubber Reconnaissance Craft, which is 15 feet long and six feet wide and powered by a 55-horsepower water jet engine to reduce noise. For missions requiring a submerged approach, the Mark 25 Draegar Underwater Breathing Apparatus, which contains 240 minutes' worth of oxygen, is issued to divers. This is a closed-circuit system that does not leave a telltale trail of bubbles along the water's surface. Finally, airborne insertion is achieved by either the MC-5 Static Line/Free Fall Ram Air Parachute System or the MC-1C Low Level Static Line Parachute. Distinct improvements over the traditional T100-10 parachute first issued in the 1950s, these devices permit high-altitude, high-opening or high-altitude, low-opening descents, depending on mission necessities. Both devices also afford jumpers good degrees of control while descending, hence greater flexibility when choosing where to land. For all the firepower and exotica packed into marine reconnaissance teams, their primary weapon—and best defense—is remaining undiscovered by a vigilant enemy. Their tactical situation, perilous enough from the onset, only worsens once triggers get pulled.

Known Operations

Marine reconnaissance units are treated like all special forces, and their endeavors are highly classified and little advertised. Information relative to specific incidents is hard to obtain let alone verify. However, they were known to be active during the siege of Fallujah,

Iraq, November 8–December 24, 2004. Here, the Force Recon platoon under Captain Jason Schauble, attached to the 1st Battalion, 8th Marines, worked its way into the northern parts of the town and neutralized scores of insurgents by directing sniping, artillery, and air attacks in their immediate proximity. Schauble lost one man killed, and 13 of 24 men were wounded but they executed a very difficult and dangerous task with consummate skill. Extended service during Operation IRAQI FREEDOM has also forced the Marine Corps to take a long look at traditional roles as it relates to Force Recon. In high-density, urban areas, cover and obscurity while moving are almost impossible to achieve, particularly in counter-insurgency warfare. It has since been deduced that long-term occupation, at least in Iraq, precludes the very kind of clandestine reconnaissance they excel at, so greater emphasis is being placed on direct-action missions. A celebrated incident reflecting this trend occurred off the northern coast of Somalia when a group of nine pirates seized a German container ship, the *Magellan Star*, on September 9, 2010. The following day, the vessel was boarded by a Force Recon detachment from a nearby U.S. Navy warship; the pirates were subdued, and the 11-man crew was rescued without firing a shot. Given the rise of piracy in this part of the world and the necessity for direct action by marine reconnaissance units, such events will probably occur with greater frequency until root problems of terrorism and lawlessness can be addressed regionally.

Bibliography

Afong, Milo S. *HOGs in the Shadows: Combat Stories from Marine Snipers in Iraq*. New York: Berkley Caliber, 2007.

Afong, Milo S. *Hunters: U.S. Snipers in the War on Terror*. New York: Berkley, 2011.

Cavallaro, Gina, with Matt Larsen. *Sniper: American Single-Shot Warriors in Iraq and Afghanistan*. Guilford, CT: Lyons Press, 2010.

Coughlin, Jack, Casey Kuhlman, and Don Davis. *Shooter: The Autobiography of the Top-Ranked Marine Sniper*. New York: St. Martin's Press, 2005.

Cox, Thomas. *The Last Wolf: A Vivid Quest through the Eyes of a Marine Corps Chief Scout Sniper*. Philadelphia: Xlibris, 2010.

Darack, Ed. *Victory Point: Operations Red Wings and Whalers: The Marine Corps' Battle for Freedom in Afghanistan*. New York: Berkeley Caliber, 2009.

Hollis, John H. *Enter Iraq: A Pictorial of U.S. Marine Force Recon on the Syrian Border*. New York: Aegeon Press, 2007.

Mast, Gregory. *To Be a Military Sniper*. St. Paul, MN: Zenith Press, 2007.

Piedmont, John P. *Det One: U.S. Marine Corps U.S. Special Operations Command Detachment, 2003–2006*. Washington, DC: History Division, U.S. Marine Corps, 2010.

Pushies, Fred J. *Marine Force Recon*. St. Paul, MN: MBI, 2000.

Pushies, Fred J. *MARSOC: U.S. Marine Corps Special Operations Command*. Minneapolis: Zenith Press, 2011.

Raab, J. Michael. *Every Day is Monday: U.S. Marine Snipers in Iraq*. Pottstown, PA: Scout Writer Books, 2009.

Roberts, Craig. *Crosshairs on the Kill Zone: American Combat Snipers, Vietnam Through Operation Iraqi Freedom*. New York: Pocket Star Books, 2004.

Tucker, Mike. *Ronin: A Marine Scout/Sniper Platoon in Iraq*. Mechanicsburg, PA: Stackpole Books, 2008.

Wright, Evan. *Generation Kill: Devil Dogs, Iceman, Captain America, and the New Face of American War*. New York: Berkley Caliber, 2005.

13

Navy SEALs

The only easy day was yesterday.

Having achieved considerable success during the Vietnam conflict and up through the end of the Cold War in 1991, the Naval Special Warfare Command (SWCC) arose on April 16, 1987, at Naval Amphibious Base Coronado, California. This became the over-arching command structure that controls the SEALs and two subordinate units, the SEAL Delivery Vehicle Teams (SDVTs) and the Special Boat Teams (SBT). Thus situated, the SWCC is capable of conducting small-unit, littoral operations launched from the ocean, a river, swamp, delta, or coastline, and recovering them safely. Among their litany of mission profiles is unconventional warfare, direct action, counterdrug operations, antiterrorism, foreign internal defense, personnel recovery, and hydrographic reconnaissance. The significance of these activities is significant, considering that half the world's population and infra-structures reside within one mile of a large body of water. Moreover, SEALs are capable of operating effectively in virtually any kind of environmental setting, be it temperate, arctic, desert, jungle, or urban. Tactically, they train to fight and win and are exceptionally lethal in action. SEAL teams in Naval Special Warfare Squadrons, or Special Operations Task Forces, are thus ready for service anywhere around the globe. To that end, they usually oper-ate under the aegis of a Joint Task Force or a Combined Special Operations Task Force (CJSOTF). Collectively, all SWCC personnel constitute roughly 1 percent of all U.S. Navy personnel, yet they return military dividends far out of proportion to their actual number.

Organization

Presently, the SWCC consists of eight SEAL teams and four support teams and are organ-ized into five distinct groups at assigned global locales. The actual number of combatants is approximately 2,000 out of a combined personnel roster of 6,500. It must be stressed that

(Courtesy of the U.S. Navy)

these "facts" are more or less speculative; the actual number of men and teams remains highly classified and hence not accurately known.

United States Special Warfare Development Group (Dam Neck, Virginia)

Known as SEAL Team Six until 1987, this outfit serves as an operational testing unit for new concepts and equipment for the Naval Warfare Development Group. They are considered the elite of a very elite group, and are discussed at length in Chapter 15. The Group consists of:

Naval Special Warfare Group 1 (Naval Amphibious Base, Coronado, California)
SEAL Teams One (Southeast Asia), Three (Southwest Asia), Five (Northern Pacific), and Seven (global)
Naval Special Warfare Group 2 (Naval Amphibious Base Little Creek, Virginia)
SEAL Teams Two (Europe), Four (Central/South America), Eight (Caribbean, Africa, Mediterranean), and 10 (global)
Naval Special Warfare Group 3 (Pearl Harbor, Hawaii)
SEAL Team Delivery Vehicle Team 1 (Detachments at Pearl Harbor and Little Creek)
Naval Special Warfare Group 11 (Naval Amphibious Base, Coronado, California)
SEAL Teams 17, 18

The basic tactical unit of the SEALs is the team, with each consisting of a Staff Headquarters detachment and three 40-man troops. Troops individually contain a command element of two officers and 14 enlisted men. For combat purposes, SEAL teams are generally divided up into eight four-man squads, or fire teams, although larger units can also deploy. The smallest tactical combat formation is the two-man team, or "swim buddies." All SEAL team members display mastery of a variety of troop core skills of various sorts, including sniper, breacher, communicator, maritime engineers, close air support, corpsman, point man (land)/navigator (sea), heavy weapons operator, lead diver/navigator, interrogator, ordnance disposal, technical surveillance, and advanced special operations. Moreover, all SEALs are highly cross trained to possess several relevant skills pertinent to individual missions. Teams are sometimes delivered to their tactical zones by crack SDVTs employing Mark 8 miniature submarines to ensure a clandestine approach. These vehicles are, in turn, either carried piggyback submarines and manned by scuba-rigged SEALs while submerged or launched from special holding facilities from within the sub. For missions above the surface, SEALs are conveyed by SBTs who operate a variety of small, high speed craft, to facilitate hidden deployment. In addition to direct-action missions at sea, the SBTs themselves can likewise conduct visit, board, search, and seizure; special reconnaissance; coastal patrol and interdiction; counterterrorism and antipiracy operations; riverine warfare; and search-and-rescue operations. The two branches of SWCC train and work closely together to fulfill any or all special and maritime missions they may be assigned.

Michael P. Murphy (1976–2005).
Michael Patrick Murphy was born in Smithtown, New York, on May 7, 1976, and in September 2000 he accepted a slot with the U.S. Navy Officer Candidate School at Pensacola, Florida. That December, he received his ensign's commission and transferred over to the Basic Underwater Demolition/SEAL school at Coronado, California, from which he graduated in January 2001. Murphy earned his trident as a Navy SEAL in July 2002, and in the spring of 2005, he arrived in Afghanistan as assistant officer in charge of ALFA Platoon and part of Operation ENDURING FREEDOM. In June 2005, Murphy participated in Operation RED WINGS, conceived to locate and eliminate a noted Taliban leader called Ahmad Shah. His four-man reconnaissance team was helicoptered into the rugged mountains of Kunar Province, but while performing their mission, they were discovered by a goat herder who alerted nearby

Michael Murphy, a distinguished SEAL officer, won a posthumous Congressional Medal of Honor for valuable service in Afghanistan. (Courtesy of the U.S. Navy)

Taliban units. Murphy and his three men deployed in rough terrain and engaged an estimated 100 to 200 fighters for several hours, all the while calling for reinforcements. When Murphy discovered that his cell phone could not operate properly from behind cover, he deliberately exposed himself and eventually contacted the relief team. However, he and three SEALs died in the firefight, and days passed before the lone survivor, Leading Petty Officer Marcus Lutrell, could be rescued. For sacrificing himself to save his team, Murphy became the first American soldier awarded a posthumous Congressional Medal of Honor in Afghanistan. On May 7, 2008, Secretary of the Navy Donald C. Winter announced that the Arleigh Burke class destroyer *DDG-112* would be christened the USS *Michael Murphy* in his honor.

Recruitment and Training

SEALS are expected to perform effectively in a wide variety of environments and under extremely stressful, dangerous conditions. Therefore, the training regimen to prepare them for their labors is among the most arduous, challenging, and difficult ever imposed on military personnel, anywhere. Volunteers must first pass basic training at the Recruit Training Command in Great Lakes, Illinois, and the Naval Special Warfare Course at the same locale. Nonetheless, before a prospective candidate is even allowed near a SEAL training facility, he must first endure a five-week indoctrination period, which includes the Physical Screening Test. This qualification routine is definitely not for slouches. It includes swimming 1,500 feet in 12 minutes and 30 seconds using breaststrokes or sidestrokes, 42 push-ups in under two minutes, 50 sit-ups in two minutes, and a 1.5-mile run in under 11 minutes and 30 seconds while wearing heavy combat boots. Survivors have scant time to congratulate themselves before being shunted off to Coronado, California, for the justly dreaded Basic Underwater Demolition/SEAL (BUD/S) Training. This six month ordeal of highly orchestrated abuse is calculated to cull as many as 80 percent of applicants—and usually does.

First Phase

The first round of training concentrates on intense basic conditioning over the ensuing seven weeks. Trainees are expected to participate in running, swimming, and calisthenics, all designed to improve water competency, teamwork, and mental agility. In addition, recruits are subject to weekly two-mile timed swims wearing fins and four-mile runs in boots. Small-boat seamanship is also stressed. One particular exercise, underwater acclimation, involves students being plunged into pools with their wrists tied behind their back, whereby they have to remain afloat for 20 minutes and retrieve face masks from the bottom of the pool with their teeth! But all this pales in comparison with the fourth week of training, aptly deemed "Hell Week"—and for good reason. Candidates are subject to five and a half days of continuous training, while granted only four hours of sleep per night. One particularly nightmarish practice goes by the misleading title of "sugar cookie," whereby dripping wet students are rolled around in beach sand until totally covered, then ordered to continue with their assignments. This systematic stress demonstrates that human beings are capable of strength and endurance they never thought possible and reinforces a quintessential military principle: teamwork. Significantly, at any time during Hell Week, members less disposed to pass can quit by ringing a brass ship's bell three times. The survivors gain little respite and spend the remaining three weeks training hard to master the arts of hydrographic surveys and chart making.

Second Phase

The next phase of SEAL instruction focuses on diving and lasts eight weeks. Here candidates learn to become competent combat swimmers through extensive use of scuba equipment, including open circuit (compressed air) and closed circuit (pure oxygen) systems. In addition to extensive and continuous physical conditioning, trainees must perform long-distance swimming while submerged, with demonstrated mastery of specialized diving and recovery techniques from a variety of surface and submerged platforms. This relentless emphasis on flexibility, in terms of clandestine movements to and from combat objectives, that really distinguishes SEALs from other special forces.

Third Phase

The final phase of SEAL training imparts basic and advanced land warfare skills on all candidates. These skills include weapons, demolitions, patrolling, ambushes, rappelling, land navigation, marksmanship, and a host of small-unit reconnaissance tactics. Over the next

U.S. Navy SEALs on the beach at North Island Naval Air Station in California, 2004. SEALs train continuously to operate under any weather or terrain conditions. A stealthy ingress from the sea, followed by a violent strike, remains their operational forte.
(Jim Sugar/Corbis)

nine weeks, all students continue their physical training, which has now become even more intense, once minimum passing time lowers for runs, swims, and obstacle course clearance. Successful candidates spend their final three and a half weeks on San Clemente Island, putting all their newly acquired skills to work into highly demanding mock missions. Those SEALs intending to act as corpsmen are also required to pass the 37-week U.S. Army Special Forces Medical Sergeant Course, another grueling regimen.

Having successfully completed the BUD/S course, candidates are next required to attend the army's three-week parachute qualification course at Fort Benning, Georgia, to earn their Silver Wings. Considering what they have endured, many SEALs find airborne training much akin to a vacation. The men then transfer to the Naval Special Warfare Center to attend SEAL Qualification Training (SQT). This entails a further 15 weeks to acquire all the nuances of communications, small-boat handling, close-quarter combat, sniping, and parachuting. Passage here finally elevates a recruit to an operational standard, and in a muted ceremony, each receives the coveted NSW insignia, the golden trident, along with his SEAL Naval Enlisted Classification Code. Immediately afterward, all new SEALs head off for Kodiak, Alaska, for three more weeks of cold-weather training. Others may attend the Defense Language Institute in Monterey, California, to learn exotic dialects such as Arabic, Farsi, or Mandarin. Their training may be complete, but SEALs are still perpetually required to take new courses and polish up old skills throughout their tenure with the unit. In fact, once an individual SEAL is paired up with his team, his six-month active-duty deployment is followed by up to 18 months of additional training and leave. It is no

The SEAL Delivery Vehicle allows a covert ingress by naval commandos to any objective with a shoreline. The operators are highly skilled and capable of operating under a variety of adverse sea conditions. (Library of Congress)

exaggeration to say that a SEAL is expected to give a 110 percent effort all the time. Thanks to their training, they invariably can and do.

Equipment

SEALs employ the many standard weapons and systems issued to other special operations units. The usual sidearm in the M-4 carbine, a shortened, lightened version of the venerable M-16, and fitted with a 40-mm M-203 grenade launcher to enhance firepower. However, for small-unit groups on hostile terrain, point men carry any number of different 12-gauge shotguns that spread 00 "buckshot" with lethal effect out to 100 meters. Rear-guard security is emphasized by SEALs carrying a shortened, lightened version of the old M-60 machine gun, which can lay down a steady stream of 7.62-mm fire from belts. SEAL teams are presently undergoing conversion to the newer M240 light machine guns, which is lighter and more reliable. Claymore mines, teargas grenades, and white-hot phosphorous grenades are carried in theater, contingent upon the mission. For overland operations, SEALs also handle the Desert Patrol Vehicle (DPVs), a modified dune buggy outfitted for three men. These are powered by a 200-horsepower, four-cylinder engine and can carry 2,000 pounds of additional gear. The DPV also hauls a standard .50-caliber Browning M2 machine gun or a Mark 19 40-mm grenade launcher as armament. The SEAL Delivery Teams now operate the new Mark 8 SEAL Delivery Vehicle, a miniature, free-flooding submersible with open compartments. These are launched from designated dry-deck shelters on top of nuclear submarines and are flooded and released once a team of four SEALs has clambered aboard with their equipment. The craft themselves are electric powered and capable of executing missions lasting eight hours long. It is estimated that only 200 SEALs are qualified to competently operate and navigate a Mark 8 craft underwater and in complete darkness. For ingress into littoral regions, the less dramatic Combat Rubber Raiding Craft, propelled by a short-range outboard motor, is usually deploys from smaller surface vessels offshore.

Special Boat Teams

On time! On target! Never quit!

These sailors constitute a vitally important adjunct to any naval special warfare operation for SWCC personnel, and vessels focus solely on infiltration and exfiltration of SEAL teams in shallow-water regions where larger ships cannot deploy. In addition to transporting SEALs, they must also prove adept at coastal patrolling, surveillance, armed escort, interdiction, and search-and-rescue operations. Men of the SBTs, while not combat capable in the same sense as the SEALS, are nonetheless highly trained in their duties and endure the same rigorous level of physical training as their commando counterparts. Their heritage draws heavily from the motor torpedo boats (PTs) of World War II and the "brown water navy" of the Vietnam War. Two significant developments have transpired for crewmen since the war against terror commenced in September 2001. First, the new rating of Special Warfare Boat Operator arose to grant greater recognition from the rest of the special operations community while allowing members to advance in rank like the rest of the navy. The second was adoption of the new SWCC warfare specialty within the naval community, now denoted by a formal military service badge. All told, crewmen no longer live in the shadow of their illustrious stable mates, and their essential contributions have since gained wider recognition.

Organization

Naval Special Warfare Group 4

SBT 12 (Coronado, California)

SBT 20 (Little Creek, Virginia)

SBT 22 (Hancock County, Mississippi)

SBTs 12 and 20 usually conduct insertion and extraction of SEALS from the littoral and operate mostly from maritime environments. SBT Team 22, by contrast, trains exclusively on the Mississippi River and specializes in riverine tactics and warfare.

Recruitment and Training

Like the SEALs they transport, all sailors of the SWCC are volunteers and subject to thorough physical and instructional training before becoming a candidate. Unlike the SEALs, which prefers young men, the SWCC accepts candidates as old as 30 provided that they are in exemplary physical condition. Prospective trainees first endure two weeks of indoctrination at the Naval Amphibious Base in Coronado, California, then pass through the SWCC Basic Crewman Training School. Students must also successfully navigate the Physical Screen Test (PST) with the minimum standards, such as a 500-yard swim using the breaststroke or sidestroke in under 10 minutes, 79 push-ups in two minutes, 79 sit-ups in two minutes, no fewer than 11 pull-ups from a dead hang, and a 1.5-mile run with boots in under 10 minutes. Basic Crewman Training lasts five weeks and is designed to test and develop water competency, teamwork, and mental endurance. For this reason, exercises such as swimming, running, and calisthenics incrementally grow harder with each successive week. The challenge concludes in a 72-hour exercise featuring little sleep, exposure to the elements, and boating, swimming, and navigation events.

Successful candidates are next admitted to Crewman Qualification Training to introduce them to the finer points of weapons handling, seamanship, first aid, and small-unit tactics. For 14 weeks, prospective sailors endure additional physical challenges, along with instruction in maritime navigation, communications, waterborne patrolling, marksmanship, and engineering. The Naval Special Warfare Mission Planning Cycle is also introduced to enable crewmen to experience all the nuances of planning, briefing, executing, and debriefing a special operation. The harsh training regimen and difficult environments allow all SWCC to qualify for joint operations with other special forces, including Green Berets, Marine Corps SOC, and Air Force SOC. All hands must have demonstrated competence while operating in inclement weather and heavy seas or while performing such routine maritime special operations as direct action, reconnaissance, ship boarding, and vessel boarding, search, and seizure. After receiving their SWCC insignia, personnel continue on with additional specialty training relative to boat propulsion, desert and jungle survival, medic training, air assault, and other skills deemed relative to their particular boat squadron.

Equipment

SBTs operate a variety of small, state-of-the-art, high-speed boats like the Mark V Special Operations Craft, an inflatable yet rigid device for quick ingress or egress around danger zones. This 81-foot-long craft is capable of hitting speeds of 48 knots in calm seas and can carry 16 fully equipped SEALS in addition to its five-man crew. Also used is the smaller, equally agile Seafox, a twin-engine fiberglass-hulled boat. It is capable of carrying a team of SEALs to an infiltration zone, then protecting itself with two M2 .50-caliber machine guns. Of special note is the Maritime Craft Aerial Deployment System, an elaborate parachute device allowing an 11-meter rigid inflatable boat (RIB) to be airdropped from a C-130 or C-17 transport aircraft. Four SWCCs also jump out after the plane with a view of landing in its proximity boarding, then getting unpacked and ready for action at sea within 20 minutes. Also noteworthy is the Maritime External Air Transportation System, a special sling attached to the belly of an MH-47 Chinook helicopter allowing an RIB and its crew to be transported by air for either insertion or extraction purposes. With this device, SWCC assets can be deployed quicker and much farther at sea than before.

Known Operations

SEAL operations since the end of the Cold War in 1991 remain classified and tightly under wraps. However, since the commencement of the War on Terror in the early 21st century, a basic outline of their activities is generally known. SEAL teams began participating in

Operation ENDURING FREEDOM in October 2001 in response to terrorist attacks against New York City's World Trade Center. SEALs are known to have figured prominently in roles designated by the Central Command, and Captain Raymond Harward actually led a JSOTF throughout Afghanistan. This was Task Force K-Bar, which lasted from October 2001 through April 2002 and involved several SEAL teams and scores of special operations forces from a dozen countries. During this period, they killed over 100 al-Qaeda and Taliban fighters and uncovered 500,000 pounds of weapons and explosives. In December 2001, SEALs and Danish commandos are also known to have seized Khairkha after being flown their by air force special operations helicopters. Between November 25 and December 1, 2001, a British Special Boat Service team was apparently part of coalition forces that crushed a Taliban uprising at Qala-i-Jangi Prison, where Chief Petty Officer Stephen Bass, a SEAL exchange soldier, received a Navy Cross for heroism under fire. The SEALs have performed well but not without cost. On March 4, 2002, a SEAL team was participating in Operation ANACONDA in eastern Afghanistan when Aviation Boatswain's Mate First Class Neil C. Roberts fell from his helicopter and was surrounded by Taliban fighters. He fought them off alone before his compatriots were driven off by ground fire, and he was finally captured and killed; Roberts was the first SEAL to die there. On March 27, 2002, he was joined by Chief Hospital Corpsman Matthew J. Bourgeois, who stepped on a mine during a small-unit training exercise. A bigger disaster loomed on June 28, 2005, during Operation RED WINGS in Kunar Province when Taliban militia were tipped off as to the presence of a four-man SEAL reconnaissance team under Lieutenant Michael P. Murphy and attacked. Murphy and three SEALs were killed in the ensuing fire-fight, and only Petty Officer Marcus Luttrell survived; Murphy received a posthumous Congressional Medal of Honor. Worse, a rescue attempt was mounted to save the SEALs, and Taliban ground fire brought down an MH-47 Chinook helicopter of the Army's "Night Stalkers," killing eight more SEALs and several special forces troops.

The greatest number of SWCC and SEAL forces deployed to date occurred during Operation IRAQI FREEDOM. On March 20, 2003, several SEAL teams, accompanied by Royal Marines and Polish GROM special forces, departed from U.S. Navy vessels and approached the Mina al Bakar and Khawr al Amaya oil terminals in the northern Persian Gulf. It was deemed essential to acquire these structures intact before the Iraqis could destroy them and pour millions of gallons of oil into gulf waters. Several teams arrived by helicopter to secure the onshore pumping locales at al Faw, and these were stormed after killing five Iraqis and wounding 16. Other teams boarded inflatable boats and Mark 8 submersibles to attack offshore platforms. Republican Guard troops guarding these facilities quickly surrendered, and both objectives were secured without loss. Other SEALs went ashore near al Faw to assist marines of the 5th Regimental Combat Team prior to the push north toward the Rumaila oil fields. Despite their protests, helicopters landed their DPV vehicles on soil too soggy to operate safely, and they became stuck. The SEALs were then set on by 300 Iraqi soldiers, but fortunately an embedded air Force Combat Controller called in precision air strikes that kept the enemy at bay until they were relieved by the Royal Marines 42 Commando. Yet another SEAL team was conveyed by MH-53 Pave Low helicopters to the site of the Mukaraya Dam, which was to be taken intact. Despite ground conditions that stalled their DPVs, the SEALS and some GROM elements successfully seized this objective, and they were relieved by U.S. Army troops advancing north. The only other known SEAL activity during Operation IRAQI FREEDOM occurred during the battle for Ramadi on September 9, 2006. A party of four SEAL snipers under Petty Officer Michael A. Moorsom had positioned themselves on a rooftop when an insurgent lobbed a grenade onto their position. Moorsom selflessly threw himself on the grenade and absorbed the blast; he saved his three compatriots but was himself mortally wounded. Moorsom subsequently received a posthumous Congressional Medal of Honor. Happily, not all SEAL mission are restricted to the military. On July 7, 2010, crewmen from SBT 20 employ a Mark V Special Operations Craft to rescue nine people after their DUKW amphibious truck was struck by a barge on the Delaware River and sank. The SWCC just happened to have two vessels moored near Penn's Landing at the time of the accident, and both quickly swing into action.

Bibliography

Bahmanyar, Mir. *SEALs: The U.S. Navy's Elite Fighting Force*. New York: Osprey, 2008.

Boehm, Roy. *First SEAL*. New York: Pocket Books, 1997.

Bonner, Carol, and Kit Bonner. *U.S. Navy SEALs: Quiet Professionals*. Atglen, PA: Schiffer, 2010.

Bravedy, Chuck. *Iraq in My Eye: Memoirs of a Navy SEAL*. Baltimore: PublishAmerica, 2007.

Cannon, Jon, and Jeff Cannon. *Leadership Lessons of the Navy SEALs: Battle-Tested Strategies for Creating Successful Organizations and Inspiring Extraordinary Results*. New York: McGraw-Hill, 2003.

Chalker, Dennis C. *The United States Navy SEALs Workout Guide: The Exercises and Fitness Programs of the U.S. Navy SEALs and BUD/S Training*. New York: William Morrow, 1998.

Chalker, Dennis C. *Hell Week: SEALS in Training*. New York: Avon Books, 2002.

Chalker, Dennis C., and Kevin Dockery. *One Perfect Op: One Man's Extraordinary Account of His Involvement in the Navy's Elite and Top-Secret Special Forces Teams*. New York: Morrow, 2002.

Constance, Harry. *Good to Go: The Life and Times of a Decorated Member of the U.S. Navy's Elite SEAL Team Two*. New York: Morrow, 1997.

Couch, Dick. *The Warrior Elite: The Forging of Seal Class 228*. New York: Crown, 2001.

Couch, Dick. *The Finishing School: Earning the Navy SEAL Trident*. New York: Crown, 2004.

Couch, Dick. *Downrange: Navy SEALs in the War on Terrorism*. New York: Crown, 2005.

Couch, Dick. *The Sheriff of Ramadi: U.S. Navy SEALs and the Winning of al-Anbar*. Annapolis, MD: Naval Institute Press, 2008.

De Lisle, Mark. *The Navy SEAL Workout: The Complete Total-Body Fitness Program*. Lincolnwood, IL: Contemporary Books, 1998.

Deuster, Patricia A. *The U.S. Navy SEAL Guide to Fitness and Nutrition*. New York: Skyhorse, 2007.

Divine, Mark. *The Navy SEALs Handbook: History, Training, and Equipment of America's Elite Naval Commando Units*. Encinitas, CA: NavySEALs.com, 2006.

Dockery, Kevin. *Navy Seals: A History, Part III: Post-Vietnam to the Present*. New York: Berkley Books, 2003.

Dockery, Kevin. *Navy Seals: A Complete History: From World War II to the Present*. New York: Berkley Books, 2004.

Dockery, Kevin. *Weapons of the Navy SEALs*. New York: Berkley Books, 2004.

Dockery, Kevin, and Bill Fawcett. *The Teams: An Oral History of the U.S. Navy SEALs*. New York: William Morrow, 1998.

Enoch, Barry W. *Teammates, SEALs at War*. New York: Pocket Books, 1996.

Gardner, Bill. *Hell Week: U.S. Navy SEALs*. Victoria, BC: Trafford, 2004.

Gormly, Robert A. *Combat Swimmer: Memoirs of a Navy SEAL*. New York: Dutton, 1998.

Greitens, Eric. *The Heart and the Fist: The Education of a Humanitarian and the Making of a SEAL*. Boston: Houghton Mifflin Harcourt, 2011.

Halberstadt, Hans. *U.S. Navy SEALs*. St. Paul, MN: Zenith Press, 2006.

Hollenbeck, Cliff, and Dick Couch. *To Be a U.S. Navy SEAL*. St. Paul, MN: MBI, 2003.

Jordan, David. *The U.S. Navy SEALs: Sea, Air, and Land Specialists*. San Diego: Thunder Bay Press, 2003.

Keith, Thomas H., and J. Terry Riebling. *SEAL Warrior: The Only Easy Day Was Yesterday*. New York: St. Martin's Griffin, 2010.

Luttrell, Marcus. *Lone Survivor: The Eyewitness Account of Operation Redwing and the Lost Heroes of SEAL Team 10*. New York: Little, Brown, 2009.

Marcinko, Richard. *Rogue Warrior: The Real Team*. New York: Pocket Books, 1999.

McNab, Chris. *Survive at Sea with the U.S. Navy SEALs*. Broomall, PA: Mason Crest, 2003.

Miniter, Richard. *Some Gave All: The Untold Story of the U.S. Navy SEALs' Bloodiest Battle against al Qaeda in Afghanistan*. New York: Threshold Editions, 2007.

Office of Naval Research, et al. *Naval Forces under the Sea: The Rest of the Story*. Flagstaff, AZ: Best Publishing, 2007.

Needham, Robert. *Team Secrets of the Navy SEALs: The Elite Military Force's Leadership Principles for Business*. Kansas City, MO: Andrews McMeel, 2003.

Nickelson, Richard G. *Hooyah! UDT/SEAL Stories of the 1960s: Routine and Offbeat Exploits That Team Members Have Been Talking and Laughing about for Years*. Westminster, MD: Eagle Editions, 2006.

Pfarrer, Chuck. *Warrior Soul: The Memoir of a Navy SEAL*. New York: Random House, 2004.

Pushies, Fred J. *Weapons of the Navy Seals*. St. Paul, MN: MBI, 2004.

Roat, John C. *Class-29: The Making of U.S. Navy SEALs*. New York: Ballantine Books, 2000.

Sasser, Charles W. *Encyclopedia of the Navy Seals*. New York: Facts on File, 2002.

Schoenberg, Richard D. *The Only Easy Day Was Yesterday: An Inside Look at the Training of the Navy SEALs*. Annapolis, MD: Naval Institute Press, 2006.

Smith, Stewart. *The Complete Guide to Navy Seal Fitness*. New York: Hatherleigh Press, 2008.

Stublefield, Gary. *Inside the U.S. Navy SEALS*. Osceola, WI: Motorbooks International, 1995.

Wasdin, Howard E., and Stephen Templin. *SEAL Team Six: Memoirs on an Elite Navy SEAL Sniper*. New York: St. Martin's Press, 2011.

Williams, Gary. *SEAL of Honor: Operation Red Wings and the Life of Lt. Michael P. Murphy, USN*. Annapolis, MD: Naval Institute Press, 2010.

Wood, Michael P. *U.S. Navy SEALs in San Diego*. Charleston, SC: Arcadia, 2009.

Zimmerman, Dwight J. *Uncommon Valor: The Medal of Honor and the Six Warriors Who Earned it in Afghanistan and Iraq*. New York: St. Martin's Press, 2010.

14

Special Activities Division (Central Intelligence Agency)

The Central Intelligence Agency (CIA), long viewed as one of the most successful and sophisticated intelligence-gathering networks in espionage history, is also capable of performing direct-action missions in the pursuit of national policy and security, principally through its Special Activities Division (SAD). This highly classified organization is part of the broader National Clandestine Service within that agency, whose purview is covert operations and other "black" activities. The SAD only recruits former American special forces operatives into its ranks and is paramilitary by nature but enjoys considerable operational overlap with military counterparts. It constitutes the military wing of this otherwise civilian agency and, as such, can be considered part of the national special operations continuum. SAD operatives are essential for providing the American government with plausible deniability while conducting missions in areas that military units are be denied by law. More significantly, while they frequently cooperate with special forces in the field, SAD can only be ordered into action by either the president or his National Security Council, a command distinction different from "conventional" special forces.

Specifically, SAD is capable of executing all levels of direct action, including deep reconnaissance, sabotage, assassinations, and more purely military-style activities, such as raids and ambushes, within environments deemed extremely hostile. All Special Operations Group (SOG) units are also capable of working closely with other units of the U.S. Special Forces Command when the occasion arises. Moreover, all Paramilitary Operations Officers (PMOO) are fully versed in the arts of gathering clandestine human intelligence for more traditional espionage purposes. In the context of nonmilitary, psychological operations, SAD also maintains an elite political action group especially trained to exert "covert influence"

(Courtesy of the Central Intelligence Agency)

to modify the behavior of hostile governments. Activities here include propaganda, financial support for opposition figures, public relations for favored candidates, poll watching, and other politically oriented intervention. The CIA can activate either group or both in the furtherance of U.S. policy goals around the globe. Given their broadly defined mission, SAD operatives are probably the best-trained and most accomplished special forces anywhere. The ongoing war against terrorism has led only to bigger and more protracted deployments abroad than at any time in the agency's history. It is also quite clear that they do not, by any measure, "play by the rules" in executing their mission directives.

Organization

As far as is known, SAD consists of four distinct elements, each composed of former and highly talented special forces members and all of which are completely interchangeable within various SOGs as required. Furthermore, all members are fully capable of working and fighting alongside conventional special forces on select missions where their skills are needed or overlap.

Air Branch
Throughout the Cold War, the CIA maintained several clandestine air transportation services, such as Air America, Southern Air Transport, and Evergreen Air, all of which flew extensively around the world in various conflicts. The Air Branch is the latest in a long line of similar organizations and operates all aircraft in the CIA aerial inventory, be they fixed wing or rotary, American made or foreign. Personnel pride themselves on being able to operate virtually any kind of aircraft in the world short of spaceships. Not surprisingly, many members formerly hail from the U.S. Army's elite 160th Special Operations Aviation Regiment, the "Night Stalkers," which specializes in light aircraft and helicopters.

Maritime Branch
As its name implies, the Maritime Branch focuses on clandestine missions on the open sea or other bodies of water. Appreciably, the bulk of personnel consists largely of retired SEALs and Naval Warfare Development Group (DEVGRU) operatives, with a sprinkling of Marine Corps Force Reconnaissance veterans. Their training also places higher emphasis on amphibious and waterborne actions, including combat diver and scout swimmer missions, jet-ski reconnaissance, and hostage rescue operations near coastlines.

Ground Branch
This is the largest subdivision within SAD, their "boots on the ground," with many former Green Berets, Delta Force commandos, and rangers fighting in the ranks. All personnel are

extensively cross trained in a variety of military and civilian courses, especially marksmanship and lethal applications of weaponry. Other areas of expertise include threat type assessment, covert tactical communications, personal combat with bare fists, edged weapons and batons, team leadership and movement, structure penetration, prisoner snatching and evacuation, hostage situation management, long-range reconnaissance, and extreme environmental survival, among many others. While air and maritime operations are also covered, the bulk of Ground Branch activity fall on land, so a premium is placed on advanced automobile handling, especially with a view toward high-speed emergency maneuvers. All operational facets of driving fall under the purview of Tactical Vehicle Commandeering, which all prospective operatives must pass. Thus situated, students can operate virtually any kind of motor vehicle in the world and under all weather conditions, day or night, and also employ their vehicle as a weapon if the necessity arises. Not every aspirant to SAD masters the laundry list of requisite skills, but those who do represent the finest clandestine operatives in existence.

Armor and Special Programs Branch

This is the least known or advertised subdivision of SAD, whose members are capable of literally knocking out or destroying any type of vehicle, aircraft, vessel, or building as needed. To accomplish this, they are tasked with acquiring, testing, or covertly obtaining the latest personal and armor systems as well as stockpiling various ordnance and weapons for operatives in the field.

Because all SAD activities receive stratospheric levels of secret classification, details respecting its organization remain unknown and consigned to speculation. For field operations, a SOG is called on to provide men and materiel for each requisite mission. Individuals associated with these activities are technically referred to as Paramilitary Operations Officers, or PMOOs. Facts are sketchy, but the suspected personnel complement of SAD numbers 120 men, making it far smaller than either Delta Force or SEAL Team Six, its closest military equivalents. Moreover, the sizes of individual teams are likewise estimated to run between one and six members, with each operative enjoying skills and aptitudes custom-made for their particular mission.

Recruitment and Training

Consistent with its elite status, the SAD hires only former special forces members from across the spectrum of the special operations community. Additionally, all must conform to the basic CIA requirement of owning at least a bachelor's degree from a certified college. Prospective applicants, no matter how promising, must also pass SAD's preliminary selection phase, a modified version of the Delta Force course. While the men from Army's Delta Force and the navy's DEVGRU (formerly SEAL Team Six) predominate, personnel can also be drawn from Air Force Special Tactics forces and pararescuers, Green Berets, rangers, Marine Fleet Reconnaissance, and even current CIA operatives. These recruits enjoy sterling credentials in their former trades, being highly versed in their respective professions and extraordinarily competent in planning, staging, and executing missions. Successful candidates are next subject to additional 12 months in the Clandestine Service Trainee Program at Camp Peary, Virginia (also known as "The Farm"), and Harvey Point, North Carolina, to enhance and

Johnny Micheal Spann (1969–2001) Johnny Micheal "Mike" Spann was born in Winfield, Alabama, on March 1, 1969, and he joined the Marine Corps Reserve while attending Auburn University in 1991. After graduating he attended the Marine Corps Officer Candidate School at Quantico, Virginia, where he was assigned to the 2nd Air Naval Gunfire Liaison Company. This was an elite unit tasked with directing naval gunfire and close air support for marines in the field. Spann served six years and rose to captain, whereupon he transferred to the CIA's Special Activity Division in June 1999. In this capacity, he was one of the first field officers deployed in Afghanistan during the initial phases of Operation Enduring Freedom, where he teamed up with other special forces operators. The Taliban were quickly routed by air power alone, and on November 25, 2001, he was interrogating prisoners,

Johnny Spann was the first special operations fatality of the Afghanistan War. (Getty Images)

including the American turncoat John Walker Lindh, at the ancient Qala-i-Jangi prison when rioting erupted. He was attacked by a mob, drew his pistol and killed several assailants before dying in the onslaught. Spann thus enjoys the melancholy distinction of being the first American combat fatality in Afghanistan. He was posthumously awarded the CIA's Intelligence Star and the Exceptional Service Medallion, and is further commemorated by a small memorial erected at the Qala-i-Jiangi fortress.

expand on existing skills. Here, so-called black ops predominate, and all prospective PMOO are drilled and redrilled in the application of modern weaponry, explosives, sniping, and firearms handling until high levels of proficiency are attained. Other skills imparted include Krav Maga (hand-to-hand combat); on- and off-road high-performance driving; avoiding and escaping apprehension; free-fall parachuting; scuba and close circuit diving; foreign language instruction; survival, escape, resistance, and evasion instruction; emergency combat medical training; and advanced tactical communications and tracking. Only then are individuals judged competent to serve in this most elite of U.S. special operations units.

Equipment

Unlike more conventional special forces, whose specialized equipment sometimes carries a high-visibility profile, SAD personnel are issued high-tech, low-visibility devices more relevant to espionage. In this profession, low visibility is tantamount to survival itself, so the less obtrusive a doohickey, the better. These items include satellite GPS systems for ground navigation, advanced "whispering" telecommunications, miniaturized infrared and microwave transmitters, and a host of long-range tracking devices planted on cars and other vehicles. Operators are also capable of utilizing wide varieties of local weaponry, of both foreign and domestic manufacture, but in most Third World nations the ubiquitous Kalashnikov AK-47 assault rifle is used. Undoubtedly, other classified technologies, breathtaking in their capacities, might also exist, but these have never been and, in all likelihood, will never be made public.

A Central Intelligence Agency (CIA) agent known as Dave (C) and a U.S. Special Forces soldier (R) speak with a Northern Alliance commander (L), 2001, in Mazar-e Sharif, Afghanistan. Although not as well known as conventional special forces, the CIA's Special Activities Division (SAD) operators are extremely capable and bring a wide range of talents and skills not found elsewhere. (Getty Images)

Known Operations

SAD has been extremely active in hot spots around the world since the end of the Cold War. Teams were sent into Somalia ahead of arriving U.S. forces, and on December 23, 1992, Paramilitary Officer Larry Freedman was killed in the line of duty during a special reconnaissance mission. He subsequently received a posthumous Intelligence Star by the CIA, the highest award granted by that entity. However, SAD teams remained active in the region over the next decade, primarily to combat both the rise of warlords and the threat posed by al-Qaeda terrorist networks. In 1992, they are known to have planted a beacon device into the cane of Osman Ito, a noted businessman and warlord supporter, that led to his apprehension by Little Bird helicopters flown by special forces. Apparently, SAD operatives have bribed other warlords to monitor al-Qaeda activities throughout Somalia, and on January 9, 2007, SAD operatives directed a missile strike that killed 10 militants. Saleh Ali Saleh Nabhan, a noted leader of the violent Islamic faction Shabaab, was killed in similar fashion on September 14, 2009, when two AH-6 Little Birds strafed his car, and SEALs then recovered his body. SAD operatives continue working the Horn of Africa quietly and effectively, especially given the rising tide of Islamic-based piracy in the region.

The CIA also maintained a strong presence in Afghanistan following the Soviet withdrawal in 1989, and throughout ensuing decades they made concerted attempts to locate and kill Saudi fugitive and terrorist Osama bin Laden. President Bill Clinton refused to grant authorization to execute these missions because of the dangers they posed to the SOG teams, but their operational dynamic radically changed in the wake of the 9/11 terrorist attacks against the World Trade Center. Capitalizing on some decade-old ties with dissident groups in Afghanistan, SAD teams initiated Operation JAWBREAKER by arriving from Uzbekistan on their own aircraft in advance of U.S. Special Forces. Here they consolidated a working relationship with the opposition Northern Alliance and spent several weeks observing and evaluating Taliban strengths and positions prior to the outbreak of Operation ENDURING FREE-DOM. A Green Beret Operational Detachment Alpha (A-Team) from the 5th Special Forces Group arrived in theater on October 19, 2001, and SAD personnel functioned as the liaison and facilitator between the two groups.

Moreover, the military intelligence and targeting information they allowed for a speedy defeat of the Taliban with a minimum loss of American lives. PMOO, like other special operations teams, failed to find and capture bin Laden in 2002, but since then, they have played active roles in fighting al-Qaeda and Taliban forces behind the scenes, usually in concert with highly trained and motivated indigenous forces as well as in tandem other special forces.

Neighboring Pakistan, officially off limits to U.S. military forces, has also been an intense object of SAD attention. Paramilitary officers are known to have infiltrated the wild northwestern tribal areas in search of Taliban and al-Qaeda members, and they frequently team up with Pakistani Special Service Group commandos in executing quick and lethal raids against safe houses. However, given the sensitivity of the local government to foreign operatives, SAD usually employs an extensive series of unmanned aerial vehicles to scout, monitor, and kill known enemy leaders. On July 22, 2009, it is believed that Saad bin Laden, son of Osama bin Laden, was eliminated in such a missile strike. This successful program remained relatively modest under the administration of President George W. Bush, but his successor, Barack Obama, greatly expanded SAD-directed missile attacks since 2009. This activity continues exacting a heavy toll on suspected insurgents and terrorists throughout the region, but has generated considerable resentment within Pakistan itself. Missile technology has also been exploited in another al-Qaeda hotbed, Yemen, where, on November 5, 2002, a Hellfire attack killed Al-Haitham al-Yemeni, a senior operative thought to have been behind the October 2000 bombing of the USS *Cole*. President Obama has since ordered these operations enlarged with a view toward decapitating regional al-Qaeda leadership, with special effort toward apprehending or killing the American-born imam Anwar al-Aulaqi.

Not surprisingly, SAD operatives bore a prominent role in the preinvasion buildup to Operation IRAQI FREEDOM. Teams of operatives were inserted into northern Iraq months before the outbreak of hostilities, where they were embedded among local Kurdish *pesh-merga* fighters. The two groups then conducted Operation VIKING HAMMER and wiped out Ansar al-Islam, a violent terrorist group, prior to the coalition invasion. In February 2003, SAD teams proved essential in working with Green Berets of the 10th Special Forces Group and indigenous forces to tie down 13 Iraqi divisions and prevent them reinforcing the southern sector. Subsequently, SAD members helped to plan and execute Operation RED DAWN, which captured fugitive dictator Saddam Hussein, in concert with Delta Force and Intelligence Support Activity operatives. They have also served on point in the struggle against al-Qaeda in Iraq, assisting in the deaths and capture of several senior figures. On October 26, 2008, SAD teams and other armed operatives are known to have descended upon Abu Kamal, Syria, to raid a safe house, and they killed several leaders responsible for smuggling terrorists into Iraq. The affair was conducted with the apparent blessing of the Syrian government, which subsequently warned local inhabitants not to discuss the matter—or else. Similar operations are reported to have occurred in Georgia and the Philippines, where known al-Qaeda bands have also been operating. SAD has proven relentless in its pursuit and neutralizing of targets around the globe, and its successes, while seldom heralded, constitute a vital component in the ongoing struggle against terrorism worldwide. To that end, on July 22, 2010, CIA Director Leon Panetta appointed John D. Bennett, formerly of SAD, to head up the National Clandestine Service.

Defining Activity

All facets of the CIA's war against terror, including clandestine activities of SAD, have been in several cases extremely successful and rewarding over the past decade. However, no objective was more fitfully or relentlessly pursued than Osama bin Laden—the criminal mastermind behind the attacks of 9/11—while producing fewer results. A decade of intense sleuthing and analysis lapsed before the desired results were achieved. In October 2001, it became apparent that bin Laden was in Afghanistan at the commencement of Operation ENDURING FREEDOM and that coalition forces nearly bagged him in the Tora Bora Mountains in the early spring of 2002. After that time, his whereabouts remained strictly conjectural, and the agency was forced to operate on very little information. To many intelligence analysts, his most probable locale was somewhere in the rugged northwestern tribal areas of Pakistan, adjacent to Afghanistan, where he could seek seclusion and protection from a sympathetic populace. But, otherwise, the trail there was cold, and in light of balky cooperation from an already wobbly Pakistani government, direct action in this region, in the absence of absolute proof, was impractical. The problem was further compounded by a lack of radio intelligence, for the wily terrorist realized that the United States could pinpoint any single phone call placed to his minions from anywhere in the world. Analysts concluded that bin Laden eschewed communication in favor of using highly trusted couriers to relay messages either verbally or, as it turned out, by computer files downloaded and then emailed from neutral locations. The system, primitive and simple in the extreme, was nearly impossible to verify in the absence of reliable information.

The CIA's mission thus centered on one of identifying and tailing these hypothetical couriers inside one of the most remote regions on earth, the equivalent of finding one precise needle in a towering haystack. The odds of a direct breakthrough seemed remote, but gradually, through one of the most sustained, highly coordinated intelligence-gathering and deciphering programs in history, parts of this baffling jigsaw puzzle began emerging. As these slowly accumulated over the course of a decade, they were painstakingly assembled and a picture began to emerge. Fortunately for the United States, President George W. Bush considered captured terrorists and their allies as "enemy combatants" and not soldiers—a legal distinction denying them any protection granted prisoners under the Geneva Convention. Terror suspects ("detainees") were either clandestinely sent to a special detention center at Guantanamo Bay, Cuba, or farmed out to similar "black sites" in Poland, Egypt, and elsewhere for bouts of "enhanced" interrogation. This included waterboarding, or simulated drowning, an extremely traumatic experience for anyone subject to its rigors, yet the process began yielding useful results. Given the disdain for such techniques by the U.S. military, the interrogations were mostly likely conducted by the CIA or allied intelligence agencies acting under its aegis. Ironically, the first confirmation that bin Laden employed couriers came from two notorious captives, Khalid Sheik Mohammad, the al-Qaeda operational chief, and his successor, Abu Faraj al-Libi. Both gradually admitted to the use of couriers under waterboarding, one of whom they pegged as "Abu Ahmed al-Kuwaiti," an assertion that they subsequently retracted. Analysts concluded that they (and other suspects so treated) were, in fact, shielding someone closely connected to bin

Laden's innermost circle. The hunch proved correct, for at some time in 2009, the courier was positively identified as a protégé of Mohammad and al-Libi, who, in turn, functioned as bin Laden's most trusted associates.

The next phase of the hunt commenced with a search for the elusive couriers. The attention of CIA operatives working in northwestern Pakistan focused on two brothers whose telephone conversations were secretly tapped in Peshewar in August 2010. The suspects were carefully tailed over a period of months, and agency attention inexorably shifted from the rugged, poverty-stricken frontier, to the wealthy city of Abbottabad, 30 miles north of Islamabad, the Pakistani capital. Ensuing moves by the agency proved as exotic and innovative as any from a world-class spy novel. The two couriers were tailed and eventually spotted moving in and out of a walled compound on the outskirts of Abbottabad, a building conspicuously larger than nearby structures. Enhanced satellite photography was brought to bear on the suspicious, three-story building, which, by the 18-foot-high wall surrounding it and another seven-foot-high wall around its top floor, not only looked completely out of place but was apparently constructed to conceal its inhabitants. Further research on ubiquitous Google Earth maps plainly showed that the structure was absent in 2001 but was constructed in 2005, well within the proper time frame. Eventually, CIA ground teams managed to rent a safe house nearby and kept the building under tight surveillance. Of peculiar curiosity to the agents was that the two couriers apparently living there lacked any explainable sources of wealth necessary to maintain such a lifestyle. Someone else had to be footing the bill.

The emerging body of evidence, painstakingly sifted through and pieced together, still failed to yield incontrovertible proof of bin Laden's presence but was too compelling to ignore. On closer examination, the building lacked telephone wires or satellite dishes when one would reasonably expect its wealthy inhabitants would possess and flaunt both. Moreover, the three families residing there invariably burned their garbage instead of having it collected. High-resolution photographic satellites of the U.S. National Geospatial Intelligence Agency and enhanced eavesdropping by the National Security Agency were brought to bear for additional details. By September 2010, their revelations induced high-level discussions in Washington about how to proceed next, and Director Panetta authorized newly developed stealthy drones—RQ-170 Sentinels—to slip unseen past Pakistani radar and carefully photographic the building from all possible angles. A four-dimensional model of the entire compound could then be constructed, and the results only deepened their suspicions. The seven-foot-high wall mysteriously constructed around the third-story terrace proved precisely high enough to obscure the six-foot, four-inch bin Laden from view as he walked about the structure, and it was deduced that he resided it. Ultimately, the presence of a "high-value target" was the only rational explanation for the building and its unusual construction. Bin Laden himself was never photographed or observed from the ground, but minute analysis of all available intelligence suggested that the probability of his hiding there, with his several wives and children, was in the range of 60 to 80 percent. President Obama was kept fully informed of all developments, and on the weekend of May 1, 2011, he authorized a special forces "direct-action."

Under normal circumstances, military units committed to action fall under the purview of the Pentagon, but in this instance, Defense Secretary Robert M. Gates yielded the palm to CIA Director Panetta, who played a direct role in planning the mission in all its minute details. Apparently, it was Panetta who vetoed alerting the Pakistani intelligence agency of the impending raid for fear of sympathizers tipping bin Laden off. Moreover, SEALs of the Naval Warfare Development Group committed to Operation NEPTUNE SPEAR remained under the tactical control of the SAD operatives accompanying them. The neighborhood in question experienced an inexplicable power outage than evening, conveniently timed to assist the raid, which points to CIA subterfuge elsewhere. On balance, NEPTUNE SPEAR was also sweet revenge. On May 29, 2011, it was revealed that two CIA agents, Tom Shah and Molly Huckaby Hardy, were among 44 U.S. embassy employees killed on the 1998 terrorist attack in Kenya, and for the past 13 years, agency members were adamant on extracting vengeance. SAD operatives at Abbottabad achieved exactly that. But, diplomacy being what it is, Pakistani anger over the raid did not preclude CIA agents from subsequently gaining access bin Laden's compound following a visit to Islamabad by Deputy Director Michael J. Morell. Accordingly, on May 26, 2011, it was publicly announced that the CIA, whose persistence, skill, and imagination culminated in bin Laden's demise, would now revisit the scene for DNA evidence arising from their handiwork. The agency and its SAD operatives had a score to settle and did so with imagination and aplomb.

Bibliography

Baer, Robert. *See No Evil: The True Story of a Ground Soldier in the CIA's War on Terrorism.* New York: Crown, 2002.

Berntsen, Gary, and Ralph Pezzullo. *Jawbreaker: The Attack on Bin-Laden and al-Qaeda. A Personal Account by the CIA's Key Field Commander.* New York: Crown, 2005.

Geraghty, Tony. *Black Ops: The Rise of Special Forces in the C.I.A., the S.A.S., and the Mossad.* New York: Pegasus Books, 2010.

Haas, Roland W. *Enter the Past Tense: My Secret Life as a CIA Assassin.* Washington, DC: Potomac Books, 2007.

Kessler, Ronald. *The CIA at War: Inside the Secret Campaign against Terror.* New York: St. Martin's Press, 2003.

Kiriakou, John. *The Reluctant Spy: My Secret Life in the CIA's War on Terror.* New York: Bantam Books, 2010.

Mahoney, Richard D. *Getting Away With Murder: The Real Story Behind American Taliban John Walker Lindh and What the U.S. Government Has to Hide.* New York: Arcade Publishers, 2004.

Riedel, Bruce O. *The Search for al-Qaeda: Its Leadership, Ideology, and Future.* Washington, DC: Brookings Institution Press, 2008.

Schroen, Gary C. *First In: An Insider's Account of How the CIA Spearheaded the War against Terrorism in Afghanistan.* New York: Presidio Press, 2005.

Scott, Peter S. *Drugs, Oil, and War: The United States in Afghanistan, Columbia, and Indonesia.* Lanham, MD: Rowman and Littlefield, 2003.

Suskind, Ron. *The One Percent Doctrine: Deep Inside America's Pursuit of Its Enemies since 9/11.* New York: Simon and Schuster, 2006.

Tenet, George. *At the Center of the Storm: The CIA during America's Time of Crisis.* New York: Harper Perennial, 2008.

Tucker, Mike, and Charles S. Faddis. *Operation Hotel California: The Clandestine War inside Iraq.* Guilford, CT: Lyons Press, 2009.

15

Naval Special Warfare Development Group (SEAL Team Six)

To the Naval Special Warfare Development Group, informally known as DEVGRU or SEAL Team Six, goes the distinction of pulling off one of the most audacious special operations of this or perhaps any other century. Men of this shadowy top-secret unit have since become the toast of the nation, a status that they decline to embrace, which only accentuates that so little is verifiably known about them. What few facts that are available may very well be official disinformation to further muddy the waters. Nonetheless, in terms of training, numbers, and performance, DEVGRU is quite possibly the quintessential American special forces outfit, with three decades of antiterrorist action on their ledger. In the field, they are frequently paired with assets from the Central Intelligence Agency (CIA)—and usually with spectacular results. Accordingly, their mission profiles exceeds the highest levels of classification, which, for this same reason, can place them beyond the boundaries of international law.

Recruitment and Training

DEVGRU is one of the most obscure organizations in the American military arsenal, and what passes as accepted belief is more or less based on conjecture. They are known to be headquartered at Dam Neck, astride Naval Air Station Oceana, Virginia. Rumor also has it that they are organized along the lines of the British Special Air Service (SAS), and into four squadrons designated Red, Blue, Silver, and Gold, with a specially trained boat unit designated as Gray. Total manpower is suspected in the vicinity of 300 rank and file, rendering them appreciably smaller than the "acknowledged" 3,000 men of the line SEALs. Moreover, unlike their regular counterparts, which accepts volunteers from across the U.S. Navy, DEVGRU recruits potential candidates only from among existing SEAL teams.

(Courtesy of the U.S. Navy)

No "ordinary" SEALs will do, either, for those allowed into training are among the best in service. DEVGRU members are therefore seasoned men in their early 30s, a decade older and wiser by experience than other SEALs. Prospective candidates are initially handed off to the "Green Team" to survive a ramped-up version of traditional SEAL training. This fierce regimen is no harbinger of spring under the best of circumstances; this time, the ordeal is even more intense and demanding. Among the many skills requiring mastery now include the ability to parachute accurately from 30,000 feet, strapped to an oxygen tank, to avoid detection. For seven months, DEVGRU trainees are pushed to even greater physical and mental limits, and the attrition rate among volunteers is estimated at 50 percent—those failing are invariably reassigned back to their previous unit. Keep in mind that these "dropouts" are already active SEALs in peak physical and mental condition. Nor do service conditions get any friendlier following graduation. Once on active duty with DEVGRU, all hands continue to train 300 days a year while awaiting deployment, and their various close-quarter scenarios are constantly rehearsed to become almost reflexive. Rumors also abound that DEVGRU operators fire off at least 2,500 to 3,000 rounds per week to maintain shooting proficiency—more than the rest of the SEALs combined. Another important distinction between DEVGRU and line SEAL companies is their literal blank check to obtain the very latest war-fighting technologies or, as they are quaintly deemed, "toys." Training remains incessant and grueling throughout their tenure with the unit, and any member feeling his age or unable to keep pace is unceremoniously nudged along to greener pastures.

True to its name, DEVGRU is principally tasked with originating, developing, and evaluating new tactics and weaponry for naval special operations. These methodologies, once verified and refined, are passed on to other SEAL teams. For all these reasons, DEVGRU represents America's premier antiterrorist outfit, a distinction shared only with the army's Combat Operations Group—the deadly Deltas. Like the Deltas, DEVGRU remains the only other unit with presidential authority to conduct preemptive strikes on terrorist assets, legally and without prior approval.

Known Operations

The original SEALs greatly distinguished themselves in South Vietnam and other hot spots throughout Southeast Asia between 1962 and 1974, but like all special forces, they were reduced in numbers, funding, and reputation following the American withdrawal. It was not until October 1980, following the failed Iran hostage rescue mission, that the navy was authorized to recruit, train, and deploy a dedicated antiterrorist unit of its own.

Commander Richard Marcinko, the officer tasked with its creation, personally screened and handpicked a number of outstanding SEALs already in the ranks, along with some talented Underwater Demolition Team members, then mercilessly whipped them into an elite unit. Curiously, he christened them SEAL Team Six to confuse Soviet intelligence (there being only two other companies extant). Marcinko trained them, led them, and honed them to knife-edge proficiency, becoming an elite unit within an already elite establishment. SEAL Team Six experienced its baptism under fire during Operation URGENT FURY in 1983, with mixed results. They carried their objectives of the governor's mansion and the island radio station, only to be left unsupported by poor communications and chased out to sea by larger Grenadian forces. In 1987, the designation SEAL Team Six

U.S. Navy SEAL members emerge from the water during tactical warfare training. The SEAL member in the foreground is armed with an M-16A1 rifle equipped with an M-203 grenade launcher. The SEAL member on the right is armed with an HK-33KA1 rifle. SEALs from DEVGRU are older and more experienced than regular SEALs and constitute a literal "elite within an elite." Despite this coveted status, they rehearse every day to sharpen their skills to a knife's edge. (Corbis)

was changed in favor of its current and unspectacular designation of DEVGRU. The men next saw action in Somalia in 1992–1993 during Operations RESTORE HOPE and GOTHIC SERPENT, performed well, and avoided the heavy losses experienced by other special units engaged there. Concurrently, other teams fought alongside British SAS units in Bosnia and helped track down and apprehend individuals charged with war crimes.

Commencing in 2001, DEVGRU has actively served in Afghanistan and Iraq, both in combat and in anti-insurgent roles, with spectacular successes but also some losses. On September 3, 2008, DEVGRU members formed part of a 45-man special forces group that surreptitiously helicoptered into South Waziristan, Pakistan, that night and successfully raided a Taliban safe house at Angoor Ada. This marked the first known instance of Americans fighting on Pakistani soil, and the raiders accounted for several armed individuals, including women. However, a tragedy occurred on October 8, 2010, when DEVGRU operators staged a rescue operation attempting to free Linda Norgove, a kidnapped Scottish aid worker, from Taliban captors in Kunar Province. During a confused firefight, one SEAL tossed a grenade at insurgents, unaware that Norgrove was lying nearby; she died of her injuries. Some of the SEALs failed to report the incident afterward, and they were summarily dismissed. DEVGRU also displayed their military prowess at sea. Somali pirates seized the American freighter *Maersk Alabama* in April 2009, took Captain Richard Phillips hostage in a small craft, and threatened to kill him. Fortunately, the destroyer USS *Bainbridge* was nearby with a DEVGRU sniper unit, which moved into assist. On April 12, the marksmen dropped three of four pirates with a single volley from the ship's deck, then moved in to apprehend the sole survivor. That Phillips and his crew emerged unscathed from such terrible circumstances highlights the lethality of DEVGRU in action, even with small numbers.

Defining Operation

Its prior accomplishments notwithstanding, DEVGRU gained a measure of immortality on May 1–2, 2011, when it ably executed Operation NEPTUNE SPEAR. By the fall of 2010, an intense intelligence-gathering effort orchestrated by the CIA proffered convincing proof that terrorist mastermind Osama bin Laden was sequestered in a safe house on the outskirts of Abbottabad, Pakistan, only 30 miles from the capital of Islamabad. The one-acre compound hiding him was carefully photographed by satellites and reconnaissance drones to the extent that a life-sized three-dimensional model was constructed at an undisclosed location in North Carolina, and DEVGRU SEALs began training maneuvers there. On April 26 2011, the Red Squadron secretly transferred to Jalalabad, Afghanistan, where they continually rehearsed assaults until every facet of their three-story target was memorized. Consistent with the nature of special operations, the DEVGRU operators were neither informed why they were training there nor to what end. The reason was revealed shortly before they departed to take on one of history's most wanted criminals, and produced cheers. For operational purposes, command of the raid was also transferred from the Joint Special Operations Command to the CIA, whose SAD agents wielded tactical control on the spot.

Operation NEPTUNE SPEAR unfolded late Sunday night on May 1, 2011 as two DEVGRU assault teams, one trained dog, a Belgian Malinois named Cairo, a Pakistani interpreter, and a handful of SAD clambered onto five helicopters of the army's 160th Special Aviation Regiment, the elite "Night Stalkers." The plan called for 24 SEALs, representing the best culled from the entire force, to ride two HH-60 Black Hawks from

Camp Alpha, Bagram Air Base, Afghanistan, across 90 miles of Pakistani airspace to Abbottabad. Supporting elements of the "quick reaction force," consisting of another 24 SEALs and men of other detachments, accompanied them in three MH-47E Chinooks, although these landed in a dry river bed about two-thirds of the way in and remained on standby until needed. This dangerous incursion, conducted on a moonless night at extremely low altitude, successfully dodged Pakistani radar, and the Night Stalkers finally hovered over their objective around 1 a.m. in the morning

The assault plan called for one team of SEALs to "fast rope" (rappel) down into the deserted courtyard while the other landed on the rooftop to catch bin Laden in a "squeeze play." It is perhaps indicative of special operations that, despite constant preparation and rehearsals, even the best-laid plans of mice and SEALs can go awry. On approach, one HH-60 lost its lift

To DEVGRU (SEAL Team Six) goes the distinction of bagging the world's most wanted criminal: Saudi expatriate and terror mastermind Osama bin Laden. (AFP/Getty Images)

to a "vortex" effect from the compound's 18-foot-high walls, struck one on the way down, and made a "hard" landing to keep from rolling over. No SEALs were injured, but plans for a simultaneous assault were scrapped and the remaining chopper touched down outside the compound. On the spot improvisation, always a special operations contingency, now became essential to success. The SEALs hastily departed their stricken craft and fanned out into along the outer wall before entering. Those in the court yard also moved forward, encountering false security doors, and knocked them down with explosives before forcing their way inside. Light resistance was encountered, and three armed males, two trusted couriers and bin Laden's son, were killed while resisting. Several women and children were also present, complicating the rules of engagement and resulting in the unintended death of one female. Forging ahead room to room, the SEALs quickly worked their way up to the third story, where bin Laden was suspected of hiding, and crashed inside. One team member was rushed by another female—apparently one of bin Laden's wives—who sustained a leg injury and was shoved aside. Moving quickly, they suddenly confronted this highest of "high-value targets" in a darkened hallway, unarmed and apparently confused by the onslaught. A SEAL fired at bin Laden and missed, and the latter instantly ducked into a nearby room. Three SEALs leapt in after him, and when it appeared that their quarry might be reaching for a gun, he was brought down with a "double tap" to the chest and head, killing him instantly. Only 15 minutes had lapsed since the raid commenced. Bin Laden's body was quickly photographed and tested for DNA, while SEALs and SAD operators ransacked his computers, thumb drives, and disks. Anything that was not nailed own, was hauled off in an operation lasting only 40 minutes. There were no American casualties. The SEALs departed as silently as they had approached, with bin Laden's body a prized trophy. An MH-47 had to be brought up from reserves to carry them off; the crippled Black Hawk could not be flown off and was deliberately destroyed with explosives. The SEALS arrived safely back at Jalalabad around 3 a.m., jubilant, triumphant—and inexpressively relieved.

The world awoke that morning with the incredible news of bin Laden's demise, which sparked joyous celebration in the United States. President Barack Obama, who authorized the raid, quickly pronounced that "justice has been done," and he thanked the men involved in the action for their heroism. A minor row erupted among Native Americans when it was learned that the code name for bin Laden was "Geronimo," the noted Chiricahua Apache chief, and they resented his being equated with a terrorist. Pakistani leaders, moreover, were mortified by what they deemed a gross violation of national sovereignty by not being informed of events beforehand. They even threatened to fire on any American forces violating their airspace. Worse for them, however, was that their government had to explain how one of the world's most wanted fugitives was comfortably ensconced in a military garrison town for several years without detection. The entire situation points to complicity by the ISI, the national intelligence service, but its officials strenuously denied any knowledge of bin Laden's whereabouts.

The vagaries of war being what they are, triumph and tragedy invariably function as different sides of the same coin. This truism was painfully underscored on August 6, 2011, during a routine airlift of a SEAL "Immediate Reaction Force" to assist a party of the 75th Rangers who were taking fire from enemy combatants in the Tangi Valley, Wardak Province, Afghanistan. As the action unfolded, the army CH-47 Chinook conveying them to the scene was struck by a Taliban rocket-propelled grenade and crashed, killing all 38 passengers. Among the tally were 15 members from DEVGRU's Gold Team (an entire troop), eight other SEALS, three Air Force tactical air controllers, the army five-man air-crew, and seven Afghan commandos. The incident represents the largest single loss of American life in the 10-year history of Operation ENDURING FREEDOM, and the largest single tally extracted from the special forces community. None of those killed had participated in the raid that killed Osama bin Laden, however. The SEALs, like all special forces, take their losses, mourn their dead, then carry on. In the words of Leon Panetta, now Secretary of Defense, "This is a reminder, a reminder to the American people that we remain a nation at war." Casualties are inevitable in all special operations, but successes like NEPTUNE SPEAR underscore a singular reality in the war against global terror: no matter where they hide or how elaborately they conceal themselves, terrorists remain within the deadly grasp of America's fighting elites.

Bibliography

Cawthorne, Nigel. *Warrior Elite: 31 Heroic Special-Ops Missions from the Raid on Son Tay to the Killing of Osama bin Laden*. Berkeley, CA: Ulysses, 2011.

Donahue, Raymond V. *The Death of Osama bin Laden and Related Operations*. Happauge, NY: Nova Science Publishers, 2011.

Mann, Don, and Ralph Pezzullo. *Inside SEAL Team Six: My Life and Missions with America's Elite Warriors*. Boston: Little, Brown, 2011.

Pfarrer, Chuck. SEAL *Target Geronimo: The Inside Story of the Mission to Kill Osama bin Laden*. New York: St. Martin's Press, 2011.

Pfarrer, Chuck. *Warrior Soul: The Memoir of a Navy SEAL*. New York: Random House, 2004.

Phillips, Richard. *Captain's Duty: Somali Pirates, Navy Seals, and Dangerous Days at Sea*. New York: HarperCollins, 2011.

Runkle, Benjamin. *Wanted Dead or Alive: Manhunts from Geronimo to Bin Laden*. New York: Palgrave Macmillan, 2011.

Scheuer, Michael. *Osama bin Laden*. New York: Oxford University Press, 2011.

Wasdin, Howard E. *SEAL Team Six: Memoirs of an Elite Navy Seal Sniper*. New York: St. Martin's Press, 2011.

16

U.S. Special Operations Command

The U.S. Special Operations Command (SOCOM) has functioned as the overarching command structure imposed on all American special forces units since its creation at MacDill Air Force Base, Tampa, Florida, on April 16, 1987. It constitutes the fifth regular military command (along with the army, navy, marines, and air force) and, with only 57,000 regulars and reserve members in the ranks, is also the smallest. However, it is the only entity authorized to combine special operations units from all four services as a matter of course, and its famously trained troops employ the devices encompassing a host of the latest military technologies. This fact, coupled with a strategic reach best be described as global, allows SOCOM to project American military power in a devastating manner that belies its small numbers. Operational flexibility is also a major component to this organization's role in the War on Terror. To accomplish this, most special operations units are especially trained and equipped to execute nine distinct mission profiles, whether in overt or covert fashion:

Direct Action
These are small-scale tactical assaults against specified targets or individuals and can be conducted by ambush, raiding, or mining; with standoff missiles; or simply through an all-out ground assault. These encounters are relatively small and precise by nature, although the target eliminated may harbor wider strategic or tactical implications. If a quick, stealthy ingress to the target is employed, an equally speedy ingress or extraction usually follows once finished. Generally, direct action usually transpires deep behind enemy lines and beyond the range of conventional forces or weapons.

Combating Terrorism
This is a more prolonged form of special operations, consuming more time, personnel, and resources than generally allocated to direct-action attacks. Mission profiles might

(U.S. Department of Defense)

include antiterrorism, counterterrorism, hostage rescue, enhanced security for a given area or installation, or a large-scale attack on known terrorist infrastructures. Under most circumstances, the units best trained for this work are the army's Delta Force and the navy's DEVGRU unit (SEAL Team Six). Larger targets, however, may require the assistance of the 75th Ranger Regiment who function as elite light infantry and not quick-strike commandos.

Foreign Internal Defense

This constitutes a still larger, more protracted special force effort whereby operatives serve as training cadres at the behest of foreign governments for the purpose of suppressing subversion, crime waves, or insurgencies. Units so involved are tasked with building the defensive capabilities of host nation military or paramilitary forces. The nature of this work is sometimes culturally sensitive, so language fluency is a major requisite for the personnel chosen. For this reason, Green Berets, given their emphasis on cultural training, are the troops most likely chosen for this task. In addition to training functions, designated operatives may accompany combat operations in an advisory capacity where required.

Unconventional Warfare

These activities are a step above foreign internal defense in terms of scope and longevity and may require considerable amounts of funding, equipment, and manpower. Units so committed usually find themselves in direct conflict with irregular or proxy forces sponsored by a hostile government or secessionist movement, especially when a direct application of conventional military force needed may be diplomatically impractical. Such protracted but low-intensity warfare mission profiles include ambushes, patrolling, security, political subversion, clandestine intelligence gathering, and other "below-the-radar" activities that are potentially lethal but conducted to attract little attention. Technically savvy outfits like the Intelligence Support Activity would excel in these capacities.

Special Reconnaissance

This activity consists of inserting special forces teams (or even individuals) in hostile situations whereby they provide superiors with real-time military intelligence. The data sought may involve the presence of certain individuals at a given locale or the strength and possible intent of hostile enemy forces. The technical reconnaissance term used is SALUTE, for size, activity, location, unit, time, and equipment. A wide variety of sophisticated equipment detection and communication equipment may be involved in addition to cooperation with indigenous forces. These endeavors usually unfold on or near an active battlefield or behind enemy lines as situations warrant. SEALs and Marine Force Reconnaissance units would most likely be assigned to areas adjoining large bodies of water, but all special operations units may be assigned here.

Psychological Operations

These actions are conducted to influence or persuade a foreign government's behavior to be favorable to the operator's national or strategic interests. Designated units may be involved in publishing campaigns, radio or television broadcasts, or any other manipulation of public media deemed relevant and effective. The CIA Special Operations Division would most likely coordinate these critical functions.

Civil Affairs

A useful corollary here would be "public relations," whereby special operations personnel undertake various civilian-oriented actions to improve relations, boost morale, or cement relations between units in question and local populations. This is less subtle and more proactive and visible than psychological operations but produces similar results.

Information Operations

Computers and the Internet have become a de facto military arena, and these activities are designed to either secure intelligence for a hostile power or sabotage their ability to use advanced technology for communications and intelligence gathering. This "cyberwarfare" could also be utilized for compromising national power grids, entire communication networks, or any societal activity that relies on automated technology to function.

Counterproliferation

This little-known but extremely vital facet of special operations include elements of all the previously mentioned missions, usually for either seizing or destroying highly dangerous weapons of mass destruction or preventing them from falling into the wrong hands. The direct application of military force in this instance may entail units from across the spectrum of special forces available given the stark urgency of their mission.

In sum, SOCOM is demonstrably the most successful organization in the history of special operations warfare. Its ability to plan, mount, and execute dramatic operations like NEPTUNE SPEAR places them at the forefront of the war against global terror. SOCOM's litany of successes almost appears surreal and certainly lends credence to an unofficial meme coined by the present writer: "America's special forces: always there when you *least* expect them!"

History

SOCOM arose in the wake of Operation EAGLE CLAW, the failed Iranian hostage rescue attempt of April 24–25, 1980. The ensuing disaster and national embarrassment triggered deep-seated introspection at the Department of Defense, along with a determination to get at the root of failure—and correct it. Clearly, new and better methods of funding, training, and deploying special forces were necessary to reconstitute special forces since their heady days of the Vietnam War. Congress, for its part, instituted the Holloway Commission to review facts and make suggestions. Their revelations were startling. It was ascertained that units assigned to EAGLE CLAW, while individually well trained, had no prior experience working in tandem with each other, and their equipment was incompatible in the field. The fact that Marine Corps helicopters were not equipped for flying long-distance missions or their pilots versed in nighttime operations almost ensured its failure. Nor were they fitted with special air filters to prevent systems failures that arose from encountering unexpected sand storms. Moreover, lapses manifested at all levels of mission planning, intelligence, and weather analysis, further eroding the odds of success. Compounding all these deficiencies were entrenched attitudes of the regular military establishment, which traditionally looked askance at special operations and the handpicked elite units performing them. In fact, during testimonies before Congress, special forces officers candidly admitted that many senior military leaders were biased against their employment and, when allowed to engage, they were invariably misused and took unnecessary losses. Fortunately, the special operations found its avatar in the Goldwater-Nicholas Act of 1986, the first major overhaul of military policy since the seminal National Security Act of 1947. Heretofore diverse responsibilities were now amalgamated into a single, unified entity, with clearly delineated chains of command divided among regional commanders in chief. A year later, the bill was amended by U.S. Senators Sam Nunn and William Cohen, who felt that special forces themselves needed an institutional makeover. They felt that this change was justified given the rise of unconventional warfare throughout the Third World and the growing menace of politically or religiously based terrorism. Specifically, Nunn and Cohen argued that units required better training, leadership, and equipment, that the military should be obliged to invest manpower and capital in developing better special operations procedures, and, above all, that the sticky matter of operational command and control between varying services needed to be systematized and formalized—whether the services liked it or not.

By 1987, the internal and political wrangling ceased with creation of the U.S. Special Force Command, which represented a complete departure from earlier approaches to unconventional warfare. To counter long-standing opposition toward special operations, the new command was earmarked for a four-star general or admiral, while an assistant secretary of defense for special operations and low-intensity warfare also arose at the Pentagon. These two offices guaranteed that special operations exerted an equal voice in Department of Defense decision-making and proffered input at the highest councils. General James Lindsay was appointed the first leader of the U.S. Special Operation Command, which now enjoyed equal footing with the other four services in terms of budgeting priorities. Another welcome development is that long-standing interservice rivalries among the four branches was now replaced by infraservice coordination. Today's special operations units now train incessantly with each other, know each other's capabilities and limitations, and depend on each other in a crunch. Despite the sometimes clandestine nature of special operations, SOCOM is still not authorized to conduct covert (e.g., spy) missions with personnel out of uniform. This task remain the purview of the Special Activities Division (SAD) of the Central Intelligence Agency—a civilian concern. However, operatives from both organizations are frequently brigaded together on specific missions or objectives, sometimes with spectacular results. Consequently, SAD chooses all its new personnel from former SOCOM members who have bunked with them in the past.

Organization

SOCOM currently consists of five independent but closely synchronized service commands, each with its own tactical specialties but all capable of integrated military maneuvers to achieve given objectives. It should be acknowledged that while all American special forces units display certain degrees of operational overlap, some are more highly trained in specific functions than others, are consequently more proficient in those undertakings, and would therefore be more likely be chosen in certain scenarios for that reason. SOCOM itself is divided into five distinct geographical regions/combat commands, including Special Operations Command, South (South America); Special Operations Command, Atlantic (North America); Special Operations Command, Europe (Europe, West Africa, southern Africa, and Israel); Special Operations Command, Central (Southwest Asia, eastern Africa, and the Middle East); and Special Operations Command, Pacific (East Asia and the Pacific).

Joint Special Operations Command

The Joint Special Operations Command (JSOC) constitutes America's premier antiterrorist organization and, as its name implies, incorporates the talents and training of so-called Tier One Special Mission Units, the most elite antiterrorist formations within the military establishment. In the field, two or three differing units can be lumped together and deployed abroad under the designation "Task Force." The bulk of these are described in detail under their respective service chapters:

Army 1st Special Forces Operational Detachment—Delta (Delta Force)

Naval Special Warfare Development Group (DEVGRU or SEAL Team Six)

Intelligence Support Activity

Air Force 24th Special Tactics Squadron

U.S. Army Special Forces Command

The U.S. Army Special Forces Command was established at Fort Bragg, North Carolina, on December 1, 1989, and is the military's sixteenth major military command and, numerically, the largest component of JSOC. Its lineage traces back to the foundation of the U.S. Army Special Force Group in 1954 and, with a six-decade history, is also the most senior arm of special operations. The units contained are all multimission capable, although the overwhelming proportion of their assignments are consigned to land, especially in rear-area capacities.

75th Ranger Regiment

U.S. Army Special Forces (Green Berets)

160th Special Operations Aviation Regiment (SOAR)

4th Psychological Operations Group (Airborne)

95th Civil Affairs Brigade (Airborne)

Sustainment Brigade (Special Operations) (Airborne)

John F. Kennedy Special Warfare Center

U.S. Naval Special Warfare Command

The U.S. Naval Special Warfare Command arose at Coronado, California, on April 16, 1987, as the naval component of SOCOM. Its purpose is to provide highly qualified naval assistance to special operations around the world, with equal capabilities for operating on land. Their operational specialty is undetected ingress from the sea, lightning-quick elimination of objectives, and an equally stealthy extraction before local defenses can materialize.

> Sea/Air/Land (SEALS)
> SEAL Delivery Vehicle Teams
> Special Warfare Combatant-Craft Crewmen

Marine Corps Forces Special Operations Command

The Marine Corps possessed special operations–capable units since the Vietnam War, and, coupled with a fiercely guarded tradition for independence, it declined to become a formal part of SOCOM until March 24, 2004, with headquarters at Camp Lejeune, North Carolina. Although numerically the smallest component of American special forces, only 2,500 marines, it is capable of a wide variety of activities, including direct action, counter-terrorism, special reconnaissance, and foreign internal defense. Covert reconnaissance and sniping are Marine Corps operational specialties, but they are also capable of training military and paramilitary forces of other nations in these skills.

> Marine Special Operations Regiment
> Marine Special Operations Intelligence Battalion
> Marine Special Operations Support Group
> Marine Corps Special Operations School

Air Force Special Operations Command

The Air Force Special Operations Command (AFSOC) was founded on May 22, 1990, at Hurlburt Field, Florida, and constitutes a major air force command. In addition to providing SOCOM with classified aerial capabilities on a global basis, it also administers all special operations formations within the U.S. Air Force, Air Force Reserve, and Air National Guard. Like all modern special forces units, the airmen of AFSOC can perform a variety of mission profiles, including aerial fire support, commando-style direct-action raids, clas-sified reconnaissance, and the infiltration and exfiltration of other special units behind enemy lines. One particularly valuable activity is directed radio and television broadcasting from aerial platforms as part of psychological warfare.

> 23rd Air Force
> 1st Special Operations Wing
> 27th Special Operations Wing
> 193rd Special Operations Wing
> 352nd Special Operations Group
> 353rd Special Operations Group
> 919th Special Operations Wing

Known Operations

No sooner had SOCOM been fully activated in 1987 than it deployed near the scene that occasioned its rise—the Persian Gulf. Operation EARNEST WILL had commenced in September of that year as helicopters of the 160th SOAR and SEAL elements were successfully employed against Iranian vessels that had been illegally laying mines in gulf waters. In two small encounters, the threat was completely neutralized. Over the next 12 months, the SEALs were also called in to demolish several Iranian oil platforms in retaliation for attacks on neutral shipping. The fact that small army helicopters now operated from the decks of navy frigates demonstrates the viability of interservice cooperation as far as special operations are concerned. In the fall of 1992, several SOCOM units partook in Operations RESTORE HOPE in war-torn Somalia, which began as a humanitarian mission but ended up in several bloody encounters with local hostiles. Nonetheless, the collection of U.S. Army Rangers, Delta Force, SEAL Team Six, 160th SOAR, and Air Force Special Tactics units assembled for Operation GOTHIC SERPENT captured a number of subordinates associated with warlord Mohamed Farrah Aidid. However, on October 3, 1993, insurgents brought down two helicopters, the crews of which had to be rescued by rangers at a cost of 17 killed and 106 wounded. Somali casualties are estimated in the range of 1,000.

In October 2001, SOCOM assumed its largest role to date by figuring centrally in Operation ENDURING FREEDOM, which toppled the brutal Taliban regime there in only two months and with only a handful of casualties to friendly fire. It has since been revealed that fanatical mujahideen fighters, which had previously defied the Soviet Union for a decade, quickly succumbed to only 200 A-teams of four to 12 men from the 5th Special Forces Group and handfuls of accompanying operatives from the air force's 720th Special Tactics Group. Elements of the SEALs, rangers, air force combat controllers, and pararescuemen subsequently distinguished themselves the following spring at Takur Ghar Mountain, again with considerable success and great loss to the enemy. On June 28, 2005, disaster struck when a four-man SEAL patrol under Lieutenant Michael Murphy was gradually overpowered by superior Taliban forces, who also managed to shoot down a rescue helicopter, killing 16 service members. Operations in Afghanistan are still ongoing by SOCOM units, and details remain either sketchy or classified. Presently, around 10,000 SOCOM personnel are active in Afghanistan, and it is suspected that they conduct, on average, 300 classified operations per month. There are usually nighttime assault against suspected safe houses or other strong points, usually with great success. It is known that, between April to July 2011, 2,832 special forces raids were conducted, which captured 2,941 suspected insurgents and killed 834 more. The full extent of special operations remains classified and the exact statistics may never be known.

In March 2003, SOCOM deployed the 10th Special Force Group to Iraq during Operation IRAQI FREEDOM, and they achieved signal success acting in concert with local Kurdish guerillas. Together, these handful of men tied down several Iraqi divisions up north and prevented them from being redeployed to meet the coalition invasion. Scores of SEALs and other units were active elsewhere, locating SCUD missile launchers and seizing oil platforms in the Persian Gulf. They remain active in Iraq to present times and have spearheaded the largely successfully fight against al-Qaeda terrorists and other insurgents in the shadows. But SOCOM's most celebrated achievement—and possibly the most heralded special forces action of all time—happened on May 2, 2011, when helicopters of the 160th

William H. McRaven (1955–). William H. McRaven was born in San Antonio, Texas, the son of an air force colonel, and he majored in journalism at the University of Texas. In 1976, he was commissioned through the NROTC program, gained admittance into the SEAL training program, and at some indeterminate time he commanded SEAL Team Four. Throughout his ensuing career, McRaven was indelibly drawn to special operations, and while obtaining his master's degree from the Naval Postgraduate School, he pioneered the Special Operations/Low Intensity Conflict curriculum there, of which he was also the first graduate. McRaven quickly emerged as one of the leading authorities on counterterrorism theory and practice, penning a seminal text on the subject. He subsequently joined a special operations team in Iraq under General Stanley McChrystal and is credited with eliminating the noted terrorist Musab

U.S. Navy Vice Admiral William H. McRaven helped orchestrate the successful raid against Osama bin Laden and has since been appointed commander of the U.S. Special Operations Command. (Courtesy of the U.S. Navy)

al-Zarqawi in 2006. He also influenced the planning and execution of many "direct action" raids in Afghanistan by Task Force 714, which accounted for several hundred al-Qaeda and Taliban insurgents. McRaven is no armchair general, and he frequently accompanied covert actions as an observer. His expertise led to a berth as commander, Naval Special Warfare Group 1 and Special Operations Command Europe. However, it was as head of the 4,000-strong Joint Special Operations Command that Vice Admiral McRaven electrified the world by planning and executing the clandestine raid that killed Osama bin Laden on May 2, 2011. He was subsequently nominated for promotion to admiral by Defense Secretary Robert M. Gates and also to serve as ninth commander of the U.S. Special Operations Command. This quintessential warrior-scholar is positioned to leave his personal stamp on the war against global terror, backed by the 57,000 "quiet professionals" at his disposal.

SOAR and SEALs of DEVGRU stormed a safe house at Abbottabad, Pakistan, and killed Osama bin Laden, the world's most wanted criminal. As spectacular and celebrated as this achievement is, the lines of continuity are clear: another of America's most inveterate enemies, Metacomet (King Philip), also met his demise at the hands of a highly skilled band of special operations troops in 1676. In this context, Colonel Benjamin Church has cast a very long shadow, indeed, and perhaps the story of U.S. Special Forces, having come full circle will occasion even greater legacies yet to come.

SOCOM continues to function as the world's foremost antiterrorist organization by combining unparalleled intelligence gathering, unsurpassed mobility—and unimaginable firepower—for units their size. As large-scale conventional warfare becomes increasingly impractical and asymmetrical (guerilla) warfare reigns as a bargain-basement alternative, America's "quiet professionals" will undoubtedly expand in numbers and capabilities, all the while exhibiting the superb training, tactical discipline, and operational excellence that are their hallmarks—and calling card.

Bibliography

Allen, Patrick H. F. *U.S. Special Operations Command in Action*. Shrewsbury: Airlife, 2002.

McRaven, William H. *Spec Ops: Case Studies in Special Operations Warfare: Theory and Practice*. Noavto, CA: Presidio Press, 1996.

Sapolsky, Harvey M., Benjamin H. Friedman, and Brendan R. Green. *U.S. Military Innovation since the Cold War: Creation without Destruction*. New York: Routledge, 2009.

Shelton, Henry H. *Without Hesitation: The Odyssey of an American Warrior*. New York: St. Martin's Press, 2010.

United States Special Operations Command History: 20 (1987–2007), Proven in the Past, Vigilant Today, Prepared for the Future. MacDill Air Force Base, FL: U.S. Special Operations Command, 2007.

Worley, D. Robert. *Shaping U.S. Military Forces: Revolution or Relevance in a Post-Cold War World*. Westport, CT: Praeger Security International, 2006.

U.S. Special Forces Chronology

1676

July 5   In Plymouth, Massachusetts, Governor Winslow grants Captain Benjamin Church permission to raise a half-English, half-Indian company. This unit, partly recruited from Christianized "Praying Indians" and trained in the "skulking way of war," constitutes the origins of America's special forces.

August 2   In Rhode Island, an elite half-English/half-Indian party under Captain Benjamin Church captures the wife and son of Wampanoag Chief Metacomet.

August 12   Near Mount Hope (Bristol), Rhode Island, Indian scouts working for Captain Benjamin Church's elite company ambush and kill Chief Metacomet, effectively ending King Philip's War.

1755

September 24–29   At Crown Point, New York, Captain Robert Rogers leads his first, four-man scouting expedition to examine French fortifications in the vicinity.

1757

January 22   Below Crown Point, New York, a ranger company under Captain Robert Rogers ambushes a French sled convoy, then is attacked in turn by 200 Canadians and Indians; the rangers suffer 20 dead and wounded, and the French and Indians sustain 37 wounded and 116 dead.

1758

March 13   Near Lake George, New York, a ranger scouting party under Captain Robert Rogers is heavily ambushed by more numerous French and Indians; the rangers sustain heavy loss but outwit their pursuers and manage to escape.

1759

October 6   In Lower Canada, a party of 180 rangers under Major Robert Rogers surprises the Indian village of St. Francis by inflicting heavy casualties and burning the settlement.

1774

October 26   In Worcester, Massachusetts, the Massachusetts Provincial Congress passes a resolution requiring all town and towns to better train and organize "Minutemen" for anticipated hostilities with Great Britain.

1775

April 19   At Concord, Massachusetts, American Minutemen and other militia troops surround and badly shoot up a British column under Colonel William Smith as it withdraws back to Boston. The British lose 274 men killed and wounded to a colonial tally of 49 killed and 97 injured. Collectively, they have fired "the shots heard 'round the world."

December 31   At Quebec, Lower Canada, three companies of elite Virginia riflemen under Major Daniel Morgan fight their way into the city before being surrounded and overwhelmed.

1776

September 6   Off New York City, Sergeant Erza Lee pilots David Bushnell's radical new submersible *Turtle* against the flagship HMS *Eagle*. The attack fails when the screws designed to attach a floating bomb fail to penetrate the British craft's copper sheathing.

1779

September 19   In New York, the elite formation of 500 riflemen under Colonel Daniel Morgan shoots down scores of British officers and others in the battle of Freeman's Farm, ensuring an American victory.

1780

August 3   In South Carolina, a small band of guerillas under Francis Marion attempts to join the Continental Army of General Horatio Gates. Gates, who has no use for irregulars, sends Marion off on an extended scouting mission.

August 20   At Great Savannah, South Carolina, partisans under General Francis Marion ambush and overrun a British detachment, freeing 150 Americans previously captured at Camden.

September 4   At Blue Savannah, South Carolina, partisans under General Francis Marion attack a 250-man Loyalist detachment under Major Micajah Ganey, routing them at a cost of three casualties.

September 29 At Black Mingo Creek, South Carolina, General Francis Marion and 50 partisans routs a Loyalist force of similar size under Colonel John Ball, capturing 20 for a loss of two killed and eight wounded.

October 7 At King's Mountain, South Carolina, a large gathering of American riflemen under Colonel William Campbell and others destroy a large Loyalist force under Major Patrick Ferguson and attack.

November 1 In New Jersey, the "Lee's Legion" forms under Colonel Henry Lee; it is partly mounted with several light infantry companies attached. It gains renown as an elite unit.

1781

January 1 Colonel Henry Lee's Legion is officially renamed the "2nd Partisan Corps." It consists of three troops of cavalry and three companies of infantry and becomes one of the most feared formations in the Continental Army.

January 17 At Cowpens, North Carolina, Brigadier General Daniel Morgan uses highly unorthodox tactics employing riflemen, cavalry, and militiamen to overcome and destroy an elite British force under Lieutenant Colonel Banastre Tarelton.

January 24 At Georgetown, South Carolina, cavalry under Colonel Henry Lee and partisans under General Francis Marion raid a British garrison; they capture Colonel William Campbell but cannot storm the British fort and withdraw.

February 13 In North Carolina, the 2nd Partisan Corps under Lieutenant Colonel Henry Lee engages and routs a detachment of the dreaded Tarleton's Legion at Dix's Ferry, killing 18 troopers.

February 25 At the Haw River, North Carolina, Lieutenant Colonel Henry Lee's 2nd Partisan Corps attacks Colonel John Pyle's Loyalist militia, who mistakenly believe they are British; 300 men are either killed or wounded.

March 2 At Clapp's Mill, North Carolina, the 2nd Partisan Corps of Colonel Henry Lee again bests Lieutenant Colonel Banastre Tarleton's British Legion in a hot skirmish, taking eight casualties and inflicting 21.

April 15–23 Despite their lack of artillery, cavalry under Colonel Henry Lee and partisans under General Francis Marion besiege Fort Watson, South Carolina; the British surrender 114 men.

May 8–12 Fort Motte, South Carolina, surrenders a 150-man garrison to partisans under General Francis Marion following a four-day siege during which the Americans pelted the defenders with fire arrows.

May 15 Fort Granby, South Carolina, is captured by the 2nd Partisan Corps of Colonel Henry Lee, along with 352 prisoners. Acrimony ensues among the victors as the garrison marches is allowed to march with honors of war.

May 21   At Fort Galphin, South Carolina, the 2nd Partisan Corps of Colonel Henry Lee attacks and captures 126 Loyalists attempting to reinforce that important outpost; it also capitulates.

May 23   In Augusta, Georgia, the 2nd Partisan Corps of Colonel Henry Lee joins up with partisans under Colonel Elijah Clarke and captures Fort Grierson and its 80-man Loyalist garrison.

August 13   At Parker's Ferry, South Carolina, a combined partisan force led by General Francis Marion and Colonel William Hardin attack a force of 200 British dragoons under Major Thomas Fraser; nearly 100 British are killed or captured.

1782

February 25   At Wambaw Bridge, South Carolina, partisans under General Francis Marion attack a large British force under Colonel Benjamin Thompson but are repulsed with 20 killed and 12 captured.

1805

March 6   At Alexandria, Egypt, Consul William Eaton and Marine Corps lieutenant Presley N. O'Bannon lead a motley assortment of eight marines, 70 Greek mercenaries, 107 camels, and 300 Arab cavalry on a 500-mile desert journey to Derna, Libya.

April 27   Derna, Libya, falls to a determined attack by Consul William Eaton and Marine Corps lieutenant Presley N. O'Bannon. Two marines are killed two wounded along with nine Greek Christian mercenaries injured.

1808

April 8   In Washington, D.C., Congress approves a military expansion act that includes, among other things, creation of the Regiment of Riflemen and the Regiment of Light Artillery, the first elite formations of the U.S. Army.

1812

July 30   At Sackets Harbor, New York, Captain Benjamin Forsyth's company of the Regiment of Riflemen becomes the first regular army troops deployed in northern New York.

September 21 Captain Benjamin Forsyth takes 70 of his riflemen and 34 New York militia on a successful raid up Lake Ontario against the village of Gananoque, Upper Canada.

1813

February 7   Major Benjamin Forsyth orders his rifle company and 130 New York militia on a raid from Ogdensburg, New York, to Elizabethville, Upper Canada. They seize 48 prisoners and 120 muskets.

February 22 A column of 800 British an Canadian troops dash across the frozen St. Lawrence River and attack Ogdensburg, New York; Major Benjamin Forsyth's rifle company is forced to retreat to Sackets Harbor with three killed and 17 wounded to a British tally of six dead and 48 wounded.

August 13 Outside Fort George, Upper Canada, a company of the Regiment of Riflemen under Lieutenant Colonel Benjamin Forsyth ambushes a detachment of British Iroquois, who lose 15 killed and 13 captured in a matter of moments.

November 1–2 At French Creek, New York, Captain Robert MacPherson's company of the Regiment of Light Artillery drives off a force of British gunboats intending to capture American transports.

1814

February 10 In Washington, D.C., Congress authorizes creation of three additional regiments of riflemen for a total of four.

March 28 At Horseshoe Bend, Alabama Territory, a battalion of Cherokee warriors under Junaluska assist General Andrew Jackson in delivering a crushing blow to the Creek Indians.

May 30 At Sandy Creek, New York, a detachment of riflemen under Major Daniel Appling, assisted by 130 Oneida Indians, captures two British gunboats and five armed barges in a startling ambush.

June 28 Near Odletown, New York. Lieutenant Colonel Benjamin Forsyth is killed in a minor skirmish after he refuses to retreat and lure enemy forces into an ambush.

August 4 Along Conjocta Creek, New York, Major Ludowick Morgan and his combined battalion of the 1st and 4th Riflemen decisively repel a larger British force attempting to cross a bridge to capture Buffalo. This action spares the American garrison at Fort Erie.

1815

March 2 In Washington, D.C., Congress finalizes a peacetime military establishment that consolidates the four wartime rifle regiments into a single Regiment of Riflemen.

1821

March 2 In Washington, D.C., Congress votes the Regiment of Riflemen and the Regiment of Light Artillery out of existence for reasons of economy. Both units had served with distinction during the War of 1812.

1836

June 21 In Georgia, the Creek Volunteer Regiment is recruited for service in the Second Seminole War. They are led by Major David Moniac, the first Native American to graduate from the U.S. Military Academy (1822).

November 21 In southern Florida, Territorial Governor Richard K. Call wins the battle of Wahoo Swamp; among the slain is Major David Moniac, head of the Creek Volunteer Regiment.

1845

December 9 A scouting party led by Lieutenant John C. Fremont enters California and goes into winter quarters near San Jose with secret orders to foment a revolution against Mexican authority.

1846

May 19 In Washington, D.C., Congress authorizes the creation of a new mounted rifle regiment to patrol the Oregon Trail. This elite unit is capable of fighting on foot or from the saddle with their Model 1841 rifles.

July 4 At Sonoma, California, the so-called California Battalion is raised, along with the Bear Flag Republic. Lieutenant John C. Fremont is appointed its colonel, and it presently musters 242 riflemen and 34 Native Americans.

September 20–24 Detachments of Texas Rangers perform valuable services as scouts prior to the battle of Monterey, Mexico, then distinguish themselves in bloody fighting to take the city.

1847

February 11 In Washington, D.C., Congress authorizes creation of the Regiment of Voltigeurs and Foot Riflemen. This is an elite, gray-clad, light infantry formation.

September 13 At Chapultepec, Mexico, the Regiment of Voltigeurs and Foot Riflemen under Lieutenant Colonel Joseph E. Johnston garner distinction, losing 98 men of 341 present.

November 23 South of Puebla, Mexico, Captain Jacob Robert's company of Texas Rangers is set on by a 500 Mexican lancers; they gun down their opponents with new Colt revolvers, driving them off.

1848

February 25 At Zacualtipan, Mexico, a force of 130 U.S. dragoons and 250 Texas Rangers attacks a town held by Mexican irregulars under Padre Jarauta, routing them with losses of 150 killed and 50 captured.

August 23 At Fort McHenry, Maryland, the Regiment of Voltigeurs and Foot Riflemen is disbanded after accruing distinction in the Mexican War.

1861

June 14   In Washington, D.C., Congress authorizes creation of the 1st United States Sharpshooters under Colonel Hiram Berdan. A second regiment arises on September 28, 1861.

August 3   In Washington, D.C., the War Department's all-mounted regiments to be formally classified as cavalry. Hence, the elite Regiment of Mounted Riflemen becomes the 3rd U.S. Cavalry.

1862

April 12   At Big Shanty, Georgia, a group of seven Union spies under James J. Andrews hijacks a Confederate engine named *The General* and leads the owners on a 90-mile chase toward Chattanooga, Tennessee. They are eventually captured and executed.

July 1   At Malvern Hill, Virginia, men of the 1st U.S. Sharp Shooters pick numerous Confederate snipers out of the treetops at long range, then shoot up a rebel howitzer battery in quick order.

1863

March 9   At Fairfax Court House, Virginia, Major John S. Mosby and 29 of his raiders steal past Union sentries and capture Brigadier General Edwin H. Stoughton in his bed, along with 100 soldiers.

June 10   At Rector's Cross Roads, Virginia, Major John S. Mosby organizes his raiders into Company A, 43rd Battalion, Virginia Cavalry.

July 2   At Gettysburg, Pennsylvania, the 1st and 2nd U.S. Sharpshooters drop scores of Confederates attacking the Union center and left, allowing Union troops there time to shore up their defenses.

1864

October 14   Outside Baltimore, Maryland, Confederate raiders under Lieutenant Colonel John S. Mosby halt a Baltimore & Ohio train near Harpers Ferry, then plunder a Federal payroll worth $173,000.

October 27   On the Roanoke River, North Carolina, a small steam launch under Lieutenant William B. Cushing attacks and sinks the powerful Confederate ram CSS *Albermarle* as it lay at anchor.

November 18 At Kabletown, Virginia, Confederate partisans from Lieutenant Colonel John S. Mosby's command lure Captain Richard Blazer's elite command into a clever ambush, routing them.

1865

April 21   In Salem, Virginia, Colonel John S. Mosby disbands his raider detachment rather than surrender to Union authorities. The "Gray Ghost" enjoyed the finest partisan record of any Confederate officer.

1866

In Washington, D.C., Congress passes legislation allowing for the recruitment of Native Americans to be used as scouts. These perform with distinction over the next three decades.

1883

May 1   At San Bernardino Springs, New Mexico, General George Crook's cavalry column departs with 193 Apache scouts in tow; these are being paid to help locate the elusive fugitive Geronimo and his band.

1891

March 9   In Washington, D.C., the War Department issues General Order No. 28, which reduces the number of Indian scouts employed on the Great Plains to only 150.

1918

October 26   In France, Colonel A. W. Bloor, 142nd U.S. Infantry, arranges for Choctaw-speaking Native Americans to serve as radio code talkers; they completely befuddle Germans intelligence agents.

1941

July 11   In Washington, D.C., President Franklin D. Roosevelt signs an executive order creating the new Office of the Coordinator of Information to collect and analyze intelligence of national security interest.

August 1   Outside Toungoo, Burma, Colonel Claire L. Chennault assembles his motley group of mercenaries, the American Volunteer Group, and divides them into three squadrons.

December 20 Over Kunming, China, a force of 10 Japanese Ki-48 light bombers is attacked and savaged by four P-40s of the American Volunteer Group; four bombers are downed.

December 23 Over Rangoon, Burma, the 3rd Pursuit Squadron, American Volunteer Group, assist RAF fighters in a raging battle with a large Japanese bomber force escorted by fighters; the American shoot down six Ki-21 Sallys for a loss of three P-40s.

1942

January 9   On Luzon, a large Japanese force attacks part of the II Corps defensive line guarded by the 57th Infantry, Philippine Scouts; the Japanese are driven off with a loss of 300 soldiers killed.

January 12   On Luzon, Lieutenant Alexander R. Nininiger Jr. of the Philippine Scouts single-handedly wipes out several Japanese machine gun positions, winning the first posthumous Congressional Medal of Honor of World War II.

February 16   The 1st Marine Raider Battalion is formed under Lieutenant Colonel Merritt A. Edson.

February 19   The 2nd Marine Raider Battalion is formed under Lieutenant Colonel Evans F. Carlson.

April 14   In the China-Burma-India theater, the COI activates Detachment 101 for service in Japanese-occupied Burma. This Kachin-recruited unit is their most successful unconventional operation of the war.

May   At Camp Pendleton, California, the first group of Navajo Indians reports for duty as code talkers; these serve with distinction throughout the war in the Pacific.

May 26   Colonel Lucian K. Truscott pens a draft proposal for an American military unit based on the famous British commandos; this is the origin of the 1st U.S. Ranger Battalion.

June 13   In Washington, D.C., the new Office of Strategic Services under Colonel William Donovan arises from the Office of the Coordinator of Information.

June 13   Over Kweilin, China, a squadron of P-40s belonging to the American Volunteer Group intercepts a force of 20 Japanese bombers, flaming 11 aircraft for a loss of two fighters.

June 19   At Carrickfergus, Ireland, the 29 officers and 488 enlisted men of the 1st Ranger Battalion is organized under Major William O. Darby assemble and transfer to the Royal Commando School at Achnacarry, Scotland.

July 4   At Kunming, China, the American Volunteer Group disbands, although some personnel elect to join the China Air Task Force under Colonel Claire L. Chennault.

July 9   At Fort William Henry Harrison, Montana, the joint American/Canadian 1st Special Service Force is organized by Colonel Robert T. Frederick.

August 7   In the Solomon Islands, the 1st Marine Raider Battalion under Lieutenant Colonel Everett A. Edson wipes out the Japanese garrison on Tulagi.

August 15   At the Amphibious Training Base, Little Creek, Virginia, specially selected army and navy personnel arrive for training as scouts and raiders.

August 17–18 On Makin Island, the 2nd Marine Raider Battalion under Lieutenant Colonel Evans F. Carlson lands from submarines and eliminates the 85-man Japanese garrison. Several marines are accidentally left behind and executed.

August 19 At Dieppe, France, a force of 50 men from the 1st Ranger Battalion comes ashore as part of larger British/Canadian raiding force to destroy German artillery position; they suffer seven killed and seven wounded.

August 27 In Washington, D.C., the proposed "crossed arrows" insignia of the 1st Special Service Force is approved by Secretary of War Henry Stimpson. It was formerly issued to the U.S. Army's Indian Scouts.

September 1 At Little Creek, Virginia, the new Amphibious Scout and Raider School (Joint) opens for business at the Naval Amphibious Base there.

September 13–14 On Guadalcanal, the 1st Marine Raider Battalion under Lieutenant Colonel Everett A. Edson staunchly defends a ridge near strategic Henderson field; it becomes known as the battle of Bloody Ridge.

September 16 At Camp Pendleton, California, Company E (Scouts), 3rd Tank Battalion, is activated. This is the parent unit of the future 3rd Reconnaissance Battalion.

November 4 On Guadalcanal, the 2nd Marine Raider Battalion under Lieutenant Colonel Evans F. Carlson commences a 150-mile running engagement with the Japanese 228th Regiment; the enemy loses 500 killed to an American tally of 16 dead and 13 wounded.

November 8 In the Mediterranean, Operation TORCH unfolds as Allied forces storm ashore at Algiers and Morocco, supported by scout and raider personnel.

December 24 Over Tunisia, two C-47 transports drop 32 paratroopers from the 2nd Battalion, 503rd Parachute Infantry behind German lines in order to destroy the El Djem Bridge; only eight men survive the 100-mile trek back to Allied lines.

1943

January 23 Over Burma, Office of Strategic Services Detachment 101 agents jump into the Kachin region to begin recruiting an indigenous tribal army. The Kachins, resenting Japanese brutality toward them, are receptive.

January 31 On Mindanao, the Philippines, guerillas led by Colonel Wendell Fertig use a jerry-rigged radio set to contact a U.S. Navy monitoring station in San Francisco, California. This act constitutes the first tangible evidence of partisan activity in the islands.

February 11 In North Africa, Major William O. Darby leads his 1st Ranger Battalion against Italian positions at Sened Station, killing 50 enemy soldiers and seizing 11 captives.

February 23   At Camp Macknall, North Carolina, the 187th Glider Infantry Regiment is activated and assigned to the then-still-forming 11th Airborne Division.

March 16   At the Amphibious Training Base, Camp Bradford, Virginia, the U.S. Navy forms Beach Jumper Unit One, which is trained and equipped to enact large-scale tactical amphibious deceptions.

March 21–22   In Tunisia, the 1st Ranger Battalion surprises a large Italian garrison guarding the Djebel El Ank Pass who retreat with a loss of 700 prisoners.

April 1   At Camp Forrest, Tennessee, the 2nd and 5th Ranger Battalions are raised and trained.

May 21   In Tunisia, the 3rd Ranger Battalion is activated, being partly constructed from veterans of the 1st Ranger Battalion.

May 29   At Nemours, Morocco, the 4th Ranger Battalion is activated, stiffened by veterans from the 1st Ranger Battalion.

June 6   At Fort Pierce, Florida, Lieutenant Commander Draper L. Kaufman founds the Naval Combat Demolition Unit to facilitate Allied landings in western Europe.

June 13   In France, the first Office of Strategic Services operative infiltrates behind enemy lines.

July 10–12   In Sicily, the 1st and 4th Ranger Battalions storm ashore with the 1st Infantry Division to capture the port of Gela. The 3rd Ranger Battalion also lands with the 3rd Infantry Division to seize Licata.

August 15   On Kiska, the Aleutians, the 1st Special Service Force lands, only to find that the Japanese have long evacuated the place.

September 9–29   Off Salerno, Italy, three ranger battalions come ashore on the left of the main Allied beachhead, where they are left to fend off strong German counterattacks by themselves.

October 3   In Ledo, northern India, three battalions of the 5307th Composite Unit (Provisional) are activated. Better known as Merrill's Marauders, they are the only American ground unit committed to the China-Burma-India theater.

November 20–23   In the Pacific, U.S. Marines storm Tarawa atoll, suffering heavy losses because of unpredictable tidal conditions and reef conditions. This toll inspires creation of the Underwater Demolition Teams.

November 28   Lieutenant General Walter Krueger directs Lieutenant Colonel Frederick W. Bradshaw to establish the Alamo Scout Training Center on Fergusson Island, New Guinea.

December 2   In Italy, men of the 1st Special Service Force storm German defensive positions at Monte la Difensa in only 12 hours, taking a position that had previously defied an entire division for several weeks.

December 23   In Washington, D.C., Marine Corps Commandant Thomas Holcomb orders the 1st Marine Parachute Regiment disbanded and its personnel redistributed among other units.

1944

January 4–5   From Harrington, England, B-24s of the 801st Bombardment Group (Heavy), the famous "Carpetbaggers," fly their first mission to supply partisans operating in the Loire River valley.

January 8   In India, the 5307th Composite Unit (Provisional) under Brigadier General Frank D. Merrill is assigned to the army of General Joseph Stilwell. It goes by the operation name of GALAHAD.

January 30   At Cisterna, Italy, Colonel William O. Darby and his 1st, 3rd, and 4th Ranger Battalions are ambushed by tanks of the Hermann Göring Panzer division, taking staggering losses.

January 31   The Navy's Underwater Demolition Teams undergo their baptism of fire during Operation FLINTLOCK in the Marshall Islands. Underwater Demolition Team Two's success here leads to an expansion of the program.

February 1   In Italy, the 1st Special Service Force deploys on the left flank of the Anzio landing position, which it holds with great tenacity against superior numbers of German troops.

March 5   Over Burma, Operation THURSDAY commences as aircraft of the 5318th Provisional Unit (the future 1st Air Commando Group) support the latest incursion by General Orde Wingate's "Chindits."

March 7   At Walawbum, Burma, Merrill's Marauders withdraw to safer positions after engaging superior numbers of veteran Japanese troops, killing around 800; American losses are 200.

March 25   In India, the 1st Air Commando Group is formally constituted in the China-Burma-India theater.

April 24–26   In Burma, the 1st Air Commando Group's Lieutenant Carter Harman pilots his Sikorsky YR-2 Hoverfly over the jungle and performs the first helicopter rescue of a downed aircrew.

April 9   At Nhpum Ga, Burma, the 2nd Battalion, Merrill's Marauders, is relieved by the 1st and 3rd Battalions after holding off superior numbers of Japanese for the previous 11 days.

May 14   In Burma, numerous Kachin scouts infiltrate the vicinity of Myitkyina and report back that the Japanese have taken no special defensive precaution to guard the airfield against attack.

May 17	In Burma, the 5307th Composite Unit, Merrill's Marauders, captures the Japanese airfield outside of Myitkyina in a surprise attack. However, the town itself defies them for another three months.
June 4	In Italy, the 1st Special Service Force storms across the Tiber River, capturing several bridges near Rome. They are among the first Allied units to enter the Eternal City.
June 5	Over France, men of the 82nd and 101st Airborne Divisions begin the invasion of occupied France with a massive nighttime drop at midnight.
June 6	At Normandy, France, Operation OVERLORD commences as Naval Combat Demolition Units go ashore at Utah and Omaha Beaches into the very teeth of German defenses. Losses here are 31 killed and 60 wounded, 50 percent of all personnel involved.
	At Point Du Hoc, France, the 2nd Ranger battalion uses rocket-launched grappling hooks to ascend towering beach front cliffs in the face of heavy German resistance. The 5th Ranger Battalion also distinguishes itself in savage combat on Omaha Beach.
	Among the thousands of Allied troops going ashore this day are 16 Comanche code talkers who, like the Navajo in the Pacific, perform excellent duty and save hundreds of American lives.
June 14	Off Saipan, Underwater Demolition Team Five is directed by Lieutenant Commander Draper Kauffman. Several divers are killed and injured by Japanese mortar rounds exploding in their vicinity.
June 17	At Saipan, several days of explosive work by Underwater Demolition Team Seven finally clears a functioning path through offshore coral reefs.
August 3	In Burma, the 5307th Composite Unit (Provisional) finally overruns Japanese defenders at Myitkyina with the assistance of Chinese forces.
August 10	In Burma, the 5307th Composite Unit (Provisional), also known as Merrill's Marauders, is unceremoniously deactivated; only 100 men are still regarded combat-worthy.
August 14–15	In the Mediterranean, the 1st Special Service Force lands at night on the Hyeres Islands of southern France and eliminates three German artillery batteries.
August 15	In Italy, Colonel Darby's 6615th Ranger Force (Provisional) is officially disbanded; survivors are distributed among the 1st Special Service Force.
August 16	In St. Tropez, France, Naval Combat Demolition Units use demolition charges to remove obstructions in the harbor. as part of Operation DRAGOON, the invasion of southern France.

August 20   On New Guinea, the 6th Ranger Battalion is activated; this is the only such unit to campaign in the Pacific theater.

August 25   At Osbourne, St. George, England, the 11th Corps is redesignated the 18th Airborne Corps, which consists of the 82nd and 101st Airborne Divisions and a British division.

September 17 Over the Netherlands, the XVIII Airborne Corps (82nd and 101st Airborne Divisions) participate in the ill-fated Operation MARKET GARDEN.

October 17   Off Leyte Gulf, the Philippines, the 6th Ranger Battalion spearheads an assault against Dinagat Island, which controls access to that region.

October 19   At Leyte, the Philippines, frogmen of Underwater Demolition Team Nine reconnoiter off the Tacloban landing strip White Beaches. Underwater Demolition Teams Six and Ten are also active in scouting missions ahead of the invasion.

November 6   At Camp Hale, Colorado, the 10th Infantry Division is redesignated the 10th Mountain Division (Alpine) with an authorized blue and white "mountain" tab.

December 5   At Villeneuve-Loubet, France, the 1st Special Service Force, the famous "Devil's Brigade," disbands as American and Canadian personnel transfer back to their respective services.

December 17–25   At Bastogne, Belgium, the entire 101st Airborne Division under Brigadier General Anthony McAuliffe arrives to defend that vital crossroads against superior German forces.

1945

January 9   On Luzon, the Philippines, the American land along Lingayen Gulf; this also marks the first time that all Underwater Demolition Teams present have been acting as a group under their own commander.

January 30   On Luzon, the Philippines, the 6th Ranger Battalion makes a deep penetration behind Japanese lines to storm the Cabanatuan prison camp, rescuing 500 prisoners and killing 200 enemy troops. They are greatly assisted by Alamo Scouts and Filipino guerilas.

February 18 Off Iwo Jima, the destroyer-transport USS *Blessman* takes a direct bomb hit that kills 42 men of Underwater Demolition Team 15 and wounds 34; this is the largest single loss ever sustained by frogmen in combat.

February 18–19   In northern Italy, the 10th Mountain Division surprises German defenders along the Riva Ridge and successfully storms this heavily fortified position.

February 19 Off Iwo Jima, frogmen from Underwater Demolition Team 13 assist in directing landing craft while also conducting salvage work to keep the beaches safe for incoming marines.

February 22 Over Luzon, men of the 511th Parachute Infantry regiment, 11th Airborne Division, land near the Los Banos prisoner-of-war camp, liberating 2,147 civilian captive from Japanese internment.

April 1 At Okinawa, Operation ICEBERG commences with the largest amphibious landing ever attempted in the Pacific Theater, and Underwater Demolition Teams are responsible for guiding the assault waves in.

April 16 In Burma, Office of Strategic Services agents begin training the First Chinese Commando unit.

April 30 In northern Italy, a stray artillery round kills Colonel William O. Darby, the noted ranger commander, only two days before the cease-fire.

June 15 In Burma, a force of Kachin scouts manages to capture the strategic points of Lawsawk, Pangtara, and Loilem, killing 1,200 Japanese in the process; they lose 300 dead and many more wounded.

July 4 Off Balikpapan, Borneo, navy Underwater Demolition Teams perform their final mission of World War II.

July 12 At Simlumkaba, Burma, Office of Strategic Services Detachment 101 receives a Presidential Unit Citation before being disbanded. The Kachin tribesmen particularly distinguished themselves against veteran Japanese troops.

August 30 At Atsugi Airfield, Japan, the 187th Glider Infantry Regiment becomes the first American unit to touch down for occupation duties. It adopts the Japanese moniker Rakkasan ("Falling umbrella" or parachute) as an official nickname.

September 20 In Washington, D.C., President Harry S. Truman inactivates the Office of Strategic Services, handing off its intelligence-gathering functions to the U.S. State Department.

October 11 At Coronado, California, Underwater Demolition Team 25 arrives to assist Lieutenant Commander Draper Kaufman to establish a permanent Underwater Demolition Base for the postwar period.

November 3 At Camp Kilmer, New Jersey, the 1st Air Commando Group is deactivated.

1946

May 21 Of the 34 Underwater Demolition Teams once in service, only five are maintained at Coronado, California, and Little Creek, Virginia.

May 29 The Army Air Force establishes the Air Rescue Service to rescue all aerial personnel who crash far beyond the range of helicopters at nearby air bases.

1947

July 1 The Army Air Force authorizes its first dedicated pararescue teams, which quickly evolve into an elite service.

1950

August 5   Off Yosu, South Korea, Lieutenant George Atchison and Boatswain's Mate Warren Foley of the Underwater Demolition Team go ashore from the destroyer-transport USS *Diachenko*. Foley, who is wounded, becomes the navy's first casualty of this war.

August 27   The 187th Airborne Infantry (Rakkasans) is redesignated the 187th Airborne Regimental Combat Team in preparation for service in the Korean War.

October 12   Off Wonsan Harbor, North Korea, William Gianotti conducts the first combat operation using the new aqualung by searching through the sunken minesweeper USS *Pledge*, after it struck a mine.

October 20   Over Sukchon, North Korea, the 187th regimental Combat Team makes the first successful parachute jump of the Korean War as part of the battle of Pakchon.

October 28   At Fort Benning, Georgia, the 1st Ranger Infantry Company is reactivated for service in Korea; it is disbanded there on August 1, 1951.

1951

February 15   At Paengyong, South Korea, the U.S. Army deploys Task Force William Able to coordinate guerilla activities behind communist lines.

February 23   At Andrews Air Force Base, Maryland, the Air Resupply and Communications Service is established as the first dedicated special operations unit in the U.S. Air Force.

March 23   North of Seoul, South Korea, the 187th Regimental Combat Team makes the second and final parachute assault of the Korean War, assisted by Rangers of the 2nd and 4th Companies.

July 10   In South Korea, all ranger companies present are ordered deactivated, and all jump-qualified personnel are transferred over to the 187th Regimental Combat Team.

September 27 At Fort Bragg, North Carolina, the Ranger Training Command is disbanded in favor of the new Ranger Department, which now offers ranger-style training to qualified noncommissioned and commissioned officers only.

1952

April 10   At Fort Bragg, North Carolina, the U.S. Army Psychological Warfare Center is founded.

June 19   At Fort Bragg, North Carolina, Colonel Aaron Bank officiates during ceremonies marking the activation of the 10th Special Forces Group (Airborne). However, he can muster only eight enlisted men and a warrant officer besides himself.

July 23   Off North Korea, Operation FISH unfolds as frogmen of Underwater Demolition Team Five debark from the destroyer-transport USS *Diachenko* and begin cutting the nets of local fishermen.

1953

July 27   In South Korea, an armistice is signed; for their part, frogmen of Underwater Demolition Teams One, Three, and Five pioneered several new techniques for operating inland, assisted 61 landings.

September 25 In the United States, the 77th Special Forces Group activates.

1954

January 1   At Andrews Air Force Base, Maryland, the Air Resupply and Communications Service, which provided excellent special operations capabilities during the Korean War, is deactivated.

July 1   At Camp Pendleton, California, Marine Corps Test Unit #1 is activated; over the next three years, it goes on to pioneer helicopter insertion and other techniques used by special operations troops today.

1955

March 27   In the United States, the 300th Special Forces Operational Detachment is activated.

1956

July 9   At Sewart Air Force Base, Tennessee, the 20th Helicopter Squadron is activated as part of the 18th Air Force. This is the origin of the 20th Special Operations Squadron, the "Green Hornets."

December 10 At Fort Bragg, North Carolina, the U.S. Army Psychological Warfare Center is redesignated the U.S. Army Special Warfare School.

1957

June 19   The U.S. Marine Corps establishes its Force Reconnaissance Companies to provide better reconnaissance capabilities for the Fleet Marine Force.

July 17   On Okinawa, the 14th Special Forces Operational Detachment is ordered merged with the 8231st Army Special Operation Detachment in Korea to form the new 1st Special Forces Group (Airborne).

October 21   In South Vietnam, Captain Harry G. Cramer, 77th Special Force Group, becomes the first American military adviser killed in hostile action.

1958

April 15   At Camp Schwab, Okinawa, the 3rd Reconnaissance Battalion, 3rd Marine Division, is activated.

1959

July 25   In Laos, the first Special Forces A-teams arrive to train local defense forces.

1961

January 5   In Washington, D.C., President John F. Kennedy begins the process of founding two special operations units of consequence, the Navy SEALs and the Army Green Berets.

January 6   The 24th Special Force Group is activated.

March 10   In Washington, D.C., Rear Admiral William Genter Jr., director of the Strategic Plans Division, approves the acronym SEAL for the new Sea-Air-Land concept of elite naval infantry that arises the following year.

May 11   In Washington, D.C., President John F. Kennedy authorizes deploying an additional 400 Special Forces to South Vietnam.

May 25   In Washington, D.C., the new Freedom Doctrine is promulgated by President John F. Kennedy, which encourages the U.S. military to develop counterinsurgency units and tactics.

September 21 At Fort Bragg, North Carolina, Colonel Aaron Bank establishes the 5th Special Forces Group (Airborne), which is destined for far-flung, hard-won fame in Vietnam.

October 12   At Fort Bragg, North Carolina, President John F. Kennedy reviews members of the 77th Special Force Group, arrayed in technically nonregulation green berets. He subsequently orders that berets become an official part of their uniform.

1962

January 1   SEAL Team One is organized at the Naval Amphibious Base, Coronado, California, while SEAL Team Two forms at the Naval Amphibious Base, Little Creek, Virginia.

January 4   Off South Vietnam, the transport vessel USS *Cook* deploys hydrographic surveyors from Underwater Demolition Team 12 to examine the beach, the tides, and any underwater obstacles.

January 16   In Saigon, South Vietnam, the highly classified Studies and Observations Group is established by the Military Assistance Command—Vietnam.

1963

February 21 Off South Vietnam, men from the 3rd Marine Reconnaissance Battalion assist Underwater Demolition Team 12 onboard the USS *Weiss*.

March 10 In Saigon, South Vietnam, the first two SEAL instructors are tasked with training members of the South Vietnamese navy in the tricks of clandestine maritime operations.

March 26 On Okinawa, the 173rd Airborne Brigade (Separate) is activated under Brigadier General Ellis W. Williamson. In time, they acquire the nickname "Sky Soldiers" from the Taiwanese.

1964

January 24 In South Vietnam, the Military Assistance Command—Vietnam established the Special Operations Group, a precursor to the Studies and Observations Group.

April 1 At Udorn Royal Thais Air Force Base, Thailand, Detachment 6, 1st Air Commando Wing, established Waterpump, a clandestine training program for the Royal Laotian Air Force.

May 15 In South Vietnam, highly trained, six-man, long-range reconnaissance teams begin participating in Operation LEAPING LENA behind communist lines.

May 16 In South Vietnam, the 5th Special Forces Group activates Detachment B-52 to oversee the major clandestine reconnaissance effort dubbed Project Delta.

July 6 At Nam Dong, South Vietnam, Vietcong units attack the special forces base commanded by Captain Roger H.C. Donlon. He is badly wounded but repels them, winning the first Congressional Medal of Honor awarded during the Vietnam War. He is also the first Green Beret so honored.

December 21 In South Vietnam, a forward air controller calls in an air force FC-47 gunship to perform an air support mission. It completely demolishes an enemy building, killing 21 Vietcong.

1965

June 9 In South Vietnam, communist forces attack the special forces border camp at Dong Xoai; Lieutenant Charles Q. Williams wins the Congressional Medal of Honor for heroism under fire.

August 9 In the United States, the U.S. Air Force's Detachment Eight is activated, being the first unit equipped with FC-47 gunships; it eventually deploys abroad as the 4th Air Commando Squadron.

October 8 At Tan SonNhut Air Base, South Vietnam, the Air Force 20th Helicopter Squadron arrives; they begin flying clandestine insertion missions throughout Southeast Asia as the "Pony Express."

December 18 In South Vietnam, the U.S. Navy institutes its "brown water navy" to patrol the Mekong Delta and other riverine systems for Vietcong activity.

1966

March 9–10 In the A-Shau Valley, South Vietnam, communist forces attack a special forces base camp; the defenders are safely evacuated after a stout fight, and the camp is abandoned to the enemy.

March 26 In the Rung Sat Special Zone, South Vietnam, SEALs and Underwater Demolition Teams undertake Operation JACKSTAY, their first joint venture marking beaches for navy, marine, and Vietnamese forces.

April 27 In Thua Thien Province, South Vietnam, frogmen of Underwater Demolition Team 11 reconnoiter the Phu Loc region looking for Vietcong units that can be attacked by marine amphibious assaults.

July 30 Along the Demilitarized Zone between North and South Vietnam, special forces observe communist regulars infiltrating southward for the first time.

August 19 In the Rung Sat Special Zone, South Vietnam, Petty Officer Billy W. Machen espies a group of enemy troops preparing to ambush his fellow SEALs, so he opens fire and is killed during the exchange.

November 10 In the I Corps Tactical Zone, South Vietnam, the Marine Corps institutes its Kit Carson program, employing Vietcong defectors as informants and combatants. It proves highly successful.

October 7 In the Rung Sat Special Zone, South Vietnam, two squads from SEAL Team One are ambushed when a mortar round scores a direct hit on their Mike boat, wounding 16 of 19 SEALs.

1967

January 6 In South Vietnam, frogmen from Underwater Demolition Team 12 conduct extensive surveys and reconnaissance missions of the Than Phu Secret Zone between the Co Chien and Ham Luong Rivers.

January 16 In the Rung Sat Special Zone, two fire teams from SEAL Team One arrive by helicopter and uncover a small Vietcong base camp with huts storing 17 tons of unhusked rice.

January 17 The U.S. Navy Test Station assigns eight Stoner 63 light machine guns to be combat tested by SEALs in Vietnam. An iconic weapon of this conflict, it fires the same 5.56-mm round as the M16 rifle and remains in service up through the early 1980s.

February 2 In the Rung Sat Special Zone, South Vietnam, SEALs from SEAL Team One Detachment Golf accompany a Mike boat up a river, where they land and ambush four sampans, killing five enemy troops.

February 27   Over South Vietnam, the 173rd Airborne Brigade (Separate) makes the only combat parachute jump of the war.

March 21   In the III Corps Tactical Zone, South Vietnam, Special Forces Master Sergeant Charles E. Hosking Jr. grapples with a Vietcong prisoner who has grabbed a grenade, both men die in the ensuing blast, and Hosking wins a posthumous Congressional Medal of Honor.

March 28   In Bolivia, special forces under Major Ralph Shelton arrive to train local troops in counterinsurgency operations. His target is guerrilla leader Ernesto "Che" Guevara.

April 7   In the Mekong Delta, South Vietnam, Operation JACKSTAY concludes; the SEALs have accounted for 69 Vietcong dead and captured, along with numerous supplies and bases destroyed.

May 18   In South Vietnam, a SEAL team under Lieutenant Richard Marcinko attacks a Vietcong enclave on Ilo Ilo Island, killing several communists and burning six enemy sampans.

June 18   In Kien Hoa Province, South Vietnam, the Fourth Platoon, SEAL Team Two, splits into two squads, then successfully ambushes a Vietcong force, killing three and capturing four.

September 16 In Ving Long Province, South Vietnam, the Fourth, Fifth, and Sixth Platoons, SEAL Team Two, sweep across Tan Dinh Island; 100 sampans are destroyed, along with scores of weapons.

September 21 Over the Ho Chi Minh Trail, South Vietnam, the first AC-130 gunship, or Specter, completes its initial sortie during an evaluation tour. It enjoys spectacular success over the next three months and accounts for 94 trucks destroyed and 38 damaged.

October 8   In Bolivia, the Machengo Number 2 Bolivian ranger force, trained by U.S. Special Forces, kills the bloody Argentine terrorist Ernesto "Che" Guevara.

November 27 In South Vietnam, the Fifth Platoon, SEAL Team Two, is heavily attacked as they attempt to extract themselves; they kill six communist soldiers while suffering no losses.

December 13 In South Vietnam, the 3rd Battalion, 187 th Infantry Regiment (Rakkasans), arrives for duty; they will depart with nine decorations and 12 battle streamers.

1968

January 2   In South Vietnam, the Eighth Platoon, SEAL Team Two, lands on May Island in the Bassac River, obliterating a small Vietcong detachment, killing six, and seizing 600 pounds of rice.

January 7   In Chau Doc Province, South Vietnam, Bravo Platoon, SEAL Team One, destroys 21 structures, 25 bunkers, and 3,000 pounds of rice before withdrawing.

January 20   In South Vietnam, Aviation Machinist's Mate Second Class Eugene Fraley is preparing a booby trap when it suddenly explodes, killing him. He is SEAL Team Two's first fatality of the war.

January 22   In Dinh Toung Province, South Vietnam, the Sixth Platoon, SEAL Team Two, takes up ambush positions along two canals. Several enemy sampans are eliminated while the second squad ambushes Vietcong troops marching to assist them.

January 31   In Chau Doc Province, South Vietnam, SEALs and members of a Provincial Reconnaissance Unit team rescue eight civilian workers surrounded by Vietcong in the provincial capital.

February 6   In South Vietnam, North Vietnamese troops attack the Special Forces camp at Lang Vei, using PT-76 tanks. Two-man Green Beret teams and Laotian mercenaries destroy seven of the interlopers once they penetrate the perimeter, but the camp itself is overrun and abandoned.

February 17 In Ba Xuyen Province, South Vietnam, a Provincial Reconnaissance Unit, lead by a SEAL adviser, defeats a Vietcong formation, killing 20 and wounding 23 more.

March 6   In Vinh Binh Province, South Vietnam, Detachment Alpha, Seventh Platoon, SEAL Team Two, engages a superior force of Vietcong, killing six and wounding 20 in a seven-hour battle.

March 13   In South Vietnam, Squad 7B, Seventh Platoon, SEAL Team Two, encounters large Vietcong forces attacks, being nearly overrun before Seawolf helicopters extracts the team.

April 29   In Kien Hoa Province, Mike Platoon, SEAL Team One, a new Stoner gun belonging to Boatswain's Mate First Class Walter Pope falls to the deck and begins firing; Pope jumps on the weapon to block it and is killed by 40 bullets.

May 12   In Vinh Binh Province, South Vietnam, SEAL adviser Storekeeper Second Class Ronald Zillgitt, assisting a Provincial Reconnaissance Unit, is killed in action, along with 17 communists.

May 14   Near the Cambodian border, the Eighth Platoon, SEAL Team Two, ambushes a small Vietcong unit; the enemy retreats, leaving 24 dead on the ground.

May 16   Near the city of Chau Doc, South Vietnam, a squad from the Eighth Platoon, SEAL Team Two, calls in helicopter air strikes that kill 36 communists.

May 19   In Kien Giang Province, a squad from SEAL Team One trips a booby trap, killing Chief Machinist's Mate Gordon Brown and wounding six Provincial Reconnaissance Unit soldiers.

June 29   In Vinh Long Province, South Vietnam, Mike Platoon, SEAL Team One, runs headlong into his company-sized escort; several communists are killed, 10 huts are destroyed, and several sampans are captured.

August 11   In Dinh Tuong Province, South Vietnam, Detachment Alpha, SEAL Team Two, ambushes some Vietcong with small arms fire and claymore mines, killing five.

August 23   In Go Cong Province, South Vietnam, a patrol from the Tenth Platoon, SEAL Team One, lands and searches for a Vietcong grenade factory; 36 communists are killed, 40 huts are destroyed, and several weapons are seized.

October 10   In the Mekong Delta, South Vietnam, Yeoman Third Class Gary Gallagher wins a Navy Cross after his squad encounters fights off superior Vietcong forces.

1969

January 1   The new 75th Infantry Regiment (Ranger) is accepted into the U.S. Army Combat Arms Regimental System. It is reconstituted from the 15 companies of Long Range Reconnaissance Patrol units then operating in South Vietnam.

January 10   At Fort Bragg, North Carolina, the U.S. Army Special Warfare School is redesignated the U.S. Army Institute for Military Assistance.

January 14   In Vinh Long Province, South Vietnam, Charlie Platoon, SEAL Team One, encounters a sampan that the defector identifies as belonging to the Vietcong, and the SEALS open fire, sinking it.

January 19   In Dinh Tuong Province, South Vietnam, seven SEALs from Alfa Platoon, SEAL Team One, open fire, sinking three Vietcong boats, then call in for their extraction.

January 21   Off the coast of South Vietnam, frogmen from Underwater Demolition Team 11 begin testing new Swimmer Delivery Vehicles for hydrographic reconnaissance purposes.

February 1   In South Vietnam, all long-range reconnaissance patrol units are redesignated as ranger companies.

February 5   In Kien Hoa Province, South Vietnam, a squad from the Fifth Platoon, SEAL Team Two, arrives at the My Tho River, attack a nearby house, and kill five communist troops.

February 11 In Washington, D.C., the Department of the Army orders that all existing long range reconnaissance companies be redesignated as lettered companies of the new 75th Infantry Regiment (Ranger).

March 14   In South Vietnam, a SEAL Team under Lieutenant Joseph R. "Bob" Kerrey lands on an island in the bay of Nha Trang, scales a 350-foot cliff, and then surprises a Vietcong unit, winning a Congressional Medal of Honor.

April 12	On the Duong Keo River, South Vietnam, Vietcong forces ambush a swift boat patrol, forcing Patrol Boat PCF 43 to the beach itself. Members of Underwater Demolition Team 13 help man the defenses and beat off enemy attacks until the crew can be rescued.
May 10–20	In South Vietnam, the 506th Infantry Regiment, 101st Airborne Division, makes repeated and costly assaults on Hill 937. The Screaming Eagles suffer 56 dead and 420 wounded in the struggle for "Hamburger Hill."
June 3–4	South of Khe Sanh, South Vietnam, Recon Team "Flight Time," 3rd Marine Reconnaissance Battalion, is attacked by superior numbers of Vietcong. The six-man team is wiped out in hand-to-hand fighting.
July 6	In the Mekong Delta, South Vietnam, the Eighth Platoon, SEAL Team Two, boats up the Song My Tho River and kills several Vietcong before being extracted.
October 1	In Washington, D.C., the U.S. Navy adopts the "trident" insignia for SEAL and Underwater Demolition Team units. This badge can be obtained only after passing the demanding Basic Underwater Demolition/SEAL course, or BUD/S.

1970

January 11	In the Mekong Delta, South Vietnam, SEAL Team Two lieutenant John C. Brewerton, despite two severe wounds, refuses to be evacuated and calls in a helicopter gunship for support. He becomes the last member of SEAL Team Two killed in the war.
March 2	In Dinh Tuong Province, South Vietnam, a squad from Fifth Platoon, SEAL Team Two, kills 10 Vietcong along with large amounts of ammunition, weapons, and documents.
April 9	In Ba Xuyen Province, South Vietnam, a SEAL team comes under intense Vietcong rocket fire, and Chief Petty Officer Barry W. Enoch organizes an effective defense perimeter; he wins a Congressional Medal of Honor.
April 22	The U.S. Navy accepts production of the Convair Model 14 swimmer delivery vehicle, which enters service as the Mark VII Mod 2 SEAL Delivery Vehicle.
June 1	In South Vietnam, the final 37 Civilian Irregular Defense Group camps begin conversion to Republic of Vietnam ranger encampments.
June 23	Over Can Tho, South Vietnam, 10 men from SEAL Team One die when the army helicopter in which they are riding inexplicably crashes into the jungle below.
June 30	In South Vietnam, Detachment B-52, which orchestrated Project Delta, is inactivated.

July 1   At Firebase Ripcord, Ashau Valley, South Vietnam, Vietcong forces begin a 23-day siege of soldiers belonging to the 101st Airborne Division. A total of 250 Screaming Eagles die during the contest, including Colonel Andre Lucas of the 2nd Battalion, 506th Airborne Infantry.

November 21   Outside of Hanoi, North Vietnam, Operation KINGPIN unfolds as helicopters of the 1st Special Operations Wing fly 25 hours to support a prisoner-of-war rescue mission at Son Tay. Colonel Arthur D. "Bull" Simons lead a Green Beret team into the camp, but the captives are not present.

December 20   In South Vietnam, a five-man SEAL patrol comes under heavy fire, and Radioman Second Class Harold L. Baker administers aid to two wounded SEALS, winning the last Navy Cross awarded during the Vietnam War.

1971

March 1   At Nha Trang, South Vietnam, the 5th Special Forces Group concludes its presence in Southeast Asia, boards C-141s, and returns to the United States. The group colors were conducted by an honor guard of 94 men.

December 7   In South Vietnam, Mike Platoon, SEAL Team One, is the last remaining SEAL unit to depart for the United States, ending a highly successful five-year tour of Southeast Asia.

1972

April 10   In Quang Tri Province, SEAL adviser Lieutenant Thomas R. Norris spends the next three days conducting a ground rescue of two downed American pilots; he wins a Congressional Medal of Honor.

April 23   Over South Vietnam, a unit of the Army of the Republic of Vietnam calls in an air strike against a North Vietnamese column of 30 tanks and other vehicles. An Air Force AC-130E Specter gunship destroys one tank and damages others.

June 5   In the Gulf of Tonkin, North Vietnam, the submarine USS *Grayback* cancels its prisoner-of-war rescue. Several SEALs are rescued by helicopter, and Lieutenant Melvin S. Dry is the last SEAL fatality of the Vietnam War when he jumps too high from a helicopter and drowns.

October 31   In South Vietnam, SEAL Petty Officer Michael E. Thornton, advising three Vietnamese SEALs, rushes in to rescue a wounded SEAL officer under fire; he receives a Congressional Medal of Honor.

1974

January 28   At Fort Bragg, North Carolina, the 1st Battalion, 75th Ranger Regiment, is formally constituted.

1975

May 15   Over Koh Tang Island, Cambodia, an AC-130 Specter gunship of the 16th Special Operations Squadron flies close support missions for marines attempting to free the hijacked American vessel *Mayaguez*.

1976

July 1   At Hurlburt Air Force Base, Florida, the 20th Special Operations Squadron is reactivated as part of the Tactical Air Command's 1st Special Operations Wing. The "Green Hornets" are now flying HH-53 Pave Low helicopters.

1977

November 19 In the United States, Colonel Charles Beckwith receives permission to activate his secret antiterrorist unit, the First Special Forces Operational Detachment, Delta.

1979

December 24 At Macrihanish, Scotland, Naval Special Warfare Unit Two deploys as a forward operating unit tasked with supporting SEAL operations in Europe or the Arctic Circle.

1980

April 25   In Iran, Operation EAGLE CLAW goes awry at the Desert One landing zone as a marine CH-53 helicopter collides with an air force MC-130 on the ground; five members of the 8th Special Operations Squadron lose their lives, as do three marines.

1981

October 16   At Fort Campbell, Kentucky, the 160th Aviation Battalion forms; this is the precursor to the 160th Special Operations Aviation Regiment (Airborne).

1982

January 28   In Guizza, Italy, Italian commandos storm an apartment where Brigadier General James Dozier had been held captive by Red Brigade terrorists; they had been guided there by signal intelligence gathered by men of what emerges as the Field Operations Group.

April 1   The 160th Aviation Battalion is designated by the U.S. Army as a special operations aerial unit to support rangers and Delta Force. In combat, it is known as Task Force 160.

1983

March 3   The Field Operations Group under Colonel Jerry King is formally established; it is eventually renamed the Intelligence Support Activity and remains one of the nation's most clandestine special operations outfits.

May 1   After four decades of distinguished service, the navy's last remaining Underwater Demolition Teams are absorbed, along with their missions, into the SEALs.

July 21   At Fort Bragg, North Carolina, the U.S. Army Institute for Military Assistance is redesignated the U.S. Army John F. Kennedy Special Warfare Center and School.

October 23   During Operation URGENT FURY in Grenada, eight SEALs are dropped over open oceans, along with their boats, by MC-130s; four SEALs drown in very rough water.

October 24   Off Grenada, a detachment from SEAL Team Four goes ashore in a driving rain from Seafox boats to reconnoiter landing conditions, which prove unsuitable for marines awaiting offshore.

October 25   On Grenada, detachments of SEALs go ashore to free Governor General Sir Paul Scoon from captivity and capture the Radio Free Grenada radio station. The 75th Ranger regiment and 82nd Airborne Division also secure various strongpoints on the island.

1984

May 24   In San Salvador, El Salvador, Lieutenant Commander Albert A. Schaufelberger II, a SEAL, is assassinated by the communist Farabundo Marti National Liberation Front.

August 14   In Washington, D.C., three officers and 11 enlisted men from the SEALs form the new Navy Security Coordination Team OP-6D (call sign Red Cell) under Commander Richard Marcinko.

October 3   At Fort Benning, Georgia, the 3rd Battalion and Headquarters Company, 75th Ranger Regiment, is activated.

1985

January 16   Men and helicopters of Task Force 160 transfer from the 101st Airborne Division to the 1st Special Operations Command.

February 13   At Fort Drum, New York, the 10th Mountain Division (Light) is reactivated; this is the army's first such formation since 1975 and the first based in the Northeast since World War II.

December 12 Near Gander, Newfoundland, a civilian airliner contracted from Arrow Air crashes, killing eight crew members and 248 men of the 3rd Battalion, 502nd Infantry, 101st Airborne Division.

1986

October 16 Task Force 160 is redesignated the 160th Special Operations Aviation Regiment.

1987

April 9 The special forces is established as an official branch of the U.S. Army for officers. They receive a unit badge consisting of a crossed-arrow insignia.

April 16 At McDill Air Force Base, Tampa, Florida, the U.S. Special Operations Command activates to unite all special operations units in the U.S. military establishment under a single command.

September 21 In the Persian Gulf, helicopters from Task Force 160 uncover the Iranian ship *Iran Ajr* illegally laying mines in international waters. They fire in the vessel to disable it, and SEAL teams subsequently board the vessel and discover a cache of Soviet mines.

October 8 In the Persian Gulf, four Iranian speedboats open fire on U.S. Army helicopters of Task Force 160; the helicopters fire back, sinking one vessel and damaging two others.

October 19 In the Persian Gulf, a SEAL platoon swarms onboard an Iranian oil platform that had been partially destroyed by U.S. Navy vessels.

1988

March 8 Over Fort Campbell, Kentucky, two helicopters belonging to the 101st Airborne Division (Air Assault) collide, killing all 17 servicemen onboard.

1989

December 1 The U.S. Army Special Forces Command activates as the military's 16th major army command.

December 19 Over Panama, Operation JUST CAUSE unfolds as aircraft of the 1st Special Operations Wing delivers U.S. Army Rangers and Delta troops in a bid to overthrow dictator Manuel Noriega.

December 20 At Paitilla Airfield, Panama, SEALs of Task Unit Papa advance to destroy the presidential Lear jet and are taken under fire by local defense forces, suffering four dead and eight wounded. Meanwhile, Delta Force operators rappel down helicopters to the roof of Modell Prison to rescue radio announcer Kurt Muse, while the 82nd Airborne Division also makes its first combat air assault since World War II by seizing Torrijos International Airport with the 75th Ranger Regiment.

1990

May 16   At Fort Campbell, Kentucky, the 160th Special Operations Aviation Regiment (Airborne) is formally activated.

May 22   At Hurlburt Field, Florida, the 23rd Air Force is redesignated the Air Force Special Operations Command, which is also a subdivision of the U.S. Special Operations Command.

September 5 In Saudi Arabia, SEALs manning listening posts along the Kuwaiti border are replaced by operators of the 5th Special Force Group (Airborne).

1991

January 17 Over Kuwait, Operation DESERT STORM begins as MH-53J Pave Low helicopters of the 20th Special Operations Squadron ("Green Hornets") leads a detachment of AH-64 Apache helicopters, 101st Airborne Division, in an attack against Iraqi air defense radars.

January 18 In the Persian Gulf, SEALs help capture several offshore Iraqi oil platforms being used to fire shoulder-launched antiaircraft missiles at coalition warplanes.

January 21 Over Iraq, a Pave Low helicopter from the 20th Special Operations Squadron ("Green Hornets") rescued U.S. Navy pilot Lieutenant Devon Jones. This is also the first combat air rescue behind enemy lines since the Vietnam War.

January 22 Over southern Iraq, a helicopter flies a team from the Intelligence Support Activity to within 30 miles of Baghdad to recover a large segment of Iraqi fiber-optic cable for analysis.

January 31 Over Kuwait, an AC-130 Specter gunship from the 16th Special Operations Squadron ("Spirit 03") is shot down by an Iraqi ground-to-surface missile; all 14 crew members are killed.

January 30 In Kuwait, SEALs of Naval Special Warfare Task Group One are ordered to begin the first of 15 classified reconnaissance missions behind Iraqi lines.

February 6 With Operation DESERT STORM in play over Kuwait, MC-130Hs of the 8th Special Operations Squadron drop two 15,000-pound BLU-82 Daisy Cutter bombs on Iraqi minefield and defensive berms.

February 14 In Saudi Arabia, SEALs begin training Kuwaiti swimmers in maritime infiltration tactics. They are instructed for six days, then dropped off south of Kuwait City to contact resistance forces.

February 15   In the northern Persian Gulf, SEALs from the Naval Special Warfare Task Group One perform 15 close reconnaissance missions along the Kuwaiti shoreline to establish a military deception for Operation DESERT STORM.

February 21   In Kuwait, two companies of the 1st Battalion, 187th Airborne Infantry, attack and take Objective Weber, securing 434 Iraqi prisoners without loss.

February 23   Off Kuwait, a team of eight SEALs under Lieutenant Tom Deitz come ashore at Mina Saud towing 20-pound C-4 explosive haversacks for a tactical diversion.

February 24   In Kuwait, as the ground war phase of Operation DESERT STORM commences, helicopters of the Third Battalion, 160th Special Operations Regiment, retrieve three special forces men from Iraqi soil.

February 25   Over Iraq, the 187th Airborne Infantry conducts the deepest air assault in history by striking 155 miles into the Euphrates River valley by helicopter.

February 27   In Kuwait City, a fast column of SEALs and men of the 3rd Special Forces Group (Airborne) form a convoy around the former's Fast Attack Vehicles to recapture the U.S. embassy compound.

April 19   In northern Iraq, two SEAL platoons assist thousands of Kurdish refugees during Operation PROVIDE COMFORT by erecting refugee camps along the Turkish border.

1992

December 8   Off Mogadishu, Somalia, Operation RESTORE HOPE commences as SEALs and Marine Force Reconnaissance units wade ashore on a scouting mission just ahead of the main landing.

December 28   In Somalia, U.S. Special Forces arrive from Kenya to support Operation RESTORE HOPE. They are tasked with building intelligence ties with local Somalis to keep tabs of various rebel groups.

1993

August 30   In Mogadishu, Somalia, the 75th Ranger Regiment, with a contingent of Delta Force operators, deploy for active duty.

October 1   The Air Force 1st Special Operations Wing is redesignated the 16th Special Operations Wing.

October 3   In Mogadishu, Somalia, an army UH-60 Black Hawk helicopter is downed by Somali rocket fire, and rangers and Delta Force soldiers are called in to rescue the crews. By the time the smoke clears, 18 Americans have died, 70 are wounded, and an estimated 1,000 Somalis are also casualties. Delta operators Master Sergeant Gary Gordon and Sergeant First Class Randall Shugart win posthumous Congressional Medals of Honor.

1994

March 14   Off the Kenyan coast, an AC-130 Specter gunship ("Jockey 14") supporting Operation CONTINUE HOPE in Somalia crashes, killing eight of the 14 crewmen onboard.

September 14 Off Cap Haitian, Haiti, a SEAL detachment performs a hydrographic reconnaissance of landing beaches as part of Operation RESTORE DEMOCRACY. The 82nd Airborne is also activated for duty in Haiti.

September 19 Off Cap Haitian, Haiti, the 3rd Brigade, 10th Mountain Division, is conveyed by 54 helicopters from a navy aircraft carrier to secure Port-au-Prince International Airport in the first-ever shipborne aerial assault by army troops.

1996

June 18   In the Adriatic Sea, special forces partake of Operation SHARP GUARD to prevent unauthorized vessels from plying the waters of Yugoslavia.

1997

January 1   In Lima, Peru, a small-team Delta Force deploys in response to the seizure of the Japanese ambassador's residence by terrorists. They are holding 200 hostages.

July 10   Near Lake Gradine, Serbia, British Special Air Service commandos arrest Serbian war criminals Mialn Kovecevic, Sisa Drljaca, and Spiro Milanovic. They had been guided by a team from the Intelligence Support Activity.

1998

September 27 In the Zlatibor region of western Serbia, commandos of a British Special Air Service team snatches war criminal Stevan Todorovic. They had been assisted by a signal intelligence team provided by the Intelligence Support Activity.

2000

June 12   At Vicenza, Italy, the 173rd Airborne Brigade (Sky Soldiers) reactivates for the first time since 1972.

November 24 In Kosovo, the 75th Ranger Regiment deploys Regimental Reconnaissance Detachment Team Two as part of Task Force Falcon.

2001

October   Over Afghanistan, the 16th Special Operations Wing begins flying support missions for Operation ENDURING FREEDOM.

October 7	In Uzbekistan, the first elements of the 10th Mountain Division (Light) arrive to provide security an airfield; this is also the first American unit to deploy on territory of the former Soviet Union.
October 19	Over Afghanistan, the first A-teams of Green Berets begin arriving on the Shomali Plain to establish contacts with units of the anti-Taliban Northern Alliance.
October 19–20	Southwest of Kandahar, Afghanistan, 100 men of the 75th Ranger Regiment participate in Operation ENDURING FREEDOM by conducting a raid on a house previously occupied by Mullah Omar.
November 2	Over Afghanistan, an MH-53J Pave Low helicopter of the 20th Special Operations Squadron swoops in to rescue the crew another Pave Low that crashed in bad weather.
November 9	The city of Mazar-i-Sharif, Afghanistan, falls to Northern Alliance forces, closely assisted by Green Berets and other Western special forces.
November 14	In Kunduz, Afghanistan, men of the 75th Ranger Regiment rescue eight foreign aid workers who had been held captive by the Taliban.
November 25–27	At Mazar-i-Sharif, Afghanistan, Green Berets are active in helping suppress a Taliban prisoner uprising, although five soldiers are wounded by an errant "smart" bomb dropped by the U.S. Air Force.
November 28	Elements of the 10th Mountain Division (Light) begin to deploy at Mazar-i-Sharif, Afghanistan; they are the first regular army units to deploy in that theater.
December 5	Near Tarin Kot, Afghanistan, bombs dropped by B-52s on Taliban positions accidentally kill three Green Berets and five Northern Alliance allies. A further 19 Americans and 11 Afghans are wounded.

2002

January 7	In Afghanistan, a combined Special Operations Command unit, Task Force K-Bar, begins an anti-Taliban sweep through the Zawar Kili cave complex.
January 29	At Kandahar, Afghanistan, Task Force Rakkasan, consisting of three battalions of the 187th Infantry Regiment, 101st Airborne Division, deploys to replace marines stationed there.
February 21	On Basilan Island, the Philippines, an MH-47E helicopter from the 160th Special Operations Aviation Regiment crashes, killing two crewmen and eight soldiers.
March 4	Over the Shahi-Kot valley, Afghanistan, two MH-47E Chinook helicopters participate in Operation ANACONDA by touching down in a hot landing zone. Aviation Boatswain Mate First Class Neil C. Roberts, a SEAL, falls from a chopper to the ground and dies in combat fighting the Taliban.

March 27   Near Kandahar, Afghanistan, SEAL Chief Hospital Corpsman Matthew J. Bourgeois dies after stepping on a land mine, becoming the second SEAL to die in Operation ENDURING FREEDOM.

April 19   At the Naval Amphibious Base, Little Creek, Virginia, the navy commissions SEAL Team 10.

June 12   In Afghanistan, an MC-130 Combat Talon transport from the 15th Special Operations Squadron crashes at a desert airstrip, killing two crew members. Staff Sergeant Anissa Shero becomes the first female air commando to die in action.

July   In Afghanistan, the 82nd Airborne Division replaces members of the 187th Airborne Regiment, the "Rakkasans," then on detached service from the 101st Airborne Division (Air Assault).

August 2   In Puerto Rico, an MC-130H Combat Talon of the 15th Special Operations Squadron crashes during an aerial exercise, killing all 10 crew members onboard.

August 18–26   Operation MOUNTAIN SWEEP commences in southeastern Afghanistan, as men of the 82nd Airborne Division and 75th Ranger Regiment begin combing the area for terrorists.

September 7–11   The 1st Battalion, 504th Parachute Infantry (82nd Airborne Division), begins sweeping through the Bermel Valley, Afghanistan, seizing several suspected Taliban operatives.

September 29   In Afghanistan, men of the 82nd Airborne Division and the 75th Ranger Regiment commence Operation ALAMO SWEEP near the Pakistani border to root out Taliban or al-Qaeda fighters.

November 2   Outside Marib, Yemen, a signal intelligence team belonging to the Intelligence Support Activity destroys a Toyota land cruiser driven by al-Qaeda leader Qa'ed Sunyan al-Harethi with a Hellfire missile.

2003

January 28   Near Spin Boldak, Afghanistan, Green Berets, Afghan militia, and soldiers of the 82nd Airborne Division clear caves in the Adi Ghar Mountains; 18 al-Qaeda terrorists are reported killed.

February 19–March 3   In the Baghran Valley, Afghanistan, the 2nd Battalion, 504th Parachute Infantry (82nd Airborne Division), begin air assaults and sweep through the region seeking Taliban and al-Qaeda terrorists.

March 18–19   Over Iraq, aircraft of the 16th Special Operations Wing EC-130 Command Solo begin transmitting messages to alert Iraqi citizens to take cover.

March 20   In the Persian Gulf, Navy SEALs commence their largest single operation by deploying off the Iraqi coastline and helping to seize the Al Basrah and Khawr Al Amaya oil platforms.

March 20–27   Operation VALIANT STRIKE commences in the Sami Ghar Mountains of Afghanistan as the 2nd Battalion, 504th Parachute Infantry (82nd Airborne Division), begins sweeping through the area.

March 28   In Iraq, the 3rd Battalion, 75th Ranger Regiment, performs its first airborne assault to secure Objective Serpent.

March 21   In southern Iraq, the 101st Airborne Division (Air Assault) under Major General David H. Petraeus crosses the border in a mass of helicopters and ground vehicles.

March 25   Over northwestern Iraq, rangers, men of the 82nd Airborne Division, and assorted special forces parachute onto an airfield designated H-2.

March 26   In northern Iraq, the 173rd Airborne Brigade parachutes in as part of the Joint Special Operations Task Force—North and seizes Bashur Airfield in concert with Green Beret of the 10th Special Force Group.

March 27   In the Kohe Safi Mountains, Afghanistan, Operation DESERT LION commences as the 2nd Battalion, 505th Airborne Infantry (82nd Airborne), begins sweeping the region around Bagram air base.

March 30–31   In Iraq, units of the 101st Airborne Division (Air Assault) seize the airfield at al-Najaf while the 82nd Airborne Division maintains American lines of communication back to Kuwait.

April 2   At Nasiriya, Iraq, a quick raid on a hospital by Delta Force operators, SEALs, Force Recon units, and the 75th Ranger Regiment rescues Private First Class Jessica Lynch.

April 3   In Iraq, units of the 82nd and 101st Airborne Divisions provide rear-area security for the 3rd Infantry Division (Mechanized) as it rumbles through the Karbala Gap.

April 6   In the Karbala Pass, Iraq, Operation Detachment—Alphas 391, 392, and 044, engage superior Iraqi conventional forces in the Debecka Pass for several hours. Amazingly, no Americans are killed.

April 10   In northern Iraq, the 173rd Airborne Brigade helps secure oil-gas separation plants and oil wells in the vicinity of Kirkuk. Green Berets also strike up a close working relationship with Kurdish *peshmerga* fighters.

May 28   In Iraq, a roving band of special forces seizes the al-Asad airfield, discovering 15 undamaged Iraqi fighter jets camouflaged from view.

June 9–13   In Balad, Iraq, men of the 173rd Airborne Brigade assist the 4th Infantry Division and 7th Cavalry in rounding up militants and former Baath Party members.

July 22   Near Tikrit, Iraq, members of the 101st Airborne Division (Air Assault), assisted by undisclosed special forces, corner and kill Saddam Hussein's murderous sons Uday and Qusay thanks to information provided by the Intelligence Support Activity.

November 23 Over Afghanistan, a helicopter of the 20th Special Operations Squadron crashes in support of Operation ENDURING FREEDOM; three crew members are killed.

December 4 In Abu Gjurayb, Iraq, the 325th Airborne Infantry (82nd Airborne Division) participates in Operation BULLDOG mammoth to track down terrorist suspects.

December 13 In the village of al-Dawr, Iraq, men of the 101st Airborne Division find and arrest Iraqi dictator Saddam Hussein. They had been led there by accurate information acquired by the Intelligence Support Activity.

2004

March 28 In Ghazni, Afghanistan, units of the 10th Mountain Division (Light) uncover a large cache of Taliban weapons.

April 16 Over Kharbut, Iraq, an Air Force Special Operations MH-53J helicopter swoops in to rescue the crews of two CH-47 Chinooks that crashed in a sandstorm.

November 8–13 In Fallujah, Iraq, Marine Corps Force Recon units distinguish themselves in infiltrating terrorist positions throughout the city and calling air and artillery strikes down on them.

2005

May 30 Over Iraq, an aircraft belonging to the 6th Special Operations Squadron crashes, killing Major William Downs.

June 28 In Afghanistan, a four-man SEAL team is surrounded and attacked by Taliban militia; only one sailor survives. Lieutenant Michael P. Murphy, the SEAL detachment leader, receives a posthumous Congressional Medal of Honor. Meanwhile, a CH-47 helicopter dispatched with reinforcements is shot down in the mountains, killing eight additional SEALs and eight special forces troops.

October To combat terrorism worldwide, the 3rd Special Operations Squadron and the 319th Special Operations Squadrons are activated with unmanned MQ-12 Predator and U-28A pilotless aircraft.

December 30 In Ninevah and Dahuk Province, Iraq, Task Force Band of Brothers (101st Airborne Division) assumes responsibility for conducting security operations and training Iraqi forces.

2006

February 24 At Camp Lejeune, North Carolina, the Marine Special Operations Command formally activates. It designates 2,500 men to serve under U.S. Special Operations Command jurisdiction.

May 15   At Camp Lejeune, North Carolina, the 2nd Marine Special Operations Battalion is activated as part of the Marine Special Operations Command.

June 7   In Baquba, Iraq, Delta Force operators use a laser to "paint" a safe house used by notorious terrorist Abu Musab al-Zarqawi. Two orbiting F-16s drop then drop guided smart bombs on the locale, killing him.

June 8   At Vicenza, Italy, the Special Troops Battalion, 173rd Airborne Combat Brigade (Sky Soldiers), is formally activated.

July 17   The 75th Ranger Regiment activates its Regimental Special Troops Battalion for the purpose of conducting intelligence, reconnaissance, and maintenance missions.

August 10   At Hurlburt Field, Florida, the 8th Special Operations Squadron turns in its MC-130 Combat Talons and begin training on new, CV-22 tilt-rotor Ospreys.

September 9   In Ramadi, Iraq, a SEAL sniper team positions itself on a rooftop, and Petty Officer Second Class Michael A. Monsoor throws himself on an insurgent grenade to absorb the blast; he receives a posthumous Congressional Medal of Honor.

October 11   At Vincenza, Italy, the 173rd Airborne Brigade (Sky Soldiers) is redesignated the 173rd Airborne Brigade Combat Team.

October 17   At Hurlburt Field, Florida, the 73rd Special Operations Squadron, flying MC-130W Combat talons, is activated.

October 26   At Camp Pendleton, California, the 1st Marine Special Operations Battalion is activated as part of the Marine Special Operations Command.

2007

January 7   Over Somalia, an Air Force Special Operations AC-130H Specter gunship levels a suspected al-Qaeda training facility.

January 24   Air Force Special Operations AC-130H Specter gunships pay a second call on suspected al-Qaeda training camps in Somalia.

2008

January 25   In Kunar Province, Afghanistan, a patrol of four Green Berets and 18 Afghan militia are ambushed in mountains astride the Pakistani border. Staff Sergeant Robert Miller receives a posthumous Congressional Medal of Honor for saving his men.

April 6   In the Shok Valley, Afghanistan, soldiers from the 3rd Battalion, 3rd Special Force Group, under Captain Kyle Walton attacks 200 dug-in Taliban, defeating them; 10 Silver Stars are awarded for this violent action.

May 26   In Paktia Province, Afghanistan, a patrol of the 2nd Battalion, 75th Ranger Regiment, is ambushed by superior Taliban forces. Sergeant 1st Class Leroy A. Petry charges ahead to rescue several wounded compatriots and loses his right hand while tossing back a Taliban grenade. Undeterred, Petry advanced and killed several enemy combatants with his rife. In 2011, he receives a Congressional Medal of Honor.

July 13   In Nuristan Province, Afghanistan, Taliban fighters attack Wanat, then guarded by the 2nd Platoon, Chosen Company, 2nd Battalion, 503rd Infantry Regiment (Airborne). They are driven off but not before nine Americans are killed and 27 wounded.

September 3   Over Angoor Ada, Waziristan, Pakistan, a force of 45 special forces soldiers, including SEALS, attacks a Taliban safe house, killing several occupants. This is the first known instance of Americans operating on Pakistani soil.

October 26   Over Abu Kamal, Syria, operatives of the CIA's Special Activities Division conduct a helicopter raid against a terrorist safe house, killing several suspected al-Qaeda terrorists, including Abu Ghadiya, who had been funneling men and supplies into neighboring Iraq. The Syrian government subsequently disavowed the action, but it could not have transpired without their implied consent.

December 18 The Marine Corps activates its elite Force Reconnaissance Company to reestablish force-level reconnaissance capabilities within the 2nd Marine Expeditionary Unit.

2009

January 26   Over Kirkuk, Iraq, a pair of OH-58D Kiowa helicopters belonging to the 10th Mountain Division (Light) collide, killing all four crewmen.

April 12   Off Somalia, a detachment of DEVGRU SEAL snipers firing from the deck of the destroyer USS *Bainbridge* kills three of four pirates holding the captain of the freighter *Maersk Alabama* hostage.

June 15   In Afghanistan, General Stanley McChrystal, a special forces leader, arrives to replace General David McKiernan as overall commander of U.S. and NATO forces in that country.

June 21   At Bagram air base, Afghanistan, a Taliban missile attack kills two soldiers of the 82nd Airborne Division and wounds eight more.

July 24   In Washington, D.C., President Barack Obama awards Staff Sergeant Jared Monti, 10th Mountain Division (Light), a posthumous Congressional Medal of Honor for service in Afghanistan.

August 19   Over Leadville, Colorado, an MH-60 Blackhawk belonging to the 160th Special Operations Aviation Regiment (Airborne) crashes, killing four Nightstalkers.

September 8 At an undisclosed area of Afghanistan, three Chinook helicopters from the 4th Battalion, 160th Special Operations Regiment (Airborne), are called in to help pick up a high-value target at night. En route, they encounter a large enemy force that pelts them with an estimated 50 rocket-propelled grenades as they land and complete their mission. A total of 18 Distinguished Flying Crosses are awarded to all crewmen involved, along with two Air Medals for Valor apiece.

October 22 Off Fort Story, Virginia, a helicopter belonging to the 160th Special Operations Aviation Regiment (Airborne) crashes into a naval vessel, killing one soldier and injuring eight more.

2010

April 9 Over southern Afghanistan, an Air Force Special Operations CV-22 Osprey troop transport crashes with the loss of four crewmen and one civilian employee. Mechanical failure is suspected.

June 23 In Afghanistan, it is announced that General Stanley McChrystal is being relieved of command because of some ill-considered remarks he made during an interview with *Rolling Stone* magazine.

August 4 In southern Afghanistan, Green Beret ODA 3116, 3rd Special Forces Group, is ambushed by superior Taliban forces and sustains several casualties. Sergeant 1st Class Chad E. Lawson sprang forward to rescue a fallen teammate, then organized a defense for incoming MEDEVAC helicopters, winning a Silver Star.

September 10 In Washington, D.C., it is announced that Staff Sergeant Salvatore Giunta of the 503rd Infantry Regiment (Sky Soldiers) will receive a Congressional Medal of Honor for repelling a Taliban attack on October 27, 2007.

October 11 In Kunar Province, Afghanistan, DEVGRU SEALs launch a failed rescue attempt to secure British aid worker Linda Norgrove, age 36. Although Taliban commanders Mullah Basir and Mullah Keftan are killed in the raid, Norgrove died of her wounds. Three SEALS, who failed to completely report their actions in the raid, are expelled from the unit.

2011

April 23 In Afghanistan, Green Beret Master Sergeant Benjamin Franklin Bitner is killed by an improvised explosive device. He was a member of Company C, 3rd Battalion, 3rd Special Force Group (Airborne).

April 27 At Arlington National Cemetery, Virginia, the remains of Green Beret Sergeant 1st Class Douglas J. Glover, who was killed in a helicopter crash over Laos on February 19, 1968, are laid to rest. He apparently died in a classified mission to rescue a reconnaissance team trapped behind communist lines; his remains were not recovered and identified until October 2007.

April 29   At Arlington National Cemetery, Virginia, the remains of Green Beret Sergeant 1st Class Donald Shue are laid to rest. He was last seen alive in Laos in November 1969, gathering intelligence along the Ho Chi Minh Trail.

May 1–2   Over Abbottabad, Pakistan, four helicopters operated by the U.S. Army 160th Special Operations Aviation Regiment (Airborne) convey a party of 40 commandos from SEAL Team Six to a high-walled compound, shortly after midnight. Two helicopters land and disgorge their occupants, led by an undisclosed number of Central Intelligence Agency operatives, and storm the complex. The struggle ends in the death of Osama bin Laden, the world's most wanted criminal, and a handful of male compatriots. The Americans ransack the compound for 40 minutes before successfully departing without a single American casualty, although one HH-60 Black Hawk helicopter malfunctions and is deliberately destroyed. Within hours, bin Laden's body is deposited in the Arabian Sea from a navy aircraft carrier, fitfully concluding one of history's greatest manhunts.

May 29   In Wardak Province, Afghanistan, a special operations vehicle is struck by an improvised explosive device, killing three Green Berets from the 3rd Special Forces Group.

August 6   Over Wardak Province, Afghanistan, an army CH-47 Chinook en route to assist a ranger detachment taking fire is struck by a rocket-propelled grenade and crashes in flames, killing 22 SEALs, three air force air controllers, five army flight crew, and eight Afghan commandos. This is the largest single loss to special forces since the war on terror commenced a decade ago.

September 27 In Paktia Province, Afghanistan, American and Afghan special forces operators capture Haji Mali Khan, a senior, high-ranking member of the Haqqani terrorist network.

September 30 In al-Jawf Province, Yemen, a CIA-directed Predator drone fires a Hellfire missile that kills American-born terrorists Anwar al-Awlaki and Samir Khan. The surgical nature of the strike suggests the presence of SAD operatives nearby.

October 3   At Cannon Air Force Base, New Mexico, the first MC-130J Combat Shadow II aircraft deploys with the 27th Special Operations Wing.

October 7   Over Hohenfels, Germany, 1,000 members of the 173rd Airborne Brigade conduct their first full-scale parachute drop since 2003. Owing to difficult wind conditions, 47 Sky Soldiers were reported as injured, although the loss rate of three percent is regarded as normal for this kind of exercise.

Bibliography

General

Adams, Thomas K. *U.S. Special Operations Force in Action: The Challenge of Unconventional Warfare*. Portland, OR: Frank Cass, 1998.

Allen, Patrick D. *U.S. Special Operations in Action*. Shrewsbury: Airlife, 2002.

Barker, Geoffrey T. *A Concise Story of U.S. Army Special Operations Forces, with Lineage and Insignia*. Tampa, FL: Anglo-American Publishing, 1993.

Beaver, William. *Practical Martial Arts for Special Forces*. Boulder, CO: Paladin Press, 1996.

Bessette, Adrian. *Special Operations Forces: Background and Issues for the U.S. Military's Elite Units*. Happauge, NY: Nova Science Publishers, 2009.

Black, Jeremy. *Elite Fighting Forces: From the Praetorian Guard to the Green Berets*. New York: Thames and Hudson, 2011.

Bohrer, David. *America's Special Forces*. Osceola, WI: MBI, 1998.

Bonds, Ray. *America's Special Forces: The Organization, Men, Weapons, and the Actions of the United States Special Operations Forces*. London: Salamander Books, 2001.

Brooks, Judith E., and Michelle M. Zazanis, eds. *Enhancing U.S. Army Special Forces: Research and Applications*. Alexandria, VA: U.S. Army Research Institute for the Behavioral Social Sciences, 1997.

Busch, Briton C. *Bunker Hill to Bastogne: Elite Forces and American Society*. Washington, DC: Potomac Books, 2006.

Campbell, James D. *"Making Riflemen from Mud:" Restoring the Army's Culture of Irregular Warfare*. Carlisle, PA: Strategic Studies Institute, U.S. Army War College, 2007.

Cawthorne, Nigel. *The Mammoth Book of Inside the Elite Forces: Training, Equipment, and Endeavors of British and American Elite Combat Units*. Philadelphia: Running Press, 2008.

Cawthorne, Nigel. *Special Forces War on Terror*. London: John Blake, 2009.

Cawthorne, Nigel. *Heroes on the Frontline*. London: John Blake, 2011.

Cerasini, Marc. *The Complete Idiot's Guide to U.S. Special Ops Forces*. Indianapolis: Alpha, 2002.

Clancy, Tom, and John Gresham. *Special Forces: A Guided Tour of U.S. Army Special Forces*. New York: Berkley Books, 2001.

Clancy, Tom, Carl Stiner, and Tony Koltz. *Shadow Warriors: Inside the Special Forces*. New York: G. P. Putnam's Sons. 2002.

Collins, John M. *Special Operations Forces: An Assessment*. Washington, DC: National Defense University Press, 1994.

Conference of Army Historians. *The U.S. Army and Irregular Warfare, 1775–2007: Selected Papers from the 2007 Conference of Army Historians*. Edited by Richard G. Davis. Washington, DC: Center of Military History/United States Army, 2008.

Couch, Dick. *Chosen Soldier: The Making of a Special Forces Warrior*. New York: Three Rivers Press, 2007.

Dockery, Kevin. *Special Forces in Action: Missions, OPS, Weapons, and Combat, Day by Day*. New York: Kensington Publishing, 2004.

Dunnigan, James F. *The Perfect Soldier: Special Operations, Commandos, and the Future of U.S. Warfare*. New York: Citadel Press, 2003.

Ervine, Quintin V. *Special Operations Forces*. New York: Nova Science, 2009.

Finlan, Alastair. *Special Forces, Strategy, and the War on Terror: Warfare by Other Means*. New York: Routledge, 2007.

Godbee, Dan C., comp. *Special Forces Bibliography: An Indexed Guide to References about the U.S. Special Forces*. Houston: Radix Press, 1996.

Irvin, David W. *Special Operations*. Paducah, KY: Turner, 2002.

Isby, David C. *Leave No Man Behind: Liberation and Capture Missions*. London: Cassell, 2005.

Kaplan, Robert D. *Imperial Grunts: The American Military on the Ground*. New York: Random House, 2005.

Kelley, Ross S. *Special Operations and National Purpose*. Lexington, MA: Lexington Books, 1989.

Landau, Alan M., et al. *U.S. Special Forces: Airborne Rangers, Delta and U.S. Navy Seals*. Osceola, WI: MBI, 1999.

Lanning, Michael L. *Blood Warriors: American Military Elites*. New York: Ballantine Books, 2002.

Malvesti, Michele L. *Time for Action: Redefining SOF Missions and Activities*. Washington, DC: Center for a New American Security, 2009.

Malvesti, Michele L. *To Serve the Nation: U.S. Special Operations Forces in an Era of Persistent Conflict*. Washington, DC: Center for a New American Security, 2010.

Markham, George. *Guns of the Elite: Special Forces Firearms, 1940 to the Present*. London: Arms and Armour Press, 1995.

Marquis, Susan L. *Unconventional Warfare: Rebuilding U.S. Special Operations Forces.* Washington, DC: Brookings Institution Press, 1997.

Martin, Joseph J., and Rex Dodson. *Get Selected! For Special Forces: How to Successfully Train for and Complete Special Forces Assessment and Selection.* Fayetteville, NC: Warrior Mentor, 2006.

McCullough, Jay. *Ultimate Guide to U.S. Special Forces Skills, Tactics, and Techniques.* New York: Skyhorse, 2011.

McNab, Christopher. *The World's Best Soldiers.* Broomall, PA: Mason Crest, 2003.

Micheletti, Eric. *Special Forces: War against Terrorism.* Paris: Histoire & Collections, 2003.

Neillands, Robin. *In the Combat Zone: Special Forces since 1945.* New York: New York University Press, 1998.

North, Oliver, and Chuck Holton. *American Heroes in Special Operations.* Nashville: Fidelis Books, 2010.

Pushies, Fred J. *U.S. Army Special Forces.* St. Paul, MN: MBI, 2001.

Pushies, Fred J. *Special Ops: America's Elite Forces in the 21st Century.* St. Paul, MN: MBI, 2003.

Pushies, Fred J. *The Complete Book of U.S. Special Operations Force.* St. Paul, MN: MBI, 2004.

Robinson, Linda. *Masters of Chaos: The Secret History of the Special Forces.* New York: Public Affairs, 2004.

Roseneau, William. *Special Operations Forces and Elusive Enemy Ground Targets: Lessons from Vietnam and the Persian Gulf War.* Santa Monica, CA: RAND, 2001.

Schemmer, Benjamin F., and John Carney, eds. *U.S. Special Forces Operations.* Westport, CT: Hugh Lauter Levin Associates, 2003.

Schultz, Richard H., Robert L. Pfaltzgraff, and W. Bradley Stock, eds. *Special Operations Forces: Roles and Missions in the Aftermath of the Cold War.* Fort MacDill, FL: U.S. Special Operations Command, 1995.

Simmons, Anna. *The Company They Keep: Life inside the U.S. Army Special Forces.* New York: Free Press, 1997.

Southworth, Samuel A., and Stephen Tanner. *U.S. Special Warfare: The Elite Combat Skills of America's Modern Armed Forces.* Cambridge, MA: Da Capo Press, 2004.

Sullivan, George. *Elite Warriors: The Special Forces of the United States and Its Allies.* New York: Facts on File, 1995.

Tallon, J. Paul de B. *The Evolution of Special Forces in Counter-Terrorism: The British and American Experiences.* Westport, CT: Praeger, 2001.

Tierney, John J. *Chasing Ghosts: Unconventional Warfare in American History.* Washington, DC: Potomac Books, 2006.

Tomajczyk, Stephen F. *U.S. Elite Counter-Terrorist Forces.* Osceola, WI: Motorbooks International, 1997.

Tucker, David, and Christopher J. Lamb. *United States Special Operations Forces.* New York: Columbia University Press, 2007.

U.S. Department of the Army. *U.S. Army Special Forces Handbook*. New York: Skyhorse, 2008.

Walter, Douglas C. *The Commandos: The Inside Story of America's Secret Soldiers*. New York: Simon and Schuster, 1994.

Zedric, Lance Q. *Elite Warriors: 300 Years of America's Best Fighting Troops*. Ventura, CA: Pathfinder, 1996.

Zimmerman, Dwight Jon, and John Gresham. *Beyond Hell and Back: How America's Special Operations Forces Became the World's Greatest Fighting Unit*. New York: St. Martin's Press, 2007.

Afghanistan

Bradley, Rusty, and Kevin Mauer. *Lions of Kandahar: The Story of a Fight against All Odds*. New York: Bantam Books, 2011.

Briscoe, Charles H., et al. *U.S. Army Special Operations in Afghanistan*. Boulder, CO: Paladin Press, 2006.

Brown, B. Diggs. *Your Neighbor Went to War: Reality and the War on Terror*. Fort Collins, CO: Clifton House, 2005.

Camp, Richard D. *Boots on the Ground: The Fight to Liberate Afghanistan from al-Qaeda and the Taliban, 2001–2002*. Minneapolis, MN: MBI Publishing, 2011.

Carney, John T., and Benjamin Schemmer F. *No Room for Error: The Covert Operations of America's Special Tactics Units from Iran to Afghanistan*. New York: Ballantine Books, 2002.

Hardcastle, Nate. *American Soldier: Soldiers of Special Forces from Iraq to Afghanistan*. New York: Thunder's Mouth Press, 2002.

Jones, Seth G. *Counterinsurgency in Afghanistan: Prepared for the Office of the Secretary of Defense*. Santa Monica, CA: RAND, 2008.

Mayer, Bob. *Hunting al-Qaeda: A Take-No-Prisoners Account of Terrors, Adventure, and Disillusionment*. St. Paul, MN: Zenith Press, 2005.

Micheletti, Eric. *Special Forces in Afghanistan: 2001–2003: War against Terrorism*. Paris: Histoire & Collections, 2003.

Moore, Robin. *The Hunt for Bin Laden: Task Force Dagger*. New York: Random House, 2003.

Naylor, Sean. *Not a Good Day to Die: The Untold Story of Operation Anaconda*. New York: Berkley Books, 2005.

Neville, Leigh. *Special Operations, Forces in Afghanistan*. New York: Osprey, 2008.

Neville, Leigh. *Special Operations Patrol Vehicles, Afghanistan and Iraq*. New York: Osprey, 2011.

Rothstein, Hy S. *Afghanistan and the Troubled Future of Unconventional Warfare*. Annapolis, MD: Naval Institute Press, 2006.

Shaffer, Anthony. *Operation Dark Heart: Spycraft and Special Ops on the Frontlines of Afghanistan—and the Path to Victory*. New York: Thomas Dunne Books, 2010.

Shelton, Henry H., and Ronald Levinson. *Without Hesitation: The Odyssey of an American Warrior*. New York: St. Martin's Press, 2010.

Telep, Peter. *Critical Action: Special Forces Afghanistan*. New York: Berkley, 2009.

Weiss, Mitch, and Kevin Maurer. *No Way Out: A Story of Valor in the Mountains of Afghanistan*. New York: Berkeley Caliber, 2012.

Zapata, Regulo. *Desperate Lands: The War on Terror through the Eyes of a Special Forces Soldier*. Gilroy, CA: Nadores Publishing & Research, 2007.

Iraq

Alexander, Matthew. *Kill or Capture: How a Special Operations Task Force Took Down a Notorious al Qaeda Terrorist*. New York: St. Martin's Press, 2011.

Briscoe, Charles H., et al. *All Roads Lead to Baghdad: Army Special Forces in Iraq*. Fort Bragg, NC: USAOC History Office, 2006.

Bruning, John R. *The Devil's Sandbox: With the 2nd Battalion, 162nd Infantry at War in Iraq*. St. Paul, MN: Zenith Press, 2006.

Frederick, Jim. *Black Hearts: One Platoon's Plunge into Madness in the Triangle of Death and the American Struggle in Iraq*. New York: Harmony Books, 2010.

Hardcastle, Nate. *American Soldier: Soldiers of Special Forces from Iraq to Afghanistan*. New York: Thunder's Mouth Press, 2002.

Lansford, Tom. *9/11 and the Wars in Afghanistan and Iraq: A Chronology and Reference Guide*. Santa Barbara, CA: ABC-Clio, 2011.

Micheletti, Eric. *Special Forces in Iraq: The War against Saddam*. Paris: Histoire & Collections, 2006.

Moore, Robin. *Hunting Down Saddam: The Inside Story of the Search and Capture*. New York: St. Martin's Press, 2004.

Neville, Leigh. *Special Operation Forces in Iraq*. New York: Osprey, 2008.

Pirnie, Bruce, and Edward O'Connell. *Counterinsurgency in Iraq (2003–2006)*. Santa Monica, CA: RAND, 2008.

Russell, Steve. *We Got Him!: A Memoir of the Hunt and Capture of Saddam Hussein*. New York: Threshold Editions, 2011.

Ryan, Mike. *Special Operations in Iraq*. Barnsley: Pen & Sword Military, 2004.

Schultheis, Rob. *Waging Peace: A Special Operation's Team's Battle to Rebuild Iraq*. New York: Gotham Books, 2005.

Index

About the Author

John C. Fredriksen is an independent historian and the author of 30 reference books on various subjects. He received his doctorate in military history from Providence College. His books include ABC-CLIO's *The United States Marine Corps: A Chronology, 1775 to the Present* (2011) and *American Military Leaders: From Colonial Times to the Present* (2001).